Laos

Joe Cummings
Andrew Burke

Contents

Northern Laos
p108

Vientiane &
Around
p63

Southern
Laos p188

Destination Laos

Known in antiquity as the Land of a Million Elephants, and to Indochina War–era journalists as the Land of a Million Irrelevants, Laos boasts a rich cultural tapestry woven of ethnic strands from all over the region. French influences – morning coffee and baguettes, and stylish *tailleur* (tailor) shops – survive in the ex-colonial districts along the Mekong River, while the great Angkor empire has left behind striking, still-revered stone temples on the slopes of the country's most sacred peak.

Perhaps most remarkable of all are the great expanses of wilderness Laos has been able to preserve. Despite external demand for Lao timber and hydropower, Laos today boasts some of the most exciting ecotravel options in the region, including caving and kayaking in the Khammuan Limestone, and trekking to remote hill-tribe villages in the north.

Such unique assets have been hard won, following four centuries of intermittent war with neighbouring countries and Cold War superpowers. With the Soviet-installed hammer and sickle removed from the national seal, Laos now charts its own course, and its free-market economy attracts a steady trickle of investors from all over the world. Yet it remains perhaps the most enigmatic and least visited country in Southeast Asia.

From the placid shores of the Mekong to the rugged Annamite highlands, from the shimmering spires of Pha That Luang to the moss-covered stones of Wat Phu Champasak, travellers who have made it to Laos are almost unanimous in their admiration of the country. Many visitors have found Laos to be a highlight of their Southeast Asian journeys. As a well-travelled Lao said after staying away for over 20 years, 'This is one of the last quiet countries on earth.'

JERRY GALEA

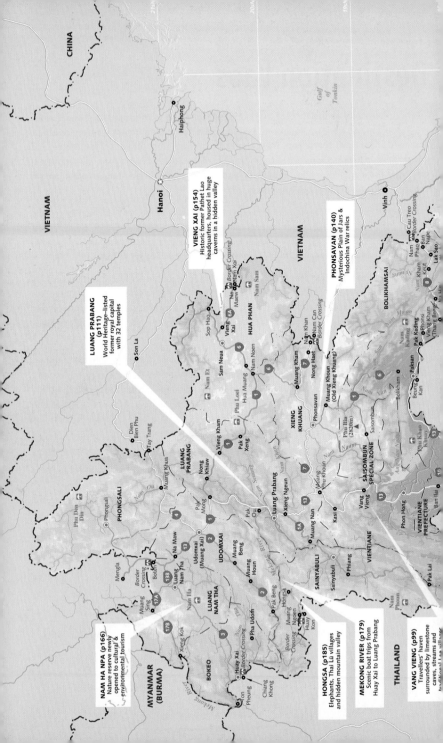

LUANG PRABANG (p111)
World Heritage–listed former royal capital with 32 temples

VIENG XAI (p154)
Historic former Pathet Lao headquarters, housed in huge caverns in a hidden valley

PHONSAVAN (p140)
Mysterious Plain of Jars & Indochina War relics

NAM HA NPA (p166)
Nature reserve newly opened to cultural & environmental tourism

HONGSA (p185)
Elephants, Thai Lü villages and hidden mountain valley

MEKONG RIVER (p179)
Scenic boat trips from Huay Xai to Luang Prabang

VANG VIENG (p99)
Travellers' haven surrounded by limestone caves, streams and traditional Lao villages

CHINA

VIETNAM

Hanoi

Haiphong

Gulf of Tonkin

Vinh

Son La

Dien Bien Phu

Tay Trang

PHONGSALI

Phongsali

Phu Dou Din

Muang Khua

Nong Khiaw

LUANG PRABANG

Vieng Kham

Pak Xeng

Luang Prabang

Pak Mong

Pak Ou

Xieng Ngeun

Muang Nan

Sop Hao

Vieng Xai

Sam Neua

Nam Et

Nam Noen

HUA PHAN

Hua Muang

Phu Loei

Muang Kham

Nong Haet

Nam Can Border Crossing

Nam Khan

XIENG KHUANG

Phonsavan

Muang Khoun (Old Xieng Khuang)

Phu Bia (2820m)

Sasomsai

SAISOMBUN SPECIAL ZONE

Vang Vieng

Kasi

Phon Hong

VIENTIANE PREFECTURE

Pak Lai

Ban Na

Cau Treo Border Crossing

Nam Phao

Ban Nape

Keut

Lak Sao

BOLIKHAMSAI

Pak Kading

Phonsi

Vieng Kham

Thang Beng

Paksan

Beung Kan

Bolikham

Muang Feuang

THAILAND

VIETNAM

Nam Nageum

MYANMAR (BURMA)

Mengla

Muang Sing

Nam Ha

Luang Nam Tha

Na Maw

Udomxai (Muang Xai)

UDOMXAI

Muang Beng

Muang Houn

Boten Border Crossing

LUANG NAM THA

Xieng Kok

Huay Xai

Pha Udom

Pak Beng

Hongsa

Muang Ngeun

Huay Kon

Pha Udom

BOKEO

Ton Pheung

Chiang Khong

SAINYABULI

Sainyabuli

Phiang

Pak Lai

Nam Phoun

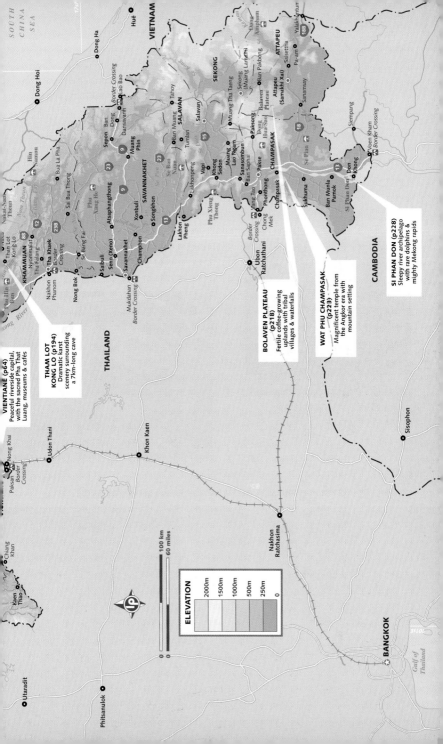

Most travel in Laos revolves around history and nature. The former royal kingdoms of **Vientiane** (p64) and **Champasak** (p221) are home to stunning antique temples, while the **Plain of Jars** (p145) holds more mysterious ancient remains. Traditional villages and one of the least disturbed ecosystems in Southeast Asia can be seen while boating on the **Nam Tha** (p165) or **Mekong River** (p179), hiking through **Nam Ha National Protected Area** (p166), or riding an elephant through the mountains and forests of **Hongsa** (p185). Laos's karst countryside is also studded with caves, including a cave city in **Vieng Xai** (p154), while its engaging folk culture has produced the musical drama **măw lám** (p42).

LINDY HICKMAN

Chill out in a sleepy river archipelago with rare freshwater dolphins in Si Phan Don (p228)

Experience Laos's diverse cultures (p34) in hill-tribe villages and cosmopolitan towns

FRANK CARTER

Wander through historic temples in World Heritage–listed Luang Prabang (p111)

JOHN BANA

ANDERS BLOMQVIST

Gaze at the mountainside Angkor-era temple of Wat Phu Champasak (p223)

BETHUNE CARMICHAEL

Discover the waterfalls of the Bolaven Plateau (p218)

Take home Lao textiles of hand-woven silk or cotton with seductive colours and intricate designs (p260)

BERNARD NAPTHINE

BILL WASSMAN

Sample *làap,* the quintessential Lao dish, made with minced fish or meat, fresh mint, lime and chillies (p52)

MARTIN LLADÓ

Admire Vientiane's sacred Pha That Luang (p70)

Explore caves and waterways among spectacular karst terrain in Vang Vieng (p99)

JOHN ELK III

Getting Started

Travel in Laos is easier than many people might expect, especially with the relatively recent upgrading of the country's main roadways, the easing of visa regulations and the increasing variety of accommodation. Still, it's a country that will appeal more to those who don't need an air-con room and a hot-water shower every night, and to those who can tolerate long bus rides into the hinterlands.

WHEN TO GO

The best overall time for visiting most of Laos is between November and February – during these months it rains the least and is not too hot. This is also Laos's main season for both national and regional *bun* (festivals; see Top Tens p11).

If you plan to focus on the mountainous northern provinces, the hot season (from March to May) and early rainy season (around June and July) is not bad either, as temperatures are moderate at higher elevations. Southern Laos, on the other hand, is best avoided from March to May, when daytime temperatures break into the 40s and nights aren't much cooler.

Extensive road travel in remote areas like Attapeu, Phongsali and Sainyabuli may be impossible during the main rainy season from July to October, when roads are often inundated or washed out for weeks, even months, at a time. River travel makes a good alternative during these months. If you intend to travel extensively by river, November is the best; flooding has usually subsided yet river levels are still high enough for maximum navigability throughout the country at this time. Between January and June boat services on some rivers – or certain portions of some rivers – may be irregular due to low water levels.

See Climate Charts p249 for more information.

Peak months for tourist arrivals are from December to February, and August.

COSTS & MONEY

Laos is an inexpensive country to visit by almost any standards. Not including transport, a budget of US$15 a day brings with it decent food and comfortable, but basic, lodgings. When you add air-con, hot water and *falang* (Western) food, costs are around US$25 per day if you economise, and around US$75 for top-end hotels and food. Of course, you can spend even more if you stay in the best suites in the best hotels and eat at the

---

DON'T LEAVE HOME WITHOUT ...

- checking government travel advisories for Laos (see Government Travel Warnings p252)
- contraceptives and tampons if needed – they can be hard to find in Laos
- light wash-and-wear clothes
- medical items, see p279 for a list of recommended items
- slip-on shoes or sandals – cool to wear and easy to remove before entering a Lao home or temple
- a small torch (flashlight) – power blackouts are common everywhere in Laos
- sunscreen and mosquito repellent
- a sweater/pullover or light jacket for the cool season and for mountainous provinces

most expensive restaurants in town, although such a scenario exists only in Vientiane and Luang Prabang.

For those on a tight budget, in Vientiane or Luang Prabang you can squeeze by on about US$8 a day if you stay in the cheaper guesthouses and eat local food; in remote areas where everything's less expensive you can whittle this figure down to around US$6 a day.

Add to these estimates the cost of transport, which varies considerably depending on how fast you're moving through the country. Flying with Lao Airlines, the only domestic air carrier, costs from US$50 to US$90 per leg. Most bus trips cost between US$2.50 and US$7.

TRAVEL LITERATURE

In 1952 Norman Lewis narrated his trip through French Indochina in *A Dragon Apparent: Travels In Cambodia, Laos and Vietnam*, a book that contained this passage on Laos: 'Europeans who come here to live, soon acquire a certain recognisable manner. They develop quiet voices, and gentle, rapt expressions'.

One Foot in Laos (1999) by Dervla Murphy is worth reading for the impressionistic detail it contains on travel in rural Laos and the passion the Irish writer feels for the Lao people, all as a result of a single bicycle trip through the country.

No other personal account of contemporary Laos is as informative, under-the-surface and well written as *Another Quiet American* (2003) by Brett Dakin, who spent two years working at the National Lao Tourism Authority. By paying close attention to the Lao and *falang* lives around him, Dakin makes Vientiane jump off the printed page.

Several classic travel narratives by 19th-century French visitors to Laos have been translated into English, including Henri Mouhot's *Travels in Siam, Cambodia, and Laos*. The book covers the 1858 to 1860 Southeast Asia trip which resulted in the explorer's death. Mouhot shows his ambivalence about the Lao in such contradictory estimations as 'They appear to be more industrious than the Siamese and possess a more adventurous and mercantile spirit' while later on he says, 'A race of children, heartless and unenergetic; the enervating climate makes them apathetic'.

First published in 1912 with original photographs, *In Laos and Siam* (Au Laos et Au Siam) was written by Marthe Bassenne, one of the few women of this era to have recorded her impressions of Southeast Asia.

INTERNET RESOURCES

Websites concerned with Laos are few, and generally of rather low quality. Most are commercial sites that are selling hotel rooms or tours, and contain very little hard information about the country. Here are the best we've found this time around:

Lao Embassy in Bangkok (www.bkklaoembassy.com) The best online source for information on visa options.

LaoPDR.com (www.laopdr.com) A commercial site with an assortment of travel information, including on accommodation and nightlife.

Laos-Travel.net (www.laos-travel.net) One of the better commercial sites, with information on hotels, tours and general travel.

Travel.LaoPDR.com (www.travel.laopdr.com) For independent travellers, this is the meatiest site in terms of ground-researched travel information, although it's out of date.

Vientiane Times (www.vientianetimes.org.la) Website of the country's only English-language newspaper, and operated by the government. In addition to daily news stories about Laos, this is the only place online to get accurate exchange rates for the Lao kip.

Visit Laos (www.visit-laos.com) Similar in content to Laos-Travel.net.

HOW MUCH?

Eggs & baguette breakfast
US$1

Luang Prabang budget room
US$3-5

Vientiane mid-range room
US$24

Slow boat, from Pak Beng to Luang Prabang
US$7.50

One-way airfare, Vientiane to Pakse
US$86.50

LONELY PLANET INDEX

One litre of petrol
US$0.50

One litre of bottled water
US$0.25

660mL bottle of Beerlao
US$0.50

Bowl of *föe* (rice noodles)
US$0.40

Souvenir T-shirt
US$2.50

TOP TENS
FABULOUS FESTIVALS

Laos boasts a couple of festivals a month year round, not to mention public holidays. Here are the most impressive.

- Makha Busa (Full Moon) (national) February (p254)
- Bun Wat Phu (Champasak) February (p226)
- Vietnamese Tet & Chinese New Year (Vientiane, Pakse and Savannakhet) February–March (p254)
- Bun Pi Mai Lao (Lao New Year) (Luang Prabang) April (p116)
- Bun Pha Wet (national) March (p254)
- Bun Bang Fai (Rocket Festival) (national) May (p254)
- Bun Khao Phansa (national) July (p254)
- Bun Awk Phansa (national) October (p254)
- Bun Nam (Boat Racing Festival) (Vientiane, Savannakhet, Huay Xai) October (p254)
- Bun Pha That Luang (Vientiane) October–November (p80)

GREAT BOOKS

Compared to other countries in Southeast Asia, not that many books have been written about Laos, but we think you'll find these 10 to be enjoyable and enlightening reads.

- *Another Quiet American* Brett Dakin
- *A Dragon Apparent: Travels In Cambodia, Laos and Vietnam* Normal Lewis
- *A History of Laos* Martin Stuart-Fox
- *Mekong* Milton Osborne
- *The Politics of Ritual and Remembrance: Laos since 1975* Grant Evans
- *Poppies, Pipes, and People: Opium and Its Use in Laos* Joseph Westermeyer
- *The Ravens: Pilots of the Secret War of Laos* Christopher Robbins
- *Shooting at the Moon* Roger Warner
- *The Spirit Catches You and You Fall Down* Anne Fadiman
- *Stalking the Elephant Kings: In Search of Laos* Christopher Kremmer

GREAT THRILLS

Sometimes you just need to get a little wild with it.

- Braving the road from Sainyabuli to Hongsa (p247)
- Climbing Phu Asa by elephant (p166)
- Crossing the Lao-Vietnamese border at Nam Khan (see p147)
- Eating a full-power *tạm màak-hung* (green papaya salad) with your fingers (p52)
- Kayaking the Khammuan (p247)
- Riding a longtail down the Nam Tha (p165)
- Rock-climbing at Pak Ou (see p135)
- Scaling a cliff to reach Muang Sui's coffin cave (p149)
- Sharing a jar of *lào-hǎi* (jar liquor; home-brewed rice wine; p55)
- Trekking in the Nam Ha National Protected Area (see p166)

Itineraries
CLASSIC ROUTES

NORTHERN LOOP
One to Two Weeks / Huay Xai to Vientiane

Travellers have been doing this circuit since before the 1975 revolution, and it's still one of the best samplers for anyone who wants a good dose of Laos in a relatively short time-span.

Entering Laos via ferry from Chiang Khong, Thailand, to **Huay Xai** (p176), board one of the slow boats that ply the Mekong between Huay Xai and Luang Prabang. This two-day voyage requires an overnight in the small riverside district of **Pak Beng** (p159), a trading nexus for hill tribes where one can arrange short treks. Along the Mekong River is terrific scenery consisting of villages, limestone cliffs and intermittent forest.

Boats may stop at **Pak Ou** (p134) so that passengers can visit Buddha-filled caves there. Sightseeing in and around **Luang Prabang** (p111), Laos's atmospheric former royal capital, can easily occupy a week.

From here, continue southward to Vientiane by bus or van along Rte 13, stopping in **Vang Vieng** (p99), a modern-day travellers centre surrounded by craggy, cave-studded limestone peaks. After a few days of river-tubing and cave hikes, head to **Vientiane** (p64), Laos's semibustling capital city.

Pass quiet village ports and rugged gorges on the Mekong to Luang Prabang, then follow Rte 13, which winds high into the mountains between Kasi and Vang Vieng toward Vientiane, to complete this 700km route.

SOUTHERN LOOP   One to Two Weeks / Vientiane to Si Phan Don

This circuit takes you through the heartland of lowland Lao culture, a world of broad river plains planted with rice and home-made looms shaded by wooden houses on stilts.

Start your trip in **Vientiane** (p64), the country's capital city, now easily accessed via the Thai-Lao Friendship bridge. After enjoying the food, nightlife and historical sights of here, head south to **Tha Khaek** (p196), where you can stroll the sleepy urban riverside and explore nearby caves in the **Khammuan Limestone** (see the Loop p201), best accessed from **Tham Lot Kong Lo** (p194).

Your next stop heading south will be **Savannakhet** (p202), where you'll get an architectural taste of how postcolonial Vientiane looked before it was gussied up by the Lao PDR government and international aid. Chowhounds can sniff around for the country's best *fǒe* (rice noodles) and *sîn sawǎn* (literally 'heavenly beef'; dried beef).

From Savannakhet continue southward to Champasak Province, home to **Wat Phu Champasak** (p223). The Angkor-style temple ruins at Wat Phu extend stepwise of the slopes of Phu Pasak, itself a sacred site due to a rock-shelter spring flowing near the phallus-shaped summit.

By either bus or riverboat, make a final short hop to **Si Phan Don** (Four Thousand Islands; p228), an archipelago of river islands where the southern Lao farming and fishing life continues much as it has for a century or more. Here you can enjoy a relaxed pace of life and take a boat trip to see the rare freshwater Irawaddy dolphin before heading back to Thailand via Chong Mek or on to Cambodia via Voen Kham.

This route covers 730km of river plains and rolling hills, bridging clear streams and tracing traditional Lao villages via Rte 13 before arriving at Pakse, from where you can go by road or river to the relaxed islands of Si Phan Don.

ROADS LESS TRAVELLED

NORTHERN WILDERNESS

Two to Three Weeks /
Luang Nam Tha to Xieng Khuang

This route explores the mountains and plateaus of the north. In **Luang Nam Tha Province** (p161) visit the **Nam Ha National Protected Area** (p166) or trek through hill-tribe villages near **Muang Sing** (p167) and **Muang Long** (p171).

Head southeast from Luang Nam Tha and kick back in **Nong Khiaw** (p136), soaking up northern Lao life along the Nam Ou and taking hikes to limestone caves. Crossing the Nam Ou, climb higher into the Annamite Chain through Hmong villages till you reach remote **Sam Neua** (p150). Near here the communist Pathet Lao, with help from the North Vietnamese Army, took shelter in huge caverns in **Vieng Xai** (p154) and mounted a successful campaign to seize the former Royal Government of Laos. Sam Neua is also known for intricately patterned, hand-woven textiles.

South of Sam Neua en route to **Nam Noen** (p155) stands **Suan Hin** (p153), where ancient megaliths are arranged in patterns that remain a total enigma to locals and scholars alike.

From Sam Neua a lengthy road trip southwest leads to **Phonsavan** (p140), the fast-growing capital of Xieng Khuang Province. Here one of the main attractions is a large plateau scattered with hundreds of monumental lidded stone jars known as the **Plain of Jars** (p145).

Visit caverns, traditional villages and mysterious relics on this adventure which takes you along 588km of high, winding road which crosses many rivers and streams. Add 92km for the detour to Sam Neua.

BOLAVEN AND BEYOND

10 to 14 days / Pakse to Pakse

This trip into the remote provinces of southern Laos can be done by bus and truck, by private vehicle or motorbike – a 100cc variety will do – and is best in the dry season.

After a day or two getting organised in **Pakse** (p211), head up onto the **Bolaven Plateau** (p218) and Laos's most impressive waterfall at **Tat Fan** (p218), from where treks into the rustic **Dong Hua Sao NPA** (p218) can be arranged. At the coffee capital of **Paksong** (p219) you could stop to buy some Java before continuing on to **Sekong** (p240), passing through Laven, Katang and other villages en route. Use Sekong as a base to visit the renowned weavers in nearby Alak villages and waterfalls including the breathtaking **Nam Tok Katamtok** (p242).

If the river is full enough, head down the **Se Kong** (see Down the Se Kong by Longtail Boat p241) for an unforgettable trip into **Attapeu Province** (p242). Sleepy **Attapeu** (p242) is an easy place to hang out, interrupting your sunsets-by-the–Se Kong with bumpy day trips out to the **Ho Chi Minh Trail** (p209) villages of **Pa-am** (p245) and **Phu Vong** (p245).

Head back up Rte 16, through Sekong and turn north at Muang Tha Taeng on a long, downhill laterite road to Beng. Check out **Salavan** (p238) for a day and arrange transport along the rarely travelled road to **Tahoy** (p239), once an important marker on the Ho Chi Minh Trail and now a more peaceful home of the Ta-oy (Tahoy) people, plus a few noisy tigers.

Beautiful **Tat Lo** (p220) and its inevitable backpackers will be a shock after days with little, if any, contact with Westerners, and **Phasoume Resort** (p219) makes an attractive lunch spot before the trip back to Pakse.

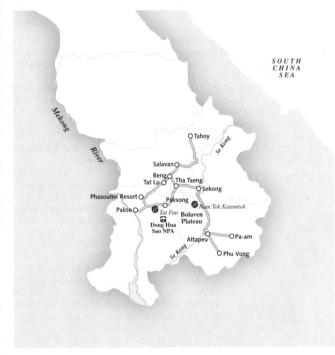

On this roughly 650km journey you'll climb into the coffee-growing districts of the Bolaven Plateau, see spectacular waterfalls, and visit villages little-changed since the Ho Chi Minh Trail passed.

TAILORED TRIPS

LAOS FOR KIDS   Two Weeks

Assemble the family for an all-out assault on everything kids will like about Laos. In Vientiane they'll be awed by the bizarre Hindu-Buddhist sculptures at **Xieng Khuan** (Buddha Park; p76) – once they're in the 'pumpkin' monument you may have to drag them away.

Head north to Luang Prabang, waking the brood when you pass through the spooky finger peaks near **Muang Phu Khoun** (p107), which resemble a

scene out of Disney's *Sorcerer's Apprentice*. In Luang Prabang, swimming at **Tat Sae** (p136) and **Tat Kuang Si** (p135) waterfalls is a sure bet, as is the half-day boat trip to the **Pak Ou caves** (p134).

From Luang Prabang, fly, drive or bus to Xieng Khuang Province and let them loose among the mysterious stone jars on the **Plain of Jars Site 1** (p145). For a cultural interlude, hike to nearby villages. Other activities the team might enjoy here include a visit to the new hot springs near **Ban Thak** (p148) and the easy clamber up a cliff to see **Tham Piu** (p147), a cave now famous as a Second Indochina War memorial.

GRAND TEMPLE TOUR   Two to Three Weeks

Start in Vientiane with this trio of must-sees: **Pha That Luang** (p70) for its spiky stupa, where Buddhist doctrine is numerologically encoded; **Wat Si Saket** (p71) for the thousands of niches holding tiny Buddhas; and **Haw Pha Kaew** (p71) for the best collection of Lao Buddhist art in the country.

In Luang Prabang head first to the city's showcase temple, **Wat Xieng Thong** (p118), a collection of Buddhist chapels delicately decorated with the best gold stencil work in the country. Virtually every other wat in the old temple district is also worth stopping by, as each is unique, but don't miss the massive bronze seated Buddha image at **Wat Manolom** (p120), the unique watermelon-shaped stupa and faux-lathed windows at **Wat Wisunarat** (p119) and the Buddhist art school at **Wat Xieng Muan** (p121).

Saving the most ancient and venerated for last, drop south to the small, unassuming town of **Champasak** (p221). Just 4km outside of town at **Muang Kao** (see Champasak in Antiquity p222) lie the ruined city walls of Kuruksetra, where the oldest surviving Sanskrit inscription in Southeast Asia was recently found. This defunct kingdom was almost certainly linked to nearby **Wat Phu Champasak** (p223), an Angkor-style temple ruin and the grandest archaeological site in Laos. If you can visit in time for the **Wat Phu Festival** (p226) in February, you'll be treated to one of the country's most visually impressive and spiritually significant festivals.

The Authors

JOE CUMMINGS

**Coordinating Author &
Northern Laos**

Born in the subtropical port of New Orleans, Joe became accustomed to hot weather and spicy food at a young age. After college he headed straight for Southeast Asia, where he worked as a university English lecturer in Thailand and Malaysia. Heading back to school, Joe earned a master's degree in Southeast Asian studies, and later wrote Lonely Planet's first guidebook to Thailand.

Joe began travelling in Laos in 1989, the first year the country opened to tourism following the 1975 Pathet Lao liberation. He has been writing on Laos for Lonely Planet ever since.

My Favourite Trip

I like to slip into Laos at Huay Xai (p176), then catch a boat down the Mekong (p165) to Pak Tha at the mouth of the Nam Tha. In Pak Tha I'll pick up a longtail boat headed northwest up the Nam Tha, stopping off in Na Lae (p165) for a night before getting another boat on to Luang Nam Tha (p161).

After exploring the quirky sights of Luang Nam Tha Province, I'll quickly transit Udomxai, then take it slow heading north into the hills. Stopping in the Thai Lü villages of Muang La (p174) or Boun Tai (p174) breaks the journey nicely and lets me wander around admiring the Thai Lü architecture. The final stop, at Laos's northernmost tip, is Phongsali (p173), a town where the blend of Yunnanese, Lao and Phu Noi cultures still has me scratching my head.

ANDREW BURKE

**Vientiane & Around,
Southern Laos, Transport**

Andrew has lived in Asia since 2001 and during many visits to Laos he's developed a deep affection for the country and its people. Whether working as a journalist and photographer for newspapers in Hong Kong, Australia and London, as a guidebook author, or in his favourite mode of traveller-without-deadline, he has endeavoured to get off the beaten track as often as possible, particularly in southern Laos. Andrew plans to continue exploring Laos from his base in Phnom Penh, Cambodia.

My Favourite Trip

There is nothing new or particularly difficult about this route, but I find this meander down the Mekong as relaxing and romantic today as when I first travelled it. I take a bus from Pakse (p211) south to Champasak (p221) and spend the afternoon wandering around town at a very leisurely pace. Early next morning I take a motorbike taxi to Wat Phu Champasak (p223), at its most glorious in the dawn light. I'm back in Champasak by 10am to pick up the slow boat for its zigzagging journey along the Mekong to Don Khong (p230). After circling the island by motorbike, a longtail boat navigates me through the maze of islands to Don Det, and then Don Khon (p233). Does it get any better…?

CONTRIBUTING AUTHOR

Dr Trish Batchelor is a general practitioner and travel medicine specialist who works at the CIWEC Clinic in Kathmandu, Nepal, as well as being a Medical Advisor to the Travel Doctor New Zealand clinics. Trish teaches travel medicine through the University of Otago, and is interested in underwater and high-altitude medicine, and in the impact of tourism on host countries. She has travelled extensively through Southeast and East Asia and particularly loves high-altitude trekking in the Himalayas. Dr Batchelor wrote the Health chapter.

Snapshot

Laos has become the latest darling of the travel scene in Southeast Asia, with positive word of mouth fuelling a growing influx of aspiring 'lotus-eaters', as the French used to call the colonials who 'dissipated' themselves when stationed here. With the lowering of travel restrictions and proliferation of guesthouses and hotels, it's easier and cheaper to travel in Laos now than it ever has been since the nation first opened its doors to tourists in 1989.

The government recently declared that tourist visas (see p263) may be granted on arrival at all official border entry points, a great leap forward from the previous policy which required advance visas except for Vientiane and Luang Prabang international airport arrivals, and at the Thai-Lao Friendship Bridge near Vientiane. New border crossings from Thailand and Vietnam have been added to the official list, so there are now more ways than ever to get into Laos quickly.

Following the surrender of between 700 and 800 Hmong insurgents in February 2003, road travel along Rte 13 – previously plagued by the occasional Hmong attack but apparently now safe – will surely increase.

On the other hand Lao government officials obviously feel ambivalent about the increased international attention, which has brought to the surface various sticky issues related to tourism. Operators of bars and nightclubs, for example, are currently resisting a government push to close such venues an hour earlier than the previous 11.30pm standard, an effort on the government's part to curb perceived corruption of Lao youth. Riverfront restaurants and cafés in Vientiane and Luang Prabang have been torn down by the government three times – and rebuilt four times so far – due to concerns over 'naval security'.

Ecotourism continues to enjoy modest success in Laos, with the Nam Ha NPA trekking-project model being exported to other parts of the country, particularly southern Laos. Via the Mekong River Commission (MRC), the governments of Cambodia, Laos, Thailand and Vietnam have recently agreed to notify each other before undertaking any Mekong River projects that might have an impact on their neighbours, a positive development in the eyes of environmentalists and Mekong-oriented tour operators as well. However, the one MRC member that hasn't signed this agreement, China, continues to blast away at shoals and rapids in the Upper Mekong River in an effort to allow 500-tonne ships to navigate the river (see Development of the Mekong p45). The blasting has already negatively affected fish species native to the Mekong, including the rare giant Mekong catfish.

Although finding mind-blowing Lao cuisine remains as big a challenge as ever, a new Lao-made beer on the scene, made from sugar-palm sap and called Golden Palm, is turning heads. Also tickling local and visiting palates are several new Lao coffee ventures competing to capture a growing market for the good life; see p54.

This burgeoning elite market can be linked to the steady growth of tourism and unflagging influx of foreign-aid projects, as Laos becomes less isolated and more reliant on the outside world.

FAST FACTS

Area: 236,800 sq km

Border countries: Cambodia, China, Myanmar, Thailand, Vietnam

Population: 6 million

Literacy: 52.8%

GDP per capita (purchasing power parity): US$1700

Inflation: 7.8%

Number of written laws: around 50

Original name: Lan Xang Hom Khao (Million Elephants, White Parasol)

Number of elephants in Laos today: around 2000

Laos's share of the Mekong River: 1865km

History

PREHISTORY & AUSTRO-THAI MIGRATION

The Mekong River valley and Khorat Plateau areas which today encompass parts of Laos, Cambodia and Thailand were inhabited at least 10,000 years ago. Although data on these early cultures is scant, ceramic and bronze production began here significantly earlier than elsewhere in the world.

The earliest inhabitants of Laos were part of a group that occupied areas in a vast zone of the Austro-Thai river valley following migrations stretching from the Red River in southern China and Vietnam to the Brahmaputra River in Assam, northeast India. The Mekong River valley between Thailand and Laos may have received such migration as early as the 8th century AD, and most certainly had by the 10th century. These river-valley states were organised along traditional Tai (the Austro-Thai group) lines according to *meuang* (principalities or city-states) under the hereditary rule of *jao meuang* (chieftains or sovereigns). One of the largest contributors to early *meuang* is thought to have been northwestern Vietnam's Dien Bien Phu.

In Lao legend, the mythical figure Khun Borom (Bulom) cut open a gourd somewhere in the vicinity of Dien Bien Phu and out came seven sons who spread the Tai family from east to west. Although previous theory had placed the original centre of Tai culture in southwestern China or even Indonesia, recent evidence suggests it may have been in northern Vietnam and part of the Dongson/Tonkin culture – a theory supported by the Khun Bulom myth.

Meanwhile, southern Laos had been an early centre of the Mon-Khmer Funan kingdom (1st to 6th centuries AD) and the Chenla kingdom (6th to 8th centuries), both of which extended from Champasak into Cambodia. Further north two Mon kingdoms called Sri Gotapura (centred at present-day Tha Khaek) and Muang Sawa (at Luang Prabang) flourished from the 8th to the 12th centuries. These kingdoms were superseded by the Angkor Empire and later by Lao and Siamese principalities.

LAN NA THAI & LAN XANG

In the mid-13th century, a Tai rebellion against the Khmers resulted in the consolidation of a number of *meuang* to create the famous Sukhothai kingdom in northern Thailand. Sukhothai's King Ramkhamhaeng supported Chao Mengrai of Chiang Mai and Chao Khun Ngam Muang of Phayao (both in northern Thailand) in the formation of Lan Na Thai (Million Thai Rice Fields), often written simply as Lanna. Lanna extended across northcentral Thailand to include Muang Sawa (Luang Prabang) and Wieng Chan (Vientiane).

Debate about whether Lanna was essentially Lao or Thai remains a hot topic in Laos today. There is evidence that both 'Lao' and 'Thai' were terms used by the people of this kingdom to describe themselves.

In the 14th century, as Lanna declined under pressure from the kingdom of Ayuthaya in central Siam, an exiled Lao warlord named Chao Fa Ngum

DID YOU KNOW?

The Tai tended to base their *meuang* along river valleys. Small vassal states developed in roughly concentric circles – known as mandala after the Sanskrit for circle, pronounced 'monthon' in Thai and Lao – around stronger principalities.

1353	1421
Fa Ngum declares himself king of Lan Xang	Lan Xang lapses into warring factions

ROYAL TREACHERY

As a child, Chao Fa Ngum was expelled from Muang Sawa along with his father, Chao Phi Fa, because the latter had seduced one of his own father's wives. The pair took refuge at the Angkor court of Jayavarman Paramesvara, where Fa Ngum eventually married the Khmer king's daughter, Nang Kaew Kaeng Nya, and became a favourite of the Angkor monarchy.

Upon the Khmer-sponsored invasion of Laos, Chao Phi Fa's plan to become the new ruler evaporated when he was killed during the conquest of Muang Sawa (Luang Prabang). Instead, Fa Ngum exiled his own grandfather and took the royal throne in 1353.

(also spelt Fa Ngoum) came to power seemingly out of nowhere. With the help of 10,000 Khmer troops, Fa Ngum seized Wieng Chan, the Phuan kingdom of Xieng Khuang, the Khorat Plateau (in northeastern Thailand) and finally Muang Sawa. In 1353 he declared himself king of the three territories, which he collectively renamed Lan Xang Hom Khao (Million Elephants, White Parasol).

Within 20 years of its founding, Lan Xang had expanded eastward to Champa and along the Annamite mountains in Vietnam. Fa Ngum became known as 'the Conqueror' because of his constant preoccupation with warfare. Unable to tolerate his ruthlessness any longer, Fa Ngum's ministers finally drove him into exile to the present-day Thai province of Nan in 1373, where he died five years later.

Fa Ngum's eldest son, Oun Heuan, succeeded him and took the title of Phaya Samsenthai (the Lord of 300,000 Thai; derived from a census of adult males living in Lan Xang in 1376). After marrying Thai princesses from Chiang Mai and Ayuthaya, Samsenthai reorganised and consolidated the royal administration of Lan Xang along Siamese lines, building many wat (temples) and schools. During Samsenthai's 43-year reign, Lan Xang became an important trade centre.

Theravada Buddhism became the state religion in Lan Xang when Samsenthai's successor King Visounarat accepted the Pha Bang, a gold Buddha image, from his Khmer sponsors. The image was initially kept in Muang Sawa, prompting the city's later name change to Luang Phabang (Great Pha Bang, more commonly spelt 'Luang Prabang' following an older Thai/Lao pronunciation). See Luang Prabang (p111) for further history related to this venerated image, which became the palladium of Lao sovereignty.

In 1421, Lan Xang lapsed into warring factions for the next 100 years. Twelve rulers succeeded one another during this period, most lasting only a year or two. Seven of these monarchs were installed by Samsenthai's daughter Nang Kaew Phimpha, who then took the throne herself to become Lan Xang's only female ruler. Deposed by her own ministers after a few months, she was tied to a stone and 'abandoned to the crows and vultures', according to Lao archives.

In 1520 King Phothisarat came to the throne and moved the capital to Wieng Chan to avoid Burmese aggression from the west. In 1545 he subdued the kingdom of Lanna and gained the throne of that kingdom for his son, Setthathirat. Five years later, after Phothisarat was crushed to death while trying to impress visiting ambassadors with his elephant-

DID YOU KNOW?

Surviving inscriptions from the Lan Xang era refer to inhabitants of the state as 'Thai', further fuelling the debate as to when the distinction between 'Thai' and 'Lao' began.

1520	1637
King Phothisarat moves the capital to Vientiane	King Suriya Vongsa takes the throne and rules for 57 years

roping talent, Setthathirat inherited the Lan Xang kingship. From Lanna he brought with him the Pha Kaew, or so-called Emerald Buddha (Lanna's equivalent to Lan Xang's Pha Bang). Setthathirat built Wat Pha Kaew in Wieng Chan to house the image and also ordered the construction of Pha That Luang, the country's largest Buddhist stupa (see p70).

Although Lan Xang was a large and powerful kingdom, its rulers were never able to fully subjugate the highland tribes of Laos. Xieng Khuang and Sam Neua in the mountainous northeast remained independent of Lan Xang rule, and subject to Chinese or Annamese influence. In 1571, King Setthathirat disappeared in the mountains on his way back from a military expedition into Cambodia, most likely a victim of rebellious highlanders.

Leaderless, Lan Xang declined rapidly over the next 60 years, dissolving into warring factions and subject to intermittent Burmese domination. Finally, in 1637 King Suriya Vongsa ascended the throne following a dynastic war. He ruled for 57 years, the longest reign of any Lao king, and was able to further expand Lan Xang's frontiers. These years are regarded as Laos's 'golden age', a historic pinnacle in terms of territory gains, prestige and power.

FRAGMENTATION & WAR WITH SIAM

Breaking New Ground in Lao History (2002) by Mayoury Ngaosrivathana and Kennon Breazeale (eds) includes writing by nine internationally recognised scholars, bringing Lao history up to date.

When King Suriya Vongsa died without an heir in 1694, a three-way struggle for the throne led to the break-up of Lan Xang. By the early 18th century, Suriya's nephew, under the stewardship of Annam (in Vietnam), had taken control of the middle Mekong River valley around Wieng Chan. A second, independent kingdom emerged in Luang Prabang under Suriya's grandsons. A third kingdom, Champasak, was established in the lower Mekong River area under Siamese influence.

Between 1763 and 1769 Burmese armies overran northern Laos and annexed the kingdom of Luang Prabang, while the Siamese took Champasak in 1778.

By the end of the 18th century, the Siamese had expanded their influence to include the kingdom of Wieng Chan and were also exacting tribute from Luang Prabang. The Siamese court installed Chao Anou, a Lao prince educated in Bangkok, as the vassal king of Wieng Chan. Anou restored the capital, encouraged a renaissance of Lao fine arts and literature, and improved relations with Luang Prabang.

Pressured by the Vietnamese into paying tribute to the Annamite empire, Chao Anou rebelled against Siam in the 1820s. The unsuccessful challenge resulted in the virtual razing of the Wieng Chan capital and the resettlement of many of its residents to Siam. Eventually the same fate overtook Luang Prabang and Champasak. By the late 19th century, almost the entire region between the Mekong and the Annamite Chain had been defeated and depopulated by the Thais, and Wieng Chan, Luang Prabang and Champasak had become Siamese satellite states.

In 1885, after successive invasions by the Annamese and the Chinese Haw (actually a loose affiliation of looting mercenaries of various ethnicities, including Yunnanese, Thai Dam, and French army deserters), the neutral states of Xieng Khuang and Hua Phan also agreed to Siamese protection. For their part, the Siamese desired these states as buffers against the expanding influence of the French in Vietnam.

1694	1885
The break-up of Lan Xang begins	The Lao kingdoms come under Siamese control

FRENCH RULE

After creating French protectorates in Tonkin and Annam in the late 19th century, France established a consulate at Luang Prabang – with Siamese permission – and soon convinced hat state to ask for protectorate status as well. Though Luang Prabang monarch Oun Kham is painted as a villain for having agreed to French protectorship, it's probable that his only feasible choice was between French or Siamese rule.

Through a succession of Siamese-French treaties between 1893 and 1907, the Siamese eventually relinquished control of all the territory east of the Mekong River, retaining everything to the west. The French united the remaining Lao principalities as one colonial territory and gave the country its modern name, Laos, the plural of Lao, in reference to the several Lao kingdoms that existed side by side. It was also under colonial rule that the French spelling of 'Vientiane' for Wieng Chan took hold.

Before they became part of French Indochina, none of the Lao kingdoms had ever been surveyed or mapped. The nation's present boundaries took shape between 1896 and 1897 through joint commissions with China, Britain and Siam.

Laos was never very important to France except as a buffer state between British-influenced Thailand (and British-occupied Burma) and the more economically important Annam and Tonkin. An 1866 French survey concluded that the Mekong was useless for commercial navigation, that no precious metals were readily available and that the country was too mountainous for large-scale plantations.

Nevertheless the French installed *corvée,* a system of draft labour in which every Lao male was forced to contribute 10 days of manual labour per year to the colonial government. In spite of producing tin, rubber and coffee, Laos never accounted for more than 1% of French Indochina's exports (opium was by far the most lucrative) and by 1940 only 600 French citizens lived in Laos.

The presence of the French undermined the traditional flexibility of Lao interstate relations and severed the most populous part of the Champasak kingdom by conceding Isan (northeastern Thailand, predominantly Lao in population) to Siam. Hence the French involvement in Laos resulted in a weakening of Lao states that probably could not have been achieved even by warfare.

The French also stifled the indigenous modernisation of Laos by imposing a Vietnamese-staffed civil service. The Lao government still labours under this legacy. In retrospect France's disregard for differences between the cultures west and east of the Annamite Chain – the historic dividing line between the Indianised and Sinicised cultures of Southeast Asia – was a major blunder, for almost as soon as the French left, the country was at war.

WWII & INDEPENDENCE

In 1945, the Japanese occupied French Indochina with the support of the Vichy regime. The Lao mounted little resistance, but were able to gain more local autonomy than they had enjoyed under the French.

Towards the end of the war, the Japanese forced the French-installed King Sisavang Vong to declare independence in spite of his loyalty to

DID YOU KNOW?

Throughout the Francophone world Laos was known as the land of the lotus-eaters, and resident *fonctionnaires* (civil servants) were regarded as among the most dissolute in the French Empire for their adoption of native mores.

1893–1907	1896–97
Siamese-French treaties give the French control of all territory east of the Mekong River	China, Britain and Siam create Laos's current boundaries

France. The prime minister and viceroy, Prince Phetsarat, not trusting Sisavang Vong, formed the resistance movement Lao Issara (Free Lao) to ensure that the country remained free of French colonial rule once the Japanese left.

When French paratroopers arrived in Vientiane and Luang Prabang in 1945, they had Sisavang Vong relieve Prince Phetsarat of his official positions and once again declared Laos to be a French protectorate. Phetsarat went underground, and with the Lao Issara in October 1945 drew up a new constitution proclaiming Laos independent of French rule. When Sisavang Vong refused to recognise the new document, he was deposed by the National Assembly.

Eventually, Sisavang Vong came around to the Lao Issara view of things and was reinstated as king in April 1946. This was the first time a Lao monarch actually ruled all of what is today called Laos. Two days after the coronation, French and Lao guerrillas (who called themselves the 'Free French') took Vientiane and smashed the Lao Issara forces, as well as resistance forces sent from Vietnam by Ho Chi Minh. Phetsarat and many of the Lao Issara fled to Thailand, where they set up a government-in-exile with Phetsarat acting as regent. This brutal suppression of the Lao Issara sent many recruits in Ho Chi Minh's direction.

By late 1946, the French were willing to concede autonomy to Laos and invited the Lao Issara to enter into formal negotiations. But the Lao Issara split into three factions. One faction, under Phetsarat, refused to negotiate with the French, insisting on immediate independence on Lao Issara terms. The second faction was headed by Phetsarat's half-brother, Prince Souvanna Phouma, who wanted to negotiate with the French in forming an independent Laos. The third was led by another half-brother, Prince Souphanouvong, who wanted to work out a deal with the Viet Minh under Ho Chi Minh.

The French proceeded without the cooperation of the Lao Issara and in 1949 held a French-Lao convention in which Laos was recognised as an 'independent associate state' that remained part of the French Union. The treaty gave Laos the right to become an independent member of the United Nations and for the first time Laos was recognised by the world as a separate nation. The Lao Issara dissolved, and Phetsarat remained in Thailand for most of the rest of his life.

Four years later, France granted full sovereignty to Laos via the Franco-Laotian Treaty of October 1953. By this time, the French were heavily preoccupied with the Viet Minh offensives in Vietnam and were looking to reduce their colonial burden.

DID YOU KNOW?

Born to a Lao mother and a Vietnamese father in Savannakhet in 1920, Kaysone Phomvihane spent much of his early life in Hanoi, where he studied law.

RISE OF THE PATHET LAO

In 1948, Prince Souphanouvong had gone to Hanoi to gain support from the Viet Minh for a Lao communist movement. Around this time, a young Lao named Kaysone Phomvihane was making headway among tribal minorities in the mountain districts of eastern Laos on behalf of Ho Chi Minh's Indochinese Communist Party (ICP).

In 1950, the Viet Minh–supported Free Lao Front (FLF; Neo Lao Issara) and the Lao Resistance Government under Prince Souphanouvong were founded in eastern Laos to fight the French.

1945	1945–49
The Japanese occupy Laos; King Sisavang Vong forced by the Japanese to declare independence	WWI ends; resistance to French rule widens

The next 25 years, until the Lao communist takeover in 1975, encompassed a somewhat bewildering succession of political changes. First, the ICP reconstituted itself as the Vietnamese Workers Party in 1951, with plans to organise separate covert parties in Laos and Cambodia as well. The first use of the term Pathet Lao (PL; Land of the Lao) came in an international communiqué released by the FLF in 1954 and referred specifically to the tactical forces of the FLF (and later the Patriotic Lao Front). In 1965, the name was changed to the Lao People's Liberation Army (LPLA) but, in international media, the term Pathet Lao became generally applied to the Vietnamese-supported liberation movement in Laos.

In 1953 and 1954, the kingdom of Laos was governed by a constitutional monarchy along European lines. A French-educated elite ran the government, but Lao resistance in the countryside increased, especially following the defeat of the French by Viet Minh troops at Dien Bien Phu in 1954.

The US government, anxious to counter the Viet Minh influence in Southeast Asia, began pouring aid into Laos to ensure loyalty to the 'democratic cause'. During this same period, Viet Minh and PL troops claimed the Northeastern Lao provinces of Hua Phan and Phongsali following the Geneva Conference of 1954, which sanctioned the takeover 'pending political settlement'.

In 1955, a clandestine communist party was officially formed in Sam Neua (Hua Phan Province). It was named the Lao People's Party (LPP) and consisted of 25 former ICP members. The LPP set up a tactical arm in early 1956 called the Lao Patriotic Front (LPF; known in Lao as Neo Lao Hak Sat or NLHS). Like its counterpart in Cambodia, the LPP was a member of the Indochinese United Front, which was led by the Vietnamese Workers Party.

COALITION & DISSOLUTION

By 1957, the participants at the Geneva Conference had finally reached a settlement. The LPF and the Royal Lao Government (RLG) agreed to a coalition government (under the RLG's Prince Souvanna Phouma) known as the Government of National Union. Two LPF ministers and their deputies were admitted at the national level.

According to the Geneva agreement, the 1500 PL troops in the northeast were to be absorbed into the Royal Lao Army, but disagreements over rank precluded a successful merger. When a 1958 National Assembly election in two northeastern provinces demonstrated unexpected LPF support among the general populace (13 out of 21 seats), there was a right-wing reaction that led to the arrest of LPF ministers and deputies, and the re-entrenchment of PL troops in the countryside. This government action was undoubtedly fuelled by the US government's withdrawal of all aid to Laos (which by this point made up the bulk of the Lao national budget) following the electoral results.

The fall of the Government of National Union left the Vientiane government under the dominance of the Committee for the Defence of National Interests (CDNI), which was made up of extreme right-wing military officers and French-educated elites. With powerful US backing, Phoui Sananikone was installed as prime minister and Souvanna Phouma was made the Lao ambassador to France. But within a year of their arrest,

DID YOU KNOW?

Laos's national seal features six symbols of the productive proletarian state: Vientiane's Pha That Luang (religion); rice fields (agriculture); gear cogs (industry); a dam (energy); a highway (transport); and a grove of trees (forestry).

1949	1950
Laos recognised as an 'independent associate state' of France	Communist-inspired Pathet Lao (PL) resistance government formed with Vietnamese support

Prince Souphanouvong and his LPF colleagues had escaped and were again leading the resistance in the countryside.

When a 1959 UN investigation declared that the PL was not using regular North Vietnamese troops, the Vientiane government was advised to adopt a more neutral policy towards the LPF.

It soon came out that the NVA were in fact helping the PL subjugate tribal mountain dwellers in the northeast. To counter the North Vietnamese presence, the USA renewed aid to Laos, this time for direct military use. In the summer of 1959 fighting broke out between the PL (and its North Vietnamese military advisers) and the RLG at the strategic Plain of Jars. The US dispatched Special Forces teams to train government troops in Laos, and in March 1960 the Central Intelligence Agency's (CIA's) infamous Air America took delivery of four helicopters in Laos.

Air America (1990) stars Mel Gibson and Robert Downey Jr, who squeeze comedy out of the exploits of the infamous CIA airline.

COUP & COUNTER-COUP

In August 1960, a neutralist military faction led by Kong Le seized Vientiane in a coup d'etat and recalled Souvanna Phouma from France to serve as prime minister. Rightist General Phoumi Novasan at first agreed to support the new government and to allow LPF participation, but later withdrew with his troops to southern Laos. In December, supplied with US guns and ammunitions, he launched an attack on Vientiane and wrested control from the neutralists in a CIA-rigged election. Kong Le and his troops retreated to Xieng Khuang, where they joined forces with the PL and North Vietnamese. The USSR supplied this coalition with armaments and by 1961 they held virtually all of Northern and eastern Laos.

A superpower confrontation threatened to erupt when US president John F Kennedy, in his first enunciation of the famous 'domino theory', announced that he would intervene with US troops to prevent a communist takeover of Laos. A 14-nation conference convened in Geneva in May 1961 to try to halt the crisis. In July 1962, after lengthy negotiations, a set of agreements was signed which provided for an independent, neutral Laos. The observance of these agreements was to be monitored by the International Commission for Supervision and Control (ICSC).

A second Government of National Union was formed the following month, a coalition of Prince Boun Oum (representing the rightist military), Souphanouvong (for the PL) and Souvanna Phouma (for the neutralist military). The US pulled out all 666 of its military advisers and support staff. Seven thousand North Vietnamese ground troops, on the other hand, remained in Laos, completely ignoring Geneva and the ICSC.

The second attempt at a coalition government didn't last long. Minor skirmishes occurred between PL and neutralist troops over the administration of the northeast. The PL seriously upset the tripartite balance of power with an unprovoked attack on Kong Le's neutralist headquarters in Xieng Khuang; Kong Le reacted by forming an alliance with the rightists.

In 1964, a rapid series of coups and counter-coups resulted in the final alignment of the PL on the one side and the neutralist and right-wing factions on the other. From this point on, the PL leadership refused to participate in any offers of coalition or national elections, believing they would never be given a voice in governing the country as long as either of the other two factions were in power. Instead they continued to look

1953	1957
Franco-Laotian Treaty grants full sovereignty to Laos	Formation of coalition Government of National Union

towards the North Vietnamese, allowing seven North Vietnamese Army (NVA) divisions into Northeastern Laos, in direct contravention of the Geneva accords.

WAR OF RESISTANCE

From 1964 to 1973, the war in Indochina intensified. US air bases were established in Thailand, and US bombers were soon crisscrossing eastern and northeastern Laos on bombing missions in North Vietnam and along the Ho Chi Minh trail. So that their orders to release all bombs would be fulfilled, B-52 captains would empty their bomb bays over eastern Laos when returning from Vietnamese air strikes. Secret saturation bombing of PL and NVA strongholds was carried out, but the PL simply moved its headquarters into caves near Sam Neua.

As guerrilla resistance in South Vietnam increased, the US military leadership began forming a special CIA-trained army in Laos to counter the growing influence of the PL. At first this army of 10,000 was largely made up of Hmong tribesmen under the direct command of the Royal Lao Army (RLA) General Vang Pao, himself a Hmong. A division of the RLA trained for mountain warfare, these troops were US- and Thai-trained, and US-paid. However, by the end of the 1960s, there were more Thais and Lao Thoeng than Hmong in the RLA.

A rotating number of US Air Force pilots, stationed in Long Cheng (spelt Long Tieng by the French) and Savannakhet, flew missions in northern and eastern Laos as forward air controllers (FACs), spotting PL and NVA targets for Lao- and Thai-piloted tactical bombers.

By 1971 Chinese troops were also engaged in Laos with an air defence force of between 6000 and 7000, mostly concentrated along the 'Chinese Road' (actually a complex of roads the Chinese were building in Luang Nam Tha, Udomxai and Phongsali Provinces). The Chinese maintained as many as 16,000 Chinese road workers in Laos throughout the war.

REVOLUTION & REFORM

In 1973, as the USA began negotiating its way out of Vietnam (via the Paris agreements), a ceasefire agreement was reached in Laos. The country was effectively divided into PL and non-PL zones, just as it had been in 1954, only this time the communists controlled 11 of the 13 provinces, instead of two. A Provisional Government of National Union (PGNU) was formed and the two sides began trying to form yet another coalition government. Meanwhile popular support for the PL was growing as the non-PL Vientiane leadership showed signs of corruption and manipulation by the US. The US finally began drawing back from Laos, and the last Air America aeroplane flew across the Mekong River to Thailand in June 1974.

The unexpectedly rapid fall of Saigon and Phnom Penh following US withdrawal in April 1975 led the PL to attack Muang Phu Khun, a strategic RLG- and Hmong-defended crossroads between Vientiane and Luang Prabang. It was a crushing defeat for the US-backed forces, and a symbolic final battle in the PL's long struggle.

On 4 May 1975, following concerted LP pressure, four non-LP ministers and seven generals resigned and an exodus of the Lao political and

Bombies (2002) is a poignant Canadian film documentary about the devastating after-effects of unexploded cluster bombs ('bombie' in Lao slang) dropped during the Second Indochina War.

The Ravens: Pilots of the Secret War of Laos (1989), by Christopher Robbins, is an impressive work on the US-directed Secret War, with plenty of historical context as well as tactical specifics.

THE SECRET WAR

From 1964 to 1973 Laos was a battlefield in a war that most of the Western world didn't know about. Basically a continuation of a struggle whose roots extended back centuries, the historical antagonists were the relatively peaceful Indianised cultures west of the Annamite Chain and the more expansionist Sinicised Vietnamese. These enemies were superseded by modern opponents playing native pawns (the Hmong and the Pathet Lao) against one another, while committing thousands of their own troops in support.

Both the USA and North Vietnam (along with China) acted in direct contravention of the Geneva Accord of 1962, which recognised the neutrality of Laos and forbade the presence of all foreign military personnel. To evade the Geneva agreement, the USA placed CIA agents in foreign-aid posts and temporarily turned air force officers into civilian pilots. The war was so secret that the name of the country was banished from all official communications; participants simply referred to operations in Laos as the 'Other Theater'.

As Christopher Robbins, in his book *The Ravens* (a code name for US pilots in Laos), has described:

> The pilots in the Other Theater were military men, but flew into battle in civilian clothes: denim cutoffs, T-shirts, cowboy hats and dark glasses…They fought with obsolete aircraft… and suffered the highest casualty rate of the Indochina War, as high as 50%…Each pilot was obliged to carry a small pill of lethal shellfish toxin, especially created by the CIA, which he had sworn to take if he ever fell into the hands of the enemy.

US military 'technicians' were in Laos as early as 1959, when they began training the Royal Lao Army (RLA) as well as Hmong hill tribe guerrillas under the charismatic Vang Pao. First used as anti-insurgent armies by the French in Vietnam, the Hmong became perhaps the most important human component of the US-financed Secret War. The so-called Armée Clandestine grew to 9000 troops by mid-1961 with nine CIA specialists, nine Special Forces officers ('Green Berets') and 99 CIA-trained Thai 'special service' officers in command of a force of Hmong, Lao and Thai foot soldiers. To this day the CIA effort in Laos remains the largest and most expensive paramilitary operation ever conducted by the USA.

The American forward air controllers ('Ravens') flew only small, slow prop planes used to fire white phosphorous smoke rockets to mark North Vietnamese Army (NVA) and PL targets for Lao pilots, who flew American-made jets.

Long Cheng was the clandestine headquarters for the Other Theatre. Its name didn't appear on any maps even though the American-Hmong military presence made it the second-largest city in the country and one of the busiest airports in the world. Sitting high in the mountains about halfway between Vientiane and the Plain of Jars, Long Cheng was usually referred to by the Air America code name 'Alternate', the Raven nickname 'Shangri-La' or the USAF designation LS ('Lima Site' or Landing Site) 20A.

commercial elite to Thailand began. PL forces seized the southern provincial capitals of Pakse, Champasak and Savannakhet without opposition and on 23 August they took Vientiane in a similar manner.

Lao People's Democratic Republic

Over the following months, the PGNU was quietly dismantled, and in December the Lao People's Revolutionary Party (LPRP) was declared the ruling party of the Lao People's Democratic Republic (LPDR). The takeover was bloodless; even the US embassy closed down for only one day.

1961	1962
US President Kennedy announces he will intervene to stop communist takeover of Laos	Vietnamese army defies Geneva Convention by remaining in Laos

Other towns and villages around the country with military landing strips were also called 'Lima Sites' and numbered (eg LS 32), and by the early 1970s there were over 400. Today Long Cheng is surrounded by the Saisombun Special Zone, a new administrative unit carved out of Luang Prabang and Xieng Khuang Provinces by the Lao military due to continuing 'security problems' related to Hmong army remnants in the area who have yet to yield ground to the Pathet Lao (PL).

Of the Americans who volunteered to serve in Laos as pilots, intelligence operatives or reconnaissance troops, an estimated 400 died in combat while over 400 others have been classified as 'missing in action' (MIA). The American presence in the western part of Laos, however, paled beside that of the NVA in eastern Laos, a side of the war most Western journalists never saw.

The illegal Vietnamese occupation was far greater than the US presence from beginning to end. By 1969 the entire North Vietnamese 316th Division was deployed in Laos, fielding a total of 34,000 combat troops, 18,000 support troops, 13,000 army engineers and 6000 advisers for the purpose of placing Long Cheng under siege.

Outnumbered and outmanoeuvred, the US-Hmong-Thai forces lost Long Cheng and scored few strategic victories during the nine-year Secret War, despite their superior firepower. They were also able to ignore virtually all the 'rules of engagement' (aka ROEs, nicknamed 'Romeos') that had to be observed in Vietnam (where they were often cited as an excuse for the US defeat). In Vietnam, for example, the ROEs prohibited bombing within 500m of a temple or hospital; in Cambodia there was a 1km limit. In Laos, bombardiers were free to decimate any building in their sights.

In support of Vang Pao's army alone, the Ravens and their native cohorts flew 1.5 times the number of air sorties flown in all of Vietnam. Totalling 580,944 sorties by 1973, the secret air force dropped an average of one planeload of bombs every eight minutes, 24 hours a day, for nine years! This cost US taxpayers around US$2 million per day.

After US President Lyndon Johnson halted all bombing raids on North Vietnam in November 1968, the bombing of Laos increased as more air power became available. In 1970 US President Richard Nixon, on the advice of Henry Kissinger, authorised massive B-52 air strikes in Laos, actions which remained highly classified until years later. Between 1964 and 1969 about 450,000 tonnes of ordnance had been let loose on the country, and afterwards that amount was fielded every year through to the end of 1972. By the war's end the bombing amounted to approximately 1.9 million metric tonnes in all, or over a half-tonne for every man, woman and child living in Laos. This makes Laos the most heavily bombed nation, on a per capita basis, in the history of warfare.

Defoliants and herbicides were also dropped on Laos by the secret air force. During 1965 and 1966, 200,000 gallons of herbicides were deposited along the Ho Chi Minh Trail near Sepon, laying bare all vegetation, poisoning civilian crops and rendering the water system unusable even for irrigation, much less drinking. Dubbed 'Agent Orange' and 'yellow rain' in the modern media, this toxic substance is responsible for a large number of infirmities suffered by the inhabitants of eastern Laos. The Lao government itself allegedly used Agent Orange captured from the RLG against its own citizens in Central Laos for two years following the 1975 PL takeover.

Kaysone Phomvihane, a longtime protégé of the Vietnamese communists who had helped to organise the Lao Issara resistance movement in the 1940s, served as prime minister until his death in November 1992. Kaysone's role in modern Lao politics cannot be overestimated; he was fluent in Lao, Vietnamese, Thai, Shan, French and English, and was considered a highly pragmatic ruler who learned from his mistakes.

The harsh political and economic policies of the LPRP's first two years of rule caused thousands to flee the country. The government followed the Vietnamese policy of 'accelerated socialisation' through a

1964	1964–73
Series of coups divides country into PL and neutralist / right-wing zones	Indochina War intensifies; US carpet-bombs eastern Laos

rapid reduction of the private sector and a steep increase in agricultural collectivisation. As well, the practice of Buddhism was severely curtailed (see Post-Revolution Buddhism p38).

Military campaigns by the government against its own citizens quickened the exodus of ethnic minorities. Although the war had technically ended in 1975, fighting in the interior continued for another two years, most of it pitting North Vietnamese and PL troops against highlanders in Luang Prabang and Xieng Khuang. The Phu Bia Plateau, a defiant Hmong homeland, was barraged with Soviet artillery, napalm bombs and chemical weaponry (including trichothecene or 'Agent Orange'). An estimated 10% of all Hmong in the country were killed during the course of the war, while others escaped to Thailand.

Bua Deng (Red Lotus; 1988) is a tale of an ordinary Lao family buffeted by events leading to the PL liberation of Vientiane, by Lao director Som-ok Southiphone. One of only a dozen or so Lao films produced since 1975, *Bua Deng* is the only one to have seen release outside of Laos.

Former King Imprisoned

After being forced to abdicate the throne – despite an earlier PL proposal endorsing a constitutional monarchy for post-Revolution Laos – Savang Vatthana was given a figurehead role in the new government as Supreme Adviser to the President. However, in early 1977 anticommunist rebels briefly seized Muang Nan, located 50km southwest of Luang Prabang. When government forces regained the village, the captured rebels supposedly implicated the former monarchy, and the king and his family were banished to a remote area of northern Laos on the Vietnamese border.

Although it was announced that the king, queen, and crown prince would be attending a *samana* (re-education camp), they were actually consigned to the cave prisons of Hua Phan – see Samana (Re-Education Camps) p152 – where they perished within four years due to inadequate food rations and the denial of medical treatment.

The Exodus

DID YOU KNOW?

The word 'communism' doesn't appear in any Lao government documents, not even the constitution, and the hammer and sickle were removed from the national seal in the early 1990s.

By mid-1979 repression had resulted in widespread unrest among the peasants, the traditional power-base for Lao communism. Liberal reforms were undertaken (see Post-Revolution Buddhism p38), but were too late to prevent the further reduction of an already small population. By the end of the 1970s, Lao refugees (including hill tribes), who had simply to cross the Mekong to escape, constituted 85% of all Indochinese with official refugee status in Thailand.

The Thai government eventually set a deadline for all Lao living in Thailand to return to their homeland or leave for a third country by 1 January 1995. All Lao refugee camps in Thailand were officially closed by the end of the 1990s.

LAOS IN THE 1980S & 1990S
Samana

As many as 40,000 people were sent to re-education camps called *samana* (*sǎmmanáa*, from the English seminar); see Samana (Re-Education Camps) p152. Some 30,000 were imprisoned for 'political crimes' following the 1975 PL takeover (the Union of Lao Organizations in the USA estimates the total number imprisoned at 160,000). A person's position in the old regime's hierarchy determined the length of stay; the higher the position,

1973	1975
Negotiations lead to ceasefire; Provisional Government of National Union (PGNU) formed	Royal government leaders flee Laos; Lao People's Democratic Republic (LPDR) formed

the longer they were subjected to manual labour and daily lectures on the glories of communism.

Since 1989 nearly all camps are reported to have closed and most political prisoners have been released. However, seven prisoners of conscience have received lengthy sentences in Hua Phan camps since 1992.

The influence of the former USSR's *glasnost* (public frankness and accountability) and *perestroika* (economic reconstruction) policies contributed to further reform in the LPDR during the 1980s in the form of *jintanáakqan mai* (new thinking; fancifully translated by some journalists as 'new economic mechanism'). Ever since then there has been a power struggle between the old hardliners and the younger and non-Party leadership, who seek further liberalisation.

In Laos, this is compounded by two conflicting tendencies for policy development. One tendency has been for the Lao leadership to follow the Vietnamese example, the other to implement policies that are developed specifically for the Lao situation. The second tendency has gained increasing strength during recent years. But the flourishing of a truly Lao system, if such a thing is possible, is still hampered by the Vietnamese ideological influence on Lao affairs, via high-ranking hardliners in the Lao government who received their military and political training in Hanoi. Younger pragmatists who push for liberalisation always run the risk of being labelled *pátíkqan* (reactionaries).

Bamboo Palace: Discovering the Lost Dynasty of Laos (2003) by Christpher Kremmer is a tightly written and well researched account of the Lao royal family's fate after the 1975 communist takeover.

Relations with Thailand

Another very significant influence on modern Laos is its relationship with Thailand. Immediately following the Revolution the Lao government banned practically all things Thai – including Thai university and Buddhist texts, previously central components of educational and religious literature in Laos. Friction grew as Thailand provided resources for huge camps housing thousands of Lao refugees. The conflict culminated in a three-month border war in late 1987 and early 1988 between the Lao and Thai armies in which over 100 Lao and Thai soldiers died.

The battle seemed to clear the air and the two neighbours have been closer than ever since the end of the 1980s. Thai investment remains by far the largest component of the country's foreign portfolio. Some Lao worry that Laos will be overwhelmed by Thai culture and by the Thais' business acumen, and that Laos will eventually become an 'economic province' of Thailand. Others say they would prefer living under Thai economic hegemony to remaining a political vassal of Vietnam.

As greater regional economic integration draws Laos into the larger Southeast Asian marketplace, the dual influences of Vietnam and Thailand should become more diffuse. Laos became a member of the Association of Southeast Asian Nations (Asean) in 1997.

DID YOU KNOW?

After 1975 around 300,000 Lao citizens – about 10% of the population – officially resettled abroad. Countless others simply blended into largely Lao-speaking northeastern Thailand.

CHALLENGES FOR THE FUTURE

Compared to the country's long history of civil and international conflict, the current state of Lao affairs seems relatively peaceful and stable. However, Lao party officials continue to maintain that absolutely no non–Communist Party members will ever be allowed a share in governing any part of Laos, and discontent among Lao is growing.

1975–77	1997
Policy of 'accelerated socialism' and curtailed practice of Buddhism prompts a huge exodus of Lao citizens	Laos becomes Association of Southeast Asian Nations (Asean) member

On 26 October 1999, during the annual Awk Phansa (end of the Buddhist rains retreat) festival, members of the Lao Students Movement for Democracy organised a demonstration in front of the Presidential Palace in Vientiane. No sooner had the demonstrators raised banners calling for peaceful political change than they were surrounded by police and either dispersed or arrested. Five student organisers remain imprisoned and the government fired a large number of secondary school teachers suspected of encouraging the protest.

In July 2000, 60 armed rebels captured an immigration office and border police station at Ban Wang Tao village in southern Laos, raising a Royal Lao flag and holding 15 Lao officials and civilians hostage. The ensuing clash with Lao government forces left five rebels dead, and sent 27 fleeing into Thailand, where they were arrested by Thai police. The group appeared to have launched the attack from within Thailand, leading to Lao accusations that the Thais were harbouring resistance forces, thus straining Thai-Lao relations for many months afterward.

A further setback in the perceived stability of the LPDR occurred that same year with a series of 15 minor bombings or attempted bombings in Vientiane, Savannakhet and Pakse. All involved hand grenades or small, handmade explosive devices tossed or placed in public venues, possibly the work of a group called Underground Government in Exile. See Terrorist Bombings p251 for further details on these explosions, plus an additional one in October 2003.

DID YOU KNOW?

The national flag consists of two horizontal bars of red (symbolising courage and heroism), above and below a bar of blue (nationhood) on which is centred a blank white sphere (the light of communism), sometimes also interpreted as a moon.

In February 2004 around 700 Hmong insurgents in Luang Prabang and Xieng Khuang provinces surrendered to Lao PDR authorities, who resettled them in lowland districts.

At the moment the situation in Laos seems relatively quiet but until the Lao government provides an escapé valve for public dissent, it can be assumed that trouble will brew from time to time.

The Vietnamese influence on Lao political affairs is still strong, thanks to continuing connections between ageing hardliners educated in Vietnam and their ideological mentors. The current president, 73-year-old Khamtay Siphandone was trained in Hanoi and has close links with the Vietnamese military establishment. The prime minister, Bounyang Vorachit, formerly served as the country's Finance Minister and is also considered a hardliner who is primarily influenced by Vietnamese political ideology, having graduated from the Institute of Political Economics in Vietnam.

2000	2004
15 minor bombings in Vientiane, Savannakhet and Pakse	700 Hmong insurgents surrender to the government

The Culture

THE NATIONAL PSYCHE

To a large degree 'Lao-ness' is defined by Buddhism, specifically Theravada Buddhism, which emphasises the cooling of the human passions. Thus strong emotions are a taboo in Lao society. *Kamma* (karma), more than devotion, prayer or hard work, is believed to determine one's lot in life, so the Lao tend not to get too worked up over the future. This trait is often perceived by outsiders as a lack of ambition.

The cultural contrast between the Lao and the Vietnamese is an example of how the Annamite Chain has served as a cultural fault line dividing Indic and Sinitic zones of influence. The French coined this saying: 'The Vietnamese plant rice, the Cambodians watch it grow and the Lao listen to it grow.'

The Lao commonly express the notion that 'too much work is bad for your brain' and they often say they feel sorry for people who 'think too much'. Education in general isn't highly valued, although this attitude is rapidly changing with modernisation. Avoiding any undue psychological stress, however, remains a cultural norm. From the typical Lao perspective, unless an activity – whether work or play – contains an element of *múan* (fun), it will probably lead to stress.

The Lao have always been quite receptive to outside assistance and foreign investment, since it promotes a certain degree of economic development without demanding a corresponding increase in productivity. The Lao government wants all the trappings of modern technology – the skyscrapers seen on socialist propaganda billboards – without having to give up any of the Lao traditions, among them the *múan* philosophy. The challenge for Laos in the future is to find a balance between cultural preservation and the development of new attitudes that will lead the country towards a measure of self-sufficiency.

Laos: Culture and Society (2000), by Grant Evans (ed), brings together a dozen essays on Lao culture, among them a profile of a self-exiled Lao family that eventually returned to Laos, and two well-researched studies of the modernisation and politicalisation of the Lao language.

LIFESTYLE

Due to Laos's ethnic diversity, 'Lao culture' only exists among the lowland Lao or Lao Loum, who represent about half the population. Lao Loum culture predominates in the cities, towns and villages of the Mekong River valley, ie in western Laos from Huay Xai to Pakse.

The Lao tend to live in extended families, with three or more generations sharing one house or compound. Women tend to control the family finances.

Most Lao don some portion of the traditional garb during ceremonies and celebrations – the men only a *phàa biang* (shoulder sash), the women a similar sash, tight-fitting blouse, and *phàa nung* (sarong). In everyday life a man dispenses entirely with traditional Lao clothing, dressing in the

---

DOS & DON'TS

- Always ask permission before taking photos.
- Don't prop your feet on chairs or tables while sitting.
- Never touch any part of someone else's body with your foot.
- Refrain from touching people on the head.
- Remove your shoes before entering homes or temple buildings.

international shirt-and-trousers style, as long as his clothing contributes to a neat and clean appearance, and as long as his hair is neat and short.

Women, on the other hand, often wear the *phàa nung* while going about their daily lives. Other ethnicities living in urban Laos – particularly Chinese and Vietnamese women – forego the *phàa nung* as daily wear, but even they must don the Lao sarong when they visit a police or prefecture office, or risk having any civic requests denied.

Lao women are more or less equal in the workforce, inheritance, land ownership and so on, often more so than in many Western countries. Lao Buddhism, however, commonly teaches that women must be reborn as men before they can attain nirvana, hence a woman's spiritual status, in general, does not equal that of a man.

As in neighbouring Thailand, gays and lesbians are usually accepted without much comment in Lao society. Transvestism, on the other hand, is much less common, perhaps reflecting the society's more conservative nature.

Because incomes are rock-bottom for virtually every occupation in Laos – US$100 per month could be considered middle-class in Laos – the Lao typically socialise as families, pooling their resources to enjoy a *bun wat* (temple festival) or picnic at the local waterfall together.

In fast-modernising Vientiane, lifestyles are evolving quickly, especially among Lao under the age of 35. In the capital the beginnings of the kind of age stratification typically seen in Thailand's larger cities or in the West are appearing – where teenagers hang out in one group, 20-somethings in another. Drug abuse and prostitution are beginning to enter the scene as well, with amphetamine use in particular becoming increasingly common throughout Vientiane Province.

POPULATION

One third of Laos's total population live in cities in the Mekong River valley, chiefly Vientiane, Luang Prabang, Savannakhet and Pakse. Another third live along other major rivers such as the Nam Ou, the Nam Seuang and Set Don.

DID YOU KNOW?

Foreign ethnographers who have carried out field research in Laos have identified anywhere from 94 to 132 different ethnic groups.

About one in 10 Lao fled the country after the 1975 communist takeover, half of them lowland Lao and the remainder a mixture of minorities. Vientiane and Luang Prabang lost the most inhabitants, with approximately a quarter of the population of Luang Prabang going abroad. Over the last decade or so this emigration trend has been reversed so that the influx of immigrants – mostly repatriated Lao, but also Chinese, Vietnamese and other nationalities – now exceeds the number of émigrés.

Most expatriate Westerners living in Laos are temporary contract employees of multilateral and bilateral aid organisations. A smaller number are employed by foreign companies involved in mining, petroleum and hydropower.

ETHNIC GROUPS

Laos is often described as less a nation state than a conglomeration of tribes and languages. The Lao traditionally divide themselves into four categories – Lao Loum, Lao Thai, Lao Thoeng and Lao Soung – roughly classified according to the altitude at which they live, and, by implication (not always accurate), their cultural proclivities.

About half the population are ethnic Lao or Lao Loum. Of the rest, 10% to 20% are tribal Thai, 20% to 30% are Lao Thoeng (lower mountain dwellers, mostly of proto-Malay or Mon-Khmer descent) and 10% to 20% are Lao Soung (Hmong or Mien tribes who live higher up).

The Lao government has an alternative three-way split, in which the Lao Thai are condensed into the Lao Loum group. This triumvirate is represented on the back of every 1000 kip bill, in national costume, from left to right: Lao Soung, Lao Loum and Lao Thoeng.

Small Tibeto-Burman hill-tribe groups in Laos include the Lisu, Lahu, Lolo, Akha and Phu Noi. They are sometimes classified as Lao Thoeng, but like the Lao Soung they live in the mountains of northern Laos.

Lao Loum

The Lao Loum (Lowland Lao) are the ethnic Lao who have traditionally resided in the Mekong River valley or along lower tributaries of the Mekong, and who speak the Lao language. Under the official government classification they are found at elevations of between 200m and 400m above sea level.

The Lao Loum culture has traditionally consisted of a sedentary, subsistence lifestyle based on wet-rice cultivation. The Lao, like all Austro-Thais, were originally animists who took on Theravada Buddhism as their main religion in the middle of the 1st millennium AD.

The distinction between 'Lao' and 'Thai' is a rather recent historical phenomenon, especially considering that 80% of all those who speak a language recognised as 'Lao' reside in northeastern Thailand. Even Lao living in Laos refer idiomatically to different Lao Loum groups as 'Thai', for example, Thai Luang Phabang (Lao from Luang Prabang).

Lao Thai

Closely related to the Lao, these Thai subgroups have resisted absorption into mainstream Lao culture and tend to subdivide themselves according to smaller tribal distinctions. Like the Lao Loum, they live along river valleys, but the Lao Thai have chosen to reside in upland valleys rather than in the lowlands of the Mekong floodplains.

The Lao Thai cultivate dry or mountain rice as well as wet, or irrigated, rice. In general, they have maintained animist beliefs and eschewed conversion to Buddhism or Christianity.

The various Lao Thai groups are distinguished from one another by the predominant colour of their clothing, or by general area of habitation; for example, Black Thai (Thai Dam), White Thai (Thai Khao), Forest Thai (Thai Pa), Northern Thai (Thai Neua) and so on.

To distinguish between the Siamese Thai and other Austro-Thai ethnic subgroups, some English-speaking Lao scholars use the spelling Tai to distinguish the Austro-Thais in general from the Siamese Thai subgroup in spite of the fact that the origins and pronunciation for this word differ not in the slightest from the word 'Thai'. The spelling 'Tai' also poses potential confusion with the Lao-Thai word *tai* (south), as in the Lao Tai (or Thai Tai) of Southern Laos.

Lao Thoeng

The Lao Thoeng (Upland Lao) are a loose affiliation of mostly Austro-Asiatic peoples who live on mid-altitude mountain slopes (officially from 300m to 900m) in northern and southern Laos. The largest group is the Khamu, followed by the Htin, Lamet and smaller numbers of Laven, Katu, Katang, Alak and other Mon-Khmer groups in the south. The Lao Thoeng are also known by the pejorative term *khàa*, which means 'slave' or 'servant'. This is because they were used as indentured labour by migrating Austro-Thai peoples in earlier centuries and more recently by the Lao monarchy. They still often work as labourers for the Lao Soung.

Ethnic Groups of Laos, Vols 1-3 (2003) by Joachim Schliesinger is, of all the modern ethnographies of Laos, the most complete and up to date. Schliesinger's scheme enumerates and describes 94 ethnicities in detail.

The Lao Thoeng have a much lower standard of living than any of the three other groups described here. Most trade between the Lao Thoeng and other Lao is carried out by barter.

The Htin (also called Lawa) and Khamu languages are closely related, and both groups are thought to have been in Laos long before the arrival of the lowland Lao, tribal Thai or Lao Soung. During the Lao New Year celebrations in Luang Prabang the lowland Lao offer a symbolic tribute to the Khamu as their historical predecessors and as 'guardians of the land'.

Lao Soung

The Lao Soung (High Lao) include those hill tribes who make their residence at altitudes greater than 1000m above sea level. Of all the peoples of Laos, they are the most recent immigrants, having come from Myanmar, Tibet and southern China within the last century.

The largest group is the Hmong, also called Miao or Meo, who probably number around 200,000 in four main subgroups, the White Hmong, Striped Hmong, Red Hmong and Black Hmong (the colours refer to certain clothing details). They are found in the nine provinces of the north plus Bolikhamsai in central Laos.

The agricultural staples of the Hmong are dry rice and corn raised by the slash-and-burn method. They also breed cattle, pigs, water buffalo and chickens, mostly for barter rather than for sale. The one Hmong cash crop is opium; they grow and manufacture more than any other ethnic group in Laos. The Hmong are most numerous in the provinces of Hua Phan, Xieng Khuang and Luang Prabang.

The second-largest group are the Mien (also called Iu Mien, Yao and Man), who number between 30,000 and 50,000 and live mainly in Luang Nam Tha, Luang Prabang, Bokeo, Udomxai and Phongsali. The Mien, like the Hmong, cultivate opium poppy.

The Mien and Hmong have many ethnic and linguistic similarities, and both groups are predominantly animist. The Hmong are considered more aggressive and warlike than the Mien, however, and as such were perfect for the CIA-trained special Royal Lao Government forces in the 1960s and early 1970s. Large numbers of Hmong-Mien left Laos and fled abroad following the 1975 revolution. A few Hmong resistance groups still exist in the mountains of Xieng Khuang and Sainyabuli Provinces.

'A few Hmong resistance groups still exist in the mountains of Xieng Khuang and Sainyabuli Provinces.'

Other Asians

As elsewhere in Southeast Asia, the Chinese have been migrating to Laos for centuries to work as merchants and traders. Most come direct from Yunnan but more recently many have also been arriving from Vietnam. Estimates of their presence varies from 2% to 5% of the total population. At least half of all permanent Chinese residents in Laos are said to live in Vientiane and Savannakhet. There are also thousands of temporary Chinese immigrants from Yunnan working as skilled labourers in the far north.

In southern Laos, especially in Champasak Province, live small numbers of Cambodians. Most commonly they work as truck drivers and boatmen and are involved in legal and illegal trade between Laos, Cambodia and Thailand.

Substantial numbers of Vietnamese live in all the provinces bordering Vietnam and in the cities of Vientiane, Savannakhet and Pakse. For the most part, Vietnamese residents in Laos work as traders and own small businesses, although there continues to be a small Vietnamese military presence in Xieng Khuang and Hua Phan Provinces. Many of the Vietnamese in urban areas are of ethnic Chinese origin.

SPORT

Football (soccer) and other stadium sports can occasionally be seen at the National Stadium in Vientiane. Interprovincial matches take place on fields or stadiums in each provincial capital.

Boxing

Though very popular, *múay láo* or Lao kickboxing is not nearly as developed a sport in Laos as its counterpart in Thailand and is mostly confined to amateur fights at upcountry festivals.

All surfaces of the body are considered fair targets and any part of the body except the head may be used to strike an opponent. Common blows include high kicks to the neck, elbow thrusts to the face and head, knee hooks to the ribs and low crescent kicks to the calf. A contestant may even grasp an opponent's head between his hands and pull it down to meet an upward knee thrust.

International boxing *(múay sàakọn)* is gaining popularity in Laos and is encouraged by the government in spite of the obvious Lao preference for the bang-up Southeast Asian version. At local festival programmes, an eight-match line-up might include three matches in the international style and five in the Lao-Thai style.

Kátâw

Kátâw, a contest in which a woven rattan – or sometimes plastic – ball around 12cm in diameter is kicked around, is almost as popular in Laos as it is in Thailand and Malaysia.

The traditional way to play *kátâw* is for players to stand in a circle (the size of the circle depends on the number of players) and simply try to keep the ball airborne by kicking it soccer-style. Points are scored for style, difficulty and variety of kicking manoeuvres.

A variation on *kátâw* – and the one used in local or international competitions – is played with a volleyball net, using all the same rules as in volleyball except that only the feet and head are permitted to touch the ball. It's amazing to see the players perform aerial pirouettes, spiking the ball over the net with their feet.

RELIGION
Buddhism

About 60% of the people of Laos – mostly lowland Lao, with a sprinkling of tribal Thais – are Theravada Buddhists. Theravada Buddhism was apparently introduced to Luang Prabang (then known as Muang Sawa) in the late 13th or early 14th centuries, though there may have been contact with Mahayana Buddhism during the 8th to 10th centuries and with Tantric Buddhism even earlier.

Lao Buddha: The Image & Its History (2000), by Somkiart Lopetcharat, is a large coffee-table book containing a wealth of information on the Lao interpretation of the Buddha figure.

King Visounarat – a successor of the first monarch of Lan Xang, King Fa Ngum – declared Buddhism the state religion after accepting the Pha Bang Buddha image from his Khmer sponsors. Today the Pha Bang is kept at Wat Manolom (p120) in Luang Prabang. Buddhism was fairly slow in spreading throughout Laos, even among the lowland peoples, who were reluctant to accept the faith instead of, or even alongside, *phïi* (earth spirit) worship.

Theravada Buddhism is an earlier and, according to its followers, less corrupted school of Buddhism than the Mahayana schools found in east Asia or in the Himalayan lands. It's sometimes referred to as the 'Southern' school since it took the southern route from India, its place of origin, through Sri Lanka and Southeast Asia (Myanmar, Thailand, Laos

POST-REVOLUTION BUDDHISM

During the 1964–73 war years, both sides sought to use Buddhism for their own propaganda purposes.

By the early 1970s, the Laos Patriotic Front (LPF) was winning the propaganda war in the religious sphere, as more and more monks threw their support behind the communist cause.

But major changes were in store for the Sangha (monastic order) following the 1975 takeover. Initially, Buddhism was banned as a primary school subject and people were forbidden to make merit by giving food to monks. Monks were also forced to till the land and raise animals in direct violation of their monastic vows.

Mass dissatisfaction among the faithful prompted the government to rescind the ban on the feeding of monks in 1976. By the end of that year, the government was not only allowing traditional alms-giving, it was offering a daily ration of rice directly to the Sangha.

In 1992, in what was perhaps its biggest endorsement of Buddhism since the Revolution, the government replaced the hammer-and-sickle emblem that crowned Laos's national seal with a drawing of Pha That Luang, the country's holiest Buddhist symbol.

Today the Department of Religious Affairs (DRA) controls the Sangha and ensures that the teaching of Buddhism is in accordance with Marxist principles. All monks now have to undergo political indoctrination as part of their monastic training. All the canonical and extracanonical Buddhist texts have been subject to 'editing' by the DRA, which makes sure that everything contained therein is congruent with the development of socialism in Laos. Monks are also forbidden to promote *phïi* (spirit) worship, which has been officially banned in Laos along with *säinyasqat* (magic). The cult of *khwăn* (the 32 guardian spirits attached to mental/physical functions), however, has not been tampered with.

One major change in Lao Buddhism was the abolition of the Thammayut sect. Formerly, the Sangha in Laos was divided into two sects, the Mahanikai and the Thammayut (as in Thailand). The Thammayut is a minority sect that was begun by Thailand's King Mongkut. Although the number of precepts or vows followed is the same for both sects, discipline for Thammayut monks has always been more strictly enforced.

The Pathet Lao objected to the Thammayut sect because it was seen as a tool of the Thai monarchy (and hence US imperialism – even though the Thammayut were in Laos long before the Americans were in Thailand) for infiltrating Lao political culture. For several years the new government also banned all Buddhist literature written in the Thai language. This severely curtailed the teaching of Buddhism in Laos, since Thailand has always been a major source of religious material. The Thammayut ban has also resulted in a much weaker emphasis on meditation, considered the spiritual heart of Buddhist practice in most Theravada countries. Overall, monastic discipline in Laos has become a great deal more lax than it was before 1975.

Nowadays there is only one monastic sect, the Lao Sangha *(sŏng láo)*. The ban on Thai Buddhist texts has been rescinded, however, and the government even allows Lao monks to study at Buddhist universities throughout Thailand.

and Cambodia), while the 'Northern' school proceeded north into Nepal, Tibet, China, Korea, Mongolia, Vietnam and Japan.

Theravada doctrine stresses the three principal aspects of existence: *dukkha* (suffering, unsatisfactoriness, disease), *anicca* (impermanence, transience of all things) and *anatta* (nonsubstantiality or nonessentiality of reality – no permanent 'soul'). Comprehension of *anicca* reveals that no experience, no state of mind, no physical object lasts. Trying to hold onto experience, states of mind, and objects that are constantly changing creates *dukkha*. *Anatta* is the understanding that there is no part of the changing world can we point to and say 'This is me' or 'This is God' or 'This is the soul'.

The ultimate goal of Theravada Buddhism is *nibbana* (Sanskrit: *nirvana*), which literally means the 'blowing-out' or 'extinction' of all causes of *dukkha*. Effectively it means an end to all corporeal or even heavenly existence, which is forever subject to suffering and which is conditioned from moment to moment by *kamma* (action). In reality, most Lao Buddhists aim for rebirth in a 'better' existence rather than the supramundane goal of *nibbana*. By feeding monks, giving donations to temples and performing regular worship at the local wat, Lao Buddhists acquire enough 'merit' (Pali *puñña*; Lao *bun*) for their future lives.

Lao Buddhists visit the wat on no set day. Most often they'll visit on *wán pha* (literally, 'excellent days'), which occur with every full, new and quarter moon, ie roughly every seven days. On such a visit typical activities include the offering of lotus buds, incense and candles at various altars and bone reliquaries around the wat compound, offering food to the monks, meditating, and attending a *thêt* (*Dhamma* talk) by the abbot.

MONKS & NUNS

Socially, every Lao Buddhist male is expected to become a *khúu-bạa* (monk) for a short period in his life, optimally between the time he finishes school and starts a career or marries. Men or boys under 20 years of age may enter the Sangha as *néhn* (novices) and this is not unusual since a family earns merit when one of its sons takes robe and bowl. Traditionally the length of time spent in the wat is three months, during the *phansǎa* (Buddhist lent) beginning in July, which coincides with the rainy season. However, nowadays men may spend as little as a week or 15 days to accrue merit as monks or novices.

There is no similar hermetic order for nuns, but women may reside in temples as *náang sǐi* (lay nuns), with shaved heads and white robes.

Spirit Cults

In spite of the fact that *phǐi* worship has been officially banned, it remains the dominant non-Buddhist belief system in the country. Lao citizens openly perform the ceremony called *su khwǎn* or *bạasǐi* (*baci* in the common French transliteration) in which the 32 *khwǎn* or guardian spirits are bound to the guest of honour by white strings tied around the wrists.

Each *khwǎn* is thought to act as a guardian over a specific organ or faculty – mental and physical – in a person's body. *Khwǎn* occasionally wander away from their owner, which is really only a problem when that person is about to embark on a new project or on a journey away from home, or when they're very ill. Then it's best to perform the *bạasǐi* to ensure that all the *khwǎn* are present and attached to the person's body.

Another obvious sign of the popular Lao devotion to *phǐi* can be witnessed in Vientiane at Wat Si Muang. The central image at the temple is not a Buddha figure but the *lák méuang* (city pillar), in which the guardian spirit for the city is believed to reside. Many local residents make daily offerings before the pillar.

Outside the Mekong River valley, the *phǐi* cult is particularly strong among the tribal Thai, especially the Thai Dam, who pay special attention to a class of *phǐi* called *then*. The *then* are earth spirits that preside not only over the plants and soil, but over entire districts as well. The Thai Dam also believe in the 32 *khwǎn*. The *mǎw* (master/shaman), who are specially trained in the propitiation and exorcism of spirits, preside at important Thai Dam festivals and ceremonies.

The Khamu tribes have a similar hierarchy of spirits they call *hrooi*. The most important *hrooi* are those associated with guardianship of house and village. Ceremonies involving the *hrooi* have been closed to non-Khamu observers, so very little has been written about them.

The Hmong-Mien tribes also practise animism, plus ancestral worship. Some Hmong groups recognise a pre-eminent spirit that presides over all earth spirits; others do not. The Akha, Lisu and other Tibeto-Burman groups mix animism and ancestor cults.

Other Religions

A small number of Lao – mostly those of the remaining French-educated elite – are Christians. A very small number of Muslims live in Vientiane, mostly Arab and Indian merchants whose ancestry as Laos residents dates as far back as the 17th century. Vientiane also harbours a small community of Chams, Cambodian Muslims who fled Pol Pot's Kampuchea in the 1970s. The latter now have their own mosque in Vientiane. In Northern Laos there are also pockets of Muslim Yunnanese, known among the Lao as *jiin háw*.

ARTS

The focus of most traditional art in Lao culture has been religious, specifically Buddhist. Yet, unlike the visual arts of Thailand, Myanmar and Cambodia, Lao art never encompassed a broad range of styles and periods, mainly because Laos has a much more modest history in terms of power and because it has only existed as a political entity for a short period. Furthermore, since Laos was intermittently dominated by its neighbours, much Lao art was destroyed or carried off by the Chinese, Vietnamese, Siamese or Khmer.

Unlike its neighbour to the east, Vietnam, Laos lacks a strong tradition of contemporary art.

Architecture

Traditional housing in Laos, whether in the river valleys or in the mountains, consists of simple wooden or bamboo-thatch structures with leaf or grass roofing. Among lowland Lao, houses are raised on stilts to avoid flooding during the monsoons, while the highlanders typically build directly on the ground.

L'Art du Laos (1954), by Henri Parmentier, is a thick, hard-to-find folio containing rare photographs of early Lao architecture and sculpture.

Colonial architecture in late 19th- and early 20th-century urban Laos consisted of thick-walled buildings with shuttered windows and pitched tile roofs in the classic French provincial style. Although many of these structures were torn down or allowed to decay following independence from France, today they are much in demand.

Buildings erected in post-Revolution Laos followed the socialist realism school that was enforced in the Soviet Union, Vietnam and China. Straight lines, sharp angles and an almost total lack of ornamentation were the norm for much of the 1970s and early 1980s.

More recently, a trend towards integrating classic Lao architectural motifs with modern functions has taken hold. Prime examples of this movement include Vientiane's National Assembly hall (Map pp68–9) and the Luang Prabang airport, both of which were designed by Havana- and Moscow-trained architect Hongkad Souvannavong. Other design characteristics, such as those represented by the Siam Commercial Bank on Th Lan Xang in Vientiane, seek to gracefully reincorporate French colonial features ignored for the last half-century.

Sculpture

Of all the traditional Lao arts, perhaps most impressive is the Buddhist sculpture of the period from the 16th to 18th centuries, the heyday of the kingdom of Lan Xang. Sculptural media usually included bronze,

TEMPLE ARCHITECTURE

The uposatha (Lao *sĭm*; ordination hall) is always the most important structure in any Theravada Buddhist wat. The high-peaked roofs are layered to represent several levels (always odd in number – three, five, seven or occasionally nine), which correspond to various Buddhist doctrines. The edges of the roofs almost always feature a repeated flame motif, with long, fingerlike hooks at the corners called *chaw fâa* (sky clusters). Umbrella-like spires along the central roof-ridge of a *sĭm*, called *nyâwt chaw fâa* or 'topmost *chaw fâa*', sometimes bear small pavilions or *naga*s (mythical water serpents) in a double-stepped arrangement representation of Mt Meru, the mythical centre of the Hindu-Buddhist cosmos.

There are basically three architectural styles for such buildings – the Vientiane, Luang Prabang and Xieng Khuang styles. The front of a *sĭm* in the Vientiane style usually features a large veranda with heavy columns which support an ornamented, overhanging roof. Some will also have a less-ornamented rear veranda, while those that have a surrounding terrace are Bangkok-influenced.

In Luang Prabang, the temple style is akin to that of the northern Siamese or Lanna style, hardly surprising as for several centuries Laos and northern Thailand were part of the same kingdoms. Luang Prabang temple roofs sweep very low, almost reaching the ground in some instances. The overall effect is quite dramatic, as if the *sĭm* were about to take flight. The Lao are fond of saying that the roof line resembles the wings of a mother hen guarding her chicks.

Very little remains of the Xieng Khuang style of *sĭm* architecture because the province was so heavily bombed during the Second Indochina War. Fortunately for admirers of temple art, a few examples of the Xieng Khuang style remain in Luang Prabang. As in the Vientiane style, the *sĭm* is raised on a multilevel platform, and the roof sweeps wide and low, as in the Luang Prabang style, but isn't usually tiered. Cantilevered roof supports play a much more prominent role in the building's overall aesthetics, giving the *sĭm*'s front profile a pentagonal shape. The pediment is curved, adding a grace beyond that of the pediments of the typical Luang Prabang and Vientiane pediments.

A fourth, less common style of temple architecture in Laos has been supplied by the Thai Lü, whose temples are typified by thick, whitewashed stucco walls with small windows, two- or three-tiered roofs, curved pediments and *naga* lintels over the doors and steps. Though there are examples of Thai Lü influence in a few Luang Prabang and Muang Sing temples, their main location is in Sainyabuli Province.

stone or wood and the subject was invariably the Lord Buddha or figures associated with the Jataka (*sáa-dók*; stories of the Buddha's past lives). Like other Buddhist sculptors, the Lao artisans emphasised the features thought to be peculiar to the historical Buddha, including a beaklike nose, extended earlobes, tightly curled hair and so on.

Two types of standing Buddha images are distinctive to Laos. The first is the 'Calling for Rain' posture, which depicts the Buddha standing with hands held rigidly at his side, fingers pointing towards the ground. This posture is rarely seen in other Southeast Asian Buddhist art traditions. The slightly rounded, 'boneless' look of the image recalls Thailand's Sukhothai style, and the way the lower robe is sculpted over the hips looks vaguely Khmer. But the flat, slablike earlobes, arched eyebrows and very aquiline nose are uniquely Lao. The bottom of the figure's robe curls upward on both sides in a perfectly symmetrical fashion that is also unique and innovative.

The other original Lao image type is the 'Contemplating the Bodhi Tree' Buddha. The Bodhi tree, or 'Tree of Enlightenment', refers to the large banyan tree that the historical Buddha purportedly was sitting beneath when he attained enlightenment in Bodhgaya, India, in the 6th century BC. In this image the Buddha is standing in much the same way as in the 'Calling for Rain' pose, except that his hands are crossed at the wrists in front of his body.

The finest examples of Lao sculpture are found in Vientiane's Haw Pha Kaew (p71) and Wat Si Saket (p71), and in Luang Prabang's Royal Palace Museum (p117).

Handicrafts

Among the Hmong and Mien hill tribes, silversmithing plays an important role in 'portable wealth' and inheritances. Silversmithing and goldsmithing are traditional lowland Lao arts as well but in recent years these have been in decline.

Mats and baskets woven of various kinds of straw and reed are also common and are becoming a small but important export to Thailand. Among the best baskets and mats are those woven by the Htin (Lao Thoeng).

Paper handcrafted from *sǎa* (the bark of a mulberry tree) is common in northwestern Laos, and is available in Vientiane and Luang Prabang. Environmentally friendly *sǎa* is a renewable paper resource that needs little processing compared with wood pulp.

See Shopping p260 for more on handicrafts in Laos.

Music & Dance

Lao classical music was originally developed as court music for royal ceremonies and classical dance-drama during the 19th-century reign of Vientiane's Chao Anou, who had been educated in the Siamese court in Bangkok. The standard ensemble for this genre is the *sep nyai* and consists of *khâwng wóng* (a set of tuned gongs), the *ranyâat* (a xylophonelike instrument), the *khui* (bamboo flute) and the *pii* (a double-reed wind instrument similar to the oboe) – the same instruments are used in the Thai *pii-phâat* ensemble.

The practice of classical Lao music and drama has been in decline for some time – 40 years of intermittent war and revolution has simply made this kind of entertainment a low priority among most Lao. Generally, the only time you'll hear this type of music is during the occasional public performance of the *Pha Lak Pha Lam,* a dance-drama based on the Hindu Ramayana epic.

Not so with Lao folk and pop, which have always stayed close to the people. The principal instrument in folk, and to a lesser extent in pop, is the *kháen* (common French spelling: *khene*), a wind instrument that is devised of a double row of bamboolike reeds fitted into a hardwood soundbox and made air-tight with beeswax. The rows can be as few as four or as many as eight courses (for a total of 16 pipes), and the instrument can vary in length from around 80cm to 2m. An adept player can produce a churning, calliope-like dance music. The most popular folk dance is the *lám wóng* (circle performance) in which couples dance circles around one another until there are three circles in all: a circle danced by the individual, a circle danced by the couple, and one danced by the whole crowd.

MǍW LÁM

The Lao folk idiom also has its own musical theatre, based on the *mǎw lám* tradition. *Mǎw lám* is difficult to translate but roughly means 'master of verse'. Led by one or more vocalists, performances always feature a witty, topical combination of talking and singing that ranges across themes as diverse as politics and sex. Very colloquial, even bawdy, language is employed. This is one art form that has always bypassed government censors, whether the French or the Lao People's Revolutionary Party (LPRP), and has provided an important outlet for grass-roots expression.

TEXTILES

Laos boasts over a dozen weaving styles across four regions. Southern weavers, who often use foot looms rather than frame looms, are known for the best silk weaving and for intricate *mat-mii* (ikat or tie-dye) designs that include Khmer-influenced temple and elephant motifs. In these provinces, beadwork is sometimes added to the embroidery. One-piece *phàa nung* (sarongs) are more common than those sewn from separate pieces.

In northeastern Laos, tribal Thai produce weft brocade *(yìap kǫ)* using raw silk, cotton yarn and natural dyes, sometimes with the addition of *mat-mii* techniques. Large diamond patterns are common.

In central Laos, typical weavings include indigo-dyed cotton *mat-mii* and minimal weft brocade *(jók* and *khit)*, along with mixed techniques brought by migrants to Vientiane.

Gold and silver brocade is typical of traditional Luang Prabang patterns, along with intricate patterns and imported Thai Lü designs. Northerners generally use frame looms; the waist, body and narrow *sín* (bottom border) of a *phàa nung* are often sewn together from separately woven pieces.

Natural sources for Lao dyes include ebony (both seeds and wood), tamarind (seeds and wood), red lacquer extracted from the *Coccus iacca* (a tree-boring insect), turmeric (from a root) and indigo. A basic palette of five natural colours – black, orange, red, yellow and blue – can be combined to create an endless variety of other colours. Other unblended, but more subtle, hues include khaki (from the bark of the Indian trumpet tree), pink (sappanwood) and gold (jackfruit and breadfruit woods).

Diverse other instruments, including electric guitar, electric bass and drums, may supplement the basic *kháen*/vocalist ensemble. Versions that appear on Lao national television are usually much watered down to suit 'national development'.

There are several different types of *mǎw lám*, depending on the number of singers and the region the style hails from. *Mǎw lám khuu* (couple *mǎw lám*), for example, features a man and woman who engage in flirtation and verbal repartee. *Mǎw lám jót* (duelling *mǎw lám*) has two performers of the same gender who 'duel' by answering questions or finishing an incomplete story issued as a challenge – not unlike free-style rap.

Northern Lao *kháen*-based folk music is usually referred as *kháp* rather than *lám*.

Authentic live *mǎw lám* can be heard at temple fairs and on Lao radio. CDs and audio cassettes can be purchased in larger towns and cities. Among the most notable Lao *mǎw lám* artists are Daomuang Tai, Noy Vilaset, Chantho Sopha and Phou Vieng.

LAO POP

Mainstream Lao pop owes much to Thai-style *lûuk thûng*, with syrupy arrangements that combine cha-cha and bolero rhythms with Lao-Thai melodies. Popular mainstays of Lao *lûuk thûng* include singers Bua Ngoen and Sombat Keokamdi.

Over the last five or so years more international influences have crept into Lao pop, creating such local stars as Thidavanh Bounxouay, a Lao-Bulgarian singer more popularly known as 'Alexandra', and Overdance, the country's first dance-oriented rap/funk/hip-hop band.

Traditional Music of the Lao (1985), by Terry Miller, although mainly focused on northeast Thailand, is the only book-length work yet to appear on Lao music, and is very informative.

Literature

Of all classical Lao literature, *Pha Lak Pha Lam,* the Lao version of the Indian epic the Ramayana, is the most pervasive and influential in the culture. The Indian source first came to Laos with the Hindu Khmer approximately 900 years ago as stone reliefs which appeared on Wat Phu Champasak and other Angkor-period temples built in what is now Central and Southern Laos. Oral and written versions may also have been available; eventually, though, the Lao developed their own version of the epic, which differs greatly both from the original and from Thailand's *Ramakian*.

Of the 547 Jataka tales in the *Pali Tipitaka* (tripartite Buddhist canon) – each chronicling a different past life of the Buddha – most appear in Laos almost word-for-word as they were first written down in Sri Lanka. A group of 50 'extra' or apocryphal stories – based on Lao-Thai folk tales of the time – were added by Pali scholars in Luang Prabang between 300 and 400 years ago. Laos's most popular Jataka is an old Pali original known as the Mahajati or Mahavessandara (Lao: Pha Wet), the story of the Buddha's penultimate life. Interior murals in the *sǐm* of many Lao wat typically depict this Jataka as well as others.

Contemporary literature has been hampered by decades of war and communist rule. Only in 1999 was the first collection of contemporary Lao fiction, Ounthine Bounyavong's *Mother's Beloved: Stories from Laos*, published in a bilingual Lao and English edition.

Detailed information on Lao *mǎw lám*, including audio samples can be found at http://wattay -pro.com/morlum.html.

Environment

THE LAND

Covering an area slightly larger than Great Britain, landlocked Laos shares borders with China, Myanmar, Thailand, Cambodia and Vietnam. Rivers and mountains dominate, folding the country into a series of ridges and valleys extending westward from the Lao-Vietnamese border.

Mountains and plateaus cover well over 70% of the country. Running about half the length of Laos, parallel to the course of the Mekong River, is the Annamite Chain, a rugged mountain range with peaks averaging between 1500m and 2500m in height. Roughly in the centre of the range is the Khammuan Plateau, an area of striking limestone grottoes and gorges. At the southern end of the Annamite Chain stands the 10,000-sq-km Bolaven Plateau, an important area for the cultivation of high-yield mountain rice, coffee, tea and other crops that flourish at higher altitudes.

The larger, northern half of Laos is made up almost entirely of broken, steep-sloped mountain ranges. The highest mountains are found in Xieng Khuang Province (p140), including Phu Bia, the country's highest peak at 2820m. Just north of Phu Bia stands the Xieng Khuang plateau, the country's largest mountain plateau, which rises 1200m above sea level.

DEVELOPMENT OF THE MEKONG

The 12th-longest river in the world, and 10th-largest in terms of volume, the Mekong is also one of the world's most untamed waterways. Before the completion of the Thai-Lao Friendship Bridge in 1993, not a single span crossed its Southeast Asian length, and in Laos it is still undammed. Except in Vietnam's Mekong Delta, there are no large cities or industrial zones anywhere along its banks. Long the main artery of travel within Laos, especially by ferry and speedboat, the Mekong is now increasingly giving way to the all-weather roads that run north and south of Vientiane.

Marco Polo was probably the first European to cross the Mekong, a feat he accomplished in the 13th century. In the 16th century a group of Portuguese emissaries forded the river at Vientiane, and in the following century the Dutch merchant Geritt van Wuystoff arrived by boat. The Treaty of Bangkok, signed by the French and Siamese on 30 October 1893, officially designated the river as the border between Siam and French Indochina.

Now with peace and relative stability in Laos, the nation's hydroelectric and navigation potential is being tapped. Up to dozen hydroelectric facilities and dams are planned, and there is talk of blasting the upper Mekong (north of Luang Prabang) to make it navigable year-round. The river's hydroelectric potential alone is equivalent to the entire petroleum production of Indonesia. Pa Mong, a yet-to-be-built 210m-long dam planned north of Vientiane, would flood at least 609 sq km and result in the relocation of 43,000 people. Upstream, the Chinese government plans to build over 20 dams along the Mekong and its tributaries over the next 25 years, much to the chagrin of the countries further downstream. So far two have been completed and a third (which will be the second-largest dam in China after the Three Gorges project) is under construction.

The Mekong Committee (Committee for Coordination of Investigations of the Lower Mekong Basin), set up in 1957 under UN auspices to coordinate development of irrigation, electricity, flood control, fishing and navigation, has been revived as the Mekong River Commission. Member states include Thailand, Cambodia, Laos, Vietnam, China and Myanmar.

Although the six countries each have their own set of priorities, the Chiang Rai Accord signed by the members of the Commission in 1995 allows five of the six the means to settle disputes – an important step in coordinating regional development. Cambodia and Vietnam have the most to lose from exploitation of the Mekong, since they are last in line for its resources. In the meantime Beijing has refused to sign the accord, and thus China holds the key to the Mekong's future.

The most famous part of the plateau is the Plain of Jars (p145), an area dotted with huge prehistoric stone jars of unknown origin.

Springing forth over 4000km from the sea, high up on the Tibetan Plateau, the Mekong River so dominates Lao topography that, to a large extent, the entire length of the country parallels its course. Although half of the Mekong's length runs through China, more of the river courses through Laos than through any other Southeast Asian country. At its widest, near Si Phan Don in the south, the river can measure 14km across during the rainy season. The Mekong's middle reach is navigable year-round, from Heuan Hin (north of the Khemmarat Rapids in Savannakhet) to Kok Phong, Luang Prabang.

DID YOU KNOW?

The Mekong River is known as Lancang Jiang (Turbulent River) in China; Mae Nam Khong in Thailand, Myanmar and Laos; Tonle Thom (Great Water) in Cambodia and Cuu Long (Nine Dragons) in Vietnam.

The fertile Mekong River flood plain, running from Sainyabuli to Champasak, forms the flattest and most tropical part of Laos. Virtually all of the domestic rice consumed in Laos is grown here, and most other farming takes place here as well. The Mekong and its tributaries are also an important source of fish, a mainstay of the Lao diet. The two largest valley sections surround Vientiane and Savannakhet, which, not surprisingly, are the major population centres.

Major tributaries of the great river include the Nam Ou and the Nam Tha, both of which flow through deep, narrow limestone valleys from the north, and the Nam Ngum, which flows into the Mekong across a broad plain in Vientiane Province. The Nam Ngum is the site of a large hydroelectric plant that is a primary source of power for Vientiane area towns and a secondary source for neighbouring Thailand.

All the rivers and tributaries west of the Annamite Chain drain into the Mekong, while waterways east of the Annamites (in Hua Phan and Xieng Khuang Provinces only) flow into the Gulf of Tonkin off the coast of Vietnam.

WILDLIFE

Laos boasts one of the least disturbed ecosystems in Asia due to its overall lack of development and low population density.

Animals

As in Cambodia, Vietnam, Myanmar and much of Thailand, most of the fauna in Laos belong to the Indochinese zoogeographic realm (as opposed to the Sundaic domain found south of the Isthmus of Kra in southern Thailand or the Palaearctic to the north in China).

Wildlife Trade in Laos: The End of the Game (2001), by Hanneke Nooren & Gordon Claridge, is a frightening description of animal poaching in Laos.

Nearly half of the animal species native to Thailand are shared by Laos, often in greater numbers due to higher forest cover and fewer hunters. Notable mammals endemic to Laos include the concolour gibbon, snub-nosed langur, lesser panda, raccoon dog, pygmy slow loris, giant muntjac, Lao marmoset rat and Owston's civet. Other exotic species, common to an area that overlaps neighbouring countries in mainland Southeast Asia, are a number of macaques (such as pig-tailed, stump-tailed, Assamese and rhesus), Phayre's leaf monkey, François' leaf monkey, Douc langur, Malayan and Chinese pangolins, Siamese hare, six species of flying squirrel, 10 species of nonflying squirrel, 10 species of civet, marbled cat, Javan and crab-eating mongoose, spotted linsang, leopard cat, Asian golden cat, bamboo rat, yellow-throated marten, lesser mouse deer, serow (sometimes called Asian mountain goat), goral (another type of goat-antelope) and 69 species of bats.

Between 200 and 500 wild Asiatic elephants roam open-canopy forest areas throughout the country, mainly in Sainyabuli Province west of Vientiane and along the Nakai Plateau in central eastern Laos. In the lat-

---

CRUELTY TO ANIMALS

Live frogs in large metal bowls with their legs sewn together; a live cow tied to the back step of a *sǎwngthǎew* (passenger truck); a river turtle plucked from the Nam Ou and slung over a fisherman's shoulder by a rope strung through its shell; and live turkeys or chickens carried upside down by their feet: would you consider any of the foregoing as 'cruelty to animals'? If so then you're in for a theatre of cruelty in Laos, since – with only the rare slaughterhouse or butcher shop in existence – many rural people themselves deal with all the messy bits involved in transporting and processing animal protein.

Harder to understand, at least for many Westerners, is the taking of monkeys and other animals from the jungle to be kept as pets, usually tied by a rope or chain to a tree, or confined to cages. Yet this, too, is an inevitable part of the Lao scene.

---

ter region Vietnamese poachers kill elephants for their meat and hides. Around 1000 to 1300 captive or domesticated elephants – used for logging and agriculture – can be found around the country, mostly in Sainyabuli, Udomxai, Champasak and Attapeu Provinces. In total number of work elephants, Laos ranks fourth in Asia after Myanmar, Thailand and India, but in its ratio of elephants to people it ranks first with one elephant per 3920 people; the second closest, Myanmar, has only one per 7130. The Lao government keeps a rare albino elephant in Vientiane as a legitimator of its power – just as all Lao kings since Fa Ngum have done. This elephant is rarely seen in public.

Herpetofauna include numerous snake varieties, of which six are venomous: the common cobra, king cobra (hamadryad), banded krait, Malayan viper, green viper and Russell's pit viper. The country's many lizard species include two commonly seen in homes and older buildings, the *káp-kǎe* (gecko) and the *jî-jîan* (smaller house lizard), as well as larger species like the black jungle monitor.

The forests and mountains of Laos harbour a rich selection of resident and migrating bird species. Surveys carried out by a British team of ornithologists in the 1990s recorded 437 species, including eight globally threatened and 21 globally near-threatened species. Notable among these are Siamese fireback pheasant, green peafowl, red-collared woodpecker, brown hornbill, tawny fish-owl, Sarus crane, giant ibis and the Asian golden weaver. The urban bird populations are noticeably thin as a result of bird hunting; in the city centres of Vientiane or Savannakhet it's not uncommon to see someone pointing a long-barrelled musket at upper tree canopies, even on monastery grounds where killing is supposedly not permitted.

DID YOU KNOW?

The spindlehorn was one of only three land mammals to earn its own genus in the 20th century.

ENDANGERED SPECIES

An exciting regional zoological discovery made in 1992 in Vietnam was the presence of the spindlehorn (*Pseudoryx nghethingensis;* known as the *saola* in Vietnam, *nyang* in Laos), a horned mammal found in the Annamite Chain along the Lao-Vietnamese border. Surveys in 1993 and 1994 confirmed the existence of the animal in Laos. The spindlehorn, which was described in 14th-century Chinese journals, was long thought not to exist. Unfortunately horns taken from spindlehorn are a favoured trophy among certain groups on both sides of the Lao-Vietnamese border and it is very much an endangered species.

The Wildlife Conservation Society has also found new species of muntjac, rabbit, squirrel and warbler. Like the *nyang*, some of these have also been found in Vietnam, but according to the International Union for Conservation of Nature and Natural Resources (IUCN), 'the prospects for continuing species survival would appear to be better in the Lao PDR [People's Democratic Republic] than in Vietnam'. A case in point is the presence in Laos of Vietnam warty pig *(Sus bucclentes),* a species last recorded in Vietnam in 1892 and until recently considered extinct.

A few Javan one-horned and/or Sumatran two-horned rhinos, probably now extinct in Thailand, are thought to survive in the Bolaven Plateau area (p218). Sightings of kouprey, a wild cattle extinct elsewhere in Southeast Asia, have been reported in Attapeu (p242) and Champasak (p211) Provinces as recently as 1993.

Becoming increasingly rare, due to habitat loss, hunting and collecting, are the endangered Eld's deer, black-cheeked gibbon, Asiatic jackal, Asiatic black bear, Malayan sun bear, Malayan tapir, barking deer, sambar (a type of deer), gaur, banteng (gaur and bantengs are types of wild cattle), Siamese crocodile, leopard, tiger and clouded leopard.

Another of the creatures thought to be most seriously endangered in Laos is the Irrawaddy dolphin, native to the southern Mekong. At present around 50 dolphins are thought to survive, but experts say they will have disappeared in 10 years or less if gill-net fishing on the Cambodian side of the border is not halted or controlled.

DID YOU KNOW?

The giant Mekong catfish may grow up to 3m long and weigh as much as 300kg. Due to Chinese blasting of shoals in the Upper Mekong, it now faces extinction in the wild.

Plants

As in other parts of tropical mainland Southeast Asia, with distinctive dry seasons of three months or more, most indigenous vegetation is associated with monsoon forests. In such forests many tree varieties shed their leaves during the dry season to conserve water. Rainforests – which are typically evergreen – don't exist in Laos, although nonindigenous rainforest species such as the coconut palm are commonly seen in the lower Mekong River valley.

Monsoon forests typically grow in three canopies. Dipterocarps – tall, pale-barked, single-trunked trees that reach as high as 30m – dominate the top canopy of the deciduous monsoon forest, while a middle canopy consists of teak, padauk (sometimes called 'Asian rosewood') and other hardwoods. Underneath is a variety of smaller trees, shrubs, grasses and – along river habitats – bamboo. In certain plateau areas of the south are dry dipterocarp forests in which the forest canopies are more open, with less of a middle layer and more of a grass-and-bamboo undergrowth. Parts of the Annamite Chain are covered by tropical montane evergreen forest, while tropical pine forests can be found on the Nakai Plateau and Sekong area to the south.

DID YOU KNOW?

Opium has been cultivated and used in Laos for centuries but the country didn't become a major producer until the passing of the 1971 Anti-Narcotics Law, a move that helped drive up regional prices steeply.

According to the IUCN, natural unmanaged vegetation covers 85% of Laos and about half the country bears natural forest cover. Of these woodlands about half can be classified as primary forest – a very high proportion in this day and age – while another 30% or so represents secondary growth. In Southeast Asia, only Cambodia boasts a higher percentage of natural forest cover; worldwide Laos ranks 11th.

In addition to teak and padauk, the country's flora includes a toothsome array of fruit trees, bamboo (more species than any country outside Thailand and China) and an abundance of flowering species such as the orchid. In the high plateaus of the Annamite Chain, extensive grasslands or savanna are common.

NATIONAL PROTECTED AREAS (NPAs)

Laos boasts one of the youngest and most comprehensive protected area systems in the world. In 1993 the government set up 18 National Biodiversity Conservation Areas, comprising a total of 24,600 sq km, or just over 10% of the country's land mass. It did this following sound scientific consultation rather than creating areas on an ad hoc basis (as most other countries have done). Two more were added in 1995, for a total of 20 protected areas covering 14% of Laos.

Recently the Lao PDR government renamed as these National Protected Areas (NPAs). International consulting agencies have recommended an additional nine sites but these have yet to materialise.

Most NPAs are in southern Laos, which, contrary to popular myth, bears a higher percentage of natural forest cover than the north. These units are not preserves: forests encompassed by this designation, for example, are divided into production forests for timber, protection forests for watershed and conservation forests for pure conservation. The largest of the NPAs, Nakai-Nam Theun, covers 3710 sq km and is home to the recently discovered spindlehorn (see p47) as well as several other species unknown to the scientific world a decade ago.

Among the most accessible and rewarding NPAs for wilderness travel are the Nam Ha NPA (see Nam Ha National Protected Area, p166) in Luang Nam Tha, the Nakai-Nam Theun NPA (p191) on the Vietnamese border and the Phu Hin Bun (Khammuan Limestone; p194) NPA to the east of Tha Khaek. The wildlife in these areas – from rare birds to wild elephants – is abundant, and the best overall time to view wildlife in all three NPAs is just after the monsoon season has ended, in November. Local tour operators can assist in organising visits to these three NPAs.

Laos has one officially declared national park, Phu Khao Khuay NPA (p98), near Vientiane. What sets Phu Khao Khuay apart from the NPAs is that it is preserved for public recreation, complete with opening hours and a nominal admission fee.

DID YOU KNOW?

Around 85% of Laos is mountainous terrain, and less than 4% is considered arable.

ENVIRONMENTAL ISSUES

Although major disruptions were wreaked on the eastern section of Laos along the Ho Chi Minh Trail, where herbicides, defoliants and bombs were used in abundance during the Second Indochina War, and logging in central Laos is proceeding at a sometimes alarming rate, Laos has one of the most pristine ecologies in mainland Southeast Asia. This makes it of major importance for world wildlife conservation. Many of the plant and animal species found within its borders, though decreasing in numbers, face less risk of extinction than in neighbouring countries, mainly due to the comparative lack of population pressure in Laos.

The majority of Lao citizens derive most of their protein from food culled from nature, not from farms or ranches. How threatening this is to species survival in Laos is debatable given the nation's extremely sparse population. In the more densely populated areas of the country such as Savannakhet Province, the overfishing of lakes and rivers is posing a danger to certain fish species.

The cross-border trade in wildlife is also potentially serious. Much of the poaching that takes place in Laos's NPAs is allegedly carried out by Vietnamese hunters who have crossed into central Laos illegally to round up such species as pangolins, civets, barking deer, goral and raccoon dogs to sell back home.

One of the biggest obstacles facing environmental protection in Laos is corruption among those in charge of enforcing conservation regulations. Illegal timber felling, poaching and the smuggling of exotic wildlife species would decrease sharply if corruption among officials was properly tackled. Even Lao military personnel are known to use explosives to catch fish in lakes and rivers.

Mekong (2000), by Milton Osborne, is a fascinating cultural history of the Mekong that spans 2000 years of exploration, mapping and war.

Other threats facing Laos's environment include a widespread lack of awareness of world conservation issues, an absence of legal frameworks, poor definition of authority in conservation areas, lack of communications between national and local governments, and limited funds for conservation purposes. Yet most Lao still live at or just above a subsistence level, and this frugal country has one of the lowest per-capita energy-consumption rates in the world.

Thus the major challenges facing Laos's environment are the internal pressures of economic growth and external pressures from the country's more populated and affluent neighbours – particularly China, Vietnam and Thailand – who would like to exploit Laos's abundant resources as much as possible.

Numerous hydroelectric projects, some of which would be contained in the National Protected Areas (NPAs), are slated for development in the near future, though there is still time for the government to consider cancelling at least some of the projects proposed for the more ecologically sensitive areas (see Development of the Mekong, p45).

One of the more disturbing aspects of the hydroelectric industry is the way in which companies deliberately apply for concessions in areas zoned for dams, confident in the knowledge that – even if the facility is never constructed – they can usually stall for time long enough to log the valleys intended for inundation. Hence the main profit comes from timber, whether or not the dams go ahead. Like solar and wind power, hydropower is a potential source of sustainable and renewable energy when coupled with responsible land/resource planning. The question is, does Laos have the latter?

Deforestation is another major environmental issue in Laos. Although the official export of timber is tightly controlled, no-one really knows how much teak and other hardwoods are being smuggled into Vietnam, Thailand and especially China. The policy in northern Laos has been to allow the Chinese to take as much timber as they want in return for building roads. The Lao army is still removing huge chunks of forest in Khammuan Province, much of it going to Vietnam. The national electricity-generating company also profits from timber sales each time it links a Lao town or village with the national power grid, clear-cutting a wider-than-necessary swath along Lao highways.

Essentially, the Lao authorities express a seemingly sincere desire to conserve the nation's forests – but not at the cost of rural livelihoods. Yet in most rural areas 70% of nonrice foods comes from the forest. Thus forest destruction will lead to increased poverty and reduced local livelihoods.

DOING YOUR PART

Visitors to Laos can do their bit to conserve the environment in many ways, including: proper disposal of rubbish; avoidance of restaurants serving threatened or endangered wildlife species; hiking only on established trails; as much as possible patronising hotels, guesthouses and restaurants that employ 'green' methods of construction and waste disposal; and finally by reporting any illegal or unethical environmental practices to international environmental observer groups such as the **Wildlife Conservation Society** (☎ 021-215400; WCS-lao@wcs.org; PO Box 6712, Vientiane) and the **International Union for Conservation of Nature & Natural Resources** (IUCN; ☎ 021-216401; cro@iucnlao.org; 15 Th Fa Ngum, Vientiane).

If you come across endangered wildlife for sale, or if anyone in Laos offers to sell you endangered wildlife, you can inform (take photos if possible) **Traffic East Asia** (☎ 852-2530 0864; tea@asiaonline.net; 20/F Double Bldg, 22 Stanley St, Central, Hong Kong).

Other pressures on the forest cover come from swidden (slash-and-burn) methods of cultivation, in which small plots of forest are cleared, then burnt for nitrogenation of the soil, and farmed intensively for two or three years, after which they are infertile and unfarmable for between eight and 10 years. Considering the sparse population, swidden cultivation is probably not as great an environmental threat as logging.

Tourism, growing steadily in post-1975 Laos, has had no major impact on the environment thus far. Until recently the government has avoided giving contracts to companies wanting to develop large-scale resorts. Plans for a huge hotel-casino complex in Champasak Province, financed by a Lao-Thai joint venture and intended for a previously undeveloped area next to the beautiful Khon Phapheng Falls (see p237) have been cancelled for the time being. Proponents of the project claimed it would provide job alternatives to local villagers who currently make their living cutting timber to make charcoal or overfishing the Mekong River to the detriment of the rare Irrawaddy dolphin. Opponents said it would increase overall human activity in the area and lead to environmental degradation. The World Bank finally issued a report that concluded the negative ecological consequences of the proposal would outweigh any benefits.

Laos has not yet ratified the UN Convention on International Trade in Endangered Species of Wild Flora and Fauna (Cites), although it does have 'accession' status, meaning it subscribes in principle to the convention. While Cites and other legal measures have been somewhat effective in protecting species endangered as a direct result of international trade, habitat destruction remains the principal cause of species loss worldwide.

'Tourism, growing steadily in post-1975 Laos, has had no major impact on the environment thus far.'

Food & Drink

Although Lao food has yet to develop the variety and depth of the more famous cuisines of neighbouring China, Thailand and Vietnam, you can eat well in Laos if you take the time to learn a little about the cuisine while you're there. While few people travel to this country with food as their prime objective, a little experimentation can take you a long way towards appreciating the cuisine.

STAPLES & SPECIALITIES

Outside of the Mekong River valley, where most of the country's wealth is concentrated and people have more sophisticated palates, you will probably find the culinary offerings in most of the country limited to the same dozen or fewer dishes.

Ant Egg Soup (2004), by Natacha du Pont de Bie, is a well-written account of the author's encounters with food while travelling through Laos, garnished with recipes and line drawings.

Travellers already hip to Thai cuisine will experience *déjà vu* in the Lao emphasis on simple, fresh ingredients coarsely blended into rustic dishes. The herbal tones of basil, mint, coriander and lemongrass lend bright tones to the mix, balanced by the spicy bitterness of roots and rhizomes (the thick, underground stem of certain plants), the tang of lime juice and Kaffir lime leaves, the pungent salt of fish sauce or shrimp paste and the fire of fresh chillies.

Staple ingredients include locally raised *phák* (vegetables), *pąa* (fish), *kai* (chicken), *pét* (duck), *mŭu* (pork) and *sìin ngúa* (beef) or *sìin khwái* (water buffalo). Because of Laos's distance from the sea, freshwater fish is more common than saltwater fish or shellfish. When meats are used, Lao cooks prefer to emphasise savoury tones imparted by grilling, roasting or mixing with cooked ingredients that are inherently savoury, such as roasted rice.

In rural areas wild rather than domestic animals – especially deer, wild pigs, squirrels, civets, monitor lizards, jungle fowl/pheasants, dhole (wild dogs), rats and birds – provide most of the meat in local diets, though the eating of endangered species causes much consternation among international wildlife conservationists. In part this practice is due to the expense involved in animal husbandry, and partly due to the Lao preference for the taste of wild game.

Fish and Fish Dishes of Laos (2003), by Alan Davidson, is a thorough description of Laos's diverse freshwater fish cookery. The late Davidson was British ambassador to Laos in the 1970s and author of the esteemed *Oxford Companion to Food*.

To salt the food, various fermented fish concoctions are used, most commonly *nâm pąa*, which is a thin sauce of fermented anchovies (usually imported from Thailand), and *pąa dàek*, a coarser, native Lao preparation that includes chunks of fermented freshwater fish, rice husks and rice 'dust'. *Nâm pąa dàek* is the sauce poured from *pąa dàek*. See the Health chapter (p282) for warnings on eating *pąa dàek*. *Phŏng sûu lot* – *ajinomoto* or MSG – is also a common seasoning, and in Laos you may even see it served as a table condiment in noodle restaurants.

Fresh *nâm màak náo* (lime juice), *sìi-khái* (lemongrass), *bąi sálanae* (mint leaf) and *phák hăwm* (coriander leaf) are added to give the food its characteristic tang. Other common seasonings include *khaa* (galingale), *màak phét* (hot chillies), *nâm màak khăam* (tamarind juice), *khìng* (ginger) and *nâm màak phâo* or *nâm káthí* (coconut milk). Chillies are sometimes served on the side in hot pepper sauces called *jąew*. In Luang Prabang, *năng khwái hàeng* (dried skin of water buffalo) is quite a popular ingredient.

One of the most common Lao dishes is *làap*, which is a Lao-style salad of minced meat, fowl or fish tossed with lime juice, garlic, *khào khûa* (roasted, powdered sticky rice), green onions, mint leaves and chillies. It can be very hot or rather mild, depending on the cook. Meats mixed into *làap* are sometimes raw *(díp)* rather than cooked *(súk)*. *Làap* is typically served with a large plate of lettuce, mint, steamed mango leaves and various other fresh herbs depending on season and availability. Using your fingers you wrap a little *làap* in the lettuce and herbs and eat it with balls of sticky rice which you roll by hand.

For *pîng kai* (grilled chicken), cooks take whole chickens or chickens cut into pieces and rub them with a marinade of garlic, coriander root, black pepper and salt or fish sauce before cooking them slowly over hot coals.

Another dish you'll come across often is *tạm màak-hung* (more commonly known as *tạm sòm* in Vientiane), a spicy, tangy salad made by pounding shredded green papaya, lime juice, chillies, garlic, *pạa dàek*, *nâm phàk-kàat* (a paste of boiled, fermented lettuce leaves) and various other ingredients together in a large mortar. This is a favourite market and street-vendor food – customers typically inspect the array of possible *tạm màak-hung* ingredients the vendor has spread out on a table next to the mortar, then order a custom mix. For something different, ask the pounder to throw in a few *màak kàwk*, a sour, olive-shaped fruit.

Many Lao dishes are quite spicy because of the Lao penchant for *màak phét*. But the Lao also eat a lot of Chinese and Vietnamese food, which is generally less spicy. *Fõe* (rice noodle soup) is popular as a snack or even for breakfast, and is almost always served with a plate of fresh lettuce, mint, basil, coriander, mung bean sprouts and lime wedges to add to the soup as desired. Especially in the south, people mix their own *fõe* sauce of lime, crushed fresh chilli, *kápí* (shrimp paste) and sugar at the table using a little saucer provided for the purpose. In Luang Prabang, some *fõe* shops may add *jạew ngáa*, a sesame paste.

Another common noodle dish, especially in the morning, is *khào pịak sèn*, a soft, round rice noodle served in a broth with pieces of chicken or occasionally pork. A popular condiment for this noodle soup is crushed fresh ginger. Many *khào pịak sèn* vendors also sell *khào-nõm khuu*, small deep-fried, doughnut-like Chinese pastries. Some vendors even leave a pair of scissors on each table so that you can cut the pastries up and mix them into your soup. It may sound strange, but it's very tasty.

Khào pũn, flour noodles topped with a sweet and spicy *nâm káthí* (coconut sauce), is another popular noodle dish. These noodles are also

Simple Laotian Cooking (2003), by Penn Hong-thong, is a collection of nearly 200 recipes along with straightforward expositions on the tools and techniques required to closely approximate Lao cuisine.

NUTRITION

If your food is poor or limited in availability, if you're travelling hard and fast and therefore missing meals or if you simply lose your appetite, you can soon start to lose weight and place your health at risk.

Make sure your diet is well balanced. Cooked eggs, tofu, beans, lentils and nuts are all safe ways to get protein. Fruit you can peel (eg bananas, oranges or mandarins) is usually safe and a good source of vitamins, but melons are best avoided as they can harbour bacteria in their flesh. Try to eat plenty of grains (including rice) and bread. Remember that although food is generally safer if it is cooked well, overcooked food does lose much of its nutritional value. If your diet isn't well balanced or if your food intake is insufficient, it's a good idea to take vitamins and iron pills.

---

eaten cold with various Vietnamese foods popular in urban Laos, particularly *năem néuang* (barbecued pork meatballs) and *yáw* (spring rolls).

Rice is the foundation for all Lao meals (as opposed to snacks), as with elsewhere in Southeast Asia. In general, the Lao eat *khào nǐaw* ('sticky' or glutinous rice), although *khào jâo* (ordinary white rice) is also common in the major towns.

In Vientiane, Savannakhet, Pakse and Luang Prabang, French bread *(khào jìi)* is popular for breakfast. Sometimes it's eaten plain with *kạa-féh nóm hâwn* (hot milk coffee), sometimes it's eaten with *khai* (eggs) or in a baguette sandwich that contains Lao-style pâté, and vegetables. Or you can order them *sai nâm nóm*: sliced in half lengthwise and drizzled with sweetened condensed milk. When they are fresh, Lao baguettes can be superb. Croissants and other French-style pastries are also available in the bakeries of Vientiane.

DID YOU KNOW?

The teapots commonly seen on tables in Chinese and Vietnamese restaurants are filled with *nâm sáa* (weak Chinese tea); ask for a *jàwk pao* (glass) and you can drink as much as you'd like at no charge.

DRINKS
Nonalcoholic Drinks
WATER

Water purified for drinking purposes is simply called *nâm deum* (drinking water), whether it is boiled or filtered. *All* water offered to customers in restaurants or hotels will be purified, so don't fret about the safety of taking a sip. In restaurants you can ask for *nâm pao* (plain water, which is always either boiled or taken from a purified source) served by the glass at no charge, or order by the bottle. A bottle of carbonated or soda water costs about the same as a bottle of plain purified water but the bottles are smaller.

COFFEE & TEA

Lao-grown coffee is known to be one of the world's best. Traditionally, pure Lao coffee is roasted by wholesalers, ground by vendors and filtered through a sock-like cloth bag just before serving. On occasion, restaurants or vendors with the proper accoutrements for making traditional filtered coffee keep a supply of Nescafé just for foreigners. To get authentic Lao coffee ask for *kạa-féh láo* (Lao coffee) or *kạa-féh bọh-láan* (old-fashioned coffee).

The usual brewed coffee is served mixed with sugar and sweetened condensed milk – if you don't want either be sure to specify *kạa-féh dạm* (black coffee) followed with *baw sai nâm-tạan* (without sugar).

In central and southern Laos coffee is almost always served with a chaser of hot *nâm sáa* (weak Chinese tea), while in the north it's typically served with a glass of plain hot water.

Both Indian-style (black) and Chinese-style (green or semicured) teas are served in Laos. An order of *sáa hâwn* (hot tea) usually results in a cup (or glass) of black tea with sugar and condensed milk. As with coffee you must specify beforehand if you want black tea without milk and/or sugar. Chinese tea predominates in Chinese restaurants and is also the usual ingredient in *nâm sáa,* the weak, often lukewarm, tea traditionally served in restaurants for free. For stronger fresh Chinese tea, request *sáa jîin.*

Alcoholic Drinks

BEER
Lao Brewery Co (LBC), located on the outskirts of Vientiane, produces the very drinkable Bia Lao, the Romanised name for which is Beerlao. A draught version (*bịa sót*: fresh beer) is tastier yet, but it's only available in Vientiane. Beerlao contains 5% alcohol.

Beerlao comes standard in 630mL bottles, but is also available in 330mL cans. Heineken and Tiger beer, which are imported from Singapore, come in 330mL cans, but typically cost the same as a 660mL bottle of Beerlao.

DISTILLED SPIRITS
Rice whisky (*lào-láo)* is a popular drink among lowland Lao. The best *lào-láo* is said to come from Phongsali and Don Khong, the northern and southern extremes of the country, but it's available virtually everywhere, usually for between US$0.15 and US$0.30 per 750mL bottle.

Lào-láo is usually drunk neat, with a plain water chaser. See the Spirit of Spirits (below) for further detail on drinking customs.

Tourist hotel bars in the larger cities carry the standard variety of liquors.

WINE
In Vientiane there are decent French and Italian wines abundantly available at restaurants, in shops specialising in imported foods and in a few shops which sell nothing but wine. You will also find a limited selection in Luang Prabang, Savannakhet and Pakse. Wines of Australian, American, South African, Chilean and other origins are more scarce. Whatever the origin, wines in Laos are much cheaper than in neighbouring Thailand because the import tax is much lower.

Luang Prabang is famous for a type of light rice wine called *khào kam,* a red-tinted, somewhat sweet beverage made from sticky rice. It can be quite tasty when properly prepared and stored, but rather mouldy-tasting if not.

In rural provinces, a rice wine known as *lào-hǎi* (jar liquor) is fermented by households or villages. *Lào-hǎi* is usually drunk from a communal jar using long reed straws.

DID YOU KNOW?

Mon-Khmer tribal villages on the Bolaven Plateau periodically hold special ceremonies where water buffalo are sacrificed to appease local spirits. Once the rituals have been performed, the villagers share the buffalo meat, washed down with copious moonshine.

THE SPIRIT OF SPIRITS

In a Lao home the pouring and drinking of *lào-láo* at the evening meal takes on ritual characteristics. Usually towards the end of the meal, but occasionally beforehand, the hosts bring out a bottle of the stuff to treat their guests. The usual procedure is for the host to pour one jigger of *lào-láo* onto the floor or a used dinner plate first, to appease the house spirits. The host then pours another jigger and downs it in one gulp. Jiggers for each guest are poured in turn; guests must take at least one offered drink or risk offending the house spirits.

LAOS'S TOP FIVE RESTAURANTS

- The Apsara (p126), Luang Prabang
- The Boat Landing Guest House & Restaurant (p164), Luang Nam Tha
- Bunmala Restaurant (p84), Vientiane
- Hay Thien (p206), Savannakhet
- Samsenthai Fried Noodles (p84), Vientiane

CELEBRATIONS

Temple festivals *(bun wat)* make good opportunities to taste real home-cooked Lao food as temple regulars often bring dishes from home to share with other temple visitors. At the same time vendors may set up foodstalls offering everything from *khûa fõe* (fried rice noodles) to *pîng kai* (grilled chicken).

The annual boat races, held near the end of October in Huay Xai, Vientiane, Savannakhet and other Mekong River towns, is another great chance to graze at long lines of vendor booths; *năem khào* is particularly popular at these events.

During *tut jiin* (Chinese New Year), also know by its Vietnamese name Tet, Laos's Chinese population celebrates with a week of house-cleaning, lion dances, fireworks and feasting. The most impressive festivities take place in Vientiane's Chinatown (at the north end of Th Chao Anou). Favourite foods eaten during Tet include 'mooncakes' – thick, circular pastries filled with sweet bean paste or salted pork – and lots of noodles.

WHERE TO EAT & DRINK

The most economical places to eat and the most dependable are *hâan fõe* (noodle shops) and *talàat sâo* (morning markets). Most towns and villages have at least one morning market (which often lasts all day despite the name) and several *hâan fõe*. The next step up is the Lao-style café (*hâan kheuang deum;* drink shop) or *hâan kịn deum* (eat-drink shop), where a more varied selection of dishes is usually served. Most expensive is the *hâan ạahăan* (food shop), where the menu is usually posted on the wall or on a blackboard (in Lao).

Many *hâan ạahăan* serve mostly Chinese or Vietnamese food. The ones serving real Lao food usually have a large pan of water on a stool – or a modern lavatory – somewhere near the entrance for washing the hands before eating (Lao food is traditionally eaten with the hands).

Many restaurants or food stalls, especially outside Vientiane, don't have menus at all, so it's useful to memorise a standard 'repertoire' of dishes. Those restaurants that do offer written menus don't always have an English version. Most provinces have their own local specialities in addition to the standards and you might try asking for *ạahăan phisèht* (special food), allowing the proprietors to choose for you.

VEGETARIANS & VEGANS

Almost all Lao dishes contain animal products of one kind of another. Two principal seasonings, for example, are fish sauce and shrimp paste. Some dishes also contain lard or pork fat.

Vegetarian or vegan restaurants are virtually nonexistent although you may come across a couple of Chinese vegan foodstalls in Vientiane's Chinese neighbourhood.

Menus at tourist-oriented restaurants in larger towns and cities such as Vientiane and Luang Prabang will often have a small list of vegetarian dishes available.

Outside of tourist areas, vegetarians and vegans will have to make an effort to speak enough Lao to convey their culinary needs. The best all-around phrase to memorise is 'I eat only vegetables' *(khàwy kịn tae phák)*. If you eat eggs you can add *sai khai dâi* (it's OK to add egg) to your food vocabulary. Dairy products such as cheese won't be much of a concern since they're rarely served in Lao restaurants.

WHINING & DINING

Children are usually well looked-after at Lao restaurants, where cooks will usually be very flexible about creating dishes tailored to young tastes. Of course dishes that make Lao kids happy might not always coincide with what make your kids happy, but in general the Lao will automatically prepare less spicy versions of Lao food for youngsters.

Baby food is available at minimarkets in Vientiane and to a lesser extent Savannakhet and Luang Prabang. Elsewhere you'll have to bring your own. See p249 for more detail on travelling with children in Laos.

HABITS & CUSTOMS

Eating in Laos is nearly always a social event and the Lao avoid eating alone whenever possible. Except for the 'rice plates' and the noodle dishes, Lao meals are typically ordered 'family style', which is to say that two or more people order together, sharing different dishes. Traditionally, the party orders one of each kind of dish, for example, one chicken, one fish, one soup, etc. One dish is generally large enough for two people.

Eating alone is something the Lao generally consider to be rather unusual; but then as a *falang* (Westerner) you are an exception anyway. In Chinese or Thai restaurants a cheaper alternative is to order dishes *làat khào* (over rice).

Most Lao dishes are eaten with *khào nĭaw* (glutinous or sticky rice). *Khào nĭaw* is served up in lidded baskets called *típ khào* and eaten with the hands. The general practice is to grab a small fistful of rice from the *típ khào*, then roll it into a rough ball which you then use to dip into the various dishes. Watching others is the best way to learn. At the end of the meal it is considered bad luck not to replace the lid on top of the *típ khào*.

If *khào jâo* (normal steamed rice) is served with the meal, then it is eaten with a fork and spoon. The spoon, held in the right hand, is used to scoop up the rice and accompanying dishes and placing it in the mouth. The fork, held in the left hand, is merely used to prod food onto the spoon.

Chopsticks *(mâi thuu)* are reserved for dining in Chinese restaurants (where rice is served in small Chinese bowls rather than flat plates) or for eating Chinese noodle dishes. Noodle soups are eaten with a spoon

---

THE RIGHT TOOL FOR THE JOB

If you're not offered chopsticks, don't ask for them. When *falang* (Westerners) ask for chopsticks to eat Lao food, it only puzzles the restaurant proprietors. An even more embarrassing act is trying to eat sticky rice with chopsticks. Use your right hand instead. For ordinary white rice, use the fork and spoon provided (fork in the left hand, spoon in the right, or the reverse for left-handers).

in the left hand (for spooning up the broth) and chopsticks in the right (for grasping the noodles and other solid ingredients).

Dishes are typically served all at once rather than in courses. If the host or restaurant staff can't bring them all to the table because of a shortage of help or because the food is being cooked sequentially from the same set of pots and pans, then the diners typically wait until all the platters are on the table before digging in.

The Lao don't concern themselves with whether dishes are served piping hot, so no one minds if the dishes sit in the kitchen or on the table for 15 minutes or so before anyone digs in. Furthermore it's considered somewhat impolite to take a spoonful of food that's steaming hot as it implies you're so ravenous or uncivilised that you can't wait to gorge yourself.

COOKING COURSES

In Luang Prabang you can take a course in Lao cooking from the Lao native chef at **Tum Tum Cheng Restaurant & Cooking School** (☎ 252019; Th Sakkarin). See p130 for details.

EAT YOUR WORDS

Want to know *làap* from *lào láo*? *Khào kam* from *khào nĭaw*? Get behind the cuisine by getting to know the language. For pronunciation guidelines see p292.

Useful Phrases

What do you have that's special?	*mîi nyǎng phi-sèt baw*	ມີຫຍັງພິເສດບໍ່
Do you have ...?	*mîi ... baw*	ມີ ... ບໍ່
I didn't order this.	*khàwy baw dâi sang náew nîi*	ຂ້ອຍບໍ່ໄດ້ສັ່ງແບບນີ້
I eat only vegetables.	*khàwy kĭn tae phák*	ຂ້ອຍກິນແຕ່ຜັກ
(I) don't like it hot and spicy.	*baw mak phét*	ບໍ່ມັກເຜັດ
(I) like it hot and spicy.	*mak phét*	ມັກເຜັດ
I'd like to try that.	*khàwy yàak láwng kĭn boeng*	ຂ້ອຍຢາກລອງກິນເບິ່ງ
Please bring (a) ...	*khǎw ... dae*	ຂໍ ... ແດ່
menu	*láai-kqan qa-hǎan*	ລາຍການ ອາຫານ
plate	*jqa*	ຈານ
bowl	*thùay*	ຖ້ວຍ
glass	*jàwk*	ຈອກ
spoon	*buang*	ບ່ວງ
fork	*sâwm*	ສ້ອມ
chopsticks	*mâi thuu*	ໄມ້ທູ່
knife	*mĭit*	ມີດ
bill	*saek*	ແຊັກ

Menu Decoder

DRINKS

water	*nâm*	ນ້ຳ
drinking water	*nâm deum*	ນ້ຳດື່ມ
boiled water	*nâm tôm*	ນ້ຳຕົ້ມ

hot water	*nâm hâwn*	ນ້ຳຮ້ອນ
cold water	*nâm yén*	ນ້ຳເຢັນ
soda water	*nâm sòh-dqa*	ນ້ຳໂສດາ
orange juice/soda	*nâm màak kîang*	ນ້ຳໝາກກ້ຽງ
plain milk	*nâm nóm*	ນ້ຳນົມ
ice	*nâm kâwn*	ນ້ຳກ້ອນ
glass	*jàwk*	ຈອກ
bottle	*kâew*	ແກ້ວ
hot Lao coffee with milk & sugar	*kqa-féh nóm hâwn*	ກາເຟນົມຮ້ອນ
hot Lao coffee with sugar, no milk	*kqa-féh dqm*	ກາເຟດຳ
iced Lao coffee with sugar, no milk	*kqa-féh nóm yén*	ກາເຟນົມເຢັນ
iced Lao coffee with milk & sugar	*òh-lîang*	ໂອລ້ຽງ
hot tea with sugar	*sáa hâwn*	ຊາຮ້ອນ
hot tea with milk & sugar	*sáa nóm hâwn*	ຊານົມຮ້ອນ
iced tea with sugar	*sáa wǎan yén*	ຊາທວານເຢັນ
iced tea with milk & sugar	*sáa nóm yén*	ຊານົມເຢັນ
Ovaltine	*oh-wantin*	ໂອວັນຕິນ
beer	*bja*	ເບຍ
draught beer	*bja sót*	ເບຍສົດ
rice whisky	*lào láo*	ເຫົ້າລາວ

EGG DISHES

fried egg	*khai dqo*	ໄຂ່ດາວ
hard-boiled egg	*khai tôm*	ໄຂ່ຕົ້ມ
plain omelette	*jqun khai*	ຈືນໄຂ່
scrambled egg	*khai khùa*	ໄຂ່ຂົ້ວ

FISH & SEAFOOD

crisp-fried fish	*jqun pqa*	ຈືນປາ
fried prawns	*jqun kûng*	ຈືນກຸ້ງ
grilled prawns	*pǐing kûng*	ປີ້ງກຸ້ງ
steamed fish	*nèung pqa*	ໜຶ້ງປາ
grilled fish	*pǐing pqa*	ປີ້ງປາ
sweet & sour fish	*pqa sòm-wǎan*	ປາສົ້ມທວານ
catfish	*pqa dúk*	ປາດຸກ

MEAT SALADS (LÀAP)

beef laap	*làap sìin*	ລາບຊີ້ນ
chicken laap	*làap kai*	ລາບໄກ່
fish laap	*làap pqa*	ລາບປາ
pork laap	*làap mǔu*	ລາບໝູ

RICE DISHES

steamed white rice	*khào nèung*	ເຂົ້າໜຶ້ງ
sticky rice	*khào nĭaw*	ເຂົ້າໜຽວ
curry over rice	*khào làat kqeng*	ເຂົ້າລາດແກງ
'red' pork (char siu) with rice	*khào mŭu dqeng*	ເຂົ້າໝູແດງ
roast duck over rice	*khào nàa pét*	ເຂົ້າໜ້າເປັດ
fried rice with ...	*khào phát (khào khùa) ...*	ເຂົ້າຜັດ (ເຂົ້າຂົ້ວ) ...
chicken	*kai*	ໄກ່
pork	*mŭu*	ໝູ
shrimp/prawns	*kûng*	ກຸ້ງ
crab	*pŭu*	ປູ

NOODLE DISHES

rice noodle soup with vegetables & meat	*fŏe*	ເຝີ
rice noodles with vegetables & meat, no broth	*fŏe hàeng*	ເຝີແຫ້ງ
rice noodles with gravy	*làat nàa*	ລາດໜ້າ
fried rice noodles with meat & vegetables	*fŏe khùa*	ເຝີຂົ້ວ
fried rice noodles with soy sauce	*phát sá-yîu*	ຜັດສະອິ້ວ
yellow wheat noodles in broth, with vegetables & meat	*mii nâm*	ໝີ່ນ້ຳ
yellow wheat noodles with vegetables & meat	*mii hàeng*	ໝີ່ແຫ້ງ
white flour noodles served with sweet-spicy sauce	*khào pûn*	ເຂົ້າປຸ້ນ

SNACKS

fried peanuts	*thua dĭn jęun*	ຖົ່ວດິນຈືນ
fried potatoes	*mán fa-lang jęun*	ມັນຝລັ່ງຈືນ
fresh spring rolls	*yáw díp*	ຍໍດິບ
fried spring rolls	*yáw jęun*	ຍໍຈືນ
grilled chicken	*pĭng kai*	ປີ້ງໄກ່
shrimp chips	*khào khìap kûng*	ເຂົ້າຂຽບກຸ້ງ
spicy green papaya salad	*tąm màak-hung*	ຕຳໝາກຫຸ່ງ

SOUP

mild soup with vegetables & pork	*kqeng jèut*	ແກງຈືດ
mild soup with vegetables, pork & bean curd	*kqeng jèut tâo-hûu*	ແກງຈືດເຕົ້າຮູ້
fish & lemongrass soup with mushrooms	*tôm yám pqa*	ຕົ້ມຍຳປາ
rice soup with ...	*khào pìak ...*	ເຂົ້າປຽກ ...
chicken	*kai*	ໄກ່
fish	*pqa*	ປາ
pork	*mŭu*	ໝູ

STIR-FRIED DISHES

chicken with ginger	*kai phát khǐing*	ໄກ່ຜັດຂີງ
sweet & sour pork	*mǔu sòm-wǎan*	ໝູສົ້ມຫວານ
beef in oyster sauce	*ngúa phàt nâm-mán hǎwy*	ງົວຜັດນ້ຳມັນຫອຍ
stir-fried mixed vegetables	*phát phák*	ຜັດຜັກ

Food Glossary

BREAD & PASTRIES

plain bread (usually French-style)	*khào jìi*	ເຂົ້າຈີ່
baguette sandwich	*khào jìi páa-tê*	ເຂົ້າຈີ່ປາເຕ
croissants	*khúa-sawng*	ຄົວຊ່ອງ
'Chinese doughnuts' (Mandarin youtiao)	*pá-thawng-kó* *(khào-nǒm khuu)*	ປະຖ່ອງໂກະ (ເຂົ້າໜົມຄູ່)

CONDIMENTS, HERBS & SPICES

chilli	*màak phét*	ໝາກເຜັດ
dipping sauces	*jaew*	ແຈ່ວ
fish sauce	*nâm pqa*	ນ້ຳປາ
ginger	*khǐing*	ຂີງ
lemongrass	*hǔa sǐng khái*	ຫົວສິງໄຄ
lime juice	*nâm màak náo*	ນ້ຳໝາກນາວ
salt	*keua*	ເກືອ
soy sauce	*nâm sá-ìu*	ນ້ຳສະອິ້ວ
sugar	*nâm-tqan*	ນ້ຳຕານ
sweet basil	*bqi hǒh-la-pháa*	ໃບໂຫລະພາ
tamarind	*màak khǎam*	ໝາກຂາມ
vinegar	*nâm sòm*	ນ້ຳສົ້ມ

FOOD TYPES

beef	*sìin ngúa*	ຊິ້ນງົວ
butter	*bqe*	ເບີ
chicken	*kai*	ໄກ່
egg	*khai*	ໄຂ່
fish	*pqa*	ປາ
pork	*sìin mǔu*	ຊິ້ນໝູ
rice	*khào*	ເຂົ້າ
seafood	*qa-hǎan tha-léh*	ອາຫານທະເລ
shrimp/prawns	*kùng*	ກຸ້ງ
vegetables	*phak*	ຜັກ
yogurt	*nóm sòm*	ນົມສົ້ມ

FRUITS

banana	*màak kûay*	ໝາກກ້ວຍ
coconut	*màak phâo*	ໝາກພ້າວ
guava (year-round)	*màak sïi-dqa*	ໝາກສີ່ດາ
jackfruit	*màak mïi*	ໝາກມີ້
lime	*màak náo*	ໝາກນາວ
longan (dragon's eyes)	*màak nyám nyái*	ໝາກຍຳໃຍ
lychee	*màak lîn-jii*	ໝາກລີ້ນຈີ່
mandarin orange	*màak kîang*	ໝາກກ້ຽງ
mango	*màak muang*	ໝາກມ່ວງ
pineapple	*màak nat*	ໝາກນັດ
papaya	*màak hung*	ໝາກຫຸ່ງ
rambutan	*màak ngaw*	ໝາກເຄາະ
sugarcane	*âwy*	ອ້ອຍ
watermelon	*màak móh*	ໝາກໂມ

VEGETABLES

bamboo shoots	*naw mâi*	ໜໍ່ໄມ້
beans	*thua*	ຖົ່ວ
bean sprouts	*thua ngâwk*	ຖົ່ວງອກ
cabbage	*ká-lam pji*	ກະລ່ຳປີ
cauliflower	*ká-lam pji dàwk*	ກະລ່ຳປີດອກ
Chinese radish (daikon)	*phák kàat hǔa*	ຜັກກາດຫົວ
cucumber	*màak tqeng*	ໝາກແຕງ
eggplant	*màak khẽua*	ໝາກເຂືອ
garlic	*hǔa phák thíam*	ຫົວຜັກທຽມ
lettuce	*phák sá-lat*	ຜັກສະລັດ
long green beans	*thua nyáo*	ຖົ່ວຍາວ
onion (bulb)	*hǔa phák bua*	ຫົວຜັກບົ່ວ
onion (green 'scallions')	*tôn phák bua*	ຕົ້ນຜັກບົ່ວ
peanuts (groundnuts)	*màak thua djn*	ໝາກຖົ່ວດິນ
potato	*mán fa-lang*	ມັນຝລັ່ງ
tomato	*màak len*	ໝາກເລັ່ນ

Vientiane & Around

CONTENTS

HIGHLIGHTS

- Gaze up at the tapered golden stupa of **Pha That Luang** (p70), the symbol of Lao nationhood in Vientiane

- Check out the concrete folly that is **Xieng Khuan** (p76), the bizarre park full of dozens of giant Buddhist and Hindu sculptures, 20km from Vientiane

- Treat yourself to a traditional herbal sauna and massage at Vientiane's **Wat Sok Pa Luang** (p75)

- Trek to waterfalls, weave baskets or spy on wild elephants at **Phu Khao Khuay National Protected Area** (p98)

- Tube, climb, raft, kayak, cycle or walk through the rivers and imposing karst terrain around **Vang Vieng** (p99)

You'll seldom see the words 'hustle' or 'bustle' used to describe Vientiane, which could mount a strong case for being the most relaxed capital city on earth. But the typically easygoing pace of life masks rapid growth – as fast as any in Asia – spurred on by investment from Thailand and the presence of thousands of foreign aid workers.

Vientiane means Sandalwood City, and is actually pronounced Wieng Chan (Wieng means 'city' or 'place with walls' in Lao; Chan is the Lao pronunciation of the Sanskrit 'Chandana' meaning sandalwood); the French are responsible for the modern transliteration. Parts of the town are quite attractive, particularly the older section along the Mekong River. The tree-lined boulevards and dozens of temples impart an atmosphere of timelessness in a city whose kaleidoscopic architectural styles reflect an intriguing mix of Lao, Thai, Chinese, Vietnamese, French, US and Soviet influences.

As Laos continues to open itself to the world, Vientiane is a fascinating place from which to watch the struggle between the communist past and inevitably more capitalist future, for it is here that change happens first. Wander along the river front on a Friday afternoon, for example, and you'll see Beerlao-drinking teenagers chatting on mobile phones. Later in the day you might adjourn from one of the city's excellent French restaurants to see the same youth cheering once-decadent rock music in On The Rock Pub. The Lao National Museum is another giveaway; it was once the dour Lao Revolutionary Museum, but fading pictures of gun-wielding cadres are gradually giving way to more conventional displays.

Of course, Vientiane is not only about witnessing change. The 6400 Buddhas at Wat Si Saket, the religious art of Haw Pha Kaew, and the lotus-inspired lines of Laos's gilded national symbol, Pha That Luang, speak to the historical importance of the city. Patuxai and the surreal Xieng Khuan (Buddha Park) may have less artistic merit, but like the city itself, they're not short of appeal.

VIENTIANE

ວຽງຈັນ

☎ 021 / pop 201,000

HISTORY

Set on a bend in the Mekong River, Vientiane was originally one of the early Lao valley *meuang* (city-states) that were consolidated around AD 1000. The Lao who settled here did so because the surrounding alluvial plains are so incredibly fertile. Early on, the Vientiane *meuang* prospered and enjoyed a fragile sovereignty.

At various times over the 10 or so centuries of its history, however, Vientiane lost its standing as an independent kingdom and was controlled by the Vietnamese, Burmese, Siamese and Khmers. When the kingdom of Lan Xang was founded in the 14th century by the Khmer-supported conqueror Fa Ngum, it was centred in Muang Sawa (Luang Prabang). By the mid-16th century, however, the capital had shifted to Vientiane.

When Laos became a French protectorate in the late 19th and early 20th centuries, Vientiane was named as the capital city, and it remains so under communist rule today.

ORIENTATION

Vientiane curves along the Mekong River following a meandering northwest–southeast axis, with the central district of Muang Chanthabuli at the centre of the bend. Most of the government offices, hotels, restaurants and historic temples are located in Chanthabuli, near the river. Some old French colonial buildings and Vietnamese-Chinese shophouses remain, set alongside newer structures built according to the rather boxy social realist school of architecture.

The Wattay International Airport (Map pp68-9) is located about 4km northwest of the centre, while the Northern Bus Station (Map pp68-9), where most of the long-distance services begin and end, is about 2km northwest of the centre. The border with Thailand at the Thai-Lao Friendship Bridge (Map p96) is 20km southeast of the city.

There are very few street signs anywhere in Vientiane. Where they do exist, the English and French designations for street names vary (eg route, *rue*, road and avenue) but the Lao script always reads *thanǒn* (Th). Therefore, when asking directions it's always best to just use *thanǒn*.

Th Samsenthai, which is the pre-eminent shopping area, and Th Setthathirat, where several of the most famous temples are located, are the main streets in central Vientiane. Both eventually lead to Rte 13 north at their northwest ends. These streets also cross Th Lan Xang, a boulevard leading from the presidential palace (see p78) past Talat Sao (the Morning Market) to Patuxai (Victory Gate) and, after turning into Th Phon Kheng, to Rte 13 south.

The *meuang* of Vientiane are broken up into *bâan* (Ban), which are neighbourhoods

or villages associated with local wats. Wattay International Airport, for example, is in Ban Wat Tai – the area in which Wat Tai is located.

Maps

There is no recently published definitive map of Vientiane. 'Advertising maps', however, are everywhere – in 2004 there were at least nine such plans of Vientiane published, all with a fairly relaxed approach to details like scale and perspective, but still quite useful. You'll find them in hotels, shops and restaurants, sometimes for sale for about US$1, sometimes free.

At the **National Geographic Service** (Map pp68-9; ☼ 9am-noon & 2-4pm Mon-Fri) just west of Patuxai, a new Vientiane is slowly emerging from the computer screen and should be completed by 2005.

INFORMATION
Bookshops

Vientiane's bookshops sell second-hand novels in English and French, travel guides, maps and years-old reports by development organisations.

Bookshop Sapasin Tha (Map pp72-3; ☎ mobile 020-2241590; Talat Sao; ☼ 8am-4pm Mon-Sat) In the air-conditioned Vientiane Department Store at Talat Sao.

Kosila Bookshop 1 (Map pp72-3; ☎ 241352; Th Chanta Khumman; ☼ 9am-5pm Mon-Fri)

Kosila Bookshop 2 (Map pp72-3; ☎ 241352; Th Nokeo Khumman; ☼ 9am-5pm Mon-Fri)

Lao Plaza Hotel Bookshop (Map pp72-3; Th Setthathirat) Wide selection of coffee-table books at five-star prices.

VIENTIANE IN...

Two days

Start with Lao coffee and the *Vientiane Times* before making your way to **Patuxai** (p75) to begin the **Monument to Mekong Walking Tour** (p78). This will take you through most of Vientiane's main sights, including **Wat Si Saket** (p71), **Haw Pha Kaew** (p71) and **Talat Sao** (p92). On day two check out the myriad concrete Buddhas and Hindu deities at **Xieng Khuan** (p76). On the way back stop in at **Salakham Beer Garden** (p89) for the freshest Beerlao, then head over to **Pha That Luang** (p70). Enjoy a fine French meal at **Le Côte D'Azur Restaurant** (p86) and finish it off with some jazz and drinks in **Snow White & One Dwarf** (p90) and/or **Deja Vu** (p89).

Four days

Start day three at the **Lao National Museum** (p76) then hire a bike and pedal out to **Bunmala Restaurant** (p85) for an authentic Lao lunch. Keep on to **Wat Sok Pa Luang** (p75) for a herbal sauna and massage. Enjoy sunset at **Sala Sunset Khounta** (p89) before adjourning to **On The Rock Pub** (p90) for rock, Lao style. On day four just take it easy in the morning before unleashing yourself on the **handicraft and textile shops** (p91) of Th Nokeo Khumman.

State Book Shop (Map pp72-3; ☎ 212472; cnr Th Setthathirat & Th Manthatulat; ⏰ 8am-noon & 1-4pm Mon-Fri) No light reading here, but the political comic books and posters are entertaining.

Vientiane Book Center (Map pp72-3; ☎ 212031; laobook@hotmail.com; Th Pangkham; ⏰ 8.30am-5.30pm Mon-Sat) Best selection of novels, postcards and books on Laos.

Cultural Centres

Centre Culturel et de Coopération Linguistique

(Map pp72-3; ☎ 215764; www.ambafrance-laos.org /centre; Th Lan Xang; ⏰ 9.30am-6.30pm Mon-Fri & 9.30am-noon Sat) The French Centre, as it's known, has a busy schedule of movies, musical and theatrical performances, a library and, of course, French and Lao language classes.

Emergency

Ambulance (☎ 195)
Fire (☎ 190)
Police (☎ 191)
Tourist Police (Map pp72-3; ☎ 251128; Lan Xang Ave)

Internet Access

There are several places on Th Setthathirat between Nam Phu and Th Nokeo Khumman, and on Th Nokeo Khumman itself. Rates are usually about US$1.20 an hour. Some have international telephone call facilities (see p67 for details).

A1 Computer (Map pp72-3; ☎ 2612129; Th Setthathirat; ⏰ 8.30am-11.30pm)

i-net (Map pp72-3; ☎ 262799; Th Heng Boun; per hr US$0.75; ⏰ 8.30am-11pm) Eight fast terminals, each with webcam, headphones, and Windows XP. International calls.

Lanexang Internet (Map pp72-3; cnr Th Setthathirat & Th Manthatulat; per hr US$0.60; ⏰ 8am-11pm) Cheapest in town. Has a booth for laptop connections. Sells prepaid Internet cards for remote access.

PlaNet Online (Map pp72-3; ☎ 218972; Th Setthathirat; per hr US$1.20; ⏰ 8.30am-11pm) Sells prepaid Internet cards for remote access, US$10/20/40.

Sokxay Internet (Map pp72-3; ☎ 218370; Th Khun Bulom; per hr US$0.90; ⏰ 8am-midnight) Very fast machines, Windows XP, printer, CD burning.

Star-Net Internet (Map pp72-3; ☎ 243209; Th Nokeo Khumman; per hr US$1.20; ⏰ 7.30am-11pm) Burns CDs; international calls; webcams.

Laundry

Most hotels and guesthouses offer laundry services. Otherwise, several laundries and dry-cleaners are on Th Samsenthai just east of Th Chao Anou. Typical rates are about US$1.50 per kg.

Media

Laos's only English-language newspaper is the government-run *Vientiane Times* (US$0.30). The paper is maturing fast and now publishes five times a week – from Monday to Friday – and even carries the odd story critical of the government. Look for the What's On page and bus-fare table.

Medical Services

HOSPITALS

Vientiane's medical facilities can leave a lot to be desired, so for anything serious strongly consider making a break for the border and the excellent hospitals in Thailand. Among those, the **Aek Udon International Hospital** (☎ 0066-4234 2555) can dispatch an ambulance to take you to Udon Thani. You could also use the services of Lao Westcoast Helicopter (p280).

Less serious ailments can be dealt with in Vientiane.

Australian Embassy Clinic (Map pp68-9; ☎ 413603; ⏰ 8.30am-12.30pm & 2-5pm Mon-Thu, 8.30am-12.30pm Fri) For residents of Australia, Britain, Canada, PNG and NZ only, this clinic's Australian doctor treats minor problems by appointment. In an emergency, just turn up.

International Clinic (Map pp68-9; ☎ 214021–2; Th Fa Ngum; ⏰ 24hr) Part of the Mahasot Hospital, this is probably the best place for minor to moderate medical conditions. English-speaking doctors.

Mahasot Hospital (Map pp68-9; ☎ 214023; Th Mahasot)

Setthathirat Hospital (☎ 450197, 413720) A Japanese-funded overhaul means this hospital, located northeast of the city, is fairly well equipped.

PHARMACIES

Vientiane's better pharmacies are on Th Nong Bon near Talat Sao.

Pharmacie Kamsaat (Map pp72-3; ☎ 212940; Th Mahasot; ⏰ Mon-Sat)

Pharmacie Sengthong Osoth (Map pp72-3; ☎ 213732; Th Mahasot; ⏰ 24hr) English and French is spoken.

Money

Licensed moneychanging booths can be found in Talat Sao and a few other locations around town. You can also change at various shops, hotels or markets for no commission or from the unofficial moneychangers hanging out near Talat Sao. The latter have particularly good rates but count your money carefully. See p257 for more information.

Several banks in Vientiane change cash and travellers cheques. A few, including those listed following, issue cash advances against Visa and MasterCard, usually for a commission of between 3% and 4%. All are open 8.30am to 3.30pm Monday to Friday unless otherwise stated.

Bangkok Bank (Map pp72-3; 28/13-15 Th Hatsady)

Bank of Ayudhya (Map pp72-3; ☎ 214575; 79/6 Th Lan Xang) Also the Western Union Money Transfer agent.

Banque pour le Commerce Extérieur Lao (BCEL; Map pp72-3; ☎ 213200; cnr Th Pangkham & Th Fa Ngum; ☸ 8.30am-7pm Mon-Fri, 8.30am-3pm Sat & Sun) Best rates. Longest hours. Exchange booth on Th Fa Ngum.

Joint Development Bank (Map pp72-3; ☎ 213535; 75/1-5 Th Lan Xang) Usually charges the lowest commission on cash advances.

Lao-Viet Bank (Map pp72-3; ☎ 214377; Lan Xang Ave)

Siam Commercial Bank (Map pp72-3; ☎ 227306; 117 Th Lan Xang)

Thai Military Bank (Map pp72-3; ☎ 216486; 69 cnr Th Samsenthai & Th Khun Bulom)

Post

Post, Telephone & Telegraph (PTT; Map pp72-3; cnr Th Lan Xang & Th Khu Vieng; ☸ 8am-noon & 1-5pm Mon-Fri, 8am-noon Sat & Sun) Come here for post restante.

COURIERS

Several international courier services operate out of Vientiane:

DHL (Map pp68-9; ☎ 214868; www.dhl.com; Th Nong No) Near the airport.

Fedex (Map pp72-3; ☎ 223278; www.fedex.com; Th Khu Vieng) Beside the PTT office.

TNT Express Worldwide (Map pp68-9; ☎ 261918; 2nd fl, Thai Airways Bldg, Th Luang Prabang)

Telephone & Fax

The **Lao Telecom Numphu Centre** (Map pp72-3; ☎ 250123; Th Setthathirat; ☸ 9am-10pm) has fax and international-call facilities to Europe/US for US$1.40 per minute, and to Australia for US$0.65 per minute. Fax services are in a separate room. The cardphone booths are outside the building; cards can be purchased inside or at the PTT office.

Cheaper international calls are available in many Internet cafés (see p66), with approximate per-minute rates: Australia (US$0.30), Canada (US$0.25), EU countries (from US$0.30 to US$0.50), Japan (US$0.30) and USA (US$0.20).

Local calls can be made from any hotel lobby, often for free.

Tourist Information

Between Talat Sao and Patuxai, the ground-floor office of the **Lao National Tourism Authority** (NTAL; Map pp72-3; ☎ 212251; fax 212769; Th Lan Xang; ☸ 8am-noon & 1-4pm, Mon-Fri) has a few brochures and English-speaking staff who are most knowledgeable about trips to Phu Khao Khuay and other day-trips from Vientiane. Ask for the glossy *Official Lao PDR Tourism Guidebook*.

Travel Agencies

For a list of reputable agencies able to organise tours, see p276. These agencies will book air tickets, and in some cases Thai train tickets fairly efficiently:

A-Rasa Tours (Map pp72-3 ☎ 213633; www.laos-info .com; Th Setthathirat; ☸ 8.30am-5pm Mon-Sat) Happy to answer questions, runs some tours. Beside Lao Travellers Café.

Lao American Airport (☎ 512232; ☸ Mon-Sun); Th Luang Prabang (Map pp68-9; ☎ 215623; Th Luang Prabang; ☸ 8am-5.30pm Mon-Sat) Big place just past the Novotel.

Visa Extensions

The **Immigration Office** (Map pp72-3; ☎ 212520; Th Hatsady; ☸ 8am-4pm Mon-Fri) handles visa extensions with a minimum of fuss. Take your passport, one photo, and US$2 for each extra day to this office across from the Talat Sao. If you lodge the application early, you can collect it the same day. See p264 for more on visa extensions.

Guesthouses and travel agencies will also arrange extensions, usually for US$3 per day.

DANGERS & ANNOYANCES

Vientiane has a very low crime rate, but you should still take the usual commonsense precautions and remain aware of potential dangers, especially at night. Public pavements (sidewalks) remain a danger, albeit lessening by the year, as there is still the occasional open sewer big enough to swallow you – a thoroughly shitty end to any day.

All businesses in Vientiane are supposed to close by 11.30pm, though some stay open an extra hour or so. It's not dangerous to be out beyond midnight, but you could be annoyed by military types if you're away from central Vientiane in an area where *falang* (Westerners) are seldom seen. If you are somewhere you shouldn't be (around the airport, for example) you might be told to go back to your hotel, or even escorted.

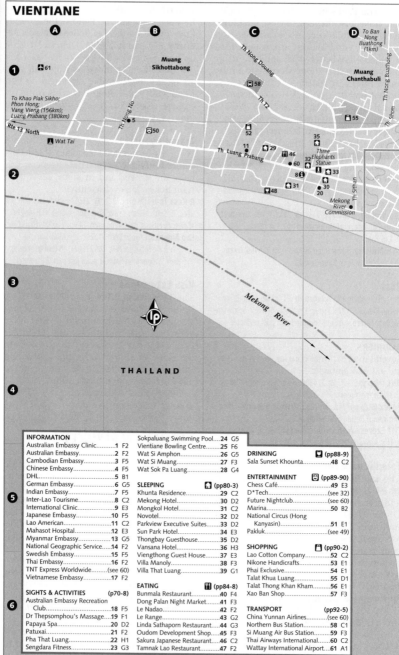

VIENTIANE

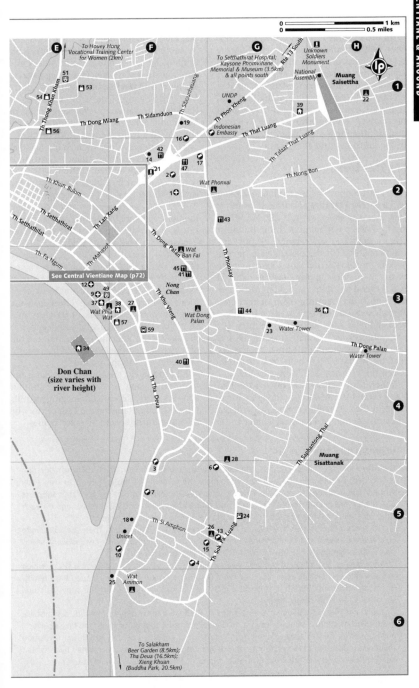

0 ——— 1 km
0 ——— 0.5 miles

To Houey Hong
Vocational Training Center
for Women (2km)

To Setthathirat Hospital;
Kaysone Phomvihane
Memorial & Museum (3.5km)
& all points south

Rte 13 South

Unknown
Soldiers
Monument

National
Assembly

Muang
Saisettha

51
54
53
56

Th Thong Khan Kham
Th Sibounheuang
Th Dong Miang
Th Sidamduon
Th Phon Kheng
Th That Luang

UNDP
Indonesian
Embassy

19
16

39

22

42
14
21
2
1

47
17

Wat Phonxai
Th Talaat That Luang
Th Nong Bon

Th Khun Bulom
Th Setthathirat
Th Setthathilat
Th Lan Xang
Th Mahasot
Th Fa Ngum

43

See Central Vientiane Map (p72)

Th Dong Palan
Wat
Ban Fai

Th Phonsay

45
41

12
9
37
38
27
57

49

Wat Phia
Wat

Nong
Chan

Th Khu Vieng

Wat Dong
Palan

44

36

59

23
Water Tower

34

Don Chan
(size varies with
river height)

40

Th Dong Palan
Water Tower

Th Tha Deua

Th Saphantong Thai

Muang
Sisattanak

3
6

28

7

18

Th Si Amphon

Unicef

10

26
13

24

15

4

25

Wat
Ammon

Th Sok Pa Luang

To Salakham
Beer Garden (8.5km);
Tha Deua (16.5km);
Xieng Khuan
(Buddha Park, 20.5km)

VIENTIANE & AROUND

SIGHTS

With urban sprawl a fairly recent phenomenon in Vientiane, it's no surprise that the bulk of sights are concentrated in a small area in the centre of the city. Except for the Kaysone Phomvihane Memorial & Museum and Xieng Khuan (Buddha Park), all sights are easily reached by bicycle and, in most cases, on foot. Most wats welcome visitors after the monks have collected alms in the morning until about 6pm.

Pha That Luang

ພະທາດຫລວງ

The most important national monument in Laos, **Pha That Luang** (Great Sacred Reliquary or Great Stupa; Map pp68-9; admission US$0.20; ☺ 8am-4pm Tue-Sun) is a symbol of both the Buddhist religion and Lao sovereignty. Its full official name, Pha Chedi Lokajulamani, means World-Precious Sacred Stupa, and an image of the main stupa appears on the national seal. Legend has it that Ashokan missionaries from India erected a *thâat* or reliquary stupa here to enclose a piece of the Buddha's breastbone as early as the 3rd century BC. Excavations have found no trace of this, but did find suggestion of a Khmer monastery that might have been built near here between the 11th and 13th centuries AD.

When King Setthathirat moved the Lan Xang capital from Luang Prabang to Vientiane in the mid-16th century, he ordered the construction of Pha That Luang in its current form on the site of the Khmer temple. Construction began in AD 1566 and in succeeding years four wats were built around the stupa, one on each side. Only two remain today, **Wat That Luang Neua** to the north and **Wat That Luang Tai** to the south. Wat That Luang Neua is the residence of the Supreme Patriarch (Pha Sangkhalat) of Lao Buddhism. The main building is a reconstruction from the early 20th century.

The monument looks almost like a gilded missile cluster from a distance. Surrounding it is a high-walled cloister with tiny windows, added by King Anouvong in the early 19th century as a defence against invaders. Even more aggressive-looking than the thick walls are the pointed stupas themselves, which are built in three levels (see Viewing Pha That Luang below).

In 1641, Gerrit van Wuystoff, an envoy of the Dutch East India Company, visited Vientiane and was received by King Suriya Vongsa in a reportedly magnificent ceremony at Pha That Luang. The Lan Xang kingdom was at the peak of its glory and van Wuystoff wrote that he was deeply impressed by the 'enormous pyramid, the top of which was covered with gold leaf weighing about a thousand pounds'.

Unfortunately, the glory of Lan Xang and Pha That Luang was only to last another 60 years or so. Repeated damaging assaults were carried out during the 18th century by invading Burmese and Siamese armies.

VIEWING PHA THAT LUANG

Each level of Pha That Luang has different architectural features in which Buddhist doctrine is encoded; visitors are supposed to contemplate the meaning of these features as they walk around. The first level is an approximately square base measuring 68m by 69m that supports 323 *siimáa* (ordination stones). There are also four arched *háw wái* (prayer halls), one on each side, with short stairways leading to them and beyond to the second level.

The second level is 48m by 48m and is surrounded by 120 lotus petals. There are 288 *siimáa* on this level, as well as 30 small stupas symbolising the 30 Buddhist perfections *(páalamíi sáam-síp thâat)*, beginning with alms-giving and ending with equanimity.

Arched gates again lead to the next level, a 30m by 30m square. The tall central stupa, which has a brick core that has been stuccoed over, is supported here by a bowl-shaped base reminiscent of India's first Buddhist stupa at Sanchi. At the top of this mound the superstructure, surrounded by lotus petals, begins.

The curvilinear, four-sided spire resembles an elongated lotus bud and is said to symbolise the growth of a lotus from a seed in a muddy lake bottom to a bloom over the lake's surface, a metaphor for human advancement from ignorance to enlightenment in Buddhism. The entire *thâat* was regilded in 1995 to celebrate the LPDR's 20th anniversary, and is crowned by a stylised banana flower and parasol. From ground to pinnacle, Pha That Luang is 45m tall.

Then, in 1828, a Siamese invasion ransacked and depopulated Vientiane to such an extent that Pha That Luang remained abandoned, and eventually dismantled by treasure seekers, until it was (badly) restored by the French in 1900.

In 1867 French explorer and architect Louis Delaporte had stumbled on the abandoned and overgrown Pha That Luang and made a number of detailed sketches of the monument. Between 1931 and 1935, a French university department tore down the much-criticised French reconstruction of 1900 and rebuilt the stupa in the original Lao-style lotus-bud shape depicted in Delaporte's sketches.

Pha That Luang is about 4km northeast of the centre of Vientiane at the end of Th That Luang. Facing the compound is a statue of King Setthathirat. The temple is the site of a major festival, held in early November (see p80).

Wat Si Saket

ວັດສີສະເກດ

Built in 1818 by Chao Anou, **Wat Si Saket** (Wat Sisaketsata Sahatsaham; Map pp72-3; cnr Th Lan Xang & Th Setthathirat; admission US$0.20; 8am-noon & 1-4pm, closed public holidays) is perhaps Vientiane's oldest surviving temple.

Chao Anou, who was educated in the Bangkok court and was more or less a vassal of the Siamese state, had Wat Si Saket constructed in the early Bangkok style but surrounded it with a thick-walled cloister similar to – but much smaller than – the one that surrounds Pha That Luang (p70). The stylistic similarity to their own wats might have motivated the Siamese to spare this monastery when they crushed Chao Anou's rebellion (p22), even as they razed many others. The French restored the temple in 1924 and again in 1930.

In spite of the Siamese influence, Wat Si Saket has several unique features. The interior walls of the cloister are riddled with small niches that contain over 2000 silver and ceramic Buddha images. Over 300 seated and standing Buddhas of varying sizes and materials (wood, stone, silver and bronze) rest on long shelves below the niches, most of them sculpted or cast in the characteristic Lao style (p40). Most of the images are from 16th- to 19th-century Vientiane but a few hail from 15th- to 16th-century Luang Prabang.

A slightly damaged Khmer-style Naga Buddha – which depicts the Buddha seated on a coiled cobra deity, sheltered by the *naga*'s multiheaded hood – is also on display; it was brought from a Khmer site at nearby Hat Sai Fong. Along the western side of the cloister is a pile of broken and half-melted Buddhas from the 1828 Siamese-Lao war.

The *sim* (ordination hall) is surrounded by a colonnaded terrace in the Bangkok style and topped by a five-tiered roof. The interior walls bear hundreds of Buddha niches similar to those in the cloister, as well as beautiful – but decaying – Jataka murals depicting stories of the Buddha's past lives. Portions of the Bangkok-style murals are unrestored 1820s originals, while others are a 1913 restoration.

The flowered ceiling was inspired by Siamese temples in Ayuthaya, which were in turn inspired by floral designs from Versailles. At the rear interior of the *sim* is an altar with several more Buddha images, bringing the total number of Buddhas at Wat Si Saket to 6840. The standing Buddha to the left on the upper altar is said to have been cast to the same physical proportions as Chao Anou. The large, gilt wood candlestand in front of the altar is an original, carved in 1819.

On the veranda at the rear of the *sim* is a 5m-long wooden trough carved to resemble a *naga* (serpent deity). This is the *háang song nâm pha* (image-watering rail), which is used during Lao New Year to pour water over Buddha images for ceremonial cleansing.

To the far left of the entrance to the cloister, facing Th Lan Xang, is a raised *hăw tại* (Tripitaka library) with a Burmese-style roof. The scriptures once contained here are now in Bangkok.

The grounds of the wat are planted with coconut, banana and mango trees. *Thâat kádụuk* (small stupa-shaped monuments containing the cremated remains of temple devotees) line the northern and western walls.

Haw Pha Kaew

ຫໍພະແກ້ວ

Once a royal temple built specifically to house the famed Emerald Buddha, **Haw Pha Kaew** (Map pp72-3; Th Setthathirat; admission US$0.20; 8am-noon & 1-4pm, closed public holidays) is today a museum of religious art. It is about 100m southeast of Wat Si Saket.

VIENTIANE & AROUND

CENTRAL VIENTIANE

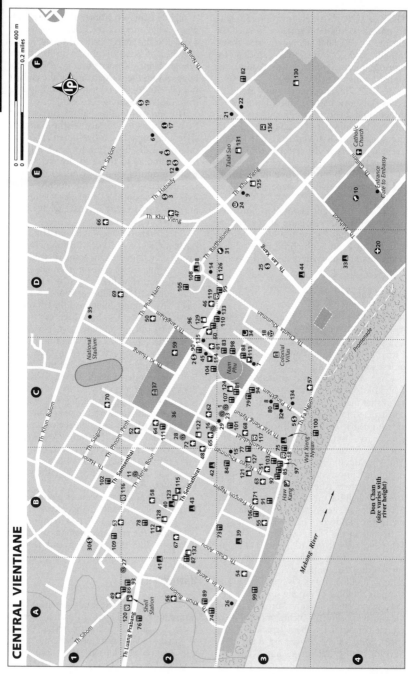

According to the Lao, the temple was originally built in 1565 by command of King Setthathirat, who on inheriting the Lan Xang throne moved the capital from Luang Prabang to Vientiane and brought with him the so-called Emerald Buddha (Pha Kaew in Lao, which means Jewel Buddha Image – the image is actually made of a type of jade). Wat Pha Kaew also served as Setthathirat's personal place of worship. Following a skirmish with the Lao in 1779, the Siamese stole the Emerald Buddha and installed it in Bangkok's Wat Phra Kaew. Later, during the Siamese-Lao war of 1828, Vientiane's Wat Pha Kaew was razed.

The temple was finally rebuilt with French help between 1936 and 1942, supposedly following the original plan exactly. However, the 'original' 16th century plan looks nothing like its contemporaries, instead bearing an uncanny resemblance to 19th-century Bangkok-style *sim*. Perhaps the architects used the 19th-century style because they didn't have the original plans after all.

At any rate, today's Haw Pha Kaew is not particularly impressive, except in size. The rococo ornamentation that runs up and down every door, window and base looks unfinished. But some of the best examples of Buddhist sculpture found in Laos are kept here, with a dozen or so prominent sculptures displayed along the surrounding terrace. These include Dvaravati-style stone Buddha from between the 6th and 9th centuries; several bronze standing and sitting Lao-style Buddhas – including the 'Calling for Rain' (standing with hands at his sides), 'Offering Protection' (palms stretched out in front) and 'Contemplating the Tree of Enlightenment' (hands crossed at the wrist in front) poses; and a collection of inscribed Lao and Mon stelae. Most of the Lao bronzes are missing their *usnisa* (flame finial).

Inside the *sim* are royal requisites such as a gilded throne, more Buddhist sculpture (including a wooden copy of the Pha Bang), some Khmer stelae, various wooden carvings, palm-leaf manuscripts and bronze frog drums. A bronze 'Calling for Rain' Buddha, tall and lithe, is particularly beautiful; also unique is a 17th-century Vientiane-style bronze Buddha in the 'European pose', ie with the legs hanging down as if seated on a chair or bench.

The *sim* is surrounded by a landscaped garden. A French- and English-speaking guide is occasionally available.

Wat Ong Teu Mahawihan

ວັດອົງຕື້ມະຫາວິຫານ

This **temple** (Temple of the Heavy Buddha; Map pp72-3; Th Setthathirat) is one of the most important in Laos. It was originally built in the mid-16th century by King Setthathirat, but like almost every other temple in Vientiane it was destroyed in later wars with the Siamese, then rebuilt in the 19th and 20th centuries. The Hawng Sangkhalat (Deputy Patriarch) of the Lao monastic order has his official residence here and presides over the Buddhist Institute, a school for monks who come from all over the country to study *dhamma* (the Buddha's teachings).

The temple's namesake is a 16th-century bronze Buddha of several tonnes that sits in the rear of the *sim*, flanked by two standing Buddhas. This *sim* is famous for the wooden façade over the front terrace, a masterpiece of Lao carving.

Wat Si Muang

ວັດສີເມືອງ

The most frequently used grounds in all of Vientiane are those of the **Wat Si Muang** (Map pp72-3; cnr of Th Setthathirat, Th Samsenthai & Th Tha Deua; ⊗ 6am-7pm daily, until 10pm on special days). The grounds are the site of the *lák meuang* (city pillar/phallus), which is considered the home of the guardian spirit of Vientiane (see No Sacrifice Too Great below).

The *sim* (destroyed in 1828 and rebuilt in 1915) was constructed around the *lák meuang*, which forms the centre of the altar. The stone pillar is wrapped in sacred cloth, and in front of it is a carved wooden stele with a seated Buddha in relief.

Several other Buddha images surround the pillar. One worth noting is on a cushion to a little to the left and in front of the altar. This rather crude, partially damaged stone Buddha survived the 1828 inferno and locals believe it has the power to grant wishes or answer troubling questions. The practice is to lift it off the pillow three times while mentally phrasing a question or request. If your request is granted, then you are supposed to return later with an offering of bananas, green coconuts, flowers, incense and candles (usually two of each). This is why so many platters of fruit, flowers and incense sit around the *sim*.

NO SACRIFICE TOO GREAT

Legend has it that a group of sages selected the site for Wat Si Muang in 1563, when King Setthathirat moved his capital to Vientiane. Once the spot was chosen, a large hole was dug to receive the heavy stone pillar (probably taken from an ancient Khmer site nearby) that would become the *lák meuang* (city pillar). When the pillar arrived it was suspended over the hole with ropes. Drums and gongs were sounded to summon the townspeople to the area and everyone waited for a volunteer to jump in the hole as a sacrifice to the spirit. A pregnant woman finally leapt in and the ropes were released, establishing the town guardianship.

Some people mistakenly believe the name of the wat is somehow related to the name of the legendary human sacrifice, but in fact 'wat sii meuang' simply means 'holy city monastery'.

Behind the *sĭm* is a crumbling laterite *jēhdii* (stupa), probably of Khmer origin. Devotees deposit broken deity images and pottery around the stupa's base so the spirits of the stupa will 'heal' the bad luck created by the breaking of these items. In front of the *sĭm* is a little public park with an un labelled statue of King Sisavang Vong (1904–59) – the identifying plaque was taken off after the 1975 Revolution.

Wat Sok Pa Luang
ວັດໂສກປ່າຫລວງ

In a shaded, almost semirural setting that is entirely in keeping with its name (*wat paa* means forest temple), **Wat Sok Pa Luang** (Wat Mahaphutthawongsa Pa Luang Pa Yai; Map pp72-3; Th Sok Pa Luang) is famous for its herbal saunas and expert massage. The masseurs are usually lay people who reside at the temple. After a relaxing sauna, you can take herbal tea on the veranda while cooling off; then opt for a massage. You're not supposed to wash away your accumulated perspiration for two or three hours afterwards, apparently to allow the herbs to soak into your pores. The sauna (US$1) and massage (US$2 for 40 minutes, US$3 for one hour) operate from 1pm to 7pm daily. Nearby **Wat Si Amphon** (Map pp68-9; Th Si Amphon) also does herbal saunas.

Wat Sok Pa Luang is also known for its course of instruction in *vipassana* (Lao *vi-patsanáa*), a type of Buddhist meditation that involves careful mind-body analysis. See p79 for details.

GETTING THERE & AWAY

Taxi, jumbo (motorcycle taxi) and tuk-tuk drivers all know how to get to Wat Sok Pa Luang. If you're travelling by car or bicycle, take Th Khu Vieng south past Talat Sao for about 2.5km until you come to a fairly major road on the left (this is Th Sok Pa Luang, but it's unmarked). Turn left here; the ornamented entrance to the wat is about 500m on the left. For Wat Si Amphon, go a few hundred metres further and turn right on Th Si Amphon.

Patuxai
ປະຕູໄຊ

A large monument reminiscent of the Arc de Triomphe in Paris, the **Patuxai** (Map pp68-9; Th Lan Xang; admission US$0.10; ☺ 8am-5pm) is known by a variety of names. The official Lao name is approximately equivalent to Arch (*pátuu*, also translated as door or gate) of Triumph (*xái*, from the Sanskrit *jaya* or victory). Unlike its Paris namesake, the Patuxai boasts four, rather than two, archways. It was built in the 1960s with US-purchased cement that was supposed to have been used for the construction of a new airport. Hence foreign residents sometimes refer to it as 'the vertical runway'.

From a distance, Patuxai looks much like its French source of inspiration. Up close, however, the Lao design is revealed. The bas-relief on the sides and the temple-like ornamentation along the top and cornices are typically Lao, though the execution is at times shoddy. Don't miss the painted description on the southwest corner, which in a few lines reflects both Laos's endearing honesty and naivety to 'First World' pre-occupations like marketing. One sentence reads: 'From a closer distance, it appears even less impressive, like a monster of concrete'. A stairway leads through two levels stuffed with souvenir T-shirts (seriously, there are thousands) to the top levels of the monument, from where the views are grand.

This huge arch is within walking distance of the town centre and work in recent years has transformed the surrounding muddy field into the most popular park in Vientiane – a good place to soak up the atmosphere of modern Laos in the late afternoon.

That Dam
ທາດດຳ

Now known as the 'Black Stupa', or **That Dam** (Map pp72-3; Th Bartholomie), local legend has it this stupa near the centre of Vientiane was once coated in a layer of gold. The gold is said to have been carted off by the Siamese during their pillaging of 1828, after which the stupa took the 'black' sobriquet in memory of the dastardly act. However, another myth is slightly at odds with this. It says That Dam is the abode of a dormant seven-headed dragon that came to life during the 1828 Siamese-Lao war and protected local citizens, though apparently not the stupa's gold...

Either way, the stupa appears to date from the Lanna or early Lan Xang period and is very similar to stupas in Chiang Saen, Thailand.

Lao National Museum

ພິພິດທະພັນປະຫວັດສາດແຫ່ງຊາດລາວ

The **Lao National Museum** (Map pp72-3; Th Sam-senthai; admission US$0.50; ☉ 8am-noon & 1-4pm) used to be known as the Lao Revolutionary Museum, and much of the collection retains an unmistakable revolutionary zeal. It is housed in a well-worn mansion originally built in 1925 as the French governor's residence. There are many artefacts and photos from the Pathet Lao's (PL) lengthy struggle for power, as well as enough historic weaponry to arm all the extras in a Rambo film. The museum is worth a look, and with temporary (and nonrevolutionary) exhibitions also beginning to appear in the museum, it's worth checking even if you've visited before. The number of labels in English is also rising.

The rooms near the entrance feature small cultural and geographical exhibits. The more interesting items include several Khmer sandstone sculptures of Hindu deities and a display of traditional musical instruments.

Inner rooms are dedicated to the 1893–1945 French colonial period, the 1945–54 struggle for independence, the 1954–63 resistance to American imperialism, the 1964–69 provisional government and the 1975 communist victory.

Lao National Culture Hall

ຫໍວັດທະນະທໍາແຫ່ງຊາດ

Opposite the Lao National Museum, and dwarfing it, is the monumentally proportioned **Lao National Culture Hall** (Map pp72-3; Th Samsenthai). The hall hosts cultural events as varied as French cinema and Lao classical dance. There is no publicly available schedule of events at the hall, not even a phone number, although the *Vientiane Times* does print occasional announcements.

Kaysone Phomvihane Memorial & Museum

ອະນຸສາວະລີໄກສອນພົມວິຫານ

Opened in 1995 to celebrate the late president's 75th birthday, the **Kaysone Phomvihane Memorial & Museum** (☉ 8am-noon & 1-4pm, closed Mon & holidays), near Km 6 on Rte 13 south, serves as a tribute to Indochina's most pragmatic communist leader. It's worth visiting if you are interested in the Lao revolution or want to see the relatively modest

building – an American-built single-storey house – where the great man lived after the revolution.

Exhibits include a bronze bust of Kaysone, fashioned by a North Korean sculptor, pictures of Laos's most important cultural and historic sites and a mock-up of Kaysone's childhood home in Savannakhet Province. You can also view his desk from the French school he attended at Ban Tai, surmounted by family pictures; and many a picture and artefact chronicling the founding of the Lao Issara and the Indochinese Communist Party. A model of a portion of 'Kaysone Cave' in Hua Phan Province contains a revolver, binoculars, radio and other personal effects.

The museum-memorial is inside the former Usaid/CIA compound, a self-contained headquarters known as 'Six Klicks City' because of its location from central Vientiane. It once featured bars, restaurants, tennis courts, swimming pools, a commissary and assorted offices from where the Secret War (see the Secret War p28) was orchestrated. During the 1975 takeover of Vientiane, the PL forces ejected the Americans and occupied the compound. Kaysone lived here until his death in 1992.

The museum is within easy cycling distance; the entrance is just before the Children's Home as you head along Rte 13. A shared tuk-tuk (US$0.20) from Talat Sao will drop you here, or hire one outright for about US$1.30 one way.

Xieng Khuan (Buddha Park)

ຊຽງຂວັນ

In a field by the Mekong River, off Th Tha Deua, 24km south of central Vientiane, **Xieng Khuan** (Buddha Park or Suan Phut; admission person US$0.30, camera US$0.20; ☉ 8am-4.30pm, sometimes longer) is, as the name suggests, a park full of Buddhist and Hindu sculpture that is a monument to one eccentric man's quite bizarre ambition.

Xieng Khuan was designed and built in 1958 by Luang Pu (Venerable Grandfather) Bunleua Sulilat, a yogi-priest-shaman who merged Hindu and Buddhist philosophy, mythology and iconography into a cryptic whole. Originally, Bunleua is supposed to have studied under a Hindu *rishi* (sage) who lived in Vietnam. Legend has it that their meeting was fortunate, to say the least, as while Bunleua was walking in the mountains he fell through a sinkhole and landed in the *rishi*'s lap. As you do. Bunleua developed a large following in Laos and northeastern Thailand, and moved to Thailand around the time of the 1975 Revolution. In 1978, he established the similarly inspired Wat Khaek in Nong Khai, Thailand.

The concrete sculptures at Xieng Khuan (which means Spirit City) are bizarre but compelling in their naive confidence. They include statues of Shiva, Vishnu, Arjuna, Avalokiteshvara, Buddha and just about every other Hindu or Buddhist deity imaginable, as well as a few secular figures, all supposedly cast by unskilled artists under Luang Pu's direction. The style of the figures is remarkably uniform. Children will enjoy cavorting around some of the more fantastic shapes, such as the deity with tentacles.

The large pumpkin-shaped concrete monument in the grounds has three levels joined by interior spiral stairways. The three levels are said to represent hell, earth and heaven, and lead to the roof and panoramic views of the park.

A few food vendors offer fresh coconuts, soft drinks, beer, *ping kai* (grilled chicken) and *tạm màak-hung* (spicy green papaya salad).

GETTING THERE & AWAY

Buses for Xieng Khuan (US$0.30, 45 minutes) leave the Talat Sao terminal every 20 minutes or so throughout the day. Alternatively, charter a jumbo (about US$5 return) or hop on a shared jumbo (US$0.30) as far as the old ferry pier at Tha Deua and walk or take a *sǎam-lâaw* (three-wheeled taxi) the final 4km to the park. You could cycle here fairly easily as the road is relatively flat all the way.

ACTIVITIES
Bowling

Vientiane's two bowling alleys make a fun diversion, especially watching some of the local form.

Lao Bowling Centre (Map pp72-3; ☎ 218661; Th Khun Bulom; per frame US$1.50; ☺ 9am-midnight) Bowling and music.

Vientiane Bowling Centre (Map pp68-9; ☎ 313823; 58/1 Th Tha Deua)

Gyms & Aerobics

There is a free aerobics session on the riverfront just east of Haw Kang most weekend afternoons at about 5pm. If that doesn't do it for you, the following places might:

Sengdara Fitness (Map pp68-9; ☎ 414061; 5/77 Th Dong Palan; ☺ 5am-10pm) Vientiane's first Western-style mega-gym, with dozens of machines, sauna, pool, massage, juice bar and restaurant.

Tai-Pan Hotel (Map pp72-3; ☎ 216906; 22/3 Th François Nginn; per visit US$4) Small fitness room and sauna; central location; see p83.

Hash House Harriers

The Vientiane Hash House Harriers welcome runners to their weekly hash on Monday at 5pm; it starts from Nam Phu and is followed by food and Beerlao. Many of the same harriers run a more challenging route on Saturday afternoons, usually starting about 3.45pm; transport is provided. Look for details of upcoming hashes at the Scandinavian Bakery (p84), Phimphone Market (p88) or Asia Vehicle Rentals (p274), where owner **Joe Rumble** (☎ mobile 020-5511293) has all the info.

Massage/Sauna

Good massage comes cheap in this town.

Dr Thepsomphou's Massage (Map pp68-9; ☎ 223564; Th Sibounheuang; ☺ 4-9pm) Cheap but good sauna (US$0.60) and massage (US$2) with the locals.

Papaya Spa (Map pp68-9; ☎ mobile 020-5610565; www.papayaspa.com; ☺ 1-8pm) In an old French villa west of town (follow the many signs), this is definitely the classiest and priciest massage operation. Services include massage (US$6), facial (US$10), leg wax (US$10), sauna (US$2) and on Mondays aromatherapy (US$12).

Wat Sok Pa Luang (Th Sok Pa Luang) The traditional Lao experience; see p75.

White Lotus Massage & Beauty (Map pp72-3; ☎ 217492; Th Pangkham; ☺ 10am-10pm) Just north of Nam Phu; foot massage (US$4), aromatherapy body massage (US$10).

Swimming

There are several places in Vientiane where you can work on your strokes or simply take a cooling dip. For laps, the 25m-long **Sokpaluang Swimming Pool** (Map pp68-9; ☎ 350491; Th Sok Pa Luang; adult/child US$0.60/$0.40; ☺ 9am-8pm Tue-Sun) in southeastern Vientiane is one of the best choices. It also has a shallow children's pool and changing rooms; leave your stuff with the woman taking your money.

The pool at the **Australian Embassy Recreation Club** (AERC; Map pp68-9; ☎ 314921; Km 3 Th Tha Deua; ☼ 9am-8pm) is good, and several hotels welcome nonguests:

Lane Xang Hotel (Map pp72-3; ☎ 214102; Th Fa Ngum; per day US$3) See p82.

Lao Plaza Hotel (Map pp72-3; ☎ 218800; 63 Th Samsenthai; per visit US$5) See p83.

Settha Palace Hotel (Map pp72-3; ☎ 217581; Th Pangkham; US$6) This decadent pool and surrounding bar is very nice indeed; see p83.

MONUMENT TO MEKONG WALKING TOUR

This walking tour can be done on foot or bicycle. It covers about 6km and will take between four and six hours, depending on how often you stop, eat, drink and shop. When deciding how long to spend in Talat Sao, and where to stop, remember Wat Si Saket and Haw Pha Kaew close between noon and 1pm.

To start, take a jumbo ride to **Patuxai (1**; p75) and climb this concrete edifice for unbeatable views of the city. From here, head back into town along Th Lan Xang, a street whose recent renovation has seen it labelled by some as the 'Champs Elysées of the East'. Use this chance to stop in the **Lao National Tourism Authority office (2**; p67) and pick up maps and descriptions of the Phu Khao Khuay National Protected Area (NPA) walks, before continuing to Vientiane's biggest market, **Talat Sao (3**; p92). Wander among textiles, TVs and pirated

Thai pop to the **goldsmiths (4**), who craft their precious metal over a long line of fiery work benches at the southeast edge of the market. You could eat here, or head across to **Khouadin Vegetarian (5**; p88), on the northern side of the labyrinthine **Talat Khua Din (6**; p92) for some cheap but tasty fare before cutting through the market back to Th Khu Vieng.

Cross Th Lan Xang and walk past the high walls of the **US Embassy (7)** to **That Dam (8**; p75), one of Vientiane's oldest Buddhist stupas. If you manage to pass here without being swallowed by the dragon that lurks beneath, turn left (southwest) on Th Chanta Khumman and head for the Mekong. Consider ducking up Th Samsenthai to **PVO (9**; p84) for some of Vientiane's best *khào jìi páa-tê* (French baguette stuffed with Lao-style pâté and assorted vegetables and dressings), before continuing down to the shaded Th Setthathirat. Turn left (east) and you'll see the **Presidential Palace (10)**, a vast beaux-arts–style chateau originally built to house the French colonial governor. After independence King Sisavang Vong (and later his son Sisavang Vatthana) of Luang Prabang used it as a residence when visiting Vientiane; these days it is used only on ceremonial occasions.

Opposite the palace is the ochre-painted **Wat Si Saket (11**; p71), with its ancient Buddha figures and fading temple murals. Further along is the striking **Haw Pha Kaew (12**; p71), the temple first built for royalty in the

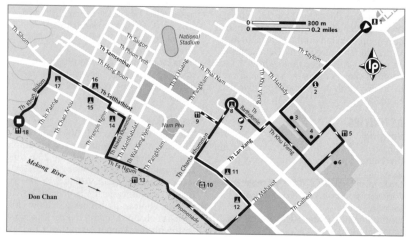

16th century and now a national museum for religious objects.

Turn down Th Mahasot and cross Th Fa Ngum to reach a modest, brick-paved riverside promenade that has benches for the weary or the romantic and, during the rainy season, views of the river. As you head northwest you'll pass under more than 25 tall, wide-girthed teak trees, each of them at least 200 years old, and two very old banyan trees. The **Riverside Restaurant** (**13**; p85) is a good place to stop for food or a drink.

You could finish up here but if time permits kick on along Th Fa Ngum, passing several alternative eateries on the way, and turn up Th Nokeo Khumman, one of Vientiane's best shopping streets. Step left into **Wat Mixay** (**14**), with its Bangkok-style *sǐm* and heavy gates, flanked by two *nyak* (guardian giants). Walk through the wat and further along Th Setthathirat to **Wat Ong Teu Mahawihan** (**15**; p74). On the opposite side of the road is **Wat Hai Sok** (**16**) and its impressive five-tiered roof (nine if you count the lower terrace roofs), which is topped by an elaborate set of *nyâwt saw fâa* (roof-ridge spires).

Finally, Vientiane's temple district closes out with **Wat In Paeng** (**17**), which is famed for the artistry displayed in the *sǐm*'s stucco relief. A rough translation of its name is 'Assembled by Indra'. Finish the day by heading down Th Khun Bulom to the Mekong, find a seat at one of the **outdoor drink vendors** (**18**) and watch the sun set with as much Beerlao and *pîng kai* as you dare.

COURSES
Language Courses
For details on Vientiane language schools that teach Lao see p250.

Cooking
As well as being a good place to stay (p81), **Thongbay Guesthouse** (Map pp68-9; ☎ /fax 242292; www.thongbay.laopdr.com; US$10) offers cooking courses at 10am and 4pm, arranged by appointment, which involve a trip to the market, brief kitchen work and sampling your creation.

Garden Fresh Restaurant (Map pp72-3; ☎ mobile 020-7711034; Th Manthatulat) specialises in vegetarian food, but is able to cater to carnivores as well (see p88). Garden Fresh was establishing a cooking course when we visited. It was expected to cost US$7 or US$8.

Weaving & Dyeing
You can learn how to dye textiles using natural pigments and then weave them on a traditional loom at the **Houey Hong Vocational Training Center for Women** (☎ 560006; hhtw@laotel.com; Ban Houey Hong; ☼ 8am-5pm Mon-Sat). The NGO group, run by a Lao-Japanese woman, established this centre about 20 minutes north of Vientiane to train unemployed Thai Dam women from Xieng Khuang Province and Sam Neua in the dying art of natural dyeing and traditional silk-weaving practices. Visitors are welcome to just look around, but can also partake in the dyeing process (US$12, two hours, two stoles) or weaving (US$15, whole day). You keep the fruits of your labour. One American woman spent a whole month learning to weave.

To get there, you can take a No 33 bus from Talat Sao, getting off at the first gasoline stand past the Houey Hong market, then following a small road 200m west. Much simpler is calling the centre, who will collect and return you for US$1. The centre's store in Vientiane is **True Colour** (Map pp72-3; ☎ 214410; Th Setthathirat).

Vipassana Meditation
Every Saturday from 4pm to 5.30pm monks lead a session of sitting and walking meditation at **Wat Sok Pa Luang** (Th Sok Pa Luang); see p75. The session is held in a small pavilion (to the left of the *sǐm*) and garden. All are welcome – about half the participants are Lao, while the other half are foreigners – and there is no charge. There is a translator for the question period held after the meditation.

Twice a year, once in February or March and again in September or October, the respected Buddhist teacher and abbot Ajahn Sali holds intensive meditation workshops at the monastery.

VIENTIANE FOR CHILDREN
While children are welcome almost wherever you are in Vientiane, there is little in the way of traditional child-friendly attractions to keep them occupied. The concrete wonders of Xieng Khuan (Buddha Park, p76) and Patuxai (p75) should keep them looking for an hour or so each, with the climbing giving these places a slightly more participatory aspect.

FESTIVALS & EVENTS

That Luang Festival (Bun Pha That Luang), usually in early November, is the largest temple fair in Laos. Apart from the religious fervour, the festival also features a trade show and a number of carnival games. The festivities begin with a *wíen thíen* (circumambulation) around Wat Si Muang, followed by a procession to Pha That Luang, which is illuminated all night for a week. The festival climaxes on the morning of the full moon with the *ták bàat* ceremony, in which several thousand monks from across the country receive alms food. That evening there's a final *wíen thíen* around Pha That Luang, with devotees carrying *pǫasàat* (miniature temples made from banana stems and decorated with flowers and other offerings). Fireworks cap off the evening and everyone makes merit or merry until dawn.

Another huge annual event is **Bun Nam** (River Festival) at the end of *phansǎa* (the Buddhist rains retreat) in October, during which boat races are held on the Mekong River. Rowing teams from all over the country, as well as from Thailand, China and Myanmar, compete, and the river bank is lined with food stalls, temporary discos, carnival games and beer gardens for three nights.

SLEEPING

Vientiane's dozens of guesthouses and hotels range from US$2-a-night cells to opulent colonial-era affairs where no luxury is spared. Most rooms, particularly those at the cheaper end of the market, suffer from capital-city syndrome – meaning you'll pay

twice as much here as you would for the same room elsewhere in Laos.

Most accommodation is within walking distance of the centre of town and comparing options is easy enough on foot. Some midrange and top-end places are a little further away, but it's usually only a couple of kilometres. Many places quote US dollar rates and some of the more expensive require payment in US currency. Others will take kip, US dollars or Thai baht, though expect currency conversions to add to your bill.

Budget

GUESTHOUSES

Saysouly Guest House (Map pp72-3; ☎ 223757, mobile 020-517609; saysouly@hotmail.com; 23 Th Manthatulat; r US$5-12; 🗙) In a quiet location two minutes from Nam Phu, this three-storey place offers spacious, clean rooms with bathrooms (single/double US$9/12) and fan rooms with shared bathrooms (US$5/7). There's a relaxed atmosphere, with acres of communal space on the balconies. Good choice.

Joe Guest House (Map pp72-3; ☎ /fax 241936; 112 Th Fa Ngum; s/d US$5/8) In a prime position on the river, this new and welcoming place has simple but spotless rooms and shared bathrooms on top of an open-fronted coffee shop, where breakfast is US$1.50.

Syri 1 Guest House (Map pp72-3; ☎ 212682; Th Saigon; r US$5-10; 🗙) The family-run Syri 1 (not to be confused with the Syri 2) is a relaxed, enjoyable place in a quiet location near the National Stadium. Some rooms in this old house are enormous, others smaller; all are clean and comfortable. The communal balcony is a good place to hang out. Look for the vintage Mercedes limo in the garage.

Chindamay Guest House (Map pp72-3; ☎ 262 165; chindamayph@yahoo.com; Th Sihom; r US$6-8; 🗙) This new place just west of the centre has small but very clean rooms with three beds. It's popular because it's outstanding value. Opt for fan instead of air-con for US$6.

Khamvongsa Guest House (Map pp72-3; ☎ 223 257; Th Khun Bulom; souriyo_a@hotmail.com; r US$4-7; 🗙) Double rooms with cold-water bathroom and fridge in Lao-style wooden buildings are excellent value at US$4, while the air-con rooms share a hot-water bathroom (single/double US$6/7). There is some English spoken.

THE AUTHOR'S CHOICE

Vayakorn Guest House (Map pp72-3; ☎ 241 911; vayakone@laotel.com; 91 Th Nokeo Khumman; s/d US$12/15; 🗙) In a quiet street two blocks west of Nam Phu, Vayakorn is a new guesthouse where smart, stylish and spacious rooms are a bargain. All rooms have polished floors, satellite television and spotless bathrooms, and those at the front boast views over the leafy garden and colonial-era building of Carol Cassidy's Lao Textiles. Service is friendly and professional, and rooms are cleaned daily. Breakfast, coffee and snacks are served downstairs.

Praseuth Guest House (Map pp72-3; ☎ 217932; 312 Th Samsenthai; r US$5-6; 🔀) Next door to the Xayoh Café, the basic rooms here are clean and the management is helpful. The upstairs shared bathroom is best. Fan rooms are US$5.

Saylomyen Guest House (Map pp72-3; ☎ 214 246; Th Saylom; r US$3-9; 🔀) Not far from Talat Sao in the north of town, this place has rooms ranging from windowless boxes with shared bathrooms to air-con and bathroom. The US$6 rooms with bathroom overlooking the courtyard are good value. There's a convenient noodle joint next door.

RD Guesthouse (Map pp72-3; ☎ 262112; ☎ mobile 020-7719401; Th Nokeo Khumman; dm/s/tw US$2/4/6) Popular with Japanese and Korean travellers, who have contributed extensively to the visitors' book, the windowless rooms and shared bathrooms are clean. The big, airy dormitory is the best in town.

Mixay Guesthouse (Map pp72-3; ☎ 262210; 39 Th Nokeo Khumman; dm US$2, r US$3-5) The English-speaking management here is both friendly and helpful, which makes up for the clean but mostly windowless rooms, some with hot-water bathrooms (US$5).

If money (or a lack of it) is your primary consideration, then the cheapest beds in the capital are found just west of Nam Phu in the **Sabaidy Guest House** (Map pp72-3; ☎ 213929; sabaidy_gh@hotmail.com; 203 Th Setthathirat; dm/d US$1.50/3), the **Ministry of Information & Culture Guest House** (MIC; Map pp72-3; ☎ 212362; 67 Th Manthatulat; tr US$5) and **Mixok Guest House** (Map pp72-3; ☎ 251606; Th Setthathirat; s/d/tr US$3.50/4.50/5.40). There is little else to recommend them.

HOTELS

Saysana Hotel (Map pp72-3; ☎ 213580; fax 218636; Th Chao Anou; r US$5-12; 🔀) Singles/doubles with air-con, hot water, phone and TV are US$10/12. The four flights of stairs can be trying, but the spacious fan rooms with balcony (US$5) and fine views over Wat Ong Teu Mahawihan are a bargain. Air-con rooms have TV and phone, and those on the lower floors are dangerously near to the nightclub.

Mid-Range

Most mid-range hotels accept Visa and MasterCard, but the cheaper guesthouses probably won't.

GUESTHOUSES

Vientiane has an abundance of mid-range guesthouses catering to NGO staffers and long-term visitors who prefer the family atmosphere these places provide. Discounts for long-term stays are usually available.

Villa Manoly (Map pp68-9; ☎ /fax 218907; manoly20@hotmail.com; r US$20-30; 🔀 🛱) In a quiet street off Th Fa Ngum between Wat Si Muang and the Mekong, the Manoly is a large French-era villa (plus a newer building) in a landscaped garden. The house is all hardwood floors and high ceilings with tasteful furnishings (look for the collection of antique typewriters) and a sitting terrace on the 2nd floor. Service is subtle but attentive. Recommended.

Lani I Guest House (Map pp72-3; ☎ 216103; lanico@ laotel.com; 281 Th Setthathirat; s/d/tr US$25/35/40; 🔀) Down a lane just west of Wat Hai Sok, this distinctive old house has 12 comfortable rooms and the antique and Lao handicraft decorations give it a vaguely historic atmosphere. The welcome is warm and the terrace dining area is a great place to end the day.

Mali Namphu Guest House (Map pp72-3; ☎ 215 093; 114 Th Pangkham; r US$13-16; 🔀) Just metres from Nam Phu, this new place is built around a pleasant courtyard and has attractive medium-sized rooms with satellite TV. Management is professional and eager to please. Good value.

Chanta Guest House (Map pp72-3; ☎ 243204; Th Setthathirat; r US$7-15; 🔀) The friendly Chanta has eight rooms, all of them different, in a converted French-era shophouse. The pick are the two with bathrooms and balconies (US$12) overlooking Wat Mixay, though these can be frightfully noisy in the mornings. All rooms have satellite TV and are cleaned daily, and laundry is free.

Thongbay Guesthouse (Map pp68-9; ☎ /fax 242292; www.thongbay.laopdr.com; r US$10-15; 🔀) A couple of kilometres west of town on a quiet block, the Thongbay is a large house on leafy grounds. Rooms are large and cool, with low beds and modern bathroom (US$15). Fan-rooms (US$12) and rooms without bathrooms (US$10) are also available. The food here is excellent and the English-speaking owners also organise a cooking class.

Soukchaleun Guest House (Map pp72-3; ☎ 218 723; soukchaleun_gh@yahoo.com; 121 Th Setthathirat; r US$10-13; 🔀) Soukchaleun is a friendly and very popular new place where the clean rooms have TV and air-con, but you can choose the fan for US$10. The front rooms have views over Wat Mixay. There's a free airport shuttle and discounts for returning guests.

Villa That Luang (Map pp72-3; ☎ 413370; fax 412953; 307 Th That Luang; d/tw with breakfast US$15/18; ﹖) Not far from Pha That Luang, this clean and comfortable guesthouse has rooms with wooden floors, fridge, phone, satellite TV and a free daily laundry service. Staff are very friendly and English and French are spoken. Huge discounts are available for long stays.

Dragon Lodge (Map pp72-3; ☎ 250112; dragon lodge2002@yahoo.com; Th Samsenthai; r US$12-15; ﹖) Just west of the Cultural Centre, the spotless and comfortable rooms and welcoming bar downstairs (full of handy travel information) make this a good choice. Fan rooms are US$12. The only drawback is that many rooms have no windows.

Viengthong Guest House (Map pp68-9; ☎ /fax 212095; 8 Th Fa Ngum; s/tw US$12/15; ﹖) In a quiet *soi* (alley) along the northwest side of Wat Phia Wat, the Viengthong is two buildings and a garden dining area. The brick building houses rooms with satellite TV, refrigerators and soft beds, plus some quite colourful wat-style murals.

Located a few metres north of Nam Phu, the **Phonepaseuth Guest House** (Map pp72-3; ☎ 212263; day inn@laotel.com; Th Pangkham) and the neighbouring **Pangkham Guest House** (Map pp72-3; ☎ 217053; pangkham_gh@yahoo.com; Th Pangkham) are in fact run as one guesthouse, where windowless rooms with TV (US$10) outnumber the large front rooms with balcony (US$15).

HOTELS

Inter Hotel (Map pp72-3; ☎ 242843–4; www.laointer hotel.com; 24-25 Th Fa Ngum; r US$15-40; ﹖ 🖳) For so long a soulless middle-of-the-road place, albeit with unbeatable Mekong River views, the Inter has received a marvellous makeover with a touch of class. Huge, bright rooms with high ceilings, polished wood floors, tasteful Asian furnishings and antique decorations cost US$30 to US$40 for a river view and breakfast, while smaller rooms are US$15 without breakfast. The only drawback is the lack of a lift, though further expansion should rectify this.

Day Inn Hotel (Map pp72-3; ☎ 222985; dayinn@ laotel.com; 59/3 Th Pangkham; s/d US$25/30; ﹖) Just north of the Lao Plaza Hotel, the Day Inn is two renovated buildings with large, airy rooms with attractive rattan furnishings, TV, stocked fridge and, in most rooms, large bathrooms with bathtubs. However, be sure to ask for a room in the smaller building (out the back) as some of those in the main building have outside bathrooms but are the same price. Discounts are readily available.

Asian Pavilion Hotel (Map pp72-3; ☎ 213430; asianlao@loxinfo.co.th; 379 Th Samsenthai; r US$25; ﹖) In the heart of town, the Asian Pavilion's aging but comfortable rooms with satellite TV and minibar are decent value, especially when the routine hefty discount is thrown in. However, the history is more of a draw than the rooms themselves. In its pre-Revolutionary incarnation, this was the Hotel Constellation (immortalised in John Le Carré's *The Honourable Schoolboy*) and was frequented by all sorts of secret-agent types during the '60s and '70s. The original owner, a former Royal Lao Army colonel who had been trained in the USA, was sent to a re-education camp from 1975 until 1988; he reopened the hotel in 1989. Staff are efficient and the place is surprisingly quiet.

Lane Xang Hotel (Map pp72-3; ☎ 214102; fax 214108; Th Fa Ngum; s/d/ste US$22/25/45; ﹖ 🖳) Once the classiest place in town, this vast four-storey wonder facing the Mekong is good value partly for the retro-cool of its socialist-era feel, something that is almost extinct elsewhere in Southeast Asia. All rooms have satellite TV and minibar, and other amenities include a bar, fitness centre, baby cots, sauna and the sort of nightclub that would have Karl Marx turning in his grave. Karl probably wouldn't agree with the capitalist pricing policy, either, as rates in kip are 15% more than those in dollars. Prices include buffet breakfast.

Hotel Lao (Map pp72-3; ☎ 219280; hotellao@laotel .com; 53/9 Th Heng Boun; s/d US$20/25; ﹖) In the heart of Chinatown, the welcoming Hotel Lao is a three-storey building with a Thai-style wooden platform added to the front. The large rooms have two beds, TV, fridge and some have balconies.

Vansana Hotel (Map pp68-9; ☎ 413894; www.van sana.laopdr.com; d/tw US$25/30; ﹖ 🖳) Out in the suburbs east of Wat Sok Pa Luang, off Th Phon Than, the Vansana is well-run and has spacious, clean rooms with satellite TV set around a swimming pool, making it popular with families. Prices include breakfast. There is a restaurant and the hotel car will ferry you into town for US$1.

Mongkol Hotel (Map pp68-9; ☎ 216244; mkrvs@ laopdr.com; 25 Th Kham Khong; r US$13-21; 🈺 🖳) Formerly called the River View Hotel, this place west of town seems to have fallen through some sort of sinkhole to a place with no character whatsoever. For a riverside hotel, the opaque windows are hard to fathom, but some of the large rooms at the front have see-through glass to go with the antique phones, satellite TV and a quiet location.

Douang Deuane Hotel (Map pp72-3; ☎ 222301; DD_hotel@hotmail.com; Th Nokeo Khumman; s/d US$18/ 23; 🈺) Near the river, Douang Deuane is a four-storey place with simple but clean, medium-sized rooms with fridge, phone and satellite TV, but no lift. Prices include breakfast.

Also recommended:

Mekong Hotel (Map pp68-9; ☎ 212938; www .mekonghotel.com; Th Luang Prabang; tw/d US$35/50, apt US$40-80; 🈺 🖳) Vast apartment complex which once housed Vientiane's Soviet bloc residents, now popular with Chinese businessmen. Unattractive but fair value.

Lao-Paris Hotel (Map pp72-3; ☎ 222229; laoparishotel@hotmail.com; 100 Th Samsenthai; s/d US$15/20; 🈺) In the centre of town with large but unremarkable rooms and good service.

Chaleunxay Hotel (Map pp72-3; ☎ 223407; Th Khou Vieng; r US$10-18; 🈺) Vietnamese-run place where rooms get cheaper as you climb the five storeys.

Top End

There aren't many top-end places in Vientiane, though the number is rising. The Sun Park Hotel is due to open on the Mekong River island of Don Chan in 2005, reportedly with a casino and sundry other extravagances. It somehow managed to bypass Vientiane's seven-storey limit to become the tallest building and greatest eyesore in Laos.

HOTELS

All places listed here have business centres, pool and at least one restaurant. Rooms have IDD phones, satellite television and minibar. Major credit cards are accepted; tax is included in the price quoted here.

Settha Palace Hotel (Map pp72-3; ☎ 217581; www.setthapalace.com; 6 Th Pangkham; standard/deluxe US$106/142; 🈺 🖳 🛋) This French-colonial landmark at the upper end of Th Pangkham just breathes class and is *the* place to stay in Vientiane. It has been beautifully restored, with custom-made rosewood furniture, plank floors and landscaped gardens. The 29 tastefully appointed rooms have wireless Internet connections and black-and-white Venetian marble bathrooms, the deluxe rooms with bathtubs. Having a drink from the poolside bar while sitting under the surrounding frangipanis is a delight, as is the food from Le Belle Epoque continental restaurant (p86).

Tai-Pan Hotel (Map pp72-3; ☎ 216906; www.trav elao.com; 22/3 Th François Nginn; r US$49-150; 🈺 🖳 🛋) Near the riverfront, the tranquil Tai-Pan is the best value for money among the top-end places. Many rooms feature individual balconies – be sure to request one. Rooms also have Internet connection (US$3 per day) and polished wooden floors. Prices include breakfast.

Lao Plaza Hotel (Map pp72-3; ☎ 218800, in Bangkok 0066-2653 9972; www.laoplazahotel.com; 63 Th Samsenthai; r US$120-168, ste US$264-384; 🈺 🖳 🛋) This 142-room complex, occupying an entire block east of the Lao National Museum, boasts plush rooms with views across the city. Discounts are available if you book online. You must pay in US dollars or by credit card.

Novotel (Map pp68-9; ☎ 213570; www.novotel .com; Th Samsenthai; r US$85-462; 🈺 🖳 🛋) This is Vientiane's largest hotel, a four-storey, 168-room establishment 2km east of the centre. The attractive rooms have Internet connections on demand. Lower corporate rates are casually dispensed. Prices include breakfast.

APARTMENTS

Vientiane also has a couple of luxury apartment complexes dedicated to the long stay. The huge new **Parkview Executive Suites** (Map pp68-9; ☎ 250888; www.laos-hotels.com; Th Luang Prabang; apt per day US$100-360, per month US$1500-2750; 🈺 🖳 🛋) and the French-run **Khunta Residence** (Map pp68-9; ☎ 251199; www.ahlao.com; 1-/2-bedroom apt per day US$45/70, per week US$280/400; 🈺 🖳 🛋), off Th Luang Prabang, which is smaller and more personal. Prices here include tax.

EATING

Vientiane's ever-growing number of cafés, street vendors, beer gardens and restaurants now embrace much of the world's cuisine. The many simple eateries serving fresh and tasty Lao dishes are complemented by establishments offering food as diverse as French provençale, sushi, Tex-Mex and Indian. Prices are higher than elsewhere in Laos, but it's hard to argue with paying US$4 or $5 for a meal that would probably cost five times as much at home. Most eateries are a walk or short jumbo ride from Nam Phu.

Breakfast

Most hotels offer set 'American' breakfasts (known as ABF; two eggs, toast and ham or bacon) usually for between US$1 and US$2. Or you could get out on the streets and eat where the locals do. One popular breakfast is *khào jìi páa-tê*, a split French baguette stuffed with Lao-style pâté (which is more like English or American luncheon meat than French pâté) and various dressings. These vendors also sell plain baguettes (*khào jìi*) – there are several regular bread vendors around town, but especially on Th Heng Boun between Th Chao Anou and Th Khun Bulom.

Namphou Coffee (Map pp72-3; Th Pangkham; 6am-10pm) This Lao Chinese place serves very good *kàa-féh nóm hâwn* (Lao-style milk coffee) and *khào jìi khai dạo* (two fried eggs with sliced baguette). Also on offer are plain French bread with coffee and some excellent noodle soups. The baguettes tend to disappear before 10am.

Restaurant Santisouk (Map pp72-3; ☎ 215303; 105 Th Nokeo Khumman; meals US$1-3; 7am-10pm) Opposite the Lao National Museum, the breakfasts here include tasty potato omelettes, pastry plates and good coffee.

All of the bakeries and cafés following also serve breakfast.

Bakeries & Delis

There's a string of at least half a dozen cake shops along Th Saylom, off Th Lan Xang, all with selections of inexpensive Lao interpretations of European cakes and pastries.

JoMa Bakery Café (Map pp72-3; ☎ 215265; Th Setthathirat; pastries US$0.80-2; 7am-9pm Mon-Sat;) Formerly known as Healthy & Fresh, JoMa does a brisk trade in pastries, sandwiches, quiche, muesli, fruit, shakes and ex-

cellent coffee. The combination breakfasts and lunches are justifiably very popular.

Scandinavian Bakery (Map pp72-3; ☎ 215199; Nam Phu; pastries US$0.80-1.50; 7am-7pm;) Long a favourite of expats and travellers, this place on Nam Phu sells fresh bread, pies, sandwiches (US$2), real Scandinavian-style pastries, cakes and ice cream. Seating is inside or out, and the upstairs room has satellite TV tuned to BBC or CNN.

Liang Xiang Bakery House (Map pp72-3; ☎ 212284; 54/10 Th Chao Anou; pastries US$0.30-0.70; 7am-9pm) Liang Xiang is one of a couple of places on this stretch that sell decent pastries and breakfasts of *khào jìi khai dạo* and other egg dishes. It's a good place to sit outside and people-watch.

Noodles, Chinese & Vietnamese

Several *óp pét* (roast duck) restaurants can be found along the eastern side of Th Khun Bulom towards the river, while further north on the western side are four *fŏe* stands in a row. This is the best area in town for *fŏe*, especially at night when it's very busy. At these eateries, dishes typically cost US$1 or less.

Noodles of all kinds are popular in Vientiane, especially in the unofficial Chinatown area bounded by Th Heng Boun, Th Chao Anou, Th Khun Bulom and the western end of Th Samsenthai. The basic choice is *fŏe* (a rice noodle that's popular throughout mainland Southeast Asia), *mii* (traditional Chinese egg noodle) and *khào pûn* (very thin wheat noodles with a spicy Lao sauce). *Fŏe* and *mii* can be ordered as soup (eg *fŏe nâm*), fried (eg *khùa fŏe*) or dry-mixed in a bowl (eg *fŏe hàeng*), among other variations.

Samsenthai Fried Noodle (Map pp72-3; ☎ 214993; Th Samsenthai; meals US$0.70-1.50; 10am-11pm) Delicious *khùa fŏe* with chicken, pork or shrimp is the dish of choice, and if you say *phi-sẹht* (special) the staff will add more green vegies to the mix. The fruit shakes outside are also good.

PVO (Map pp72-3; ☎ 214444; 314 Th Samsenthai; meals US$0.50-1; 8am-8pm) The large glass cabinet out front stuffed with baguettes is the source of the best *khào jìi páa-tê* in town (US$0.70/1.40 half/whole baguette). The garage-style restaurant behind also serves good, inexpensive Vietnamese (the spring rolls are divine) and Lao food. Motorbikes can be hired here, see p274.

Vieng Sawan (Map pp72-3; ☎ 213990; Th Heng Boun; meals US$1.50-3.50; ⏱ 11am-10pm) In the middle of Chinatown, Vieng Sawan specialises in *nǎem néuang* (barbecued pork meatballs) and many varieties of *yáw* (spring rolls), usually sold in 'sets' *(sut)* with *khào pûn*, fresh lettuce leaves, mint, basil, various sauces for dipping, sliced starfruit and green plantain. You can also order *sìin ja* here, thinly sliced pieces of raw beef which customers boil in small cauldrons of coconut juice and eat with dipping sauces, or some of the many varieties of spring rolls. Recommended.

Café Indochine (Map pp72-3; ☎ 216758; 199 Th Setthathirat; meals US$3-5; ⏱ 10.30am-10.30pm Sun-Fri; ⊠) This smart-looking restaurant in the middle of town serves decent Vietnamese cuisine and has efficient service, though you can eat the same for a lot less elsewhere.

Guangdong Restaurant (Map pp72-3; ☎ 217364; 91-93 Th Chao Anou; meals US$2-4; ⏱ noon-10pm; ⊠) The menu here resembles a small phone book of Chinese dishes, with dim sum and fresh *mii* to round out the options. Won't disappoint.

On the riverfront just east of Th Nokeo Khumman are three little shophouse restaurants serving a mix of reliable Asian dishes mostly for less than US$1.50; look for **Nok Noy Restaurant** (Map pp72-3; ⏱ 6am-11pm) and **Addy** (Map pp72-3; ☎ 241354; ⏱ 6am-11pm) in particular.

Lao

The long stretch of **open-air food and drink vendors** (⏱ 5-11pm) that convenes along the levee beside the Mekong River is a great place to watch the sunset and the river eating excellent *pîng kai*. Apart from chicken, you'll find dishes such as *tàm màak-hung* or *nǎem* (minced sausage mixed with rice, herbs and roasted chillies with a plate of greens on the side) designed to accompany, and to promote, your consumption of Beerlao.

Dong Palan night market (Map pp68-9; ☎ 250836; Th Dong Palan; ⏱ 5-11pm) For authentic, cheap Lao meals, Vientiane's night markets and street vendors are your best source. The Dong Palan, near Wat Ban Fai east of the centre, has the largest number of food vendors selling the widest selection of Lao standards, including *làap* (spicy minced meat salad) and *pîng kai*.

Bunmala Restaurant (Map pp68-9; ☎ 313 249; Th Khu Vieng; meals US$2-4; ⏱ 11am-11pm) It's a little out of town, but this open-sided, timber-floored restaurant is about as archetypal Lao as you can find – and the food is great, too. There are all manner of Lao favourites (all about US$1.50), including *pîng pét* (roast duck), *pîng pqa* (grilled fish), *pîng lîn* (roast cow tongue) and *pîng kai* made from particularly plump chickens. For a classic Lao meal, order the (very hot) *tqm màa-hung* (papaya salad), *kqeng naw mâi* (soupy bamboo-shoot salad), sticky rice and draught beer. Delicious. Bunmala is busiest at dinner, when the full range of *pîng* is on offer.

That Dam Wine House (Map pp72-3; ☎ 222647; Th Chanta Khumman; meals US$3-5; ⏱ lunch & dinner; ⊠) As the name suggests, this is something of a cross between a wine bar and a restaurant, with both Lao and Western dishes. The Lao food is particularly good, as is the outdoor seating overlooking That Dam.

Nang Khambang (Map pp72-3; 97 Th Khun Bulom; meals US$1-3; ⏱ noon-9pm; ⊠) The cheap and friendly Nang Khambang, not far from the river, serves a wide selection of Lao specialities include *kóp yat sài* (stuffed frogs), *thàwt nok* (roast quail), *pîng pqa*, *sòm pákàat* (pickled lettuce), fish, beef or chicken *làap* and *yám sìin ngúa* (spicy beef salad). Good choice.

Riverside Restaurant (Map pp72-3; Th Fa Ngum; meals US$1.50-3; ⏱ 11am-10.30pm) Opposite the Lan Xang Hotel, this is probably the best of the riverfront eateries, with a small menu of tasty Lao staples supplemented by snacks you won't find at home; deep-fried underground singer (cricket; US$2.50) anyone?

Tamnak Lao Restaurant (Map pp68-9; ☎ 413562; Th That Luang; meals US$4-8; ⏱ lunch & dinner; ⊠) If you mention Tamnak Lao to locals, they will be impressed. It has a well-earned reputation for excellent Lao and Thai food. You can sit inside or in the manicured garden, and there is a traditional dancing show most nights.

Soukvimane Lao Food (Map pp72-3; ☎ 214441; 89/12 Ban Sisaket; meals US$1.50-3; ⏱ 11am-2pm & 6-9pm) While standards here are not quite what they once were, this is still a good place to taste a range of Lao dishes. Specialities include *kǣeng pǡa khai mot* (fish soup with ant larvae) and *làap pǡa* (spicy minced fish salad). It's at the end of an alley next to That Dam.

Ban Vilaylac Restaurant (Map pp72-3; ☎ 222 049; meals US$2-4.50; ✿ 8am-10.30pm) Hidden between Wat Ong Teu Mahawihan and Wat Chanthabuli, this cosy little place of many pot plants serves tasty Lao and Thai food. Worth a look.

French & Italian

It is no surprise that this former French colony should boast so many French restaurants, but their overall high quality is. When you consider that this fine dining experience will cost a fraction of what you'd pay at home, it gets even better.

Le Silapa (Map pp72-3; ☎ 219689; 17/1 Th Sihom; meals US$5-10; ✿ lunch & dinner Mon-Sat; ✿) The fine French cuisine at Le Silapa remains some of the best in Vientiane, and combined with the refined surrounds and discreet service you can't go too far wrong. The menu consists of classic as well as improvised dishes and changes frequently. If you drink a bottle of wine the restaurant contributes to a medical fund for economically disadvantaged children…what better excuse? The lunch set menu is the best value.

Le Côte D'Azur Restaurant (Map pp72-3; ☎ 217 252; 62-63 Th Fa Ngum; meals US$3-6; ✿ lunch Mon-Sat, dinner daily; ✿) The number of French expats eating here is encouraging, and when your food arrives you'll understand why. The inviting country-French décor, delicious provençale cuisine and understated service make this a top choice. Also on offer are pastas, salads and pizzas (order anything with fresh herbs).

Le Belle Epoque (Map pp72-3; ☎ 217581; 6 Th Pangkham; ✿ breakfast, lunch & dinner; US$8-13; ✿) For a taste of colonial-era luxury it's hard to beat this restaurant in the Settha Palace Hotel. The menu is mainly French but also has a Lao component; dishes include foie gras (US$8.50) and the delicious flat noodles with grilled eggplant and cream sauce (US$4.50).

Le Nadao (Map pp68-9; ☎ 550 4884; Th Siboun Heuang; meals US$10-17; ✿ lunch & dinner Mon-Sat; ✿) This small, softly lit place out near Patuxai is suitably popular with ambassadors and those on expenses, and the food and service is expectedly good. For the money, however, you could do better.

L'Opera Italian Restaurant (Map pp72-3; ☎ 215 099; Nam Phu; meals US$5-9; ✿ 11.30am-2pm & 6-10pm; ✿) This is the best, and for a time the only, Italian restaurant in Vientiane. The menu includes pizzas (served with fresh ground chilli and oregano on the side), seafood and salads, but it's the pasta (US$5 to US$6.50) that really stands out here. The gelati bar offers takeaway.

Saovaly Restaurant (Map pp72-3; ☎ 214490; Th Manthatulat; meals US$1.50-3.50; ✿ lunch Mon-Sat, dinner daily) This snug little place serves good French and Lao cuisine in a small but stylish dining room, and at very reasonable prices.

Le Vendôme (Map pp72-3; ☎ 216402; Th Wat In Paeng; meals US$3-6; ✿ lunch Mon-Fri, dinner daily; ✿) Tucked away in an old house in a quiet street behind Wat In Paeng, Le Vendôme is popular but retains an intimate, romantic ambience with its soft lighting and seating on the terrace. The menu features salads, French cuisine, wood-fired pizza, pasta and desserts.

The French influence is most noticeable around Nam Phu, where you'll find three small, atmospheric eateries each serving delicious Gallic cuisine. On the east side is the intimate **Restaurant-Bar Namphu** (Map pp72-3; ☎ 216248; meals US$4-10; ✿ lunch & dinner; ✿), where the menu offers a mix of French, German and Lao fare and the bar is popular with expatriates. Next door is the petite **La Cave des Chateaux** (Map pp72-3; ☎ 212192; meals US$5-8; ✿ 11am-11pm; ✿), which specialises in French cheeses (grilled to perfection) and wines; while the cosy **Restaurant Le Provençal** (Map pp72-3; ☎ 216248, mobile 020-513160; Nam Phu; meals US$2-6; ✿ lunch Mon-Sat, dinner daily; ✿) serves rustic southern French-style dishes and oven-baked pizzas.

International

More expats and travellers means a demand for a greater variety of cuisines, one that Vientiane seems to be meeting fairly well. There are also plenty of eateries offering a combination of cuisines. And while you should justifiably be wary of any kitchen purporting to know *làap* as well as lasagne, there are a few here that manage to do their multicultural menus justice.

Sticky Fingers Café & Bar (Map pp72-3; ☎ 215972; 10/3 Th François Nginn; meals US$3.50-6; ☯ 10am-midnight Tue-Sun; 🖭) Stickies, as it's known among expats, is one of the best restaurants in Vientiane. It serves a range of original and delicious dishes cooked up by the Australian chef from a menu that could be described as 'modern international'. It's in a small, informal setting just back from Th Fa Ngum and the bar is often busy late into the evening. The regular 'open mic' sessions are better than they sound.

Full Moon Café (Map pp72-3; ☎ 243373; Th François Nginn; meals US$3-5; ☯ 9am-10.30pm; 🖭) Sitting in a well-fanned outdoor area or on the colourful cushions inside, the relaxed, stylish atmosphere of the Full Moon is as attractive as the food. The food is Asian fusion (see their tapas consisting of samosa, dim sum, gyoza etc) and delicious. Set menus (US$2.50 to US$3.50) change daily, or stop in for an after-dinner cocktail (US$2.50).

Khop Chai Deu (Map pp72-3; ☎ 223022; 54 Th Setthathirat; meals US$2.50-5; ☯ noon-11.30pm; 🖭) Occupying an extensively remodelled but nonetheless beautiful colonial-era house near Nam Phu, Khop Chai Deu has become one of the most consistently good and evenly priced eateries in town. Popular with Laos, expats and travellers alike, the Lao, Thai and assorted Western dishes will satisfy without leaving you raving.

Restaurant Tex-Mex Alexia (Map pp72-3; ☎ 241 349; Th Fa Ngum; meals US$3-5; ☯ 9am-11.30pm) On two levels overlooking the Mekong, the Alexia is an upbeat place with live music at 8pm every night. The food consists of burritos (US$4.50), pizzas (US$4.50) and a range of spaghettis (US$3) and is solid without being inspirational.

Xayoh Café (Map pp72-3; ☎ 262111; cnr Th Samsenthai & Th Nokeo Khumman; meals US$2-4.50; ☯ 9am-10.30pm; 🖭) This stylish bistro opposite the Lao National Culture Hall offers an extensive menu of European dishes, sandwiches, pizza and some tasty Thai. There's a British Sunday roast (US$5) on, yes, Sundays.

Le Range (Map pp68-9; ☎ 413700; Th Phonsay; meals US$4-6; ☯ 9.30am-10pm) Run by a French-Lao couple, this big, breezy place northeast of the centre has a southwest USA feel to it, with its huge and heavy wooden furniture. The food is both tasty and reasonably priced, with steak and woodfired pizza being the speciality, and Lao food making up the menu.

Food House (Map pp72-3; Th Sihom; ☯ 11am-11pm) This stylish-looking new place has a menu of cheap dishes (steak US$2 and *pad thai*, Thai noodles, US$0.80) and beer aimed squarely at the backpacker guesthouse next door.

Thai

There are fewer Thai restaurants than you would expect considering Thailand is just over the Mekong River, though this is in part because Thai dishes also appear on the menus of many places that call themselves Lao restaurants.

Phikun (Map pp72-3; ☎ 222340; Th Sihom; meals US$1.50; ☯ 8am-9pm) Phikun doesn't look all that inspiring but who cares when the Thai food is so good and cheap. Dishes include *tôm yám kûng* (prawn and lemon grass soup) and *kai phàt bai kàphrao* (chicken fried in holy basil) and the curries – something you don't see much of in Lao cuisine – are like a drug if you're a spice nut. If it's not warm enough, they'll be happy to heat it for you. The English sign reads 'Thai Food'.

Linda Sathaporn Restaurant (Map pp68-9; ☎ 415 355; cnr Th Dong Palan & Th Phonsay; meals US$3-6; ☯ lunch & dinner; 🖭) A couple of kilometres east of the centre, Linda Sathaporn has not one but three plastic folders filled with pictures of their varied Thai dishes, and top notch fare it is. Seating is inside or in the more pleasant shaded courtyard out back, service is good and portions large. It's very popular.

Indian

Taj Mahal Restaurant (Map pp72-3; ☎ mobile 020-5610505; Th Setthathirat; meals US$2-3.50; ☯ lunch & dinner) Just west of Nam Phu, the Taj Mahal doesn't look much from the outside. However, the Indian food here is the best in Vientiane, and the prices are very reasonable. Vegetarian diners won't be disappointed. Recommended.

Fathima Restaurant (Map pp72-3; Th Fa Ngum; meals US$1-2.50; ☯ 10am-10pm) Another low-key dining area but the food more than compensates. The vegetarian dishes (US$1) are a big draw, and the chicken and meat curries (US$1.60) are also delicious. Real ice cream is sold outside.

Nazim Restaurant (Map pp72-3; ☎ 223480; 335 Th Fa Ngum; meals $1.50-3; ☯ 11am-11pm; 🖭) The menu here is huge and the North Indian cuisine and dozens of vegetarian dishes have become a travellers' favourite. Sadly, the resulting success has been accompanied by a decline in quality and especially service. It's by no means terrible, but there are other choices...

Japanese

Sakura Japanese Restaurant (Map pp68-9; ☎ 212 274; Soi 3 Khounta Thong; meals US$2-6; ☺ 10am-2pm & 5-10pm; ☒) Off Th Luang Prabang west of the Novotel, Sakura serves Japanese cuisine in an intimate setting. Good value.

Fujiwara Restaurant (Map pp72-3; ☎ 222210; Th Luang Prabang; meals US$6-10; ☺ lunch Mon-Sat, dinner daily; ☒) Just west of Wat In Paeng, Fujiwara is a bigger, flasher place with an epic menu including all the Japanese favourites and several set meals.

Vegetarian

While you can find vegetarian dishes on almost every menu, only a couple of places are marketing themselves directly to vegetarian diners. All of the Indian restaurants (see earlier) have a wide selection of vegetarian dishes.

Garden Fresh Restaurant (Map pp72-3; ☎ mobile 020-7711034; Th Manthatulat; meals US$1.50-2; ☺ 11am-10pm) This new place was described by one vegan traveller as 'a gem'. The sweet green curry (US$1.20) and 'soo-see' tofu dish (US$1.20) are both recommended. Staff are charming and are planning to run cooking courses (see p79).

Just for Fun (Map pp72-3; ☎ 213642; 51/2 Th Pangkham; meals US$1-3; ☺ 7.30am-9pm Mon-Sat) This very relaxed little shop opposite the Lao Airlines office serves a limited vegetarian menu inspired by Thai, Lao and Indian cuisine, plus Lao coffee, lots of herbal teas and...herbal shampoo.

Khouadin Vegetarian (Map pp72-3; ☎ 351615; buffet US$1; ☺ 7am-2pm) Hidden away behind Talat Sao, this simple restaurant serves precooked but thoroughly recommended vegetarian dishes, mainly for lunch. It's a bargain.

Self-Catering

For the largest selection of fresh groceries and the best prices, you should stick to the markets (see p92). But if there's something 'Western' you're yearning for, or a bottle of wine, check out the following minimarkets.

Phimphone Market (Map pp72-3; 94/6 Th Samsenthai; ☺ 7.30am-9pm) The mother of all Phimphones, this store near Nam Phu has a wide selection of imported goods, including biscuits, canned and frozen foods, magazines, and personal hygiene and women's products such as tampons. Upstairs is an excellent selection of wine.

Phimphone Market 2 (Map pp72-3; ☎ 214609; cnr Th Samsenthai & Th Chanta Khumman; ☺ 8am-8.30pm) This is a smaller branch of the Phimphone market, and it stocks a smaller range than Phimphone market.

Oudom Development Shop (Map pp68-9; Th Dong Palan; ☺ 8am-9pm) Out near the Dong Palan Night Market, this is the best-stocked of all these supermarkets and the cheapest and most popular with *falang* expats.

Vins de France (Map pp72-3; ☎ 217700; 354 Th Samsenthai; ☺ 9am-7pm) Almost opposite the Asian Pavilion Hotel, this has one of the best French wine cellars in Southeast Asia. You can sit and taste for a small fee, or just pop in for a look at a place so completely out of character with its surrounds.

DRINKING

Vientiane is no longer the illicit pleasure palace it was when Paul Theroux described it, in his 1975 book *The Great Railway Bazaar*, as a place in which 'The brothels are cleaner than the hotels, marijuana is cheaper than pipe tobacco and opium easier to find than a cold glass of beer'. Nowadays, brothels are strictly prohibited, Talat Sao's marijuana stands have been removed from prominent display and cold beer has definitely replaced opium as the nightly drug of choice. Most of the bars, restaurants and discos close by 11.30pm or midnight.

Cafés

Vientiane is home to a growing number of cafés, usually serving food and shakes along with a range of Lao and foreign coffees.

Life, Coffee, Break (Maison du Café; Map pp72-3; ☎ 214781; 70 Th Pangkham; ☺ 7am-9pm Tue-Sun) A few metres north of Nam Phu, this friendly and trendy place makes a range of coffees (US$1 to US$2) and quality sandwiches or baguettes (US$1.50), plus great shakes. There's also plenty of reading matter around.

Paradice (Map pp72-3; ☎ 312836; Th Lan Xang; ☺ 8am-8pm Mon-Sat) In the grounds of the

JULIET COOMBE

Lao people offer votive, Pha That
Luang (p70), Vientiane

FRANK CARTER

Fisher, Mekong River, Vientiane (p64)

Drink vendor, Vientiane (p64)

BERNARD NAPTHINE

Patuxai (p75), Vientiane

Riverside restaurant (p85),
Vientiane

Nun, Vientiane (p64)

Centre Culturel et de Coopération Linguistique, this airy, comfortable bar and café is, understandably, popular with Francophone expats. The coffee, sandwiches and simple meals here are good.

Lao Traveller's Café (Map pp72-3; Th Setthathirat; ⊙7.30am-7pm) A classic travellers café with passable Western breakfasts (US$2), agreeable coffee and day-old newspapers in a central location.

Café de Mamam (Map pp72-3; ☎ 261877; Th Fa Ngum; ⊙7am-11pm) Apart from great *café Lao*, this smart riverfront place does an elaborate line in 'frappe'-style brews, if that's your thing, and café-style food.

Beer Gardens

Not long ago the banks of the Mekong River were one long beer garden, with bamboo and thatch dwellings perched over the river as far west as the original of the species, the Sala Sunset Khounta. These days the Sala Sunset Khounta is the only one that remains – the government decided the others were too loud, open too late and attracting too many young people who would end up behaving badly once the Full Taste of Happiness (Beerlao) had taken its full toll. There are still plenty of drink vendors on the riverfront between Th Khun Bulom and Th François Nginn, though there's more beer than garden in these parts. If plans for a riverfront esplanade materialise, things might change again.

Sala Sunset Khounta (Map pp68-9; ☎ 251079; snacks US$0.50-1.50; ⊙11am-11pm) At the western end of a dirt road along the riverfront, this simple wooden platform made of old boat timbers has been serving beer at sunset for years. Beerlao is the main attraction, but the friendly and enterprising proprietors also offer an array of Lao and Vietnamese snacks including barbeque fish and deep-fried cricket (especially during the February and March 'cricket season'). The savoury *yáw jęun* (fried Vietnamese spring rolls) are recommended.

Salakham Beer Garden (Beerlao Brewery; ☎ 812 045; Km 12, Th Tha Deua; ⊙noon-7pm) Southeast of town, 12km from central Vientiane, the Lao Government Brewery has its own thatched beer garden where you can drink inexpensive Lao draught beer (*bįa sót*, literally fresh beer – and it doesn't get any fresher than this) and eat Lao snacks.

Bars

If you're looking for something with more of a local flavour, and which is less expensive than the expat bars, your best bet is one of the many *bįa sót* bars (selling draught beer) – look for nondescript rooms with plastic jugs of beer on the tables.

Vientiane doesn't have many pure bars – places that don't have a restaurant, nightclub or hotel alter-ego. The following places are worth a look in.

Deja Vu (Map pp72-3; ☎ mobile 020-5610735; Nam Phu; ⊙7pm-midnight Mon-Sat) This small, chic bar is run by Malisay Bodhisane, the Lao/Japanese/English/French–speaking barman who learned to mix in Tokyo. His cocktails (about US$2) are top notch.

Blue Sky (Map pp72-3; ☎ 216368; cnr Th Setthathirat & Th Chao Anou; ⊙7am-10pm) The best part of this four-storey place is the rooftop bar, which is ideal for sundowners. There's also a TV bar playing movies, and decent food.

Restaurant-Bar Namphu (Map pp72-3; ☎ 216248; Nam Phu) This tiny, well-serviced watering hole and restaurant is open most evenings and recommended for anyone pining for the surrounds of a European-style bar.

Cheetah Bar & Restaurant (Map pp72-3; ☎ mobile 020-5515820; Th Khun Bulom; ⊙11am-11pm Mon-Sat) This place has a relaxed feel to it with seating inside and out, and serves a mix of Asian meals.

Samlo Pub (Map pp72-3; ☎ 222308; Th Setthathirat; ⊙4-11.30pm) Opposite Wat In Paeng, this dark, smokey dive is a good place to watch football and other live sport.

ENTERTAINMENT

Vientiane is not exactly bursting with nightclubs, and with Thai pop dominating there is even less in the way of original live music. By law all entertainment places are supposed to close by 11.30pm, though most push it to about midnight and, depending on how zealous the police are at that time, some clubs might kick on until 3am.

Cinema

Lao cinemas died out in the video shop tidal wave of the 1990s.

Centre Culturel et de Coopération Linguistique (Map pp72-3; ☎ 215764; www.ambafrance-laos.org /centre; Th Lan Xang; movies US$1; screenings 7.45pm Tue & Thu, 5.45pm Sat) This is your best bet these days for viewing a film. The French Centre screens French films (usually subtitled in English), check the *Vientiane Times* or call the centre for information. See p66 for more on the centre.

Lao National Culture Hall (Map pp72-3; Th Samsenthai) Periodically screens foreign – usually French – films. See p76.

Circus

National Circus (Hong Kanyasin; Map pp68-9; Th Thong Khan Kham) The old Russian Circus established during the time of Soviet influence in Laos is now known as Hong Kanyasin. It performs from time to time in the National Circus venue, in the north of town. This tentlike structure also occasionally plays host to pop and classical music performances sponsored by the French embassy. Check for dates in the *Vientiane Times*.

Gay & Lesbian Venues

Despite their being a fair-sized gay community in Vientiane, there is really not much of a scene. There are no dedicated 'gay bars', but the Chess Café (p90) and neighbouring Pakluk (p90) are the most gay-and-lesbian-friendly places.

Laos Traditional Show

Laos Traditional Show (Map pp72-3; ☎ 242978; www .laostraditionshow.com; Th Manthatulat; child/adult US$4/7, still/video camera charge US$1/3; ☼ 8.30pm) The Lao National Theatre has a performance of traditional music and dancing aimed directly at the tourist market. It plays every night except the third Sunday of the month. It's quite a professional show.

Live Music

On The Rock Pub (Map pp72-3; Th Fa Ngum; ☼ 8pm-midnight) If rock is your thing, this is the best place by far to see it played live. The tiny venue means you're virtually within touching distance of the regular six-piece crammed into the corner. The patrons are almost all Lao and the music a lively mix of Thai, Lao and Western tunes, mostly covers. Recommended.

Wind West (Map pp72-3; ☎ 217275; Th Luang Prabang; ☼ 5.30pm-midnight) A Western-US–style bar and restaurant, Wind West (yes, that's not a typo) has live music most nights – not-so-wild Lao-style guitar folk when we visited. Happy hour runs from 5.30pm to 8.30pm and the food is pretty good, too.

Snow White & One Dwarf (Map pp72-3; ☎ 772617; Th Samsenthai; ☼ 8pm-midnight) Beside the Asian Pavilion Hotel, Vientiane's first jazz bar (of the post-Revolution era, at least) is indeed a cold white throughout and, yes, there is a friendly dwarf man at the door. The jazz is not quite Dave Brubeck and drink prices are high, but Snow White is an interesting change of scene.

Nightclubs

Vientiane has several 'discos', though the term is rather a misnomer because often the music is live. Although a younger Lao crowd tends to predominate, there is usually a mix of generations and the bands or disc jockeys play everything from electrified Lao folk (for *lám wóng* circular dancing) to quasi-Western pop, with the latest Thai hits likely to dominate. There is generally no charge to enter, but you'll pay about US$1.20 for a can or small bottle of Beerlao.

Pakluk (Map pp68-9; ☎ 214592; Th Sakkaline; ☼ 9pm-midnight) This cosy little place just beyond the Mahasot Hospital was one of the hippest nightspots at the time of writing. It has a timber dance floor, lofty bar stools, trippy decorations and a decent DJ. Flip-flops and singlets are banned on men.

Chess Café (Map pp68-9; ☎ mobile 020-5512303; Th Sakkaline; ☼ 8pm-12.30pm) Conveniently located next door to Pakluk, the Chess Café has been around for a while and is probably the favourite among backpackers. Bands sometimes play here.

Future Nightclub (Map pp68-9; ☼ 8pm-1am) Not far past the Novotel, the music can make stepping into the Future seem more like leaping into the past. Fun though.

Marina (Map pp68-9; ☎ 216978; Th Luang Prabang; ☼ 8pm-1am) Situated closer to the airport, Marina features plenty of Thai techno and MTV clips, not always synchronised. It's big and popular.

HOTEL CLUBS

Most top-end hotels have nightly discos that are open to all comers. Note that in some of these places a charge might be added to your bill if you are male and one of the female staff comes and sits at your table. There's often a small charge to enter that also covers your first drink.

D*Tech (Map pp68-9; ☎ 213570; Th Samsenthai) At the Novotel, this place often has a Philippine band playing covers sharing space with its DJ.

Broadway (Map pp72-3; ☎ 218800; 63 Th Samsenthai) This place at the Lao Plaza Hotel is modern, popular but none too edgy.

Victory Discotheque (Map pp72-3; ☎ 213580; Th Chao Anou) This disco, at the Saysana Hotel, is nice and central but fairly downmarket.

Anou Cabaret (Map pp72-3; ☎ 213630; cnr Th Heng Boun & Th Chao Anou) On the ground floor of the Anou Hotel, the cabaret has been swinging along for years. It's well worth a visit to slide into a booth and glimpse a piece of the past crooning its way into history.

Recreation Clubs

Australian Embassy Recreation Club (AERC or Australian Club; Map pp68-9; ☎ 314921; Km 3 Th Tha Deua; ☼ 9am-8pm) AERC is out of town on the way to the Thai-Lao Friendship Bridge. The club has a brilliant salt-water pool, right next to the Mekong River. From 6pm to 7pm on Friday there is an official Happy Hour at the snack bar. Barbecues are held every second and last Friday of the month (except in June and July), and nonmembers are welcome for an admission fee of US$2. There is also an air-con squash court (open from 6am to 8.30pm). Short-term memberships can be arranged for single/family US$10/20 per day, or you could go as the guest of a member.

SHOPPING

Just about anything made in Laos is available for purchase in Vientiane, including hill-tribe crafts, jewellery, traditional textiles and carvings. The main shopping areas in town are Talat Sao (Morning Market), the eastern end of Th Samsenthai (near the Asian Pavilion Hotel), Th Pangkham and along Th Nokeo Khumman.

Furniture & Interior Design

Several workshops around town produce inexpensive custom-designed furniture of bamboo, rattan and wood (eg teak and Asian rosewood).

Couleur d'Asie (Map pp68-9; ☎ 223008; Nam Phu; ☼ 9am-7pm) Newly relocated into the old French Cultural Centre building on Nam Phu, Couleur d'Asie carries some beautifully designed, Asian-accented furniture, along with a number of interior design accessories, household linens and clothes. Prices are very reasonable. You can drink tea or Lao coffee at a table overlooking Nam Phu.

Xao Ban Shop (Map pp68-9; ☎ mobile 020-5504661; Th Fa Ngum) A wide range of woven bamboo and rattan household accessories at very reasonable prices. Manager Mr Latanavong runs tours to a market and bamboo-weaving centre north of Vientiane.

Phai Exclusive (Map pp68-9; ☎ 214804; 3 Th Thong Khan Kham; ☼ 8am-5pm Mon-Sat) This place makes expensive bamboo furniture as well as bamboo accessories.

Handicrafts, Antiques & Art

Several shops along Th Samsenthai, Th Pangkham and Th Setthathirat sell Lao and Thai tribal and hill-tribe crafts. You might also find an increasingly rare carved opium pipe. Many of the places listed under Textiles and Clothing (p92) also carry handicrafts and antiques.

Handicraft Products of Ethnic Groups (Map pp72-3; Th Khu Vieng) Beside the PTT office and opposite Talat Sao, this market-style place sells handicrafts from around Laos. The quality is variable, but at the least this is a good place to get an idea what is out there and how much it costs. Combine it with a visit to Talat Sao.

T'Shop Lai Galerie (Map pp72-3; ☎ 223178; Th In Paeng; ☼ 8.30am-6m Mon-Sat) T'Shop Lai stocks a range of modern and traditional art in all media.

Carterie du Laos (Map pp72-3; ☎ 241401; 118/2 Th Setthathirat) This shop has the widest range of postcards, cards, posters and a few small souvenirs.

Kanchana Boutique (Map pp72-3; ☎ 213467; 102 Th Chanta Khumman; ☼ 8am-9pm Mon-Sat) Kanchana carries an extensive selection of crafts and Lao silk and can arrange visits to their Lao Textile Museum.

Jewellery

Most of the jewellery shops are along Th Samsenthai and trade primarily in gold and silver. Among the better options are **Saigon Bijoux** (Map pp72-3; ☎ 214783; Th Samsenthai), which also repairs jewellery; and **Bari Jewellery** (Map pp72-3; ☎ 212680; Th Samsenthai), which also deals in precious stones.

Talat Sao (p92) has plenty of gold and silversmiths, though many are more artisan than artist.

Textiles & Clothing

Downtown Vientiane is littered with stores selling textiles to tourists, with Th Nokeo Khumman being the epicentre. Talat Sao is also a good place to buy fabrics. You'll find antique as well as modern fabrics, plus utilitarian items such as shoulder bags (some artfully constructed around squares of antique fabric), cushions and pillows.

To see Lao weaving in action, seek out the weaving district of Ban Nong Buathong, northeast of the town centre in Muang Chanthabuli. About 20 families (many originally from Sam Neua in Hua Phan Province) live and work here, including a couple of households that sell textiles directly to the public; the **Phaeng Mai Gallery** (☎ 217341; 117 Th Nong Buathong; ☯ 10am-6pm), in a white, two-storey house is among the best.

Carol Cassidy Lao Textiles (Map pp72-3; ☎ 212123; www.laotextiles.com; 84-86 Th Nokeo Khumman; ☯ 8am-noon & 2-5pm Mon-Fri, 8am-noon Sat, or by appointment) In an old two-storey French-Lao house, Lao Textiles sells high-end contemporary, original-design fabrics inspired by older Lao weaving patterns, motifs and techniques. The American designer, Carol Cassidy, employs Lao weavers who work at the house. Prices reflect the international renown of this weaving house.

Couleur d'Asie (Map pp72-3; ☎ 223008; Nam Phu) The owner, a French-Vietnamese dress designer with Paris fashion school experience, manages to fuse Lao and Western styles into some very attractive clothes.

KPP Handicraft Promotion Enterprise of Sekong Province (Map pp72-3; ☎ 241421; pholsana@laotel .com; cnr Th Setthathirath & Th Chao Anou; ☯ 9am-9pm) It may not be flash, but it's Fair Trade and the textiles from the Bolaven Plateau province of Sekong are well worth a look.

Lao Cotton Company (Map pp68-9; ☎ 215840; ☯ 8am-5pm Mon-Sat) A UN-sponsored programme, the Lao Women's Pilot Textile Project, has this clothing factory in Ban Khunta, off Th Luang Prabang around 2.5km west of central Vientiane. It specialises in handwoven Lao cotton products in both modern and traditional designs, including shirts, dresses, handbags, place mats and table linen.

Nikone Handicrafts (Map pp68-9; ☎ 212191; nikone@hotmail.com; ☯ 9am-5pm Mon-Sat) Located out near the National Circus, this is a good place to see weaving and dyeing in action.

True Colour (Map pp72-3; ☎ 214410; Th Setthathirat; ☯ 9am-8pm Mon-Sat) This store sells textiles and clothes made in the Houey Hong Vocational Training Center for Women (p79).

Other stores on Th Nokeo Khumman worth a look include **Khampan Lao Handicraft** (Map pp72-3; ☎ 222000; ☯ 8am-9pm), with textiles from the Sam Neua area at very reasonable prices; upmarket **Mixay Boutique** (Map pp72-3; ☎ 216592; ☯ 9am-8pm); and **Camacrafts** (Mulberries; Map pp72-3 ☎ 241217; www.mulberries .org; ☯ 10am-6pm Mon-Sat), which stocks silk clothes and weavings from Xieng Khuang Province, plus some bed and cushion covers in striking Hmong-inspired designs.

Markets

Talat Sao (Map pp72-3; Th Lan Xang; ☯ 7am-4pm) Vientiane's biggest market is a sprawling collection of stalls offering fabrics, ready-made clothes, jewellery, cutlery, toiletries, bedding, hardware and watches, as well as electronic goods and just about anything else imaginable. In the centre of the area is a large building that houses the Vientiane Department Store.

Talat Khua Din (Map pp72-3; Th Khua Vieng) East of Talat Sao and beyond the bus terminal, this rustic market offers fresh produce and meats, as well as flowers, tobacco and assorted other goods.

Talat Thong Khan Kham (Map pp68-9; cnr Th Khan Kham & Th Dong Miang) This market is open all day, but is best in the morning. It's one of the biggest markets in Vientiane and has virtually everything. You'll find it north of the town centre in Ban Thong Khan Kham. Nearby are basket and pottery vendors.

GETTING THERE & AWAY
Air

Departures from Vientiane are perfectly straightforward. The Domestic Terminal is in the older, white building east left of the impressive International Terminal. There is an (often unmanned) information counter in the arrivals hall, and food can be found upstairs in the International Terminal.

See p266 for details on air transport to Laos, p270 for information on flights

CROSSING THE THAI BORDER AT THE THAI-LAO FRIENDSHIP BRIDGE

The Thai-Lao Friendship Bridge (Saphan Mittaphap Thai-Lao) spans the Mekong River bet— Nong Khai in Thailand to Tha Na Leng in Laos, 20km southeast of Vientiane. The border open between 6am and 10pm and the easiest and cheapest way to cross is on the comfortable Thai-Lao International Bus (US$0.80, 90 minutes), which leaves Vientiane's Talat Sao (Morning Market) Bus Station at 7.30am, 10.30am, 3.30pm and 6pm. From Nong Khai, it leaves at the same times for 30B. The border itself is easy, with visas issued on arrival in both countries (see p263).

Alternative means of transport between Vientiane and the bridge include taxi (US$5), jumbo (US$4), or the regular public bus from Talat Sao (US$0.30) between 6.30am and 5pm. At the bridge, shuttle buses ferry passengers between immigration posts every 20 minutes or so. On the Thai side you'll need to take a tuk-tuk between the bridge and bus or train stations. For details on trains between Nong Khai and Bangkok, see p269.

within Laos, and p94 for specifics on transport into Vientiane.

AIRLINE OFFICES
See also Travel Agencies, p67.

China Yunnan Airlines (Map pp68-9; ☎ 212300; Th Luang Prabang) In the same building as Thai Airways.

Lao Airlines (www.laoairlines.com) Airport Office (☎ 512028; 7.30am-noon & 1-4.30pm); Head Office (Map pp72-3; ☎ 212051-4; 2 Th Pangkham; 8am-noon & 1.30-5pm Mon-Sat, 8am-noon Sun) Handles domestic and international ticketing.

Thai Airways International (Map pp68-9; ☎ 222527; Th Luang Prabang; 8am-5pm Mon-Fri, 8am-noon Sat)

Vietnam Airlines (Map pp72-3; ☎ 217562; www .vietnamairlines.com; 1st fl, Lao Plaza Hotel, Th Samsenthai; 8am-noon & 1.30-4.30pm Mon-Fri, 8am-noon Sat)

Boat
Passenger boat services between Vientiane and Luang Prabang have become almost extinct as most people now take the bus, which is both faster and cheaper.

Occasional six-passenger *héua wái* (speedboats) do run to Pak Lai (US$15, 115km, four to five hours). If you can get a group of six passengers together you can hire a speedboat all the way north to Luang Prabang for US$38 per person. Count on a full day, at least, to reach Luang Prabang. To charter a speedboat you'd have to pay a fee roughly equal to six passenger fares. Speedboats leave from Tha Heua Kao Liaw (Kao Liaw Boat Landing), which is 7.7km west of the Novotel (3.5km west of the fork in the road where Rte 13 heads north) in Ban Kao Liaw. Because departures are so inconsistent it's recommended you head

out to Tha Heua Kao Liaw the day before, at least, to try and arrange it.

A rare cargo boat runs to Luang Prabang (about US$24, four or five days upriver, three or four days down).

Bus
Our table (p94) gives timetable information. Buses use three different stations in Vientiane. However, it's the new **Northern Bus Station** (Map pp68-9; ☎ 260255; Th T2) where you're most likely to enter and leave the capital. Buses leave here for everywhere from Phongsali in the far north to Attapeu in the south, and even Ho Chi Minh City for the truly masochistic. The station is huge, and food is available here. Destinations and the latest ticket prices are listed in English, and the two ticket offices are manned by helpful English-speaking staff – Nr Nom (☎ mobile 020-2243024) is a walking timetable.

The **Si Muang Air Bus Station** (Map pp68-9; Th Tha Deua) is where the more expensive **KVT** (☎ 242101) and **Laody** (☎ 2421102) operate buses heading south to Pakse, via Tha Khaek and Savannakhet. There are no facilities at this station, so buy any food or drink you want before you arrive.

The final departure point is the **Talat Sao bus station** (Map pp72-3; ☎ 216507), from where buses run to destinations within Vientiane Province and not far beyond. This is also where the **Thai-Lao International Bus** begins its trip across the Thai-Lao Friendship Bridge to Nong Kai, see p269 for details.

Train
See p269 for information on Thai trains to the Lao-Thai border.

LEAVING VIENTIANE BY BUS

These services depart every day from the Northern Bus Station, except where noted: *Talat Sao bus station and +Si Muang Air Bus Station. The bus to Huay Xai might not run in the wet season.

Destination	Fare normal/ VIP/KVT (US$)	Distance (km)	Duration (hrs)	Departures
Attapeu	9.50	812	22-24	9.30am, 5pm
Don Khong	9	788	16-19	10.30am
Huay Xai	16	869	30-35	5.30pm
Lak Sao	4.50	334	8	4am, 5am, 6am
Luang Nam Tha	11	676	19	8.30am
Luang Prabang	6/7.50	384	11/9	6.30am (VIP), 7.30am, 9am (VIP), 11am, 1.30pm, 4pm, 6pm, 7.30pm (VIP)
Paksan *	1.50	143	1½	7.30am, 10am, 11am, noon, 1.30pm, 3.30pm
Pakse	7/9/14.50	659	14-16/10/9½	Normal buses every 30 mins from 9am-5pm; VIP buses 5.15am, 7am+, 6pm, 7pm, 8pm, 8pm+; KVT bus 8.30pm+
Phongsali	12	811	26	7.15am
Phonsavan	6/8	374	10/8	6.30am, 7.30am (VIP), 9.30am, 4pm
Sainyabuli	7.50	485	16	5.30pm
Salavan	8.50	774	20	4.30pm
Sam Neua	12	612	15 via Phonsavan or 24	7am, 10am
Savannakhet	4.50/6	457	8/7	4am, 5am, 5.30am (VIP express), 6am (VIP), then every 30 mins until 9am
Tha Khaek	3.50/4.50	332	6/4½	4am, 5am, 6am (VIP), noon
Udomxai	8.30/9.10	578	15/14	6.45am, 2pm, 4pm (VIP)
Vang Vieng *	1.50	153	3½	7am, 9.30am, 10.30am, 11.30am, 1.30pm, 2pm
Voen Kham	9	818	17-20	11am
Xieng Houng (for Kunming, China)	20	784	20-24	1.30pm Thu & Sun

GETTING AROUND

Central Vientiane is entirely accessible on foot. For exploring neighbouring districts, however, you'll need transport.

To/From the Airport

Wattay International Airport is about 4km northwest of the city centre, which makes the US$5 flat fare for a taxi more than a little steep. The fare is set by the government and the US$5 takes you anywhere in Vientiane (to the Thai-Lao Friendship Bridge is US$9). Only official taxis can pick up at the airport, and even the drivers think the fare is too high because it's costing them business.

Many passengers, if they don't have too much to carry, simply walk out of the terminal, across the carpark and on for 500m to the airport gate, where jumbos and tuk-tuks loiter and will make the trip for US$1.50. A few metres further, on Th Luang Prabang, you could wait for a shared jumbo (US$0.40 per person), or even a bus (US$0.15). Prices on shared transport will rise if you're going further than the centre. There is no dedicated airport bus.

From the centre of town to the airport costs should be the same, though jumbo drivers will usually ask for twice as much. The Phon Hong bus from Talat Sao makes the journey for US$0.15.

Bicycle

This is the most convenient and economical way to get around the city, besides walking. Several guesthouses hire out bikes on a regular basis for around US$1 per day, as does a place on the corner of Th Setthathirat and Th Pangkham. The cheapest hire bikes are found outside the **Douang Deuane Hotel** (Map pp72-3; Th Nokeo Khumman; per day US$0.55).

Bus

There is a city bus system, but it's not oriented towards the central Chanthabuli district, but to outlying districts north, east and west of the centre. Most buses leave from Talat Sao bus station; to the Thai-Lao Friendship Bridge costs US$0.30.

Car & Motorcycle

Small motorbikes are a popular means of getting around Vientiane and can be hired from several places. The cheapest are from outside the **Douang Deuane Hotel** (Map pp72-3; Th Nokeo Khumman) where 110cc bikes cost about US$5.50 a day. Similar but newer bikes are available from **PVO** (Map pp72-3; ☎ 214444; 314 Th Samsenthai; per day US$10) and **Lucky Motorcycle Rental** (Map pp72-3; cnr Th Pangkham & Th Samsenthai; per day US$8). PVO is the best place to hire 250cc bikes, usually Honda Bajas, for US$20 a day, less for longer hire.

For car hire and drivers, see p274.

Jumbo

Drivers of jumbos, which are three-wheeled taxis not dissimilar to tuk-tuks, will be glad to take passengers on journeys as short as 500m or as far as 20km. They will also be glad to overcharge you, usually asking tourists for US$1 no matter how short the trip. The fare for a chartered jumbo should be no more than US$0.50 for distances of 1km or less, plus about US$0.15 for each kilometre beyond 2km. Bargaining is mandatory. Share jumbos that run regular routes around town (eg Th Luang Prabang to Th Setthathirat or Th Lan Xang to That Luang) cost a minimum of US$0.20 per person, no bargaining necessary. Prices of common routes, such as Talat Sao to Pha That Luang (US$0.20), are listed in the *Vientiane Times*.

From the Thai-Lao Friendship Bridge to the city centre a jumbo will cost about 150B (about US$4). A shared jumbo between the bridge and Talat Sao is only US$0.40.

Taxi

Car taxis of varying shapes, sizes and vintages can often be found stationed in front of the larger hotels or at the airport. A growing number of these (usually the newer models) are fitted with air-con and meters and wear a 'Taxi Meter' sign. The meters, however, are ornamental only – you'll still have to negotiate the fare, which will be higher than in a naturally cooled jumbo. For taxis, you could try **Lavi Taxi Company** (☎ 350000) or the **Taxi Meter Company** (☎ 222222).

In Vientiane, a car and driver for the day usually costs from US$25 to US$30 as long as the vehicle doesn't leave town. If you want to go further afield, eg to Ang Nam Ngum or Vang Vieng, you may have to pay from US$35 to US$45 a day.

AROUND VIENTIANE

There are several places worth seeing within an easy day trip of Vientiane. A few might detain you for longer than a day, such as Vang Vieng, Ban Pako and the new treks and elephant watching in Phu Khao Khuay NPA.

VIENTIANE TO ANG NAM NGUM

On the way to Ang Nam Ngum (Nam Ngum Reservoir) are a number of interesting stopover possibilities. **Ban Ilai**, on Rte 13 in Muang Naxaithong, has a good market for basketry, pottery and other daily utensils. The **Nam Tok Tat Khu Khana** waterfall (also called Hin Khana) is easy to reach via a 10km dirt road, leading west from Rte 13 near the village of Ban Naxaithong, near Km 17.

At Km 52 on Rte 13 is **Talat Lak Ha-Sip Sawng** (Km 52 Market), a large daily market that is often visited by Hmong and other local ethnic minorities. A bit further north is the prosperous town of Phon Hong at the junction of the turn-off for Thalat and Ang Nam Ngum; Rte 13 continues north from here to Vang Vieng. If you're looking for somewhere to eat lunch, Phon Hong is the best place between Vientiane and Vang Vieng.

At **Vang Sang**, 65km north of Vientiane via Rte 13, a cluster of 10 high-relief Buddha sculptures on cliffs is thought to date from the 16th century, although some local scholars assign it an 11th-century Mon provenance. Although this is not likely, given the absence of any other Mon sites in the area, it is possible this was a stopover for Buddhist travellers from Mon-Khmer city-states in Southern Laos or northern Thailand. Two of the Buddhas are over 4m tall. The name means Elephant Palace, a reference to an elephant graveyard once found nearby. About 20m from the main sculptures is another cluster with one large and four smaller images. To reach Vang Sang, take the signed turn-off at Km 62 near Ban Huay Thon, and follow a dirt road 1.8km to the sanctuary.

Thalat, between Phon Hong and Ang Nam Ngum, is known for its environmentally incorrect market, which sells all kinds of forest creatures – deer, spiny anteaters, rats and so on – for local consumption.

The new **Nam Lik Eco-Village** (☎ mobile 020-5508719; Ban Vang Moen; bungalows US$25, floating house US$10) sits on a hill at Ban Vang Moen overlooking the Nam Lik, and is designed as a base from which to explore the surrounding area. Activities include a 25m rock-climbing wall (grade 6a-c routes), kayaking and trekking. There are two ways to reach the eco-village: by vehicle via a turn-off 75km north of Vientiane, then a further 6km drive to Ban Vang Moen; or more interestingly by getting yourself to the south end of Hin Hoep bridge (anything going north from Vientiane or south from Vang Vieng will stop here), then paddling a kayak downriver (US$10/15 without/with a guide) to the village, your bags following by road. Call English- and French-speaking owner David at Nam Lik Eco-Village for further details.

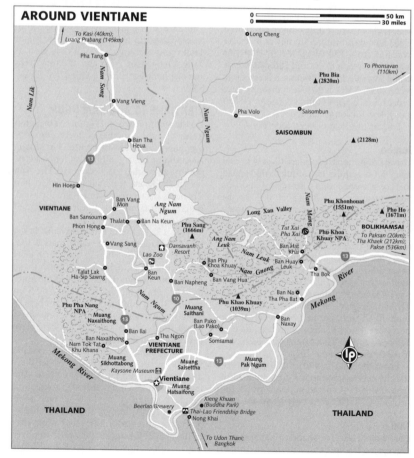

AROUND VIENTIANE

ANG NAM NGUM
ອ່າງນ້ຳງື່ມ

Ang Nam Ngum is the vast artificial lake created by the damming of the Nam Ngum. The highest peaks of the former river valley became forested islands after the valley was inundated in 1971. Following the 1975 PL conquest of Vientiane, an estimated 3000 prostitutes and petty criminals were rounded up from the capital and banished to some of these islands for several years. Today the Nam Ngum hydroelectric plant generates most of the electricity used in the Vientiane area and sells power to Thailand.

About 250 sq km of forest were flooded when the river was dammed. For years since, logging rigs have used hydraulic underwater saws to cut the submerged but still very valuable teak trees. A few towns and villages on or near the shores of the lake, such as **Ban Tha Heua** and **Ban Huay** at the northern end, specialise in crafting furniture from the salvaged teak.

Fishing is also an important local industry, and one that attracted thousands of people to the area during the '80s and '90s. Too many, perhaps. In recent years fishers have reported a drastic fall in their catch and many have been forced to find other work.

Ang Nam Ngum is dotted with picturesque little islands and it is well worth arranging a cruise. Boats holding up to 20 people can be hired from Ban Na Kheun, or any other lakeside village, for about US$10 an hour.

Sleeping & Eating

Since most people day-trip to Ang Nam Ngum from Vientiane the few guesthouses in the region are often empty and it can be difficult to find anyone with a key. You will, however, be able to find somewhere to sleep in both Ban Na Kheun and Tha Heua, usually for less than US$10.

Opened in 1999, the **Dansavanh Nam Ngum Resort** (☎ 021-217594; www.dansavanh.com; packages including meals from US$50; ❄ ▣) is a US$200 million lakeside resort – 75% owned by a Malaysian company and 25% owned by the Lao military – which harbours the only legal casino in Laos. The resort is 10 minutes by boat from the landing at Na Nam, although most visitors and guests arrive on free shuttle buses from Vientiane or Nong Khai.

The reservoir produces a sizable annual harvest of freshwater fish, and local restaurants are famous for tasty *kâwy pąa* (tart and spicy minced fish salad), *kąeng pąa* (fish soup) and *neung pąa* (steamed fish with fresh herbs). Attached to the shore are several floating restaurants where fish are kept on tethers beneath the deck. When there's an order, the cook lifts a grate in the deck and yanks a flapping fish directly into the galley.

Getting There & Away

From Vientiane's Talat Sao Bus Station you can catch a 7am service all the way to Kheun Nam Ngum (Nam Ngum Dam; US$0.70, about three hours), near Ban Na Kheun. This trip goes along Rte 13 through Thalat. If you don't make the 7am bus, you'll have to take a bus to Thalat (US$0.55, 87km, 2½ hours) and then catch a pick-up or jumbo to the lake.

Taxis in Vientiane usually charge from US$30 to US$40 return to the lake. Ask the driver to take the more scenic Rte 10 through Ban Kheun for the return trip, completing a circle that avoids backtracking.

BAN PAKO (LAO PAKO)
ລາວປາໂກ

Situated on a lushly forested bend of the Nam Ngum, **Ban Pako** (Lao Pako; ☎ 451970, in Vientiane 021-451841; fax 451844; dm US$3, r US$11-20) is no longer the backpacker magnet it was a few years ago. It is, however, still a beautiful part of the world and a relaxing getaway from Vientiane.

The rustic bamboo and thatch 'village' is in a secluded spot about 50km from the capital and chances are it will be fairly quiet when you arrive – don't expect a party. Activities include swimming and boating in the river, volleyball and badminton on the property or hiking to nearby villages, wat and waterfalls. The community-oriented proprietors were instrumental in creating a 40-hectare forest preserve on the river's opposite bank. After a hike and a swim, you can sweat a bit more in the herbal sauna in the forest. The archaeology of the site is also interesting, with 2000-year-old artefacts having been dug up nearby.

If you tire of swinging in a hammock and reading, a couple of nearby riverbank villages are worth visiting. **Ban Kok Hai**, 15 minutes away by river, is notable for its *lào-hǎi* (Lao-style jar liquor), while **Tha Sang** (Elephant Landing) is another riverside village where a local wat houses a large reclining Buddha and classic central Lao-style stupa.

Lodgings are built of native materials and consist of a few private bungalows with bathrooms and river views (US$20), a bamboo and wood longhouse contains an eight-bed dorm, plus three rooms (US$11), and a range of other double rooms with jungle views. Lao and European food is served – order well in advance. Electricity runs from 6pm to midnight.

Getting There & Away

The best way to reach Lao Pako is to drive or take the bus along Rte 13 south, turn left (north) after 24km, follow the signs to Somsamai and take a boat (US$1.50 per person one way, 30 minutes) to the lodge. Buses run between Talat Sao and Somsamai (US$0.40 one way, 90 minutes, six times daily), the first at 7am and the last at 5.30pm.

PHU KHAO KHUAY NATIONAL PROTECTED AREA

ປ່າສະຫງວນພູເຂົາຄວາຍ

Covering more than 2000 sq km of mountains and rivers to the east of Vientiane, the underrated Phu Khao Khuay NPA is easily accessible from the capital. Treks ranging in duration from a couple of hours to three days have been developed in close consul-

---

BUFFALO HORN MOUNTAIN

Phu Khao Khuay means 'buffalo horn mountain'. The name derives from a legend in which a water buffalo walking in the forest overhears a *leusǐi* (hermit sage) practising magic. The buffalo was pretty sharp and taught himself the magic before using it to kill all other male buffaloes and taking the females as his wives. From these wives came many offspring, one of whom learned of the magical massacre from his mother. She urged her son to kill his father before he himself was also killed. The young buffalo did just that and buried his father's horns in the mountains. But overcome by guilt, the young buffalo took his own life and was buried next to his father.

---

tation with two villages on the edge of the NPA, Ban Na and Ban Hat Khai.

Phu Khao Khuay boasts an extraordinary array of endangered wildlife, including wild elephants, gibbons, gaur, Asiatic black bear, tiger, clouded leopard, Siamese fireback pheasant and green peafowl. About 88% of the NPA is forested, though only 32% has been classified as dense, mature forest. Depending on elevation, visitors may encounter dry evergreen dipterocarp (a Southeast Asian tree with two-winged fruit), mixed deciduous forest, conifer forest or grassy uplands. Several impressive waterfalls are accessible on day-trips from Vientiane.

Tour operators in Vientiane (see p276) can arrange any of the trips mentioned following, or you could do it yourself. Do *not*, however, just turn up unannounced.

To organise a trek, get a Lao speaker, perhaps a staff member at the NTAL office in Vientiane (p67) or your guesthouse, to call the village to check their availability and, in the case of Ban Na, whether the elephants are around. Prices vary depending on the number of trekkers but are very reasonable; for example, a three-day trek from Ban Hat Khai is US$37/23 per person in a group of two/eight people. A one-day trip is US$18/13. From Ban Na prices are slightly lower as there is no boat trip. The prices do not include transport from Vientiane and are not negotiable. All monies go to the village or NPA. For Ban Hat Khai, get a Lao speaker to call **Mr Khammany** (☎ mobile 020-2240303), and for Ban Na **Mr Bounthanom** (☎ mobile 020-2208262).

There are additional small charges if you opt for 'luxury' items such as tents and hammocks with built-in mosquito nets. In addition trekkers need to buy a yellow trekking permit (US$4 per trip), which can be arranged in the village.

Ban Hat Khai

ບ້ານຫາດໄຂ່

The village of Ban Hat Khai is the launch point for treks into Phu Khao Khuay NPA, with destinations including the huge cliff, views and beautiful landscape of **Pha Luang** (three to four hours one way), and the forested areas around **Huay Khi Ling** (two to three hours one way). A trek taking in both these areas takes two or three days, depending on the season; you sleep in the forest.

THE SWEET-TOOTHED ELEPHANTS OF BAN NA

The farmers of Ban Na grow rice and vegetables, but a few years ago they began planting sugar-cane after being encouraged by a local sugar company. What they didn't count on was the collective sweet tooth of the herd of elephants in the nearby mountains. It wasn't long before these jumbos had sniffed out the delights in the field below and were happily eating the sugarcane, pineapples and bananas planted around Ban Na. Not surprisingly, the farmers weren't happy. They decided the only way to get rid of the elephants was to rip up the sugarcane and go back to planting boring (and less lucrative) vegetables.

It was hoped the 30-odd elephants would take the hint and return to the mountains, but they didn't. Instead, they have made the lowland forests, bamboo belt and fields around Ban Na their home. The destruction they cause is significant, affecting both the environment and finances of Ban Na. The only way the villagers can continue to live with the elephants (ie not shoot them) is by making them pay their way. The result is elephant ecotourism. Let's hope it works.

However, most people visit Ban Hat Khai en route to the area's most impressive waterfalls, **Tat Xai** and **Pha Xai**. Tat Xai cascades down seven steps, while 800m downstream Pha Xai plunges over a spectacular 50m-high cataract. The nearby **Tat Leuk** is much smaller; the main attraction being the wonderfully well-documented **Huay Bon Nature Trail** and excellent visitor centre.

Ban Na
ບ້ານນາ

The lowland farming village of Ban Na, 82km northeast of Vientiane, is home to about 600 people. The village is typical Lao, with women weaving baskets from bamboo (skills they will happily impart for a small fee) and men tending the fields. But it's the local herd of elephants that is most interesting to visitors (see The Sweet-Toothed Elephants of Ban Na above).

Village guides lead one-, two- and three-day treks to places of interest near Ban Na, including through elephant territory to Keng Khani (three to four hours one way), through deep forest to the waterfall of Tat Fa (four to five hours) and to Pung Xay, where an observation tower is due to be built to look down on the elephants' favourite salt lick. Trekkers will be able to sleep in the tower, though of course there is no guarantee the pachyderms will come to the party.

Getting There & Away

Buses from Talat Sao in Vientiane leave regularly for Tha Bok and Paksan. For Ban Na, you should get off at Tha Pha Baht Phonsan (p192) 80km northeast of Vientiane. Follow the signs to Ban Na, 1.5km north.

For Ban Hat Khai, keep on the bus until Tha Bok, 90km from Vientiane. From here, take a *săwngthăew* (passenger truck) 5km to Ban Huay Leuk. Ban Hat Khai is 2km further, but the road beyond tends to get washed out in the rainy season, meaning you might have to take a boat (40 minutes, 12km), then walk another hour to Tat Xai.

There is a good-value guesthouse in Tha Bok.

SAISOMBUN SPECIAL ZONE
ເຂດພິເສດໄຊສົມບຸນ

After 30 years as a no-go zone, off-limits due to an ongoing armed insurgency by Hmong rebels, Saisombun is slowly opening to tourism. The first tentative steps have been made by rafting operators out of Vang Vieng, who launch their Nam Ngum trips inside the zone. While it is in theory possible to take public transport to Saisombun town itself, whether you actually get there depends on the attitude of the authorities at the time. Long Cheng, the 'secret city' from where the Hmong and CIA operated during the Indochina War, remains off-limits.

VANG VIENG
ວັງວຽງ

☎ 023 / pop 25,000

The small town of Vang Vieng, nestled beside the Nam Song amid stunningly beautiful limestone karst terrain, is a place travellers have come to either love or hate. While the town is not without charm, the main attraction of Vang Vieng is the surrounding countryside and the activities that are available therein.

Honeycombed with unexplored tunnels and caverns, the limestone cliffs here are a spelunker's heaven. Several of the caves are named and play minor roles in local mythology – all are said to be inhabited by spirits. These caves and cliffs are also gaining a reputation among rock climbers.

The Nam Song, meanwhile, plays host to a growing number of kayakers, who share the river with travellers floating along on tractor inner tubes – a pastime so thoroughly enjoyable and popular that it has become one of the rites of passage of the Indochina backpacking circuit.

So what's to dislike, you might ask. The most common complaint is that in earning its stripes as a fully paid-up member of backpacker world, Vang Vieng has lost its soul. It's probably not as bad as that, but the growth of Vang Vieng has taken its toll. Inevitably, the profile of the town has changed as concrete guesthouses have gone up at a dizzying rate. This is fine in itself, but the architectural style (Greco-Laotian, perhaps?) is not endearing.

What grates most is the continued growth, in both quantity and volume, of 'TV bars' – restaurants that have their televisions blaring all day and into the night. At the time of writing it was possible to sit watching one episode of *Friends* while hearing another five (all different) episodes at the same time. A nightmare! But don't blame the locals for this, it is travellers who are driving it – when restaurants switch off their TVs, people stop coming.

The TV bars notwithstanding, Vang Vieng's attractions make it worth a visit. Accommodation is ridiculously cheap and the people seem to have accepted this influx of *falang* without losing their sense of humour. Sights include several monasteries dating from the 16th and 17th centuries, among them Wat Si Vieng Song (Wat That), Wat Kang and Wat Si Suman. Outside town are several villages to which Hmong have been relocated, including Nam Som and Nammuang, both of which are accessible by bicycle.

Note that both the market and bus station will probably have moved to locations 2km north of town by the time you arrive. The bamboo footbridges crossing the Nam Song are down from about June to October, when you'll need to take a boat.

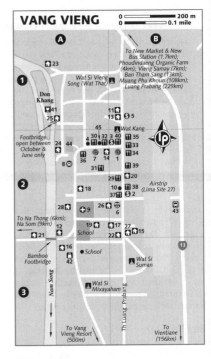

Information

A1 Internet (Map pp100-1; ☎ 511296; per hr US$1.80; ☼ 8am-11pm) Internet access.

Agricultural Promotion Bank (Map pp100-1; Th Luang Prabang) Exchanges cash only.

BCEL (Map pp100-1; ☎ 5114480; ☼ 8.30am-3.30pm Mon-Sun) Exchanges cash, travellers cheques and handles cash advances on Visa, MasterCard and JCB.

BKC Bookshop (Map pp100-1; ☎ 511303; ☼ 7am-7pm) Second-hand novels plus some guidebooks and hand-drawn maps.

Lao Development Bank (Map pp100-1; Th Luang Prabang)

PlaNet Online (Map pp100-1; ☎ 511209; per hr US$1.80; ☼ 8am-11pm) Internet access, CD burning, international phone calls.

Post office (Map pp100-1; ☎ 511009) Beside the old market.

Provincial Hospital (Map pp100-1) Avoid unless absolutely necessary. Head for Vientiane.

Dangers & Annoyances

Like any big backpacker destination, Vang Vieng has its fair share of thefts, many by fellow travellers. Take the usual precautions, and be careful about leaving valuables outside caves.

VIENTIANE & AROUND

There are two other dangers you need to be especially aware of. The first is the Nam Song, the river down which you will probably tube and which has claimed the life of at least one traveller in recent years. Most of the year the Nam Song is positively serene. But at the height of the wet season in July and August the water flows up to four times faster than normal. You're advised to wear a lifejacket at any time, and especially during these months; tubing companies should provide one. It's also worth asking how long the trip should take (durations vary depending on the time of year) and planning your trip so you get back to Vang Vieng before it gets dark. Finally, don't forget that the Nam Song is especially dangerous when you're off your head on drink and drugs.

The other trouble that tends to find travellers is the law. While Vang Vieng is no longer home to opium dens, the police are adept at sniffing out spliffs, especially late at night. Being caught can be expensive, with police usually issuing a US$500 on-the-spot fine. And, no, they don't take plastic, nor will they issue a receipt.

Sights & Activities

Most visitors spend their time strolling or biking the river bank, exploring local villages, tubing or kayaking the river and checking out the many local limestone caves.

CAVES

Following, we've described only the most accessible of the *thàm* (caves). All the caves in Vang Vieng are now signed in English as well as Lao, and an admission fee ranging from US$0.10 to US$0.90 is collected by a guide at the entrance to each cave. The guide (often a young village boy) will lead you through the cave, but it's wise to bring along a torch (flashlight).

For more extensive multicave tours, most guesthouses can arrange a guide. Trips including river tubing and cave tours cost around US$8/12 for a half/full day.

Tham Jang (Tham Chang)
ຖ້ຳຈາງ

The most famous of the caves, **Tham Jang** (Map p102; Tham Chang; admission US$0.90) is a large cavern that was used as a bunker in defence against marauding *jiin háw* (Yunnanese Chinese) in the early 19th century (*jàng* means steadfast). A set of stairs leads up to the main cavern entrance.

From the main cave chamber you can look over the river valley through an opening in the limestone wall; a cool spring at the foot of the cave feeds into the river. You can swim up this spring around 80m into the cave. Inside the cave are electric lights, which the caretakers will turn on once you've paid the admission fee. You can swim outside the cave without paying.

To get there, walk south to the Vang Vieng Resort where you must pay a US$0.10 fee to cross the grounds. The cave is signed on the far side of the hanging bridge.

Tham Phu Kham
ຖ້ຳພູຄຳ

The cavernous hall of **Tham Phu Kham** (Map p102; admission US$0.40) contains a Thai bronze reclining Buddha, and deeper galleries branch

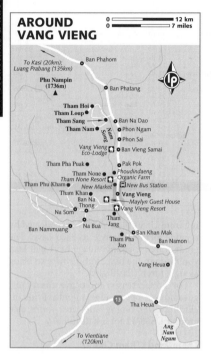

AROUND VANG VIENG

0 — 12 km
0 — 7 miles

To Kasi (20km);
Luang Prabang (135km)

Ban Phahom

Phu Nampin
(1736m)

Ban Phatang

Tham Hoi
Tham Loup
Tham Sang — Ban Na Dao
Tham Nam — Phon Ngam

Phon Sai

Vang Vieng
Eco-Lodge — Ban Vieng Samai

Tham Pha Puak — Pak Pok

Tham None — Phoudindaeng
Tham None Resort — Organic Farm
Tham Phu Kham — New Market — New Bus Station

Tham Khan — Vang Vieng
Ban Na — Maylyn Guest House
Thong — Vang Vieng Resort
Na Som — Tham
Jang

Na Bua

Ban Nammuang

Ban Khan Mak
Tham Pha — Ban Namon
Jao

Vang Heua

13

Tha Heua

Ang
Nam
Ngum

To Vientiane
(120km)

off the main cavern formation. A dip in the stream after the steep climb up and down to the cave is very inviting. To get there, cross the bamboo footbridge (US$0.20 toll) near the Hotel Nam Song, then walk or pedal 6km along a scenic, unpaved road to the village of Ban Na Thong. From Ban Na Thong, where you can park your bicycle for a small fee, follow the signs for 1km to a hill on the northern side of the village. It's a stiff 200m climb through some interesting scrub forest to the cave.

Tham Pha Jao
ຖ້ຳພະເຈົ້າ

This cave (Map p102) takes a little more effort to reach, and although the cave itself is not spectacular, the pleasant walk and natural setting make it worthwhile. Follow Rte 13 south 6km to Ban Khan Mak village, then take a side road down to the Nam Song. Hire a pirogue (dug-out canoe) to ford the river (or wade across in the driest months), and then follow a path on the opposite bank until it breaks right into a banana grove. At this point head for the giant lone dipterocarp tree (note the huge bees nests hanging high above, and the steps added to the trunk for easy honey collection) standing sentinel near the cave. Soon you'll see the heart-shaped entrance to the medium-size cavern, which contains a Buddha figure but little else.

The Tham Sang Triangle

A popular half-day trip that's easy to do on your own takes in Tham Sang plus three other caves within a short walk. Begin this caving odyssey by riding a bike or taking a jumbo 13km north along Rte 13, turning left a few hundred metres beyond the barely readable Km 169 stone. A rough road leads to the river, where a boatman will ferry you across to Ban Tham Sang (US$0.50 return). Tham Sang itself is right here, as is a small restaurant.

Tham Sang (Map p102; Tham Xang; admission US$0.10), meaning 'Elephant Cave', is a small cavern containing a few Buddha images and a Buddha 'footprint', plus the elephant-shaped stalactite that gives the cave its name. It's best visited in the morning when light enters the cave.

From Tham Sang a signed path takes you 1km northwest through rice fields to the entrances of **Tham Loup** and **Tham Hoi** (Map p102; admission for both caves US$0.30). The entrance to Tham Hoi is guarded by a large Buddha figure; reportedly the cave continues about 3km into the limestone and an underground lake. Tham Loup is a large and delightfully untouched cavern with some impressive stalactites.

About 400m south of Tham Hoi, along a well-used path, is the highlight of this trip, **Tham Nam** (Map p102; admission US$0.50). The cave is about 500m long and a tributary of the Nam Song flows out of its low entrance. In the dry season you can wade into the cave, but when the water is higher you need to take a tube from the friendly woman near the entrance; the tube and headlamp are included in the entrance fee. Dragging yourself through the tunnel on the fixed rope is a lot of fun.

From Tham Nam an easy 1km walk brings you back to Ban Tham Sang. This loop is usually included in the rafting/kayaking/trekking/tubing combo trip run by almost all the tour operators in Vang Vieng.

KAYAKING

Kayaking has taken off in a big way in Vang Vieng and operators have been slashing prices to kill off the competition. Trips typically include visits to caves and villages and traverse a few rapids, costing US$8 to US$12 per person for a whole day, depending on the season. Kayaking trips to Vientiane, advertised around town for about US$15, involve a lot of paddling and part of the trip is by road.

Although all guides are supposed to be trained, many are not. Before using a cheap operator, check the guides' credentials and that there is adequate safety equipment.

RAFTING

Rafting the Nam Ngum has taken off in the past couple of years, with two-day expeditions running down the river through untouched Saisombun Province into Ang Nam Ngum; sleeping on an island in the lake, and often finishing with a ride to Vientiane. The Nam Ngum has several Grade 4 and 5 rapids that are far more exciting, and more dangerous, than anything on the Nam Lik, and choosing a company with a good guide is the best way to maximise safety. Guides, of course, come and go, but those at Wildside Green Discovery and Vang Vieng Paddle Adventures are generally pretty good, see opposite; ask around before you sign up. The two-day trip will cost at least US$90 per person. Rafting is best and safest between October and March.

ROCK CLIMBING

The limestone peaks around Vang Vieng are starting to attract the attention of serious rock climbers. More than 50 routes have been identified by a German team and most have bolts in place. The routes have been provisionally rated at between 4 and 8b, with the majority being in or near a cave and less than 20m high. Experienced climbers should seek out Si Pou (7b+, 20m), Sok di Phi Mai (8a, 12m), Chicken Schnitzel (7b+, 17m), AK-47 (7c, 30m), and Another Day in Paradise (8a+, 15m).

The climbing season usually runs between October and May, with routes too wet at other times. Equipment can be hired from **Wildside Green Discovery** (Map pp100-1; ☎ 511440), which also sells a handy guide to the various climbs, with basic maps,

and conducts courses for beginners. The government requires all climbers to have a permit and liaison officer, though this is less hassle than it sounds. The permit costs US$5 per day, per group of climbers, and can be bought from Wildside. If you want to split costs, be at Wildside at 9am.

TUBING

Virtually everyone who comes to Vang Vieng goes tubing down the Nam Song in an inflated tractor tyre. The 3km trip from near Phoudindaeng Organic Farm, north of Vang Vieng, has become such a popular rite of passage on the Southeast Asia backpacker circuit that several 'bars' have been set up on islands and beaches along the route. The tube-hiring businesses have formed a cartel, with only one allowed to operate on any given day, so tube prices are fixed at US$3, including your trip to the launch point.

In times of high water, rapids along the Nam Song can be quite daunting; see Dangers & Annoyances p100.

Tours

More than 10 companies operate so-called adventure tours out of Vang Vieng. Prices and standards vary, though the following four have good reputations:

Nam Lao Adventure Tours (Map pp100-1; ☎ 511135; namlao@hotmail.com; Th Luang Prabang)

Riverside Tours (Map pp100-1; ☎ 511091, mobile 020-2244775)

Vang Vieng Paddle Adventures (Map pp100-1; ☎ mobile 020-2255176; paddle_adventures@hotmail .com; Th Luang Prabang)

Wildside Green Discovery (Map pp100-1; ☎ 511440; www.greendiscoverylaos.com; Th Luang Prabang) In the Xayoh Cafe, Wildside is the biggest operator with the widest selection of tours, including trekking, kayaking, rafting, rock-climbing and caving. Ask about their Secret Eden trek.

Sleeping

There are so many guesthouses in Vang Vieng that they are doing each other out of business. For the traveller, this means Vang Vieng has some of the best-value rooms in Laos. Prices often fall even further in the low season.

BUDGET

Vang Vieng Orchid (Map pp100-1; ☎ mobile 020-2202259; r US$5-10; ⌘) On the banks of the Nam Song north of the old market, this is a new three-storey place with 20 clean, spacious rooms, 12 of which have balconies and wonderful views over Don Khang and the karst peaks beyond. At US$5 without air-con, they are unbeatable value. Rooms 101–4, 201–4 and 301–4 are recommended.

Saysong Guest House (Map pp100-1; ☎ 511130; r US$4-5) This very friendly place is popular for its decent rooms, both with (US$5) and without (US$4) private bathrooms, and communal balconies with similar views to the nearby Vang Vieng Orchid.

Maylyn Guest House (Map pp100-1; ☎ mobile 020-5604095; jophus_foley@hotmail.com; r US$3-5.50) West of the bamboo footbridge across the Nam Song, the Maylyn is in a lush, butterfly-filled garden beside a stream. It's very relaxed here, with the bamboo bungalows (without private bathrooms) and rooms in a Lao-style wooden house (some with bathroom) generally offering fewer amenities than those in Vang Vieng, but far more atmosphere. Owner Jophus is an old overlander himself who can advise on various hikes and climbs in the surrounding peaks. Food is served at reasonable prices, the barbecued fish is a highlight. Recommended.

Dok Khoun 1 Guest House (Map pp100-1; ☎ 511 032; r US$3-7; 🏠) Right in the centre of town east of the old market, the Dok Khoun 1 is an oldie but a goodie, spread over three buildings. You can choose from very clean but small rooms (fan/air-con US$3/4) or larger rooms for US$5/7.

Riverside Bungalows (Map pp100-1; ☎ 511035, mobile 020-3523426; r US$3.50-12; 🏠) In the north of town where the river bends to the west, the quiet position here has made it popular even though the 12 bamboo bungalows (singles/doubles US$3.50/4.50) share a bathroom and require you to BYO hammock. There are also larger, wooden bungalows with bathroom and balcony (US$8/12).

Several places in Ban Vieng Kaew, about 250m south of the Xayoh Cafe, are quiet, cheap and well worth a look, including the following four.

Dok Khoun 2 Guest House (Map pp100-1; ☎ 511063; r US$3-8; 🏠) Down a small lane leading to the old runway, Dok Khoun 2 has clean rooms in two wings and a friendly atmosphere. Some rooms contain one large bed, others two single beds.

Vieng Savanh Guest House (Map pp100-1; ☎ 511112; r US$3-7; 🏠) The best value of the Greco-Laotian set, with clean, comfortable fan rooms from US$3.

Nana Guest House & Restaurant (Map pp100-1; ☎ 511036; r US$3-5; 🏠) Nana's is welcoming and the balcony is a good place to chill out, but the rooms are looking a bit tired.

Khamphone Guest House (Map pp100-1; ☎ 511062; r US$5-10; 🏠) Khamphone spreads across three buildings on the southern edge of town and the welcoming management speak English. Rooms in the northeast building are best.

Malany Guest House (Map pp100-1 ☎ 511083; Th Luang Prabang; r US$5-10; 🏠) This four-storey Greco-Laotian style place has clean but unremarkable rooms in the centre of town. Could be friendlier.

Chanthala Guest House (Map pp100-1; ☎ 511146; d/tr/q US$2/3/4) On a wafer-thin budget? This place and its psychedelic sheets, and free tea is for you…More bang for your two bucks.

Also recommended:

Chan-thanom Guest House (Map pp100-1; ☎ 511174; r US$3-7; 🏠) The convivial people are the draw here more than the rooms.

Khounthong Guest House (Map pp100-1; Ban Vieng Kaew; r US$2.25-3.40) This wooden house has more local character than most.

VK Guest House (Map pp100-1; ☎ 511483; r US$3-10; 🏠) Huge upstairs rooms are the best for US$6/10 fan/air-con.

Bountang Guest House (Map pp100-1; ☎ 511328; d/tw US$4/5) Small, simple fan rooms.

MID-RANGE

Xayoh Riverside Bungalows (Map pp100-1; ☎ 511088; r US$20-28; 🏠) This classy new place has modern bungalows in a serene riverside location. Some rooms have a bathtub (US$28) and there are two romantic US$20 'singles' with a double bed and balcony over a river pool. There is a bar and restaurant.

Bungalow Thavonsouk (Map pp100-1; ☎ 511096; r US$20-50; 🏠) In a scenic location beside the bamboo bridge, Thavonsouk's attractive rooms are clean and some have verandas; prices depend on their size and proximity to the river. Try Xayoh first.

Hotel Nam Song (Map pp100-1; ☎ 511016; s/d US$20/30; 🏠) Just south of Thavonsouk, this one-storey hotel is in a good position but the rooms are overpriced.

OUT OF TOWN

If Vang Vieng wasn't quite what you envisaged, you can head out of town for a quieter, and often superior, location.

Kayakers, Vang Vieng (p103)

NEIL SETCHFIELD

CLINT LUCAS

Monk, Wat Hai Sok (p79), Vientiane

Sugar-cane juice being made, Vientiane (p64)

WOODS WHEATCROFT

Street food, Vientiane (p85)

Tham Phu Kham (p101), Vang Vieng

Lao textiles (p43)

Street scene, Vientiane (p64)

Phoudindaeng Organic Farm (Map p102; ☎ 511 220; suanmone@hotmail.com; r US$5) Known locally as *sŭran máwn phúu dịn dạeng* (Phoudindaeng Mulberry Farm), this organic farm 4km north of Vang Vieng raises mulberry trees for silk and tea production. It also grows organic fruits and vegetables and plays a vital role in the surrounding community. Accommodation is in rooms with shared bathroom, or in a dorm with spectacular views, but volunteer workers can no longer get free board. The attached **restaurant** (☻ 7am-8.30pm) makes great vegetarian food, or drink a delicious mulberry shake before beginning your tubing trip.

Vang Vieng Eco-Lodge (Map p102; ☎ mobile 020-2247323; bungalows US$25) About 7km north of town (turn left/west at Ban Vieng Samai after the Km 162 stone), these nicely decorated bungalows run along the riverfront and have twin or double beds and a balcony. The Lao food is served in the main house, but order well ahead. Prices are halved from May to September.

Heritage Guest House (Morodok; ☎ /fax 511488; moradok2003@yahoo.com; r US$8-15; ☻) These 14 well-built brick, tin-roofed cottages have two rooms each with balconies. Those on the river are bigger and have air-con (US$15). It's about 1.5km north of town. Fair value.

Vang Vieng Resort (Map p102; ☎ 511050; r US$6) Slightly south of town but near the river and opposite Tham Jang, Vang Vieng Resort is quiet and the cottages are comfortable, but the welcome is less than enthusiastic.

Eating

You know by the time you sit down for your third meal that something is amiss in the Vang Vieng restaurant scene. 'This looks a lot like the menu at that other place,' is commonly heard. Usually followed by something like: 'Hang on, it *is* the same – they've just photocopied it and changed the name on the front…!' Sad, but true. Many of Vang Vieng's restaurants, especially the TV bars, sell virtually identical fare aimed squarely at perceived Western tastes. And as with any place offering such a varied selection of cuisines (usually including Lao, Thai, Chinese, Italian, American, French and even Rasta), none of it is done particularly well. There are, however, a few decent eateries.

Most restaurants are open from about 7am or 8am until about 11pm, though in the low season hours might be shorter.

Organic Farm Café (Map pp100-1; ☎ 511174; meals US$1-2.50) Probably the best food in Vang Vieng comes from the Organic Farm Café, whose innovative vegetarian menu is being quoted up and down the country. The mulberry shake (US$0.60) and pancake (US$1.10) are famous, and the meat dishes pretty good too. You can also eat at the organic farm itself (opposite).

Sabaydee Restaurant (Map pp100-1; ☎ 511408; Th Luang Prabang; meals US$2-3) Food here ranges from bangers and mash (US$1.50) through a range of fresh salads (US$1 to US$1.50), bruschetta (US$1) and 18 different pizzas. The vaguely Middle Eastern look, chilled-out music and lack of TV make this one of the better options on this strip.

Full Moon Restaurant (Map pp100-1; ☎ mobile 020-5610825; meals US$1.50-3) The usual menu plus extras such as the snickers shake (US$1) and Israeli dishes make this place popular.

Xayoh Restaurant (Map pp100-1; ☎ 511088; meals US$2-4) A typically international menu has a heavy Italian influence; pizzas (US$2.50) and pastas (US$1.20) mix with burgers (US$1.80) and a pretty good caramel flan (US$0.80) for dessert. The riverside patio is quite romantic by night and also has several sun loungers. The same menu is available at **Xayoh Café** (Map pp100-1; Th Luang Prabang).

Nam Lao Restaurant (Map pp100-1; ☎ 511135; meals US$2-3) Good Thai-style curries, vegetarian options, good service and no TV – though in this area you'll be able to follow five or six programmes without even looking.

Luang Prabang Bakery (Map pp100-1; ☎ 511145; pastries under US$1) Strong coffee, sugary pastries, great baguettes, and a range of breakfasts (US$2 to US$3.50).

Sunset Restaurant (Map pp100-1; ☎ 511096; meals US$2.50-5) This restaurant and bar at Bungalow Thavonsouk is ideally located to watch locals crossing the bamboo bridge and travellers ending their tubing trips. The menu ranges from Western breakfasts to pseudo-Lao cuisine.

Nokeo (Map pp100-1; meals US$0.80-2; ☻ 8am-8pm) Nokeo has been around for years because it serves consistently good Lao food at prices low enough that locals can afford to eat here. The beef *làap* is excellent. It's on the corner opposite the old market.

HAPPINESS IS A STATE OF MIND

'Don't worry, be happy' could be the national motto for Laos, but in a growing number of backpacker centres the term 'happy' has taken on a wholly different connotation. In the TV bars of Vang Vieng and the riverside bungalows of Si Phan Don (p228) seeing the word 'happy' in front of 'shake', 'pizza' or anything else does not, as one traveller was told, mean it comes with extra pineapple. The extra is usually marijuana, added in whatever quantity the shake-maker deems fit.

For many travellers this might seem obvious enough, but there are others who innocently guzzle down their shake or pizza only to spend the next 24 hours somewhere near the outer reaches of the galaxy paranoia, with no idea why. So if you'd prefer not to be nine miles high for your tubing trip, then avoid the 'happy' meals and steer well clear of anything described as 'ecstatic'. If you do fancy floating down both literally and figuratively, then at the very least please wear a life jacket.

Erawan Restaurant (Map pp100–1; ☎ 511093; Th Luang Prabang; meals US$2-4) This place has decent Lao and Asian dishes, in particular, and is popular for having one of its TVs constantly tuned to sports.

The three places with an Indian flavour are all predictably popular, especially with vegetarians. Near the old market, **Fathi-ma Restaurant** (Map pp100–1; ☎ 511198; meals US$1-2.50) has 25 vegetarian options (US$1 each); while up on Th Luang Prabang the tiny **Nisha** (Map pp100–1; ☎ mobile 020-5685538; meals US$2-4) and yet another branch of the empire **Nazim** (Map pp100–1; ☎ 511214; meals US$2-5) both serve their curries with a side-dish of Bollywood.

Drinking

With its pool table, indoor and outdoor seating, safe music and easy atmosphere, **Xayoh Café** (Map pp100–1), was the busiest drinking spot when we passed. Louder and, at times, more lively are the **Island Bar** (Map pp100–1; ☎ mobile 020-5623572) and **Namsong Island Café** (Map pp100–1) on Don Khang.

Getting There & Away

Buses, pick-ups and *săwngthăew* have departed from a simple shedlike **bus terminal** (Map pp100–1; ☎ 511341; Rte 13) on the eastern side of the airstrip for several years. However, a proposed move to an expanse of gravel opposite the New Market, 2km north of town, will probably have become reality by the time you arrive. Transport may or may not still stop at the airstrip, but wherever you end up jumbos will be there to take you into town.

Minibuses and VIP buses catering for *falang* offer air-conditioning and often leave from one of the guesthouses in town, but don't expect any extra leg room. Just about every guesthouse sells tickets for these services; buses fill fast so book your ticket as early as possible. Note that anyone who suffers from motion sickness should take precautions when heading in either direction from Vang Vieng, and particularly on the road to Luang Prabang.

VIENTIANE

Buses from Vientiane leave Talat Sao bus station regularly in the mornings (see p93).

Heading south from Vang Vieng, regular buses leave for Vientiane (US$1.50, 153km, four hours) at 5.30am, 5.55am, 6.20am, 7am, 12.30pm and 1.30pm. If you miss one of these, pick-ups (US$1.50, 3½ hours) leave about every 20 minutes from 5am until 3pm, and as they are often not full they make for quite an enjoyable (and cheap) trip.

A minibus (US$4.50, three hours) and a VIP bus (US$3.50, three hours) also leave in the morning, while minibuses and VIP buses stop here en route from Luang Prabang to Vientiane at about 1pm.

If you're travelling by private transport, a good place to break the journey along the way to/from Vientiane is at the scenic Hin Hoep river junction. The PL, Prince Souvanna Phouma and Prince Bounome signed a short-lived peace treaty in the middle of the bridge at Hin Hoep in 1962.

LUANG PRABANG

Buses for Luang Prabang (US$5.50, 168km, six to seven hours) stop for about five minutes en route from Vientiane about every hour between 11am and 8pm. For better departure (and arrival) times, minibuses and VIP buses (US$7) leave between about 9am and 10am, the number varying depending on demand. All these services stop at Kasi and Muang Phu Khoun, though you might need to pay the full Luang Prabang fare on some.

For transport from Luang Prabang, see p135.

PHONSAVAN

There's one bus to Phonsavan (US$5.50, 219km, six to seven hours) which leaves between about 9am and 9.30am.

Getting Around

You can easily walk anywhere in town on foot. Several shops near the market hire out bikes for US$1 a day. Some people take bikes across the river (via the bamboo bridge between Hotel Nam Song and Bungalow Thavonsouk) and ride to villages and caves west of the Nam Song.

For cave sites out of town you can charter *săwngthăew* in the market – expect to pay around US$10 per trip up to 20km north or south of town.

KASI & AROUND

ກາສີ

In the middle of a fertile valley filled with rice fields, Kasi, 56km north of Vang Vieng, is little more than a lunch stop for bus passengers and truck drivers travelling on Rte 13. If you get stuck here, the **Vanphisith Guest House** (r US$2) near the new market has simple rooms and shared bathrooms. **Nang Kham Phanh** (meals US$1-2) serves *fŏe* and simple rice

dishes and is reasonably clean. A Shell station dispenses petrol and diesel.

About 40km north of Kasi, next to the T-junction between Rte 13 and Rte 7 going east into Xieng Khuang Province, lies **Muang Phu Khoun**, site of a former French garrison. Surrounded by jagged, mist-shrouded mountain peaks, Muang Phu Khoun lies near the heart of Hmong country and it was only in the 1920s, when the French extended Rte 13 this far, that it became linked to the rest of French Indochina. During the Second Indochina War the RLA and PL constantly fought for control of the town (then known as Sala Phu Khun) because of its strategic location at the junction of Rte 7, the main artery leading to Plain of Jars battlefields. Other than a market, a few shops and a single **guesthouse** (r US$2-3), there is little to see.

The 44km section of highway between Kasi and Muang Phu Khoun, which runs along a mountain ridge with excellent views, is an area where Hmong rebel attacks have been known to take place.

Further north towards Luang Prabang the scenery becomes even more spectacular, with lots of craggy mountain peaks and among the highest limestone formations in Southeast Asia – a remote and desolate landscape tailor-made for rebels. Beginning around Km 228, you'll start getting views of Phu Phra, a craggy limestone peak considered holy to animist hill tribes and Buddhists alike, on your right (on your left going south).

See p106 for details of transport into the area and on to Luang Prabang.

Northern Laos

HIGHLIGHTS

- Wander the historic temples, brick alleys and French colonial villas of Unesco World Heritage city **Luang Prabang** (p111)
- Hop on a boat and drink up the scenery along the **Mekong River** (p179), **Nam Ou** (p133) or **Nam Tha** (p165)
- Trek to waterfalls and tribal villages in the **Nam Ha National Protected Area** (p166)
- Contemplate the huge, enigmatic stone jars at the **Plain of Jars** (p145)
- Ride elephants and visit Thai Lü villages in **Hongsa** (p185)
- Marvel at the Pathet Lao's former 'cave city' in **Vieng Xai** (p154), a legacy of the Second Indochina War.

Laos's fame as a land of mountains and rivers derives largely from the geography of its northern provinces, which contain the nation's highest peaks and lengthiest waterways. This striking natural heritage has greatly influenced the country's human history. While lowland Lao migrants favoured the flatter, rice-friendly river plains of central and southern Laos, hill-tribe cultures from the more rugged territories of Tibet and southwestern China found the mountainous north suitable for small-scale farming of corn and opium, and the raising of domestic animals.

Northern Laos's natural barriers against the outside world have allowed for an isolation not easily maintained in the broad Mekong River valley plains and plateaus of southern Laos. Thus cultural traditions of the northern tribal groups have remained relatively well preserved.

This ethnic diversity, along with the alluring natural scenery, means that tourism here has outpaced that of the south. Luang Prabang and the Plain of Jars in particular attract more tourists than anywhere outside Vientiane. Meanwhile Luang Nam Tha and Bokeo Provinces have become the focus of ecotourism endeavours that have received support from the UN and accolades from around the world.

Only 20 years ago much of northern Laos was off limits to foreign visitors due to lingering post–Second Indochina War paranoia among the northern provinces (most of which were communist enclaves during the war). Staying overnight anywhere outside a provincial capital required special permission, while trekking to hill-tribe villages was forbidden.

In 2000 the Lao government finally began to allow foreigners to visit remote minority villages on organised trips that require trekking permits, licensed guides and the advance permission of the villages involved.

Road-building has also made much of 'undiscovered Laos' more accessible to tourism, although one rarely sees foreigners outside Luang Prabang, Phonsavan, Huay Xai, Muang Sing and Muang Ngoi Neua. Road access has increased logging and mining from neighbouring countries, particularly China. The future of northern Laos may depend largely on the competing development models offered by tourism, logging and mining.

Climate

Because mountainous northern Laos has higher overall elevations than the rest of the country, and sits at higher latitudes as well, it generally boasts the coolest temperatures. In the short cool season – roughly late November through to mid-February – temperatures may easily fall into the single digits at night. During the hot season – March through to May – the more mountainous provinces (particularly Luang Nam Tha, Phongsali, Xieng Khuang and Hua Phan) are a good choice if you want to avoid the stifling heat of the Mekong River plains.

The annual southwest monsoon season generally runs a bit shorter in the north, so that while in Si Phan Don (southern Laos) it may still be raining in October, in Luang Nam Tha and Udomxai the rainy season may be finished. The northeastern provinces of Hua Phan and Phongsali, on the other hand, often receive rain from Vietnam and China during the northeastern monsoon (from November to February) while the rest of the north is dry.

Getting There & Around

Many visitors enter northern Laos via Thailand at Huay Xai (p179), then make their way southeastward to Luang Prabang and Vientiane from here. Others come northwestward by bus from Vientiane (p93), and yet others fly to Luang Prabang (see p267) from Bangkok or Chiang Mai in Thailand. You can also fly to some northern cities – namely Luang Prabang, Phonsavan, Udomxai, Luang Nam Tha and Sam Neua – from Vientiane.

Boat travel along the Mekong River is a popular way of moving between Huay Xai and Luang Prabang, and much less so between Luang Prabang and Phongsali. By far the most used means of interprovincial

transport in the north nowadays is public bus. Bus trips around the north can be quite slow due to the steep and winding nature of the roadways as well as the conditions of the roads themselves.

Săwngthăew (pick-up trucks fitted with benches in the back for passengers) do the job in less populated areas. These can often be chartered for between 10 and 15 times the individual passenger fare.

Some people travel the north by bicycle or motorcycle, now that the government has loosened restrictions on the hire of two-wheeled vehicles. Car hire is also an option, although the only cities where hire cars are readily available are Vientiane and Luang Prabang.

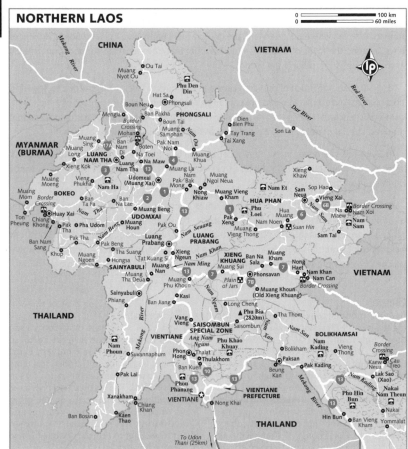

NORTHERN LAOS

LUANG PRABANG PROVINCE

For centuries isolated from the rest of Southeast Asia by a lack of reliable surface transport (even the Mekong is not navigable year-round), the Luang Prabang Province has only recently moved from a traditional subsistence foundation to develop a small but steady economy based on tourism and regional trade. With Rte 13 almost fully sealed, putting the province within a day's drive of China as well as Vientiane, Luang Prabang is well on the route to becoming one of the country's richest provinces.

The mountainous northern province harbours 12 ethnicities, of whom nearly half are Lao Thoeng, 40% Lao Loum and the remainder Lao Soung.

LUANG PRABANG

ຫລວງພະບາງ

☎ 071 / pop 26,000

Awakened from a long slumber brought on by decades of war and revolution, Luang Prabang has become Lao PDR's foremost tourist showpiece. Encircled by mountains and set 700m above sea level at the confluence of the Nam Khan (Khan River) and the Mekong River, the city's mix of gleaming temple roofs, crumbling French provincial architecture and multiethnic inhabitants tends to enthral even the most jaded travellers. Hmong, Mien and Thai tribal people can often be seen walking around town on their way to and from the markets. Orange-wrapped Buddhist monks and novices occupy 32 of the original 66 historic temples built before the era of French colonisation, including the stunning half-millennium-old Wat Xieng Thong. Luang Prabang (Muang Luang, as the locals call it) also boasts a unique palace-turned-museum.

Sealed highways linking Luang Prabang with Thailand and China have turned the city into an important relay point for commerce between the three countries. City governors have wisely provided a road bypass system that gives the city centre a wide berth. Thus the sense of calm antiquity that first brought visitors to the city when Laos opened to tourism in 1989 has been well preserved.

Although the population has more than doubled since the days when August Pavie governed the city under the French, and tourism has brought a certain prosperity to what was formerly one of the nation's poorest cities, Luang Prabang remains a relatively quiet place where most residents are sound asleep by 10pm.

History

Near Luang Prabang, archaeologists have found large, stone, drum-shaped objects bearing engraved motifs that are very similar to those of north Vietnam's Dongson bronze drums. Conclusions as to whether they are related to the Dongson culture (generally considered to have thrived from 500 BC to AD 100) – and if so whether they are pre- or post-Dongson – have yet to be drawn. There is also the possibility of a prehistoric or proto-historic connection with the stone jars of Xieng Khuang Province's Plain of Jars.

What is certain is that early Thai-Lao *meuang* (city-states) established themselves in the high river valleys along the Mekong River and its major tributaries, the Nam Khan, the Nam Ou and the Nam Seuang, sometime between the 8th and 13th centuries. Prior to this time the only inhabitants of the area appear to have been Khamu. Recent evidence also suggests the Mon may have sponsored a small kingdom centred in Sainyabuli Province.

During the ascendance of the Chenla kingdom, centred in southern Laos and northern Cambodia between the 6th and 8th centuries, the area became known as Muang Sawa, the Lao rendering of 'Java'. It is likely this name referred to Javanese sponsorship in Chenla. The Khmer-supported conqueror Fa Ngum consolidated the first Lao kingdom, Lan Xang Hom Khao (Million Elephants, White Parasol), here in 1353. See p20 for additional detail on the founding of Lan Xang.

Four years later the name was changed to Muang Xieng Thong (City of Gold), and under Fa Ngum's son, King Samsenthai, the kingdom flourished. In 1512 his successor, King Visounarat, accepted a celebrated Buddha image – the Pha Bang – as a gift from the Khmer monarchy, and the city-state became known as Luang (Great or Royal) Phabang (Prabang). Luang Prabang remained the capital of Lan Xang until King

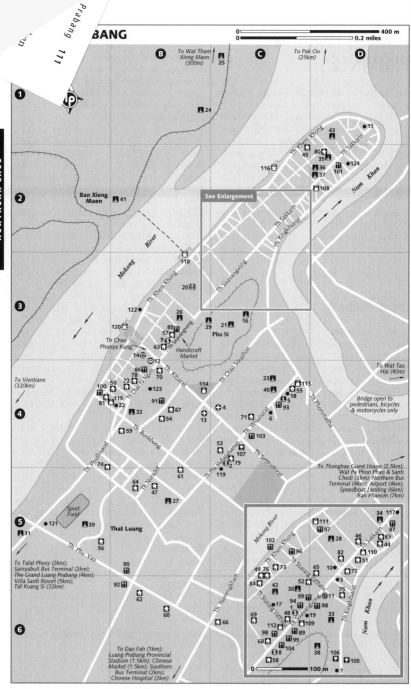

LUANG PRABANG

0   400 m
0   0.2 miles

To Wat Tham
Xieng Maen (300m)

To Pak Ou
(25km)

Ban Xieng
Maen

Mekong River

See Enlargement

Th Khem Khong

Th Sakkarin

Th Kingkitsarat

Th Sisavangvong

Nam Khan

Phu Si

Th Chao Siouphon

Handicraft
Market

Th Chao
Phanya Kang

Th Kitsarat

Th Chao Fa Ngum

Th Setthathirat

Th Phommathda

To Wat Tao
Hai (40m)

Bridge open to
pedestrians, bicycles
& motorcycles only

To Vientiane
(320km)

Th Phousi

Th Bunkhong

Th Nokeo

Th Phou Vao

Th Phothisarat

Th Wisunarat

Th Pha Mahapatsaman

Sport
Field

That Luang

Th Maniewnekham

To Thongbay Guest House (2.5km);
Wat Pa Phon Phao & Santi
Chedi (3km); Northern Bus
Terminal (4km); Airport (4km);
Speedboat Landing (6km);
Ban Phanom (7km)

To Talat Phosy (2km);
Sainyabuli Bus Terminal (2km);
The Grand Luang Prabang (4km);
Villa Santi Resort (5km);
Tat Kuang Si (32km)

To Dao Fah (1km);
Luang Prabang Provincial
Stadium (1.5km); Chinese
Market (1.5km); Southern
Bus Terminal (2km);
Chinese Hospital (2km)

Mekong River

Th Khem Khong

Th Sisavang Vatthana

Th Sisavangvong

Th Sakkarin

Th Kingkitsarat

Nam Khan

0   100 m

NORTHERN LAOS

Phothisarat moved the administrative seat to Vientiane in 1545.

Even after the capital moved to Vientiane, Luang Prabang remained the main source of monarchical power throughout the Lan Xang period. When Lan Xang broke up following the death of King Suriya Vongsa in 1694, one of Suriya's grandsons set up an independent kingdom in Luang Prabang, which competed with kingdoms in Vientiane and Champasak.

From then on, the Luang Prabang monarchy was so weak that it was forced to pay tribute at various times to the Siamese, Burmese and Vietnamese. After a particularly destructive attack by the Black Flag wing of the Chinese Haw in 1887, the Luang Prabang kingdom chose to accept French protection, and a French Commissariat was established in the royal capital.

The French allowed Laos to retain the Luang Prabang monarchy, and imported Vietnamese workers to erect the brick-and-stucco offices and villas that today give the city its faded colonial atmosphere. Luang Prabang quickly became a favourite post for French colonials seeking a refuge as far away from Paris as possible – even during French Indochina's last years, prior to WWII, a river trip from Saigon to Luang Prabang took longer than a steamship voyage from Saigon to France.

The Japanese invasion of Southeast Asia during WWII weakened France's grip on Luang Prabang, and in 1945 Laos declared its independence from France. France, for its part, stubbornly insisted that Laos remained part of the French Union until the 1954 Vietnamese triumph over the French at Dien Bien Phu, Vietnam.

When the penultimate Luang Prabang king, Sisavang Vong, died in 1959, his son Crown Prince Sisavang Vatthana was scheduled to ascend the throne. According to official Pathet Lao (PL) history the 1975 Revolution prevented the prince's actual coronation, though many Lao and foreign diplomats insist he was crowned before the PL deposed him. At any rate, after two years as 'Supreme Adviser to the President', King (or Crown Prince?) Sisavang Vatthana and his wife were exiled to northeastern Laos.

A brochure printed by the Ministry of Information and Culture reads, 'On his return to Luang Prabang, Sisavang Vatthana moved to his private residence close to Xieng Thong temple and offered the royal palace to the Government'. In reality the king, queen and crown prince of Luang Prabang were imprisoned in a cave in Hua Phan Province where they died, one by one, from lack of adequate food and medical care between 1977 and 1981. The Lao PDR government has yet to issue a full report on the royal family's whereabouts following the Revolution.

By the time Laos finally reopened to tourism in 1989, after the fall of the USSR and Soviet bloc governments, Luang Prabang had become a ghost of its former grand self due to collectivisation of the economy and the resulting exodus of nearly 100,000 businesspeople, aristocracy and intelligentsia. Over the next decade, however, as the Lao government legalised private enterprise, long-closed shops reopened and dilapidated villas were converted into hotels and guesthouses. Restaurants, handicraft shops and art galleries sprang up on practically every corner of the formerly comatose city.

The placing of the city on Unesco's World Heritage list in 1995 has played a major role in preserving and enhancing historic architecture, and in raising the city's international profile.

Orientation

Most of the longer roadways through Luang Prabang parallel the river. Shorter roads – once mere footpaths – bisect the larger roads and lead to the riverbanks, serving as dividing lines between different villages. Each village is named for its local wat, eg Ban Khili for Wat Khili, Ban Ho Xiang for Wat Ho Xiang. On the west side of the river, opposite the royal city, is a village called Ban Xieng Maen

(not to be confused with the similarly named Ban Xieng Muan on the east side).

A large hill called Phu Si (sometimes spelt Phousi or Phousy) dominates the town skyline, standing towards the middle of the peninsula formed by the confluence of the two rivers. Since it is visible from any point in town, Phu Si serves as a very helpful 'beacon' for orientating yourself. Most of the historic temples are located between Phu Si and the Mekong, while the trading district lies to the south of the hill. Virtually the whole town can be seen on foot in a day or two, though many visitors extend their stay here in order to soak up more atmosphere.

The official street names in Luang Prabang have changed at least three times over the last decade, so you'll find that naming varies widely on city maps and address cards. Until very recently, naming local streets for Lao royalty, particularly the penultimate king (Sisavang Vong) and his son (Sisavang Vatthana), were definitely out of government favour. All of that appears to have changed since the city was granted Unesco World Heritage status, and the city government now seems to acknowledge its royal patrimony.

Currently the main street heading northeast up the peninsula is called Th Phothisarat (Phothisalat according to the modern Lao spelling) at its southwestern end, Th Sisavangvong in its middle reach and Th Sakkarin towards the northeastern end. Th Sakkarin (Sakkalin) is also sometimes known as Th Xieng Thong. The road that runs along the Mekong waterfront is variously known as Souvannakhamphong, Oun Kham and Suvannabanlang, although most locals call it Th Khem Khong. When giving directions, the locals fortunately almost never quote street names, using landmarks instead.

Easy-to-reach attractions outside of town include the Pak Ou caves (p134) to the north, which are usually reached by river, and the waterfalls of Tat Kuang Si (p135) and Tat Sae (p136) to the south, reached by road.

The airport, speedboat landing and northern bus terminal are all northeast of the city, while the southern bus terminal and Sainyabuli terminal are to the southwest.

Information
BOOKSHOPS
L'Etranger Books & Tea (Th Kingkitsarat; booksinlaos@ yahoo.com; ⏰ 8am-10pm Mon-Sat, 10am-10pm Sun)

This shop offers new and used nonfiction about Laos and Southeast Asia, as well as some fiction. It buys used books for cash or trade credit, and also lends books. Art is showcased on the 2nd floor, which doubles as a tea lounge.

EMERGENCY
Ambulance (☎ 195)
Fire (☎ 190)
Police (☎ 191)

IMMIGRATION
Immigration & Foreigners Management (☎ 212435; Th Wisunarat; ☻ 8.30am-4.30pm Mon-Fri) Staff can deal with any immigration problems you might have, however, for visa extensions you must go to Vientiane. See p264 for further information.

INTERNET ACCESS
Several small Internet cafés can be found along Th Sisavangvong in the historic district, including the nationwide chain **PlaNet Online** (☎ 218972; cnr Th Sisavangvong & Th Sisavang Vatthana).

MEDICAL SERVICES
Visitors with serious injuries or illnesses are almost always flown to Vientiane for emergency transit to hospitals in northeastern Thailand, or put on direct flights to Chiang Mai or Bangkok. Some services in the area:
Boua Phanh Pharmacie (☎ 252252; Th Sakkarin) Across from an old French school, this is one of the better pharmacies in town.
Chinese hospital (☎ 254026; Ban Phu Mok) This large new hospital has modern medical equipment and supplies, yet is short of trained personnel who know how to make use of it all. It's a couple of kilometres south of the centre.
Provincial Hospital (☎ 252049, 212123; Th Setthathirat) Neither this hospital nor the Chinese hospital receive high marks from foreign medical observers.

MONEY
Banque pour le Commerce Extérieur Lao (BCEL; Th Mahapatsaman; ☻ 8.30am-3.30pm Mon-Sat) Situated next to Lao Airlines, the BCEL also has a branch on Th Sisavangvong near the Boupha Guest House. BCEL will exchange Thai baht, US, Australian and Canadian dollars, euros and UK pounds – cash or travellers cheques – for kip. The bank normally won't change in the other direction because of a claimed shortage of these currencies. BCEL also offers cash advances, in kip only, for Visa credit cards.
Lao Development Bank (65 Th Sisavangvong; ☻ 8.30am-3.30pm Mon-Sat) This bank, near the New Luang Prabang Hotel, offers foreign exchange services, but

does not accept Visa or other credit cards. There is a second branch on Th Sisavangvong, near Nisha Restaurant.

POST
Post office (cnr Th Chao Fa Ngum & Th Setthathirat; ☻ 8.30am-3.30pm Mon-Fri, 8.30am-noon Sat) Opposite the Phousi Hotel.

TELEPHONE
Several Internet cafés along Th Sisavangvong offer Internet phone services at rates well below regular long-distance phone rates.

Domestic and international phone calls can be made at a window inside the post office (see above), down a corridor to the right inside the entrance, and at a phonecard booth at the front of the post office. Cards may be purchased inside the post office or at sundries shops around town.

TOURIST INFORMATION
Department of Commerce and Tourists (☎ 212019; Th Wisunarat) This office, opposite Wat Wisunarat, stocks a few brochures but in general is of limited use to most visitors. Opening hours are unposted and erratic.

LAO URBAN PLANNING

When migrating Thai-Lao settled the peninsular junction between the Mekong River and the Nam Khan (Khan River), they brought with them a new, and seemingly more democratic, form of social organisation than was common in mainland Southeast Asia. Instead of structuring a city in a radial plan at the disposal of an emperor who presided over the centre with his subjects and slaves at the perimeter (as at Chenla, Funan or Angkor), they organised their *meuang* (city-states) by linking small communities of houses, each centred on a Buddhist temple. Rather than bending to a central government, these *muu bâan* (villages) within the *meuang* set their own rules of civil conduct. Only in times of crisis, eg war or agricultural shortages, would the villages join together to act as a unit.

Luang Prabang is the most intact example remaining in Southeast Asia of this once-common urban plan. The current village clusters are thought to date back to the 14th century, and many residents still identify more with their village neighbourhoods than with Luang Prabang as a city.

UNESCO WORLD HERITAGE INFORMATION
Unesco World Heritage office (French customs house; Th Sakkarin; ☺ 8.30am-4.30pm Mon-Fri) One of the anterooms in an old French customs house at the northeastern tip of the peninsula contains posted public information on the Unesco project being conducted in Luang Prabang.

Dangers & Annoyances

During the late dry season – roughly from February to May – the air over Luang Prabang can become very smoky due to slash-and-burn agriculture in the hills and mountains around the city. It becomes so bad in March and April that even local

BUN PI MAI LAO (LAO NEW YEAR)

In the middle of April the three-day Songkan (water festival) celebrates the start of Lao New Year. Songkan, from the Sanskrit *samkranta* (fully passed over), signifies the passage of the sun from the sign of Pisces into the sign of Aries in the zodiac. All of Laos observes this festival, but it is particularly well celebrated in Luang Prabang, where many people dress in traditional clothes for the major events and stretch the event out to a full seven days.

On a spiritual level, the Lao traditionally believe that during this period the old Songkan spirit departs and the new one arrives. On the first day of the festival, when the old spirit departs, people give their homes a thorough cleaning. At Hat Muang Khoun, a Mekong River island beach near Ban Xieng Maen, locals gather to build and decorate miniature sand stupas for good luck, amid much playful throwing of river water. On the second day civic groups mount a colourful, costumed parade down Luang Prabang's main avenue from Wat Pha Mahathat to Wat Xieng Thong. The third day is a 'rest day', when all parading stops and the devout take time to wash Buddha images at their local wat.

In the early morning of the fourth day people climb Phu Si to make offerings of sticky rice at the summit stupa. Then in the afternoon they participate in *bqasii* (sacred string-tying) ceremonies with family and friends. On the fifth day the Pha Bang (the Khmer-style standing Buddha figure kept in the Royal Palace Museum) leaves the Royal Palace Museum and is taken to Wat Mai Suwannaphumaham (Wat Mai) in a solemn procession, while on the sixth day the new spirit arrives. This day is considered especially crucial, and cleansing rituals extend to the bathing of Buddhist holy images – particularly the Pha Bang, in a temporary pavilion erected in front of Wat Mai – by pouring water onto them through wooden sluice pipes shaped like *nagas* (mythical water serpents). Senior monks receive a similar treatment, and younger Lao will also pour water over the hands (palms held together) of their elderly relatives in a gesture of respect. On the last day a final procession carries the Pha Bang from Wat Mai back to the museum.

During the most important processions you may notice three figures wearing large red-hued wooden heads with thick hairlike material draped over the rest of their bodies. Two of the wooden heads are round and display big teeth and heavy eyebrows, features meant to portray the Lao Thoeng who lived in Luang Prabang before the Lao arrived. Although from one perspective the exaggerated features would appear to be disrespectful of Luang Prabang's Lao Thoeng antecedents (thought to have been Khamu), the lowland Lao consider these Lao Thoeng spirits – called Grandfather Nyeu and Grandmother Nyeu – to be guardians of the environment and thus worthy of veneration. A third figure, Sing Kaew Sing Kham, wears the same hairy robe but is topped by a stylised lion head and is possibly a representation of a Khamu king. The three figures receive offerings at Wat Aham and then begin their procession to Wat That Luang, Wat Wisunarat and Wat Xieng Thong, stopping to dance at each. The festival – or at least its spiritual aspect – ends when the Pha Bang is returned to the palace museum. A hundred years ago the festivities used to include an elephant procession and even an elephant *bqasii* ceremony but Laos's elephant population has become too small.

Although the true meaning of the festival is kept alive by ceremonies such as these, nowadays it's mainly a festival of fun. As in Thailand and Myanmar, this is the height of the hot and dry season, and the locals revel in being able to douse one another with cold water to cool off. Activities don't usually get quite as rowdy as in these neighbouring countries but you still have groups of teenagers standing along the roadside and dousing every person or vehicle that passes by with bowls or buckets of water. Foreigners are not exempt from the soaking, so watch out!

residents will complain of red, watery eyes and breathing difficulties. Landscape photography is hopeless, except on the rare day when a strong breeze flushes out the smoke from the valley. With the arrival of rain in late May or June, the air clears and generally stays that way until the following year. One hopes the authorities will get a handle on the situation before all the surrounding forests are gone, and extensive erosion and flooding result.

Sights

ROYAL PALACE MUSEUM (HO KHAM)
ຫໍພິພິດຫະພັນພະລາດຊະວັງ (ຫໍຄຳ)

Start your tour of Luang Prabang with a visit to this quaint museum to get a sense of local history. The **Royal Palace Museum** (Haw Kham or Golden Hall; ☎ 212470; Th Sisavangvong; admission US$2; ⏲ 8-11am & 1.30-4pm) was built in 1904 during the early French colonial era as a residence for King Sisavang Vong and his family. The site for the palace was chosen so that official visitors to Luang Prabang could disembark from their river journeys directly below the palace and be received there.

Architecturally, the building features a blend of traditional Lao motifs and French beaux-arts styles, and has been laid out in a double-cruciform shape with the entrance on one side of the lower crossbar. The steps leading to the entrance are Italian marble. Most of the private chambers of the royal family are preserved as they were the day the Pathet Lao forced the royals into exile. Many locals believe the palace to be haunted by the spirits of the royal family, and few Lao will venture into the building after dark.

The large entry hall displays royal religious objects, including the dais of the former Supreme Patriarch of Lao Buddhism; an ancient Buddha head presented to the king as a gift from India; a reclining Buddha with the unusual added feature of sculpted mourners at his side; an equally uncommon Buddha seated with a begging bowl (the bowl is usually only depicted with a standing figure); and a Luang Prabang–style standing Buddha sculpted of marble in a 'Contemplating the Bodhi Tree' pose.

To the right of the entry hall is the king's reception room, where busts of the

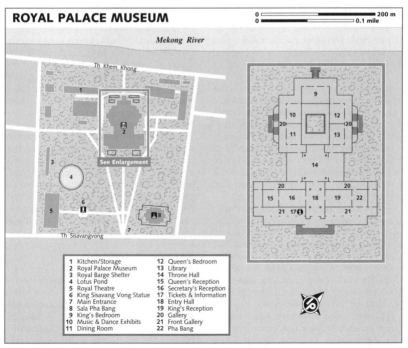

ROYAL PALACE MUSEUM

1	Kitchen/Storage	12	Queen's Bedroom
2	Royal Palace Museum	13	Library
3	Royal Barge Shelter	14	Throne Hall
4	Lotus Pond	15	Queen's Reception
5	Royal Theatre	16	Secretary's Reception
6	King Sisavang Vong Statue	17	Tickets & Information
7	Main Entrance	18	Entry Hall
8	Sala Pha Bang	19	King's Reception
9	King's Bedroom	20	Gallery
10	Music & Dance Exhibits	21	Front Gallery
11	Dining Room	22	Pha Bang

NORTHERN LAOS

Lao monarchy are displayed along with two large gilded and lacquered Ramayana screens crafted by local artisan Thit Tanh. The walls of the room are covered with murals that depict scenes from traditional Lao life. French artist Alix de Fautereau painted these in 1930, intending that each wall be viewed at a different time of day – according to the light that enters the windows on one side of the room – to correspond with the time of day depicted.

The right front corner room of the palace, open to the outside, contains a collection of the museum's most prized art, including the Pha Bang. Cast of a gold, silver and bronze alloy, this Buddha stands 83cm tall and is said to weigh 53.4kg. Legend has it the image was cast around the 1st century AD in Sri Lanka and later presented to Khmer King Phaya Sirichantha, who in turn gave it to King Fa Ngum in 1359 (other accounts have it that his successor, King Visounarat, received it in 1512) as a Buddhist legitimiser of Lao sovereignty. Since stylistically it is obviously of Khmer origin, most likely its casting took place nearer to the latter date. The Siamese twice carried off the image to Thailand (in 1779 and 1827) but it was finally restored to Lao hands by King Mongkut (Rama IV) in 1867. Persistent rumours claim that the actual image on display is a copy and that the original is stored in a vault either in Vientiane or Moscow. The 'real' one supposedly features a bit of gold leaf over the eyes and a hole drilled through one ankle.

Also in this room are large elephant tusks engraved with Buddhas, including Khmer-crafted sitting Buddhas and Luang Prabang–style standing Buddhas; an excellent Lao frieze taken from a local temple; and three beautiful *saew mâi khán* (embroidered silk screens with religious imagery) that were crafted by the queen.

To the left of the entry hall, the secretary's reception room is filled with paintings, silver and china that have been presented to Laos as diplomatic gifts from Myanmar, Cambodia, Thailand, Poland, Hungary, Russia, Japan, Vietnam, China, Nepal, the USA, Canada and Australia. The objects are grouped according to whether they're from 'socialist' or 'capitalist' countries.

The next room to the left was once the queen's reception room. Large royal portraits of King Sisavang Vatthana, Queen Kham

Phouy and Crown Prince Vong Savang, painted by the Russian artist Ilya Glazunov in 1967, are hung on the walls. Also on display in this room are friendship flags from China and Vietnam, and replicas of sculpture from New Delhi's Indian National Museum.

Behind the entry hall is the throne hall where royal vestments, gold and silver sabres, and the king's elephant chair (or saddle) are exhibited. Glass cases hold a collection of small Buddhas made of crystal and gold that were found inside the That Makmo (Makmo Stupa). Intricate wall mosaics, placed on a deep red background, took eight craftsmen 3½ years to complete and are a highlight of the palace's art.

Beyond the throne room are the halls or galleries that lead to the royal family's residential quarters. The royal bedrooms have been preserved as they were when the king departed, as have the dining hall and a room that contains royal seals and medals. One of the more interesting displays in the museum is a room in the residential section that now contains Lao classical musical instruments and masks for the performance of Ramayana dance-drama – just about the only place in the country where you see these kinds of objects on display.

Towards the southeastern corner of the compound stands a large, unlabelled bronze statue of King Sisavang Vong. Behind the statue is a palace building now designated as the **Royal Theatre**. See p131 for more information.

Sala Pha Bang

A project planned before the monarchy was abolished in 1975, construction on this highly ornate pavilion (which stands in the northeast corner of the palace compound) began in 1993. Completion is scheduled for the end of 2004, and at that point the highly revered Pha Bang will be moved from the palace museum to an altar in the centre of the pavilion.

WAT XIENG THONG
ວັດຊຽງທອງ

Near the northern tip of the peninsula formed by the Mekong River and the Nam Khan is Luang Prabang's most magnificent temple, **Wat Xieng Thong** (admission US$1; ☿ 8am-5pm). King Setthathirat ordered the construction of Wat Xieng Thong's *sĭm* (ordination hall) in 1560, and the compound remained under royal patronage until 1975. Like the royal palace, Wat Xieng Thong was placed within easy reach of the Mekong. The *hăw tại* (Tripitaka library) was added in 1828, and the *haw kạwng* (drum tower) in 1961.

Along with Wat Mai Suwannaphumaham this was the only Luang Prabang wat spared by the 1887 Black Flag Haw sacking of the city. The Black Flag's leader, Deo Van Tri (a Thai Khao or White Thai from the north Vietnam province of Lai Chau), had studied here as a monk earlier in his life, and he used the desecrated, if not destroyed, temple as his headquarters during the invasion.

The *sim* represents what is considered classic Luang Prabang temple architecture, with roofs that sweep low to the ground. The rear wall of the *sim* features an impressive 'tree of life' mosaic set in a red background. Inside, the elaborately decorated wooden columns support a ceiling stencilled in gold with *dhammachakka* (dharma wheels). Other gold-stencilled designs on the interior walls depict the exploits of legendary King Chanthaphanit, about whom there exists no verifiable written history.

To one side of the *sim*, towards the east, stand several small halls *(haw)* and stupas containing Buddha images of the period. The *hăw tại pha sai-nyàat* (reclining Buddha sanctuary; dubbed La Chapelle Rouge – Red Chapel – by the French) contains an especially rare reclining Buddha that dates from the construction of the temple. This one-of-a-kind figure is exquisitely proportioned in classic Lao style (most Lao recliners imitate Thai or Lanna styles), with the monastic robes curling outward at the ankle like rocket fumes. Instead of merely supporting the head, the unique right-hand position extends away from the head in a simple but graceful gesture. In 1931 this image was taken to Paris and displayed at the Paris Exhibition, after which it was kept in Vientiane until its return to Luang Prabang in 1964.

Gold-leaf votives line the upper walls of the sanctuary on either side of the reclining image. In front of the image are several seated bronze Buddhas of different styles and ages, and on either side of the altar are small embroidered tapestries depicting a stupa and a standing Buddha. A mosaic on the back exterior wall of this chapel was done in the late 1950s in commemoration of the 2500th

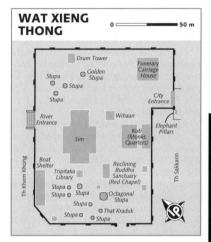

WAT XIENG THONG

0 ———————— 50 m

anniversary of the Buddha's attainment of *parinibbana* (final nirvana, or passing away). The mosaic is unique in that it relates the exploits of Siaw Sawat, a hero from a famous Lao novel, along with scenes of local village life, rather than a religious scene.

Near the compound's eastern gate stands the *hóhng kép mîen* (royal funerary carriage house). Inside is an impressive funeral carriage (crafted by local artisan Thit Tanh), standing 12m high, and various funeral urns for the members of the royal family. (The ashes of King Sisavang Vong, the queen and the king's brother, however, are interred not here but at Wat That Luang at the southern end of Luang Prabang.) Glass cabinets hold royal puppets that were once used for performances of *la-kháwn lek*. Gilt panels on the exterior of the chapel depict semierotic episodes from the Ramayana epic.

WAT WISUNARAT (WAT VISOUN)
ວັດວິຊຸນນະຣາດ

Originally built in 1513 during the reign of Chao Wisunarat, **Wat Wisunarat** (Th Wisunarat; admission US$1; ☯ 8am-5pm) is the oldest operating temple in Luang Prabang. It was rebuilt between 1896 and 1898 following an 1887 fire set by Black Flag Haw raiders. The original was wooden, and in the brick and stucco restoration the builders tried to make the balustraded windows of the *sim* appear to be fashioned of lathed wood (an old South Indian and Khmer contrivance that is uncommon in Lao architecture). The front roof that slopes sideways over the terrace is another unique feature. Inside the high-ceilinged *sim* is a collection of gilded wooden 'Calling for Rain' Buddhas and 15th- to 16th-century Luang Prabang *sĭimáa* (ordination-precinct stones). These were placed here by Prince Phetsarat after the Haw invasion. The Pha Bang was kept here from 1507 to 1715 and from 1867 to 1894.

Standing well in front of the *sim* – instead of in the usual spot for a large stupa, immediately behind the *sim* – stands the 34.5m That Pathum (Lotus Stupa). Locally the stupa is more commonly known as That Makmo (Watermelon Stupa) because of its semispherical shape. Work on the stupa began in 1503 by order of Nang Phantin Xieng, wife of King Wisunarat, and was completed 19 months later. Workmen filled the interior of the stupa with small Buddha images made of precious materials and other sacred items. Many of these were stolen when the Haw destroyed the temple, while those recovered can be seen on display in the Royal Palace Museum. The stupa underwent reconstruction in 1895 and again in 1932 after a partial collapse due to rain.

WAT AHAM
ວັດອາຮາມ

Between Wat Wisunarat and the Nam Khan stands **Wat Aham** (admission US$1; ☉ 8am-5pm), which was formerly the residence of the Sangkharat (Supreme Patriarch of Lao Buddhism). Two large banyan trees grace the grounds, which are semideserted except for the occasional devotee who comes to make offerings to the town's most important spirit shrine at the base of the trees.

WAT MAI SUWANNAPHUMAHAM
ວັດໃໝ່ສຸວັນນະພູມອາຮາມ

Inaugurated in 1821 (some sources claim 1797), **Wat Mai** (Th Sisavangvong; admission US$0.50; ☉ 8am-5pm) succeeded Wat Aham as the residence of the Sangkharat until that position moved to Pha That Luang in Vientiane. The five-tiered roof of the wooden *sim* follows the standard Luang Prabang style, but the roofed front veranda, with its gables angled towards the sides of the chapel rather than towards the front, is an anomaly. This unusual plan may have been influenced by local vernacular architecture, as exemplified in the old wooden house just across the street

from Wat Mai. The front veranda is also remarkable for its decorated columns and the sumptuous gold relief walls that recount the tale of Vessantara (Pha Wet in Lao), the Buddha's penultimate birth, as well as scenes from the Ramayana and village life.

Behind the main *sim* stands an open-sided shelter housing two long racing boats. These slender, graceful craft are brought out during Bun Pi Mai Lao (Lao New Year) in April and again in October during Bun Nam (Water Festival). Heavily decorated with flower garlands, each boat will hold up to 50 rowers, plus a coxswain.

Wat Mai was spared destruction by the Chinese Haw, who reportedly found the *sim* too beautiful to harm. Most of the other 20 or so buildings are newer.

The Pha Bang, which is normally housed in the Royal Palace Museum, is brought here and put on public display in a temporary pavilion in front of the *sim* at Wat Mai during the Bun Pi Mai Lao celebrations.

WAT THAT LUANG
ວັດທາດຫລວງ

Legend has it that **Wat That Luang** (Th Phu Vao) was originally established by Ashokan missionaries from India in the 3rd century BC. However, there is no evidence whatsoever to confirm this and the current *sim* was built in 1818 under the reign of King Manthaturat. The ashes of King Sisavang Vong and his brother are interred inside the large central stupa, which was erected in 1910. A smaller *thâat* (stupa) in front of the *sim* dates back to 1820. Inside the huge *sim* are a few Luang Prabang Buddha images and other artefacts.

WAT MANOLOM
ວັດມະໂນລົມ

Although its outer appearance isn't very impressive, **Wat Manolom** (Wat Mano; Th Pha Mahapatsaman) stands just outside the barely visible city walls and occupies possibly the oldest temple site in Luang Prabang. City annals say it was founded in 1375 on the site of a smaller temple established by King Fa Ngum. The decaying *sim* held the Pha Bang from 1502 to 1513 and still contains a sitting bronze Buddha cast in 1372. This image is about 6m high and weighs an estimated two tonnes – some parts of the bronze are 15mm thick. An important city talisman, the image would probably be moved to another temple if anyone could figure out how!

The Buddha's arms reportedly came off during a battle between French and Thai armies in the late 19th century. After the battle the colonialists allegedly made off with the appendages except for a portion of one forearm now placed beside one of the feet. The Lao later reconstructed the missing arms with cement. Near the *sim* are the scant remains of an older temple, Wat Xieng Kang, allegedly constructed in 1363.

PHU SI
ພູສີ

The temples on the upper slopes of 100m-high **Phu Si** (Th Sisavangvong; admission US$1; 🕙 8am-6pm) were recently constructed, but it is likely there were once other temples located on this important hill site. There is an excellent view of the town from the top of the hill.

On the lower slopes of the hill are two of the oldest (and now abandoned) temples in Luang Prabang. The decaying *sim* at **Wat Pa Huak** – on the lower northern slope near the Royal Palace Museum – has a splendid carved wood and mosaic façade showing Buddha riding Airavata, the three-headed elephant of Hindu mythology (in which he is usually depicted as Lord Indra's mount). The gilded and carved front doors are often locked, but during the day there's usually an attendant nearby who will open the doors for a tip of a couple of hundred kip. Inside, the original 19th-century murals have excellent colour, considering the lack of any restoration. The murals show historic scenes along the Mekong River, including visits by Chinese diplomats and warriors arriving by river and horse caravans. Three large seated Buddhas and several smaller standing and seated images date from the same time as the murals or possibly earlier.

Around on the northeastern flank of the hill are the ruins of **Wat Pha Phutthabaht**, originally constructed in 1395 during the reign of Phaya Samsenthai on the site of a 'Buddha footprint'. The ruins are of mixed style but are said to show a definite Lanna or Chiang Mai influence, as well as some later Vietnamese augmentation.

The fee to climb to the summit of the hill is collected at the northern entrance near Wat Pa Huak (you do not have to pay the fee to reach Wat Pa Huak, however).

The 24m-high **That Chomsi**, erected in 1804 and restored in 1914, stands at the summit, clearly visible from most ground-level points in the city. This stupa is the starting point for a colourful Lao New Year procession in mid-April. If you continue over the summit and start down the path on the other side you'll come to a small **cave shrine** (sometimes called Wat Tham Phu Si, although without monks it's not officially a wat). Plopped down in the middle of the cave is a large, fat Buddha image – called Pha Kasai in Lao – and a sheltered area for worshippers. On a nearby crest is a Russian anti-aircraft cannon that children use as a makeshift merry-go-round.

WAT XIENG MUAN
ວັດຊຽງມວນ

The *sim* at **Wat Xieng Muan** dates back to 1879, though no doubt the monastery site is much older. The sculpture inside is better than average and the ceiling is painted with gold *naga*s, an uncommon motif in this position – possibly a Thai Lü influence. Also notable is the elaborate *háang thíen* (candle rail) with *naga*s at either end.

With backing from Unesco and New Zealand, Wat Xieng Muan has restored the monks' quarters as a classroom for training young monks in the artistic skills needed to maintain and preserve Luang Prabang's temples. Among these skills are wood-carving, painting and Buddha-casting, all of which came to a virtual halt after 1975. If you step into the grounds of Wat Xieng Muan during the day you'll see the monastic residents learning or teaching these arts.

OTHER TEMPLES
In the northeastern corner of town near the meeting of the Nam Khan and the Mekong River is a string of historic, still active temples. Facing Th Sakkarin just northeast of Villa Santi (see p128) is **Wat Saen**, a Thai-style wat built in 1718 and restored in 1932 and 1957. The name reportedly refers to its founding on an initial 100,000 kip donation. The abbot, Ajahn Khamjan, ordained here in 1940, is one of the most revered monks in Luang Prabang, perhaps in all of Laos. Behind Villa Santi near the river road, the simple **Wat Nong Sikhunmeuang** was built in 1729, burned in 1774 and rebuilt in 1804.

Southwest of Villa Santi and set back off the street is **Wat Pa Phai**, whose classic

Thai-Lao fresco over the gilded and carved wooden façade is at least 100 years old; the picture depicts scenes from everyday Lao life from the era in which it was painted.

Wat Pha Mahathat, the third wat southwest of the Phousi Hotel, is named for a venerable Lanna-style *thâat* erected in 1548. The *sĭm* in front – built in 1910 – is quite ornate, with carved wooden windows and portico, rosette-gilded pillars, exterior Jataka (stories of the Buddha's past lives) reliefs and a roof in the Luang Prabang style lined with temple bells. The massive *nagas* along the steps, also Lanna in style, resemble those at Wat Phra That Doi Suthep in Chiang Mai, Thailand.

An easy 3km walk or bicycle ride north-east of town is **Wat Pa Phon Phao**, a forest meditation wat famous for the teachings of the late abbot, Ajahn Saisamut. Saisamut's 1992 funeral was the largest and most well attended monk's funeral Laos had seen in decades. The monastery's **Phra That Khong Santi Chedi** (Peace Pagoda; donation expected; ☉ 8-10am & 2-4pm Mon-Fri), built in 1988, has become a favourite Lao tourist attraction. This large yellow stupa contains three floors inside plus an outside terrace near the top with a view of the surrounding plains. The inside walls are painted with all manner of Buddhist stories and moral admonitions.

On the Mekong River near the north-western end of Th Phu Vao is a modern Vietnamese-Lao temple, **Wat Pha Baht Tai**. The temple itself is rather garish but behind the temple is a shady terrace overlooking the Mekong; on a hot afternoon this is a good place to cool off and watch the sunset.

ACROSS THE MEKONG RIVER

Across from central Luang Prabang are several notable temples in Ban Xieng Maen. Ban Xieng Maen itself played an important role as the terminus of the historic road between Luang Prabang and various north-ern Thai kingdoms, eg Nan and Phayao.

Wat Long Khun (admission US$0.50; ☉ 8am-5pm), almost directly across the Mekong River from Wat Xieng Thong, is the best place to disembark by boat for Xieng Maen explorations if you're chartering a boat. This wat features a nicely decorated portico of 1937 vintage, plus older sections from the 18th century and a few fading Jataka murals. When the coronation of a Luang Prabang king was pending, it was customary for him to spend three days in retreat at Wat Long Khun before ascending the throne. A res-toration project, completed in 1995 by the Department of Museums and Archaeology with the assistance of the Ecole Française d'Extrême Orient, has brought new life and beauty to the monastery buildings.

Founded in 1889 and since abandoned, **Wat Tham Xieng Maen** (admission US$0.50; ☉ 8am-5pm) is in a 100m-deep limestone cave called Tham Sakkarin Savannakuha, a little to the northwest of Wat Long Khun. Many Buddha images from temples that have been torched or otherwise fallen into decay are kept here; during Bun Pi Mai Lao many local worshippers come to Wat Tham to pay homage and cleanse the images. The large stone-block entrance built around the mouth of the cave displays good relief work on stair pedestals, and is flanked by two large ruined spirit houses and a couple of plumeria (frangipani) trees. An iron gate across the cave mouth is usually locked; inquire at Wat Long Khun for someone to come and unlock the gate and guide you through the cave. The cave is very long and dark, and parts of the cave floor are slippery, so it's a good idea to go with a guide. Bring a torch (flashlight). There are several other caves nearby that are easily found and explored with local help, although none are quite as extensive as Tham Sakkarin Savannakuha.

At the top of a hill above Wat Long Khun and Wat Tham is peaceful **Wat Chom Phet** (admission US$0.50), built by the Thai army in 1888 and offering an undisturbed view of the town and river. A small *thâat* here contains the bones of Chao Thong Di (wife of King Sakkarin), who died in 1929.

Southwest of Wat Chom Phet in the village of Xieng Maen, **Wat Xieng Maen** was founded in 1592 by Chao Naw Kaewkumman, son of Setthathirat, but it fell into ruin and had to be rebuilt in 1927. The newer *sĭm* contains a few artefacts dating from the original temple, including the original doors. This spot is especially sacred to Xieng Maen residents because it once housed the Pha Bang – on its way back to Luang Prabang in 1867 following a lengthy stay in Vientiane – for seven days and seven nights.

Ban Xieng Maen itself is worth a wander since, like Luang Prabang, it has maintained its original urban plan, possibly dating back to the 14th century. Unlike Luang

Prabang, for the most part the main roads (paralleling the river) and byways (leading to the river) haven't been paved over, so the plan is technically more intact.

Getting There & Away

You can charter boats from Luang Prabang's charter boat pier to Wat Long Khun or Ban Xieng Maen for US$3 return, or you can wait for the infrequent ferry boats, at the ferry boat pier further south, which charge around US$0.25 per passenger.

HERITAGE HOUSE

ເຮືອນມໍລະດົກ

A Unesco-sponsored exhibit and information centre called **Heritage House** (La Maison de Patrimoine; 8.30am-4pm Mon-Fri) occupies an old wooden Lao house on teak pillars in Ban Xieng Muan. Other than the very impressive wood and colombage (bamboo lattice daubed with natural mortar) house itself, there is little to take in here. Occasional weaving demonstrations are held in the house.

Activities

MASSAGE & SAUNA

You can take a traditional herbal sauna and/ or an hour-long Swedish-Lao massage at the **Lao Red Cross** (Th Wisunarat; sauna US$1, massage per hr US$3; 3.30-9pm). The Lao Red Cross is housed in a nicely preserved Lao-French building with half-timbered walls.

Lotus de Laos (212777; Th Sisavangvong; per hr US$5-6), Luang Prabang's first day spa, offers a more upmarket massage experience.

THE PRESERVATION OF LUANG PRABANG

Marthe Bassene, a French woman married to a colonial doctor, wrote in her published journal of 1909:

> Oh! What a delightful paradise of idleness this country protects, by the fierce barrier of the stream, against progress and ambition for which it has no need! Will Luang Prabang be, in our century of exact sciences, of quick profits, of victory by money, the refuge of the last dreamers, the last lovers, the last troubadours?

As if to answer Bassene's rhetorical question with a resounding affirmative, Unesco's World Heritage programme and its many independent supporters began lobbying in the early 1990s to have the city added to the World Heritage list. In a preliminary survey Unesco pronounced Luang Prabang 'the best preserved city in South-East Asia' and on 2 December 1995 the organisation placed the Luang Prabang's name on the register, which makes the city eligible for UN funds for preservation. Luang Prabang's future now seems to be relatively assured.

The historical and cultural heart of the city straddles a peninsula measuring 1km long by 250m wide inside the confluence of the Nam Khan (Khan River) and the Mekong River. Here are found the city's most important religious edifices along with the residences of the former nobility and trading aristocracy. It is a graceful neighbourhood of ponds and coconut palms, with old wooden or colombage (bamboo lattice daubed with natural mortar) homes in the traditional Lao style; brick-and-stucco colonial buildings with tiled roofs; and neocolonial houses that mix Lao and French motifs, with ground-floor walls of brick and plaster and upper-floor walls of wood. Although a few French administrative buildings near the junction of Th Phothisarat and Th Kingkitsarat date to between 1909 and 1920, most of the old colonial buildings now standing were constructed between 1920 and 1925.

Unesco has one French architect, one Japanese architect and five Lao architects working full-time in Luang Prabang. So far they have identified over 700 historic structures in the city and classified them by construction methods and materials. The Lao government has recently bestowed legal protective status on many types of historic structures in the city. In addition to the preservation and restoration of local architecture, the programme calls for a careful review of any new construction and for the restoration and conservation of natural wetlands within the city limits.

If the Unesco team is successful in its endeavours to preserve and even enhance Luang Prabang's charm, it will have helped Laos's most important tourist attraction attain a level of sustainability that few places in Asia have been able to maintain. In this the city can truly be called a 'refuge of the last dreamers'.

RAFTING & CYCLING

(☎ 252372; indochina1@yahoo.com; Th Phothisa... rganises single- and multiday trips involving trekking, rafting and cycling – or a combination of these – on trails and rivers around Luang Prabang. A typical excursion involves pedalling from Luang Prabang to a put-in point on the Nam Khan, Nam Ming or Nam Pa, followed by whitewater rafting downriver to a pick-up point. Longer trips may go as far north as Muang Ngoi or Muang Khua. Some treks include elephant riding. Prices range around US$20 to US$40 per day, including use of bikes and rafts imported from Germany.

Action Max Laos (☎ 253489; http://actionmax asia.com; 02/169 Ban Xieng Muan) offers trips of a similar nature to Tiger Trails, but using completely separate routes, starting at US$36 per person for two days and US$52 for three days.

Wildside Laos (☎ 212093; www.wildside-laos.com; 43 Th Sisavangvong) offers similar trekking and rafting excursions around the province and further afield as well.

For cycling around town, guesthouses and shops in the historic district hire out bicycles of varying quality for US$1 to US$2 per day.

Walking Tour

A simple walking circuit around Luang Prabang's northeastern quarter will take you to most of the historic attractions and sightseeing spots. You might want to do this circuit in two stages – one part in the coolness of early morning and another in the late afternoon – with time off in between for lunch and a rest. Most of the highlighted sights mentioned here are described in detail earlier in this chapter.

An easy morning walk might start at the bustling **Talat Dala** (**1**; p132). The area surrounding this market is Luang Prabang's commercial nerve centre, and you'll find all sorts of intriguing as well as very mundane shops and vendors here. From the market, head southeast along Th Setthathirat, passing the Provincial Hospital on the right and more shops on the left.

At the next big crossroads, turn left and continue past the Rama Hotel. On the left about 150m past the hotel stands **Wat Wisunarat** (**2**; p119), one of the city's oldest

temples. At the eastern end of the temple's compound is the bulbous That Makmo – the Watermelon Stupa. Adjacent to the northern side of the temple is another older temple, **Wat Aham** (**3**; p120), which is known for its two large and venerable banyan trees.

Exiting from the east entrance to Wat Aham, bear left (northwest) onto the somewhat busy road that parallels the Nam Khan. Continue northwest until this road terminates and bear right, following the road that winds its way between the Nam Khan below on the right and Phu Si above on the left. As you continue northeast along this road you'll pass several views of river life below. If you're hungry, look out for informal eating places along the riverbank nearby. Or you can walk up the steep, zigzagging *nâa-kha* (*naga* – water serpent) stairs to **Wat Thammothayalan (4)**, one of the few active monasteries on Phu Si, for good views of the Nam Khan.

For the second half of this walking circuit, start at the **Royal Palace Museum** (**5**; p117). From the museum, go northeast on Th Sisavangvong towards the eastern end

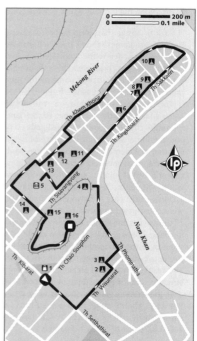

of the peninsula formed by the confluence of the Mekong River and the Nam Khan. Along this road you'll pass several temples of minor note, including **Wat Saen** (**6**; p121), **Wat Sop** (**7**), **Wat Sirimungkhun** (**8**) and **Wat Si Bun Heuang** (**9**), all lined up along the left (northern) side of the street. These are interspersed with a number of charming brick-and-stucco French colonial buildings on both sides of the street, along with some of the traditional wood-and-mortar houses and hybrid French-Lao brick dwellings. Most of the colonial buildings were built during the 1920s and 1930s.

When you reach the end of the road, bear left and follow the river bend around to **Wat Xieng Thong** (**10**; p118), one of the town's premier temples and well worth spending some time at. After you've had your fill of this wat, exit towards the river and head west (left) on the river road. On your left you'll pass side streets that lead to small, older temples that the usual guided tour itineraries don't include – **Wat Pa Phai** (**11**; p121), **Wat Xieng Muan** (**12**; p121) and **Wat Chum Khong** (**13**). Wat Xieng Muan is home to an arts' school for monks.

When you pass the rear side of the Royal Palace Museum on your left, take the next left turn and follow the short road south back to Th Sisavangvong, where you'll come to **Wat Mai Suwannaphumaham** (**14**; p120) – noted for its exterior gilded relief – on your right. On the other side of the street, opposite the front of the Royal Palace Museum, is a set of steps that leads up the northwestern side of Phu Si. To the right of the steps above the road is the abandoned *sĭm* of one of Luang Prabang's oldest temples, **Wat Pa Huak** (**15**; p121), whose interior murals are not to be missed – if you can find someone with a key.

If you're ready for a climb, ascend the steps to the summit of **Phu Si** (p121), where you'll find good views of the town. Sunset vistas from the western side of the hill next to the 19th-century **That Chomsi** (**16**; p121) can be superb, except in the late dry season when even the sun's intensity is strongly muted.

Festivals & Events

The two most important annual events in Luang Prabang are **Bun Pi Mai Lao** (Lao New Year) in April (see Bun Pi Mai Lao p116) and the **boat races** during Bun Awk Phansa (the End of the Rains Retreat) in October.

Both events draw large numbers of both Lao and foreigners to the city, so be sure to book a room in advance if you're coming to town then.

Sleeping
BUDGET
Near the Mekong
The old silversmithing district near the Mekong, a neighbourhood known as Ban Wat That (named for nearby Wat Pha Mahathat, or 'Wat That' for short), and the adjacent Ban Ho Xiang, have become a centre for a cluster of modest guesthouses.

Vanvisa Guest House (☎ /fax 212500; 42/2 Ban Wat That; s/d US$6/10) Vanvisa features six rooms at the back of a shop that sells textiles, antiques and handicrafts. The owner, a cultured Lao lady, sometimes makes breakfasts and family-style dinners for guests and can even arrange an informal cooking workshop.

Chanthy Banchit Guest House (☎ 252538; 26/2 Ban Wat That; r with/without bathroom US$5.50/4.50) This friendly, family-run spot in a two-storey wooden house offers well-kept rooms and the use of a safety deposit box. Discounts are available in the low season.

Suankeo Guest House No 2 (☎ 252804; Ban Ho Xiang; s/d US$2.50/4) In a white two-storey house with blue shutters and a terrace, friendly and efficient Suankeo No 2 has 10 rooms with shared hot-water showers. Breakfast and laundry service are available.

Historic Temple District
In the most concentrated area of colonial architecture and historic monasteries on and off Th Sisavangvong/Th Sakkarin are a few places with cheap rooms.

Phoun Sab Guest House (☎ 212975; Th Sisavangvong; r US$3-6) In an old shophouse (a two-storey building designed to have a shop downstairs and a residence upstairs) not far from the Royal Palace Museum, Phoun Sab offers simple but clean two-bed rooms; the more expensive ones have private bathrooms. There's a basic café downstairs and bikes are available for hire.

Bou Pha Guest House (☎ 252405; Th Sisavangvong; r US$3-6) Between Phoun Sab Guest House and the Scandinavian Bakery, Bou Pha offers a similar standard to the Phoun Sab.

Phousi Guest House (☎ 212973; r US$5-7) On the road that runs along the northern side of the Royal Palace Museum, off Th Sakkarin, this guesthouse occupies a nice-looking two-storey colonial-style building with a restaurant downstairs serving Lao and vegetarian food. The cheaper rooms feature shared bathroom.

Pa Phai Guest House (Paphay; ☎ /fax 212752; Th Sisavang Vatthana; s/d US$5/8) Situated opposite Wat Pa Phai, the friendly Pa Phai occupies an historic two-storey French-Lao house and has a small garden at the front. Bamboo walls separate the rooms.

Heritage House (☎ 252537; fax 252562; Th Sisavang Vatthana; r US$8-10; 🕮) Almost opposite Pa Phai Guest House, this old Lao-French house with wood shutters is friendly and clean; the more expensive upstairs rooms have air-con.

Chittana Guest House (Th Sakkarin; r US$3-7) Down a pedestrian alley opposite Villa Santi, this century-old Lao house offers well-kept rooms at bargain prices. Rates vary depending on the size of the room but all rooms come with private bathroom.

Chaliny Guest House (☎ 252377; 53/7 Th Khem Khong; r with breakfast US$4-8) Next door to Mekong Guest House, the friendly Chaliny offers good rooms in a building with a wooden upper storey, and a brick and stucco lower storey. The cheaper rooms have shared bathroom.

Near Talat Dala

Opposite Talat Dala and behind the Phousi Hotel is a quiet street with a few newer guesthouses of good standard. The neighbourhood is known as Ban Thong Chaleun, and it's convenient to the post office, bank and Talat Dala.

Phonethavy Guest House (☎ 253213; Ban Thong Chaleun; r US$4-5) Situated on a road beside the Phousi Hotel, this one-storey guesthouse has 10 clean rooms with either shared or attached bathroom.

Koun Savan Guest House (☎ 212297; Ban Thong Chaleun; r US$4-10; 🕮) Next to the Phonethavy, the quiet Koun Savan has rooms in a couple of two-storey houses. In the cheaper rooms bathroom facilities are shared, while the most expensive rooms have air-con.

Th Pha Mahapatsaman

This area is centrally located for trips to Talat Dala, the immigration office, Lao Airlines, Lao Red Cross and restaurants on Th Wisunarat, but is otherwise uninspiring.

Jaliya Guest House (☎ 252154; Th Pha Mahapatsaman; r US$3-10; 🕮) Opposite Lao Airlines, this guesthouse offers clean rooms, a nice garden out the back and the use of a safety deposit box. The cheapest rooms come with shared bathroom and fan, the mid-priced ones have private bathroom and the most expensive are in separate cottages with air-con. Motorbikes and bicycles are available for hire.

Thavisouk Guest House (☎ 252022; Th Pha Mahapatsaman; r US$4-10; 🕮) The friendly Thavisouk features fatter-than-usual mattresses in clean, sunny rooms; the more expensive rooms have air-con.

MID-RANGE
Historic Temple District

Sala Luang Prabang (☎ 252460; http://salalao.com; 102/6 Th Khem Khong; r with breakfast US$35-55; 🕮) This artistically refurbished, century-old mansion facing the river is joined by two newer wings built in similar style, all painted in earth tones. Service is very friendly and efficient. Rooms come with both fan and air-con (most air-con rooms in Laos do not have fans), hairdryer and IDD phone. Visa credit cards are accepted.

Apsara (☎ 212420; www.theapsara.com; Th Kingkitsarat; r with breakfast US$45; 🕮) Formerly the Duang Champa, the seven large rooms here have been completely redone and redecorated with antiques and handicrafts.

Luang Prabang Bakery Guest House (☎ 252499; Th Sisavangvong; r with breakfast US$25; 🕮) Efficiently run, awkwardly named LPBGH offers small, spotless rooms with satellite TV, along with a good restaurant downstairs.

Le Tam Tam Garden Hotel (☎ /fax 253300; 91/8 Th Sisavangvong; r US$8-15) This modern, three-storey hotel, reminiscent of the latest generation of Khao San Rd hotels in Bangkok, offers a variety of rooms escalating in price with the size of the room. Downstairs there's a large indoor-outdoor restaurant.

Saynamkhan Hotel (☎ 212976; Th Kingkitsarat; r US$20-35; 🕮) Saynamkhan is housed in a restored two-storey colonial building near the banks of the Nam Khan, right opposite Wat Phu Phutthabaht, on the street that wraps around the peninsula parallel to the river. The exterior of the building is very attractive, but the upstairs interior restoration could have been better. Downstairs looks more inviting, with a cosy bar and slim outdoor terrace.

Phousi Hotel (☎ 212192; www.phousihotel.lao pdr.com; cnr Th Chao Fa Ngum & Th Kisarat; r US$33-38; family US$55; ✹) The 40-room Phousi occupies the former French commissariat in the centre of town. All of the rooms are equipped with TV, fridge, minibar and phone. It's a quiet place to stay in spite of its central location.

Tum Tum Cheng Guest House (☎ 253262; tumtum cheng@yahoo.com; Ban Wat Xieng Thong; r US$25-35; ✹) A Hungarian woman and her Lao husband offer 10 clean rooms in a newly built, faux-colonial style building very close to Wat Xieng Thong. Discounts are available in the low season.

Xieng Mouane Guest House (☎ /fax 252152; 86/6 Ban Xieng Muan; r US$15-35; ✹) Near Wat Xieng Muan a block east of the Mekong River, this white two-storey French colonial mansion has spacious rooms with wood floors. The more expensive rooms come with air-con.

Sayo Guest House (☎ 252614; sayo@laotel.com; Ban Xieng Muan; r US$15-35; ✹) Just north of Xieng Mouane Guest House, Sayo is housed in an old French mansion with even larger rooms – those inside the house have 4.8m-high ceilings. The most expensive here are the two huge corner rooms with louvered windows on three sides and wood floors, as well as a separate seating area and a refrigerator. Out the back are the former servants' quarters where you'll find the less expensive rooms.

Senesouk Guest House (☎ 212074; sensouk@lao tel.com; 2/4 Ban Wat Saen; s/d US$20/25; ✹) In a re-novated colonial-era shophouse, all rooms at the friendly, well-run Senesouk have air-con. The proprietor speaks French.

New Luang Prabang Hotel (☎ 212264; fax 212804; Th Sisavangvong; s/d US$25/30) This plain three-storey hotel offers 15 medium-sized rooms, all with fridge. It's an OK place, if a bit sterile.

Elsewhere

Rama Hotel (☎ 212247; Th Wisunarat; ramahotel@ hotmail.com; r US$10-13; ✹) Recently renovated, the centrally located Rama is one of the city's older hotels, boasting a friendly, efficient staff and 27 large rooms with good beds. The cheaper rooms have fan only.

Lane Xang Guest House (☎ 212749; Th Wisunarat; r US$20-25; ✹) Seven very large rooms, div-ided between two Lao-French colombage houses, come with fridge, closets and large bathrooms. During the low season you can sometimes rent rooms here for half the normal rate.

Ban Lao Guest House (☎ 252078; fax 212438; Ban That Luang; r US$15-20; ✹) Housed in a white two-storey building a bit west of Wat Manolom on a shady *soi* (lane) leading towards the river, Ban Lao offers spacious rooms, some with air-con. The friendly owner speaks English and French.

Muangsua Hotel (☎ 212192; Th Phu Vao) The Muangsua has 17 rooms that are currently being renovated. When it reopens, expect rates in the US$25 to US$35 range. The popular disco out the back is noisy until 11.30pm.

Manoluck Hotel (☎ 212250; fax 212508; 14/3 Th Phu Vao; r with breakfast US$45) Constructed in the modern Lao style, Manoluck offers 30 rooms with fridge, satellite TV and phone. Most guest rooms are at the back of the building, hence they're protected from street noise, while the restaurant and reception are at the front. The restaurant serves Lao, Chinese, Thai, Vietnamese and European food.

Noix d'Arec Guest House (☎ 252775; noixdarec _gh@yahoo.com; 089 Th Noradet; r US$10-20) Yet another colonial villa–turned-guesthouse, the Noix d'Arec offers large, comfortable suites upstairs in the old house, or less expensive rooms in a newer row-house wing. All rooms are fan only.

Rattana Guest House (☎ 252255; 4/2 Ban Wat That; s/d US$8-15) Off Th Phothisarat near Indochina Spirit restaurant, this modern guesthouse has eight very clean rooms, six with fan and two more expensive ones with air-con. The two upstairs rooms are quieter. There's a pleasant outdoor sitting area and a clothesline if you'd like to do some laundry. The owners usually lower the room rates during low season months (May, June, September and October).

Out of Town

Thongbay Guest House (☎ 219686; Ban Vieng Mai; s/d US$10/15; ✹) This guesthouse features traditional Lao thatched-roof bungalows, each with a terrace, in a quiet, secluded spot by the Nam Khan. Amenities include a swimming pool, room service, phone, fax, minibar, laundry, and bicycle and canoe hire.

TOP END

Historic Temple District

Auberge les 3 Nagas (☎ 253888; www.3nagas.com; r US$90-150; ⚡) This large, two-storey colombage villa boasts one of the most inspired restoration jobs in Luang Prabang, with exposed roof beams left beautifully intact. All seven suites come with fridge and spacious private verandas; the two more expensive suites also have their own private stairway entries. The downstairs café-restaurant offers excellent Lao-French cuisine.

Villa Savanh (☎ 212420; Th Sakkarin; s/d US$80/120; ⚡) The Apsara manages these two self-contained Lao colombage villas. Discounts are available for long-term stays.

Villa Santi (☎ 252157; http://villasantihotel.com; Th Sakkarin; r US$65-150; ⚡) Villa Santi, about midway between the Royal Palace Museum and Wat Xieng Thong, was the first place in Luang Prabang to take advantage of the abundant French-Lao colonial architecture after Luang Prabang opened to tourism in 1989. Formerly the residence of King Sisavang Vong's wife, then inherited by Princess Manilai, the villa was taken over by the government in 1976, but finally returned to the princess and her family in 1991. The 120-year-old residence has been extensively remodelled and decorated with Lao art and antiques. A 14-room newer wing closely mimics Luang Prabang's classic French-Lao architecture. All rooms and suites feature IDD phone, minibar and hairdryer. Facilities and services include a herbal sauna, traditional massage and fitness club.

Auberge Le Calao (☎ 212100; www.calaoinn.laopdr .com; Th Khem Khong; s/d with breakfast US$60/75; ⚡) A restored 1930-vintage Sino-Portuguese–style mansion facing the Mekong, Auberge Le Calao has five capacious rooms, some with verandas overlooking Th Khem Khong and the river. Originally built by a Chinese-Lao, the house was occupied by a French merchant from 1936 to 1968.

Ban Wat That

Satri House (☎ 253491; satrilao@hotmail.com; 057 Th Phothisarat; r with breakfast US$120; ⚡ ⚡) Built at the turn of the last century as a royal villa, Satri House's seven rooms are beautifully furnished with Southeast Asian antiques. During the low season the proprietors knock US$50 off the normal rates.

Maison Souvannaphoum (☎ 212200; reservations@ angsana.com; Th Phothisarat; r US$60-120; ⚡) Once the official residence of Prince Souvanna Phouma, the rambling Souvannaphoum became a French-managed hotel in the 1990s. The government required the owners to drop the final 'a' from the name so as not to evoke the monarchy. In December 2004 it will be reopening under the Thailand-based Angsana Resorts Hotel group. Rooms in the old wing are quite spacious and well decorated, while a newer two-storey wing has private terraces facing a garden.

Mouang Luang Hotel (☎ /fax 212790; Th Bunkhong; r US$40-60; ⚡ ⚡). Mouang Luang is a large, two-storey, palacelike building with an intricate Lao-style roof and polished dark wood floors throughout. The 35 spacious high-ceilinged rooms come decked out with minibar and marble bathrooms, while the two suites feature sitting areas. An open-air restaurant offers a menu of Lao and European dishes, and there's a swimming pool on the grounds. Credit cards are accepted.

Th Phu Vao

Pansea Phou Vao Hotel (☎ 212194; www.pansea .com; Th Phu Vao; r with breakfast US$200-290; ⚡ ⚡) Sitting on the crest of Phu Vao (Kite Hill) on the southern edge of town, the Pansea Phou Vao has gone by several names, including Ratchathirat, Luang Prabang and Mittaphap. Since the Pansea took over in 2002, the hotel has undergone major renovations and is now the top hotel address in Luang Prabang. The hotel features two huge suites, 12 large superior rooms with sweeping views and 20 upgraded standard rooms, all with satellite TV, minibar and IDD telephone.

Le Parasol Blanc Hotel (☎ 252124; fax 252159; Th Phu Vao; s/d US$45/50; ⚡) Surrounded by lushly landscaped grounds, this hotel features tastefully designed rooms with balconies, minifridge and modern bathrooms. Outdoor restaurant seating overlooks a picturesque pond. There's a free shuttle to town or the airport.

Out of Town

Two resorts south of town on the way to Tat Kuang Si (see p135) are set to provide luxury retreats away from the city's slowly increasing buzz.

The Grand Luang Prabang (☎ 253851; http:// grandluangprabang.com; Ban Xieng Kaew, 4km south of town on the Mekong River; r US$80-150; ☒) Built around the former villa of local hero Prince Regent Phetsarat, this 78-room resort features French Indochina–inspired architecture spread over a large, well-landscaped area with reflecting pools, lotus ponds and superb views of the Mekong.

Villa Santi Resort (☎ 253470; villasantihotel.com; r US$65-100; ☒ ☒) This resort branch of the Villa Santi, 5km south of town en route to Tat Kuang Si, features 55 rooms decorated in Luang Prabang style. Recreational facilities include tennis courts, badminton, aerobics, herbal sauna, herbal massage, fitness club and horseback riding. Regular shuttle service is provided between the airport and the resort.

Eating

BAKERIES

Strong Lao coffee and sweet European pastries tempt foreign visitors at several bakeries along Th Sisavangvong and Th Chao Fa Ngum. Normally the pastry selection is better during the high season when consumption is as its peak, and supplies are fresh. During the low months such as May, June and September the variety may be less than impressive.

JoMa Bakery Café (☎ 252292; Th Chao Fa Ngum; meals US$1-2; ☒ breakfast, lunch & dinner, closed Sun) Arguably the best bakery in town, JoMa has alfresco tables along the street as well as in a spacious air-con dining room indoors. In addition to the large bread and pastry selection, the café offers a menu of sandwiches, soups and salads.

Luang Prabang Bakery (Th Sisavangvong; pastries US$0.30-1.20; ☒ breakfast & lunch) At two locations about one block apart, Luang Prabang Bakery offers all kinds of home-made pastries, yogurt, cheese, sandwiches, ice cream and coffee at moderate prices. There are tables inside as well as a few on the pavement. The original location on the western side of the road contains a small bookshop.

Scandinavian Bakery (Th Sisavangvong; pastries US$0.30-1.50; ☒ breakfast, lunch & dinner) This is a branch of the Vientiane bakery of the same name, and although the quality is not nearly as high, the tiny air-con eating area is popular in the hot season.

Bakery Bar (Th Sisavangvong; meals US$0.70-2; ☒ breakfast, lunch & dinner) In addition to the usual baked goods, this newer spot near the Royal Palace Museum specialises in pizzas and burgers.

EUROPEAN

Café des Artes (Th Sisavangvong; meals US$1-3; ☒ breakfast, lunch & dinner) In the heart of the tourist district, Des Artes serves a long list of breakfasts, along with French fare, soups (the pumpkin soup is delicious), sandwiches, tartines, burgers, brochettes and set menus. The menu also features one page of Luang Prabang cuisine.

Le Café Ban Vat Sene (Th Sakkarin; snacks US$1-3; ☒ breakfast, lunch & dinner) Opposite a picturesque old French school, this café in a restored colonial building nicely decorated with Lao antiques serves Lao coffee and an assortment of pastries, sandwiches and salads.

Restaurant Brasserie L'Elephant (☎ 252482; Ban Wat Nong; meals US$3-10; ☒ lunch & dinner) One of Luang Prabang's most elegant Western eateries occupies a choice corner spot near Wat Nong Sikhunmeuang with wooden floors, subdued lighting and Lao antiques. The menu is French, the wine list international.

Le Potiron (☎ 212780; Th Sisavangvong; meals US$3-5; ☒ lunch & dinner) Pizza is the house speciality, but you'll also find salads and standard French fare.

INDIAN

Nazim Indian Food (Th Wisunarat; meals US$1-2.50; ☒ breakfast, lunch & dinner) Two branches of Vientiane's popular Nazim serve a broad range of North and South Indian food, with plenty of vegetarian dishes. The second branch is on Th Sisavangvong.

Nisha Restaurant (Th Sisavangvong; meals US$1-2; ☒ breakfast, lunch & dinner) This tiny place serves Indian specialities, Western breakfasts and Lao dishes, both veg and nonveg.

LAO, THAI & VIETNAMESE

The Apsara (☎ 212420; Th Kingkitsarat; meals US$2.50-10; ☒ lunch & dinner) Chefs at The Apsara, in the hotel of the same name, whip up an excellent fusion of Lao, Thai and Pacific Rim cooking. The reasonably priced wine list is one of the best in town, and the tasteful Chinoiserie décor in the open-air bar and dining room makes a pleasant change from the usual Lao wall hangings.

View Khaem Khong (Th Khem Khong; meals US$0.80-2; ☺ lunch & dinner) As in Vientiane, the local government continues to flip-flop on whether to allow restaurants to operate along the Mekong River, with the situation changing every three months or so. When the restaurants are operating, this one has the best river view and best Lao food.

Tum Tum Cheng Restaurant & Cooking School (☎ 252019; Th Sakkarin; meals US$1-3; ☺ lunch & dinner) The Lao chef at Tum Tum Cheng – now in its third Luang Prabang location, next to Wat Khili – not only prepares an interesting menu of Lao and Lao-European fusion, he is also one of the only teachers of Lao cuisine. As the chef lived in Hungary for some years, some of the dishes display a European touch.

Samsara (Th Sisavangvong; meals US$2-4; ☺ lunch & dinner) The best part about this small and chicly Indochinese restaurant is the rooftop bar.

Yongkhoune Restaurant (Th Wisunarat; meals US$1-2; ☺ breakfast, lunch & dinner) Yongkhoune makes a good 'Salad Luang Prabang', a savoury arrangement of watercress, sliced boiled eggs, tomatoes and onions with a unique dressing. The stir-fried long beans are also good, as are egg sandwiches made with baguettes; chicken curry with potatoes; and fruit smoothies. A second branch is on Th Sisavangvong.

Restaurant Indochine (☎ 252333; 9/7 Th Sisavangvong; meals US$1-4; ☺ breakfast, lunch & dinner) This clean restaurant serves reliable if unremarkable Lao and Vietnamese food.

Pak Huay Mixai Restaurant (☎ 212260; Th Sisavang Vatthana; meals US$1-4; ☺ breakfast, lunch & dinner) In a little shophouse off Th Sisavangvong, this pleasant restaurant serves slightly Westernised Lao cuisine at tables covered with tablecloths and cloth napkins. Popular with Lao as well as *falang* (Westerners).

Mr Hong's Coffeeshop & Restaurant (71/6 Ban Thongchaleun; meals US$0.60-1.20; ☺ breakfast, lunch & dinner) Mr Hong draws a steady clientele with his long menu of reasonably priced Lao dishes designed for *falang* palates; potent cocktails; and easy conversation.

Nang Sengdao (Th Phu Vao; meals US$0.60-0.80; ☺ 6am-9pm) This is one of the best noodle shops along Th Phu Vao, a street known for its many wooden eateries selling noodles. In addition to *fŏe* (rice noodles), Nang Sengdao offers *khào jįi khai dạo* (fried eggs and baguettes), *khào sáwy* (noodles in a mildly spicy sauce) and a variety of other simple dishes.

LUANG PRABANG

Luang Prabang has a unique cuisine all its own. One of the local specialities is *jąew bạwng*, a jamlike condiment made with chillies and dried buffalo skin. A soup called *áw lám*, made with dried meat, mushrooms, eggplant and a special bitter-spicy root, is also a typical Luang Prabang dish (roots and herbs with bitter-hot effects are a force in Luang Prabang cuisine). Other local delicacies include *phák nâm*, a delicious watercress that's rarely found outside the Luang Prabang area, and *khái pâen*, dried river moss fried in seasoned oil, topped with sesame seeds and served with *jąew bạwng*. *Khào kam*, a local red, sweet, slightly fizzy wine made from sticky rice, is abundantly and inexpensively available by the bottle in Luang Prabang. It can be good or bad depending on the brand.

Somchanh Restaurant (☎ 252021; Th Suvannabanlang; meals US$1-2; ☺ breakfast, lunch & dinner) Another good spot for local cuisine is this simple but pleasant outdoor place near the cluster of guesthouses in Ban Wat That. Dining areas are divided between tables on a slight bluff near the kitchen and seating across the road on the riverbank. The menu features a large selection of Lao and Luang Prabang dishes, including the best choice of vegetarian Lao food in town.

Drinking

Most of Luang Prabang is sound asleep, or at least nodding off behind a bottle of *khào kam*, by 10pm, but there are a few bars around. We found that the usual closing time here is still 11.30pm, despite a new national law mandating a 10.30pm closing.

Cruisin Gate (Th Kingkitsarat) Nestled in a curve in the road, near the Nam Khan, this lively spot is the town's first openly gay bar, although the crowd is mixed and both women and couples are welcome.

Hive Bar (Th Kingkitsarat) Next door to L'Etranger Books & Tea, the aptly named Hive Bar consists of a honeycomb of brick-lined, candlelit rooms and corridors, plus a cluster of alfresco tables out the front. Sample the bar menu's amusing list of drinks based on home-brewed liquors while listening to a subdued mix of trance, trip-hop and tribal.

Maylek Pub (cnr Th Pha Mahapatsaman & Th Setthathirat) This French-managed pub is stylishly decorated with modern furniture of original design. The fully stocked bar includes such hard-to-find items as pastis, Southern Comfort and Bailey's. Snacks and sandwiches are also available.

The long wooden bars at Restaurant Brasserie L'Elephant (p129) and The Apsara (p129) restaurants are good choices for quiet drinks and conversation.

Entertainment
LAO CULTURAL PERFORMANCES

Royal Theatre (Th Sisavangvong; admission US$3-12; ⏱ 5pm Mon, Wed & Sat) Inside the Royal Palace Museum compound, local performers put on a show that includes a *bąasìi* ceremony, traditional dance and folk music.

DANCE CLUBS

Luang Prabang thus far has only two places where dancing is permitted. Both close at 11.30pm sharp.

Dao Fah (⏱ 9-11.30pm) A young Lao crowd packs this cavernous club, located off the road to the southern bus terminal. Live bands playing Lao and Thai pop alternate with DJs who spin rap and hip-hop. The bar serves Beerlao as well as mixers for patrons bringing their own liquor.

Muangsua Hotel (☎ 212263; Th Phu Vao; ⏱ 9-11.30pm) In a low-ceilinged room behind the hotel, a Lao band plays the usual mix of Lao and Thai pop. Only Beerlao is sold.

Shopping
HANDICRAFTS, ART, TEXTILES & ANTIQUES

Baan Khily Gallery (☎ 212611; Th Sakkarin) This beautiful old building, formerly the Alliance Française during colonial times, carries a collection of unique and carefully selected Lao crafts, including handmade *săa* (mulberry bark) paper. This gallery started the revival of *săa* arts in Laos, and its huge *săa*-paper stars, to be lit from the inside and hung outdoors, have become famous here and abroad. Also on hand are books on Laos and Southeast Asia, local and international artwork, and an upstairs gallery with rotating exhibits. The very knowledgeable owner speaks German, English, Italian and French, and is happy to answer questions about the area. An upstairs veranda offers tea service with views of the street below.

Thithpeng Maniphone (Ban Wat That) Thithpeng crafted silverware for Luang Prabang royalty before 1975 (Thailand's royal family are now some of his best customers). He has 15 apprentice silversmiths working under him to create his designs, but still does the most delicate work himself, including ceremonial swords and spears. To get here follow the signs opposite the Hotel Souvannaphoum.

OckPopTok (☎ 253219; 73/5 Ban Wat Nong) This unique textile gallery and workshop offers a selection of naturally dyed housewoven Lao silk and cotton from which is produced custom-tailored clothing as well as household decorative items. Lengths of fabric can also be purchased. There is a second branch on Th Sisavangvong.

Pathana Boupha Antique House (☎ 212262; 29/4 Ban Visoun) In an impressive old French mansion, Pathana Boupha carries antique statuary, jewellery, silverwork (especially antique silver betel-nut sets), Royal Lao government currency and old photos, mostly from the Lao owners' private collection. It also sells high-quality textiles (originals as well as reproductions) from the various ethnic groups around Laos. The late patriarch of the family designed many of the costumes and ornaments used in the former Royal Palace, and until his death he also furnished costuming for the local Miss Pi Mai Lao pageant.

Heritage (Moladok; Th Sisavangvong) In a narrow but nicely restored shophouse, Heritage stocks one of the more unique yet practical collections of Lao handicrafts, for the most part styled for use in interior design, including silk-lined cushions and embroidered rice mats.

Mekong Art Gallery (Th Sakkarin, opposite Villa Santi) Contemporary Lao artists display their work in an old French villa.

MARKETS

Talat Dala (Dara Market; cnr Th Setthathirat & Th Chao Sisuphon) Luang Prabang's oldest market, collects together an impressive array of hardware, cookware, dried and preserved foodstuffs, textiles and handicrafts. Sitting right at the centre of town, it is by far the most conveniently located market for most visitors.

Handicraft market (cnr Th Sisavangvong & Th Kitsarat; ⏱ 5-11pm) Every evening this market assembles along Th Sisavangvong from the Royal Palace Museum to Th Setthathirat, closing this section of the street off to motor vehicles. Hmong appliqué blankets and hangings comprise most of the goods on display, along with a few ceramics, bamboo lamps and some jewellery. Many of the shopowners along Th Sisavangvong have been complaining that blocking off the street nightly is costing them business, so the market may be cut back to one or two nights a week.

A huge warehouselike structure built by the Chinese, **Talat Phosy**, located on the road to the Sainyabuli bus terminal, encompasses the biggest market for fresh produce, meats, herbs and just about any other basic requisite of Lao life. It has totally replaced the old Talat Naviengkham in the town centre.

A recently built large **Chinese market**, located opposite the Luang Prabang Provincial Stadium on the outskirts of town towards the southern bus terminal, emphasises dry goods, textiles and hardware. Thought it threatens to eclipse the Talat Dala, the atmosphere is lacking by comparison.

Getting There & Away
AIR

Lao Airlines (☎ 212172; Th Pha Mahapatsaman) operates three daily flights between Luang Prabang and Vientiane (one way/return US$57/108, 40 minutes). During the high season, flights to/from Phonsavan (Xieng Khuang) may be added (one way/return US$37/70, 40 minutes). In the past, Lao Airlines (formerly Lao Aviation) also linked

Luang Prabang with Udomxai, Huay Xai and Luang Nam Tha, but with the current lack of aircraft these services are not likely to be resumed anytime soon.

Even if you have a return reservation from Luang Prabang, you should confirm it the day before your departure. Lao Airlines in Luang Prabang accepts credit cards and can book flights on THAI (between Laos and Thailand only).

For information on international flights to Luang Prabang from Asia see p267.

When flying into Luang Prabang, try to get a window seat – as the plane descends over the mountains in preparation for landing the view of the town is excellent.

The **Luang Prabang International Airport** (☎ 212173), 4km from the city centre, has a restaurant, phonecard telephone, post office, exchange booth, a branch of Lao Development Bank, an air-con departure lounge and modern toilets.

BOAT

Ferries are a major form of transport between Luang Prabang and Huay Xai on the Thai border to the northwest, but are much less so to other towns. In Luang Prabang the main landing for long-distance Mekong River boats, at the northwestern end of Th Chao Phanya Kang, is called Tha Heua Meh (literally, mail boat pier; ferry pier on our map). A blackboard at the Navigation Office announces long-distance boat departures, eg to Nong Khiaw and Vientiane – it's all in Lao. A second pier near the Royal Palace Museum is sometimes used when the river level is too low for the main pier.

Speedboats use a landing at Ban Don, 6km north of Luang Prabang. To charter a speedboat the pilots usually ask that you pay the equivalent of six passenger fares but they'll usually go if you pay for four spaces – often they have paid cargo to carry, too. If you want to share the cost of hiring a speedboat with other passengers it's best to show up at the speedboat pier in Ban Don the day before you want to leave and see what your prospects are. Then show up again around 6am on the morning of your intended departure to queue up. Speedboat fares are often quoted in Thai baht, though either kip or US dollars are acceptable payment.

Speedboat passengers are required to wear life vests and helmets but the helmets are very often substandard. See p252 for warnings on travelling by speedboat.

Pak Beng, Tha Suang & Huay Xai
As there is no direct road between Huay Xai and Luang Prabang, this is the most popular way for visitors to travel between the Thai border and Luang Prabang. The Lao border crossing at Huay Xai in Bokeo Province, across the Mekong River from Chiang Khong, Thailand, grants visas on arrival to most nationalities. Pak Beng, on the Mekong roughly halfway between Huay Xai and Luang Prabang, is a common place to break the trip in either direction or to use as a starting point for road trips northeast to Udomxai.

See p179 for details on Mekong River boat travel between Huay Xai, Pak Beng and Luang Prabang.

If you're heading to Hongsa in northern Sainyabuli Province, coming from Luang Prabang, take the slow boat from the ferry pier as far as Tha Suang (US$6, half day), where you can continue on to Hongsa by bus. You can also, of course, choose to get off in Pak Beng (US$7.50) and head north to Udomxai and Luang Nam Tha.

Smaller, faster speedboats from the pier in Ban Don pound up the Mekong to Tha Suang (US$12, two hours), Pak Beng (US$16, three hours) and Huay Xai (US$26, six hours) in double the time.

Nong Khiaw & Muang Khua
Most passengers and cargo going to Nong Khiaw travel by road nowadays as it's much quicker than by boat. Slow boats still head up the Nam Ou to Nong Khiaw (US$6.50, four or five hours) a couple of times a month from the ferry pier, and the dates are posted on a chalkboard in front of the Navigation Office in Luang Prabang about a week in advance of the departures. The Nong Khiaw landing is sometimes referred to as Muang Ngoi, or as Nam Bak, a larger village to the west.

The same situation applies to Muang Khua, further up the Nam Ou – it's more quickly reached by road than by slow boat. Slow boats do travel to Muang Khua (US$12, eight hours) on posted dates.

When there are sufficient passengers, speedboats travel from Luang Prabang to Nong Khiaw (US$12, two hours) and Muang Khua (US$22, four hours).

Be sure to inquire thoroughly as to river conditions before embarking on a Nam Ou trip; from mid-February on it's not unusual for speedboat pilots to get stranded in Nong Khiaw, unable to bring their boats back until the rains arrive in May or June.

Tha Deua, Pak Lai & Vientiane
Several times a month slow cargo boats travel between Luang Prabang and Vientiane (US$24, four days upriver, three days down) via Tha Deua (US$4, six hours downriver, one day upriver). Passenger travel on these boats, except for merchants accompanying fragile cargo, is rare now that Rte 13 is sealed and fast.

When there are sufficient passengers, or more commonly when chartered, speedboats travel downriver to Vientiane (US$38, eight or nine hours) via Tha Deua (US$10, one hour) and Pak Lai (US$21, four to five hours).

BUS & TRUCK
Interprovincial buses and trucks – large *săwngthăew* – operate out of three bus terminals in Luang Prabang. In general, vehicles going to destinations north of Luang Prabang leave from the northern bus terminal (on Rte 13 about 4km north of the town centre, past the turn-off for Luang Prabang International Airport) while those going south normally leave from the southern bus terminal (a few kilometres south of the town centre near the Luang Prabang Provincial Stadium). There are a few exceptions to this, due to the fact that different transport companies operate each terminal, and on certain routes they compete.

A third terminal, south of town on the road to Tat Kuang Si, serves buses going to Sainyabuli Province.

Vientiane
From Luang Prabang buses to Vientiane (ordinary/air-con US$6/7, 11 hours, six daily/two in the morning) leave from the southern bus terminal. The same buses stop in Vang Vieng (ordinary/air-con US$4.50/5, six to seven hours).

For quicker and more comfortable transport, try the travel agents in town, who can also arrange minivan transport (US$7, eight hours, four daily) and VIP bus (US$7, nine hours, four daily) to Vientiane.

See p94 for details on buses from Vientiane to Luang Prabang.

Udomxai, Luang Nam Tha & Huay Xai

Luang Prabang is linked with Udomxai and Luang Nam Tha Province via paved roads. Passenger trucks and buses to Udomxai leave once a morning (US$3, five hours) from both the southern bus terminal and the northern bus terminal. Buses bound for Luang Nam Tha (US$5, eight hours) leave once a day from both the southern terminal and the northern terminal (for Huay Xai–bound journeys).

Buses or passenger trucks to Huay Xai (US$6.50, eight hours in dry weather), on the Thai-Lao border, leave every evening from the northern bus terminal. Much of the road between Luang Nam Tha and Huay Xai is unsealed, so the trip can take up to two or even three days in the rainy season. In the rainy season it's best to take a Mekong River boat if you need to reach Huay Xai in two days or less.

These travel times are only estimates – in Laos such factors as number of passengers, number of stops, the weather, and road conditions affect travel times.

For further details on transport to and from these places, see the Getting There & Away sections for Udomxai (p158), Luang Nam Tha (p165) and Huay Xai (p178).

Nong Khiaw, Phonsavan & Sam Neua

Săwngthăew head north to Nong Khiaw (US$1.60, four hours, five daily) and northeast to Vieng Kham (US$2.50, six hours, five daily), departing from the northern bus terminal.

Buses leave for Phonsavan (US$6, 10 hours, one daily) and for Sam Neua (US$7, 10 hours, two a week) from the southern bus terminal.

Sainyabuli

Buses bound for Pak Khon (US$1.40, three hours, four daily), the Mekong River crossing for Sainyabuli Province, depart from a separate bus terminal off the road south to Tat Kuang Si. After crossing the Mekong by ferry to Tha Deua, buses on the other side continue on to Sainyabuli (US$0.60, one hour). See p183 for further details.

Getting Around

TO/FROM THE AIRPORT

From the airport into town jumbos (motorised three-wheeled taxis) or mini-trucks charge a uniform US$5.50 per vehicle, and up to six can share the ride. In the reverse direction you can usually charter an entire jumbo for between US$3 and US$4.

TO/FROM THE SPEEDBOAT LANDING

A shared jumbo into town from the speedboat landing in Ban Don costs around US$1 per person depending on your bargaining skills. To charter one, figure on US$4 to US$6.

LOCAL TRANSPORT

Most of the town is accessible on foot. Jumbos charge US$0.40 per kilometre in town, although they often ask foreigners for US$1 a ride.

Luang Prabang authorities have finally rescinded the ban on local motorcycle and bicycle hire. Motorcycles can now be hired from several shops in the town centre for US$5 a day. Bicycles are available from many of the same shops, as well as from guesthouses, for between US$1 and US$3 a day depending on the condition of the bike.

AROUND LUANG PRABANG

Pak Ou Caves

ກ້ຳປ່ອກອູ

About 25km by boat from Luang Prabang along the Mekong River, at the mouth of the Nam Ou, are the famous **Pak Ou caves** (admission US$1). Two caves in the lower part of a limestone cliff facing the river are crammed with Buddha images of all styles and sizes (but mostly classic Luang Prabang standing Buddhas). The lower cave, known as Tham Ting, is entered from the river by a series of steps and can easily be seen in daylight. Stairs to the left of Tham Ting lead around to the upper cave, Tham Phum, which is deeper and requires artificial light for viewing – be sure to bring a torch (flashlight) if you want to see both caves.

On the way to Pak Ou, most people have the boat stop at small villages on the banks of the Mekong. Opposite the caves at the mouth of the Nam Ou, in front of an impressive limestone cliff called Pha Hen, is a favourite spot for local fishers.

ROCK CLIMBING AT PAK OU

In 1999 a team of professional rock climbers developed over 20 bolted routes on huge limestone rock faces near Ban Pak Ou, across the Mekong River from the Pak Ou caves. The area should be visited only by experienced rock climbers and has routes for all levels, although most of the routes are in the 5.11 to 5.12 range (US grading system). Please be respectful to the local villagers and ask permission to climb. They are ready to show any visiting climbers the routes for a small fee.

VILLAGES NEAR PAK OU

The most common village stop on the way to the caves is **Ban Xang Hai**, which means Jar-Maker Village because at one time that was the cottage industry here. Nowadays the jars come from elsewhere, and the community of around 70 fills them with *lào-láo* made in the village. Australian archaeologists have excavated pots beneath the village that may be 2000 or more years old.

At **Ban Thin Hong**, opposite the jar village and close to Pak Ou, a cave excavated in early 2000 has yielded artefacts dating back 8000 years, including stone, bronze and metal tools, pottery, skeletons and fabrics.

During the late dry season (from January to April) villagers paddle out to sand bars in the middle of the Mekong and pan for gold using large wooden platters.

GETTING THERE & AWAY

You can hire boats to Pak Ou from Luang Prabang's charter boat landing on the Mekong River. A longtail boat costs US$15 for one to three people, US$20 for four to five people, including petrol. The trip takes two hours upriver, and one hour down, not including optional stops at villages. Speedboats from Ban Don (US$15, 30 minutes upriver and 20 to 25 minutes down) can carry up to six passengers and take up to two hours for the total trip.

Travel agencies and guesthouses around town advertise tours for US$5 per person.

You can also get to Pak Ou by jumbo. To the village of Ban Pak Ou it costs US$7 for one or two people, US$10 for three to four, or US$12 for up to eight. From here, you then take a ferry (US$1.50) to the caves.

Ban Phanom & Mouhot's Tomb

ບ້ານພະນົມ ແລະ ສຸສານທ່ານມູຫົດ

This Thai Lü village east of Luang Prabang, around 4km past Wat Pa Phon Phao to the northeast of town, is well known for cotton and silk hand-weaving. You can wander around the village to watch the weavers in action on their hand looms, or stop in at the textile centre to view a variety of potential purchases. For a while Ban Phanom prices were higher than in Luang Prabang, but these days Luang Prabang has gone much more upmarket and Ban Phanom textiles can be a good bargain.

Beyond Ban Phanom near the river stands the tomb of the French explorer Henri Mouhot, best known as the person who 'discovered' Angkor Wat. Mouhot perished of malaria in Luang Prabang on 10 November 1861, and the French erected a tomb over his grave six years later. The last entry in his journal was 'Have pity on me, O my God' and his engraved tomb was neglected until found by foreign aid staff in 1990. Mouhot's simple monument is about 4km along the Nam Khan from Ban Phanom; follow the road along the river until you see a sign on the left, descend a track towards the river, then walk about 300m along a path (upriver from the sign) to reach the whitewashed tomb.

GETTING THERE & AWAY

Many visitors ride hired bikes or motorbikes to Ban Phanom and Mouhot's tomb. If you're pedalling, note that the terrain is hilly, so don't forget to bring a bottle of drinking water. By motorbike it takes only around 40 minutes.

Săwngthăew from Luang Prabang to Ban Phanom leave from Talat Dala several times a day for US$0.70 per person.

Tat Kuang Si

ນ້ຳຕົກຕາດກວາງຊີ

This beautiful spot 32km south of town has a wide, many-tiered waterfall tumbling over limestone formations into a series of cool, turquoise pools. The lower level of the falls has been turned into a well-maintained **public park** (parking US$0.25, admission US$1.50) with shelters and picnic tables; some of the trees near the waterfall have been labelled. Vendors sell drinks and snacks. As you pass the entrance you'll notice a tall fence being erected to enclose part of the forest – this is to house a tiger that was confiscated from a poacher while still a cub.

A trail ascends through the forest along the left side of the falls to a second tier that is more private (most visitors stay below) and has a pool large enough for swimming and splashing around. A cave behind the falls here goes back 10m. For a view of the stream that feeds into the falls you can continue along a more slippery extension of the trail to the top of the falls. The best time to visit is between the end of the monsoon in November and the peak of the dry season in April.

On the way to Kuang Si you'll pass Ban Tat Paen, a scenic Khamu village with a cool stream, rustic dam and several miniature waterfalls. **Vanvisa 2 Guest House** (r US$1-3) is a simple Lao-style guesthouse in this village, operated by the owner of the Vanvisa Guest House in Luang Prabang.

GETTING THERE & AWAY

Freelance guides in Luang Prabang offer trips by jumbo for US$5 per person for two people, US$4 per person for three to five people, or US$3 for six to eight. An alternative to going by jumbo all the way would be to take a boat an hour (25km) down the Mekong and do a shorter jumbo ride over to the falls. Freelancers can arrange the latter trip for about the same cost as a straight jumbo trip.

Many visitors make their way to Tat Kuang Si by hired bicycle or motorcycle, stopping in scenic villages along the way.

Tat Sae
ບ້ວຕົກຕາດແຊ່

Found at a conjunction of the Huay Sae and the Nam Khan, the falls at Tat Sae feature multilevel limestone formations similar to those at Kuang Si except that the resulting pools are more numerous, the falls are shorter in height, and the site is much closer to Luang Prabang. Popular with local picnickers on weekends, this place is almost empty during the week.

A 35-minute, 15km jumbo ride south of town will take you to the turn-off from Rte 13, then 2km to the pristine Lao village of Ban Aen on the Nam Khan. Jumbo drivers will travel to Ban Aen for US$6.75 for one to two persons, US$8 for three to four, or

US$9 for up to eight persons, including waiting time in the village while you visit the falls for a few hours. You could also easily reach Ban Aen by bicycle – there's a sign reading 'Tat Se' at the Rte 13 turn-off.

From the riverbanks at Ban Aen you can hire a boat to the falls – only five minutes upstream – for US$1 return.

The falls are best visited from August to November when there is still an abundance of water in the pools.

NONG KHIAW
ໜອງຂຽວ
☎ 071

Anyone going by road or river between Luang Prabang and Phongsali Provinces stands a good chance of spending some time in Nong Khiaw, a market village on the west bank of the Nam Ou in northern Luang Prabang Province. Many travellers breeze through Nong Khiaw in favour of longer stays at Muang Ngoi Neua, although Nong Khiaw offers much of the same scenery yet fewer tourists.

Locals sometimes refer to Nong Khiaw as Muang Ngoi (the name of the surrounding district). As a result many visitors confuse this Muang Ngoi with the Muang Ngoi Neua – a town found about an hour north of Nong Khiaw by boat. The village on the opposite side of the river from Nong Khiaw, at the confluence of the Nam Ou and Nam Houn, is Ban Sop Houn.

In addition to Tham Pha Thok (see below), there are other caves in the vicinity of Nong Khiaw, and also a few Hmong villages within easy trekking distance.

Nong Khiaw and Ban Sop Houn have electricity from 6pm to 10pm.

Tham Pha Thok
ຖ້ຳຜາທົກ

The range of wooded karst around Nong Khiaw means there's more to do in the area than just wait for the next boat or bus out of town. A 40-minute walk will take you to Tham Pha Thok, a limestone cave where villagers lived during the Second Indochina War, and to a nearby waterfall. To find the cave, walk 2.5km east of the bridge along Rte 1, then look for a clearly visible cave mouth in a limestone cliff to your right, about 100m from the road. Descend along a path from the road to reach the cave.

Girl in traditional dress, Pha That Luang Festival (p80), Vientiane

Tuk-tuk (p275), Vientiane

Xieng Khuan (p76), near Vientiane

Luang Prabang (p111)

PETER TH

Novice monks, That Xieng Tung Festival (p169), Muang Sing

JULIET COOMBE

Endangered tiger (p48)

Boys playing, Muang Khua (p175)

BERNARD NA

RYAN FOX

Wat Xieng Thong (p118), Luang Prabang

Sleeping & Eating

Near the bridge and river landing are a number of rustic but charming and cheap guesthouses. Most of them are strung out along a short road that parallels the west riverbank. Typical opening hours for eateries are listed on p249.

NONG KHIAW

Phayboun Guest House (r US$1.50) Phayboun consists of a few rooms in a two-storey wooden house that's in better condition than most of the others in town. Each room has two beds, mosquito nets and fans. Toilet and cold shower facilities are shared.

Manypoon Guest House (r US$1.50) The friendly Manypoon offers rooms with mosquito net and shared bathroom downstairs. Its restaurant boasts one of the better local guesthouse kitchens.

Songnot Guest House (r US$1.50) Opposite the road that leads down to the boat landing, Songnot has simple rooms with shared facilities in a colourfully painted one-storey house.

Chittavong Guest House (r US$2) On the left just before crossing the bridge over the Nam Ou, you'll find this collection of thatched-roof huts behind Sengdao Restaurant.

Bouavieng Restaurant (meals US$1-2) This simple restaurant on Rte 1, not far from Chittavong Guest House, serves a variety of fairly good Lao rice and noodle dishes.

There are noodle stands across the road from Bouavieng, near the river.

BAN SOP HOUN

Sunset Guest House (s/d US$1.50/2) This simple Lao-style wooden house on stilts stands on the east bank of the Nam Ou, a short walk from the bridge. Simple rooms in a rickety bamboo-thatch house come with mattresses on the floor, mosquito nets and shared outside bathroom. There's a common sitting area with floor cushions where you can watch the sunset. Good Lao and Thai food is available.

Sunrise Guest House (r US$1) The relatively new Sunrise consists of a wooden longhouse next to the Nam Ou Bridge. The simple veranda offers perhaps the best Nam Ou and mountain views on either side of the river.

Pha Noi Guest House (r US$1) and **Paradise Bamboo Guest House** (US$1) nearby are second-

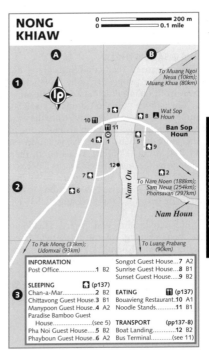

choice spots to be considered only if everything else is full.

Chan-a-Mar (www.wowlao.com; bungalow US$100) Owned by a collector of rare Bhutanese textiles, this semiexclusive resort consists of two spacious open-air 'jungalows' overlooking the Nam Houn – a tributary of the Nam Ou for which Ban Sop Houn is named – with private open-air hot-water bathrooms. Rates include a large breakfast along with evening cocktails and appetisers in the Dragon Room, a hexagonal building poised at the junction of the Nam Ou and Nam Houn.

Getting There & Away

Rte 1 crosses the river here via a steel bridge. Rte 13 north from Luang Prabang meets Rte 1 about 33km west of town at Pak Mong.

BOAT

Boat travel along the Nam Ou south of Nong Khiaw has been eclipsed by travel along the improved Rte 13. See p133 for information on chartered river boats between Luang Prabang and Nong Khiaw.

Slow boats to Muang Khua (US$7, 12 hours) leave once or twice in the morning.

BUS & SĂWNGTHĂEW

With improved road conditions along Rte 13, far more people arrive by bus than by boat from Luang Prabang and Udomxai.

Săwngthăew going to Udomxai (US$2.50, three hours, three daily) leave from the west end of the bridge. You can also take one of the more frequent *săwngthăew* southwest to Pak Mong (US$1.80, two hours), then change to another *săwngthăew* to Udomxai (US$1.50, two to three hours from Pak Mong). There are also buses heading to and arriving from Luang Prabang (US$1.60, four hours, two daily).

If you're heading east towards Hua Phan or Xieng Khuang, you can get a *săwngthăew* as far as Vieng Kham (US$1.30, three hours, six daily), from where you can connect to a *săwngthăew* to Sam Neua (US$3, six hours) or Nam Noen (US$1.50, three hours), or all the way to Phonsavan (US$7.50, 12 hours, one daily).

MUANG NGOI NEUA
ເມືອງງອຍເໜືອ

An hour north of Nong Khiaw via river, tucked away on a river peninsula cut off from regular roadways by a steep mountain range, the village of Muang Ngoi Neua has become a traveller centre known for its cheap accommodation and do-it-yourself trekking. The village's natural isolation means there are no motor vehicles. Narrow dirt footpaths lined with coconut palms, along with the common sight of fisherfolk mending their nets, create an anomalous South-Seas ambience.

Many of the people who settled Nong Khiaw to the south originally hailed from here. After Rte 1 was built by the Chinese, and especially after the construction of a bridge allowed the roadway to span the Nam Ou, residents moved downriver to Nong Khiaw to take advantage of easier access to markets for their annual crops and fishing catch.

Originally known simply as Muang Ngoi, nowadays it's often referred to as Muang Ngoi Neua (Northern Muang Ngoi) to distinguish the village from the 'new' Muang Ngoi, ie Nong Khiaw. In size, it hardly qualifies as a *meuang* any more, and

hence it is also sometimes referred to as 'Ban Ngoi' or 'Ban Ngoi Neua'. The word *ngoi* itself means 'cape' or 'small peninsula', a reference to its geographic situation.

Like most river villages in Laos, Muang Ngoi Neua's basic layout parallels the river on which the village depends for its traditional livelihoods, fishing and farming. A new addition to the local economy is tourism, and, in fact, when we asked the locals what was the main source of income they all replied 'guesthouses'.

Electric power is available only from 7pm to 10pm. There's a private moneychanging service in the village but the exchange rates are much lower than what you can get in Vientiane, Luang Prabang or Huay Xai.

Sights & Activities
TEMPLES

Muang Ngoi, which may date back to the 15th century, once had three Buddhist monasteries – Wat Neua at the northern end of town, Wat Kang in the middle and Wat Tai in the south. All three were destroyed during the Second Indochina War, but among the remains of **Wat Tai** you can still see the main pediment for the original *sĭm*, as well as a pedestal for an old Buddha that once sat at one end of the *sĭm*. That image has long disappeared, to be replaced by a cement Buddha and a few smaller wooden Buddhas beneath a little tin-roof shelter at one end of the pediment. The original brick-and-stucco entry stairway to the slightly elevated wat grounds is also still standing.

Of Wat Kang there appears to be virtually no trace.

Wat Neua, at the northern end of the village not far from the main boat landing, has been rebuilt. As at Wat Tai, the ground supporting the monastery was artificially raised to protect the facilities from flooding. Here again you can see the original steps ascending the raised earth. It appears the current *sĭm* may have been rebuilt atop the original brick-and-stucco pediment. Now the only functioning wat in the village, it has been renamed Wat Okat Muang Ngoi.

CAVES

Behind the village and its rice fields, away from the river, undulates a curtain of mountain and cliffs riddled with caves, streams and forest. Two caves can easily be visited in under an hour's walk. At the southern end of the village, turn left (east) in front of Kaikaew Restaurant, and follow the path through a large rural schoolyard and into an area of brush and secondary forest. Just past the schoolyard is a shelter where village volunteers collect an admission fee of US$0.25 from each person.

After a pleasant 30- to 40-minute walk you'll come to a crystal-clear stream running into **Tham Kang** (Middle Cave), a large limestone cavern entrance on your left. You can either wade into the cave via the stream – which can become rather deep in spots during the rainy season – or climb a limestone bank along the left side of the stream. The roof of this cave is at least 30m high for some distance, after which the floor descends into darkness.

About an additional five minutes' walk along the same trail is **Tham Pha Kaew** (Holy Image Cave), with a much smaller entry and a small stone Buddha image to one side. According to Speleo Nederland, a Dutch caving group that has explored both caves, Tham Kang and Tham Pha Kaew are connected via a subterranean passageway.

Beyond the caves you can easily walk to mixed Lao and Khamu villages of **Huay Bo** (one hour's walk), **Huay Sen** (1½ hours) and **Ban Na** (20 minutes from Huay Sen). If you fancy a village stay, try the **Jungle Face Guest House** (US$0.50) in Huay Bo.

TAT MOK

Twenty minutes downriver by boat is a trail that leads to a series of falls called Tat Mok. The walk from the landing to the falls takes about an hour. The third in the series reaches 40m tall but you'll find pools for a cool dip at all three.

Sleeping & Eating

Most guesthouses here are strung out along the main footpath that leads from the landing and down through the centre of the village. All consist of either bamboo-thatch huts or bamboo-thatch cubicles side by side in a longhouse. All are basic, and none offer hot water or private toilet and shower. Typical opening hours for eateries are listed on p249.

Lattanavongsa Guest House (s/d US$0.70/1) One of the first guesthouses you come to after

getting off at the boat landing, this is also one of the cleaner ones, and has a decent restaurant.

Poupha Guest House (US$1) This is a good choice, with bamboo-thatch huts on stilts overlooking the river.

River View Bungalows & Restaurant (US$1) This is a another good choice that's similar to Poupha, plus it's newer than the other choices in Muang Ngoi Neua and thus in better condition.

Chanthalee (r US$0.50) Past the Lattanavongsa, walking into the village, you'll come to Chanthalee, which is about as cheap and basic as it gets in Muang Ngoi.

Kaikeo Guest House (r US$1) This guest house has moved to a new set of bungalows with the best river view in Muang Ngoi, near the mouth of the Nam Ngoi.

Three places clustered near each other, the **Aloun** (US$0.50), the **Wassana** (r US$0.50) and the **Vita** (r US$0.50), all have basic wooden rooms.

A few eateries have opened in the village to serve basic Lao and Western fare for travellers, including **Sky** (meals US$0.60-0.80) and **Shanti** (meals US$0.60-0.80). **Sengdala** (meals US$1.50-2) supplements the usual rice, noodles and omelette menus with cheese-filled baguettes.

Getting There & Away

Regular boats ply between Nong Khiaw and Muang Ngoi Neua (US$1.50, one hour). Departures are most frequent in the morning, with the last boat leaving Nong Khiaw at around 3pm or 4pm.

NAM BAK & PAK MONG

ບ້ານບາກ ແລະ ປາກມອງ

These two towns, respectively 23km and 33km west of Nong Khiaw, are little more than supply depots along Rte 1 between the Nam Ou and Udomxai. Pak Mong at the junction of Rtes 1 and 13 has eclipsed Nam Bak since the sealing of Rte 13 north from Luang Prabang. Both towns have post offices, guesthouses (one in Pak Mong, two in Nam Bak) and noodle shops, but Pak Mong is the place to make bus connections: west to Udomxai (US$1.50, two to three hours) and Luang Nam Tha (US$2.50, six hours); east to Hua Phan and Xieng Khuang Provinces; and south to Luang Prabang (US$1.20, two hours).

XIENG KHUANG PROVINCE

Flying into Xieng Khuang Province, one is first struck by the beauty of high green mountains, rugged karst formations and verdant valleys. But as the plane begins to descend, you notice how much of the province is pockmarked with bomb craters in which little or no vegetation grows. Along with Hua Phan, Xieng Khuang is one of the northern provinces that was most devastated by the war. Virtually every town and village in the province was bombed at some point between 1964 and 1973. It has also been the site of numerous ground battles over the last 150 years.

The province has a total population of around 200,000 people, mostly comprised of lowland Lao, Vietnamese, Thai Dam, Hmong and Phuan. The original capital, Xieng Khuang, was almost totally bombed out, so the capital was moved to Phonsavan (often spelt Phonsavanh) after the 1975 change of government. Near Phonsavan is the mysterious Thong Hai Hin (Plain of Jars).

The altitude (average 1200m) in central Xieng Khuang, including Phonsavan and the Plain of Jars, means an excellent climate – not too hot in the hot season, not too cold in the cool season and not too wet in the rainy season. The coldest months are December and January, when visitors should come with sweaters or pullovers, plus a light jacket for nights and early mornings.

History

Although briefly a part of the Lan Xang kingdom in the 16th century, Xieng Khuang has more often than not been an independent principality or a vassal state of Vietnam called Tran Ninh. From the early 19th century until 1975, central Xieng Khuang – including the Plain of Jars – was a recurring battle zone. In 1832 the Vietnamese captured the Phuan king of Xieng Khuang, publicly executed him in Hué and made the kingdom a prefecture of Annam, forcing people to adopt Vietnamese dress and customs. Chinese Haw also ravaged Xieng Khuang in the late

19th century, which is one of the reasons that Xieng Khuang accepted Siamese and French protection later that century.

Major skirmishes between the Free Lao and the Viet Minh took place from 1945 to 1946, and as soon as the French left Indochina the North Vietnamese commenced a build-up of troops to protect Hanoi's rear flank. By 1964 the North Vietnamese and Pathet Lao had at least 16 anti-aircraft emplacements on the Plain of Jars, along with a vast underground arsenal. By the end of the 1960s this major battlefield was undergoing almost daily bombing by American planes as well as ground combat between the US-trained and supplied Hmong army and the forces of the North Vietnamese and Pathet Lao. Among the US military in Laos the area was known as 'PDJ', an acronym for the French term Plaine de Jarres.

A single 1969 air campaign – part of the secret war waged in Laos by the US Air Force and the CIA – annihilated at least 1500 buildings in the town of Xieng Khuang, along with some 2000 more on the Plain of Jars, permanently erasing many small towns and villages off the map. Continuous saturation bombing forced virtually the entire population to live in caves; 'The bombs fell like a man sowing seed' according to one surviving villager.

North Vietnamese troops did their share of damage on the ground, destroying nearby Muang Sui, a city famous for its temples, and virtually all towns or villages held by the Royal Lao Army (RLA) in the west of the province.

Now that eastern Xieng Khuang is peaceful, village life has returned to a semblance of normality, although the enormous amount of war debris and unexploded bombs (UXO) spread across the central and eastern areas of the province are a deadly legacy that will remain here for generations to come.

PHONSAVAN

ໂພນສະຫວັນ

☎ 061 / pop 57,000

Xieng Khuang's new capital district grew tremendously in the 1990s. It's now a large town crisscrossed with paved and unpaved streets lined with relatively new concrete structures, two markets, a rash of government buildings and a bank, and several modest hotels and guesthouses. The town itself holds virtually nothing of interest but serves as a centre for anyone visiting the Plain of Jars or other sights in the area.

Traditionally, the area surrounding Phonsavan and the former capital of Xieng Khuang has been a centre of Phuan language and culture (part of the Thai-Kadai family, like Lao, Siamese and Thai tribal). The local Vietnamese presence continues to increase and you'll hear the Vietnamese language in the streets almost as frequently as Lao and Phuan.

On some current Lao maps, Phonsavan is labelled 'Muang Pek' *(meuang pąek)*; outside the province most Lao (including Lao Airlines) still call the capital 'Xieng Khuang'.

Information
EMERGENCY
Ambulance (☎ 195)
Fire (☎ 190)
Police (☎ 191)

INTERNET ACCESS
There's an Internet café east of the Phonsavanh Hotel. Rates here are a little higher in Phonsavan than in Vientiane or Luang Prabang.

MEDICAL SERVICES
The Lao-Mongolian Hospital on the road to the airport is not too bad as far as Lao provincial hospitals go, although it doesn't really have the facilities for a major trauma.

MONEY
You can cash travellers cheques at the Lao Development Bank (opposite the Phu Doi Hotel), but cash advances against credit cards are not available. The bank also has a more convenient exchange office opposite the post office in the town centre.

POST
The post office (on the main road near the two markets) has a domestic phone service that has improved greatly since a satellite connection was established.

TOURIST INFORMATION
Contrary to its official-sounding name, the 'Provincial Tourist Office' is run by a private concession attempting to corner all tourism out of Phonsavan. If you ask about visiting the Plain of Jars, for example, they'll try to persuade you that you can only go as part of a tour organised by their office. This is untrue; anyone may visit the Plain of Jars via private vehicle, public transport or with any travel agency in town. The agency does distribute a useful free map of Phonsavan.

TRAVEL AGENCIES
Indochina Travel (☎ 312121; Phoukham Guest House)
Sousath Travel (☎ 312031; www.malyht.laotel.com; Maly Hotel) The best single source of information on local sights and travel logistics, Sousath also provides excellent guide services.

UXO IN XIENG KHUANG

Unexploded munitions, mortar shells, white phosphorous canisters (used to mark bomb targets), land mines and cluster bombs of French, Chinese, American, Russian and Vietnamese manufacture left behind by nearly 100 years of warfare have affected up to half of the population in terms of land deprivation and accidental injury or death. A preponderance of the reported unexploded ordnance (UXO) accidents that have occurred in Xieng Khuang happened during the first five years immediately following the end of the war, when many villagers returned to areas of the province they had evacuated years earlier. Today about 40% of the estimated 60 casualties per year are children, who continue to play with found UXO – especially the harmless-looking, ball-shaped 'bomb light units' (BLUs, or bombies) left behind by cluster bombs – in spite of public warnings.

Hunters also open or attempt to open UXO to extract gunpowder and steel pellets for their long-barrelled muskets – a risky ploy that has claimed many casualties. Several groups are working steadily to clear the province of UXO, including the Lao National UXO Programme (UXO Lao), financed by a UN trust fund that has significantly increased the availability of multi-lateral aid for this purpose.

NORTHERN LAOS

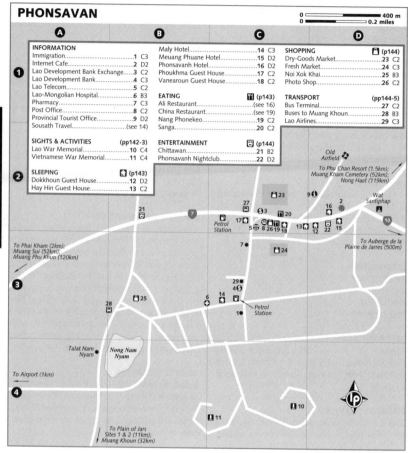

PHONSAVAN

0 ——— 400 m
0 ——— 0.2 miles

INFORMATION	
Immigration.........................1 C3
Internet Cafe......................2 D2
Lao Development Bank Exchange.....3 C2
Lao Development Bank................4 C3
Lao Telecom........................5 C2
Lao-Mongolian Hospital..............6 B3
Pharmacy............................7 C3
Post Office........................8 C2
Provincial Tourist Office..........9 D2
Sousath Travel....................(see 14)

SIGHTS & ACTIVITIES	(pp142-3)
Lao War Memorial...................10 C4
Vietnamese War Memorial............11 C4

SLEEPING	(p143)
Dokkhoun Guest House...............12 D2
Hay Hin Guest House................13 C2

Maly Hotel........................14 C3
Meuang Phuane Hotel................15 D2
Phonsavanh Hotel...................16 D2
Phoukhma Guest House...............17 C2
Vanearoun Guest House..............18 C2

EATING	(p143)
Ali Restaurant....................(see 16)
China Restaurant..................(see 19)
Nang Phonekeo......................19 C2
Sanga.............................20 C2

ENTERTAINMENT	(p144)
Chittawan.........................21 B2
Phonsavanh Nightclub...............22 D2

SHOPPING	(p144)
Dry-Goods Market...................23 C2
Fresh Market.......................24 C3
Noi Xok Khai......................25 B3
Photo Shop.........................26 C2

TRANSPORT	(pp144-5)
Bus Terminal.......................27 C2
Buses to Muang Khoun...............28 B3
Lao Airlines......................29 C3

Old Airfield

To Phu Chan Resort (1.5km);
Muang Kham Cemetery (52km);
Nong Haet (119km)

Wat Santiphap

To Phai Kham (2km);
Muang Sui (52km);
Muang Phu Khun (120km)

Petrol Station

To Auberge de la
Plaine de Jarres (500m)

Petrol Station

Talat Nam Nyam

Nong Nam Nyam

To Airport (1km)

To Plain of Jars
Sites 1 & 2 (11km);
Muang Khoun (32km)

Dangers & Annoyances

Take care when walking in the fields around Phonsavan as UXO are common. Muddy areas are sometimes dotted with 'bomblets' – fist-sized explosives that are left over from cluster bombs dropped in the 1970s.

The western third or so of Xieng Khuang Province – mainly west of the Nam Ngum river – remains one of the nation's few hotspots of Hmong guerrilla activity. However, Rte 7 west of Muang Sui, which until recently was considered unsafe for ordinary travel, appears to be safe nowadays. If you plan to travel along Rte 7 west to Muang Phu Khun (at the junction of Rte 13, which goes to Vientiane and Luang Prabang), check locally to ensure it remains safe.

Sights

Just south of town are two major war memorials, each standing on a different hill-top about 1km apart. One is Lao and the other Vietnamese, both in the shape of Lao-style stupas. The hill-top with the **Lao War Memorial** (☼ sunrise-sunset) affords sweeping views of Phonsavan. Built in 1998, the monument is inscribed with the slogan 'The nation remembers your sacrifice'. Large, polished, granite slabs standing nearby bear the inscribed names of PL soldiers who died in the area. The stupalike monument allegedly contains the bones of 4500 war dead.

At the **Vietnamese War Memorial** (☼ sunrise-sunset), the faux stupa contains the bones of Vietnamese soldiers who died in battle in northeastern Laos, and is emblazoned with the inscription 'Lao-Vietnamese solidarity and generosity forever'. If the gates are locked, wait for a caretaker to come along and unlock them.

East of town is the large **Muang Khan Cemetery** that is unique in that it mixes together Thai Dam animist tombs, Catholic headstones and Lao *thâat kádµuk* (Buddhist reliquary).

Sleeping

BUDGET

Hay Hin Guest House (☎ 312252; tw/tr US$3) The simple but dependable Hay Hin, a wooden place on the main street near the market, has basic two-bed rooms and one three-bed room with mosquito nets and shared cold-water bathroom. The mattresses and walls are thin, but the bathrooms are clean.

Vanearoun Guest House (☎ 312070; r US$4-5) Near the post office, this two-storey guest-house is clean and relatively quiet.

Dokkhoun Guest House (☎ 312189; r US$4-10) This two-storey white building with a bal-cony offers a small number of rooms with mosquito nets and good mattresses. The more expensive rooms have private showers.

Meuang Phuane Hotel (☎ 312046; r US$6) This L-shaped hotel now rents only a few rooms in the front to foreigners, with those in the back reserved for Lao.

Saing Tavanh (☎ 211131; r US$4-5) This large two-storey building east of the Meuang Phuane offers 10 fairly clean rooms with hard mattresses. The more expensive rooms have attached bath, and of those, some have hot water, some don't – the asking price is the same. You can negotiate a discount for rooms without bathroom, especially for a single.

Phonsavanh Hotel (☎ 312206; r US$5) The three-storey Phonsavanh has a fancy marble front, but ordinary rooms. Those in the interior of the hotel are windowless. There's an Indian restaurant downstairs.

Phoukham Guest House (☎ 312121; r US$4-5) The rooms in this shophouse-style building are nothing special but the staff can be very helpful with travel info. Ground-floor rooms are less expensive than those upstairs.

MID-RANGE & TOP END

Maly Hotel (☎ 312031, mobile 020-561031; www.malyht .laotel.com; r US$8-30) A kilometre southwest of the market/bus-terminal area, towards the airport and the Plain of Jars (Site 1), the well-run Maly offers 30 comfortable rooms. The Maly Hotel is the only place in Xieng Khuang Province that accepts credit cards (Visa only). Rates vary according to the size of the room and whether they have a TV and/or balcony. A cosy restaurant downstairs has some of the best Lao and Western cooking in town, especially if you order in advance. The owner speaks good English, German and French, and can arrange tours to the Plain of Jars, local villages, Tham Piu, Muang Sui, Sam Neua and Long Cheng (former site the CIA's infamous mountain base during the Second Indochina War).

Auberge de la Plaine de Jarres (Phu Pha Daeng Hotel; ☎ /fax 312044; s/d/tr US$40/50/60) On a ridge above the town and surrounding valley is the Auberge de la Plaine de Jarres, a quiet spot with 15 two-room cottages with fireplace and hot-water bathroom. A separate dining/ sitting area with a fireplace and European-lodge ambience overlooks the valley.

Phu Chan Resort (☎ 312264; s/d US$35/40) Also perched on a hill on the outskirts of town, the Phu Chan features spacious two-room pine bungalows on a hill-top, some with a good view of the cemetery and town.

Eating

Typical opening hours for eateries are listed on p249.

Maly Hotel (meals US$1-5) This hotel has the best food in town, especially during the rainy season when *hét wâi* (wild matsutake mushrooms) are plentiful.

Sanga Restaurant (Sa-Nga; ☎ 312318; meals $1-4) The clean and well-run Sanga, near the market and post office, offers an extensive menu of Chinese, Thai and Lao food, including good *yám* (a tart, spicy Thai-style salad), *tôm yám* (spicy lemon grass–based soup), *khào khùa* (fried rice) and *fŏe*, plus a few Western food items.

Nang Phonekeo (☎ 312292; meals US$0.50-1) This friendly noodle shop serves the best *fŏe* in town.

China Restaurant (☎ 312220; meals US$0.80-2) Near Nang Phonekeo stands this relatively new, nondescript-looking restaurant with good Chinese fare.

Ali Restaurant (meals US$0.70-1.60) On the ground floor of the Phonsavanh Hotel, Ali prepares a long menu of Indian dishes.

Entertainment

Three typically Lao *bąnthóeng* (nightclubs) in town feature Lao bands that play a mixture of Lao, Thai, Chinese and Vietnamese pop. **Phonsavanh Nightclub**, opposite the hotel of the same name, is the most popular due to its central location. **Phai Kham**, 2km west of the bus terminal, is smaller and cosier but can be rather dead on weeknights. **Chittawan**, a little closer in on the same road, attracts the most youthful Lao crowd.

Shopping

Dry-goods market (7am-6pm) At this market, near the bus stop, you'll find a small but sometimes interesting selection of textiles and other handicrafts, particularly silver, much of it turned out by the Hmong. Diminutive Phuan umbrellas, made of oiled paper and bamboo, can also be seen here, along with woven grass 'raincoats'. A huge Chinese market under construction on the highway west of town is supposed to subsume this market eventually.

Noi Xok Khai, a small handicraft shop near the Maly Hotel, on the way to the Plain of Jars, sells textiles, silver, woodcarvings and various other locally made items.

The **fresh market** behind the post office stocks exotic fruits you won't typically see elsewhere in Laos, such as Chinese pear. Other local delicacies include *nok ąen dąwng* (swallows stored whole in jars until they ferment), and *hét wâi* (wild matsutake mushrooms), which grow wild around Xieng Khuang and fetch high prices in Japan.

Getting There & Away

AIR

Lao Airlines (312027), located next to Lao Development Bank, flies to/from Vientiane (one way/return US$46/87, 30 minutes, daily). During high-season months (December to March), it may add flights to/from Luang Prabang (US$37/70, 40 minutes). It's a good idea to reconfirm your return ticket upon arrival.

BUS

At the moment all buses leave from a bus terminal opposite the dry goods market, but both the market and the terminal for interprovincial buses are slated to be moved about 5km west of town along Rte 7 within a year or two.

All buses with single daily departures leave between 7.30am and 8am.

Sam Neua

Buses run regularly between Phonsavan and Sam Neua (US$4, seven hours, two daily) along Rte 7 and Rte 6. You can also take a bus as far as the junction of Rte 6 and Rte 1, near the town of Nam Noen (US$2, three hours, four daily), and change to another bus going to Sam Neua, for about the same total cost.

Vientiane & Luang Prabang

Rte 7 is paved all the way now, so travel times have improved immensely. You can reach Xieng Khuang by road from Vientiane (ordinary US$6, 11 hours; VIP US$8, eight hours, one daily) or Luang Prabang (US$6, 10 hours, one daily) via Rtes 13 and 7. The junction for the two roads is at Muang Phu Khun, about 38km north of Kasi. There is a guesthouse in Muang Phu Khun (US$3, four to five hours) so you could break your journey here.

Paksan

Phonsavan is linked with Paksan in Bolikhamsai Province by a road in deplorable condition – especially south of Tha Thom (102km from Phonsavan), where it's only passable in the dry season.

From February to June it's possible to go by road to Tha Thom, then by boat to Paksan (chartered boat US$75, three days downriver, five or six upriver) along the Nam San.

Buses Within Xieng Khuang Province

From the bus terminal opposite the dry-goods market, there are public buses to Muang Kham (US$1.50, two hours, 52km, four daily) and Nong Haet (US$2, three hours, 119km, four daily), plus Russian or Chinese trucks to Muang Sui (US$1, one hour, 52km, three daily) and Nam Noen (US$3, four hours, 138km, two daily).

Other destinations include Lat Khai (Plain of Jars Site 3; US$0.80, 30 minutes, 25km, one daily) and Muang Khoun (US$0.70, 30 minutes, 32km, six daily).

There are also share taxis – mostly old Volgas or Toyotas – to/from Muang Kham (US$1 per person) and Muang Khoun (US$1). All of these prices fluctuate with the availability of petrol from Vietnam (the petrol upon which Phonsavan depends).

Getting Around

Jumbos are the main form of public transport in town. The price anywhere within a 3km radius is US$0.50 per person. A ride to the airport will cost US$1.50 per person.

Cars and 4WDs can also be hired through the guide services at Sousath Tourism at the Maly Hotel or through just about any guesthouse or hotel for jaunts outside of town.

At the moment it's forbidden to hire motorcycles and bicycles in Phonsavan but locals suggest this may change soon. If so, you could easily visit all three Plain of Jars sites by bike or motorcycle.

PLAIN OF JARS

ທົ່ງໄຫຫີນ

The Plain of Jars is a large area extending around Phonsavan from the southwest to the northeast, where huge jars of unknown origin are scattered about in over a dozen groupings. Despite local myth (see Plain of Jars below), the jars have been fashioned from solid stone, most from a tertiary conglomerate known as molasse (akin to sandstone), and a few from granite. 'Quarries' (actually boulder fields) west of Muang Sui have been discovered containing half-finished jars. Apparently the jars were carved from solid boulders of varying sizes, which goes a long way to explain the many difference sizes and shapes.

Many of the smaller jars have been taken away by various collectors, but there are still several hundred or so on the plain in the five major sites (out of the 20 or so known to exist) that are considered worth visiting.

Site 1 (Thong Hai Hin; admission US$0.70), the biggest and most accessible site, is 15km southwest of Phonsavan and features 250 jars that weigh mostly from 600kg to one tonne each. The largest jar weighs as much as six tonnes and is said to have been the

PLAIN OF JARS

Among the most enigmatic sights in Laos are several meadowlike areas close to Phonsavan littered with large stone jars. Quite a few theories have been advanced as to the functions of the jars – that they were used as sarcophagi, or as wine fermenters or for rice storage – but there is no evidence confirming one theory over the other. Lying around are the stone lids for a few of the jars. White quartzite rocks have also been found lying next to some of the jars, along with vases that may have contained human remains.

Madeleine Colani, a noted French archaeologist who spent three years studying the Plain of Jars in the 1930s, found a human-shaped bronze figure in one of the jars at Site 1, as well as tiny stone beads. The current whereabouts of these cultural artefacts and other Colani discoveries – photographs of which exist in her 1935 *Megalithes du Haut Laos (Megaliths of Highland Laos)* – are unknown. You can see the relief of a human figure carved onto jar No 217 at Site 1 – a feature Colani missed. Aerial photographic evidence suggests that a thin 'track' of jars may link the various jar sites in Xieng Khuang, and some researchers hope future excavations will uncover sealed jars whose contents may be relatively intact.

The jars are commonly said to be 2000 years old, but in the absence of any organic material associated with the jars – eg bones or food remains – there is no reliable way to date them. The jars may be associated with the equally mysterious stone megaliths ('menhirs' in Colani's words) found off Rte 6 on the way north to Sam Neua, and/or with large Dongson drum-shaped stone objects discovered in Luang Prabang Province. All of the unanswered questions regarding the Plain of Jars make this area ripe for archaeological investigation, a proceeding that has been slowed by years of war and by the presence of unexploded bombs (UXO).

Meanwhile, local legend says that in the 6th century a cruel chieftain named Chao Angka ruled the area as part of Muang Pakan. Sensitive to the plight of Pakan villagers, the Lao-Thai hero Khun Jeuam supposedly came down from southern China and deposed Angka. To celebrate his victory, Khun Jeuam had the jars constructed for the fermentation of rice wine. According to this version, the jars were cast from a type of cement that was made from buffalo skin, sand, water and sugar cane, and fired in a nearby cave kiln. A limestone cave on the Plain of Jars that has smoke holes in the top is said to have been this kiln (the Pathet Lao used this same cave as a shelter during the war).

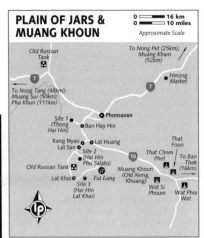

PLAIN OF JARS & MUANG KHOUN

0 ——— 16 km
0 ——— 10 miles
Approximate Scale

must hike around 2km along rice paddy dykes and up the hill.

Many smaller sites can also be seen in Muang Kham district, but none of them contain more than 40 or so jars. Only Sites 1, 2 and 3 are considered to be reasonably free of UXO. Even at these sites you should take care to stay within the jar areas and stick to worn footpaths.

Getting There & Away

You can charter a jumbo from Phonsavan to Site 1, 15km from the Phonsavan market, for US$5 return including waiting time, for up to six people. For Sites 2 and 3 your best bet is to arrange a 4WD and driver through one of the guesthouses or hotels. There is a bus from Phonsavan to Site 3 (US$0.80, 30 minutes, one daily).

Sousath Travel (p141) at the Maly Hotel in Phonsavan charges US$50 for all-day transport and guiding to Site 1 plus Muang Khoun (old Xieng Khuang) for up to four people. For a bit more, you can choose a programme that takes you to Sites 2 and 3, with stops along the way at Ban Sieng Di near Site 3 and a Hmong village in the area of Muang Kham.

PHONSAVAN TO NONG HAET

Rte 7 heads east from Phonsavan to north Vietnam via Muang Kham and Nong Haet (see Map left).

Near Km 27 en route to Muang Kham (northern side of the road) is **Nong Pet**, a picturesque spring surrounded by rice fields; it's said to be the source of the Nam Ngum.

A sizable **Hmong market** (7am-7pm Sun) is held about 30km east of Phonsavan on the way to Muang Kham. Between Muang Kham and Nong Haet you may notice Thai Dam funerary shrines along the way – large white tombs with prayer flags, offerings of food and a pile of the departed's worldly possessions.

Muang Kham is little more than a rustic highway trading post, but there are several jar sites in the vicinity (see p145). About 56km from Phonsavan on the way to Nong Haet, the large Hmong village of **Ban Na Sala** lies on a hillside 2km off the road. Further east along Rte 7, 119km from Phonsavan, is the market town of Nong Haet, which is situated only 13km short of the Vietnamese border.

victory cup of mythical King Jeuam and so is called Hai Jeuam. The site has two pavilions and restrooms that were built for a visit by Thailand's crown prince.

Near Site 1 is a Lao air force base. Large bottle-shaped clearings on surrounding hill slopes have traps at the 'bottle top' for snaring *nok qen* (swallows) – the birds are apparently attracted by the opportunity to take dust baths. The captured swallows are fermented whole in earthen jars and eaten as a local delicacy (see the fresh market p144).

Two other jar sites are readily accessible by road from Phonsavan. **Site 2** (Hai Hin Phu Salato; admission US$0.70), about 25km south of town, features 90 jars spread across two adjacent hillsides. Vehicles can reach the base of the hills, so it's only a short if steep walk to the jars.

More impressive is 150-jar **Site 3** (Hai Hin Lat Khai; admission US$0.70). It's about 10km south of Site 2 (or 35km from Phonsavan) on a scenic hill-top near the charming Lao village of Ban Xieng Di in Lat Khai district, southeast of Phonsavan. Ban Xieng Di contains a small monastery where the remains of Buddha images that were damaged in the war have been displayed. The villagers, who live in unusually large houses compared with those of the average lowland Lao, grow rice, sugar cane, avocado and banana. Villagers can lead you on a short hike to a local waterfall called **Tat Lang** (admission US$0.50). To reach the jar site you

See p144 for information on bus and share taxi travel to Muang Kham and Nong Haet.

Mineral Springs

ບໍ່ນ້ຳຮ້ອນ

Two hot mineral springs can be visited near Muang Kham. **Baw Nyai** (admission US$.50; ☺ 9am-7pm) is the larger of the two and lies 18km east of Muang Kham, 51km from Phonsavan. It has been developed as a resort with bungalows and bathing facilities, and was originally built by Kaysone Phomvihane's wife for visiting politicians. The spring source is in a heavily wooded area where several bamboo pipes have been rigged so that you can bathe nearby. The bungalows here are currently undergoing renovation but the baths are open.

Baw Noi (Little Spring) feeds into a stream just a few hundred metres off Rte 7, a couple of kilometres before Baw Nyai on the way from Muang Kham. You can sit in the stream where the hot spring water mixes with the cool stream water and 'adjust' the temperature by moving from one area to another.

Tham Piu

ຖ້ຳປິ່ວ

At this cave near the former village of Ban Na Meun, an estimated 200 to 400 people were killed when a fighter plane fired a single rocket into the cave during the Second Indochina War. A plaque identifies the date as 24 November 1968 but other accounts claim the incident occurred in December 1969. The floor of the large cave, in the side of a limestone cliff, is littered with rubble from the partial cave-in caused by the rocket, as well as with minor debris left from the two-storey shelter built into the cave. Government propaganda says many of those who died in the bombing were Lao women and children, but another version of events says that it was a makeshift Vietnamese hospital where troop casualties were treated. Adding credence to the latter story is the fact that Vietnamese officials visited the cave in the 1980s, removed virtually all of the human remains and artefacts, and took them back to Vietnam.

Although Tham Piu is certainly a moving sight, the journey to the cave is the main attraction, since it passes several Hmong and Thai Dam villages and involves a bit of hiking in the forest. From the cave mouth

---

CROSSING THE VIETNAMESE BORDER AT NAM KHAN & NAM CAN

The Nam Khan–Nam Can crossing became an official international border crossing in 2003, but so far few people aside from Lao and Vietnamese seem to use it. Coming up to Nam Can (200km north of Vinh) from the Vietnamese side is quite a journey, with winding mountain roads as you approach the lip of the Plain of Jars. After exiting Vietnam, you'll enter Laos at Nam Khan, 13km east of Nong Haet via Rte 7. Tourist visas are available on arrival for US$30. There is no accommodation in either Nam Khan or Nong Haet, so count on moving westward to Phonsavan by bus (US$2, three to four hours, four daily). Between bus departures you may be able to charter a private car for between US$30 and US$40.

---

is a view of the forest and the plains below. A stream and small irrigation dam at the base of the cliff is picturesque. Another cave known as **Tham Piu Song** (Tham Piu 2) can be found a little higher up on the same cliff. This one has a small entrance that opens up into a large cavern; since it wasn't bombed, the cave formations can be seen in their original state. Don't forget your torch (flashlight).

Tham Piu is just a few kilometres east of Muang Kham off Rte 7.

GETTING THERE & AWAY

You can hire a 4WD and driver in Phonsavan for around US$30 a day for trips to Tham Piu and back.

To get to Tham Piu by public transport, you'd have to take a Nong Haet bus and ask to be let out at the turn-off for Tham Piu. From the turn-off, start walking towards the limestone cliff north of the road until you're within a kilometre of the cliff. At this point you have to plunge into the woods and make your way along a honeycomb of trails to the bottom of the cliff and then mount a steep, narrow trail that leads up to the mouth of the cave. It would be best to ask for directions from villagers along the way or you're liable to get lost; live ordnance is another danger. Better still, find someone in Phonsavan who knows the way and invite them to come along for an afternoon hike.

MUANG KHOUN (OLD XIENG KHUANG)
ເມືອງຄູນ (ຊຽງຂວາງເກົ່າ)
pop 14,000

Muang Khoun's ancient capital was so heavily bombarded during the Second Indochina War (and ravaged in the 19th century by Chinese and Vietnamese invaders) that it was almost completely abandoned by 1975. More than 20 years after war's end the old capital is once again flourishing. Officially the town has been renamed Muang Khoun. Many of the residents are Thai Phuan, Thai Dam or Thai Neua, along with a smattering of lowland Lao and Vietnamese.

Only one French colonial building still stands, a former commissariat now used as a social centre, and the former palace of a Thai Phuan prince, now in ruins. For the most part the town consists of nondescript wooden buildings with corrugated roofs, although outside of town you'll also see original Phuan-style stilted longhouses made of thick timber.

Several Buddhist temples built between the 16th and 19th centuries lie in ruins (see map p146). The foundation and columns of **Wat Phia Wat** are still standing at the east end of town, along with a large seated Buddha. Sadly, the only intact Xieng Khuang–style temples left in Laos today – characterised by striking pentagonal silhouettes when viewed from the front – are in Luang Prabang. More modern **Wat Si Phoum** is the town's most active Buddhist temple.

That Foun (also called That Chomsi), a tall 25m to 30m *jehdii* (Buddhist stupa) constructed in the Lan Xang/Lanna style, towers over the town. You can climb right through the foliage-covered stupa via a large cavity that Chinese Ho marauders tunnelled into the brick stupa over century ago to loot valuable Buddha images enshrined in the dome. Take a glance upwards once you're inside, and you can see the perfectly formed outline of a smaller, much older stupa that was 'entombed' by the larger one. From here you can also see historic **That Chom Phet** (reputedly built by the Cham) standing atop a nearby hill.

Ban Na Si, near Wat Phia Wat, is a sizable Thai Dam village.

In 2000 a band of disaffected Hmong tribesmen came down from the mountains and torched eight houses belonging to allegedly corrupt Lao officials. Immediately afterwards the town was closed to foreigners for a couple of weeks but all appears to be calm now.

Around 16km further east along Rte 7B, the Thai Phuan village of **Ban Thak** is worth a visit to see its terraced rice fields and stately Phuan-style homes. Between Muang Khoun and Ban Thak, **hot springs** are being developed into a local weekend tourist attraction.

There are no sleeping options in Muang Khoun, and it's best visited as a day trip from Phonsavan.

Eating
Opposite the market in the centre of town is a row of noodle shops with basic Lao fare. Typical opening hours for eateries are listed on p249.

Shopping
If you ask around you may be able to buy Thai tribal textiles (especially Phuan, Thai Dam or Thai Neua) in town, although forget about buying antique Xieng Khuang styles – these were picked over long ago by collectors from Vientiane and abroad.

Getting There & Away
Several buses a day ply the much-improved 36km route between Phonsavan and Muang Khoun (US$0.70, 30 minutes, six daily). Buses arrive and depart from the market in the centre of town.

MUANG SUI
ເມືອງສຸຍ
pop 20,200

Once a city of antique Buddhist temples and quaint provincial architecture, Muang Sui became a headquarters of the Neutralist faction and 'Lima Site 108' – a landing site used by US planes – during the Second Indochina War. The North Vietnamese Army (NVA) totally razed Muang Sui late in the war after running the Royal Lao Army out of Xieng Khuang Province.

Like Muang Khoun (Old Xieng Khuang), the town is still rebuilding and is part of a new district called Muang Phu Kut. On some government maps the town is labelled Ban Nong Tang.

Visiting Muang Sui is best done as a day trip from Phonsavan.

HMONG RESISTANCE

In the mountains of Xieng Khuang Province, pockets of Hmong resistance live on nearly 30 years after the US defeat in Laos. These rebels reportedly control the nation's primary source of agarwood (*mái kítsanáa* in Lao, less commonly 'eaglewood' in English), a highly aromatic wood that fetches high prices in Arab countries where it's used for incense. Profits from the sale of agarwood, arranged through Lao and Thai wholesalers, along with donations smuggled in from abroad, help finance Hmong armaments.

In early 2003 around 700 Hmong rebels in Xieng Khuang Province and neighbouring Luang Prabang Province surrendered to Lao authorities and have been resettled in more populated areas of these provinces. Since then rebel activity has been virtually nil. At the same time the government has appointed a Hmong as Xieng Khuang provincial governor, in the hopes that this will further soothe regional tensions.

Sights

Although the devastation wrought upon Muang Sui by the NVA seriously damaged every temple in the district, the ruins of several older temples can be seen. **Wat Ban Phong**, which still has resident monks, once contained a beautiful bronze Xieng Khuang–style Buddha called Pha Ong, said to hail from the 14th century. Lao communists reportedly transferred the image to Sam Neua in Hua Phan Province, although no-one there seems to know anything about this.

Towards the eastern end of the district, a large picturesque natural lake called **Nong Tang**, flanked by high limestone cliffs, is a favourite local picnicking site. Five caves in the cliffs to the northeast of the lake can easily be visited by following posted signs, or you may be able to hire a local guide from one of the noodle stalls near the lake. Also near the lake is a semiruined 15th-century Xieng Khuang–style stupa called **That Banmang**.

Further afield are two more limestone caves that are well worth visiting. **Tham Pha** is a large network of caverns in which hundreds of small Buddha figures were stashed away to protect them from Haw invasions a couple of centuries ago. In the main entry cavern stands a very large sitting Buddha. The cave continues deep into the hillside, with ample passageways linking one cavern with another, making it the most impressive cave we've yet seen in Laos. Reportedly the NVA used the cave as a hospital during the Second Indochina War. The local Lao have rigged electric lights in Tha Pha so that visitors can easily tour most of the accessible caverns, and will turn them on for a small donation. Near Tham Pha is a second large cave, **Tham That**, which contains an old stupa ruin.

In the same general vicinity, but less accessible, is a **coffin cave** high up in a limestone cliff. To reach this one you will have to do a little rock climbing and a lot of boulder scrambling. Inside the relatively small cave are the remains of large prehistoric wooden coffins, carved from single tree trunks. All have already been opened and raided, but human skeletal remains and potsherds are still spread over the cave floor. The coffins look very similar to ones in caves in Mae Hong Son Province, Thailand. Most likely there are several other caves near Muang Sui containing similar artefacts.

Around 32km east of Muang Sui, south of Rte 7, is a **boulder field** where you can see half-carved stone jars like those from the famous jar sites near Phonsavan.

Keep in mind that there are still a lot of UXO around Muang Sui. It's best to visit the area around Tham Pha, Tham That and the coffin cave with a guide who knows the terrain. Sousath Travel (p141) in Phonsavan can provide a 4WD vehicle (necessary to reach the coffin cave), driver and guide for up to four people for an all-day journey to sites around Muang Sui, for US$80.

Getting There & Away

Rte 7 to Muang Sui from Phonsavan has been graded and improved, and a bridge now spans the Nam Ngum just east of Muang Sui, so it now takes less than an hour to drive the 52km from Phonsavan. Buses leave Phonsavan's bus terminal (US$0.70, two daily) around 7am and again around 1pm.

WAR JUNK

War scrap has become an important part of the local architecture and economy in Xieng Khuang. Torpedo-shaped bomb casings are collected, stored, refashioned into items of everyday use or sold as scrap. Among the most valuable are the 1.5m-long casings from US-made cluster bomb units (CBUs), which split lengthways when released and scattered 600 to 700 tennis-ball-size bomblets (each containing around 250 steel pellets) over 5000-sq-m areas.

Turned on its side, a CBU casing becomes a pot for plants; upright the casings are used as fence posts or as substitutes for the traditional wooden stilts used to support rice barns and thatched houses. Hundreds of casings used like this can be seen in Xieng Khuang villages along Rte 7, which stretches northeast all the way from Phonsavan to Hanoi, or in villages in the vicinity of the old capital. Aluminium spoons sold in local markets are said to be fashioned from the remains of downed American aircraft.

Farmers from around the province keep piles of French, Russian, Chinese and American war junk – including Soviet tanks and pieces of US planes shot down during the war – beneath their stilt houses or in unused corners of their fields. They use bits and pieces as needed around the farm or sell pieces to itinerant scrap dealers who drive their trucks from village to village. These trucks bring the scrap to warehouses in Phonsavan, where it is sold to larger dealers from Vientiane. Eventually the scrap is melted down in Vientiane or across the Mekong River in Thailand as a source of cheap metal.

In Laos it is illegal to trade in leftover war weaponry – bombs, bullets, arms – of any kind. According to National Law Chapters 71 and 72, the illegal purchase, sale, or theft of these can result in a prison term of between six months and five years.

HUA PHAN PROVINCE

For much of the last 500 years the mountainous northeastern province of Hua Phan has been either an independent Thai Neua kingdom or part of an Annamese vassal state known as Ai Lao. It also came briefly under Siamese protectorship as a state called Chao Thai Neua in the 1880s. Except for a two-year interval (1891–93) when the state was under Luang Prabang suzerainty, Hua Phan really only became a Lao entity under French colonial rule. During the colonial era the French commissariat at Sam Neua gave a great deal of autonomy to the Thai Neua chiefs and village headmen. By the end of the Second Indochina War, all traces of the French presence had been erased.

Enclosed by Vietnam to the north, east and southeast, Xieng Khuang to the southwest and Luang Prabang to the west, the province has a total population of 267,000, a fifth of whom live in the provincial capital of Sam Neua ('Northern Sam', a reference to its position towards the northern end of the Nam Sam). Twenty-two ethnic groups make the province their home, predominantly Thai Khao,

Thai Daeng, Thai Meuay, Thai Neua, Phu Noi, Hmong, Khamu, Yunnanese and Vietnamese. The Vietnamese influence is very strong here as Sam Neua is closer to (and more accessible from) Hanoi than Vientiane.

As a tourist attraction the province's main claim to fame is that Vieng Xai served as the headquarters for the Pathet Lao throughout most of the war years. Textiles in the 'Sam Neua' style – of tribal Thai origins – are another drawcard. The best textiles are said to come from the areas around Muang Son and Sop Hao.

SAM NEUA (XAM NEUA)

ຊຳເໜືອ

☎ 064 / pop 46,800

Tucked away in a long, narrow valley formed by the Nam Sam at about 1200m above sea level, Sam Neua is so far one of the country's least visited provincial capitals. Verdant hills, including the pointy Phu Luang, overlook the town but other than the pleasant natural setting and the general feeling of remoteness here, there's not a lot to get excited about. Residents are mostly Lao, Vietnamese and Hmong, along with some Thai Dam, Thai Daeng and Thai Lü.

Information

MONEY
Lao Development Bank (☎ 312171; ⏲ 8am-4pm Mon-Fri) This bank can exchange Thai baht or US dollars at the same rate as in Vientiane.

POST
The post office is opposite the bus terminal and market.

TELEPHONE
IDD phone service is available at Lao Telecom, next to the post office.

TOURIST INFORMATION
Provincial Tourist Office (☎ 312171; ⏲ 8am-4pm Mon-Fri) Hua Phan Province has its own tourist office near the Lao Red Cross, and has English-speaking staff eager to help with information.

Sights

For local residents, Sam Neua boasts what is perhaps the largest and fastest-growing **market** in the region. Products from China and Vietnam line up beside fresh produce and domestic goods. Sam Neua–style textiles can be found inside the main market-building; prices can be very good, although quality is generally not up to the standard of markets in Vientiane. Local Hmong, Thai Dam, Thai Daeng and Thai Lü frequent this market. Connoisseurs agree that the Thai Daeng weave the most attractive textiles. Along with textiles you'll find field rats (live or skinned), banana leaves stuffed with squirming insects, and forks and spoons made with aluminium salvaged from war debris. One vendor can make a custom-fit a silver ring in about 10 minutes.

A 1979 **independence monument** mounted by a red star sits on a hill at the northwest edge of town; it's an easy climb, worthwhile for the modest view at the top. From this hill you can continue walking on to **Wat Pho Xai**, a distance of approximately 2km from the market. The only monastery in town, with only five monks in residence (the minimum needed for holding the monastic ordination ceremonies), the wat features a small *sĭm* that was destroyed during the war and rebuilt in 1983. The two small *thâat* you'll see on the way to the independence monument are the last remnants of local prewar temples.

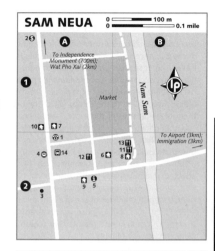

Sleeping

Kheam Xam Guest House (☎ 312111; r US$3.50-5) In front of the market, diagonally across from the Lao Houng Hotel, the three-storey Kheam Xam has clean rooms with mosquito nets, and shared hot shower facilities for the cheaper rooms, private bathroom for the more expensive ones. On the ground floor is a café with TV and VCR.

Bounhome Guest House (☎ 312223; r US$5) Behind the Kheam Xam is the brand spanking new Bounhome, where all rooms come with private hot-water shower.

Phanh Sam Guest House (☎ 312255; r US$2.50-4) On a street up from the market, around the corner from Lao Houng, the Phanh Sam is a two-storey cement building with a balcony on the upper floor. The 20 small rooms are

---

SAMANA (RE-EDUCATION CAMPS)

Hua Phan is infamous for the *samana* (re-education camps) established around the eastern half of the province immediately following the 1975 Revolution. Inspired by Vietnamese examples (several in Hua Phan were actually designed and constructed by Vietnamese architects and labourers), such camps, called *sǎamanáa* in Lao, mixed forced labour with political indoctrination to 'rehabilitate' thousands of civil servants from the old regime. Many Royal Lao Government officials were lured to the camps with promises of a two-week 'job training' session only to find themselves captives of the Pathet Lao for many years.

Although almost all of the camps were closed by 1989, Re-education Camp No 7 somewhere near Sam Neua still holds political prisoners, according to Amnesty International (AI). AI reports that three political prisoners (all former senior officials in the Lao People's Democratic Republic (PDR) government) were sentenced to 14 years' imprisonment in Hua Phan for peacefully advocating a multiparty political system in 1992. There were no defence lawyers at their trial. All three subsequently became very ill and one of the prisoners, 59-year-old Thongsouk Saysangkhi (former deputy minister of science and technology), died of alleged maltreatment in February 1998. Three more political prisoners received life sentences in 1992 after having been held without trial for 17 years. AI also reports that at Sop Hao at least two camp inductees held since 1975 were only released in 1994.

According to AI, the conditions in these camps are 'extremely harsh and fall well short of international minimum standards'. Prisoners are denied medical treatment, visits and all access to reading or writing material.

Although as many as 30,000 people were thought to have been interned by 1979 – the *samana*'s numeric peak – the Lao government has never issued a statement either confirming or denying the existence of the camps.

---

bare save for a few sticks of wooden furniture. The more expensive rooms have private bathroom. The staff are friendly and an attached restaurant serves simple one-dish meals.

Keomany Guest House (☎ 312142; s/tw US$3/4) The Keomany is a shophouse-style three-storey building with average two-bed rooms featuring shared toilet and shower.

Lao Houng Hotel (☎ 312018; r US$2.50-10) Near the western end of a bridge that spans the Nam Sam near the market, Lao Houng is a decaying Chinese/Vietnamese-style place built around a couple of courtyards by the Vietnamese in 1975 – though it looks much older. Although plenty of Lao government officials and businessmen stay here, it's difficult to understand the attraction since the guesthouses in town have better rooms at lower rates.

Eating

For cheap *fǒe*, the **market** (🕑 6am-6pm) is the place to go. Typical opening hours for eateries are listed on p249.

Chittavanh Restaurant (meals US$1-2) Next to the Kheam Xam Guest House, the friendly Chittavanh serves the usual roster of noodle and rice dishes, as well as Western breakfasts, at nice wooden tables.

Vieng Sin Chan Restaurant (meals US$1-2) Next door and very similar to the Chittavanh, the Vieng Sin Chan has the addition of decorative textiles.

Mitsampanh Restaurant (meals US$0.60-2) For a variety of Lao dishes try the Mitsampanh, about 20m down a side lane between the bus terminal and market, opposite the Bounhome Guest House.

Getting There & Away

AIR

Lao Airlines has curtailed flights to Sam Neua pending an expansion of its fleet. The airport lies around 3km from the area of town where the market and most of the guesthouses and hotels are. A motorcycle taxi from the airport to any lodging in town costs around US$1. From the market in town, however, it's easy to hire jumbos or *sǎwngthǎew* to the airport.

BUS

Sam Neua can be reached by road from both Muang Khoun and Udomxai Provinces. Rte 6 from Muang Khoun is quite good

Pétanque players, Luang Prabang (p111)

Young girl, Muang Ngoi Neua (p138)

Offering baskets, That Xieng Tung Festival (p169), Muang Sing

Wat Mai Suwannaphumaham (p120), Luang Prabang

Thai Dam women barter with a tourist, Muang Sing (p167)

JOHN

Food vendors, Luang
Prabang (p129)

WOODS WHEATCROFT

JULIET COOMBE

Stall selling cotton and silk threads, Hmong
market (p146), near the Plain of Jars

BERNARD NAP

Tham Ting (p134), Pak Ou

by Lao standards between Phonsavan and Nam Noen, a small truck stop near the junction of Rtes 6 and 1 just north of the Hua Phan Province border. Between Nam Noen and Sam Neua it's a steep, winding and rough but highly scenic dirt road that passes through numerous Lao, Hmong and Khamu villages. It's usually necessary to change buses (actually large converted Russian or Chinese diesel trucks) in Nam Noen.

See p144 for details on buses between Phonsavan, Nam Noen and Sam Neua. Southeast of Sam Neua, Rte 6 joins Rte 1 from Nong Khiaw (Luang Prabang Province) and Udomxai (Udomxai Province). See p144 for information on buses to/from Nong Khiaw. The Nong Khiaw to Nam Noen leg runs along winding roads and brilliant scenery, passing many Blue Hmong villages along the way and an international narcotics control project in the district of Vieng Thong (also known as Muang Hiam). In Nam Noen you may have to switch to a Sam Neua–bound truck – if so this may mean spending a night in Nam Noen.

The Vietnamese border at Sop Hao is open to Vietnamese and Lao nationals, and it is unlikely that a foreigner would be allowed to cross here – travel in this area is restricted probably because it's one of the last surviving nodes in the Lao PDR's post-Revolution *samana* ('re-education camp') system.

AROUND SAM NEUA

A 580-sq-km area of forested hills along the Nam Sam near Sam Tai in the southeastern section of the province was declared the **Nam Sam National Protected Area** (Nam Sam NPA) in 1993. Nam Sam NPA is thought to be a habitat for wild elephant, various gibbons, gaur, banteng, tiger, clouded leopard, Asiatic black bear and Malayan sun bear. Despite the NPA designation – and even though the area can only be reached by a 4WD track from Vieng Xai – shifting cultivation by hill tribes and cedar logging by Chinese companies threatens the forests.

Tat Saloei, about 37km south of Sam Neua off the road to Nam Noen, is a waterfall said to be very beautiful just after the rainy season.

The road northeast from Sam Neua to Sop Hao on the Vietnamese border passes by several Hmong and tribal Thai villages. A former French army camp in Sop Hao now serves as one of Laos's last remaining political prisons ('re-education camps'). Officials in this area can be very touchy about foreigners.

Suan Hin (Sao Hin Tang)
ສວນຫີນ

This 'stone garden' *(suan hin)*, far more interesting than its name makes it sound, was first described in print by French archaeologist Madeleine Colani in her 1935 thesis *Megalithes du Haut Laos (Megaliths of Highland Laos)*. The site is also known locally as Sao Hin Tang ('standing stone pillars'). Often likened to Britain's Stonehenge because of its rough-hewn, 2m stone uprights, Suan Hin is as much of a mystery as the Plain of Jars – indeed they may be historically related. The stone chosen for the megaliths coincides with that used to fashion the jars; beneath some of the pillars are tunnel-like ditches whose purpose is as enigmatic as the pillars and jars themselves – current speculation suggests a funerary function.

Large stone discs about a metre in diameter can also be seen lying among the menhirs. Local animist lore says the discs once sat atop the megaliths to form dining and drinking tables for a sky spirit named Jahn Hahn. The meaning of the discs is as lost to the world as that of the pillars.

The pillars are a 5.4km hike off Rte 6 via a road beginning at a point 55km southeast of Sam Neua. This road passes the village of Ban Pakha on the way.

You can inquire at the tourist office in Sam Neua about hiring transport out to Suan Hin. Sousath Travel (p141) in Phonsavan, the capital of Xieng Khuang

NORTHERN LAOS

CROSSING THE VIETNAMESE BORDER AT NA MAEW & NAM XOI

In April 2004 the crossing between Nam Xoi in Thanh Hoa Province, Vietnam, and Na Maew in Hua Phan Province, Laos, was opened. From Na Maew it's a relatively short bus ride to Sam Neua, where there are buses and planes onward to other points in Laos.

Province, can also provide transport and guidance to Suan Hin. It's a bit difficult by public transport because once you get off and make the hike, it could be several hours before another bus comes by.

SAM NEUA TO VIENG XAI

Whether or not you visit the famous Pathet Lao caves, Vieng Xai district is worth wandering about for its scenic beauty. Between Kms 11 and 12, coming from Sam Neua, is a fairly big Hmong Lai (Striped Hmong) village called **Ban Hua Khang**. After Km 13 you'll start seeing karst formations, many with cave entrances, along with pretty little valleys terraced in rice. At Km 20 is an intersection; the right fork reaches Vieng Xai after 9km, then continues to Na Maew on the Vietnamese border (87km from Sam Neua), while the other road goes to Sop Hao.

Six kilometres before the Vieng Xai turn-off, coming from Sam Neua, is the 80m-high **Tat Nam Neua**. You can walk to the top of the falls straight from a bridge where the road crosses the Nam Neua just after the road forks towards Vieng Xai. For an all-in-one view from the bottom, take the left fork and proceed for 2km until you see some terraced rice fields on the right-hand side of the road. A trail winds for 1km or so through the fields, along and across a stream and through bamboo thickets before reaching the bottom. You may have to ask locally for directions as the trail isn't particularly obvious. Be sure to apply insect repellent to your feet and ankles in order to keep leeches at bay. As you'd expect, the falls are most beautiful just after the rainy season, when you can swim in the lower pools.

VIENG XAI

ວຽງໄຊ
pop 32,800

The former Pathet Lao revolutionary head-quarters of Vieng Xai sits in a striking valley of verdant hills and limestone cliffs riddled with caves, several of which were used to shelter PL officers during the Second Indochina War.

The district capital itself is a small town that seems to be getting smaller as Sam Neua grows larger. The central market is a collection of poor vendors who can't afford transport to the provincial capital, 29km away.

Caves

There are 102 known caves in the district, around a dozen with war history. Only a few years ago local authorities treated them as if they were a military secret, even while the National Tourist Authority of Laos (NTAL) in Vientiane promoted the caves as tourist attractions. The book *Stalking the Elephant Kings* by Christopher Kremmer contains an enlightening chapter on the author's experiences attempting and finally succeeding in entering the caves in the mid-1990s. The book also contains some background on the royal family's short stay here during the late 1970s. Today around a dozen of the caves are open to the public as a revolutionary memorial and tourist attraction.

The setting of the caves – inside a narrow and precipitous limestone-walled valley surrounding the town of Vieng Xai – is quite impressive. The PL leadership first started using them in 1964 because the caverns are virtually unassailable by land or air. Today the caves considered the most historically important are named after the figures who once occupied them. They are within easy walking distance of town.

High in the side of a limestone cliff, **Tham Than Souphanouvong** (called Tham Pha Bong before the war) was deemed fit for royalty and housed Prince Souphanouvong, the so-called 'Red Prince'. Wooden walls and floors, as well as natural cave formations, divided the cavern into bedrooms, meeting rooms, artillery and weapons storage areas and various other spaces. Souphanouvong eventually built a house in front of the cave entrance and today the house is treated with the same mix of fear and respect as is the cave.

Tham Than Kaysone, the office and residence of the PL chief – who served as prime minister and president from 1975 until his death in 1992 – extends 140m into a cliff that was scaled by rope before steps were added. A bust of Kaysone sits inside the entry. The cave's various rooms included a political party centre, reception room, bedroom, recreation room, meeting room and a library. The rear of the cave opens onto a clearing that was used as an outdoor meeting place and kitchen. Kaysone also built a handsome two-storey house in front of his cave.

Tham Than Khamtay, named after the current president Khamtay Siphandone, is an artificial cave dug out of a limestone cliff, similarly divided into various rooms, with a Franco-Chinese–style house in front of it. Of the four main caves open to tourists, this is the only one without electric lights; labels appear in Lao only.

Tham Than Nouhak, named for Nouhak Phoumsavang, who served as Lao PDR president from 1992 to 1998, is the most recent to open to the public. Like his PL comrades, Nouhak had a house built for himself in front of the cave.

One of the deepest caves (200m) is **Tham Xieng Muang**, which was used for hospital facilities. Other caves housed weaving mills, printing presses and other facilities needed by the PL to remain self-sufficient.

VISITING THE CAVES

Before entering any of the caves, visitors must report to the **Kaysone Memorial Cave Tour Office** (admission US$1, video camera US$1, still camera US$0.50; ☺ 9am-4.30pm) to pay the necessary fees. A local Lao guide assigned by the government will then guide you to as many caves as you wish. So far only one of the guides speaks English, but there may be more in the near future.

Sleeping & Eating

Most people visit Vieng Xai as a day trip from Sam Neua since it's only 30 minutes away by bus. There are a couple of decent guesthouses here, while the two cement Vietnamese-built hotels are best avoided.

Naxay Guest House (r US$3) Rooms here are clean and the food is good (it's best if you order food in advance).

Swampside Guest House (s/d US$1.50/3) Despite the name, this guesthouse has a nice lakeside location with a restaurant on stilts out over the lake. It's generally not as clean as the Naxay, however.

Several *fŏe* shops in the market serve rice and noodle dishes.

Getting There & Away

Passenger trucks run between Sam Neua and Vieng Xai (US$0.50, 30 minutes, 29km, several daily), with departures more frequent in the morning.

The provincial tourist office (p151) in Sam Neua can arrange half-day tours to Vieng Xai for US$5 per person. You could also charter a pick-up truck to take you and up to eight other passengers from Sam Neua to Vieng Xai and back for about US$20, for a half day.

NAM NOEN
ບ້ວເນີນ

Anyone travelling by road between Nong Khiaw and Phonsavan or between Sam Neua and Phonsavan must pass through this settlement, 7km south of the junction of Rtes 6 and 1.

Nam Noen Guest House (dm US$1) offers beds with mosquito nets in dormlike rooms, while **Nang Lam Phon** (meals US$0.50-1.50) provides sticky rice and instant noodles. There are a couple of other noodle shops as well.

Buses to/from Nong Khiaw (US$4, six hours, one or two daily), Phonsavan (US$2, three hours, four daily) and Sam Neua (US$2, four hours, two daily) tend to reach Nam Noen around noon or 1pm, so if you're looking for a connection to any of these towns you'd best arrive in Nam Noen by noon. Early morning is another good time to get a passenger vehicle. After 2pm it's almost impossible unless an incoming vehicle has been delayed by a breakdown.

NONG KHIAW TO NAM NOEN

Rte 1 between Nong Khiaw and Nam Noen passes through stretches of beautiful scenery with lots of green mountains – even in the dry months when everywhere looks brown – rivers, fern-covered cliffs and villages of Striped and Blue Hmong. The districts of **Muang Vieng Kham** and **Muang Vieng Thong** are populated with Blue Hmong and other ethnicities. Vieng Kham, about 50km east of Muang Ngoi, is a fairly substantial village with a couple of wats and a couple of places to eat. **Ban Wang Wai**, the next town west after Vieng Kham, is more prosperous than many others along the road and a little bigger than Vieng Kham itself. Besides Hmong, you'll see plenty of lowland Lao here, many of whom keep looms beneath their stilted houses.

Muang Vieng Thong
ເມືອງວຽງທອງ

More than a few travellers who have found themselves stuck in Muang Vieng Thong – also known by its pre-1975 name of Muang Hiam – have opted to stay an extra night or two. This village, inhabited by a collection of hill tribes (particularly Hmong) and lowland Lao, has a very pleasant mountain setting alongside the Nam Khao.

A **hot spring**, roughly 1km north of town on the road to Ban San Tai, makes an excellent bathing alternative in the cold season. Further down the same road the visitor can find a few Lao Soung villages between the Nam Et and Phu Loei NPAs.

The road ends after 64km at **Ban San Tai** (San Teu in local dialect), a village that brings together lowland Lao, Thai tribals and Hmong-Mien groups. Several *săwngthǎew* ply this route daily from Vieng Thong.

SLEEPING & EATING
Typical opening hours for eateries are listed on p249.

Souksavan Guest House (r US$1.50) and a **no-name guesthouse** (dm US$1) supply basic rooms with two beds and mosquito nets, and shared bathing and toilet facilities.

Three modest, friendly restaurants in the centre of the village offer basic Lao fare: Boua Dom, Khamsouk and Phou That.

GETTING THERE & AWAY
Long-distance public transport is a little erratic but the general rule is that large, locally based trucks alternate routes between Luang Prabang and Sam Neua every other day. Regular buses ply between here and Nong Khiaw (US$1.60, three hours, four daily) and Luang Prabang (US$2, seven hours, five daily). You will also see buses and trucks that originated elsewhere passing through Vieng Thong, and can flag these down anywhere on the road.

UDOMXAI PROVINCE

This rugged province is wedged between Luang Prabang to the east, Phongsali to the northeast, Luang Nam Tha to the northwest and Sainyabuli to the south, with a small northern section that shares a border with China's Yunnan Province. Most of the provincial population of 211,000 is a mixture of some 23 ethnic minorities, mostly Hmong, Akha, Mien, Phu Thai, Thai Dam, Thai Khao, Thai Lü, Thai Neua, Phuan, Khamu, Lamet, Lao Huay and Yunnanese Chinese (Haw).

The Yunnanese presence continues to intensify with the influx of Chinese skilled labourers working in construction, as well as traders from Kunming. In the 1960s and early 1970s the Chinese were appreciated in Udomxai because they donated a network of two-lane paved roads radiating throughout the far north, using Udomxai as the hub. These roads were very important in moving Pathet Lao and NVA troops and supplies around the north during the war. Following the 1979 ideological split over Cambodia (China sided with the Khmer Rouge, Laos with Vietnam), the Chinese withdrew all support until the early 1990s.

The new Chinese influx is regarded by many Udomxai inhabitants as economic infiltration, since the construction and road building is no longer foreign aid but paid work for hire, using plenty of imported Chinese materials and labour.

Because Udomxai has a road system of sorts (it has deteriorated considerably since the 1970s but is still the best in the north), this province is the most accessible of the country's far northern provinces.

UDOMXAI (MUANG XAI)
ອຸດົມໄຊ (ເມືອງໄຊ)

☎ 081 / pop 80,000

The capital of Udomxai, often simply called Muang Xai, didn't amount to much before the Second Indochina War, when it became a centre for Chinese troops supporting the Pathet Lao. Today it's a booming Laos-China trade centre riding on imported Chinese wealth. Although few people visit Udomxai as a tourist destination, it's an important northern crossroads where Rtes 1, 2 and 4 intersect. Thus it's difficult to avoid if you're travelling to Luang Nam Tha or Phongsali from points south.

After roughing it through some beautiful countryside along the Mekong River and along Rte 2 from Pak Beng (or from the east via Nong Khiaw and the Nam Ou), the town can be something of a disappointment. Basically it consists of strips of asphalt or dirt flanked by modern cement buildings set in the middle of a deforested valley. However, more traditional thatched houses spread across the rim of the valley towards the base of the surrounding mountain range. If you get off the main street you can find some very picturesque villagelike sections.

The town is roughly 60% Lao Thoeng and Lao Soung, 25% Chinese and 15% Lao Loum. Thousands of Chinese workers may be in the area at any one time, and the Yunnanese dialect is often heard more than Lao in the cafés and hotels. Most of the vehicles in town bear Vietnamese or Chinese licence plates.

Information

MONEY

In town you can spend yuan, US dollars, Thai baht or kip. Lao Development Bank and BCEL have branches in town, where you can get kip for US dollars, Thai baht or Chinese yuan but not vice versa. Travellers cheques are not accepted, so bring cash.

POST

Post office (☺ 8am-4pm Mon-Fri, 8am-noon Sat) Also houses Lao Telecom.

TELEPHONE

Lao Telecom (Post office; ☺ 8-11.30am, 2-4.30pm and 6.30-9pm) Phonecards are available here for use in the international and domestic phone booth out the front.

TOURIST INFORMATION

Oudomxai Provincial Tourism Office (☎ 211797; ☺ 8am-4.30pm Mon-Fri, 8am-noon Sat) Located near the bridge in the town centre, the tourist office can answer questions about onward travel, accommodation and so forth.

Sights & Activities

A large, enclosed **Chinese market**, under construction next to the Kaysone Monument in the town centre, will supersede the charming hill-tribe market that used to convene near the river in Udomxai. The **Lao Red Cross** (☎ 312391; steam US$1, per hr massage US$3; ☺ 3-7pm), 150m behind the Phouxay Hotel, offers Lao-Swedish style massage as well as herbal steam baths.

Sleeping

Many of the guesthouses in Udomxai cater to Chinese workers and either will not accept other nationalities or will ask double the Chinese price. We've not listed any that we know are guilty of two-tier pricing.

Boua Kha Guest House (☎ 312269; r US$3-4) This modest two-storey guesthouse, only around 25m from the new bus terminal in

NORTHERN LAOS

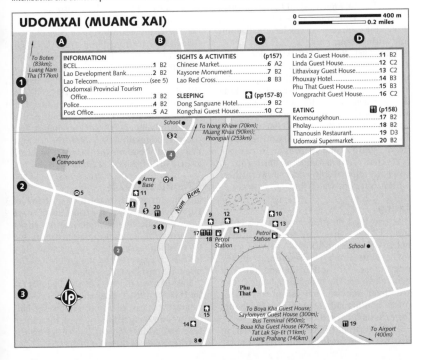

UDOMXAI (MUANG XAI)

0 — 400 m
0 — 0.2 miles

INFORMATION	
BCEL	1 B2
Lao Development Bank	2 B2
Lao Telecom	(see 5)
Oudomxai Provincial Tourism Office	3 B2
Police	4 B2
Post Office	5 A2

SIGHTS & ACTIVITIES	(p157)
Chinese Market	6 A2
Kaysone Monument	7 B2
Lao Red Cross	8 B3

SLEEPING	(pp157-8)
Dong Sanguane Hotel	9 B2
Kongchai Guest House	10 C2

Linda 2 Guest House	11 B2
Linda Guest House	12 C2
Lithavixay Guest House	13 C2
Phouxay Hotel	14 B3
Phu That Guest House	15 B3
Vongprachit Guest House	16 C2

EATING	(p158)
Keomoungkhoun	17 B2
Pholay	18 B2
Thanousin Restaurant	19 D3
Udomxai Supermarket	20 B2

To Boten (83km); Luang Nam Tha (117km)

School

To Nong Khiaw (70km); Muang Khua (90km); Phongsali (253km)

Army Compound

Army Base

Nam Beng

Petrol Station

Petrol Station

School

Phu That

To Boya Kha Guest House; Saylomyen Guest House (300m); Bus Terminal (450m); Boua Kha Guest House (475m); Tat Lak Sip-Et (11km); Luang Prabang (140km)

To Airport (400m)

the direction of Luang Prabang, has clean rooms with private facilities.

Saylomyen Guest House (☎ 211377; r US$3-5) A bit further from the bus terminal, towards the main centre of town, the Saylomyen is another good choice for visitors arriving by bus.

Vongprachit Guest House (☎ 312455; r US$4) Convenient to the town centre, featuring clean rooms with private hot-water bathroom.

Phouxay Hotel (Phuxai; ☎ 312140; r US$4-7.50) The Lao Petroleum–owned Phouxay, in the former Chinese consulate compound off the main street near the southern end of town, offers two- and three-bed rooms with mosquito nets and ceiling fans.

Phu That Guest House (☎ 211613; r US$3) The casual Phu That has only six small, ordinary rooms, but since it's well off the main street it's quieter than most.

Lithavixay Guest House (☎ /fax 212175; r US$6-15; 🖳) At one of the newest guesthouses in town all rooms come with private hot-water shower. The more expensive rooms are larger and include breakfast. Internet access is available downstairs.

Dong Sanguane Hotel (tw US$1.15, 3-bed dm per bed US$2) Dong Sanguane has very basic rooms. The three-bedroom dorms have bathroom and sitting room.

Linda Guest House (☎ 312147; r US$4) Linda Guest House has 14 fan rooms in a three-storey, ornate building on the main north–south street. There's another branch, Linda 2, right behind the Kaysone Monument, with the same price and amenities.

Kongchai Guest House (☎ 211141; r US$2.50-4) In a two-storey building 50m off the main north–south road through town, the Kongchai offers a range of basic rooms, some with shared cold-water shower, others with private hot-water shower.

Eating

The Lao food on local menus often tastes more Chinese than Lao, so you're usually better off ordering Chinese. Service tends to be quite slow. The restaurants at the guesthouses are often better but you generally need to order in advance. The Udomxai supermarket is on the main north–south road. Typical opening hours for eateries are listed on p249.

Pholay (meals US$1-3) Next to a petrol station on the main north–south street, Pholay

remains one of the most reliable places to eat in town, with an extensive menu of Chinese and Lao food.

Keomoungkoun (meals US$1-3) Near the Pholay, the Keomoungkoun has a slightly larger dining room but basically has the same menu.

Thanousin Restaurant (meals US$0.50-2) This restaurant is conveniently located near the junction of Rtes 1 and 2 and thus receives a lot of business from drivers passing through. It has the most Lao menu in town, although not everything on the menu is on hand all the time

Getting There & Away
AIR
Lao Airlines (☎ 312156; airport) flies to/from Vientiane (one way/return US$66/125, 50 minutes, three weekly).

BUS & SĂWNGTHĂEW
The Chinese-built bitumen roads that radiate from Udomxai are in fair condition (except for the road to Pak Beng on the Mekong River) and the city is the largest land transport hub in the north.

A new interprovincial **bus terminal** (☎ 212218) at the southwestern edge of town fields buses to/from Phonsavan (US$8.80, 16 to 17 hours, three weekly), Luang Prabang (US$3, five hours, two daily), Nong Khiaw (US$2.50, three hours, two daily), Pak Beng (US$2.65, four hours, two daily), Luang Nam Tha (US$2.30, four hours, two daily), Muang Khua (US$2.20, four hours, two daily), Boten (US$2, four hours, two daily), Phongsali (US$5, eight hours, one daily) and Vientiane (ordinary US$8.30, 15 hours; VIP US$9.50, 14 hours).

AROUND UDOMXAI

North and south of town is a string of Hmong villages where the tribes people have come down from higher elevations – either because of mountaintop deforestation due to swidden agriculture, or because they have been pressured by the government to integrate into lowland society.

East of town off Rte 1 at Km 11 is **Tat Lak Sip-Et** (Km 11 Waterfall; admission US$0.20), a slender cataract that cascades over a limestone cliff into a Nam Beng tributary. Look for a small blue and white sign (in Lao only) on the northern side of the road.

Baw nâm hâwn (hot springs) can be found 28km from Udomxai near Muang La, off the road to Phongsali near the banks of the Nam Pak.

TO UDOMXAI VIA PAK BENG

The river-and-road trip from Huay Xai or Luang Prabang to Udomxai is an experience in itself. Three hours by speedboat, or a day's travel by river ferry, the Mekong River journey to Pak Beng (jumping-off point for the road to Udomxai) passes craggy stone cliffs, sandy shores, undulating mountains, fishing villages, and expanses of both primary and secondary forest.

Pak Beng itself (see below) is worth an overnight stay if time allows, then it's on to Udomxai via Rte 2, an old Chinese-built road that runs parallel to the Nam Beng most of the way. The mostly sealed road is very rough in spots but is supposed to be resealed soon. Along the way you'll pass Phu Thai, Thai Lü, Hmong, Thai Dam, Lao and Khamu villages, plus primary monsoon forest alternating with secondary growth and slash-and-burn plots.

At Km 90 (about one third of the way to Udomxai) is **Muang Houn** (52km from Pak Beng), the largest village between Pak Beng and Udomxai and a convenient rest stop. Muang Houn has a few basic guesthouses, of which **Bounnam Guest House** (☎ 212289; r US$2-3) looks best. There are also a few places at which to eat, or stock up on food supplies. Around Km 18 to Km 21 (counting south from Udomxai) are at least a dozen Hmong villages.

There are a couple of scenic waterfalls not far from the main road. **Tat Yong** is said to be the largest and is a 12km hike from Km 87.

PAK BENG

ປາກແບງ

This rustic town at the junction of the Mekong River and the smaller Nam Beng (Pak Beng means Mouth of the Beng) lies about halfway between Luang Prabang and Huay Xai (Bokeo Province). Pak Beng's mostly wooden houses sit along a steep hillside. Close to the ferry and speedboat piers is a collection of makeshift shops and cafés that get more interesting the further away from the river you go. Hmong and tribal Thais are frequently seen on the main

street. A few vendors along the street sell local textiles and handicrafts. Sip espresso and peruse new and used books at the relatively new **Khok Khor Café & Bookshop**.

Dangers & Annoyances

We've heard about a local scam where groups of young local boys offer to carry your luggage up the hill from the boat, then when you reach your guesthouse they demand US$4 for the service.

If you decide to enlist the assistance of the boys, consider setting an exact tip beforehand.

PAK BENG

INFORMATION
Hospital...1 B1
Khok Khor Cafe & Bookshop.................2 B1
Post Office...3 B1

SIGHTS & ACTIVITIES   (p160)
Wat Khok Kho.....................................4 B1
Wat Sin Jong Jaeng.............................5 B1

SLEEPING   (p160)
Bounmy Guest House............................6 A2
Done Vilasak Guest House.....................7 B1
Pak Beng Guest House...........................8 A2
Phonethip Guest House..........................9 B2
Sai Kong Resort (under construction)......10 A2
Sarika Guest House.............................11 A2
Vatsana Guest House...........................12 B2
Villasak Guest House...........................13 B1

EATING   (p160)
Doi Ket Restaurant..............................14 A2
Hasan Restaurant................................15 B1
Market..16 B1
Pine Kham Restaurant..........................17 A2

TRANSPORT   (pp160-1)
Boat Landing.....................................18 A2
Boat Transport Office...........................19 A2
Bus & Sawngthaew Station......................20 B1

NORTHERN LAOS

Sights & Activities

Two wats of mild interest can be visited in town, both of which are off the left side of the road north, overlooking the Nam Beng. **Wat Khok Kho** is the newer of the two, with a *sĭm* of rather recent construction and a wooden monks' quarters.

Further up the road, a series of stairs on the right-hand side lead past a small school to **Wat Sin Jong Jaeng**, an older temple that dates back to the early French colonial period or possibly earlier. On the front exterior wall of the small but classic Lao *sĭm* is a mural that includes figures with moustaches and big noses – presumably early Dutch or French visitors. Inside there are a number of Buddha images of varying ages. The Lao-style *thâat* on the premises was constructed in 1991; it's gilded at the top, and the base is said to contain a cache of *sáksít* (sacred) material (probably small Buddha images of crystal or silver, prayer cloths and rosaries from revered monks).

Nearby villages might be worth visiting if you can find a guide – ask at any of the guesthouses.

Sleeping
BUDGET

Walking up the main sloped street leading away from the boat landing, you'll come to a long string of small, inexpensive wooden guesthouses. Most offer small rooms with one or two beds that have hard mattresses and mosquito nets, and shared facilities around the back or downstairs.

Sarika Guest House (r US$7) This was the first lodging to open in Pak Beng and is still the first place you come to from the boat landing.

Pak Beng Guest House (r US$2.50) First on the left coming from the landing, the row of bamboo-thatch rooms have recently been redone and are fronted by a pleasant terrace restaurant.

Bounmy Guest House (r US$5-7) To find this one, walk a short distance down a road that branches off the main street not far from the boat landing. Since it's off the main drag, Bounmy offers a slightly quieter alternative, although the bamboo-and-wood rooms are very similar to those at most other guesthouses. All rooms have private hot-water bathroom. The attached restaurant has nice river views.

Other budget options:

Done Vilasak Guest House (tw US$2.50) Two-storey wooden place with typical two-bed rooms and shared bathroom.

Phonethip Guest House (r US$2.50-3.25) A relatively new place with simple fan rooms, five with shared bathroom and three with private bathroom.

Vatsana Guest House (☎ 212302; r US$3) Ten rooms with fan, mosquito net and shared bathroom.

Villasak Guest House (☎ 212315; r US$6) Seven rooms with fan, desk and private bathroom.

TOP END

Luang Say Lodge (☎ 212296; www.mekongcruises .com; r US$40) If you continue along the road past Bounmy Guest House, you'll come to this eco-lodge built mainly for the use of passengers cruising between Huay Xai and Luang Prabang aboard the *Pak Ou* (see p179) Built in traditional Lao style of solid wood, the lodge encompasses 19 rooms divided among a dozen or so pavilions, all with fan and private hot-water shower. A terrace restaurant overlooks the Mekong.

On the same road that leads to Luang Say Lodge, the new Sai Kong Resort (under construction) is expected to have 26 rooms in the top-end range when it opens in late 2004.

Eating

Typical opening hours for eateries are listed on p249.

Pine Kham Restaurant (meals US$1-2) The kitchen here does justice to a wide range of Thai, Chinese and Lao dishes, plus Western breakfasts.

Day market (☼ 6.30am-5pm) In the centre of town, this market has a few vendors with prepared Lao food. There are several other simple restaurants along the street leading from the pier, most serving *fŏe* and a few basic Chinese and Lao dishes.

Other options:

Doi Ket Restaurant (meals US$1-2) A popular spot with an extensive English-language menu of good Lao and *falang* food.

Hasan Restaurant (meals US$1-2) A new place with North Indian and Lao food.

Getting There & Away
BOAT

See p133 and p179 for details on river travel between Pak Beng, Luang Prabang and Huay Xai.

SĂWNGTHĂEW

From the *săwngthăew* and bus station (1.5km from the boat landing), *săwngthăew* run along pot-holed Rte 2 between Pak Beng and Udomxai (US$2.65, four hours, two daily).

If you miss one of the direct *săwngthăew* to Pak Beng from Udomxai, you can catch one of the more frequent *săwngthăew* to Muang Houn (US$1.50, two hours, eight daily), 92km southwest of Udomxai on the way to Pak Beng. In Muang Houn it's easy to pick up another *săwngthăew* on to Pak Beng (US$1, two hours). The same is true in reverse; you can take a *săwngthăew* from Pak Beng to Muang Houn, then pick up a Udomxai-bound vehicle fairly easily. There are two or three basic guesthouses in Muang Houn if you get stuck.

LUANG NAM THA PROVINCE

Bordered by Myanmar to the northwest, China to the north, Udomxai Province to the south and east, and Bokeo Province to the southwest, Luang Nam Tha (Nam Tha for short) is a mountainous province, with a high number of Lao Soung and other minorities.

In the early 1960s the western half of the province became a hotbed of CIA activity. The infamous William Young, a missionary's son raised in Lahu and Shan villages in northern Myanmar and northern Thailand, built a small CIA-financed, pan-tribal anti-Communist army in Ban Thuay, Nam Yu and Vieng Phukha (Lima Sites 118A, 118 and 109).

Much of the opium and heroin transported by the CIA's Air America and other air services either originated in or came through Luang Nam Tha. Westerners still seem to carry a romance for Nam Tha and there is a higher than average number of World Bank, UN, NGO and commercial projects under way in the province.

South of the provincial capital, a 2224-sq-km area of monsoon forest wedged between the Nam Ha and Nam Tha rivers was declared the Nam Ha National Protected Area (NPA) in 1993. Containing some of the most densely forested regions (96% primary forest cover) in Laos, the Nam Ha NPA protects a number of rare mammal species.

The provincial population is 114,500, made up of 39 classified ethnicities (the largest number in the nation), including Hmong, Akha, Mien, Samtao, Thai Daeng, Thai Lü, Thai Neua, Thai Khao, Thai Kalom, Khamu, Lamet, Lao Loum, Shan and Yunnanese. As in Udomxai Province, the Chinese presence is increasing rapidly with the arrival of skilled labourers from Yunnan.

LUANG NAM THA

ຫລວງນໍ້າທາ

☎ 086 / pop 35,400

Having risen from the ashes of war, Luang Nam Tha's capital has expanded steadily in its role as entrepôt for commerce between China, Thailand and Laos. During French colonial administration the town was centred at Ban Luang Kon, the southern section of the district near the airfield and boat landing. Since the original town was virtually destroyed during the Second Indochina War, and since this area had always been prone to flooding, the Pathet Lao moved the main market and administrative centre 7km north in 1976. The newer town centre sits on higher ground, and is close to where the highways come in from Muang Sing, Boten and Udomxai.

Aside from the airfield and boat landing, the older southern district is mostly residential and is, in general, much more interesting than the newer centre. Locals often refer to the southern centre as *meuang* (city-state) and to the northern centre as *khwăeng* (province).

Many visitors breeze through Luang Nam Tha on the way to Muang Sing and other destinations, thinking there's nothing to see or do here. However, those who take the time to investigate beyond the bland new centre of town will find there's a lot more to the town than first meets the eye. Nam Tha is best appreciated by walking or pedalling well away from the recently designed main streets.

Information
INTERNET ACCESS
PlaNet Online (☯ 8am-10pm) This Internet café operates a branch in Luang Nam Tha, opposite Palanh Guest House.

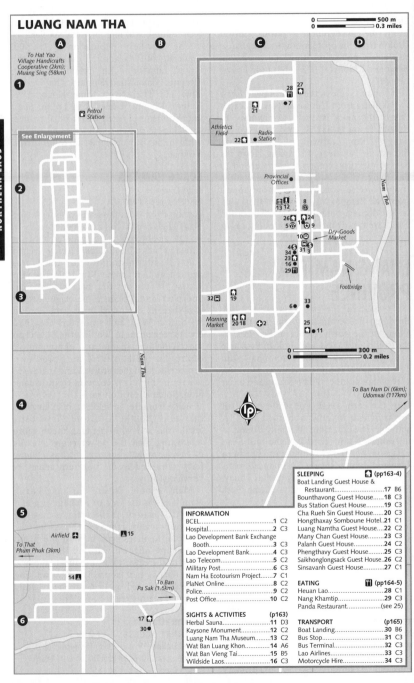

LUANG NAM THA

NORTHERN LAOS

To Hat Yao
Village Handicrafts
Cooperative (2km);
Muang Sing (58km)

Petrol
Station

See Enlargement

Athletics
Field

Radio
Station

Provincial
Offices

Dry-Goods
Market

Footbridge

Morning
Market

Nam Tha

To Ban Nam Di (6km);
Udomxai (117km)

Airfield

To That
Phum Phuk (3km)

To Ban
Pa Sak (1.5km)

INFORMATION
BCEL...1 C2
Hospital..2 C3
Lao Development Bank Exchange
    Booth.......................................3 C3
Lao Development Bank.................4 C3
Lao Telecom................................5 C2
Military Post.................................6 C3
Nam Ha Ecotourism Project........7 C1
PlaNet Online...............................8 C2
Police...9 C2
Post Office..................................10 C2

SIGHTS & ACTIVITIES   (p163)
Herbal Sauna..............................11 D3
Kaysone Monument....................12 C2
Luang Nam Tha Museum...........13 C2
Wat Ban Luang Khon................14 A6
Wat Ban Vieng Tai....................15 B5
Wildside Laos.............................16 C3

SLEEPING   (pp163-4)
Boat Landing Guest House &
    Restaurant............................17 B6
Bounthavong Guest House......18 C3
Bus Station Guest House.........19 C3
Cha Rueh Sin Guest House......20 C3
Hongthaxay Somboune Hotel..21 C1
Luang Namtha Guest House....22 C2
Many Chan Guest House.........23 C3
Palanh Guest House................24 C2
Phengthavy Guest House........25 C3
Saikhonglongsack Guest House.26 C2
Sinsavanh Guest House...........27 C1

EATING   (pp164-5)
Heuan Lao.................................28 C1
Nang Khamtip...........................29 C3
Panda Restaurant...................(see 25)

TRANSPORT   (p165)
Boat Landing............................30 B6
Bus Stop..................................31 C3
Bus Terminal............................32 C2
Lao Airlines..............................33 C3
Motorcycle Hire.......................34 C3

MONEY

BCEL (8.30am-3.30pm Mon-Fri) Almost directly opposite the telephone office is a BCEL where you can get a cash advance using your Visa card.

Lao Development Bank (8.30am-3.30pm Mon-Fri, 9.30am-12.30pm Sat) This bank will cash travellers cheques (US dollars only) for kip. Cash US dollars, Thai baht and Chinese yuan are also accepted.

Lao Development Bank Exchange Booth (8.30am-3.30pm) Located in the dry goods market.

POST

The post office is on the main north–south street through the new town centre.

TELEPHONE

Long-distance phone services are available at the Lao Telecom office just south of Saikhonglongsack Guest House.

Sights & Activities

The **Luang Nam Tha Museum** (admission US$0.50; 8.30am-noon & 1.30-3.30pm Mon-Fri) contains a collection of local anthropological artefacts, such as ethnic clothing and Khamu bronze drums, along with the usual display chronicling the revolution.

There's a Lao **herbal sauna** (sauna US$1, massage per hr US$2) behind the Panda Restaurant. Look for a bamboo bridge, which leads to a small hut on stilts next to a pond.

Near the airfield are two 50-year-old wats, **Wat Ban Vieng Tai** and **Wat Ban Luang Khon**, both of mild interest. **Ban Luang Khon** itself (the area around Wat Ban Luang Khon) is largely a Thai Kalom neighbourhood.

East across the Nam Tha from the boat landing are four or five Thai Dam villages; at **Ban Pa Sak** you can observe Thai Dam silk weaving in action.

Three kilometres west of the airfield atop a hill surrounded by rice fields stands **That Phum Phuk**, an impressively large stupa that shares stylistic similarities with That Ing Hang and other stupas more customarily found in Southern Laos. The brick-and-stucco stupa is said to have been erected in 1628, although it's likely that its current form dates to a more recent – possibly 19th century – renovation.

During the Second Indochina War a bomb explosion knocked the *jĕhdii* on its side, where it remains undisturbed. Despite its semiruined state – a large fig tree is now growing out of the base, lending a 'lost-in-the-jungle' atmosphere – the stupa is well worth visiting if you have any interest in Lao religious architecture, as it's a masterful piece of work. Much of the original stucco ornamentation is still in place; not far from the base stands a *sĭláa jáaleuk* (stele) inscribed in old Lao script. A newer replica of the stupa was erected nearby in 2003.

You can hire a jumbo from the market out to That Phum Phuk for US$5 return, including waiting time. If you decide to walk or bike, take the graded dirt road that runs west along the south side of the airport. After 700m this road ends at a T-junction. Make a right here and follow this road as it bends around to the northwest and passes rice fields. About 2.3km further on (3km total from the main paved road) you should see a hill to your right. Turn right on another dirt road just before the hill. After 100m on this road, look for a steep road on your left; this leads to the stupa at the top of the hill. Jumbos won't be able to climb this steep road, and you might not be able to pedal it either, especially when it's wet. On foot the climb takes between 10 and 15 minutes. Watch out for leeches in the rainy season.

About 6km northeast of the new town centre, off Rte 1, the Lao Huay (Lenten) village of **Ban Nam Di** is a good place to observe the process of bamboo papermaking. The villagers turn bamboo into pulp along the banks of the Nam Di adjacent to the village. They then spread the pulp into thin sheets over square cotton screens to fashion a rustic paper on which they record religious literature in a script based on Chinese characters. The paper is also much prized these days by the handicraft industry. Less than 1km away from Ban Nam Di is a **waterfall** that villagers will be glad to take you to for a small tip.

Luang Nam Tha is also the main jumping-off point for trekking, rafting and kayaking trips in the nearby Nam Ha NPA (see the boxed text p166) and for boat trips down the Nam Tha to the Mekong River (see p165). **Wildside Laos** (211484) next to Many Chan Guest House can arrange trekking, rafting and kayaking trips in the province.

Sleeping

Most lodging in Luang Nam Tha is in the newer, northern part of town. Rooms fill up fast during the December to March high season, so if you schedule a morning arrival you'll stand a better chance of getting a room.

BUDGET

Besides the places described here, there are a few less desirable Chinese guesthouses in town with overpriced rooms. We don't list them because we don't recommend them, but in a pinch they'll do until you can find something better. Often these guesthouses won't accept non-Chinese guests, and when they do they may ask double the posted tariff.

Bus Station Guest House (☎ 211090; r US$2.50-4) This aptly named spot a block north of the bus terminal offers basic but clean rooms with fan in a shophouse.

Luang Namtha Guest House (☎ 312087; r US$5-8) Three blocks north of the bus terminal, bamboo-and-wood cottages next to the adjacent pond cost less than the nicer but less charming rooms in a three-storey building. A restaurant on the pond serves simple Lao meals.

Phengthavy Guest House (☎ 312232; tw US$2) One of the newest guesthouses in town offers well-kept two-bed rooms with clean, shared facilities, along with the Panda Restaurant downstairs.

Many Chan Guest House (☎ 312209; s/d US$3/5) Many Chan, a two-storey wooden place with simple, well-kept rooms and a good restaurant downstairs, continues to be a favourite budget choice for Luang Nam Tha. Bathrooms are shared.

Saikhonglongsack Guest House (☎ 312257; s/d US$3/4) The Saikhonglongsack has basic clean rooms in Luang Nam Tha's tallest (three stories!) building.

Palanh Guest House (☎ 312439; s/d US$3/5) The reliable Palanh is a friendly two-storey place on the main drag with decent rooms and hot-water showers.

Sinsavanh Guest House (☎ 211141; r US$3) Further north up the road, Sinsavanh occupies a brightly painted two-storey wooden house. The family proprietors are friendly, the shared bathroom facilities are large and clean, and there's a pleasant sitting area on the upper terrace.

Hongthaxay Saisomboune Hotel (Hongtha; ☎ 312079; fax 312078; r US$3-5; ✕) The town's oldest hotel, Hongthaxay Saisomboune offers 28 rooms fronted by a nicely land-scaped garden area. A karaoke/disco in the compound stops by 11.30pm, after which it's a reasonably quiet place.

In the same vicinity as, and similar to, the Bus Station Guest House are:

Cha Rueh Sin Guest House (☎ 312393; r US$3)

Bounthavong Guest House (☎ 312256; r US$2.50)

MID-RANGE & TOP END

Boat Landing Guest House & Restaurant (☎ 312 398; fax 312239; www.theboatlanding.laopdr.com; r with breakfast US$25-45) Located 6km south of the new town and about 150m off the main road, this quiet lodge close to the Nam Tha boat landing offers easy access to the Nam Tha river and several Thai Dam villages. Spacious, nicely designed wooden bungalows feature verandas overlooking the river, and private bathrooms with solar-heated showers. There's also an excellent restaurant on the premises. The staff can arrange rafting or tubing excursions on the Nam Tha, fishing trips, bird-watching, mountain biking and trekking to nearby villages or to the Nam Ha NPA with English- and French-speaking guides. Bicycles are available for hire.

Eating

Typical opening hours for eateries are listed on p249.

Panda Restaurant (meals US$0.90-2.50) On the ground floor of the Phengthavy Guest House, the Panda has a long English-language menu of Lao, Chinese and *falang* dishes, plus better-than-average service.

Nang Khamtip (meals US$0.40-1; ☯ 7am-2pm) This famous shop next door to the Many Chan Guest House serves the best *fŏe*, *khào pìak* (rice soup) and *khào sǎwy* in town.

Heuan Lao (☎ 211111; meals US$1.50-3) With its open-air, 2nd-floor dining room and polished wood floors, Heuan Lao easily has the nicest atmosphere of any eatery located in the northern part of town. The mostly Lao menu is good but be prepared for slow service.

Many Chan Guest House (☎ 312209; meals US$1-2.50) The kitchen on the guesthouse's ground floor prepares very good Lao, Chinese, Thai and Western food.

Boat Landing Guest House & Restaurant (☎ 312398; US$1-4) Although it's the most ex-pensive place to eat in Nam Tha (but only by a small measure), the restaurant here serves the best and most authentic northern Lao cuisine you'll find in Nam Tha outside the market. The menu includes a good selection of vegetarian dishes.

The large morning market next to the bus terminal contains a couple of very good *fŏe* places and several *khào sáwy* stands. You can also get very inexpensive northern Lao takeaways at the market.

Shopping

Two kilometres from Luang Nam Tha on the right-hand side of the road to Muang Sing, in the Hmong village of Ban Hat Yao, is an EU-funded **Hat Yao Village Handicrafts Cooperative**. In a simple wooden structure, local villagers sell a range of handicrafts – textiles, basketry, jewellery and some clothing – at fixed prices. Some travellers will find the prices to be high compared with the markets or bargaining directly with villagers, but the project is dedicated to establishing a higher profit margin on behalf of village-based artisans. Refreshments are also available.

Getting There & Away

AIR

Lao Airlines (☎ 312180) flies a Y-12 between Luang Nam Tha and Vientiane (one way/return US$74/140, 55 minutes, four weekly). At one time there were also flights to/from Huay Xai but these have been suspended due to a lack of aircraft.

If you can't get a seat on a flight to Luang Nam Tha from Vientiane, or want to reach the town on one of the three days Lao Airlines doesn't fly to Luang Nam Tha, consider a flight to Udomxai (which fields daily flights in larger planes) and then take a bus four hours to Luang Nam Tha.

There is a second branch at the airport.

BOAT

See the Nam Tha River Trip (p165) for details on boat transport between Luang Nam Tha and the Mekong River.

BUS & SĂWNGTHĂEW

The main **bus terminal** (☎ 312164) – as usual just a large square of gravel and dirt with a wooden shack alongside – stands to the immediate north of the morning market.

Luang Nam Tha can be reached via all-weather Rte 1 from Udomxai (US$2.30,

four hours, three daily). A side road going north off Rte 1 about one-third of the way to Udomxai leads directly to Boten (US$1.50, two hours, four daily) on the Lao-Chinese border. At the intersection of Rte 1 and the road to Boten, the small town of Na Toei has one **guesthouse** (US$2), a market, health clinic and customs checkpoint.

One truck daily plies between Luang Nam Tha and Na Lae (US$3, three hours), roughly halfway to Pak Tha alongside the Nam Tha.

One bus a day also goes to/from Luang Prabang (US$5, eight hours) and Vientiane (US$11, 19 hours).

See Muang Sing (p171) and Huay Xai (p179) for public transport details for those towns.

Getting Around

From the bus terminal to the main street a jumbo costs US$0.50. Jumbos from the main street to the airport, 7km away, cost US$2. Shared pick-ups also ply this route several times daily for just US$0.20 per person.

To the Nam Tha boat landing, or the nearby Boat Landing Guest House, figure on US$3 to charter a jumbo from the bus terminal, or US$0.20 per person on a shared jumbo as far as the turn-off for the boat landing. From that intersection it's only around 150m to the boat landing or the guesthouse.

You can hire motorcycles from a shop next door to Many Chan Guest House. A few guesthouses also hire out bicycles (US$2 per day).

NAM THA RIVER TRIP

When the water is high enough, open-topped, longtail passenger boats navigate the Nam Tha between Pak Tha (where the Nam Tha feeds into the Mekong River) and Luang Nam Tha. This is a beautiful two-day river trip.

Along the way you can stop off and visit **Tham Davadeung**, a cave complex containing a large Buddha and several caverns. The cave is a short hike from the village of Ban Mo on the western bank of the river, about a third of the way between Pak Tha and Luang Prabang. Ask in the village for a key to the cave and a local guide to lead the way. A tip is expected for this service. Near **Ban**

NAM HA NATIONAL PROTECTED AREA

Named for the river that flows through it, the Nam Ha National Protected Area (NPA) extends 2224 sq km, from riverine plains to 2000m peaks. Running to the Chinese border and contiguous with Yunnan's Shiang Yong National Protected Area, it represents one of the most important international wildlife corridors in the region. Dense evergreen and semievergreen submontane forests and upland broadleaf woodlands harbour clouded leopard, tiger, elephants, gaur, muntjac and 288 bird species.

Several different ethnic groups inhabit the Nam Ha NPA, including Lao Huay, Akha and Khamu. The Unesco-sponsored **Nam Ha Ecotourism Project** (☎ 086-312150), begun four years ago, supervises small-group trekking and rafting in the NPA, with overnight stays in local villages. For more information or to book a trek, contact the project office, the Boat Landing Guest House (p164) or Wildside Laos (p163), all in Luang Nam Tha town.

Peng, a village further along towards Pak Tha, there are reportedly two waterfalls and two caves of interest.

Most travellers stop over in **Na Lae**, a charming village, located more or less the halfway point between Pak Tha and Luang Nam Tha.

In Pak Tha itself, you can visit an old Buddhist temple and wander through the local market.

Sleeping & Eating

Whether you manage to charter a boat for the entire trip, or have to change boats in Ban Na Lae, you will have to spend at least one night along the way.

There are two **guesthouses** (r US$1) in Na Lae, one near the boat landing, the other at the local market, and a noodle shop.

In Pak Tha your choice is the basic **Anusone Guest House** (r US$3) or the **Souphanee Guest House** (r US$1-2).

Getting There & Away

Because so many foreigners enter Laos via Huay Xai in the north, more people take this trip upstream from Pak Tha (about 36km via the Mekong River from Huay Xai) to Luang Nam Tha rather than vice versa, although the reverse direction is faster and less expensive.

Whether upriver or downriver, there is no regular boat service all the way from one end to the other. When regularly scheduled boats are running upriver, they go only as far as Na Lae, roughly halfway to Luang Nam Tha, for a per-person fare of US$5. Downriver most locals travel from Luang Nam Tha to Na Lae by bus (US$3, three hours, one daily).

When regular boats aren't scheduled, your only choice will be to charter a boat. Most boat pilots in Pak Tha will only go as far as Na Lae. Conversely, most boat pilots in Luang Nam Tha will also only take you to Na Lae. We've heard reports of boat pilots who say they will take you the whole way, but who then stop in Na Lae and refuse to go further. For this reason, you should not pay for the trip until you reach the agreed-upon destination.

Charter prices vary according to several factors, including size of the boat, amount of paid cargo, river level and current fuel costs. In the March to May dry season, boats don't run at all since the river is usually too low for navigation then.

Downriver charters cost less than upriver charters for obvious reasons. From Pak Tha (heading upriver) you can expect to pay US$50 to US$60 for a boat taking six to 10 passengers as far as Na Lae. If you can find someone willing to go all the way to Luang Nam Tha, the price should be around US$90. In the downriver direction, a charter should cost around US$35 from Luang Nam Tha to Na Lae, or around double that all the way to Pak Tha. If you manage to find a boat going with a lot of paid cargo, your charter price could come down.

BAP Guest House (☎ 084-211083) in Huay Xai (p177) is a good place to get information on the boat trip, and to arrange boat travel down the Mekong to Pak Tha, where you can then arrange for a boat up the Nam Tha. If you start from Luang Nam Tha, the best place to get information is the **Boat Landing Guest House** (☎ 312398) – see p164. You can also go straight to the boat transport offices at the respective landings and arrange travel.

So far speedboats aren't allowed on the Nam Tha. This appears to be more a case of quashing competition than harbouring concerns about noise pollution or safety, but the absence of speedboats makes the Nam Tha trip all the more pleasant.

MUANG SING

ເມືອງສິງ

☎ 086 / pop 23,500

Lying on the broad river plains of the Nam La northwest of Luang Nam Tha, Muang Sing is a traditional Thai Lü and Thai Neua cultural nexus as well as a trade centre for Thai Dam, Akha, Hmong, Mien, Lolo and Yunnanese. Two groups dominate the district population; Thai Lü comprising about 30% of the total (mostly in town and adjacent plains) and Akha at around 45% (in the surrounding hills).

One of the arms of the 'China Road' passes through Muang Sing on its way to Mengla in Yunnan Province, China, and the area has come under a lot of Chinese influence since the 1960s. Visiting Chinese soldiers can be seen strutting around the streets and even some local hill-tribe men wear olive-drab Mao hats. Most telling is the presence of Chinese tractors, often bearing Chinese licence tags and transporting goods and people back and forth from the Chinese border – sugar cane to China, garlic and onions to Muang Sing.

History

From at least the late 16th century until 1803 Muang Sing belonged to the Thai principality of Chiang Khong, after which it came under control of the Nan Kingdom. In the early 19th century much of Muang Sing's population was transferred to Chiang Kham district in Nan (now part of Thailand).

After a number of Shan princes took refuge from the British Raj here in 1885, both the Siamese and the British laid claim to the area. Both powers finally relinquished pretensions to all lands on the east bank of the Mekong in an 1896 agreement with the French, and France took Muang Sing as part of French Indochina.

As soon as the French left Laos in 1954, the area fell into the conflict between the Royal Lao Government and the Vietnamese-backed Pathet Lao. From then until the Pathet Lao takeover of Vientiane in 1975, ancient Muang Sing served as a setting for a series of international intrigues involving the Chinese, Vietnamese, Americans and Lao. The famous American 'jungle doctor' Tom Dooley, a pawn of the CIA in Laos from 1957 to 1961 and a man who courted Catholic sainthood until he was dismissed from the US Navy for his sexual orientation, founded a hospital in Muang Sing during this era. Muang Sing's oldest temple, Wat Xieng Nyeun, was destroyed during a battle between royalist Lao and communist Lao forces in 1962, and the town was virtually abandoned until after the 1975 revolution.

NORTHERN LAOS

THE STORY OF O

Muang Sing district typically produces four to five tonnes of opium per year, about 3% of all opium produced in Laos. Over two-thirds of that is thought to have been consumed in the district itself, where it is used as medicine, as food, in exchange for hired labour, for the hosting of guests and for spiritual ceremonies. A darker statistic estimates there are over a thousand opium addicts in Muang Sing, whose addiction rate as a district ranks fifth in all of Laos. As elsewhere in Southeast Asia the hill tribes appear to be most susceptible; nearly one in every 10 Akha tribes people in the district, for example, is said to be addicted. Negative effects of such high addiction rates include a reduced male labour force and corresponding increase in women's workloads (most addicts are men), and reduced overall agricultural production.

Opium is traditionally a condoned vice of the elderly, yet an increasing number of young people in the villages are now taking opium, heroin and amphetamines. In the town of Muang Sing local Yunnanese and hill-tribe addicts sometimes peddle opium openly to *falang* visitors, thus setting a poor example for unaddicted local youth, and everyone knows where the local 'dens' are. If you're tempted to experiment with a little 'O', keep in mind the effect your behaviour may have on the local culture – you may smoke once and a few weeks later be hundreds of kilometres away while the villagers continue to face the temptation every day.

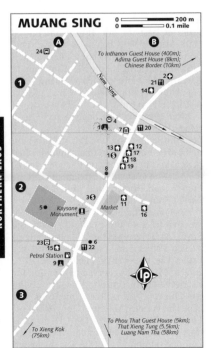

MUANG SING

0 _____ 200 m
0 _____ 0.1 mile

To Inthanon Guest House (400m);
Adima Guest House (8km);
Chinese Border (10km)

Nam Sing

Kaysone Monument

Market

Petrol Station

To Xieng Kok (75km)

To Phou That Guest House (5km);
That Xieng Tung (5.5km);
Luang Nam Tha (58km)

INFORMATION	
BCEL	1 B2
Hospital	2 B1
Lao Development Bank	3 B1
Post Office	4 B1

SIGHTS & ACTIVITIES	(pp168-9)
French Garrison	5 A2
Herbal Sauna	6 A3
Muang Sing Exhibitions	7 B1
Muang Sing Information & Trekking Guide Service Center	8 A2
Wat Nam Kaew Luang	9 A3
Wat Xieng Jai	10 A1

SLEEPING	(pp169-70)
Champa Daeng Guest House	11 B2
Daen Neua Guest House	12 B2
Muang Sing Guest House	13 B2
Sangduane Hotel	14 B1
Sing Charean Hotel	15 A3
Singsai Guest House	16 B2
Thai Lü Guest House	17 B2
Vieng Phone Guest House	18 B2
Viengxay Guest House	19 B2

EATING	(p170)
Anousone Restaurant	20 B1
Hasina Indian Restaurant	21 B1
Meuang Sing View Restaurant	22 A3

ENTERTAINMENT	(pp170)
Singsavanh Nightclub	23 A3

TRANSPORT	(p171)
Bus Terminal	24 A1

Information

Muang Sing now has two banks – a BCEL branch opposite the Viengxay Guest House and the Lao Development Bank opposite the market. They will change US dollars, baht and yuan, but at a less favourable rate than in most other parts of the country.

Electricity is available from 6.30pm to 10pm nightly. Most guesthouses give guests a thermos of hot water, which can be used to heat up cold-water scoop showers on chilly nights.

Sights & Activities

Among the buildings left standing from the French era is a 75-year-old brick and plaster **French garrison** that once housed Moroccan and Senegalese troops. It's now a Lao army outpost and some of the buildings have been restored; others stand in ruins.

Along the town's main street you'll also see hybrid Lao-French architecture where the ground floor walls are brick and stucco and the upstairs walls are wooden. The top floor usually features a long wood-railed veranda overlooking the street.

One of the better examples of the latter architectural style has been restored to contain the **Meuang Sing Exhibitions** (admission US$0.50; ⏲ 9am-4pm), a collection of cultural artefacts from the area. On display are fishing utensils, looms, cooking utensils, old gongs, bells, pottery, musical instruments, Lao-style Buddha images, local ethnic costumes and a Buddha votive. The house containing the exhibition was once occupied by a local prince named Phanya Sekong. Note that the opening hours aren't always adhered to.

Two Buddhist temples in town show Thai Lü architectural influence. At **Wat Xieng Jai** on the main street, you can see this mainly in the monastic quarters, with the massive steps and tiny windows, while in the less typical, rustic *wihǎan* (main Buddha sanctuary) you'll see classic Thai Lü–style *thóng* – long vertical prayer flags woven of colourful patterned cloth and bamboo. Red- and silver-lacquered pillars are also a Thai Lü temple design characteristic. Further north near the beginning of the road to Xieng Kok, **Wat Nam Kaew Luang** also has monastic quarters in the Thai Lü style, actually converted from a former *wihǎan*. Mud-brick antechambers before a wooden passageway leading to the *wihǎan* are unusual and may be a Yunnanese addition.

The northern end of town is the best place to see thatched Thai Lü and Thai Dam houses known as *héuan hǒng*, or swan houses.

The main **market** at Muang Sing – *talàat nyai* in Lao, *kaat long* in Thai Lü – was once the biggest opium market in the Golden Triangle, a function officially sanctioned by the French. Perhaps the most colourful market in northern Laos, today it's a venue for fresh produce and clothing staples bought and sold by a polyglot crowd mainly consisting of Thai Dam, Thai Lü, Thai Neua, Hmong, Akha, Yunnanese, Shan and Mien. Akha are the most numerous, as most villages outside the municipality are Akha. Traditional textiles – especially the simple, naturally dyed silks and cottons of the Thai Lü – are also sold in the market. Villagers also come in to town to sell textiles to foreign visitors who hang out in guesthouse restaurants.

A number of Lao Thoeng and Lao Soung **villages** in the vicinity – particularly those of the Akha – can be visited on foot from Muang Sing. In general you'll find Hmong and Akha villages to the west and northwest of Muang Sing in the hills, repatriated Mien to the northeast, and Thai Neua and Thai Dam to the south. The Thai Dam are doing the best weaving in the district these days. One of the closest Thai Dam villages is Nong Bua. The Muang Sing Information & Trekking Guide Service Center in town can provide trained guides for two- to three-day treks to remote hill-tribe villages; prices are posted at the centre. Some guesthouses sell a sketch map with information about the various villages and how to find them for about US$0.75.

The Chinese-Lao border (crossings legal for Lao and Chinese citizens only) is only 10km from Muang Sing, with a checkpoint 1km before the border. Along the way the narrow, paved road (originally constructed by the French) passes through three villages, including one called **Ban Nakham** at Km 100 (about 4km or 5km from the Chinese border) whose mud-brick homes suggest a Yunnanese population.

A traditional Lao **herbal sauna**, near the Meuang Sing View Restaurant, offers steam baths and massage.

Festivals & Events

During the full moon of the 12th lunar month, which usually occurs between late October and mid-November, all of Muang Sing and half of the province turns out for the **That Xieng Tung Festival**. Centred around a Thai Lü stupa (That Xieng Tung) on a sacred hill 5.5km south of town, the festival combines Theravada Buddhism and animistic elements of worship and includes many of the ceremonies associated with the That Luang Festival in Vientiane (which occurs at the same time).

The *thâat* is around 10m high and is constructed in the Lanna–Lan Xang style, with a stepped, whitewashed octagonal base and gilded spire. A shrine building off to one side contains a row of Buddha images on a sarcophaguslike Thai Lü altar.

The festival begins a few days before the official full moon day as merit-makers climb a broad winding path to the *thâat* grounds atop the hill and pay their respects by carrying offerings of candles, flowers and incense around the base of the stupa – a tradition called *wían thían*. On the morning of the full moon Buddhist monks from around the province gather at the stupa for *ták bàat*, the collection of alms-food. There are also traditional dance performances, carnival-style game booths, and plenty of food vendors selling *khào laam* (sweetened sticky rice baked in bamboo), noodles and other snacks. Many Chinese vendors cross over from Yunnan during the festival to sell cheap Chinese cigarettes, beer and apples. Festival activities spill over into town, where there are nightly outdoor Lao pop music performances with lots of drinking and dancing. Food vendors line the main street at night with candlelit tables.

In spite of its Thai Lü origins, the That Xieng Tung Festival is celebrated by virtually all ethnic groups in the area (including festival-goers from as far away as Xishuangbanna, the original Thai Lü homeland in China's Yunnan Province), as much for its social and entertainment value as for anything else. This is the biggest event of the year here, and one of the best times to visit Muang Sing.

Sleeping

Sing Charean Hotel (☎ 212347; r US$5-8) This is the first place you come to after entering town. It's off the main street, about 30m down a dirt road on the left just past the petrol station. The white two-storey Sing Charean features clean hotel-like rooms, all with attached cold-water bathroom. Herbal massages are available here.

Viengxay Guest House (Vieng Sai; ☎ 252630; s/d US$2/3) This a large wooden place on the main street not far from the market, with an upstairs veranda good for reading, relaxing or viewing the passing scene. Clean showers and toilets are at the rear of the building. There is a sizable restaurant downstairs.

Thai Lü Guest House (☎ 212375; r US$2-4) One of the better guesthouses in town, the Thai Lü is a two-storey French-era wooden structure. It has clean rooms with attached bathroom and a restaurant downstairs. One of its charms is the front balcony, ideal for sitting and watching the street life.

Daen Neua Guest House (☎ 212369; r US$3) Up the street from Thai Lü, this one is another good choice, with simple clean rooms and a big restaurant.

Muang Sing Guest House (☎ 212375; s/d/tr US$1/2/3) Rooms in the old, wooden two-storey building on the street have attached bathroom, while those in the new building out the back have shared facilities. Guests at the Muang Sing are provided thermoses of hot water for washing and there's a restaurant downstairs.

Singsai Guest House (☎ 212364; r US$3-7) Singsai is a concrete establishment behind the market. Food is served in a separate building. This hotel is quieter than the others as it's set back from the main street.

Saengduane Guest House (☎ 212376; r US$3-8) Further north still is the larger and well-run Saengduane. This concrete/plaster rectangular building offers six upstairs rooms and a balcony along the front. There are good views across to the mountains from the balcony, and even better views from the accessible rooftop. There's a restaurant downstairs, and toilets and showers out the back.

Phou That Guest House (☎ 312085; r US$5-7) The newest guesthouse in town is perched on the side of Phu That, the same hill 5.5km south of town where That Xieng Tung is located. The comfortable rooms come with private bathroom.

Inthanon Guest House (r US$3) In a quiet location about 400m northeast of the Saengduane hotel, this guesthouse, owned and operated by Thai Lü, consists of four bamboo-thatch-and-wood cottages plus a restaurant area. All rooms feature attached cold-water showers, mosquito nets and unlimited electricity.

Other options:

Vieng Phone Guest House (s/d US$1.50/2) Similar to the Viengxay, although not as well maintained.

Champa Daeng Guest House (☎ 212374; r US$3-7) In a two-storey L-shaped building on the way to the Singsai.

OUTSIDE MUANG SING

Adima (☎ 212372; r US$4-6) In a village 8km outside Muang Sing towards the Chinese border, the Adima's ethnic-style houses are set in the middle of rice paddies, and the guesthouse is within walking distance of several Mien and Akha villages. Adima offers free transport to/from Muang Sing twice daily, from the Viengxay Guest House (its contact in town).

Eating

Typical opening hours for eateries are listed on p249.

Most of the guesthouses have small dining areas downstairs, with the best eats generally found at the Daen Neua and Thai Lü. You can always find a few simple *fŏe* shops along the main street and in the market.

Anousone (meals US$1-3) The Anousone is diagonally opposite the Meuang Sing Exhibitions building on the northeastern corner and offers various Lao, Thai and Western dishes.

Meuang Sing View Restaurant (meals US$1.50-3) This little bamboo-thatched place, a bit off the road towards the southern end of town, overlooks rice fields. It serves Lao and Western food.

Hasina Indian Restaurant (meals US$1-2) Situated between Saengduane Guest House and the provincial hospital, this new white-tiled eatery serves up a selection of North Indian food.

Entertainment

Singsavanh Nightclub (🕒 9-11.30pm) Most of Muang Sing is dead asleep by 9pm except at the Singsavanh, near the Sing Charean Hotel, where the locals get down to live Lao and Chinese pop.

Getting There & Away

Buses ply back and forth between Muang Sing and Luang Nam Tha (US$1.50, two hours, hourly 8am to 3pm). The winding, partially sealed 58km road from Luang Nam Tha to Muang Sing parallels the Nam Tha, Nam Luang and Nam Sing rivers, crossing them at various points along the way, and passes through strikingly beautiful monsoon forest and several hill-tribe villages. The deep trench you'll see alongside the road between Nam Tha and Muang Sing is part of a hydropower and irrigation project intended to serve the Muang Sing plain.

In Muang Sing passenger vehicles are supposed to depart from a new bus terminal in the old city but most vehicles still stop in front of the market.

See Xieng Kok p172 for details on *săwngthăew* transport from Muang Sing.

CHINA

Although Muang Sing is only 10km from the Chinese border, you can't legally cross into China here without permission arranged through the Lao National Tourism Authority (NTAL) in Vientiane (see p67) or some other travel agency.

Getting Around

Bicycle hire is once again permitted in Muang Sing (US$2 per day at most guesthouses). There are no jumbos or public transport within Muang Sing.

XIENG KOK

ຊຽງກົກ

Roughly 72km from Muang Sing via a smooth, graded road that parallels the Nam Ma much of the way, this bustling river port on the Mekong River has little to attract the traveller aside from its semiremote location. Until as recently as the early 1990s up to six refineries along the Mekong between Xieng Kok and Huay Xai refined opium for world markets. Today huge Chinese barges from Yunnan Province call at Xieng Kok frequently, and it's reported that Xieng Kok is a major smuggling conduit for opium, heroin and amphetamines in both directions, depending on market destination.

Perhaps the best time to schedule a Xieng Kok visit is on the 14th and 28th of each month, when traders from Myanmar,

Thailand, China and Laos gather to buy and sell their wares. Many different hill tribes, particularly the Akha, descend on the town on these days.

Most visitors to Xieng Kok are more interested in taking a boat down the Mekong to Huay Xai. See below for details.

Some travellers stop off at **Muang Long**, a heavily Akha district a little more than halfway to Xieng Kok from Muang Sing. There are some very good forest walks near Muang Long, especially along the Nam Long. Opium is intensively cultivated between Muang Long and the Myanmar border.

Sleeping & Eating

In Xieng Kok, the **Xieng Kok Resort** (r US$5) sits on a hill and boasts simple but comfortable wooden bungalows on stilts. **Kaemkhong Guest House** (r US$3) offers basic rooms with shared facilities. Two restaurants in Xieng Kok serve simple but remarkably good Lao food – for the location.

In Muang Long, **Jony** (r US$3), **Ounseng** (r US$3) and **Thatsany** (r US$3) guesthouses all feature similarly basic accommodation.

Getting There & Away

BOAT

Speedboats holding up to six passengers ply the Mekong River between Xieng Kok and Huay Xai (US$15 per person or US$85 charter, four hours). It appears to be virtually impossible to get a slow boat out of Xieng Kok.

Via Muang Mom & Ton Pheung

You can get better rates by asking for a speedboat to Muang Mom rather than Huay Xai. Muang Mom, about two hours downriver, is a large speedboat depot near the point where the borders of Thailand, Myanmar and Laos meet. All boats must stop here anyway to allow Lao immigration and customs officers to check everyone's papers.

A speedboat from Xieng Kok to Muang Mom costs around US$6 per person (assuming there are six passengers), and another speedboat to Huay Xai – just 1½ hours further downriver – will cost around US$4 per person.

Another way to reach Huay Xai is to catch a speedboat to Ton Pheung (US$7 per person or US$40 charter), the Lao town opposite Chiang Saen. From Ton Pheung you can catch a bus onward to Huay Xai (US$1), along a decent graded road.

SÄWNGTHÄEW
A graded, unsealed road extends 72km from Muang Sing to Xieng Kok (US$1.50, two hours, three daily).

BOTEN
ບໍ່ເຕນ

This border village on the Chinese border in the northeastern corner of Luang Nam Tha Province is little more than a transit point for visitors travelling between Laos and China, since Boten is a legal border crossing for all nationalities. Although there's a basic guesthouse and noodle shops, much better facilities are available in Mengla on the Chinese side. Many Chinese visit Boten on day passes to buy imported Thai goods.

See the Luang Nam Tha (p165) and Udomxai (p158) for details on transport to/from Boten.

Information
There's a branch of Lao Development Bank in Boten where US dollars, Thai baht and Chinese yuan may be exchanged for kip, but not vice versa.

CROSSING THE CHINESE BORDER AT MOHAN & BOTEN

From Mohan in the Yunnan Province, China, you can legally enter Laos at Boten in the Luang Nam Tha Province, Laos. Fifteen-day tourist visas for Laos are available from the Lao immigration post on arrival in Boten for US$30. To cross in the opposite direction, into China, you will need to have arranged a Chinese visa in advance.

The Lao border crossing is open from 8am to 4pm, while the Chinese crossing is open from 8am to 5pm. The best time of day to cross into Laos from China is the early morning when public transport onward to Luang Nam Tha and Udomxai is most frequently available.

From Boten it's a short bus hop to the provincial capital, Luang Nam Tha, but if you arrive in Boten too late to take a bus, there are a couple of cheap guesthouses (US$1 to US$2) in the border town.

Sleeping & Eating
Boua Vanh Guest House (☎ 071-252606; r US$3) This small two-storey guesthouse is still the only place to stay. The rooms are basic and facilities are shared.

Although there's only one place to stay, Boten offers around 10 small restaurants and noodle shops. All serve very simple dishes.

PHONGSALI PROVINCE

Enclosed on three sides by China and Vietnam, Phongsali is northern Laos's most inaccessible province. Prior to the Sino-French Treaty of 1895, Phongsali was an independent Thai Lü principality attached to Xishuangbanna in southern Yunnan.

Despite efforts to counter opium poppy cultivation, poppy farms remain widespread among the Hmong, Mien and Lolo in this province. Chinese-style tea, however, stands a good chance of becoming a more significant cash crop, judging from the proliferation of tea plantations.

Phongsali's population density is 9.4 per square kilometre, the lowest in the country after Sekong and Attapeu Provinces. Twenty-two ethnicities make up the province's population of approximately 152,000, among them Kheu, Sila, Lolo, Hanyi, Hmong, Pala, Oma, Eupa, Loma, Pusang, Mien, Akha, Haw, Thai Dam, Thai Khao, Thai Lü, Phuan, Khamu, Phai, Vietnamese and Yunnanese. The Phu Noi (recognisable by their white leggings) are by far the most numerous, followed by the Thai Lü, Haw, Akha and Khamu. As in Udomxai and Luang Nam Tha, the Chinese presence has increased steeply with recent road and construction development.

Phu Den Din NPA covers 1310 sq km in the northeastern corner of the province along the Lao-Vietnamese border, adjacent to Vietnam's Muong Nhe Nature Reserve. Mountains in this area reach up to 1948m and bear 77% primary forest cover. Many threatened or endangered mammals live in the area, including elephant, tiger, clouded leopard, banteng, gaur and Asiatic black bear. Access to Phu Den Din remains difficult due to the lack of roads, and there are as yet no guided treks to the NPA.

The best areas for hill-tribe village exploration are found in the extreme northwest corner of the province, where there are also few roads. Reaching this area involves walking two or more days; guides are available in Phongsali.

PHONGSALI

ພົງສາລີ

☎ 088 / pop 25,000 / elevation 1400m

At various times in its history the provincial capital has served as a Chinese, French and Vietnamese outpost. The original name, Fongsali – changed to Phongsali by the Lao PDR – is said to be Chinese.

Built on the steep slopes of Phu Fa (1625m), Phongsali possesses a year-round cool climate that comes as a welcome relief during the hotter (March to May) season. In fact, the climate is closer to what you would find in northern Vietnam than in much of Laos. It can be quite cold during the cool season, with temperatures as low as 5°C at night and 10°C during the day. Fog and low clouds are common in the morning at any time of year. Rainfall can be intense and cold. Be sure to bring a pullover, jacket and waterproofs, even in March, April and May, just in case.

The capital district is surrounded by rolling, deforested hills. About 70% of the population is Phu Noi, who speak a Tibeto-Burman language related to Lolo. Whatever their ethnic background, most residents are trilingual in Lao, Chinese and Phu Noi. If you've come expecting to see lots of colourfully garbed minorities in the market

or around town, you'll be disappointed unless you arrive during a major holiday like Lao New Year in April, when residents from all around the province visit the capital.

Hotels and guesthouses in town can help arrange village trekking outside of town.

Information

A branch of Lao Development Bank, near the Phongsali Hotel, can change US dollars, Thai baht or Chinese yuan (but no travellers cheques) for kip.

The main post office and Lao Telecom office (card phone available) stand opposite one another in the centre of town.

Sights

The **Museum of Tribe** (admission US$0.20; ⊗ 8-11.30am & 1.30-4.30pm Mon-Fri) displays locally curated exhibits on the Phongsali Province's diverse cultures.

If you wander through the town's backstreets and alleys you'll find some interesting old Phu Noi (similar to Tibetan) and Chinese brick-and-wood architecture.

Sleeping

Yu Houa Guest House (r US$2-3) This friendly Phu Noi-owned guesthouse near the bus station has plain but clean rooms, with a very good restaurant downstairs.

Phongsali Hotel (☎ 412042; r US$2-5) The Chinese-built Phongsali Hotel, in a centrally located four-storey building said to be the highest structure in the province, offers

NORTHERN LAOS

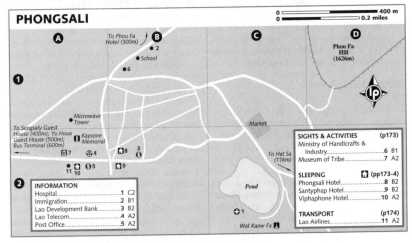

PHONGSALI

0 — 400 m
0 — 0.2 miles

To Phou Fa Hotel (300m)

Phou Fa Hill (1626m)

● 2
● School
● 6

Microwave Tower

To Sengsaly Guest House (400m); Yu Houa Guest House (500m); Bus Terminal (600m)

Kaysone Memorial

Market

To Hat Sa (11km)

Pond

Wat Kaew Fa

INFORMATION	
Hospital	1 C2
Immigration	2 B1
Lao Development Bank	3 B2
Lao Telecom	4 A2
Post Office	5 A2

SIGHTS & ACTIVITIES	(p173)
Ministry of Handicrafts & Industry	6 B1
Museum of Tribe	7 A2

SLEEPING	(pp173-4)
Phongsali Hotel	8 B2
Santyphap Hotel	9 B2
Viphaphone Hotel	10 A2

TRANSPORT	(p174)
Lao Airlines	11 A2

28 plain rooms, most with three beds; the more expensive rooms have hot water.

Santyphap Guest House (r US$2-3) Opposite the Phongsali Hotel, the rustic Santyphap is a two-storey wooden structure with a basic rooms that have mosquito nets.

Phou Fa Hotel (☎ 412057; r US$5) Standing on the hill of the same name, the walled-in Phou Fa compound was a Chinese consulate and military base in the 1960s, complete with secret tunnels crisscrossing the hill (ask to see them). The hotel commands a good view of the area and has a restaurant with a fireplace.

Viphaphone Hotel (☎ 210111; r US$2-4.50) Similar to the Phongsali Hotel in a three-storey version, the Viphaphone appears to be a favourite with truck drivers.

HAT SA

Hat Sa, a stopover for visitors heading for Phongsali via boat, has a **guesthouse** (dm US$1) with multibed rooms.

Eating

The **Yu Houa Guest House restaurant** (meals US$0.50-2; ⏰ 6am-10pm) serves delicious Yunnanese food, along with a few Lao dishes. The **Phongsali Hotel** (meals US$1-3) offers the largest menu (mostly Chinese). The **Phou Fa Hotel** (meals US$1-3) serves surprisingly good central Lao food, a relief from standard Chinese fare.

There are several noodle shops on the main street through town towards the market. Chinese beer is cheap all over town, while Beerlao is relatively expensive. The local *lào-láo* is tinted green with herbs and is quite a smooth tipple. Good Chinese-style tea is also available. Typical opening hours for eateries are listed on p249.

Getting There & Away

AIR

Lao Airlines (☎ 210032), next to the Viphaphone Hotel, operates a Y-12 to/from Vientiane (one way/return US$89/168, 1½ hours, two weekly).

BOAT

Hat Sa can be reached by boat along the Nam Ou from Muang Khua. In Muang Khua you can choose between slow boats (US$6, six hours, daily at 8.30am) and speedboats (US$6, three hours, departures depend on passenger demand). Either type of boat may be chartered from Muang Khua to Hat Sa for US$60, carrying up to 15 passengers in a slow boat or six passengers in a speedboat.

When the river level is low, particularly from March to May, the boat service may be cancelled.

BUS & 4WD

The Phongsali bus terminal, near the market at the foot of Phu Fa, fields one or two buses daily to/from Luang Prabang (US$7, 12 hours) and Udomxai (US$5, eight hours).

Hat Sa

From the boat landing at the small town of Hat Sa, passengers can share a 4WD vehicle (US$1.50 per person, US$15 charter) for the 20km journey along an unsealed road to Phongsali.

Mengla (China)

If the Yunnan-Phongsali border should open to foreign travellers in the future (it is currently open to Chinese and Lao nationals only), it will be easier to reach Phongsali from Mengla (in Yunnan), than from most points in Laos. From the Lao settlement of Ban Pakha (a village of Akha refugees who fled the communist takeover of China in the 1940s) near the Chinese border to Phongsali you could take a bus to Bun Neua, where you would change to another bus for the final leg to Phongsali.

UDOMXAI TO PHONGSALI

Sixty-two kilometres northeast of Udomxai, Rte 4 reaches a three-way junction at the village of Pak Nam Noi. From Pak Nam Noi, Rte 3 continues east-northeast to Muang Khua and to the Vietnamese border, while another (as yet unnumbered) road proceeds north-northeast to Phongsali.

From Udomxai to Pak Nam Noi about two-thirds of Rte 4 is now sealed, and before long this entire stretch no doubt will be sealed. On the way to Pak Nam Noi you'll pass through scenic **Muang La** (25km from Udomxai), a tidy Thai Lü village with a classic Thai Lü temple and a couple of restaurants built alongside a river.

In Pak Nam Noi the **Pak Nam Noy Guest House** (r US$2), near the three-way junction, can provide a room if you miss a bus connection and become stranded here.

Roughly halfway between Udomxai and Phongsali, **Boun Tai** (60km from Udomxai) is a prospering Thai Lü town popular as a base for NGOs and as a rest stop for people travelling to and from Phongsali. The **Khem Nam Lan** (r US$2-4), **Boun Tai** (r US$2-4) and **Hong Thong** (r US$2-4) guesthouses all offer decent accommodation. The Hong Thong prepares good Chinese food, while the slightly more elaborate River View Restaurant does Lao as well as Chinese.

Next comes **Ban Yo** (30km from Boun Tai), where a turn to the left leads directly to **Ban Pakha** (19km) on the Chinese border and a turn right goes to **Boun Neua** (21km) and Phongsali. Although Boun Neua is essentially a Thai Lü village, the abundance of Chinese signs and the presence of a Chinese-style guesthouse and restaurant demonstrates the close connection with China, only 40km away.

At Boun Neua the road forks into one road leading northeast to Phongsali (41km) or another heading north to **Ou Tai** (93km). Ou Tai is known to be a centre for several Phongsali Province hill tribes.

MUANG KHUA

ເມືອງຂວາ

☎ 081 / pop 20,000

This small trading town sits at the junction of the Nam Ou and Rte 4, which connects Udomxai and Phongsali Provinces with Dien Bien Phu in Vietnam. Many Vietnamese and Chinese people have migrated here to do business and it's growing steadily as a result.

Although Muang Khua is not much of a destination in itself, a quick walk around town will reveal a few older French colonial buildings amid the growing number of cement shophouses. A stroll across the old wood-plank and steel-cable suspension bridge over the Nam Phak, a Nam Ou tributary, affords some good river and mountain views and leads to the Khamu village of Ban Na Tum.

The Lao Development Bank here can change US dollars, Thai baht and Chinese yuan (cash only) for kip. Electric power comes on nightly from 6.30pm to 10pm.

There are rumours that the Lao-Vietnamese border, around 55km east of Muang Khua via Rte 4, will soon open to international travel. When it does, this route will surely become popular among those travelling to or from Dien Bien Phu in Vietnam. The border town on the Lao side is called Tai Xang; on the Vietnamese side it's Tay Trang.

Sleeping & Eating

Nam Ou Guest House & Restaurant (s/d US$2/3) This rambling wood-and-bamboo place overlooks the Nam Ou and can be accessed from the town's main road or from the main boat landing. The **restaurant** (meals US$0.50-1.50) has a good view overlooking the river, and a basic menu. The friendly owner speaks French and English. Facilities are shared.

Sernnaly Hotel (☎ 212445; r US$10) This new Chinese-built, L-shaped hotel in the town centre has clean rooms with new beds, fan and private bathroom. The downstairs **restaurant** (meals US$1-3) serves Chinese, Vietnamese, Thai and Lao food.

A few other guesthouses – Manhchany, Keophila, Sengali and Ketsana – all in two-storey buildings along the street leading to the boat landing, appear to be open only during the high season.

Other than the restaurants at the Nam Ou Guest House and Sernnaly Hotel, you'll find the usual crop of noodle stands at the market near the bus terminal. On the outskirts of town coming from Udomxai, the **Saynampak Restaurant** (meals US$0.50-2) offers a relaxed atmosphere in a wooden building overlooking the Nam Phak.

Getting There & Away

BOAT

When the river level is high enough, you can reach Muang Khua via boat on the Nam Ou. See Luang Prabang (p133), Phongsali (p174), and Nong Khiaw (p137) for details on boat travel to Muang Khua.

BUS

The bus terminal next to the town market fields buses to/from Udomxai (US$2.20, four hours, two daily) and Luang Prabang (US$4.60, eight hours, two daily).

BOKEO PROVINCE

Laos's smallest and second least populous province, wedged between the Mekong River border with Thailand and Luang

Nam Tha Province, has a population of just 113,500. In earlier times Bokeo was known as Hua Khong (Head of the Mekong); its current name means Gem Mine, a reference to minor sapphire deposits in Huay Xai district. The province borders Thailand and Myanmar, and is less than 100km from China, and so it has become a focus of the much-ballyhooed 'Economic Quadrangle', a four-nation trade zone envisioned mainly by corporate entities in Thailand and China.

Despite its diminutive size Bokeo harbours 34 ethnicities, the second-highest number of ethnic groups per province (after Luang Nam Tha) in the country. They include Lao Huay (Lenten), Khamu, Akha, Hmong, Mien, Kui, Phai, Lamet, Samtao, Tahoy, Shan, Phu Thai, Thai Dam, Thai Khao, Thai Daeng, Thai Lü, Phuan, Thai Nai, Ngo, Kalom, Phuvan, Musoe (Lahu) and Chinese people. Bokeo is the only Laos province with a significant population of Lahu, a hill-tribe common in northern Myanmar and Thailand.

For years the tourist industry in Laos has been pushing a circular overland itinerary that takes in Luang Prabang, Udomxai, Luang Nam Tha and Bokeo. In the mid-1990s a Thai company won the bid for an aid-financed road project that would eventually produce a direct land route from Thailand to China through Laos – including a new bridge over the Mekong between Chiang Khong and Huay Xai. The 1997–98 economic slump put the brakes on the project (including the bridge), although work is continuing on the road to serve a Thai coal mining enterprise in Vieng Phukha.

HUAY XAI

ຫ້ວຍຊາຍ

☎ 084 / pop 15,500

For centuries Huay Xai was a disembarkation point for Yunnanese caravans led by the Hui (Chinese Muslims) on their way to Chiang Rai and Chiang Mai in ancient Siam; today Chinese barges from Yunnan are able to navigate this far, so there is still a brisk trade in Chinese goods. Thailand's Chiang Khong, on the opposite river bank, is also a significant source of trade. Speedboats seen along Laos's northern rivers are imported from Chiang Khong, for example.

Nowadays Huay Xai is a bustling riverside town where the biggest commercial district is centred around the vehicle and passenger ferry landings for boats to Chiang Khong. Many new shophouses have been constructed along the main street, which curves along the base of a hill overlooking the river.

For most ferry arrivals from Chiang Khong, Huay Xai is just a stopover before boarding a boat southeast to Pak Beng or Luang Prabang, or catching a truck northeast to Luang Nam Tha.

Information

The **Lao Development Bank** (☺ 8am-3.30pm Mon-Fri), opposite the Arimid Guest House, also has an exchange booth at the immigration and customs office near the ferry pier. US dollars, travellers cheques, or cash in baht and Japanese yen can be changed for kip at either location, but not vice versa.

The **post office** (Th Saykhong; ☺ 8am-4pm Mon-Fri) also contains a **telephone office** (☺ 8am-10pm).

Sights & Activities

A set of *naga* stairs ascends from a point not far from the ferry landing to **Wat Jom Khao Manilat**, a thriving temple that overlooks the town and river. Constructed in 1880, the teak Shan-style temple houses a 1458 stele donated by a former Chiang Khong prince. Many of the brightly coloured Jataka paintings that decorate the exterior of the *sim* were sponsored by Lao refugees who had been repatriated from the US.

French-built, high-walled **Fort Carnot**, atop an adjacent hill and clearly visible from the Thai side of the Mekong, is occupied by Lao troops and is off limits to visitors.

Huay Xai's main morning market, **Talat Muang Bokeo Huay Xai** (Th Saykhong) – or simply Talat Sao – is situated in the southern part of town. This is also the main road-transport depot.

You can take a traditional herbal sauna and/or Swedish-Lao massage at the **Lao Red Cross** (☎ 211935; Th Saykhong; sauna US$1, massage per hr US$3; ☺ 4-8pm).

The cumbersome-sounding **Lao Natural Tourism State Enterprise Bokeo Provincial Agency** (☎ /fax 211555), near the slow boat terminal, can arrange trips to nearby villages – including Lao Huay villages – or to a sapphire mining area 12km south.

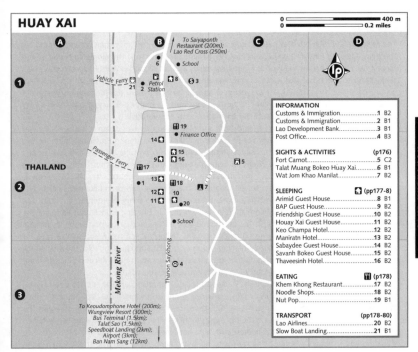

HUAY XAI

Sleeping

Most hotels and guesthouses in Huay Xai quote their rates in Thai baht.

Maniratn Hotel (Manirat; ☎ 312040; Th Saykhong; s/d US$5/6) Immediately on your right coming from the passenger ferry landing is the oldest hotel in town. Although the foyer may be cluttered and off-putting, the rooms are OK and come with fan and private hot-water shower.

BAP Guest House (☎ 211083; Th Saykhong; s/d US$2.50/5) Turn left coming from the pier, and BAP is 50m up on the left. All rooms come with fan and hot-water shower. This friendly two-storey place is perhaps the best place to find out about boats going to Luang Nam Tha via Pak Tha. There's a good restaurant downstairs.

Thaveesinh Hotel (☎ /fax 312039; Th Saykhong; r US$5-12.50 ⚒) Heading north you'll find this relatively new, clean, three-storey hotel on your right. All rooms have hot showers, and the more expensive ones have air-con and TV.

Arimid Guest House (Alimit; ☎ 211040; fax 312006; Ban Huay Xai Neua; r US$5-12.50; ⚒) This is a collection of thatched bamboo bungalows opposite a petrol station and Lao Development Bank. All bungalows have attached hot-water showers. The husband-and-wife owners speak French and English. The pier for slow boats going to Pak Beng and Luang Prabang is only about 200m away.

Sabaydee Guest House (☎ 211751; Th Saykhong; r US$5) The Sabaydee has 14 very clean rooms, all with attached hot-water shower.

Friendship Guest House (☎ 211219; Th Saykhong; s US$3, d US$5-10) Friendship lives up to its name with friendly, efficient service and comfortable rooms with attached hot-water shower. Nice rooftop view.

Keoudomphone Hotel (☎ 211405; Th Saykhong; r US$5-10; ⚒) In the opposite direction, about halfway between the town centre and the speedboat landing, this efficient three-storey hotel offers very clean rooms. All the rooms come with hot showers (the more expensive have air-con and TV).

Savanh Bokeo Guest House (Th Saykhong; r US$3-4) A bit south of Thaveesinh is this friendly two-storey place with bathrooms outside. French is spoken.

PAA BÉUK

The Mekong River stretch that passes Huay Xai was until recently an important fishing ground for the giant Mekong catfish (*pqa béuk* in Lao, *Pangasianodon gigas* to ichthyologists), probably the largest freshwater fish in the world. A *pqa béuk* takes at least six and possibly 12 years (no-one's really sure) to reach full size, when it will measure 2m to 3m in length and weigh up to 300kg. Locals say these fish swim all the way from Qinghai Province (where the Mekong originates) in northern China. In Thailand and Laos its flesh is considered a major delicacy; the texture is very meaty but has a delicate flavour, similar to that of tuna or swordfish.

These fish are only taken between mid-April and May when the river depth is between 3m and 4m and the fish are swimming upriver to spawn in Lake Tali in Yunnan Province, China. Before netting them, Thai and Lao fishers hold a annual ceremony to propitiate Chao Mae Paa Beuk, a female deity thought to preside over the giant Mekong catfish. Among the rituals comprising the ceremony are chicken sacrifices performed aboard the fishing boats. After the ceremony is completed fishing teams draw lots to see who casts the first net, and then take turns casting.

The annual catch has dwindled to almost nothing in recent years, a situation thought due to Chinese blasting of Mekong River rapids to the north. The blasting is intended to make the Mekong more navigable but it also has destroyed the underwater caves that serve as natural nurseries for the giant catfish. When a catch is made, fisherfolk sell the meat on the spot for US$40 or more per kilogram (a single fish can bring up to US$5000 in Bangkok), most of which ends up in Bangkok or Kunming restaurants, since local restaurants in Huay Xai and Chiang Khong can't afford such prices; transport to Vientiane is considered too costly.

Because of the danger of extinction, Thailand's Inland Fisheries Department has been taking protective measures since 1983, including a breed-and-release programme. Every time a female is caught, it's kept alive until a male is netted, then the eggs are removed (by massaging the female's ovaries) and put into a pan; the male is then milked for sperm and the eggs are fertilised in the pan. In this fashion over a million *pqa béuk* have been released into the Mekong since the experiment began. Although the results of releasing Pangasianodon into the wild has been very mixed, the domestic farming of *pqa béuk* in central and northern Thailand has been very successful. This means that farms on both sides of the border may one day be able to breed the fish for local consumption for little more than the cost of feed.

Houay Xai Guest House (Th Saykhong; r US$2.50-3) An older two-storey place with wooden floors and a nice little seating area that overlooks the river. All rooms have fan and attached hot-water bathroom.

Keo Champa Hotel (☎ 211505; Th Saykhong; r US$2.50-7.50; ✕) Friendly Keo Champa offers a variety of clean rooms, the cheaper ones with fan, the more expensive with air-con.

Wungview Resort (☎ 211444; Ban Huay Xai Tai; r US$7.50) Although it's a little distant from the town centre, the Wungview has separated wooden bungalows – each with TV, veranda and private hot-water shower – atop a bluff at the southern end of town. A disco in the same compound closes at 11.30pm.

Eating

Typical opening hours for eateries are listed on p249.

Khem Khong Restaurant (Riverside; ☎ 211064; meals US$0.75-3) Khem Khong, a cluster of wooden tables under a thatched roof that overlooks the Mekong passenger ferry landing, makes decent fried rice, fried noodles, Mekong fish dishes and *tôm yám*.

Nut Pop (☎ 211037; Th Saykhong; meals US$0.50-2) Choose between tables in separate, individual shelters or in an open-air garden and order from a long Lao menu.

Saiyaponth Restaurant (Th Saykhong; meals US$0.50-2) At the north end of town, just before the second bridge, on the left-hand side of the road, the Saiyaponth serves Lao food and cook-it-yourself barbecue.

About a dozen open-air food shops along Th Saykhong offer cheap noodle and rice plates.

Getting There & Away

AIR

Huay Xai's airport of US construction lies a few kilometres south of town. **Lao Airlines** (☎ 211026) flies ATR72s between Huay Xai and Vientiane (one way/return US$81/153, 50 minutes, three weekly). A few years ago Lao Airlines also fielded flights to Luang Prabang, Udomxai and Luang Nam Tha but those routes have been suspended for lack of aircraft.

BOAT

Huay Xai is a major jumping-off point for visitors planning to travel downriver to Luang Prabang by boat. It's also possible to travel upriver to Xieng Kok (see p171), where a road leads to Muang Sing.

Slow Boats South

Long-distance ferries – the *héua sáa* (slow boat) – going down the Mekong to Pak Beng and Luang Prabang leave daily at around 9am. By slow river ferry the trip to or from Huay Xai (US$15, two days) requires an overnight stay in Pak Beng. Departure times for slow boats depend largely on passenger demand, but they usually leave between 8am and 10am each morning. Be sure to carry a cushion if you have a sensitive bum, as the wooden seats can be uncomfortable and the boats are very crowded during the high season.

Several different kinds of slow boats make the journey from Huay Xai to Luang Prabang, and it's a good idea to have a look at the boat in advance. Some pack the tourists in like cattle, others have better seating, and so on. The situation is constantly changing, but BAP Guest House (p177) is a good source of info on how to select the better boats. Furthermore, if you can put together a small group of 10 or so, you can charter your own slow boat for

about the same per-person cost and travel much more comfortably.

You can also book a slow boat in advance, in Chiang Khong, before crossing to Huay Xai, for a surcharge of US$2.50. In the high season this is worth considering, as boats fill very fast.

You can also cruise to Pak Beng and Luang Prabang on the large, comfortably outfitted *Pak Ou*, a 34m, 36-seat, steel-hulled boat operated by **East West Laos** (☎ 252400; fax 252304; www.mekongcruises.com; Ban Vat Sene, Luang Prabang; per person US$199-273) three days weekly in each direction. The two-day package includes meals, guides and a night at Luang Say Lodge in Pak Beng (see p160); the exact tariff depends on the time of year.

The Mekong slow boat landing is located north of the town centre next to the vehicle ferry crossing to Thailand.

Speedboats

Six-passenger *héua wái* (speedboats) to Pak Beng (US$16, three hours) and Luang Prabang (US$26, six hours) leave from a landing about 2km south of the town centre. You can hire a whole boat for four to six times the individual fare. See (p252) for warnings on travelling by speedboat.

BUS & SǍWNGTHǍEW

The road northeast to Luang Nam Tha can be difficult because of its poor surface, but upgrading sponsored by the Asian Development Bank (ADB) is scheduled to be completed by 2005.

Buses and large *sǎwngthǎew* ply the road northeast to Vieng Phukha (US$4.30, five hours, three to four daily), Luang Nam

CROSSING THE THAI BORDER AT HUAY XAI & CHIANG KHONG

The small town of Chiang Khong, in Thailand's Chiang Rai Province, sits on the Mekong River opposite Huay Xai, Laos. The main boat landing for international crossing is Tha Bak, at the northern end of Chiang Khong. After you've legally exited Thailand via the small Thai immigration post at the landing, you can board a longtail boat (one way US$1, five minutes, 8am to 6pm) to Huay Xai. On the Huay Xai side, the pedestrian ferry landing is just below the Maniratn Hotel. At the Lao immigration post alongside the landing, 15-day tourist visas are available on arrival for US$30. On weekends or during the lunch hour (from noon to 1pm) Lao immigration usually charges 20 baht extra for 'overtime' immigration services.

If you're crossing in your own car or truck, you'll use the huge vehicle ferry (US$50) that lands at the northern end of Huay Xai.

Plans to construct a bridge from Chiang Khong to Huay Xai by late 1997 were derailed by the economic crash but it's only a matter of time before a span makes the ferry crossing obsolete.

Tha (US$7, eight hours, three daily) and Udomxai (US$8.60, four to five hours, one daily).

These time estimates apply only during dry months; during the rainy season the road can be very slow, occasionally even impassable for a day or two. A bandanna is handy for dust protection in the dry season. When the upgrading project is done, the road will be traversable year-round and buses should be able to make the Huay Xai–Nam Tha trip in four to six hours.

In Huay Xai the passenger terminal is found next to the main morning market near the provincial stadium, about 2km south of the Chiang Khong passenger ferry pier.

AROUND HUAY XAI

Various hill-tribe villages can be visited from Huay Xai, some of them within walking distance and others a short drive north or south of town. One that everyone seems to know about is the Lao Huay village of **Ban Nam Sang**. It's less than an hour east by *săwngthăew* – 17km to be exact – and you can either charter a pick-up truck from the morning market in Huay Xai for about US$6 each way, or catch the regular morning *săwngthăew* from the same market at around 8am or 8.30am for US$0.60 per person. If you go it's best to check in with the *phùu nyai bâan* (village headman) first.

A reminder: do not bring sweets, T-shirts, pharmaceuticals or any other such items to give away to the villagers as this 'generosity' threatens to interfere with their traditional way of life, and worse, threatens to foster a culture of dependency and turn Ban Nam Sang into a village of beggars. If you feel strongly about contributing to the community you might offer the headman a small monetary contribution to be used for the village school.

Huay Xai to Luang Nam Tha

Route 3 from Huay Xai to Luang Nam Tha passes through several different kinds of terrain, from river plain to high mountains. The road conditions vary accordingly from flat, graded passages to rutted, winding tracks. The road is gradually being improved, and most vehicles with high road-clearance can make the drive as long as it's not too wet.

VIENG PHUKHA

Around 120km northeast of Huay Xai, this large trading village serves traffic along Rte 3 as well as a highly visible Thai lignite (brown coal) mining enterprise a few kilometres away. The local populace, 90% Khamu, are mostly farmers or mine workers. An EU-sponsored **trekking project** (tour per person US$10-22) maintains on office on Rte 3 in the village centre. The project offers guided visits of one, two, or three days to local Khamu, Lahu and Thai Lü villages as well as to various local limestone caves,

---

LAO HUAY

Also known as Lene Tene, Lenten or Laen Taen (Dressed in Blue), the Lao Huay (Lao Stream) are classified by the government as Lao Soung despite the fact they do not – and never have – lived anywhere other than lower river valleys. Ethnolinguistically they fall within the Hmong-Mien family, most of whom live at higher elevations.

The Lao Huay build their homes – multifamily longhouses of palm and bamboo thatch – beside rivers or streams from which they irrigate rice fields using simple wooden hydraulic pumps. Unlike the closely related Mien, they do not cultivate the opium poppy for trade, only for smoking. Lao Huay women can be identified by the single large coin (usually an old Indochina piastre, sometimes accompanied by several smaller coins) suspended over the parting in their long, straight hair and by their lack of eyebrows, which are completely depilated at age 15 according to custom. Both sexes favour dark blue or black clothes – baggy shirts and trousers – trimmed in red.

The Lao Huay use Chinese characters to write their language, often on handmade bamboo paper. Their belief system encompasses a mix of Taoism, ancestor worship and animism, with spirits attached to the family, house, village, sky, forest, earth, water and birds. Around 5000 Lao Huay live in Laos; in Bokeo Province they're mostly concentrated in Nam Nyun district. This tribe isn't found in Myanmar or Thailand, though there are some Lao Huay villages in Yunnan (China) and northern Vietnam.

including the 5km-long **Tham Nam Eng**. Guides can also lead you to see the ruins of **Wat Mahapot** and the **khúu wíeng** (city walls) of an abandoned city thought to be 400 years old.

Vieng Phukha has four guesthouses, all of them simple thatched-bamboo or wooden affairs: **Phonsavath** (☎ 212397; r US$2-2.50), **Don Vieng** (☎ 212394; r US$2-2.50), **Vieng Phouka** (☎ 212390; r US$2-2.50) and **Bo Kung** (r US$2-2.50). All cater mostly to passing truck drivers, and each has its own rustic karaoke bar. Of the lot, the Bo Kung is the quietest as it's about a kilometre off the main road through town.

Buses and *săwngthăew* are available to Huay Xai (US$4.30, five hours, three to four daily), Luang Nam Tha (US$2.20, three hours, three to four daily) and Udomxai (US$4.30, five hours, three to four daily) from the market in the village centre.

SAINYABULI PROVINCE

This upside-down-L–shaped province lying between Thailand to the west and Vientiane and Luang Prabang Provinces to the east is one of the most remote provinces in Laos, despite its geographic proximity to the nation's capital. Mountains – several higher than 1000m and one as high as 2150m – define the northern half of the province, where roads are scarce, while the southern half flattens into river plains.

The province is rich in timber (particularly teak and padauk) and lignite, and is considered the 'rice basket' of northern Laos, since most other northern provinces are too mountainous to grow enough rice. Other important crops include maize, oranges, cotton, peanuts and sesame.

Sainyabuli (also spelt Xaignabouri and Sayaburi) shares a 645km border with six different Thai provinces. The northwestern section of the province is considered to be of major military and commercial importance because Pak Beng – the start of a road link (Rte 2) with northern Udomxai and the Chinese border at Boten – lies less than 50km from the Thai border.

The province was the site of a brief but heated border skirmish between the Thai and Lao in 1988. The Lao, following the border representation on a 1960 American map, claimed the border followed one tributary of the Nam Heuang while the Thai said that it should follow another branch of the river according to a 1908 Siam-France treaty. Laos sent in troops to occupy the disputed 77-sq-km territory, and in response Thailand began launching air strikes against Laos – a daring move considering that at the time 50,000 Vietnamese troops were deployed in Laos. More than 100 Thai and Lao soldiers died in battle before an agreement was reached and a compromise border was fixed.

The population totals around 300,000, including Lao, Thai Dam, Thai Lü, Khamu, Htin, Phai, Kri, Akha and Mabri; many of these groups migrate between Sainyabuli and Thailand, since the border is fairly unpoliced. Today pockets of the longtime Hmong insurgency, particularly the 2000-strong Chao Fa (Lords of the Sky), remain in the province and threaten to cause trouble for the government.

A string of rocky limestone precipices known as **Pha Xang** (Elephant Cliffs – so named because from a distance the grey-white cliffs resemble walking elephants) parallels the Mekong River on the eastern side of the province. Along the western edge of the province is the **Nam Phoun NPA**, a 1150-sq-km tract of rugged, forested hills thought to sustain elephant, Sumatran rhino, gaur, gibbon, dhole, Asiatic black bear, Malayan sun bear and tiger.

The southern part of the province harbours several scenic waterfalls, including 150m Nam Tok Na Kha (3km from Ban Nakha), 105m Nam Tok Ban Kum (5km from Ban Kum) and 35m Tat Heuang (40km from Ban Muang Phae). Unfortunately, none of these villages are easily accessible by road as yet, and this corner of the province is reputed to be a hang-out for smugglers and possibly insurgents. The Lao government considers much of the province insecure due to difficulties along the Thai border (specifically eastern Nan Province), including banditry and smuggling (drugs and timber). It's probably best if travellers avoid the border area between Muang Ngoen (to the north) and Kaen Thao (to the south).

The 30m **Tat Jao**, a 1km walk northwest of the Mekong ferry crossing at Muang Tha Deua, is a popular local picnic spot.

Sainyabuli Province has more elephants than any other province in Laos and if you get out into rural areas you may see working elephants engaged in timber or agricultural work. Two of the highest concentrations of working elephants can be found in Thong Mixai district about 40km northwest of Pak Lai at Hongsa, 85km north of the provincial capital.

Other than the fine mountain scenery and waterfalls, there are few attractions for tourists since the province never prospered under the Lan Xang or Vientiane kingdoms, nor did the Khmers reach this to leave behind any ruins or sculpture. The French had a minor presence in the capital but left little infrastructure behind.

SAINYABULI

ໄຊຍະບຸລິ
☎ 074 / pop 17,000

The capital stands on the banks of the Nam Houng, a tributary of the Mekong River towards the northern end of the province. Because of trade with Thailand, both legal and illegal, the town is much more prosperous than the typical Lao provincial capital, as evidenced by the higher-than-average percentage of new cars and motorcycles.

Other than a couple of wats there is little to interest the casual visitor. The grounds of **Wat Si Bun Huang**, south of town past the police station in an adjacent village, contain the brick foundations of Buddhist monuments that are rumoured to be over 500 years old. Nearby, **Wat Si Phan Don** contains an unusual diamond-shaped stupa with no known stylistic antecedents. In town, **Wat Sisavang Vong**, reportedly built by King Sisavang Vong on an older temple site, displays a colourful version of Buddhist hell on its front walls.

Very little English is spoken in Sainyabuli so be sure to pack your phrasebook. Attempts to over-charge for food (even for *fŏe!*) and public transport appear to be more common here than anywhere else we've been in Laos, probably because Sainyabuli has been heavily targeted by NGOs and international aid organisations. With a little gentle bargaining, the locals will usually back down to something close to normal price.

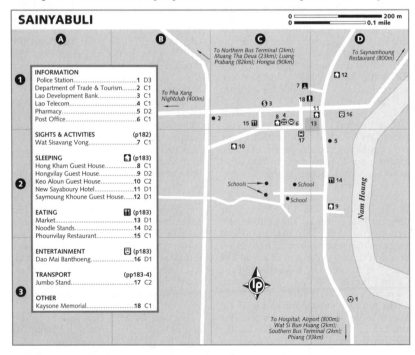

SAINYABULI

0 _____ 200 m
0 _____ 0.1 mile

INFORMATION
Police Station.................................1 D3
Department of Trade & Tourism.......2 C1
Lao Development Bank......................3 C1
Lao Telecom....................................4 C1
Pharmacy..5 D2
Post Office......................................6 C1

SIGHTS & ACTIVITIES (p182)
Wat Sisavang Vong..........................7 C1

SLEEPING (p183)
Hong Kham Guest House..................8 C1
Hongvilay Guest House....................9 D2
Keo Aloun Guest House..................10 C2
New Sayaboury Hotel......................11 D1
Saymoung Khoune Guest House......12 D1

EATING (p183)
Market...13 D1
Noodle Stands................................14 D2
Phounvilay Restaurant....................15 C1

ENTERTAINMENT (p183)
Dao Mai Banthoeng........................16 D1

TRANSPORT (pp183-4)
Jumbo Stand...................................17 C2

OTHER
Kaysone Memorial...........................18 C1

To Northern Bus Terminal (2km);
Muang Tha Deua (23km); Luang
Prabang (82km); Hongsa (90km)

To Saynamhoung
Restaurant (800m)

To Pha Xang
Nightclub (400m)

Schools

School

School

School

Nam Houng

To Hospital; Airport (800m);
Wat Si Bun Huang (2km);
Southern Bus Terminal (2km);
Phiang (33km)

Information

Lao Development Bank (☽ 8.30am- 4pm Mon-Fri) The bank accepts only cash – Thai baht or US dollars – at a lower rate than in Vientiane.

Lao Telecom (☽ 8am-10pm) You can buy international and domestic phonecards here or at the post office.

Post office (☽ 8-11am & 1-5pm Mon-Fri)

Sleeping

Keo Aloun Guest House (☎ 211311; r US$3.50) Simple rooms in a large two-storey Lao-style house come with fans and shared bathroom. Two rooms upstairs have small private balconies. Food service is available with advance notice.

New Sayaboury Hotel (☎ 211116; r US$5-8; 🏿) This huge, three-storey hotel has recently changed management and is better run than in the past. All rooms come with fans and private hot-water shower, while the more expensive rooms have air-con.

Saymoung Khoune Guest House (☎ 211176; r US$4-6; 🏿) The tidy foyer of this white split-level guesthouse makes a good first impression but inspect the rooms carefully before checking in. Rooms at the back are newer and cleaner than those at the front.

Hongvilay Guest House (☎ 211068; r US$3) South of the market next to the Nam Houng, Hongvilay has nine somewhat dingy rooms with shared facilities in a two-storey wooden building. On the plus side, out the back is a restaurant and good river views.

Hong Kham Guest House (r US$3) This Lao-style house with five guest rooms is next to Lao Telecom. Windows in the rooms aren't screened, but beds have mosquito nets. Bathroom facilities are shared.

Eating

Typical opening hours for eateries are listed on p249.

Saynamhoung Restaurant (meals US$1.50-4) This open-air, riverside spot has a nice atmosphere, good service and an extensive Lao, Thai and Chinese menu. As it's long been a favourite among local expats and Lao NGO staffers, it's more expensive than other restaurants in town.

Phounvilay Restaurant (meals US$1-2) The Phounvilay offers an English-language menu, and the Lao-Chinese food is good and reasonably priced.

There are several simple noodle shops near the market, some with rice dishes as well. You can also buy takeaway Lao food from the market.

Entertainment

At the **Dao Mai Banthoeng** (☽ 8-11.30pm) and **Pha Xang Nightclub** (☽ 8-11.30pm) live bands play Lao and Thai pop nightly. Although slow on weeknights, these venues are very popular on weekends.

Getting There & Away

AIR

The flight schedule for **Lao Airlines** (☎ 412059; airport) says a Y-12 flies four times a week between Sainyabuli and Vientiane (one way/return US$44/83, 45 minutes), but lately flights have been much more infrequent due to a lack of small planes.

BOAT

Speedboats are available between Tha Deua and Luang Prabang (US$10, one hour). From Tha Deua you can hop on a shared jumbo or *săwngthăew* into Sainyabuli.

BUS & SĂWNGTHĂEW

An all-weather, partially paved road runs southwest from Luang Prabang to a landing at Pak Khon, on the Mekong's eastern bank near Muang Nan. From here, a ferry continues to Tha Deua (pedestrian ferry US$0.30, vehicle ferry US$3.30) on the western bank and another road continues on to the provincial capital.

There are regular buses from Luang Prabang to Pak Khon (US$1.40, three hours, four daily). On the way you'll stop at Muang Nan, about 20 minutes before the river landing.

From Tha Deua there are shared *săwngthăew* and jumbos to Sainyabuli (US$0.60, one hour). If you find yourself stuck on either side of the river waiting for the next ferry, simple shacks serve *fŏe* and Lao dishes near the respective landings.

Buses from Sainyabuli to Pak Lai leave when there are enough passengers, usually between 7.30am and 10am (US$2.50, three to four hours).

There is also a road running north to Sainyabuli from Kaen Thao, which is on the Nam Heuang opposite the Thai villages of Ban Pak Huay and Ban Nong Pheu – both are legal crossing points for Thai and Lao, but not for foreigners.

In Sainyabuli there are two bus terminals, one 2km southeast of town for southbound vehicles, and one about the same distance northeast of town for northbound vehicles.

AROUND SAINYABULI
Pak Lai
ປາກລາຍ

☎ 074

This small riverside community of old French colonial buildings and traditional wooden Lao homes clustered around a village green, with the Pha Xang mountain range as a scenic backdrop, makes a pleasant stopover between Sainyabuli and Vientiane.

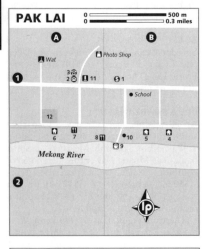

A branch of Lao Development Bank can change US dollars and Thai baht to kip.

SLEEPING & EATING

Ban Na Guest House (☎ 211995; r US$4) At this rather unusual three-storey guesthouse, where the bottom floor is cement, the middle one brick and the top one wood, the 17 rooms have screened windows and ceiling fans. Clean shower and toilet facilities are shared. Food can be ordered downstairs.

Lam Douan Guest House (r US$3-4) Run by a friendly lady who speaks Lao, Thai and a little French, the Lam Douan offers 10 basic but clean rooms with shared bucket bath and toilet. The upper floor has a balcony with a Mekong view.

Kheme Khong Guest House (☎ 071-211733; r US$4) The 15 rooms in this old wooden Lao/colonial-style house are atmospheric but not particularly clean. They come with fans and mosquito nets, while toilet and bathroom facilities are shared.

Nang Noy Restaurant (meals US$0.50-1.50) Between the boat landing and the market, Nang Noy specialises in simple rice and noodle dishes, and can do takeaway for the boat ride to Vientiane. Typical opening hours for eateries are listed on p249.

Right above the boat landing a no-name restaurant in a clean, cement pavilion with tiled floors opens early in the morning to serve thick Lao coffee and *khào-nŏm khuu* (Chinese-style fried pastry). Later in the day good rice and noodle dishes are available, and this is a good spot to take in a Mekong sunset. The eatery doubles as a snack shop for the boat passengers.

ENTERTAINMENT

Karaoke bar (☉ 7pm-midnight) Next door to the restaurant above the boat landing is a red-lanterned karaoke bar that starts rocking around 9pm or 10pm before shutting down tight at midnight.

GETTING THERE & AWAY

Săwngthăew travel between Pak Lai and Sainyabuli (US$2.80, three hours, two daily). The *săwngthăew* drops passengers off at a spot about 3km outside Pak Lai where you must continue by shared jumbo for US$0.50 per person.

Slow boats to Vientiane (US$6, seven to eight hours) leave the Pak Lai landing from

Vegetable vendors, Muang Khua (p175)

BERNARD NAPTHINE

Novice monks, Xieng Khuang Province (p140)

MARTIN LLADO

FRANK CARTER

Traditional headdress of the Akha people (p35)

Plain of Jars (p145)

JULIET COOMBE

CLINT LUCAS

That Chomsi (p121), Luang Prabang

JOHN BORT

Tat Kuang Si (p135), Luang Prabang

Kátâw match (p37)

ANTHONY PL

MYSTERY CITY

The name Hongsa (which is the Lao pronunciation of the Sanskrit word *hamsa,* the swanlike duck of Hindu-Buddhist mythology) appears to be keyed to an older principality called Hongsawadi that was once centred around present-day Hongsa. Ruins of the old city walls are still visible near the village of Vieng Kaew and the ordination hall of a temple in the old quarter of Hongsa itself bears the inscription 'Hongsawadi'. Locals know little about the history of the area, saying only that the abandoned city was called Hongsawadi and that it was founded by a people called *mâan.*

Curiously, this older city name corresponds to a Mon kingdom called Hanthawadi (Burmese and Lao names come from the Sanskrit Hamsavati, meaning 'Ruled by Swans') that once flourished in central Myanmar. Whether there was any connection between the two, no-one yet seems to know. The Mon did establish Buddhist principalities as far north as Vientiane, and in Thailand all the way to Chiang Mai, so there's a possibility that Hongsawadi may have been a Mon city.

8am to 9am but they often fill up by 7.30am so it's a good idea to be at the ticket office at 7am. The slow boat passenger service to/from Tha Deua and Luang Prabang has been discontinued, so if you're heading north from Pak Lai, you'll have to go by road to Tha Deua via Sainyabuli, then catch a river ferry across to Luang Prabang Province.

Speedboats from Pak Lai to Vientiane (US$20, four hours) leave when there are six passengers.

Hongsa

ຫົງສາ

☎ 074

This district, tucked away in the northwestern corner of Sainyabuli Province, roughly 85km northwest of the provincial capital, is a major centre for Thai Lü culture. Several villages in the area boast historic Thai Lü temples and strong local traditions. Travelling through this district, and even en route to Hongsa from Sainyabuli, you may see elephants walking along the road with their mahouts (keepers), as this part of Sainyabuli is a major centre for the logging of padauk and other timber. Elephants are also used for agricultural work in the area. So important are the pachyderms to daily life here that the Thai Lü perform yearly *bàasǐi* ceremonies on their behalf.

In Hongsa itself the main temple is **Wat Simungkhun** (also known as Wat Yai), where a very old, whitewashed *wihǎan* contains an oddly raised stone floor that allegedly covers a large hole that 'leads to the end of the world', according to locals. Women aren't allowed to enter the *wihǎan*, but from the doorway you can see the impressive collection of Lao Buddha figures on the altar inside.

In nearby **Vieng Kaew** old houses built with padauk (*Pterocarpus indicus*, a reddish-orange tropical hardwood sometimes called 'Asian rosewood') abound. On the outskirts of Vieng Kaew, a German-financed **Lao Elephant Conservation Centre** (www.help-elephants -laos.org/) has a veterinary clinic for treating ill or injured pachyderms and also strives to educate visitors about the plight of the Asian elephant. Support also comes from the sale of elephant-dung paper, which has a texture similar to mulberry bark paper. Elephant-back tours of Vieng Kaew are available here or from Jumbo House (see below).

SLEEPING & EATING

Jumbo House (Xang Luang; r US$8) Affiliated with the Lao Elephant Conservation Centre, this new one-storey guesthouse offers five large rooms. Information on Vieng Kaew and Muang Ngoen is available here, and bicycles can be hired.

Dok Tawan Guest House (Sunflower; r US$5.50-7.50) Just around the corner from the Jumbo House, Sunflower boasts 10 rooms in a two-storey house next to a lotus pond and spacious garden with café.

Villa Sisouphanh (☎ 211791; r US$3) Found opposite the market, Sisouphanh is the better of a couple of older guesthouses in Hongsa, with adequate rooms.

A Vientiane-based company called **Lao Travel – Ecotourism** (in Vientiane ☎ 021-213180; www.laoecotourism.com) maintains the slightly upscale Elephant Lodge in Hongsa but you must book a two- to three-day tour (US$100 per day) with the company in order to stay here.

Lotus Café (meals US$1-3) A pleasant new spot for a drink or a meal overlooking lotus ponds. The menu covers Lao, Italian and Korean barbecue.

In the market are several restaurant stalls. At the best, **Tui** (meals US$0.50-1.50) you can get *khào sáwy, khào píak, fŏe* and cold beer.

GETTING THERE & AWAY

You can reach Hongsa via a wild *sǎwngthǎew* ride over high mountain ridges and into deep valleys from Sainyabuli (US$8, six hours, one daily). Most of this road is unsealed and crosses several low bridges made from logs, so in the rainy season the usual six hours could easily stretch to eight or 10. During heavy rains the road may wash out entirely for several days.

Another way to reach Hongsa is by boat along the Mekong River from Luang Prabang or Huay Xai. From Tha Suang you can hop on a shared jumbo to Hongsa (US$3, one hour). See p133 for details of boat travel to Tha Suang. If you're coming downriver from Huay Xai, you'll pay just a bit above the Pak Beng fare to get dropped off in Tha Suang.

Muang Ngoen

ເມືອງເຈິນ

This Thai Lü village in the extreme northeast corner of the province, 3km from the Thai border, is worth a visit if you're in the area already or passing through from Thailand (once the border opens, that is). There are still a few houses on stilts with high-pitched roofs sloping low to the ground (similar to those found in Muang Sing and in China's Xishuangbanna District), although many of these were destroyed when the Thai air force bombed Laos during the 1988 Thai-Lao border war.

Farming is the main activity, and one made more profitable by the open Thai-Lao border at nearby Ban Huay Kon – a crossing thus far permitted for Thai and Lao nationals only. Local officials say the crossing will open to all nationalities in 2005. Once that occurs, this will become the fastest land route between Luang Prabang and Thailand.

Muang Ngoen's **Wat Ban Khon**, a traditional Thai Lü–style temple where the monks still use palm leaves for the preservation of Buddhist texts, is notable for its natural-pigment, folk-art murals, which combine animal and floral motifs with tiny mirrors to unique effect.

Another old Thai Lü wat, **Wat Salibun Nyeun**, stands on a high bluff overlooking a town, with a lovely stream winding through the valley below. Pillars inside the main *wihǎan* are cut from huge padauk trunks.

SLEEPING

Few foreign visitors choose to spend the night in Muang Ngoen, but if you feel like digging into local life, you can choose between the **Saijaloen Guest House** (r US$2-3) and **Amphawan Guest House** (r US$1-3).

THAI LÜ

Thai Lü dominate local culture and commerce in Hongsa district. Keen traders, they have been unusually successful in maintaining their traditions despite the pressures of outside Lao influence, while at the same time enjoying the relative prosperity that their district has developed as a Thailand-Laos trade centre.

The matrilineal Thai Lü practise a mix of Theravada Buddhism and animism; though traditionally endogamic (tending to marry within one's own clan) they've recently begun marrying outsiders – usually Thai Lü or Thai Neua from other districts. Women are said to enjoy greater political freedom and power than in most ethnic groups in Laos.

Typical Thai Lü villages are on the eastern bank of a stream or river, with at least one wat at the northern end and a cemetery at the west. An important folk tale says a swan deity flew down from heaven and showed the Thai Lü how to build their houses on stilts as protection from animals and flooding, and with long sloping roofs to shield the inhabitants from sun, wind and rain. Small shuttered windows known as *pong liem* allow residents to see out but restrict outsiders from seeing in. In reference to this bit of folklore, they call their traditional homes *héuan hŏng* (swan houses).

Their more distinctive customs include *suu khwǎn khuwái* (string-tying ceremony for water buffaloes) and *suu khwǎn sâang* (string-tying ceremony for elephants).

GETTING THERE & AWAY

The easiest way to reach Muang Ngoen is via a dirt road from the bank of the Mekong River opposite Pak Beng, a distance of roughly 35km. Ask in Pak Beng about the availability of transport to Muang Ngoen. Your best bet may be to hitch a ride with someone coming from here.

MABRI

Along the Thai-Lao border in Sainyabuli Province survives a single village of around 60 Mabri (sometimes spelt Mrabri or Mlabri), whom the Lao call *khàa tqwng lĕuang* (Slaves of the Yellow Banana Leaves). The men wear very little clothing, preferring nothing more than a small piece of cloth to cover the groin, while the women tend to wear castoffs from other hill tribes or from lowlanders. The most nomadic and endangered of all the minorities in Laos or Thailand, the Mabri customarily move on when the leaves of their temporary huts turn yellow – about every two weeks – hence their Lao name. Their numbers have been greatly reduced (possibly to as few as 250 – around 150 of whom live in Thailand) and experts suspect that few of the Mabri still migrate in the traditional way.

In the past the Mabri were strict hunter-gatherers but many now work as field labourers for the Lao, or for other hill-tribe groups such as the Hmong, in exchange for pigs and clothing. Little is known about the tribe's belief system except that they are animists who believe they are not entitled to cultivate the land for themselves. Their matrilineal social organisation allows serial monogamy; a Mabri woman typically changes mates every five or six years, taking any children from the previous union with her. The Mabri knowledge of medicinal plants is said to be enormous, encompassing the effective use of herbs for fertility and contraception, and for the treatment of snake or centipede poisoning. When a member of the tribe dies, the body is put in a tree top to be eaten by birds.

Unlike in Thailand, where government and nongovernment agencies are attempting to help the Mabri integrate into the modern social milieu, no-one in Laos has come forth to try to protect the Mabri from becoming an enslaved community within an increasingly capitalist rural economy. Because of their antimaterialist beliefs, the Mabri perform menial labour for the Hmong and other hill-tribes for little or no compensation.

NORTHERN LAOS

188

Southern Laos

SOUTHERN LAOS

CONTENTS

HIGHLIGHTS

- Put life on hold for a few days to better acquaint yourself with hammocks, in the laidback islands of **Si Phan Don** (p228) in the majestic Mekong

- Get up for an unforgettable sunrise at the ancient Khmer temple complex at **Wat Phu Champasak** (p223)

- Trek into the remote villages of **Dong Phu Vieng NPA** (p209), where you can witness life in the ancient spirit forests

- Gaze in awe at 100m-high waterfalls and sip the famous coffee on the cool **Bolaven Plateau** (p218)

- Make the difficult journey to **Tham Lot Kong Lo** (p194), where you'll be rewarded with a paddle through this astonishing 7km-long limestone cave

★ Tham Lot Kong Lo

★ Dong Phon Vieng NPA

Wat Phu Champasak ★ ★ Bolaven Plateau

★ Si Phan Don

After years of being little more than an afterthought in the minds of many travellers, southern Laos is beginning to attract the attention it deserves. Thanks to improved roads and a series of sensitively prepared and (hopefully) sustainable ecotourism projects, the south is more open to exploration than ever. But make no mistake, much of it is still tough and memorable travel…

Southern Laos is home to a diverse mix of ecology, environment and ethnicity that is very different to the north. The Mekong River towns of Tha Khaek, Savannakhet and Pakse, with their lowland Lao communities, slowly crumbling French histories and lethargic lifestyles, make ideal bases for exploring the mountains, rivers, caves and rugged karst terrains of the interior. This part of the country claims the most forest cover and highest concentrations of wildlife, including some species that have disappeared elsewhere in Southeast Asia.

You could do 'The Loop' (p201) through Khammuan and Bolikhamsai Provinces by motorbike, getting far off the beaten track and into the incredible 7km-long Tham Lot Kong Lo cave (p194) in the process. Or stay in a village home in the Dong Phu Vieng National Protected Area (p209) in Savannakhet province.

Parts of the Ho Chi Minh Trail that have not returned to jungle are increasingly accessible, and those few hardy souls who head into the southern highland provinces of Sekong, Salavan, and beyond to Attapeu find a mix of Thai tribal and Mon-Khmer groups for whom *falang* (Western) visitors remain a novel experience.

In Champasak Province, the Mekong flows south past the ancient Khmer religious complex at Wat Phu Champasak, before spreading out in the Si Phan Don, or Four Thousand Islands, that straddle the Cambodian border. Among this extensive and stunningly beautiful maze of waterways are the palm-lined Don Khong, Don Det and Don Khon, where you can watch the sunset from your hammock without being interrupted by endless reruns of *Friends* (unlike in Vang Vieng). Ah, bliss!

SOUTHERN LAOS

Climate
Not surprisingly, it rains a lot from May to October but the pay-off is that when it's not raining the skies are clear and the greens of the jungles and paddy fields much brighter. The further south you go the hotter it gets, and Pakse in May is uncomfortable, to put it mildly. The Bolaven Plateau, on the other hand, is relatively cool all year, and in winter it can be very chilly indeed.

The best time to visit Si Phan Don is between November and January when the weather is cool and dry. From March to May it can be very hot, most of the rice fields will be dried out and the monsoon forest will have turned brown or shed leaves. During the rainy season from June to October, smaller unsealed roads everywhere are often impassable.

National Protected Areas
Southern Laos is home to 12 National Protected Areas (NPAs) which account for almost 10% of the country's total land mass. Many have very limited if any infrastructure for tourism, but Dong Phu Vieng (p209) in Savannakhet Province, Phu Hin Bun (p194) in Khammuan Province and Dong Hua Sao (p218) on the Bolaven Plateau in Champasak Province all have plenty to offer.

Projects aimed at opening more of these areas to sustainable tourism are ongoing.

SOUTHERN LAOS

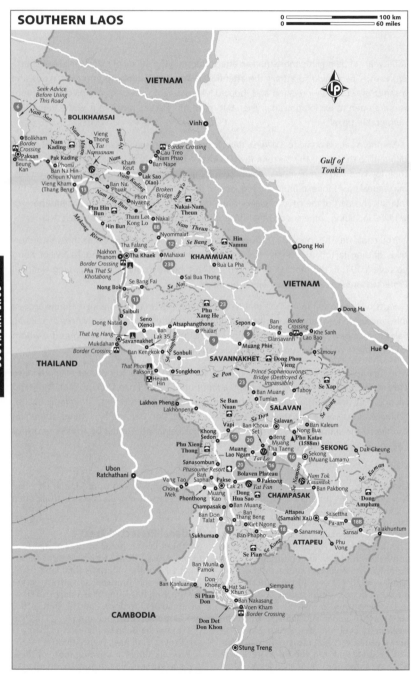

SOUTHERN LAOS

0 ─────── 100 km
0 ─────── 60 miles

Getting There & Around

Gone are the days when getting to anywhere south of Vientiane involved inordinately large amounts of time and incredible fortitude. These days Rte 13 is sealed and, somewhat surprisingly after five years, still smooth. Other roads that have, or soon will, graduate from 'bonejarring nightmare' status to 'smooth as silk' include Rte 9, from Savannakhet to the Vietnamese border at Lao Bao; Rtes 23 and 16, linking Pakse with Attapeu; and Rte 8 that links Rte 13 with the Vietnamese border at Nam Phao.

All these good roads mean many of the old buses, those big, eccentric-looking flatbed trucks with a heavy wooden cabin built on the back, have been replaced by Korean buses. Of course, wooden buses and many a *săwngthăew* (passenger truck) still service the more remote areas.

The rise of Rte 13 has also been the demise of most of the Mekong River traffic in Southern Laos. If you want a boatman to take you more than an hour or two in any direction you'll probably need a fat wad of persuasion. However, one of the few remaining 'local slow boat' experiences (p215) is still available in the south, from Pakse to Champasak and Si Phan Don.

BOLIKHAMSAI & KHAMMUAN PROVINCES

Bolikhamsai and Khammuan straddle the narrow, central 'waist' of the country, an area of moderately high mountains sloping southwest to meet the Mekong valley. Lowland Lao, who speak a dialect peculiar to these two provinces, dominate the population, followed by lesser numbers of tribal Thais, Hmong, Kri, Katang, Maling, Phuan, Ta-oy (Tahoy) and Tri.

Much of the region is relatively sparsely populated and five large swathes of forest have been declared National Protected Areas (p48), making this easily the most 'protected' part of the country. Unfortunately, accessing much of this wilderness is virtually impossible. The **Nam Kading** (p193), **Nakai-Nam Theun** and remote **Hin Namno** NPAs have practically no tourist infrastructure, and a sizeable chunk of Nakai-Nam Theun will be flooded if the enormous Nam Theun

2 dam project goes ahead, as seems likely. The **Phu Khao Khuay NPA**, part of which is in Bolikhamsai, is easily visited from Vientiane; see p98.

This leaves the rivers and serrated peaks of the **Phu Hin Bun NPA** (p194) as the big draw, and the jewel in that crown is undoubtedly **Tham Lot Kong Lo** (p194).

PAKSAN

ປາກຊັນ

☎ 054 / pop 39,000

Located at the confluence of the Nam San (San River) and the Mekong River, Paksan (Pakxan or Pakxanh) is the capital of Bolikhamsai Province and its position on Route 13 makes it marginally busier than your average Lao provincial capital. The local population is predominantly Phuan, a tribal Thai group, and many are also Christian – a combination that has traditionally made them doubly suspicious in the eyes of Lao authorities.

There's not much to see in Paksan, but a steady flow of travellers stop here en route from the south or when their *săwngthăew* from Lak Sao near the Vietnamese border ends its day here. This number is likely to increase now that the border to the Thai town of **Beung Kan**, on the opposite bank of the Mekong, is open to *falang*.

Festivals & Events

In October the boat racing festival usually comes to Paksan a week or so after it's held in Vientiane and makes a more relaxed alternative to the hordes of the capital.

Sleeping

There has been a veritable boom in the guesthouse market in Paksan; the couple of seedy brothels available a few years ago have been replaced by several mostly decent options. All the places listed here are within walking distance of the bus station, though the first two are nearest.

BK Guesthouse (☎ 212638, mobile 020-5612348; r US$4-6; 🕱) The rooms are pokey, but the ever-smiling family who run this spotless place make it easily the best atmosphere in town. Fan rooms are $4.

Saynamxan Guesthouse (☎ 212068; Rte 13; r US$4) Recently added to a building opposite the restaurant of the same name, the Saynamxan's comfortable rooms are every bit the shrine to hard woods but, with attached bathroom, they're pretty good value.

Hongxaykham Hotel (☎ 212362; r US$3–5; ❄) On the street running north from just west of the market, this big, white place on the right has musty rooms with bathroom. Fan rooms are US$3.

Vilaysack Hotel (☎ 212311; s US$3–6, d US$4–7; ❄) Rooms in the Vilaysack have TVs, but they could be cleaner. It's just past Hongxayham, on the opposite side of the road. Single/double fan rooms cost US$3/4.

Eating

You won't have any trouble finding noodle and *fŏe* (rice noodles) options around Talat Sao and Rte 13. And if you're around in the evening, the restaurants near the junction of the Mekong and the Nam Son are unbeatable for their sunset location.

Tavendang Saysane Restaurant (meals US$1.50–4; ⊙ lunch & dinner) This new waterfront restaurant is certainly the classiest option in Paksan, with Lao and a good selection of Thai food plus French red wine on the menu, attentive service and scenic views.

Paknamsane Restaurant (☎ 212829; meals US$2–3; ⊙ lunch & dinner) A few metres closer to the Mekong than Tavendang Saysane, this is a more local alternative with equally good views.

Saynamxan Restaurant (☎ 212068; meals US$2–3.50; ⊙ breakfast, lunch, dinner) At the northwest end of the bridge crossing the Nam San, this place serves Lao, Vietnamese and Chinese food with the fish dishes being the best. We recommend against the roast turtle.

BK Guesthouse run a very popular **local restaurant** (meals US$1.20) about 50m along the street from the accommodation, known for its quality Lao and Vietnamese food – the *fŏe* is wonderful.

Getting There & Away

For buses from Vientiane see the table p94. From Paksan, buses leave from outside the Morning Market for Vientiane (US$1.30, two hours, 143km) at 6am, 7am, 7.30am, 10.30am, 11am and 2.30pm. If you're heading to Vietnam, *săwngthăew* depart for Lak Sao (US$3, five to six hours, 189km) at 5am, 5.30am, 6am and 6.30am, or when they fill. After this you'll probably have to take a *săwngthăew* to Vieng Kham, usually known as Thang Beng which means

---

> ### CROSSING THE THAI BORDER AT PAKSAN & BEUNG KAN
>
> Newly opened to foreigners, this crossing of the Mekong connects Paksan with the Thai town of Beung Kan. From Rte 13, 2km west of the bridge over the Nam Son, turn south and follow the road about 300m to the port. Formalities at the **immigration office** (⊙ 8am-noon & 1.30-4.30pm) shouldn't take more than about 15 minutes. The boat (25B, 25 minutes) leaves when 10 people show up, or you can charter it for 250B. In Thailand buses leave Beung Kan for Udon Thani and Bangkok regularly.
>
> Coming from Beung Kan you can buy a 15-day visa (US$30) on arrival in Paksan. If you want to stay in Beung Kan, the **Mekong Guest House** (☎ 0 4249 1341; 200 Th Chansin; r 250-350B) is a decent option.

---

junction (US$1.80, 80 minutes), where Rte 13 joins Rte 8, then change for another *săwngthăew* along Rte 8 to Lak Sao (US$2, 3½ to five hours, 122km).

All buses heading south from Vientiane pass through Paksan about two hours after they leave the capital – wait around the Morning Market.

AROUND PAKSAN
Tha Pha Baht Phonsan

ທາພະບາດໂພນສັນ

Eighty kilometres northeast of Vientiane via Rte 13, on the way to Paksan, is a large *pha bàat* (Buddha footprint) shrine and monastery, known as **Wat Pha Baht Phonsan**, an important pilgrimage place for lowland Lao from Bolikhamsai and Vientiane. The highly stylised 'print' – along with a substantial reclining Buddha figure – sits on a low hill with older monastic structures and stands of bamboo. A well-ornamented 1933-vintage stupa is reminiscent of That Ing Hang in Savannakhet.

Recent renovations, however, have been carried out with a heavy hand, and even the footprint itself has not been spared. Once one of the most elaborate in the country, it is now hidden underneath a mountain of shining Buddhist paraphernalia, and the 108 marks believed to adorn the Buddha's foot seem to have been covered by a sea of orange paint. Still, Tha Pha Baht Phonsan is a worthy diversion if you're passing this way, especially when it hosts a large festival on the full moon of the third lunar month (around July).

GETTING THERE & AWAY
Tha Pha Baht Phonsan is one hour from Vientiane by private vehicle, 1½ hours by bus – take any Paksan-bound bus and ask to get off at the wat. Moving east or west from Tha Pha Baht Phonsan, just stand on Rte 13 and wave down anything going your way.

PAKSAN TO LAK SAO
Travellers have been complaining about the hellish 24-hour bus journey between Vientiane and Hanoi for years, but there's no reason why this trip can't be broken into smaller chunks, with the added benefit of enjoying some of central Laos along the way.

Nam Kading NPA
ປ່າສະຫງວນນ້ຳກະດິງ

Heading east along Rte 13 you'll come to the sleepy yet picturesque village of **Pak Kading**, 187km from Vientiane. Pak Kading sits just upstream from the junction of the Mekong River and the **Nam Kading**, one of the most pristine rivers in Laos. Flowing through a forested valley surrounded by high hills and menacing-looking limestone formations, this broad, turquoise-tinted river winds its way into the **Nam Kading NPA**. The river is undoubtedly the best way into this wilderness, where confirmed animal rarities include elephant, giant muntjac, pygmy slow loris, François' langur, Douc langur, gibbon, dhole, Asiatic black bear, tiger and many bird species.

As yet there are no organised kayaking or rafting trips along the Nam Kading, but a day trip is easy enough. Some travellers have reported being able to charter a boat on the Pak Kading side of the Nam Kading, underneath the bridge. However, it's simpler to continue east for 15km to the village of **Phonsi**, where a blue sign points to a promised one-hour boat ride to **Tat Wang Fong**. This small waterfall is in a wonderfully picturesque setting and is worth the trip even if the aforementioned wildlife doesn't come to the party.

From Rte 13 at Phonsi, follow the sign along a rough laterite road for a few hundred metres through the village until you reach the Nam Kading and start asking for a boat to Tat Wang Fong. It should cost about US$12 per boat, including waiting time while you swim and picnic at the falls – bring your own food, water and sun protection as the falls are mercifully free of salespeople. Depending on the season and the strength of the river, expect the boat to take one to two hours to reach the falls.

Falls or no falls, Pak Kading is a good place to stop for a meal at the **Bounxou Restaurant** (☎ 055-320046; Rte 13; meals US$1-2.50; ☷ 8am-9pm), where the fish dishes are recommended. If you need to sleep in Pak Kading, the only option is about 2km west of town directly behind a **disco** (☎ 055-320146; d US$4). Rooms are grim, guaranteed to be noisy and usually rented by the hour.

Ban Na Hin (Khoun Kham)
ບ້ານນາຫີນ (ຄຸນຄຳ)

The tiny village of Ban Na Hin (occasionally known as Khoun Kham) on Rte 8, 41km east of Rte 13, sits in a lush valley surrounded by tall karst peaks. The village itself is notable mainly for its position near the Nam Theun 1 dam operations centre; recognisable by its Lao-European–style bungalows and golf course.

Ban Na Hin is usually visited en route to Tham Lot Kong Lo (see p194). However, there is also an impressive twin-cataract waterfall known as **Tat Namsanam**, 3km north of town. The falls are in a striking location, surrounded by karst, and the upper tier is quite high. To get there from the market, head west on Rte 8 for a few hundred metres then turn north at the sign to the falls. Vehicles will need to stop after about 1km, and the ensuing 2km walk gets rocky and slippery in the latter stages; flip-flops won't do. There are plans to improve this trail.

As you approach Ban Na Hin from Rte 13, there is a **sala viewpoint** overlooking some stunning karst scenery just near Km 36. The scenery is quite dramatic.

SLEEPING & EATING
Of Ban Na Hin's guesthouses, the **Xok Xai** (☎ 051-233629; Rte 8; r US$4-6) is recommended. On the western edge of town, it has basic rooms and shared bathroom in a wooden house. For food, the **DK Restaurant** (meals US$0.75-1.50) serves simple but tasty Lao food at the east end of the street parallel to Rte 8.

GETTING THERE & AWAY

All transport plying Rte 8 between the Rte 13 towns of Paksan or Vieng Kham (also known as Thang Beng) and Lak Sao stops at Ban Na Hin market. There are occasional buses or *săwngthăew* from Tha Khaek (US$2.50, three hours, 143km). Leaving Na Hin, *săwngthăew* depart for Tha Khaek at 9am and 11am. For Paksan or Vientiane, just take anything that comes past from Lak Sao.

For Tham Lot Kong Lo, see p195.

Phu Hin Bun NPA

ປ່າສະຫງວນພູຫິນບຸນ

The Phu Hin Bun NPA, a huge (1580 sq km) wilderness area of turquoise streams, monsoon forests and striking karst topography across central Khammuan, was made a National Biodiversity Conservation Area in 1993. Although much of the NPA is inaccessible by road, the local people have nonetheless managed to reduce key forest-dependent species to very small numbers through hunting, mining and logging. The area is home to the endangered Douc langur, François' langur and several other primate species. The best, and for now one of the only ways to get into Phu Hin Bun is via Ban Na Hin (p193) and Tham Lot Kong Lo (below).

Tham Lot Kong Lo

ຖ້ຳລອດກອງລໍ

Pronounced *thàm lâwt kạwng láw*, the 7km-long **Tham Lot Kong Lo** limestone cave through which the Nam Hin Bun flows is truly one of the natural wonders of Laos. The cave-cum-tunnel is vast – up to 100m wide in some places and almost as high – and it takes a motorised canoe nearly an hour to pass through.

Boat pilots hired for the journey can also lead visitors to see natural *thâat* (stupas) inside – actually groups of glittering stupa-shaped stalagmites in one of the many dry caverns that branch off from the main tunnel. Sadly, some of the formations have been damaged by villagers looking for caches of gold and silver. Be sure to bring a torch (flashlight) and wear rubber sandals; the gravel in the riverbed is sharp and, especially during the dry season, it's sometimes necessary to disembark and wade a few metres.

Besides snaking through the tunnel, the Nam Hin Bun meanders through some spectacular scenery – Gothic mountains and cliffs of jagged black karst. Amazingly, a fair amount of hardy trees have managed to take root on the cliffs. Keep an eye out for sago palms that have attained rare heights of over 2m – in more accessible places these slow-growing trees have been dug up and sold to landscape gardeners in Thailand.

At the north end of the tunnel lies a scenic valley that once served as a refuge for lowland Lao fleeing Haw harassment during the 19th century. Temple ruins believed to date from that period can be seen in the valley. South of Kong Lo the Nam Hin Bun flows between spectacularly sheer cliffs as it follows a large arc towards the Mekong, eventually passing Rte 13 at Hinbun. If you have the time and money, this would be a truly unforgettable boat trip; ask about it at Sala Hin Bun.

Tham Lot Kong Lo is located about 40km southeast of Ban Na Hin. The best time of year to visit is from October to February, when the water is highest.

TOURS

North by North-East Tours (☎ in Thailand 0 4251 3572; www.thaitourism.com), based in Nakhon Phanom in Thailand, leads small, well-organised road-and-river tours into the Phu Hin Bun NPA, taking in Tham Lot Kong Lo and other caves in the region. Trips are designed to include positive interaction with local villagers. Four-day trips cost US$340 per person all inclusive (minimum two travellers).

SLEEPING & EATING

It's possible to visit Tham Lot Kong Lo as a day trip from Ban Na Hin, using the accommodation there (see p193), but it's a very long day. Much more fun are the options in the village of Phon Nyaeng, 8km downriver from the cave.

Sala Hin Boun (☎ in Vientiane 021-212725; www .salalao.com; s/d US$15/20, low season US$12/16) is located at the edge of Phon Nyaeng amid the scenic Nam Hin Bun valley. Rooms in this Lao-style wooden bungalow share a common veranda where you can lounge in wicker chairs overlooking the mountains and river. Rooms have attached bathroom but the hot water is not guaranteed. Lao and Western food is available for about US$3 to US$4 a meal, though you need to order in advance to allow time to get to the far-off market. Staff can arrange guided trips to Tham Lot Kong Lo as well as other caves in the area.

Cheaper and more adventurous **home-stay** options exist in Phon Nyaeng and Ban Kong Lo, about 1km west of the cave's western mouth. Ask around and you'll be offered a bed for about US$3, and will eat with your host family for a couple of dollars more. This really is mixing with the locals and is very far from luxurious; be sure to be sensitive to the cultural differences (see Dos & Don'ts p33).

GETTING THERE & AWAY

There are plans to improve the road from Ban Na Hin at least as far as Phon Nyaeng. In the meantime, getting to Tham Lot Kong Lo is not easy. From Ban Na Hin, take any transport – usually *săwngthăew* or jumbo (three-wheeled taxi) – for the 10km ride along a dirt road to the village of Ban Na Phuak (US$0.70 per person or $7 charter, 35 minutes, 10km); one service is guaranteed from Ban Na Phuak to Na Hin at 9.30am, returning at 10.30am; after this you have to wait for it to fill. From Ban Na Phuak the road becomes rough and is often impassable in the rainy season, when you'll need to take a boat (about US$15, two to 2½ hours), or a *lot thăi* (power-tiller pulling a trailer; US$12 or $1.50 per person, two to three hours) upriver to Phon Nyaeng, where Sala Hin Boun is located. During the dry season it may be possible to get a jumbo all the way from Ban Na Hin to Phon Nyaeng (about US$15, four hours).

The track between Ban Na Phuak and Phon Nyaeng extends about 12km. If you have reservations at the Sala Hin Boun and specify that you want them to do so, they'll have a motorised canoe (US$25) waiting for you at Ban Na Phuak.

From Phon Nyaeng it is another 8km to Ban Kong Lo (1km from Tham Lot Kong Lo). This could be done by bicycle (bikes can be hired from the Sala Hin Boun) but most people hire a motorised canoe for about US$10 per person, including lunch, for the return journey to and through the cave; Sala Hin Boun organises these trips, or you could

seek a better deal (without food) in the village. Some travellers have reported hiking over the mountain (and thus the cave) with a guide, then taking a boat back downstream. The walk is said to take four to six hours.

LAK SAO

ຫລັກຊາວ

☎ 054 / pop 28,000

While the forest, mountain and karst scenery along the upper stretches of Rte 8 on the way to Lak Sao (Lak Xao; literally, Kilometre Stone 20) is strikingly beautiful, the town itself is a disappointment. Located in Bolikhamsai Province between Kham Keut and the Vietnam border, Lak Sao is a frontier boomtown that has grown rapidly as the headquarters for the logging operations that continue to decimate forests in eastern Bolikhamsai and Khammuan Provinces.

The market at Lak Sao was once known for its trade in wildlife and forest products, but these days there is little on offer – no doubt due to the destruction of forests in the vicinity. Families of White Hmong and Striped Hmong can occasionally be seen trading for provisions in the market. You can hire local jumbos to investigate nearby **limestone caves** (the most accessible, Tham Mangkhon, is 17km northwest of town on Rte 8) or visit the **hot springs** (another 1km further).

Lak Sao is a good place to stop if you're travelling between Vientiane and Hanoi. It can be quite chilly from December to February.

Information

Banque pour le Commerce Extérieur Lao (BCEL; Rte 8B) Will also change local and major currencies.

Lao Development Bank (Rte 8B) Changes Thai baht, dollars, UK pounds and Vietnamese dong at the same rate as in Vientiane.

Post office (Cnr Rte 8 & Rte 8B; 8am-noon & 1-5pm Mon-Fri, 8am-noon Sat)

Sleeping & Eating

Accommodation in Lak Sao represents very good value, and you don't need 20/20 vision to see where this town made its money; there's enough high-quality timber used in these guesthouses to keep a carpenter busy for several lifetimes. All have hot water and are a short walk to the market and bus station.

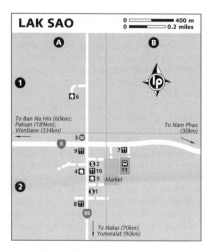

A few **small restaurants** (🕑 6am-8pm) serve Lao and Vietnamese food near the corner of Routes 8 and 8B and several *fŏe* stalls are along the outside of the market on Rte 8.

Getting There & Away

Buses leave from the east side of the market for Vientiane (US$4.50, eight hours, 334km) every day at 5am, 6am and 8am, finishing at Vientiane's Northern Bus Station. For services from Vientiane see p94. Until the painfully slow upgrading of Rte 8 is complete (probably in 2006), all other transport out of Lak Sao is by *săwngthăew*; those to Paksan (US$3.50, five to six hours, 189km) and Tha Khaek (US$3.50, five to six hours, 202km) leave hourly until 2pm. After this a couple run as far as Vieng Kham (Thang Beng; US$2, 3½ to five hours, 100km), the last at 4.30pm. From Vieng Kham get anything going your way.

THA KHAEK

ທ່າແຂກ

☎ 051 / pop 70,000

On the east bank of the Mekong River, 332km south of Vientiane, the capital of Khammuan Province is an enjoyable base from which to explore the more exciting regions east of here. Typically unhurried, Tha Khaek is a place you can soon feel comfortable in, which is appropriate considering the town name means Guest Landing, a reference to its earlier role as a boat landing for foreign traders.

The surviving Franco-Chinese architecture, mixed with newer structures, is similar to that found in Vientiane and Savannakhet. At the western end of Th Kuvoravong near the river is a modest fountain square. Today

Phouthavong Guest House (☎ 341074, mobile 020-5653251; Rte 8B; r US$4-5; 🖳) The best value in town, with clean, spacious rooms, some with desks, in a large building near the market. Slightly smaller fan rooms are US$4. No English is spoken.

Souriya Guest House (☎ 341111; Rte 8B; r US$5-7; 🖳) Opposite the Phouthavong, this three-storey guesthouse has 20 clean twin and double rooms with TV; the best are at the front with a bathtub and views of the town and mountain behind (US$7). The friendly manager speaks French and some English, and there's a good restaurant next door.

Vongsouda Guest House (☎ 341035, mobile 020-5653251; r US$5; 🖳) About 300m north of Rte 8 along a dirt road, this friendly guesthouse has eight clean and quiet rooms in a wooden house, each with fridge and TV. There's a cosy communal sitting area with a fireplace for chilly evenings. Vongsouda hires out motorbikes for US$13 a day.

Only One Restaurant (☎ 341034; Rte 8B; meals US$1-3; 🕑 6am-10pm) It's good when the most pleasant place to eat also serves the best food, with the Lao and Vietnamese dishes particularly well done. Unusually for Lak Sao, the endangered species of the surrounding forests are found on preservation posters on the wall, rather than on the menu.

Thipphavongxay (☎ 341038; Rte 8B; meals US$1-3; 🕑 6am-10pm) Next door to the Souriya Guest House, Thipphavongxay has a good range of *làap* (spicy meat salad) in its large menu. It's best to avoid the roe-deer, however.

Tha Khaek is a quiet transport and trade outpost – populated mostly by lowland Lao, Vietnamese and Thai – with a border crossing to Nakhon Phanom in Thailand.

Tha Khaek is best as a base for heading east on ropey Rte 12 (p201) into the vast Khammuan Limestone area, or all the way around The Loop (p201).

History

Once an outpost of the Mon-Khmer Funan and Chenla empires, when it was known as Sri Gotabura (Si Khotabun in Lao) and was ruled by King Suryavarman (r AD 578–614), Tha Khaek traces its present-day roots to French colonial construction in 1911–12. Before the Indochina War (and during the war until the North Vietnamese Army and Pathet Lao cut the road to Vientiane), Tha Khaek was a thriving gambling town for day-tripping Thais.

Prior to the revolution Vietnamese made up about 85% of Tha Khaek's population, having either come with the French decades earlier or having fled the Viet Minh movement in North Vietnam. Their numbers dropped drastically in the late 1970s as many left to seek their fortunes in more favourable climes.

Information

EMERGENCY
Police (cnr Th Kuvoravong & Th Unkham)
Tourist Police (Fountain Sq)
Tha Khaek Hospital (cnr Th Chou Anou & Th Champasak)

MONEY
BCEL (☎ 212686; Th Vientiane) Changes Thai baht, US dollars, euros, Vietnamese dong and Lao kip. Travellers cheques are changed, and cash advances made on Visa.
Lao Development Bank (☎ 212089; Th Kuvoravong) Changes cash, but doesn't offer cash advances. There's a second branch that changes cash located at the immigration post at the pier.

POST
Main post office (Th Kuvoravong) Also has a good range of postcards.

TELEPHONE
International calls can be made at the main post office.

TOURIST INFORMATION
Tourism Office (☎ 212512; Fountain Sq; 8am-4pm) Though not always manned, this office is worth visiting. Plans to train English-speaking local guides might have come to fruition, and if so this office will be able to help you find one.

SOUTHERN LAOS

CROSSING THE VIETNAM BORDER AT NAM PHAO & CAU TREO

The border at Nam Phao (Laos) and Cau Treo (Vietnam) is about 30km from Lak Sao and is open from 8am to 5pm, though lunch time often slows things down on the Lao side. *Săwngthăew* (US$1, 45 minutes) leave every hour or so from Lak Sao market and drop you at the typically relaxed Lao border post. There is an exchange booth on the Lao side, though the rates aren't generous. You'll need to have your Vietnamese visa arranged in advance. Laos issues 15-day visas (US$30) at the border.

Once into Vietnam you'll be welcomed by an assortment of piranhas masquerading as transport to Vinh. Contrary to their claims, a minibus to Vinh doesn't cost US$20 per person – about $5 for a seat is a more reasonable price, though you'll do very well to get that price. You can avoid these guys by taking the daily minibus from Lak Sao to Chung Thom near Vinh (40,000d, about three hours; as well as Vietnamese dong (d) you can pay in dollars or kip), which leaves about 11am. Otherwise, hook up with as many other people as possible to improve your bargaining position. Once in Vinh you can take one of the frequent buses or a sleeper on the regular **Reunification Express trains** (www.vr.com.vn) straight to Hanoi (the website lists the latest times and prices). If you have the dire misfortune of having to spend a night in Vinh, the **Bao Ngoc Hotel** (☎ 038-569999; D Le Loi; r 120,000-160,000d; 🖳) is not bad.

Coming from Vinh, buses leave for Tay Son (10,000d, 70km) regularly between 6am and 2pm. From Tay Son there are rare local buses to the border (5000d, 20km) or you could get a motorbike or minibus for about 50,000d. Expect to be ripped off on this route. Jumbos and *săwngthăew* to Lak Sao leave the border when full or cost about US$10 to charter.

There is, of course, the option of taking the 24-hour bus direct between Hanoi and Vientiane, but it's a full-blown nightmare of a trip, less fun and more expensive than doing it yourself.

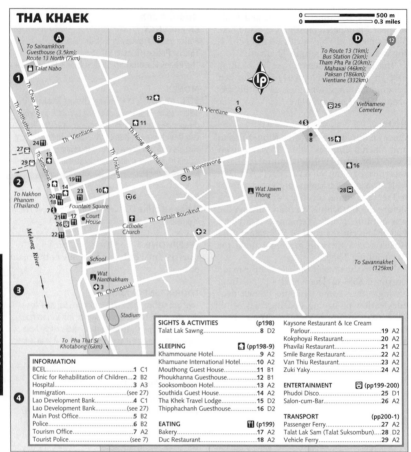

THA KHAEK

To Sainamkhon
Guesthouse (3.5km);
Route 13 North (7km)

Talat Nabo

To Route 13 (1km);
Bus Station (2km);
Tham Pha Pa (20km);
Mahaxai (46km);
Paksan (186km);
Vientiane (332km)

Vietnamese
Cemetery

Th Vientiane

Th Chao Anou
Th Sethathirat

Th Vientiane

Th Nong Bua Kham

Th Unkham

Th Kuvoravong

Th Sethathirat

Wat Jawm
Thong

To Nakhon
Phanom
(Thailand)

Fountain Square

Th Captain Bounkeut

Mekong River

Court
House

Catholic
Church

School

Wat
Nanthakham
Th Champasak

To Pha That Si
Khotabong (6km)

Stadium

To Savannakhet
(125km)

SIGHTS & ACTIVITIES	(p198)	Kaysone Restaurant & Ice Cream
Talat Lak Sawng..................8 D2		Parlour.....................19 A2
		Kokphoyai Restaurant...........20 A2
SLEEPING	(pp198-9)	Phavilai Restaurant.............21 A2
Khammouane Hotel...............9 A2		Smile Barge Restaurant.........22 A2
Khamuane International Hotel...10 A2		Van Thiu Restaurant............23 A2
Mouthong Guest House..........11 B1		Zuki Yaky......................24 A2
Phoukhanna Guesthouse........12 B1		
Sooksomboon Hotel.............13 A2		**ENTERTAINMENT** (pp199-200)
Southida Guest House..........14 A2		Phudoi Disco..................25 D1
Tha Khek Travel Lodge.........15 D2		Salon-cum-Bar.................26 A2
Thipphachanh Guesthouse.......16 D2		
		TRANSPORT (pp200-1)
EATING	(p199)	Passenger Ferry...............27 A2
Bakery........................17 A2		Talat Lak Sam (Talat Suksombun)...28 D2
Duc Restaurant................18 A2		Vehicle Ferry.................29 A2

INFORMATION
BCEL.....................................1 C1
Clinic for Rehabilitation of Children...2 B2
Hospital..................................3 A3
Immigration.........................(see 27)
Lao Development Bank.................4 C1
Lao Development Bank..............(see 27)
Main Post Office.......................5 B2
Police....................................6 B2
Tourism Office.........................7 A2
Tourist Police......................(see 7)

Sights

TALAT LAK SAWNG

ຕະຫລາດຫລັກສອງ

In town the large **Talat Lak Sawng** (Km 2 Market; Th Kuvoravong) purveys hardware, clothes, fresh produce and just about everything else the people of Tha Khaek use in daily life. In addition to the usual gold shops there are a large number of vendors selling silverwork.

Activities

A company called **North-by-Northeast Tours** (www.thaitourism.com/tours.html), based in Nakhon Phanom, Thailand (directly across from Tha Khaek), offers river trips along the Nam Hin Bun and other waterways in the Khammuan Limestone.

The physiotherapists at the **Clinic for Rehabilitation of Children** have been trained in Thai massage in an effort to earn more money for the clinic.

Sleeping

Tha Khaek is not blessed with a wide range of rooms.

Tha Khek Travel Lodge (☎ 212882; dm US$1.80; r US$4-6; ❖) Despite being far from the Mekong, this place is the best option in Tha Khaek. Run by a Lao-Danish couple who also operate a furniture factory opposite, the attractive building has nine clean rooms catering to all budgets – from a dormitory (US$1.50), through fan rooms with shared bathroom (US$3) to two air-con rooms with private bathroom (US$6). The biggest attraction, however, is the travellers' book and the local knowledge of Ejnar, the owner, and Om, the best local guide in the province. If you're thinking of doing The Loop (p201), this is the place to get the latest intelligence. They can arrange motorbike hire and offer trekking tours. And the food is good, too.

Southida Guest House (☎ 212568; Th Chao Anou; d US$8-10, tw US$9; ✹) A short walk to the river front, family-run Southida has clean rooms with TV in a modern two-storey building. Most have at least one balcony. There is one vast double with fridge for US$10. The **restaurant** (meals US$1.50-4; ✹ breakfast, lunch & dinner) is not bad either.

Phoukhanna Guesthouse (☎ 212092; Th Vientiane; r US$5-8; ✹) This new place has air-con rooms with TV in an older building, but if you can live without the TV the new fan rooms (US$5) out the back are bigger and better. Management is eager to please and one woman speaks English.

Sooksomboon Hotel (☎ 212225; Th Setthathirat; small/large rooms US$7/10; ✹) Housed in a former police station from the French era and right on the Mekong, this hotel has seen better days but its surreal faux–Art Deco interior will appeal to some. Some rooms have a bathtub and all look clean, though they are musty. Staff are friendly.

Thipphachanh Guesthouse (☎ 212762; r US$5-7; ✹) This motel-style place is super popular with Laos for its clean rooms with TV, but it's a fair way out. Fan rooms cost US$5.

Sainamkhon Guesthouse (☎ 214038; Th Chao Anou; d US$7-8; ✹) About 5km north of the fountain square this place is right on the Mekong and is popular with visiting civil servants. The rooms are clean and there's a restaurant serving Lao food, though the view is better than the food. Bigger rooms with fridge cost US$8.

Khammouane Hotel (Th Setthathirat; ✹) This four-storey hotel was being renovated when we passed but should be open by 2005. Expect to pay between US$15 and US$20. The rooms should be more appealing than the bright blue exterior of the hotel.

Samly Motel (d US$3) If you've got a few hours between buses, this motel at the bus station would suffice, with ultra-basic, windowless but clean fan rooms.

In the unlikely event that everything else is full, the **Mouthong Guest House** (☎ 212387; Th Nong Bua Kham; s/d/f US$5/6/10; ✹) has small cement rooms and one larger family room with a bathtub (US$10); while rooms in the centrally located **Khamuane International Hotel** (☎ 212171; Th Kuvoravong; s/d US$5/6; ✹) are sadly run-down and those we saw had plumbing issues.

Eating

Among hotels, the kitchens in the Southida Guest House and the Tha Khek Travel Lodge both have a reputation for well above average food; the latter is about the only place in town you'll find decent Western food. Several *khào jìi* (baguette) vendors can be found on the fountain square in the morning.

Kaysone Restaurant & Ice Cream Parlour (☎ 212563; meals US$1.50-4; ✹ lunch & dinner) With dining on the rooftop or indoors, this is a very pleasant place to eat. The Vietnamese, Lao and Chinese food is quite good and fairly reasonably priced.

Smile Barge Restaurant (☎ 212150; meals US$3-4.50; ✹ 5.30-11.30pm) This floating restaurant serves good Lao food, especially fish dishes, but the karaoke kind of kills the mood. Good for a sunset drink (before the singing starts).

Van Thiu Restaurant (☎ 212138; Th Chao Anou; meals US$1-3; ✹ lunch & dinner) This no-frills place, accessed through a shop, serves tasty Vietnamese dishes.

Zuki Yaky (☎ 212334; Th Vientiane; meals US$2-4.50; ✹ 6-10pm) This place specialises in Korean-style barbecue dishes.

Phavilai Restaurant (Fountain sq; meals US$1-2; ✹ 6am-9pm) Phavilai, not far from the river landing, serves standard Lao-Chinese rice and noodle dishes.

Bakery (✹ 5-9pm) For the best plain baguettes head for the Vietnamese bakery, a couple of blocks south of fountain square.

On the river front, the **Kokphoyai Restaurant** (☎ 213744; meals US$1.50; ✹ 6am-10pm) is noted for its fresh and filling Lao dishes, and the nearby **Duc Restaurant** (meals US$1.50; ✹ 6am-10pm) does a delicious *fǒe hàeng*, dry rice noodles served in a bowl with various herbs and seasonings but no broth.

Entertainment

Phudoi Disco (✹ 8pm-midnight) Behind the Phudoi Guest House (not recommended), this is a good place to check out the Lao nightclub scene. It's big, loud and busy, with the local youth getting down to Thai pop, Lao pop and…*Hotel California*, all while wearing the latest Linkin Park, Che Guevara or, of course, Beerlao T-shirts. Good fun.

Salon-cum-Bar (Th Setthathirat) On the river front a couple of blocks south of the fountain square, this salon often morphs into an impromptu bar when the hair-cutting stops around 5pm. It doesn't happen every day, only when the wonderfully entertaining hairdresser decides it's time; check it out.

Getting There & Away
BUS

Tha Khaek's new **bus station** (Rte 13) is about 4km from the centre of town, and has regular services going north and south. For Vientiane (US$3.50, six hours, 332km) buses originate in Tha Khaek at 4.30am, 5.30am, 6.30am and 8am. From 8.40am to 4pm, and then from 7pm to midnight try for space on buses coming through from Pakse and Savannakhet every hour or so. You can take any bus going north for Vieng Kham (Thang Beng; US$1.50, 90 minutes, 102km), Pak Kading (US$2, three hours, 149km), or Paksan (US$2.50, 2½ hours, 193km). For buses from Vientiane see p94.

Heading south, buses for Savannakhet (US$1.50, two hours, 125km) are fairly frequent, and services to Pakse (US$4, 368km, six to seven hours) stop here at about 11am, 12.30pm, 3.30pm, 4.30pm and hourly from 5pm until midnight. A 4pm bus goes all the way to Don Khong (US$5.50, about 15 hours, 452km) and Voen Kham (US$5.50, about 16 hours, 482km) on the Cambodian border, but you'd need to be in a hurry.

If you're heading to Vietnam a bus for Hanoi (US$15, 17 hours) leaves from the Talat Lak Sam (Talat Suksombun) terminal on Wednesday and Saturday at 8pm.

SĂWNGTHĂEW

Wooden buses or *săwngthăew* depart when full from the Talat Lak Sam terminal along two basic routes into the Khammuan Province interior, one going to Mahaxai (towards the Nakai-Nam Theun NPA) and the other to Nyommalat (in the vicinity of Phu Hin Bun NPA) and Rte 8B. There are simple guesthouses in Mahaxai and Nyommalat (see the Loop p201); unfortunately there is no public transport going to the NPAs from

> ## CROSSING THE THAI BORDER AT THA KHAEK & NAKHON PHANOM
>
> Crossing the Mekong from Tha Khaek to Nakhon Phanom in Thailand is simple. The boat landing and associated **immigration office** (8am-5.30pm) are about 400m north of the fountain square and boats travel in both directions every half-hour, or hourly between noon and 2pm. From Laos, the ferry costs US$1.50 or 60B, while from Nakhon Phanom it's 50B. Transporting motorbikes costs US$0.50, while larger vehicles are US$5. On weekends boats might be less frequent and you'll be asked for an extra US$1 on the Lao side, and an extra 10B in Thailand. After hours you can charter a boat for 500B.
>
> In Tha Khaek, Laos issues 15-day tourist visas on arrival (US$30) and there's a **money exchange service** (8.30am-3pm) at the immigration office. In Thailand, regular express buses leave Nakhon Phanom for Udon Thani and Bangkok. If you need to stay, try the **Windsor Hotel** (0 4251 1946; 692/19 Th Bamrung Meuang; 250-400B).

here, try engaging a local to take you. Getting to the Talat Lak Sam terminal early in the morning is your best bet. Mahaxai and Nyommalat cost around US$1.50; intermediate points cost from US$0.50 to US$1. Rte 12 is pretty rough, but expect the road and the type of transport to improve as the Nam Theun 2 hydroelectric project gathers momentum.

Getting Around

Jumbos can be hard to find early in the morning; your best bet is the eastern end of the fountain square. It should cost about US$1 to hire a jumbo to the bus terminal. Rides around town cost from US$0.20 to US$0.30 per person.

AROUND THA KHAEK
Pha That Si Khotabong
ພະທາດສີໂຄຕະບອງ

About 6km south of town, is the much-venerated **Pha That Si Khotabong** (Pha That Muang Ka; admission US$0.20; 8am-6pm) stupa which stands in the grounds of a 19th-century monastery of the same name. According to local lore the stupa was erected on the site of a 6th- to 10th-century *thâat* (Buddhist stupa or reliquary) built by King Nanthasen during a time when Tha Khaek was part of a principality called Si Khotabun. Considered one of the most important *thâat* in Laos, Si Khotabong was first renovated by King Setthathirat in the 16th century, when it assumed its current general form. It was again restored in the 1950s and later augmented in the 1970s. It's the site of a major festival each February.

A *wihǎan* (hall) on the temple grounds contains a large seated Buddha, constructed by the order of King Anouvong (Chao Anou).

Tham Pha Pa (Buddha Cave)
ຖ້ຳພະປ່າ

When Mr Bun Nong used a vine to scramble 15m up a sheer 300m-high cliff in April 2004, he was hoping to make a dinner of the bats he'd seen flying out of the rock face. Instead he discovered a 1.5m-high cave mouth and, stepping into the cavern beyond, was greeted by more than 200 bronze Buddha images. The Buddhas, ranging in height from 15cm to about 1m in height, were sitting in a cave of impressive limestone formations. After a week of silent disbelief, Mr Bun Nong told friends in the nearby village of Ban Na Kan Sarng and the cave was named Tham Pha Pa ('Buddha cave').

No-one is sure how long the Buddha images have been there, but it is agreed they are much older than the village itself, which has only been around since the 1970s. Whatever their age, the discovery of the cave drew pilgrims from as far as Bangkok. A hastily cobbled-together bamboo ladder provides access to the cave, though plans to build a stairway should have come to fruition by the time you read this (we can only hope it's not concrete).

Tham Pha Pa is about 20km from Tha Khaek along a terrible dirt road north of Rte 12. The road will be upgraded, but in the meantime you'll need to take a motorbike, tuk-tuk, *sǎwngthǎew* or *dok dok* (power-tiller pulling a trailer) to get there; ask at the tourist office (p197) for details.

East on Rte 12

Whether as a day trip or as part of The Loop (see below), the first 22km of rough Rte 12 east of Tha Khaek is an area with several caves, an abandoned railway line and a couple of swimming spots that are worth a look. Be sure to bring a torch. This is part of the vast Khammuan Limestone area, which stretches roughly between Rtes 12 and 8 and east towards Rte 8B. There are thousands of caves, sheer cliffs and jagged karst peaks, but it's difficult to get into. The best way is to visit the Tham Lot Kong Lo cave (p194).

SOUTHERN LAOS

THE LOOP

A small but growing number of travellers are taking a three-day off-the-beaten-track loop through the remote parts of Khammuan and Bolikhamsai Provinces. The trip is possible by bicycle, but is best done on a motorbike; speak to the Tha Khek Travel Lodge (p198), which also has a travellers' book with the latest Loop feedback.

Once you've got your wheels, spend day one heading east on Rte 12 (see above) visiting the caves and swimming spots on the way to Mahaxai (about 35km), where you can refuel and stay in a simple **guesthouse** (r US$3.25). Alternatively, continue north to Nakai via Nyommalat and Rte 8B, a journey of up to 90 minutes by small motorbike. There is a basic **guesthouse** (r US$3) in Nakai, and fuel.

From Nakai, continue north on 8B, taking the right fork when the road splits (the left fork will take you to the Nam Theun 2 dam site). From Nakai to Lak Sao is about 70km of rough, rocky road (about three to five hours on a 100cc bike), and the most challenging part of the trip is crossing the Nam Theun about 8km north of Nakai. In the wet season this can get very tricky and you might need to load the bike onto a small boat. Fuel is available in small *bâan* (villages) on Rte 8B.

Sleep and refuel in Lak Sao (p195) and take the smooth Rte 8 the next day to Ban Na Hin (p193) before turning south for Tham Lot Kong Lo (p194). In the wet season you might need to leave your bike in Na Hin. Spend the night at Phon Nyaeng (p195) and refuel in Na Hin before riding back to Tha Khaek (141km) on Rte 8 and Rte 13. Good luck!

The first cave is **Tham Pha Ban Tham**, a Buddhist shrine 9km from Tha Khaek. It's famous for its stalagmite 'elephant head', which is behind the large golden Buddha along a small passage way. Take Rte 12 to Km 7 and take the right fork.

Back on Rte 12, turn left (north) at Km 8 for 1km to reach the remains of a **railway line** that was abandoned unfinished during the 1920s. The line was supposed to run all the way to Vietnam, and on the Vietnamese side there is a line to the border. A road now follows the track bed, over a notable railway bridge, and all the way to Tham Pha Pa.

At Km 13 a 4WD-only trail leads 2km north to the water-sculpted rocks at **Tha Fa-lang** (French Landing) on the scenic Nam Don. Tha Falang features a wooded area on a stream where colonials used to picnic and is probably the best swimming spot in the area. In the wet season you'll need to hire a pirogue (dug-out canoe) from the Xieng Liap bridge to get there.

A track heading south at Km 14 leads to the stunning limestone cave **Tham Xieng Liap**, the entrance of which is at the base of a 300m-high cliff. The cave is 200m long and, in the dry season, you can walk through (with wet feet) and swim on the other side.

Rte 12 continues through a narrow pass, with high cliffs either side, and immediately beyond a track leads north to **Tham Sa Pha In**, a rarely visited Buddhist holy cave with a lake and opening in the roof. The water in the lake is said to have magical powers; you shouldn't swim here. At Km 18 is the touristy **Tham Nang Aen** (admission US$0.30); follow the signs.

Further afield is **Tham Pha Xang** (Tam Pha Chan) a cave 60m high and about 100m wide, and the **Nam Don Resurgence**, a cave where the Nam Don emerges from the ground, and is a good swimming spot. They are accessed via a road north from Km 14, but can be difficult to find; you're best to go with someone who knows the way (such as a tuk-tuk driver).

All these places can be reached by hired motorcycle; speak with the Tha Khek Travel Lodge (p198). Otherwise, hire a jumbo or tuk-tuk for the day, explore the caves and stop at Wat Pha That Si Khotabong on the way back for about US$25.

SAVANNAKHET PROVINCE

Home to around 15% of all Lao citizens, Savannakhet is the country's most populous province, and is a very active junction for trade between Thailand and Vietnam. The population consists of lowland Lao, Thai Dam, several small Mon-Khmer groups (Chali, Bru, Kaleung, Katang, Lave, Mangkong, Pako and Suay), Vietnamese and Chinese. The villages of Savannakhet are among the most typically Lao.

There are two NPAs in the province, Dong Phu Vieng (p209) to the south of Rte 9 and Phu Xang He to the north. Only Dong Phu Vieng is accessible to visitors, and it's well worth making the trip.

Eastern Savannakhet is the best place in Laos to see the Ho Chi Minh Trail, the primary supply route to South Vietnam for the North Vietnamese Army during the Indochina War. It is also a major gateway for visitors arriving from Vietnam via Lao Bao, a journey now completed on the luxurious new tarmac of Rte 9. With a new bridge across the Mekong due to open in 2006, the city's future as a hub for trade between Thailand and Vietnam looks bright.

SAVANNAKHET (MUANG KHANTHABULI)

ສະຫວັນນະເຂດ

☎ 041 / pop 124,000

The slowly crumbling colonial-era buildings of Savannakhet serve as reminders of the importance the French attached to what was their largest trading and administrative centre south of Vientiane. These days the city's riverside centre retains a languid ambience, with tall trees shading French-era buildings that are unfailingly appealing despite their ever-more forlorn appearance. Unfortunately many of these buildings will be lost in the coming years; the government is unsentimental about such colonial reminders and is unlikely to start spending money on their upkeep.

Outside the centre, Savannakhet (officially known as Muang Khanthabuli but more commonly called Savan) is growing fast. The expansion of Savannakhet has seen the large and lively **Talat Savan Xai** (Th Sisavangvong; ⊙ 7am-5pm), north of the centre near the bus terminal, establish itself as the

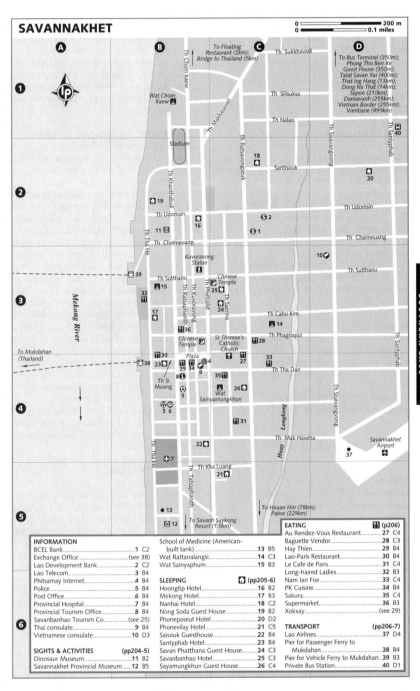

centre of much of the city's commerce; at this market you'll see Lao people mixing with Thais, Vietnamese, Chinese and a sprinkling of people from smaller ethnic groups.

Information

EMERGENCY
Police (☎ 212069; Th Ratsaphanith)
Provincial Hospital (☎ 212051; Th Khanthabuli)

FOREIGN CONSULATES
Thai consulate (☎ 212373; Th Kuvoravong; ✆ drop-off 8.30am-noon & collection 1-3pm Mon-Fri) Visas issued the same day.
Vietnamese consulate (☎ 212418; Th Sisavangvong; ✆ 7.30-11am & 1.30-4.30pm Mon-Fri) Tourist visa: US$55, one photo, three working days.

INTERNET ACCESS
Phitsamay Internet (☎ 215478; Th Si Muang; per hr US$1.50; ✆ 1am-1pm Mon-Sat & noon-10pm Sun) On the southeastern corner of the plaza, this place has three fast terminals.

MONEY
Both of the following banks will change cash or make cash advances on Visa or Master-Card. The immigration office on the pier also has an exchange office where you can change kip.
BCEL Bank (☎ 212226; Th Ratsavongseuk)
Lao Development Bank (☎ 212272; Th Udomsin)

POST
Post office (☎ 212205; Th Khanthabuli) Just south of the town centre.

TELEPHONE
Lao Telecom (☎ 212047; ✆ 8am-10pm) Long-distance phone calls.

TOURIST INFORMATION
Provincial Tourism Office (☎ 212755 or 214203; Th Ratsaphanith; ✆ 8am-11.30pm & 1.30pm-4.30pm Mon-Fri) Has several handy brochures (though no maps) and is the place to come to contact guides for treks into Dong Natad (p208) or Dong Phu Vieng NPA (p209).

TRAVEL AGENCIES
Savanbanhao Tourism Co (☎ /fax 212944; Th Saenna) In the Savanbanhao Hotel, these guys have information on local attractions and can arrange tours to Sepon and the Ho Chi Minh Trail (both p209), Heuan Hin (p208) and other spots outside the city.

Sights

Much of the charm of Savannakhet is in just wandering through the quiet streets in the centre of town, between the new and old buildings, the laughing children and, along Th Phetsalat near Wat Sainyamungkhun, among the slow-moving, *pétanque*-playing old men of the town.

SAVANNAKHET PROVINCIAL MUSEUM
ພິພິດທະພັນແຂວງ ສະຫວັນນະເຂດ

Housed in a French-era mansion near the provincial hospital off Th Khanthabuli, the **Savannakhet Provincial Museum** (admission US$0.50; ✆ 8-11.30am & 1-4pm Mon-Fri), seems to have hidden away its collection of war junk – all you can see these days are a few rusting artillery pieces aimed at Thailand and the barely recognisable remains of an American-built T-28, the main combat aircraft of the Royal Lao Army. There was some suggestion that the old displays might be returned, but in the meantime the museum is a shrine to Kaysone Phomvihane (see p29), who was born less than 1km away. There are hundreds of photos, most with basic English captions, and if you're interested in Kaysone or in the beatification of socialist heroes, then it's fascinating. If it looks closed when it shouldn't be, try asking at the curator's house – a wooden building in the southwest corner of the School of Medicine compound.

Opposite the front gate of the museum compound, on the grounds of the **School of Medicine**, is an American-built tank once used by the RLA.

DINOSAUR MUSEUM
ຫໍພິພິດທະພັນໄດໂນເສົາ

It might come as some surprise to learn Savannakhet Province is quite an exciting place for palaeontologists. In a colonial-era building, this small but well-presented **museum** (☎ 212597; Th Khanthabuli; admission US$0.10; ✆ 8am-noon & 1-4pm Mon-Fri) displays some of the finds from the five sites in the province where dinosaur bones or footprints have been found. The curators are unfailingly enthusiastic, and willing to use their limited English or French on you.

WAT SAINYAPHUM
ວັດໄຊຍະພູມ

The oldest and largest monastery in Savan, with more than 100 novices and monks in residence, **Wat Sainyaphum** (Th Tha He) is thought to have first been built in 1542, though most of what you see today dates from the 20th century. It's a pleasant place to wander and the monks may be willing to show you around and practise their English in the process. The drum tower is quite impressive, and look for the workshop near the river entrance – it's a veritable golden-Buddha production line.

WAT RATTANALANGSI
ວັດລັດຕະນະລັງສີ
Nearly as large as Wat Sainyaphum, **Wat Rattanalangsi** (Th Phangnapui) was built in 1951 and houses a monks' primary school. The *sĭm* (ordination hall) is unique in that it has glass windows (most windows in Lao temples are unglazed). Other structures include a rather gaudy Brahma shrine, a modern *săaláa lóng thám* (sermon hall) and a shelter containing a 15m reclining Buddha backed by Jataka (stories of the Buddha's past lives) paintings.

Sleeping
Savannakhet has a reasonable range of budget options but nothing too inspiring if you're looking for luxury. Most guesthouses are located in the attractive old town but there is little of quality on the Mekong itself. Thanks to an AIDS awareness project run by the local tourism office, most rooms come complete with four Number One–brand condoms. All rooms have hot water bathrooms unless otherwise stated.

BUDGET
Saisouk Guesthouse (☎ 212207; Th Phetsalat; r US$2.50-5; ✕) Just south of the centre of town, the atmosphere in this airy wooden house is hospitality personified. The rooms are clean, and those with attached cold-water bathroom are quite large. The husband-and-wife owners speak English and loan bicycles for free. Smaller rooms without bathroom are US$2.50. Recommended.

Sayamungkhun Guest House (☎ 212426; Th Ratsavongseuk; r US$4-8; ✕) One of the last colonial-era buildings being used as a guesthouse, the super-friendly Sayamungkhun has spacious, spotlessly clean rooms (some with fridge) and an inviting atmosphere. It's on the main road so rooms at the front can be noisy.

Phonevilay Hotel (☎ 212284; 172/173 Th Phetsalat; r US$3.50-7; ✕) Set around an attractive garden and courtyard in the south of town, Phonevilay has fan rooms with attached cold bathroom (US$3.50) and various-sized air-con rooms with hot water, TV and fridge (US$5 to US$7). Staff are friendly and the US$5 rooms are the best value.

Nong Soda Guest House (☎ 212522, mobile 020-5542222; Th Tha He; r US$8; ✕) About 200m north of Wat Sainyaphum, this modern house on the river's edge has reasonable if not exceptional rooms with one big bed, TV and fridge. The elevated bar in the front yard is good for sundowners.

Savanbanhao Hotel (☎ 212202; Th Saenna; s/d US$4.50/7.50, 1st class US$9.50; ✕) Centrally located in four buildings set around a soulless concrete courtyard, rooms here aren't bad but if you're seeking atmosphere, forget it. Two people are allowed to sleep in the single rooms, which have cold-water bathrooms, and there are First Class rooms (US$9.50) with hot water, TV and fridge. This is also the headquarters for Savanbanhao Tourism Co (see p204).

Santyphab Hotel (☎ 212177; Th Tha Dan; r US$2.50) This four-storey place, two blocks east of the Mekong, is the last of what was once a cluster of hotels in the older part of town near the ferry piers. The grand columns and Deco-style staircase hint at glories past, but today it's pretty grim but very cheap.

Phong Tho Ben Xe Guesthouse (r US$3) To the north of the centre is this ultra-simple guesthouse, located at the bus station.

MID-RANGE
There aren't a lot of mid-range options in Savannakhet, and nothing worthy of being called 'top end'.

Phonepaseut Hotel (☎ 212158; fax 212916; Th Santisouk d/VIP with breakfast US$25/35; ✕) A couple of blocks east of the Nanhai Hotel, the friendly Phonepaseut is a bit far from the Mekong but is your best bet for professional service. The clean, modern rooms around a courtyard and tennis court have TV, minibar and fridge. It's possible to negotiate discounts. The 25m-long swimming pool (US$2 for nonguests) was being renovated when we visited. The hotel is used as a base by US military personnel looking for the bodies of servicemen lost in Laos – hence the warehouse full of US government gear.

Nanhai Hotel (☎ 212371; fax 212380; Th Santisouk; s/d/ste with breakfast US$16/25/44; 🌀) Northeast of the town centre, the six-storey Nanhai has semiluxurious rooms with decent views, but has had something of a character bypass. There is a lift, coffee shop, and a **restaurant** (meals US$2.50-6; 🕑 breakfast, lunch & dinner) serving Chinese, Thai and French dishes. Sadly, the pool is not in working order.

Hoongtip Hotel (☎ 212262; hoongtip@laotel.com; cnr Th Phetsalat & Th Udomsin; r with breakfast US$18-25; 🌀) Rooms in the Hoongtip's two adjoining buildings have TV, minibar and aren't as good as they could be. Those in the old building (US$18) are overpriced, and many of those in the new building (US$25) are windowless.

Mekong Hotel (☎ 212249; Th Tha He; tw/f US$10/13; 🌀) This colonial-era villa on the Mekong should be one of the best places in town, but most of the character has been concreted into history or hidden behind tacky fairy lights. All rooms have TV and fridge and the two upstairs in the villa are best.

Eating

Savannakhet's culinary scene is not inspirational, but finding decent Lao, Thai and especially Vietnamese food is easy enough. Local specialities include *sìin sawǎn* (a slightly sweet, dried, roasted beef) and *jạew pạa-dàek* (a thick sauce of mashed chilli, onion, fish sauce and lotus bulb).

North of town are several floating restaurants that are popular with Laos and notable for their *khào pûn*, which are DIY rolls of spaghetti-style noodles with fish, lemongrass and herbs wrapped in lettuce and dipped in peanut sauce. You'll need a tuk-tuk to get there; ask for the *héuan pháe* (raft house).

Hay Thien (☎ 212754; Th Si Muang; meals US$0.80-2) This excellent restaurant in the centre of town specialises in Vietnamese and Chinese dishes.

Lao-Paris Restaurant (☎ 212792; Th Si Muang; meals US$1.50-4; 🕑 8am-10pm) This popular travellers' spot in an old Chinese shophouse near the river serves consistently good (though not necessarily outstanding) Lao, Vietnamese and French dishes, and sizeable breakfasts with Lao coffee. Prices are reasonable.

Le Cafe de Paris (☎ mobile 020-5518790; Th Saenna; meals US$4-7; 🕑 lunch & dinner) In a wooden house on a quiet street, this French-run restaurant

serves good pizzas (about US$6) and the best selection of European fare in town. There are plans to move to the river front…

Sakura (☎ 212882; Th Tha Dan; meals US$3-5; 🕑 lunch & dinner) An eclectic mix of sukiyaki dishes (US$3.50), fondues (US$2.50) and spicy soups (US$2.50) in an equally potpourri deep-south-saloon-meets-Korean-cinema setting. The food is good and on weekends there might be live music inside the glass room.

Au Rendez-Vous Restaurant (179 Th Ratsavongseuk; dishes US$1-3) A couple of blocks north of the Sayamungkhun Guest House, this restaurant serves decent Western breakfasts as well as the usual Chinese dishes.

Baguette vendor (cnr Th Ratsavongseuk & Th Phagnapui) Selling *khào jĩi páa-tê* (baguette sandwiches), this vendor is open all day. Besides the usual baguettes stuffed with pâté and shredded green papaya, you can get an excellent breakfast baguette filled with scrambled eggs (*khào jĩi sai khai*).

In Th Si Muang in the centre of town are several cheap eateries open for lunch and dinner: **PK Cuisine** (☎ 212022; meals US$1-2.50) is the pick and serves good-value Thai food; while **Xokxay** (☎ 213122; meals US$0.75-2) serves Chinese and Vietnamese dishes.

Opposite the Mekong Hotel and Wat Sainyaphum, riverside **snack and drink vendors** (🕑 afternoons & evenings) in this ideal sunset-viewing location. Beerlao and ice is the most common purchase, but a few make fresh *tạm màak-hung* (green papaya salad), grilled chicken and kebabs. Look for the friendly family of long-haired ladies who run one of these places; they're rightly proud of their hair (we're talking down to the calves!).

Getting There & Away

AIR

The airport is at the southeastern edge of town. In theory, **Lao Airlines** (☎ 212140; Th Makhaveha; 🕑 7.30am-4pm Mon-Fri, 7.30am-noon Sat) flies from Vientiane to Savannakhet twice weekly (US$57, one hour); in practice the flight is often cancelled due to lack of interest. The same applies to the scheduled weekly flights to Pakse (US$41.50, 50 minutes).

BUS & SĂWNGTHĂEW

Savannakhet's main **bus terminal** (☎ 212143), usually referred to as the *khíw lot*, is near the Talat Savan Xai at the northern edge

CROSSING THE THAI BORDER AT SAVANNAKHET/MUKDAHAN

As with the Mekong River borders to the north, this one is fairly hassle-free. On the Lao side, the boat pier is not far from the centre of town and ferries (US$1.20 or 50B, 30 minutes) cross the Mekong between Savannakhet and Mukdahan at 9.10am, 10am, 11.10am, 1.30pm, 2.30pm and 4.30pm from Monday to Friday, on Saturday at 9.30am, 11.10am, 2.30pm and 4.30pm, and on Sunday at 1pm and 3pm. For some reason, Lao boats only carry passengers *from* Laos, returning empty. The reverse is true of Thai boats, which run about every hour from 9am to 4.30pm Monday to Friday, with six services on Saturday and four on Sunday.

Arriving in Laos, the English-speaking immigration officers issue 15-day visas (US$30) on the spot. There is an exchange office in immigration where you can buy kip. From Mukdahan, regular buses run to Bangkok from the bus station – just ask a tuk-tuk for the 'Bangkok bus'. Otherwise, the **Mukdahan Hotel** (☎ 0 4261 1619; Th Samut Sakdarak; 200-450B) is a decent option.

When the bridge linking the two cities is complete expect to be able to enter there. The ferry is expected to continue operating even after the bridge is finished.

of town. Buses leave here for Vientiane (US$4.50, seven to nine hours, 457km) every half-hour from 6am to 9am, then about every hour until 10pm. They stop at Tha Khaek (US$2, two to three hours, 125km). VIP buses (US$6, six to seven hours) to Vientiane leave at 6am and 10pm. For buses from Vientiane, see p94.

A couple of buses to Pakse (US$2.50, five to six hours, 230km) originate here, usually departing about 6am and 2pm. Otherwise, you should be able to get a seat on one of the frequent buses passing through en route from Vientiane.

Savannakhet also has a **private bus station** (cnr Th Santyphab & Th Nalao), from which normal buses leave for Vientiane at 5.30am and 6.30am (US$4.50, seven to eight hours), and VIP express buses go to Vientiane (US$6, six to seven hours) at 11am and Pakse (US$3.50, four hours) at 2.30pm.

Buses leave the main bus terminal for Lao Bao (US$3, five to six hours, 236km) at 7am and noon (see p209), and to Sepon (US$2.50, 196km) at 8am. *Săwngthăew* leave more frequently for these destinations for about the same price, as well as for Tha Khaek (US$1.65, two to three hours).

Getting Around

Savannakhet is just big enough that you might occasionally need a jumbo; or the Savannakhet equivalent, a *sakai-làep* or 'Skylab' – like the famed space station that fell to earth. The best place to find one is in front of the passenger ferry pier. Fares usually cost from US$0.30 to US$0.60 for trips of up to 2km.

AROUND SAVANNAKHET
That Ing Hang
ທາດອີງຮັງ

Thought to have been built in the mid-16th century, this well-proportioned, 9m-high *thâat*, 3km east of the 13km marker on Rte 9, is the second holiest religious edifice in Southern Laos after Wat Phu Champasak. Built on or near the spot where Chao Fa Ngum's forces were based during the takeover of Muang Sawa in the mid-14th century, **That Ing Hang** (☯ 7am-6pm) may occupy an earlier site sacred to the Si Khotabun kingdom. The Buddha is believed to have stopped here when he was sick during his wanderings back in BC times. He rested by leaning (Ing) on a hang tree (thus Ing Hang). A relic of the Buddha's spine is reputed to be kept inside the *thâat*.

Not including the Mon-inspired cubical base, That Ing Hang was substantially rebuilt during the reign of King Setthathirat (1548–71) and now features three terraced bases topped by a traditional Lao stupa and a gold umbrella weighing 40 baht (450g). A hollow chamber in the lower section contains a fairly undistinguished collection of Buddha images (by religious custom, women are not permitted to enter the chamber). The French restored That Ing Hang in 1930.

The grounds are surrounded by high cloister walls on three sides and a low wall at the front, all with ornate gates. Some older standing Buddha images in a small *sĭm* next to the main *thâat* are worth seeing if you can get someone to unlock the door.

On the full moon of February or March there is a major festival.

SOUTHERN LAOS

GETTING THERE & AWAY

That Ing Hang is about 11.5km northeast of Savannakhet via Rte 9, then 3km east – the turn-off is clearly signed. Any northbound bus can stop here, or charter a jumbo for about US$3.50 return.

Heuan Hin

ເຮືອນຫີນ

On the Mekong River south of Savannakhet is this set of Cham or Khmer ruins (the name means Stone House), built between AD 553 and 700. Apart from a few walls, most of the stones of this pre-Angkorian site now lie in piles of laterite rubble. No carvings remain; the only known lintel from the site having been carted off to Paris.

The cheapest way to get to Heuan Hin is by săwngthăew (US$1.60, two hours, 78km), which leaves Talat Savan Xai in Savannakhet when full, usually in mid-morning. With your own transport, head south along Rte 13 and turn west at Ban Nong Nokhian, near Km stone 490. A laterite road then runs another 17km to the site. Alternatively, you could arrange transport and a guide with a tour agency (see p204).

Dong Natad

ດົງນາຕາດ

Dong Natad is a sacred, semi-evergreen forest only 15km from Savannakhet. The forest is home to two villages that have been co-existing with the forest for about 400 years; gathering forest products such as mushrooms, fruit, oils, honey, resins and insects. If you visit, there's a good chance you'll encounter villagers collecting red ants, cicadas or some other critter, all vitally important parts of their diet and economy.

It's possible to visit Dong Natad on your own, by bicycle, motorbike or in a tuk-tuk (US$2.50 charter, one way) from Savannakhet. However, it will be something of a 'forest-lite' experience. Instead, engage one of Savannakhet's English-speaking guides through the **Provincial Tourism Office** (☎ 212755) either for a day trip (US$30 total for one, two or three people, US$8 each for four or five) or an overnight stay (US$25 each for one or two people, US$15 each for five or more), sleeping in the village. The guides have been trained and will take you by public transport to the forest, where they link up with local guides. Arrange trips a day ahead.

CLAP, AND THE BUFFALO GETS IT

The Katang villagers of Dong Phu Vieng live in a starkly different world to the lowland Lao of the Mekong River Valley. They are not Buddhist, but instead believe strongly in the myriad spirits that surround them in the forest. One of the most important is the house spirit, one of which is believed to live in the home of every village family. Over the centuries a series of taboos have been developed in an effort to avoid disturbing this spirit; as a visitor it is vitally important you don't break the taboos. If the house spirit is seriously disturbed the village is obliged to call a meeting to work out how the spirit can be mollified. Usually a sacrifice must be made – ranging from a chicken all the way to a buffalo. As the villagers have little money, the unnecessary loss of a buffalo can have a dire impact both socially and economically.

So, when you're in a Katang house:

- never enter the owner's bedroom or touch the spirit place
- do not sleep beside a person of the opposite sex, even if that person is your spouse
- do sleep with your head pointed toward the nearest outside wall, and never point your feet at the outside wall or, spirits forbid, another person's head
- do not bang on the walls of the house
- never clap your hands in a house without first asking permission of the elder (who will then check with the spirit); if you do, the buffalo outside might wind up dead.

It goes without saying that these villages are extremely sensitive to outside influence, which is why you can only visit them as part of the organised trek through the Provincial Tourism Office in Savannakhet. Guides have been trained and the trek established after extensive consultation with the villagers themselves.

CROSSING THE VIETNAM BORDER AT DANSAVANH/LAO BAO

Once a potholed nightmare, Rte 9 from Savannakhet to the border (open from 8am to 5pm) at Dansavanh (Laos) and Lao Bao (Vietnam) is now one of the best roads in Laos and crossing here is a relative pleasure. From Savannakhet, buses (US$3, five hours, 255km) leave at 7am and noon for the border. Alternatively, take a *săwngthăew* to Sepon (US$3, four hours, 210km), and another from there to the border (US$1.20, one hour, 45km). If you're passing this way it's worth breaking the journey for a night in Sepon (below) as a base for seeing the Ho Chi Minh Trail.

It's a 500m walk between the border posts and formalities don't take too long, assuming you've arranged your Vietnam visa in advance. Coming into Laos you can get a 15-day visa on arrival.

Once through, take a motorbike (10,000d) 3km to Lao Bao itself, from where buses leave for Dong Ha (15,000d, two hours, 80km) on Vietnam's main north–south highway and railway. Entering Laos, *săwngthăew* to Sepon leave fairly regularly, from where you can get a bus or further *săwngthăew* to Savannakhet. If you get stuck in Lao Bao, try the **Bao Son Hotel** (☎ 053-877848; r US$12-18; 🔀).

An alternative is to take the daily 10pm bus from Savannakhet to Dong Ha (US$7, 329km), Hué (US$9, 409km) or Danang (US$11, 508km).

DONG PHU VIENG NPA
ປ່າສະຫງວນດົງພູວຽງ

One of the newest and most fascinating treks in Laos is to Dong Phu Vieng NPA, which offers a rare chance to step into a rapidly disappearing world. The park, south of Muang Phin in the centre of Savannakhet Province, is home to a number of Katang villages, where you can stay if you behave yourself during the three-day trek (see Clap, and the Buffalo Gets It opposite). The trek uses public transport to keep costs down to about US$20 to US$25 per person, per day. All food is included and eating local forest specialities after helping to gather them with the villagers is a highlight. Trekkers in Dong Phu Vieng are guided through a sacred forest, and have seen the rare silver Langur leaf monkey, hornbills and 'Lak La'puep' – clan posts placed in the jungle by village families. There is a fair bit of walking involved, but you don't need to be superman. Highly recommended.

Treks into **Phu Xang Hae NPA** (Wild Elephant Mountain) had stopped at the time of writing due to the diabolical state of the access roads.

SEPON (XEPON) & THE HO CHI MINH TRAIL
ເຊໂປນແລະເສັ້ນທາງໂຮຈິມິນ

☎ 041 / pop 35,600

One of the nearest towns to the Ho Chi Minh Trail is Sepon (often spelt 'Xepon'), about 190km east of Savannakhet via Rte 9. Sepon was destroyed during the war and rebuilt

5km to the west. Today it's an unremarkable town like so many others that suffered a similar fate during the Indochina War.

A trip to **Sepon Kao** (Old Sepon) is a sobering experience. On the banks of the Se Pon, Sepon Kao was bombed almost into the Stone Age. All that remains of the old district capital is the bomb-scarred façade of the wat, inside which a new temple has been built, a large pile of bricks around a safe – once the bank, and broken bricks scattered everywhere. If you're on foot or bike, take the first right turn heading east from Sepon, then go another 2km on a bad road. On four wheels, take the second right, just after the 199km stone.

Ban Dong, 20km east of Sepon, was on one of the major thoroughfares of the Ho Chi Minh Trail and is the easiest place to see the leftovers of war. Two American-built tanks used during Operation Lam Son 719 – a disastrous ARVN (Army of the Republic of Vietnam) assault on the Ho Chi Minh Trail in February 1971 – rust in the undergrowth a short walk from town. Despite support from US combat aircraft, the ARVN troops retreated across the border at Lao Bao after encountering seasoned North Vietnamese Army (NVA) troops at Ban Dong. The two tanks are all that is left of what locals say was once a graveyard of destroyed and abandoned tanks and jeeps. By order of the provincial government, the village headman of Ban Dong has been instructed to prevent scrap collectors from dismantling these last two reminders of the

SOUTHERN LAOS

NVA/PL victory. To see them, head 200m south from Rte 9 on the road out of Ban Dong. One of the tanks is a 50m-walk off to the left (east). It's best to get seek guidance from the local children, who will also take you a few hundred metres west to the second tank.

This north–south road was in fact one of the main branches of the **Ho Chi Minh Trail**. It is still used, and if you head another couple of kilometres south you'll come to a swing bridge built by the Vietnamese after the war ended. This area remains littered with UXO (unexploded ordnance), so don't walk too far off the road.

In **Muang Phin**, 155km east of Savannakhet and 34km west of Sepon, stands an imposing Vietnamese-built monument to

Lao-Vietnamese cooperation during the Indochina wars. Done in the 'Heroes of Socialism' style, the monument depicts NVA and PL soldiers waving an AK-47 and Lao flag aloft. You can catch a glimpse of the monument (located on the northern shoulder of Rte 9) when the bus makes its brief stop at Muang Phin.

In tiny **Ban Nabob**, 5km west of Sepon where the road runs north to Valuable and the incredibly rich Australian-operated gold and copper mines, the **Bar Beer Dokkeo Gaillard** (☎ mobile 020-2204855; meals US$2-6) is well worth a visit for the latest information on the area. French owner Vincent is a veteran traveller himself, and hires out a 4WD for about US$60 a day; motorbikes can also be arranged. His pizzas (US$5) are delicious.

HO CHI MINH TRAIL

The infamous Ho Chi Minh Trail – actually a complex network of dirt paths and gravel roads – runs parallel to the Laos-Vietnam border beginning at a point directly west of Phonsavan.

Though mostly associated with the 1963–74 Indochina War, the road network was originally used by the Viet Minh against the French in the 1950s as an infiltration route to the south. The trail's heaviest use occurred between 1966 and 1971 when over 600,000 North Vietnamese Army (NVA) troops – along with masses of provisions and 500,000 tonnes of trucks, tanks, weapons and ordnance – passed along the route in direct violation of the 1962 Geneva accords. At any one time around 25,000 NVA troops guarded the trail, which was honeycombed with underground barracks, fuel and vehicle repair depots as well as anti-aircraft emplacements.

The North Vietnamese denied the existence of the trail throughout most of the war. The USA, on their part, denied bombing it. In spite of 1.1 million tonnes of saturation bombing (begun in 1965 and reaching up to 900 sorties per day by 1969, including outings by B-52 behemoths), traffic along the route was never interrupted for more than a few days. Like a column of ants parted with a stick, the Vietnamese soldiers and supplies poured southward with only an estimated 15% to 20% of the cargo affected by heavy bombardment. One estimate says 300 bombs were dropped for every NVA casualty. The Yanks even tried bombing the trail with canned Budweiser beer (incapacitation through intoxication!), Calgonite dishwasher detergent (to make the trail too slippery for travel), and massive quantities of defoliants and herbicides.

Virtually all roads running north–south in the southeast of Laos were once part of the trail. The most accessible points are at Ban Dong (p209), east of Sepon, and the village of Pa-am in Attapeu Province, which sits almost right on the main thoroughfare. South of here the trail enters Cambodia, where (until March 1970 when a coup toppled Prince Sihanouk in Phnom Penh) it met up with the 'Sihanouk Trail', another Communist supply route running up from the Gulf of Thailand.

Along the remoter parts of the trail, such as near Muang Sui in Xieng Khuang Province, anti-aircraft emplacements, Soviet tanks and bits of other war junk can sometimes be seen. Because of the remoteness from scrap metal markets, a lot of the debris in these areas lies untouched. However, in areas near population centres the only visible remains are a few bomb craters and a tank wreck or two.

Eastern Savannakhet Province (along with Salavan, Sekong and Attapeu Provinces further south) is also one of the primary areas where joint Lao-American teams search for the remains of American MIAs. Eighty percent of the American servicemen not yet accounted for in Laos are thought to have gone down somewhere along the Ho Chi Minh Trail.

Sleeping & Eating

Nang Toon Guest House (Rte 9; r US$3-5; 🔀) Located about 1.5km east of Sepon, the US$5 air-con rooms at the Nang Toon Guest House are small but clean, and the fan rooms with hot-water bathroom are the best value in town.

Vieng Xay Guesthouse (☎ 214895; Rte 9; r US$3-5; 🔀) Just past the market on the south side of Rte 9, this is the most central place. Walls are paper-thin. The US$3 rooms have fan and no private bathroom. Look for the ordnance in the front fence.

Pa Bouaphan (🕑 6am-8pm) This is the best place to eat. It's located at the west edge of the market and the Lao food and breakfasts are recommended.

Getting There & Away

A bus leaves from outside the market for Savannakhet (US$2.50, three to four hours, 196km) at 8am. After that, take a *săwngthăew* to Muang Phin (US$1) and another to Savan. For the border at Dansavanh (US$1.20, one to two hours) buses from Savannakhet pass at about 10am and 3pm, though they're often late. It's easier to take a *săwngthăew* (US$1.20).

Coming from Savannakhet (see p206) it's possible to take the bus to Ban Dong and then hitch back to Sepon after viewing the tanks. Again though, *săwngthăew* (US$0.70) are far more frequent.

CHAMPASAK PROVINCE

Champasak is one of the most visited provinces in Laos, with Wat Phu Champasak, the Mekong River islands of Si Phan Don and the Bolaven Plateau being the main attractions, and borders to Cambodia and Thailand supplying the easy access.

The Champasak area has a long history that began with participation in the Funan and Chenla empires between the 1st and 9th centuries AD. Between the 10th and 13th centuries, it became part of the Cambodian Angkor empire. Following the decline of Angkor between the 15th and late 17th centuries, it was enfolded into the Lan Xang kingdom but then broke away to become an independent Lao kingdom at the beginning of the 18th century. The short-lived Champasak kingdom had only

three monarchs: Soi Sisamut (r 1713–37), who was the nephew of Suriya Vongsa, Sainyakuman (r 1737–91) and finally Fai Na (r 1791–1811).

Today Champasak Province has a population of about 500,000 including lowland Lao (many of them Phu Thai), Khmers and a host of small Mon-Khmer groups, most of whom live in the Bolaven Plateau region.

PAKSE

ປາກເຊ

☎ 031 / pop 66,000

Founded by the French in 1905 as an administrative outpost, Pakse sits at the confluence of the Mekong River and the Se Don and is the capital of Champasak Province. The town has grown quickly since the Lao-Japanese Bridge across the Mekong was opened in 2002, facilitating brisk trade with Thailand. Its position on the way to Si Phan Don in the far south, the Bolaven Plateau and remote provinces to the east, and Thailand to the west means anyone choosing to travel in the south will almost certainly spend time in Pakse.

The centre of Pakse retains the sort of Mekong River–town lethargy found in Savannakhet and Tha Khaek further north, though few colonial-era buildings remain. Look out for the Franco-Chinese–style **Chinese Society building** on Th 10 in the centre of town.

The vast Talat Dao Heung (New Market) near the Lao-Japanese Bridge is one of the biggest in the country, famous for its selection of fresh produce and coffee from the fertile Bolaven Plateau. This market was built after the old central market was burnt down in 1997; recently being replaced by the Western-style Champasak Plaza Shopping Centre, where after two years vendors are still to fill the retail space on the ground floor, let alone those above.

Short day trips from Pakse can be made to Ban Saphai and Don Kho (p217), weaving villages 15km north of town that produce distinctive silk and cotton *phàa salóng*, long sarongs for men.

Information

EMERGENCY

Police (☎ 212145; Th 10)

Hospital (☎ 212018; Th 10 & Th 46)

INTERNET ACCESS & TELEPHONE
@d@m's Internet (☎ 213435; www.pakse.info; Rte 13; per hr US$1.70; ⏰ 7.30am-9pm) A satellite connection makes this the fastest connection in town. It has facilities for downloading image files and burning them to CD (US$2), and for making international calls (per minute US$0.40).

Lankham Internet (☎ 212125; Rte 13; per hr US$1.80; ⏰ 7.30am-10.30pm)

SD Internet (☎ 212232; Rte 13; per hr US$1.80; ⏰ 7am-8pm) Fairly fast connections.

MONEY
On weekends, your hotel may exchange money, or try the market for better rates.

BCEL (☎ 212770; Th 11; ⏰ 8.30am-3.30pm Mon-Fri & 8.30-10am Sat) South of Wat Luang, has best rates for cash and travellers cheques and makes cash advances on Visa and MasterCard.

Lao Development Bank (☎ 212168; Rte 13; ⏰ 8.30am-3.30pm Mon-Fri) Cash and travellers cheques.

Lao Viet Bank (☎ 251470; Rte 13; ⏰ 8.30am-3.30pm Mon-Fri)

POST
Main post office (☎ 212293; cnr Th 8 & Th 1; ⏰ 8am-noon & 1-5pm) South of the town centre.

TOURIST INFORMATION
Alex at @d@m's Internet (see above) probably knows more than the NTAL people.

National Tourism Authority of Laos (NTAL; ☎ 212021; Th 11; ⏰ 8-11.30am & 1.30-4pm Mon-Fri) On the Se Don, these guys speak some English but when we visited didn't have too much information on offer.

TRAVEL AGENCIES
You can arrange tours via van or pick-up to the Bolaven Plateau, Wat Phu Champasak or Don Khong at these agencies:

Diethelm Travel (☎ 212596; fax 251491) A block north of Rte 13.

Inter-Lao Tourisme (☎ 212778; Rte 13) On the ground floor of the Champasak Palace Hotel.

Sights & Activities
CHAMPASAK HISTORICAL HERITAGE MUSEUM
ພິພິດທະພັນມໍລະດົກວັດຖຸໂບຮານຈໍາປາສັກ

Near the Hotel Residence du Champa, the **Champasak Historical Heritage Museum** (Rte 13; admission US$0.30; ⏰ 8-11.30am & 1-4pm) gathers together artefacts and documents to chronicle the history of the province. Once you get past the Lao and Communist hammer-and-sickle flags at the entrance, you'll come

to not-so-exciting historical photos detailing the glories of the 'party'. There are also black-and-white photos of Wat Phu Champasak, three Dong Son bronze drums and a couple of striking 7th-century sandstone lintels found at Um Tomo (also known as Um Muang) near Champasak town.

Also on the ground floor are musical instruments, stelae in the Tham script dating from the 15th to 18th centuries, a water jar from the 11th or 12th century, a small lingam (Shiva phallus), plus a model of Wat Phu Champasak.

The upstairs room has more of an ethnological focus, including mannequinlike figures displaying different clothing styles, along with textile and jewellery collections from the Nyaheun, Suay and Laven. The large iron ankle bracelets and ivory ear plugs are of particular interest since these are rarely worn nowadays.

The textile exhibit is informative; you can tell the southern Lao ethnicities apart by the designs of their *phàa sìn* (sarong borders). Other exhibits include bamboo implements, ceramics, basketry, bronze Buddha figures, a tiny bronze Ganesa figure, various sandstone deities, farming implements, hunting traps and an elephant saddle.

Most of the exhibits bear captions in Lao and French, or Lao and English.

WATS
There are about 20 wats in the city, of which Wat Luang and Wat Tham Fai (both founded in 1935) are the largest. A monastic school at **Wat Luang** features ornate concrete pillars, carved wooden doors and murals; the artist's whimsy departs from canonical art without losing the traditional effect. Behind the *sĭm* is an older monks' school in an original wooden building. A *thâat* on the grounds contains the ashes of Khamtai Loun Sasothith, a prime minister in the Royal Lao Government before his death in 1959.

Wat Tham Fai, near the Champasak Palace Hotel, is undistinguished except for its spacious grounds, which make it a prime site for temple festivals. It's also known as Wat Pha Baht because there is a small Buddha footprint shrine on the premises. In what might be the choice of a new generation of monks, there is a large billboard within the grounds advertising Pepsi.

PAKSE

MASSAGE & SAUNA

The professional and popular massage and sauna **Clinic Keo Ou Done** (Traditional Medicine Hospice; ☎ 251895, mobile 020-5431115; 4-9pm Mon-Fri & 10am-9pm Sat-Sun) has an air-con massage room and herbal sauna segregated by gender. A massage (highly recommended!), usually with medicated balms, costs US$2.50 per hour. Unlimited use of the herbal sauna costs US$0.80. To get there, take a jumbo east on Rte 13. About 100m before the Km 3 marker, turn right and follow the signs for another 800m. The signs usually read 'Massage Sauna'.

Sleeping
BUDGET

Sabaidy 2 Guesthouse (☎ /fax 212992; Th 24; dm US$1.50, r US$3.20-6.20;) Effervescent Mr Vong's simple by spotlessly clean and quiet rooms have become the number one backpacker haunt in Pakse; it's so busy you'll struggle to get a bed. His cheap dorm beds and singles/doubles (US$3.20/3.50) with shared bathroom are complemented with mountains of travel information; when leaving you even get a business card with your destination printed in Lao on the back. Rooms with private bathroom start at US$4.20.

Lankham Hotel (☎ 213314; Rte 13; r US$5-10; ⊠) Lankham is right in the centre of town and thus front-facing rooms (some of the few with windows that don't look onto a corridor) can be noisy. All rooms are small but clean, ranging from fan rooms with coldwater bathroom (US$5) to family rooms with TV, hot water and air-con (US$10). They hire out a range of bikes, see p217.

Narin Thachalern Hotel (☎ 212927; Th 21; s/d US$4/7; ⊠) Rooms with fridge and TV are clean and a lot quieter than the Lankham. Not all rooms are the same, so ask to see a couple. The woman manager is very friendly.

Sedone River Guesthouse (☎ 212158; tw US$4-5; ⊠) In an ideal position right on the Se Don, just north of the bridge, this place has small twin rooms with cold-water bathrooms. There's a shaded riverside communal area ideal for a sunset Beerlao or two.

Suksamlan Hotel (☎ 212002; Th 14; r US$7; ⊠) The centrally located Suksamlan has 24 decent rooms with desks and hot-water bathrooms. Switch off the air-con and save US$2. There's a **restaurant** (☯ 7am-10pm) downstairs and management can organise tours throughout the south.

Phonsavanh Hotel 1 (☎ 212842; cnr Th 12 & Rte 13; r US$2-3) Near to the bridge over the Se Don, Phonsavanh has basic fan rooms with or without cold-water bathroom.

MID-RANGE & TOP END

Pakse Hotel (☎ 212131; info@paksehotel.com; Th 5; r US$14-30; ⊠) For the money, this refurbished six-storey place in the centre of town is the best in Pakse. Rooms all come with fridge and satellite TV; the cheapest have no windows, but the US$19 rooms have Mekong views and are excellent value. There's a cafeteria downstairs, and service is professional. The only annoyance is that in some rooms water from the air-con drains onto the bathroom floor.

Hotel Salachampa (☎ 212273; fax 212646; Th 14; r US$10-15; ⊠) Just around the corner from the Pakse Hotel, this restored French villa offers huge rooms with wooden floors (tiled downstairs), high ceilings and tasteful furnishings. Rooms in the villa (US$15) are best, as those in the newer building (US$10) are smaller and altogether less appealing. There's a new restaurant in the courtyard.

Hotel Residence du Champa (☎ 212120; champa re@laotel.com; Rte 13; s/d with breakfast US$27/30; ⊠) If you don't mind being 2km out of town (near the New Market), this is a very good option. In four modern buildings of concrete, marble and teak, all 45 rooms have satellite TV, minibar and IDD phone, and some have bathtubs. French and English are spoken. Discounts are available in low season.

Lao Chaleun Hotel (☎ 251333; fax 251138; Th 10; s/d/tw US$6/10/12; ⊠) Opposite the Hotel Salachampa, rooms in this three-storey place above an informal-looking restaurant/bar are solid without being inspiring. Singles have fan only and cold-water bathrooms. The hotel hires out motos (US$10 per day), and cars and vans (about US$100 per day with driver).

Champasak Palace Hotel (☎ 212263; champa sak_palace_hotel@yahoo.com; Rte 13; r with breakfast US$25-40; ⊠) The five-storey Champasak Palace, on Rte 13 about 1km east of the town centre, was originally built as a vast palace for Chao Bounome na Champasak, the last prince of Champasak and the prime minister of the Kingdom of Laos between 1960 and 1962. Bounome started building the palace in 1968, fled to Paris in 1974 and died in 1978. It was renovated, and in some places completed, by a Thai group during the 1990s, with government help; look at the architraves above the fourth floor for the tell-tale hammer and sickle stucco work. The spacious rooms have many of the original details intact, such as tile floors and teak fittings on the bottom floor, and all include a TV and fridge. Rooms include the standard (US$30), superior (US$40) and VIP suite, which is good value at US$50 with panoramic views. In the presidential suite (US$500, or $200 in low season) you can live like a prince. There are nice views of the Se Don from the terrace restaurant and garden at the back.

Eating

The eating scene in Pakse is improving, but there are still not many places that serve good Lao food.

Delta Coffee (☎ 212488, mobile 020-5430063; Rte 13; meals US$1.50-5; ☻ 7am-10pm) The Italian menu here has some of the best non-Asian food in Southern Laos, and the Thai dishes are very tasty as well. The vegetarian lasagne (US$2.50), pizzas (US$3.50) and steaks (US$2.50) are all recommended, and the breakfasts are great value too. Owners Alan and Siriporn serve wonderful coffee from their plantation near Paksong and are happy to take people up for a look around (free) if there's room in the truck (maximum six people); Alan usually leaves about noon.

San Luck Thai Foods (☎ mobile 020-5616409; meals US$1-2.50; ☻ 10am-1am) This laid-back, welcoming place, with seating on a deck overhanging the Se Don just north of the bridge, serves a huge variety of Thai food (eight varieties of *pad thai* noodles) plus samples from several other cuisines. Its a good place for a sunset drink.

Jasmin Restaurant (☎ 251002; Rte 13; meals US$2-4; ☻ 8am-10pm) Part of the Nazim empire of Indian restaurants, this place serves the usual Indian fare and as a result has become Pakse's backpackers' favourite. It also sells bus tickets and tours.

Restaurant Sedone (☎ 212155; Th 4; meals US$1-3; ☻ 6am-10pm) Near the Pakse Hotel, the Sedone serves decent *fŏe*, rice and noodle dishes, a few stir-fried travellers favourites and a good breakfast.

Xuan Mai Restaurant (☎ 213245; Th 4; meals US$1-2.50; ☻ 6am-midnight) On the corner opposite the Pakse Hotel, Xuan Mai serves good *fŏe* (US$0.80; the chicken *fŏe* is best), *khào pûn* (white flour noodles with sweet-spicy sauce), fruit shakes and even garlic bread (US$0.50). It's the best place for a late feed.

Ketmany Restaurant (☎ 212615; Rte 13; meals US$1.50-4; ☻ 7am-10.30pm) Ketmany, situated beside @d@m's Internet, serves Chinese, Lao and European food, plus good ice cream and packed-with-processed-meat Western breakfasts (US$2).

Mai Fai Restaurant (☎ 212749; Rte 13; meals US$1-2.50; ☻ 7am-11pm) This is a simple place serving Lao dishes and noodles plus backpacker staples (banana, pineapple or chocolate pancakes for US$1.20). It's popular for breakfast.

Tour Lao Restaurant (☎ 900388; Th 9; meals US$3-5; ☻ 10am-11pm) Located on a corner behind the Champasak Plaza Shopping Centre, this place with inside and outside seating serves a mixture of Lao, Thai, Chinese and Western dishes. Cambodian visas can be arranged here, and football is often on the big screen.

Precooked Lao dishes are available from a couple of **food stands** (☻ about 10am-7pm) along Rte 13, and similar fare and *fŏe* can be had in Talat Dao Heuang from about 6am to 4pm.

Just west of @d@m's Internet a **baguette vendor** (Rte 13) sells decent *khào jìi* in the morning and afternoon. Self-caterers should head to the market and **Oulayvan Minimart** (Rte 13; ☻ 7am-10pm).

Drinking

Sinouk Coffee Shop (☎ 212553; cnr Th 9 & Th 11; coffee US$0.60; ☻ 8am-8pm) In a renovated French shophouse this café sells coffee (both in cups and by the bag – US$4 for 500g) from the plantation of the same name, one of the region's largest. They also sell Beerlao.

Getting There & Away

AIR

Lao Airlines flies between Pakse and Vientiane daily (US$87 one way, one hour), though the Tuesday flight comes via Savannakhet, taking an extra hour. The Savannakhet to Pakse leg is US$42. There are also two flights a week to Phnom Penh (US$73 one way, one hour) and three to Siem Reap (US$63, 45 minutes). It's rare that all these services actually fly, so be sure to check at the Pakse **Lao Airlines office** (☎ 212252; Th 11; ☻ 8-11.30am & 2-4pm Mon-Fri), just south of the BCEL, the day before.

The airport is 3km northwest of town and has a cafeteria and a BCEL exchange office. A jumbo should cost about US$1.

BOAT

One of the few remaining regular local boat services in Laos is the daily slow boat from Pakse to Don Khong (US$3 going south, $5 coming north, six to 10 hours), which leaves at about 8am from near the junction of the Se Don and the Mekong. The scenery is typical Mekong valley – rather flat with the riverbanks regularly punctuated by small villages. However, sharing space with bags of rice, pigs, chickens, snakes, fried insects, monks and other Lao people as the boat stops at seemingly every riverside village along the way makes the experience far more authentic than the good ships north of Luang Prabang.

The boat, with room for about 35 passengers, stops at Champasak (US$1, 1½ hours down, and 2½ hours up), and many travellers opt for this shorter part of the journey than the long, hot trip to Don Khong. If you do go all the way, you'll be dropped in Ban Hua Khong (see map p229), a small village near the north tip of Don Khong. Don't worry that none of the locals get off here – they are all continuing to islands west of Don Khong that are unreachable by road (Don Khongers themselves wouldn't dream of taking the slow boat.) From Ban Hua Khong a tuk-tuk (US$1 per person, 12km) or motorbike taxi (US$1.50, 12km) will take you to Muang Khong.

Boats heading back to Pakse usually leave Ban Hua Khong between 6.30am and 8am and take longer (up to about 11 hours in August).

When going south from Pakse or Champasak, it's important to establish exactly where the boat will terminate before you set off, as between early February and late May the river is often too low for the boat to go all the way to Don Khong. It might run as far as Ban Munla Pamok, roughly 20km from the northern tip of Don Khong; from here you may be able to charter a small boat the remainder of the way for around US$15. There is a guesthouse in Ban Munla Pamok. If it all goes pear-shaped and no amount of money will buy you a boatman, just get yourself to Rte 13 and hail anything going south.

On *wán sin dáp* (new-moon days) it may be difficult to find a boat due to the lack of passengers; the locals believe it is bad luck to travel by boat on these days.

It is also possible to charter a boat from **Mr Boun My** (☎ 251430, mobile 020-5631008), who can be found at the barbecue pork stall opposite the Mekong. His 30-seat long boats, which go faster than the public boats, can go to Champasak (US$35, one hour), to Um Muang (US$40, 90 minutes) and to Don Khong (US$100, four to five hours). These prices are for a total less than 10 people, and rise with the number of passengers.

BUS & SĂWNGTHĂEW

There are four places in Pakse from which buses and *săwngthăew* depart. The Champasak Plaza Shopping Centre (for express or VIP buses) is the most central and is the wisest choice for long-distance journeys north. The northern bus terminal has slower buses heading north, and the southern bus terminal deals with all transport heading south and east. Finally, a motley array of vehicles leaves the Talat Dao Heuang (Morning Market) for the Thai border.

Champasak Plaza Shopping Centre

This is the smallest of the stations, outside the Champasak Plaza Shopping Centre in the middle of town. The express bus to Vientiane (US$14.50 for *falang*, 9½ hours, 716km) leaves daily at about 8.30pm and boasts air-con, a toilet, a meal and a hostess; tickets can be bought in the **KVT bus office** (☎ 212228; Champasak Plaza Shopping Centre; ☺ 8.30am-8.30pm). Cheaper are the Laody VIP buses (US$9, 10 hours) that leave at 7am and 8pm daily. The **Laody bus office** (☎ mobile 020-5611252) is on the ground floor of the shopping centre. This bus also stops at Savannakhet (US$3.50, 230km, four hours), Tha Khaek (US$5.50, 6½ hours, 368km), and Paksan (US$6.50, eight hours, 572km). Tickets on either of these buses can be booked at most guesthouses.

Northern Bus Terminal

At the northern terminal (*khíw lot lák jét* or 'Km 7 bus terminal'), 7km north of town on Rte 13, you'll find more VIP buses and many agonisingly slow normal buses (without air-con) heading north. For Vientiane, express VIP buses (US$9, 9½ hours) leave at 5.30am and 8pm, while a 6pm VIP bus also stops at Savannakhet (US$3.50, four hours) and Tha Khaek (US$5.50, 6½ hours). If you have plenty of time, no money and a wide masochistic streak, normal buses leave for Vientiane (US$7, 16 to 18 hours) about every hour between 7.30am and 4.30pm, stopping wherever you want (and many places you don't) along the way. For buses from Vientiane see p94.

Southern Bus Terminal

For transport south and east, head to the southern terminal (*khíw lot lák paet* or 'Km 8 bus terminal'), south of town on Rte

JERRY GALEA

Rice-paddy workers, Sekong Province (p240)

Monk, Savannakhet (p202)

CLINT LUCAS

WOODS WHEATCROFT

Fisher, Mekong River, Si Phan Don (p228)

School girls, Tha Khaek (p196)

JOHN ELK III

ANTHONY PLL

Tat Lo (p220), Bolaven Plateau

CLINT LUCAS

Girl eating noodles (p53)

Colonial shophouses, Tha Khaek (p196)

JOHN

13; a tuk-tuk there costs about US$0.40. To Champasak buses (US$1.30, two hours, two daily) depart at 10am and noon. Other departures include: Muang Khong (US$3, three hours, 120km) at 8am and 10am; Tat Lo (US$1.20, two hours, 86km) at 9am; Sekong (US$2.50, 3½ to 4½ hours, 135km) at 7.30am, 9.30am, 11.30am and 1.30pm; Attapeu (US$3.50, 4½ to six hours, 212km) at 6.30am, 8am, 10.30am and 1pm; Paksong (US$1.50, 90 minutes) with frequent departures between 8am and 4pm; and Ban Nakasang for Don Det and Don Khon (US$2, three to four hours) at 7am, 8.30am, 10am and 11.30am.

For Salavan (US$1.70, 115km) buses depart at 7.30am, 9am, 10.30am, noon and at 1.30pm, while some buses use the more direct and smoother Rte 20 (2½ to three hours), also stopping near Tat Lo (US$1.20). Others go to Tha Taeng on Rte 23, then on a laterite road north linking with Rte 20 at Beng (3½ to four hours).

Sǎwngthǎew also leave the southern bus station regularly between about 7am and 3pm for Champasak (US$1, two hours), Don Khong (US$3, three hours), Ban Nakasang (US$2, three to four hours) and Voen Kham (US$2.50, 3½ to 4½ hours) on the Cambodian border. Trucks going to Ban Nakasang will stop at Hat Xai Khun or nearby on Rte 13, from where an 800m walk and a boat will have you at Don Khong. For Champasak, there are also a couple of sǎwngthǎew heading for Ban Don Talat that stop off in Champasak (US$1.30, two hours); they usually leave between about 8am and 1pm.

Between 8am and 10am, sǎwngthǎew head to Kiet Ngong and Ban Phapho (US$1.30, two to three hours, two daily).

Getting Around

Using any of Pakse's local transport on a shared basis costs about US$0.25 to US$0.35 to anywhere in town. A ride to either bus terminal costs US$0.40. For charter, the standard fares are US$1 (sǎam-lâaw or a tuk-tuk) or US$0.70 (jumbo).

The **Lankham Hotel** (☎ 213314) hires out bicycles (US$2.50 per day), 110cc motorbikes (US$10 per day) and, praise the patron saint of adventurers, three new Honda Baja 250cc trail bikes for US$20 per day. Discounts are possible for longer hire. The Lao Chaleun Hotel (p214) also hires out cars and vans for US$100 a day, including driver, and 110cc motos for US$10 a day.

AROUND PAKSE

There are a couple of interesting and leisurely half-day trips that can be made from Pakse.

Ban Saphai & Don Kho

ບ້ານສະພາຍ ແລະ ດອນໂຄ

About 15km north of Pakse, Ban Saphai is known locally for its cotton- and silk-weaving. Many of the village households are engaged in textile-making in some way and it's quite common to see looms set up in the shade under the houses. The villagers on Don Kho, a nearby island in the middle of the Mekong, are also involved in weaving and, as the island is crisscrossed with shady

---

CROSSING THE THAI BORDER AT VANG TAO & CHONG MEK

The crossing at Vang Tao (Laos) and Chong Mek (Thailand) is the busiest in southern Laos and is open from 5am to 8pm daily. From Pakse, sǎwngthǎew (US$0.80, 75 minutes, 40km) and some of the most battered taxis (US$2 per person or US$7 for whole vehicle, 45 minutes) you're ever likely to see run between Talat Dao Heuang (New Market) and Vang Tao regularly from about 4am until 6pm. When your transport stops, walk about 300m up the hill to the building with the green roof, where you'll be stamped in and can buy or sell kip at the exchange office.

Walk through the throngs of traders and small-time smugglers loitering around the border, then about 40m on to Thai immigration, who will issue your visa in short order. Taxi drivers will usually be waiting outside immigration and want about B600 to B700 for a whole air-con van to Ubon Ratchatani (one hour). The cheaper option is to walk to the end of the stall-lined street and find a sǎwngthǎew (B30, one hour) to Phibun Mangsahan. It will drop you at a point where another sǎwngthǎew will soon pick you up for the trip to Ubon (B30, one hour). Buses leave Ubon regularly (including overnight) for Bangkok, and there are several trains as well, including a sleeper that also stops at Dom Muang International Airport, for those in a real hurry.

trails and populated with easygoing locals, Don Kho makes for a more pleasant visit during the heat of the day. Textiles can be bought directly from the villagers for less than what you would pay at the market in Pakse.

GETTING THERE & AWAY

Săwngthăew to Ban Saphai from Pakse leave from near the boat landing on Th 11 when full. The trip takes about 45 minutes and costs about US$0.40, or you can hire a *săwngthăew* outright for about US$5 one way. Boats can be hired for the return trip from Ban Saphai to Ban Kho for US$1 per person (or US$4 per boat), which includes the boat pilot waiting a couple of hours while you wander around the island.

BOLAVEN PLATEAU

ພູພຽງບໍລະເວນ

Centred on the northeast of Champasak Province, the fertile Bolaven Plateau (sometimes spelt Bolovens, known in Lao as Phu Phieng Bolaven) is famous for its cool climate, waterfalls, fertile soil and high-grade coffee plantations. It's also known for being one of the most heavily bombed theatres of the Second Indochina War.

The area wasn't farmed intensively until the French planted coffee, rubber trees and bananas in the early 20th century. Many of

---

THE KATU & ALAK BUFFALO SACRIFICE

The Katu and Alak are well known in Laos for an annual water buffalo sacrifice (usually performed on a full moon in March) in homage to the village spirit. The number of buffaloes sacrificed – typically from one to four animals – depends on their availability and the bounty of the previous year's agricultural harvest. During the ceremony, the men of the village don wooden masks, hoist spears and wooden shields, then dance around the buffaloes in the centre of the circle formed by their houses. After a prescribed period of dancing the men converge on the buffaloes and spear them to death. The meat is divided among the villagers and each household places a piece in a basket on a pole in front of their house as a spirit offering.

---

the French planters left following independence in the 1950s and the rest followed as US bombardment intensified in the 1960s. Today the Lao have revived the cultivation of coffee beans with a gusto (see Kạaféh Láo opposite). Other local products include fruit, cardamom and rattan.

Along with the Laven, the plateau is a centre for several other Mon-Khmer ethnic groups, including the Alak, Katu, Ta-oy (Tahoy) and Suay tribes. Katu and Alak villages are distinctive because they arrange their palm-and-thatch houses in a circle. One unique Katu custom is the carving of wooden caskets for each member of the household well in advance of an expected death; the caskets are stored beneath rice sheds until needed.

Among the other tribes, the animistic-shamanistic Suay (who call themselves Kui) are said to be the best elephant handlers. Elephants were used extensively in the forests for clearing land and moving timber, though working elephants are hard to find these days.

The Alak, Katu and Laven are distinctive for the face tattoos of their women, a custom that is slowly dying out as the Lao influence in the area increases.

Several **Katu** and **Alak villages** can be visited along the road between Pakse and Paksong at the western edge of the plateau, and along the laterite road that descends steadily from Muang Tha Taeng (That Heng) on the plateau to Beng, in Salavan Province. There are also a few within walking distance of Tat Lo (p220). In **Lao Ngam** (not to be confused with Muang Lao Ngam on the road to Salavan), around 40km east of Pakse, is a large day market frequented by many tribal groups.

Of the many waterfalls scattered around, the most commonly visited are **Tat Fan**, a few kilometres west of Paksong, and **Phasoume Resort** and **Tat Lo** on Rte 23 to Salavan.

Tat Fan & Dong Hua Sao NPA

ນ້ຳຕົກ ຕາດຝານ ແລະ ປ່າສະຫງວນດົງຫົວຊາວ

Tat Fan is one of the most spectacular waterfalls in Laos, with parallel streams of the Huay Bang Lieng plunging out of dense forest and down more than 120m. Tat Fan (pronounced *tàat fáan*) is at the edge of the 1100-sq-km Dong Hua Sao NPA and the walking trails around here are the best, and perhaps the

KĄA-FÉH LÁO (LAO COFFEE)

The high, flat ground of the Bolaven Plateau is ideal for growing coffee and the region produces some of the best and most expensive bean on earth. Both Arabica and Robusta is grown, much of it around the 'coffee town' of Paksong. About 90% of the beans produced are exported; the largest share is sent to France, where drinkers are known to enjoy the smooth, slightly chocolaty taste of the Lao Arabica. The Vietnamese also import plenty of Lao coffee, despite having huge oversupply in their domestic market.

Workers on the coffee plantations tend to come from the Laven tribe, one of the largest ethnic groups native to the plateau (which is named after them – Bolaven means Place of the Laven). They usually live on the estate with their families and the going wage is less than US$1 a day. Accommodation is provided and the better employers also hire a teacher for the children of their employees.

Alak and Katu farmers also grow coffee, drying the harvested beans on the ground or on large platforms next to their villages. While production is increasingly moving toward larger estates, villagers still grow coffee and sell it to wholesalers who come by pick-up from Pakse.

The easiest way to visit a plantation is to go for free with Alan of Delta Coffee in Pakse (see p215).

only, way to get into the park. Dong Hua Sao is home to a healthy population of tigers, though you're more likely to see monkeys, gigantic butterflies and, in the wet season, dozens of great hornbills who like to hang out at the bottom of the falls.

Tat Fan is 800m south of Rte 23 – look for the signs at Km 38. A path here leads down to the falls themselves and affords fine views, though this is perilously slippery in the wet season. An easier place to view them from is Tad Fane Resort, a bungalow and ecotourism operation that looks down onto the falls from the top of a cliff opposite. The resort has a couple of highly professional English-speaking guides who can arrange treks into the NPA taking in Laven and Katu villages, coffee plantations, a dipterocarp forest and several waterfalls. Rafting is possible in the wet season. A half-day trek costs US$8, a full-day US$12 including lunch. Adventure-style sandals are appropriate in the dry season, but you should wear boots in the wet to deter leeches. As one guide told us, 'the flip-flop is not possible'.

For details on getting out to Tat Fan, see Getting There & Away, opposite.

SLEEPING & EATING

Tad Fane Resort (☎ in Bangkok 0 2953 5398; www.tad fane.com; standard/deluxe with breakfast US$20/30) This collection of well-built wooden bungalows sits atop a cliff overlooking the falls. The deluxe rooms are bigger and have the best views. All bungalows have a veranda and at-

tached bathroom. The **restaurant** (meals US$1.50-2.50; ❧ breakfast, lunch & dinner) has great views and serves sandwiches and Thai food – the green curry (US$1.60) is recommended.

Paksong

ปากซอง

Laos's coffee capital is nothing to look at, most of it having been obliterated during the Second Indochina War. But the hospitality of the Laven locals is famous, the market will keep you interested for an hour or so (longer for coffee lovers), and there is one guesthouse where you can stay if Tad Fane Resort is too pricey. The **Paksong Guest House** (r US$2-12) has rooms in three buildings, including grubby twins with shared bathroom (US$2) and better twins with bathroom (US$7). English is spoken. Coming from Pakse, turn left after the Kaysone Monument and take the second left (about 1.5km from Rte 23); the guesthouse is on the right opposite some noodle stalls.

GETTING THERE & AWAY

Buses and *săwngthăew* between Paksong and Pakse's southern (Km 8) bus terminal leave frequently between 8am and 4pm (US$1.50, 90 minutes). For Tat Fan, get off at Km 38 and follow the signs to the falls and resort (about 800m south of the turn-off).

Phasoume Resort

This new 'ecoresort' 38km northwest of Pakse is scattered through a stretch of thick jungle either side of a small but beautiful waterfall. The 10 Swiss Family Robinson–style treehouses, and especially the restaurant, are a homage to big trees – only that these trees have been cut into chairs, tables, beams, posts, floor timbers, stepping stones and just about any other use you can imagine.

There is an elevated jungle walk that leads to a model village, comprising families of Katu, Nge and Laven who are there to entertain visitors. The families seemed happy enough to be there when we visited, but some will find the village a bit too contrived.

Rooms are about US$20 and the **restaurant** (meals US$2-5; ☺ breakfast, lunch & dinner) serves tasty and reasonably priced Thai food.

GETTING THERE & AWAY

There is no direct public transport to Phasoume. You'll need to catch anything heading up Rte 20 towards Salavan (see p217), getting off at a turn-off 400m after the Houy Cham Pa bridge, about 36km from Pakse. It's then a 2km walk.

Tat Lo
ນ້ຳຕົກຕາດເລາະ

At 10m high the waterfall at Tat Lo (pronounced *tàat láw*) is not as spectacular as some, but the place has a certain serenity that sees many visitors stay longer than they planned. Accommodation is cheap, the nearby local village retains much of its Lao character and Tat Lo does have a large pool at its base that is suitable for swimming. During the dry season, dam authorities release river water in the evening, more than doubling the waterfall volume – it's worth checking out what time the release occurs (usually just after sunset) so that you're not standing at the top of the waterfall then – a potentially fatal error. There are a couple of easy walks around Tat Lo, including to Katu and Alak villages, and another waterfall about 800m upriver. Ask at Tim Guesthouse & Restaurant (opposite) for maps and information.

ELEPHANT RIDES

Tadlo Lodge (Resort) offers rides on its two elephants (US$5 per elephant, 90 minutes). The typical ride plods through streams, forests and villages, crossing terrain you wouldn't dream of crossing on foot (eg streams full of slippery rocks) and giving these domesticated elephants much-needed work. Each elephant can carry two people.

SLEEPING & EATING

Saise Guest House (☎ /fax 214180, mobile 020-2204646; r US$6-15) In lush gardens on the west bank of the river, this rambling establishment has two parts; the White House (immediately after the vehicle bridge) where small semidetached bungalows with bathrooms and inconsistent hot water cost US$6; and the much nicer Green House, upstream right next to the falls, where big, comfortable and tastefully decorated rooms in a wooden house cost US$12/15 for a twin/double. Service, however, can be slack.

Tadlo Lodge (Tadlo Resort; ☎ /fax 214184; sode tour@laotel.com; bungalows US$25) On both sides of the river overlooking the waterfall, these comfortable, well-built bungalows have balconies and clean hot-water bathrooms; big discounts are possible in low season. The large and atmospheric open-air **restaurant** (meals US$3-5; ☺ breakfast, lunch & dinner) serves pretty good Lao, Thai and European dishes. Turn left just before the bridge.

Tim Guesthouse & Restaurant (☎ 214176; www .tadlo.laopdr.com; r US$3; 🖳) The simple cane-and-wood bungalows here have shared bathroom and no views, but what they lack in luxuries is made up for in atmosphere. The English- and French-speaking owner is the semiofficial information officer for Salavan and can advise on expeditions anywhere in the province. This is usually done in his **restaurant** (meals US$1.50-2.50; ☺ 7am-midnight), where the usual range of Asian travellers' favourites is done well and augmented with seasonal specialities (ask about these), all accompanied by soft jazz music. There is a book exchange and Internet access (US$6 per hour) and the owner is working to establish a computer school for local children. You can call for a free pick-up from Ban Khoua Set, 1.8km away on Rte 20.

On the river to the right of the bridge are a couple of cheap places. The **Sephaseuth Guest House & Restaurant** (☎ 214185; d/tw US$4/6) has five clean rooms in a wooden house overlooking the river, and the **restaurant** (meals US$1.50-3) is the ideal place to have a sunset drink; while the **Saylomyen Guest House** (r US$3) has simple huts with fans and shared bathroom.

GETTING THERE & AWAY

Just say 'Tat Lo' at Pakse's southern bus station and you'll be pointed in the right direction (see p217 for details). Tat Lo is 86km northeast of Pakse off the road to Salavan; you'll be dropped at Ban Khoua Set. There might be a *dok dok* (US$0.20) to shuttle you the last 1.8km, but you'll probably have to walk or call Tim's for a lift.

If you're heading to Paksong, the main centre for the local coffee trade, buses from Pakse cost US$1 and take about 1½ hours. There are also one or two trucks a day between Salavan and Paksong; these take about two or three hours and cost US$0.35.

CHAMPASAK

ຈຳປາສັກ

☎ 031

It's hard to think of Champasak as a seat of royalty, but until only 30 years ago it was just that. These days Champasak is serenely quiet, the fountain circle in the middle of the main street alluding to a grandeur long gone. The remaining French colonial-era buildings, including one that once belonged to Chao Bounome na Champasak and another to his father Chao Ratsadanai, who was the last king of Champasak, share space with traditional Lao wooden houses. The few vehicles that venture down the narrow main street share it with buffaloes and cows who seem relaxed even by Lao standards – it's easy to spend a couple of days here.

The Angkor-period ruins of Wat Phu Champasak (p223) lie 8km southwest of town and are the main attraction; Champasak has the only accommodation in the immediate vicinity of Wat Phu.

Just about everything in Champasak is spread along the one riverside street, either side of the fountain circle. On Don Daeng (Map p226), the large island opposite Champasak, the villages (Ban) of Si Mungkhun, Xieng Vang, Bung and Sisuk support themselves by growing coconuts and fishing in the Mekong, and if tourism planners have their way, might soon be hosting sunbathers on their wide (dry-season) beaches.

Information

The **Lao Development Bank** (⏲ 8.30am-3.30pm Mon-Fri) changes US dollars, euros and baht, but won't do cash advances.

Sights

TEMPLES

Champasak has a couple of mildly interesting temples. In town, on a dirt road parallel to the main north–south street, is the late 19th-century **Wat Nyutthitham**, more commonly known as Wat Thong. An old *sim* features an arched and colonnaded veranda, and has a washed pastel stucco relief on the front. This was the wat used by Champasak's royal family, and the *thâat kádụuk* here contain the ashes of King Nyutthitham (died 1885), Chao Ratsadanai (died 1946) and Chao Bounome (died 1975), as well as an assortment of other princes and princesses.

About 8km south of town on the Mekong stands the oldest active temple in Champasak, **Wat Phuthawanaram**, more popularly known as Wat Muang Kang. Like the *sim* at Wat Thong, the intriguing *hǎw tại* (Tripitaka library) at Wat Muang Kang combines elements of French-colonial and Lao Buddhist architecture. The three-tiered roofs of the *sim* and *hǎw tại* have coloured mosaics at the corners, and a small box with coloured crystal windows at the centre of the

SOUTHERN LAOS

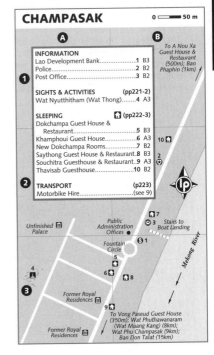

CHAMPASAK

0 ⸺ 50 m

INFORMATION
Lao Development Bank...................1 B3
Police..2 B2
Post Office..................................3 B2

SIGHTS & ACTIVITIES (pp221-2)
Wat Nyutthitham (Wat Thong)........4 A3

SLEEPING (pp222-3)
Dokchampa Guest House &
Restaurant.................................5 B3
Khamphoui Guest House................6 A3
New Dokchampa Rooms................7 B2
Saythong Guest House & Restaurant..8 B3
Souchitra Guesthouse & Restaurant..9 A3
Thavisab Guesthouse...................10 B2

TRANSPORT (p223)
Motorbike Hire.........................(see 9)

To A Nou Xa
Guest House &
Restaurant
(500m); Ban
Phaphin (1km)

Unfinished
Palace

Public
Administration
Offices

Stairs to
Boat Landing

Fountain
Circle

Mekong River

Former Royal
Residences

To Vong Paseud Guest House
(350m); Wat Phuthawanaram
(Wat Muang Kang) (8km);
Wat Phu Champasak (9km);
Ban Don Talat (15km)

Former Royal
Residences

top roof ridge – reminiscent of Burmese architecture.

Ostensibly these crystal-sided boxes hold Buddha images, but local legend ascribes a more magical purpose to the one atop the *hǎw tài*. Supposedly at a certain moment in the annual lunar calendar (most say it's during the Wat Phu Festival), in the middle of the night, a mystic light beam comes from across the river, bounces through the *kâew* (crystal) and alights atop Sri Linga-parvata, the holy mountain on which Wat Phu Champasak is situated.

You can reach Wat Muang Kang by boat from Champasak for a few thousand kip, or come by bike on the narrow dirt road along the riverbank. You could combine a boat trip to Wat Muang Kang with a visit to Um Muang (p227) across the river.

Sleeping & Eating

Champasak has a few guesthouses and you usually won't have trouble finding a room. But during the annual Wat Phu Champasak Festival (Makha Busa; usually in February; see p226) every room is likely to be taken. You could arrive days early, or look for sleeping space on the ground at Wat Phu Champasak. If you stay at the wat, it's best to ask at one of the food tents for a safe place to sleep after the nightly hubbub dies down, and take particular care of your valuables.

CHAMPASAK IN ANTIQUITY

Although you wouldn't know it from looking at today's Champasak, the town once served as the centre for a major pre-Angkor culture. The original city site – usually referred to locally as Muang Kao (Old City) – actually lies about 4km south of the current town centre, where the Huay Sawa feeds into the Mekong.

Aerial photographs show the remains of a rectangular city measuring 2.3km by 1.8km, surrounded by double earthen walls on three sides and protected on the east by the Mekong River. Other traces of the old city include a few small *baray* (a Khmer word meaning 'pond', usually used for ritual purposes), the foundations for circular brick monuments of unknown proportions, evidence of an advanced system of irrigation, various Hindu statuary and stone carvings (including a lintel in the style of 12th-century Sambor Prei Kuk), stone implements and ceramics.

The rectangular city layout bears similarities with Muang Fa Daet in northeastern Thailand and Sambor Prei Kuk in northwestern Cambodia, and may have begun as either a Mon or Cham state during the first centuries of the Christian era. A very important 5th century stele discovered in the old city bears a Sanskrit inscription saying the city was founded by King Devanika and was called Kuruksetra. The oldest surviving Sanskrit inscription in Southeast Asia, the stele mentions the auspicious Sri Lingaparvata mountain nearby, a clear reference to the mountain on which Wat Phu Champasak is found. 'Honoured since antiquity', the mountain was said to represent the phallus of the Hindu god Shiva (even today many Lao call the peak Phu Khuai or Mt Penis). An association with the Mon-Khmer kingdoms of Funan and Chenla has also been suggested.

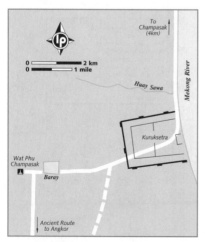

The city took on other names as well. Two Nandi (Shiva's bull mount) sculptures discovered in 1990–91 bear inscriptions calling it Sri Citrasena, and placing the city under the rule of the Khmer King Mahendravarman. It is clear that by the 8th century Champasak was under Khmer rule, and that it remained so until the 13th or 14th century. Over time the city has also been known as Samapura, Champa Nakhon and Nakhon Champasak.

A Nou Xa Guesthouse (☎ 213272, mobile 020-2275412; d US$3-10, f US$15; ☷) This welcoming place has several clean rooms with small balconies overlooking the river. They are the best in town, though the location 1km north of the fountain circle is not. There are also a couple of fan rooms (US$5), and bamboo bungalows with cold-water bathrooms (US$3). The attached riverside **restaurant** (☺ 7am-9pm; meals US$1-2) serves a mean fish soup (US$1.20).

Souchitra Guesthouse (☎ 212366; fax 212365; r US$3-10; ☷) These clean and relatively stylish double and twin rooms (some with fridge) are good value, especially the fan rooms with either hot- (US$5) or cold-water (US$3) bathrooms. The spacious common veranda, the riverside hammocks and the attached **restaurant** (meals US$1-1.50; ☺ 7am-9pm) are all good places to hang out. Motorbikes can be hired for US$5/10 for a half/full day, with or without driver.

Vong Paseud Guest House (☎ 920038; d US$1.50) About 600m south of the fountain circle, this place probably sees the most backpackers, partly because they offer free tuk-tuks to and from the car ferry, and partly because the French-speaking owners are invariably friendly and have a fairly social dining area beside the river. The 10 rooms themselves are not great, with no mosquito nets, bathrooms with dubious plumbing and paper-thin walls. The attached **restaurant** (meals US$1-2; ☺ 6am-10pm) serves up a better-than-average mix of the usual travellers' fare.

Khamphoui Guest House (r US$1.50-2) Just south of the circle, the rooms with attached cold-water bathroom (in a concrete building or two particularly good bungalows) are good value. Rooms with shared bathroom in the main house are US$1.50.

Saythong Guest House & Restaurant (Mr Sing's House; ☎ 920092, mobile 020-2209215; r US$2) English-speaking Mr Sing's **restaurant** (meals US$1-2; ☺ 6am-10pm) is one of the best locations in town, but his basic double, triple and twin rooms with cold-water bathrooms are not so praiseworthy.

Another couple of options include the overpriced **Thavisab Guesthouse** (☎ 212225; r US$5-18; ☷) a couple of hundred metres north of the circle, with negotiable prices; and the ultra-basic rooms at the **Dokchampa Guest House and Restaurant** (☎ mobile 020-2206248; r US$1.50) on the southwest corner of

the fountain circle. Dokchampa was building new bungalows just north of the bank when we passed, which will be better.

Getting There & Away

Buses and *săwngthăew* from Pakse leave between 7am and about 3pm; see p217.

Ferries (US$0.50 per person, US$0.50 for motorbikes, US$2.50 for larger vehicles) from Ban Muang on the eastern side of the Mekong to Ban Phaphin (1.8km north of Champasak) on the western side run regularly during daylight hours, and 24 hours during the Wat Phu Champasak Festival. From Ban Phaphin to Champasak by any vehicle is US$0.20 per person; US$1 charter.

You can also charter a ferry – actually two canoes lashed together with a few planks to create a rustic catamaran – from Ban Muang straight across to the Champasak boat landing for US$0.20 per person or US$1 the whole thing. Between Ban Lak 30 and the ferry landing at Ban Muang, take a motorcycle taxi or jumbo, or hitch.

Leaving Champasak, seven buses and *săwngthăew* depart for Pakse (US$1.30) between 6.30am and 8am. If you're heading south, get to Ban Lak 30 and flag down anything going past, or take the boat (p215).

Getting Around

Bicycles can be hired from several guesthouses for US$1 a day, and the **Souchitra Guesthouse** (☎ 212366) hires out motorbikes for US$5/10 per half/full day. Jumbos are available around town for about US$0.30 per kilometre.

WAT PHU CHAMPASAK

ວັດພູຈຳປາສັກ

The ancient Khmer religious complex of **Wat Phu** (admission US$3, children eight & under free; ☺ 8am-4.30pm) is one of the highlights of any trip to Laos. Spread over the lower slopes of Phu Pasak (also known more colloquially as Phu Khuai), Wat Phu is small compared with the monumental Angkor-era sites in Siem Reap in Cambodia, or Buriram in Thailand. But the tumbledown pavilions, ornate Shiva-lingam sanctuary, enigmatic crocodile stone and tall trees that shroud much of the site in soothing shade give Wat Phu an almost mystical atmosphere. The experts at Unesco obviously liked it, granting Wat Phu World Heritage status in 2001.

SOUTHERN LAOS

While their exact age remains uncertain, most scholars believe the surviving structures were begun during the Chenla kingdom (from the 6th to 8th centuries) and finished toward the end of the Angkor period (from the 9th to 13th centuries).

Talk of a full-scale project to reconstruct parts of Wat Phu has so far come to nothing. Other work has been completed, however, with Unesco overseeing Japanese-funded projects to divert water from the site and thus minimise damage caused by water erosion, and the construction of an impressive new **museum** (admission with Wat Phu ticket; ☺ 8am-4.30pm) beside the ticket office that shouldn't be missed. The low-rise building houses dozens of stunning lintels, *naga*s (mythical water serpents), Buddhas and other stone work from Wat Phu and around, and is the Unesco headquarters for Champasak. Descriptions are in English.

The Archaeological Site

Wat Phu is situated at the junction of the Mekong plain and Phu Phasak, a mountain that was sacred to local peoples centuries before the construction of any of the ruins now visible. The original Austro-Asiatic tribes living in this area undoubtedly paid respect to animist spirits associated with the mountain and its rock shelter spring.

The archaeological site itself is divided into three main levels joined by a long, stepped promenade flanked by statues of lions and *naga*s.

LOWER LEVEL

The crumbling 20th-century palace buildings that stood at the eastern end (near where vehicles now park) have recently been removed. At this point, the causeway-style promenade bisects two large ponds, known as *baray* in Khmer or *nǎwng sá* in Lao. Parts of both the northern *baray* and southern *baray* still fill with water, lotus flowers and the odd buffalo during the wet season.

MIDDLE LEVEL

The middle section features two exquisitely carved, rectangular pavilions built of sandstone, believed by some (but not the Unesco experts) to have been used for gender-segregated worship. Wat Phu was converted into a Buddhist temple in later centuries but much of the original Hindu sculpture remains in the lintels, which feature various forms of Vishnu and Shiva as well as Kali, the Hindu goddess of time and death. The rear third of the pavilion on the right reportedly dates to the 6th-century Chenla era while the front two-thirds were probably constructed during the late Angkor period (11th to 13th centuries). Over the main entrance is a relief of Shiva and Parvati sitting on Nandi, Shiva's bull mount, with what seems to be Lakulisa (an obscure, Buddha-like Shiva deity) below. This entrance is flanked by well-executed reliefs of Parvati.

Just behind the southern pavilion is a smaller **Nandi pavilion** (dedicated to Shiva's mount) and two galleries flanking a set of

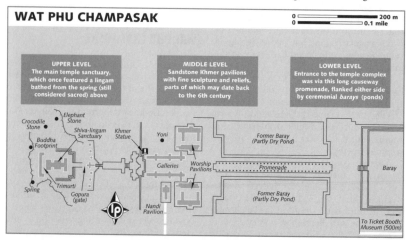

WAT PHU CHAMPASAK

0 — 200 m
0 — 0.1 mile

UPPER LEVEL
The main temple sanctuary, which once featured a lingam bathed from the spring (still considered sacred) above

MIDDLE LEVEL
Sandstone Khmer pavilions with fine sculpture and reliefs, parts of which may date back to the 6th century

LOWER LEVEL
Entrance to the temple complex was via this long causeway promenade, flanked either side by ceremonial *baray*s (ponds)

Elephant Stone
Crocodile Stone
Shiva-lingam Sanctuary
Khmer Statue
Yoni
Buddha Footprint
Galleries
Worship Pavilions
Former Baray (Partly Dry Pond)
Promenade
Baray
Spring
Trimurti
Gopura (gate)
Nandi Pavilion
Former Baray (Partly Dry Pond)
To Ticket Booth; Museum (500m)

laterite steps lead to the next level. From the Nandi pavilion an ancient royal road leads south for about 1.3km to Ho Nang Sida (see opposite), and eventually to Angkor Wat in Cambodia. Six ruined brick pavilions – only their bases remain – separate the lower two levels from the final and holiest level. Roots and mosses hold the bricks together in some places, and drive them apart in others.

Along the northern edge of the next promenade level stands an impressive **Khmer statue** that some believe to be a representation of an Angkor-era monarch, though it could just as well be a simple *dvarapala* (sentinel figure). If you step down off the walkway and onto the grassy area just north you'll come to the remains of a **yoni**, the cosmic vagina-womb symbol associated with Shaivism. Offerings of flowers and incense indicate it is now considered one of the primary worship points for Wat Phu pilgrims. Very near the yoni lie two prone, headless and armless **Khmer statues** half-buried in the grass. Local Lao tell various tall tales about what these figures mean, none of which coincide with their original functions as probable Hindu deities.

A *naga* stairway leads to the sanctuary and probably dates from the 11th century. It is lined with shade-providing *dàwk jąmpąa* (plumeria or frangipani), the Lao national tree.

UPPER LEVEL

On the uppermost level is the main temple sanctuary itself, which once enclosed a large Shiva phallus (lingam) that was bathed – via a system of stone pipes – by the sacred spring above and behind the complex. A lintel inside the southern entrance depicts the story of Krishnavatara in which Krishna kills his uncle Kamsa. This same subject was used for lintels at Prasat Meuang Khaek in Nakhon Ratchasima Province and Prasat Phanom Rung in Buriram Province, Thailand, suggesting these three temples were ritually linked. The archaeological evidence also indicates that Wat Phu was linked to Khao Phra Wihan (130km east on the Thai-Cambodian border), the personal temple of Khmer monarch Suryavarman I in the early 11th century. Reportedly the lingam at Wat Phu was used in ceremonies to 'release' the sacred power of the lingam at Khao Phra Wihan.

This sanctuary now contains a set of crude, almost clown-faced Buddha images on an altar at one end. Local worshippers have returned pieces of sculpture – mostly stone window balustrades – that had been taken from the ruins, believing that anyone who takes a piece of Wat Phu away is in for a run of bad luck.

The upper platform affords a high, wide-angle view of the surrounding plains, and in the evening monkeys cavort in the trees nearby. Behind the upper level is a shallow cave from which the sacred spring flows.

Sculpted into a large boulder behind the topmost sanctuary is a Khmer-style **Trimurti**, the Hindu triumvirate of Shiva, Vishnu and Brahma. A few monks reside at the Theravada Buddhist wat nearby. The best view of the plains below are from this wat; the cool, shady grounds are a good spot for a picnic.

East of the sanctuary and the newer wat a winding path leads north to the so-called **crocodile stone**, a boulder with a deep, highly stylised carving of a croc. The carving would happily hold a human and it has been suggested, though by no means proved, that this sculpture was used for Chenla-era human sacrifices. Further on along the same path is a huge boulder with the likeness of an elephant carved onto one side – known as the **elephant stone**. Both are important stops on the Wat Phu pilgrimage route.

Other Sites Associated with Wat Phu

South of Wat Phu are three smaller Angkor-era sites in very poor condition – probably not worth the trouble unless you're a die-hard fan of Khmer architecture and have a vivid imagination. Each of the three stands beside an ancient route that once linked Wat Phu Champasak with Angkor Wat in Siem Reap, Cambodia.

An easy 1km walk south of Wat Phu – use the trail heading south from the terraced promenade – stands **Ho Nang Sida** ('Lady Sida Hall', a reference to a local legend unrelated to the monument's original function), a pile of sandstone and laterite rubble that may have once served as a 'hospital' for Angkor pilgrims.

Another kilometre south of Ho Nang Sida along the same axis stands another rubble pile, **Hong Than Tao** (Lord Turtle Room), said to have been a Vishnu shrine built under King Jayavarman VII in the 13th century.

Another few kilometres on, close to the village of Ban That, stand three Khmer stupas reminiscent of similar tripartite monuments in Thailand's Lopburi and Sukhothai. No doubt symbolic of the Hindu Trimurti of Shiva, Brahma and Vishnu, the three *prang* (Khmer-style towers) are in poor condition; the northernmost one has collapsed entirely. This site, too, is said to have been a 13th-century construction by King Jayavarman VII. A large, dried-up *baray* can be seen nearby.

During times of heavy rain, stream crossings may make these sites unapproachable on foot from Wat Phu. Ban That can be reached by jumbo from Champasak or Ban Thong Khop.

Festivals

The highlight of the year in Champasak is the three-day Bun Wat Phu Champasak (Wat Phu Champasak Festival), held as part of Magha Puja (Makha Busa) during the full moon of the third lunar month – usually in February. The central ceremonies performed are Buddhist, culminating on the third day (the full-moon day of that lunar month) with the early-morning file of monks receiving alms food from the faithful, followed that evening by a candle-lit circumambulation *(wíen thíen)* of the lower shrines.

Throughout the three days of the festival Lao visitors wind their way up and around the hillside, stopping to pray and leave of-

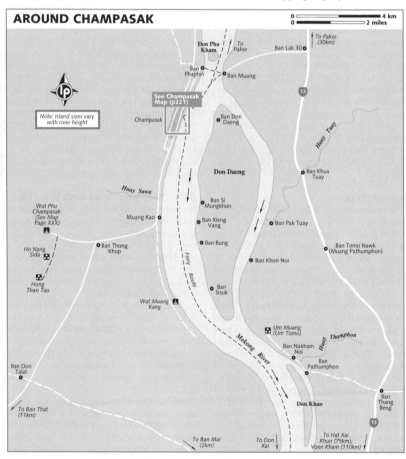

AROUND CHAMPASAK

ferings of flowers and incense. Some years a water buffalo is quietly sacrificed in a corner of the complex. Other events include daily boat races on the *baray* at the foot of the hill, Thai boxing matches, cockfights (sometimes substituted with bullfights), comedy shows, music and dancing. Food is available from vendors who set up along the road from Ban Thong Khop, and after dark several areas are cordoned off for open-air nightclubs featuring bands from as far away as Vientiane. After dark the beer and *lào-láo* (distilled rice liquor) flow freely, and the atmosphere becomes rather rowdy.

Each June the locals perform a **water buffalo sacrifice** to the ruling Champasak earth spirit, Chao Tengkham. The blood of the buffalo is offered to a local shaman serving as a trance medium for the appearance of the spirit, who is believed to preside over the rice-growing season.

Getting There & Away
Wat Phu Champasak is 46km from Pakse, 12km from Ban Phaphin and 10km from Champasak. If you can find one, a shared jumbo from Champasak to Ban Thong Khop, the village opposite Wat Phu, should cost US$0.50 per person. You can charter a jumbo direct to Wat Phu or Muang Kao (Old City) for about US$5 for a return trip. Cycling on a bike hired from a Champasak guesthouse is also popular.

UM MUANG
ອ່າງເມືອງ
Um Muang (more commonly called either Muang Tomo or Um Tomo) is a Khmer temple ruin thought to have been built late in the 9th century during the reign of the Khmer King Yasovarman I and dedicated to Rudani, an aspect of Shiva's consort. It's about 45km south of Pakse off Rte 13, in a forest on a small tributary of the Mekong. The ruins include an esplanade bordered by lingams and two crumbling laterite sanctuaries. The more intact of the sanctuaries contains a large vestibule and lintel sculpted with various Vaishnava motifs, along with a *mukhalinga* – a lingam or Shiva phallus onto which four faces *(mukha)* have been carved. A number of other sandstone lintels are displayed on rocks beneath towering dipterocarp trees. A large tin shed at the site contains a bronze Sukhothai-style

Buddha from that region of Thailand. The best lintels from this site are kept at the Champasak Historical Heritage Museum in Pakse p212.

Getting There & Away
From Ban Muang (the village on the far side of the Mekong from Champasak) or from Champasak you can charter a boat to Ban Nakham Noi (the riverbank village nearest the ruins) for US$10 return (or US$5 one way), including waiting time of an hour or so while you locate and tour the ruins.

Ban Nakham Noi, is about 1km south of the ruins. Climb the bank next to the mouth of a tributary stream (Huay Thumphon) to the village, then turn left and walk north along a smaller stream into the forest. When the path forks, stay right and walk for about 10 minutes until you see some metal-roofed sheds in the forest on your right, which shelter parts of the ruins. Children from the village will lead you for a small tip (about US$0.50 is fair).

The ruins can also be reached by vehicle from Pakse by turning west at Km 48 at Ban Thang Beng and driving to Ban Pathumphon. You can then walk about 2km from Ban Pathumphon to the ruins via Ban Nakham Noi.

If you are travelling by boat, you could combine a trip to Um Muang with a stop at Wat Muang Kang on the west bank of the Mekong. A half-day's use of a boat from Champasak or Ban Muang to both sites will cost about US$10

BAN PHAPHO & KIET NGONG
ບ້ານພະໂພແລະກຽດຄ້ອງ
The Suay village of Ban Phapho (22km east of Rte 13) in Pathumphon district is one of the last places in Southern Laos where elephants are still employed to help in agriculture. Mr Bounhome (see Sleeping p228) can take you to find elephants tethered, grazing and sometimes working, and can also arrange trips by elephant to a nearby mountain for US$7.

The better place to go for elephant rides is Kiet Ngong, which is about 13km east of Rte 13. The villagers of Kiet Ngong have a centuries-old relationship with elephants, and while the working pachyderm seems to be a dying breed they can still earn some income for the village through tourism. The elephant trek on offer here typically goes to the summit of a hill called **Phu Asa**, named for a 19th-century nationalist who fought against the Siamese. From the flat hill crest there is a good view of the village, pond and rice fields below. You can also explore the remains of a bizarre assemblage of stone on the top of the hill. The slate-brick columns, mounted by lipped slabs, stand about 2m high and are arranged in a semicircle. Some locals say the pillars date from the 19th century, and were possibly built in defence of the area. Others believe they're some sort of ritual megaliths. Like so many other archaeological sites in Laos, the origins are clouded by legend, speculation and many years of war.

A three-hour elephant trek up Phu Asa can be arranged by Mr Bounsome in Kiet Ngong. It costs US$10 per elephant, and each elephant can take two people. Alternatively, Mr Oudom can lead walks up the mountain for US$2 per person. Both Mr Oudom and Bounsome are villagers in Kiet Ngong – just ask for them when you arrive. There's no English here but the locals will know why you've come.

At either village it's worth arriving early as it takes time to fetch and prepare the elephants.

Sleeping & Eating

Boun Home Guest House (per bed US$1.50) The friendly English- and French-speaking Mr Bounhome runs the only accommodation in Ban Phapho; this very simple but unbeatably authentic wooden guesthouse. Not surprisingly, the bathroom is shared and there's no hot water. Soup and noodles (US$1) don't take long but meals of *làap* (US$2) and *khào nĭaw* must be ordered in advance.

In Kiet Ngong there are several **bungalows** (r US$4) set up for visitors. Simple Lao meals are eaten with the villagers and cost about US$1 each.

Getting There & Away

Kiet Ngong and Ban Phapho are best reached in your own transport. Both are off the laterite Rte 18 that runs east to Attapeu from Ban Thang Beng, 48km south of Pakse on Rte 13. The turn-off for Kiet Ngong is about 7km east of Rte 13, and the village is 1.6km south on a bad road. For

Ban Phapho, continue along Rte 18 and soon after the Kiet Ngong turn-off take the right fork; it's about 15km along this road. These roads are passable in most vehicles, and easily travelled on 110cc motorbikes hired in Pakse.

Cheaper and slower are the trucks (US$1.30, two to three hours, two daily) that leave between 8am and 10am from Pakse's southern (Km 8) bus terminal to Kiet Ngong and Ban Phapho. In the reverse direction there is only one truck from Ban Phapho and sometimes one from Kiet Ngong, both in the morning. If you're going to Kiet Ngong, you'll have to walk the final 1.6km or so from Rte 18.

Alternatively, you could board any transport going south on Rte 13 and get off at Ban Thang Beng, from where occasional *sǎwngthǎew* head east.

SI PHAN DON (FOUR THOUSAND ISLANDS)

ສີພັນດອນ

There must be some rule in Laos that says the further south you go the more relaxed it becomes, because just when you thought your blood pressure couldn't drop any more, you arrive in Si Phan Don...The name literally means 'Four Thousand Islands', and the few you are likely to visit on this scenic 50km-long stretch of the Mekong are so chilled you're liable to turn into a hammock-bound icicle.

During the rainy season this section of the Mekong River fills out to a breadth of 14km, the river's widest reach along its 4350km journey from the Tibetan Plateau to the South China Sea. During the dry months between monsoons the river recedes and leaves behind hundreds (or thousands if you count every sand bar) of islands and islets. The largest of the permanent islands are inhabited year round and offer fascinating glimpses of tranquil river-oriented village life – 'more detached from time than from the riverbank' as one source described it. Communities tend to be self-sufficient, growing most of their own rice, sugar cane, coconut and vegetables, harvesting fish from the Mekong and weaving textiles as needed.

The villages of Si Phan Don are often named for their position at the upriver or downriver ends of their respective islands.

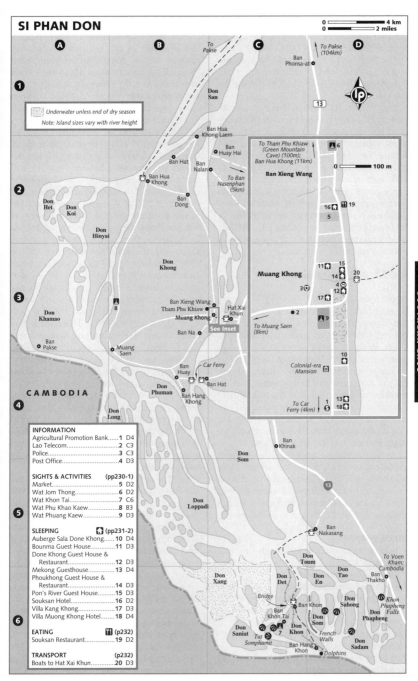

SI PHAN DON

0 — 4 km
0 — 2 miles

Underwater unless end of dry season
Note: Island sizes vary with river height

To Pakse

To Pakse
(104km)

13

Ban
Phonsa-at

Don
San

Ban Hua
Khong Laem

Ban
Huay Hai

Ban Hat
Ban
Nalan

Ban Hua
Khong

To Ban
Nasenphan
(5km)

Ban
Dong

Don
Het   Don
Koi

Don
Hinyai

Don
Khong

Don
Khamao

Ban Xieng Wang
Tham Phu Khiaw   Hat Xai
Muang Khong   Khun

Ban
Pakse

Muang
Saen

Ban Na

Ban
Huay   Car Ferry

CAMBODIA

Don
Phuman   Ban Hat
Ban Hang
Khong

Don
Long

Inset: Muang Khong

To Tham Phu Khiaw
(Green Mountain
Cave) (100m);
Ban Hua Khong (11km)

0 — 100 m

Ban Xieng Wang

6

16   19

5

Muang Khong

11   15

14

3   4

20

17   12

2

9

To Muang Saen
(8km)

Colonial-era
Mansion

10

To Car
Ferry (4km)   13
18

Ban
Khinak

Don
Som

Don
Loppadi

Ban
Nakasang

Don
Toum   To Voen
Kham;
Cambodia

13

Don
Tao   Ban
Thakho

Don
Xang   Don
Det   Don
En   Khon
Phapheng
Don Falls
Phapheng

Bridge   Ban Khon   Don
Sahong

Ban
Khon Tai   Don
Som

Don
Saniat   Tat
Somphamit   French
Walls   Don
Sadam

Ban Hang
Khon   Dolphins

INFORMATION
Agricultural Promotion Bank......**1** D4
Lao Telecom............................**2** C3
Police....................................**3** C3
Post Office.............................**4** D3

SIGHTS & ACTIVITIES   (pp230-1)
Market...................................**5** D2
Wat Jom Thong.......................**6** D2
Wat Khon Tai.........................**7** C6
Wat Phu Khao Kaew................**8** B3
Wat Phuang Kaew...................**9** D3

SLEEPING   (pp231-2)
Auberge Sala Done Khong......**10** D4
Bounma Guest House.............**11** D3
Done Khong Guest House &
    Restaurant.......................**12** D3
Mekong Guesthouse..............**13** D4
Phoukhong Guest House &
    Restaurant.......................**14** D3
Pon's River Guest House.........**15** D3
Souksan Hotel.......................**16** D2
Villa Kang Khong...................**17** D3
Villa Muong Khong Hotel.......**18** D4

EATING   (p232)
Souksan Restaurant................**19** D2

TRANSPORT   (p232)
Boats to Hat Xai Khun............**20** D3

SOUTHERN LAOS

See Inset

The upriver – usually the northern – end of the island is called *hŭa* (head), the downriver or southern end is called *hăang* (tail). Hence Ban Hua Khong would be a village at the northern end of Don Khong, while Ban Hang Khong is a village at the southern end.

The French left behind a defunct short railway (the only railway ever actually completed in Laos), a couple of river piers, and a few colonial villas on the islands of Don Khong, Don Det and Don Khon. Other attractions include some impressive rapids and waterfalls, where the Mekong suddenly drops in elevation at the Cambodian border, and a rare species of freshwater dolphin. With the border open (if you've arranged your visas in advance), the islands are becoming a popular stop for travellers between the two countries.

Don Khong (Khong Island)

ດອນໂຂງ

☎ 031 / pop 13,000

Named for the surrounding river (using the Thai pronunciation *khœng* rather than the Lao *khăwng*), this large island measures 18km along its north–south axis and 8km at its widest point. Most of the islanders live in and around two villages, Muang Khong on the eastern shore and Muang Saen on the west; an 8km road links the two. Muang Khong has most of the accommodation and eating options and is delightfully quiet; you'll seldom be disturbed by a vehicle no matter where you are on the island.

As his surname suggests, the current president of Laos, Khamtay Siphandone, was born in Si Phan Don – on Don Khong to be exact – and still spends more time in the area (no-one seems sure quite where) than he does in his palace in Vientiane.

INFORMATION

The police are a block back from the river in Muang Khong. If you get sick, head for Pakse or Thailand (see p280).

Agricultural Promotion Bank (☉ 8.30am-3.30pm Mon-Fri) South of town, this bank offers terrible rates for US dollars and Thai baht cash and travellers cheques. It doesn't have a sign in English.

Lao Telecom (☉ 8am-noon & 1.30-4pm Mon-Fri) Located on the road to Muang Saen.

Post office (☉ 8am-noon & 1.30-4pm Mon-Fri) Located south of the bridge in Muang Khong.

SIGHTS & ACTIVITIES

Don Khong is quite scenic; with rice fields and low hills in the centre and vegetable gardens around the perimeter, punctuated by small villages, most of which have their own wats. Muang Khong is dominated by **Wat Phuang Kaew** and its towering modern '*naga*-protected' Buddha image facing east. The locals believe the abbot used supernatural powers gained in meditation to defeat government efforts to oust him after the Revolution. Elsewhere in Muang Khong, the **market** is fascinating between 4.30am and 6.30am, when people come from throughout the islands to buy and sell.

At Ban Xieng Wang, a neighbourhood at the northern end of Muang Khong, is **Wat Jom Thong** the oldest temple on the island. Dating from the Chao Anou period (1805–28), the main *sĭm* features a unique cruciform floor plan in crumbling brick and stucco with a tile roof. Carved wooden window shutters are a highlight, and an old wooden standing Buddha in one-handed *abhaya mudra* (offering protection) is notable. The sandy wat grounds are shaded by coconut and betel palms and mango trees.

A kilometre or so north of Muang Khong, in some hills more or less behind the mayor's office, a trail leads to **Tham Phu Khiaw** (Green Mountain Cave). The cave – actually more of an overhanging ledge – contains some old Buddha images and is the object of local pilgrimages during Lao New Year in April. For the remainder of the year the trail becomes overgrown, so you should seek out a local guide for the stiff 30-minute walk up the hill to the cave.

At the northwestern end of the island, **Ban Hua Khong** is well known as the 1924 birthplace of Khamtay Siphandone, who rose from being a postman under French rule to the presidency. The area between Hua Khong and Ban Dong (to the east) is heavily planted in rice.

Muang Saen, on the opposite side of the island from Muang Khong, is a bustling little town with boats servicing the islands to the west of Don Khong that have no road access whatsoever. **Wat Phu Khao Kaew**, on a low hill north of Muang Saen (3km or 4km from the junction of the north–south and east–west roads), was built on the site of some Khmer ruins. Look for a stand of plumeria (frangipani) trees on the eastern side of the hill to locate the path to the temple, or better yet hire a motorcycle taxi in Muang Saen for around US$1.50 return. An unusual bronze gong in the shape of a clock hangs here. Jumbos between Muang Saen and Muang Khong cost US$2.50, by bicycle it's about 45 minutes.

Two smaller villages at the southern tip of the island worth visiting for old wats are **Ban Huay** and **Ban Hang Khong**. At the latter village, Wat Thepsulin Phudin Hang Khong, more commonly known as Wat Hang Khong, features spacious grounds and a small brick and stucco *sǐm* with a collection of Buddha images. A pair of slender wooden standing *abhaya mudra* Buddhas in front of the main image are obviously highly revered locally as they've been dressed in cloth robes.

TOURS

A three-day, two-night trip between Pakse and Don Khong is offered by **Vat Phou** (www .mekongcruises.com), including a visit to Wat Phu Champasak, Um Muang and Khon Phapheng Falls. The cruise is aboard the *Vat Phou*, a 34m steel-hulled barge converted into a floating hotel. Each of the 12 wooden staterooms has two beds, a dressing table, air-con and private hot-water bathroom. Many agencies sell this tour and fares vary, but as an idea the all-inclusive fare is US$350 from April to October, and double that at other times. In Pakse, the representative is @d@m's Internet (p212).

FESTIVALS & EVENTS

A boat racing festival (Bun Suang Heua or Bun Nam) is held on Don Khong in early December around National Day. Four or five days of carnival-like activity culminate in races next to Muang Khong along the eastern shore of the island. In times past the islanders celebrated this festival one month earlier at the end of the Buddhist rains retreat (Awk Phansa), but they now combine the boat races with government-mandated National Day celebrations to save money.

SLEEPING

Lodgings in Muang Khong are of a higher standard than those on Don Det or Don Khon, and are usually pretty good value. Most hire out bicycles for US$1 a day and have attached restaurants (see Eating p232).

Pon's River Guest House (☎ 214037, mobile 020-2270037; r US$5-10) Just north of the bridge, the savvy, English-speaking Mr Pon can arrange anything from boat trips to transport anywhere you like. His 15 clean rooms are good value and negotiable in low season. Very popular.

Souksan Hotel (☎ 212071; bungalow US$3, s/d with breakfast US$30/25; 🐱) About 300m north of the bridge, Souksan has spotlessly clean rooms in a new concrete building about 30m back from the river. They are US$5 cheaper in low season. There are also several wooden fan-conditioned bungalows that are unbeatable value at US$3 each, without breakfast. A swimming pool and Internet service are planned for 2005.

Villa Kang Khong (☎ 213539; r US$4-10; 🐱) Not far from Wat Phuang Kaew, this traditional teak house is a favourite for its convivial atmosphere, large and clean rooms and shaded communal balcony where you can enjoy breakfast. Fan rooms are US$4, or US$5 with hot water.

Auberge Sala Done Khong (☎ 212077; www .salalao.laopdr.com; s/d with breakfast US$23/28; 🐱) About 250m south of the bridge and part of the Auberges Sala Lao chain, the location in two French-era teak mansions is atmospheric but promises more than the rooms deliver; ask to see several as they can be rather different. Prices drop US$5 from May to September. The attached restaurant is quite romantic.

Done Khong Guest House & Restaurant (☎ 214 010; r US$5-15; 🐱) In a prime position just south of the bridge, the upstairs fan-rooms here open onto a balcony and are well worth the US$5; but the smaller air-con rooms downstairs are overpriced. All have cold-water bathrooms. The woman owner speaks French and a little English. The restaurant is pretty good.

Villa Muong Khong Hotel (☎ 261870; fax 261869; r US$30; 🐱) About 450m south of the bridge, these compact bungalows with wicker furniture are pleasant enough, but probably not worth the money. French and some English are spoken here.

If none of these take your fancy, the **Mekong Guest House** (☎ /fax 213668; r US$2-20; 🐱) has some very cheap and clean fan-rooms with shared bathroom (US$2/3 with a view), and some pricey air-con rooms; the **Bounma Guest House** (r US$3), about 50m down a lane north of Pon's, is a solid cheapie with a good communal balcony; while the **Phoukhong Guesthouse & Restaurant** (☎ 213673; r US$3) has small rooms with cold-water bathrooms.

Muang Saen has three guesthouses, all near the market in the centre of town, but since the slow boat no longer comes this far south they see very few guests. The **Saykhong Guest House** (r US$3) is probably the best.

EATING
Apart from the odd place selling *fŏe* and Lao snacks, all the eating options are restaurants attached to the aforementioned accommodation. In them you can try Don Khong's famous *lào-láo* (distilled rice liquor), which is often cited as the smoothest in the country. If you really get a taste for it, you can buy a bottle in the market.

Auberge Sala Don Khone (meals US$2-6; ☽ lunch & dinner) The menu of Lao and European fare is small, but the food is as enjoyable as the romantic setting; the speciality is *mók pąa* (fish steamed with herbs in banana leaves, US$3.50) and it's worth trying. Nonguests should give an hour's notice.

Done Khong Guest House & Restaurant (meals US$1.50-3; ☽ 7am-10pm) In an appealing position by the river, this place serves tasty Lao dishes such as *làap* (US$1.50), the mysterious 'soup with chicken gallingly root' (US$1.50), and *khào nĭaw* (sticky rice) and *khào jâo* (plain rice) dishes.

Souksan Restaurant (meals US$2-5; ☽ 7am-10pm) In a wooden building overhanging the river, Souksan serves a range of Chinese, Lao, Thai and Western cuisine, with a few vegetarian dishes. The homesick might find comfort in servings of fish and chips (US$2.50), roast dinners (US$5) and, if plans are fulfilled, pizzas in 2005. Cocktails are available in the evenings.

Villa Muong Khong Hotel (meals US$2-6; ☽ 7am-10pm) This airy restaurant has a more intimate ambience to go with its traditional Lao food and mix of other Asian and Western dishes. Worth the walk.

Mekong Guesthouse (meals US$1-2; ☽ 7am-9.30pm) Good value 'Lao and Canadian' food, though the 'Canadian-style banana pancake' seems to be the extent of the North American fare.

Pon's (meals US$1.50-3.50; ☽ 6.30am-10pm) Reasonable Lao, Thai and backpacker food, reasonable prices and a river-front setting make this a travellers' favourite.

Phoukhong Guesthouse & Restaurant (meals US$1-3; ☽ 7am-10pm) This place is located next door to Pon's and has an identical setting and similar food.

GETTING THERE & AWAY
Boat
The slow boat is a great way to get between Don Khong and Champasak or Pakse; see p215 for details and check the latest with Mr Pon at Pon's River Guest House.

There are regular boats between Hat Xai Khun and Don Khong; it's US$0.50 for foreign pedestrians or US$1 to charter. The boatman will take you as near as possible to your guesthouse of choice. The vehicle ferry between Ban Hat and Ban Na charges US$0.10 per pedestrian, US$0.50 per motorcycle and US$2.50 per car/van/pick-up.

Seven-seat boats (with roofs) can be hired to Don Det and Don Khon (US$12, about one hour), though getting to Don Khon in the dry season will require a smaller boat.

Bus, Săwngthăew & Minibus
Săwngthăew heading to Pakse (US$3, three to four hours, 120km) start in Muang Saen and pass Muang Khong at about 6.30am and 7am. Buses for Pakse (US$3, two to three hours) pass at 8am and 8.30am, the latter going all the way to Vientiane.

There is no direct transport to Voen Kham and the Cambodian border, but it's easy enough to get there. Just take a boat to Hat Xai Khun, walk to Rte 13 and flag down anything going south; 9am is a good time to get a ride. Alternatively, take a tuk-tuk all the way from Hat Xai Khun for about US$10 per vehicle.

Finally, Pon's River Guest House and the Souksan Hotel have air-con minibuses that can be chartered to Pakse (US$50), the Thai border at Chong Mek (US$65) or Voen Kham (ask at the hotels for current prices).

GETTING AROUND
Bicycles can be hired from several guesthouses and elsewhere along the main street for about US$1 a day. Motorbikes cost US$10 a day. Alternatively, you could strike a deal with a jumbo driver. To get to Ban Hua Khong for the boat to Pakse, it's best to arrange a ride the night before with a tuk-tuk driver (US$1 per person) or motorbike taxi (US$1.50).

Don Det & Don Khon
ດອນເດດແລະດອນຄອນ

No cars, no electricity, no TVs...no worries. The untouched ambience of Don Det and Don Khon is hard to beat, with the lack of such mod-cons being one of the islands' most endearing qualities. Unlike in Vang Vieng, there's not much chance of watching endless episodes of *Friends* here. Instead you can expect to ride a bicycle around the few sights, swing in a hammock, read books, converse with locals and travellers alike and just relax. How refreshing! Of course, with electricity expected to arrive in 2006, the pristine atmosphere will be at risk – you can do your bit for the islands' future by just saying 'no' to Vang Vieng–style TV bars.

Located south of Don Khong near the Cambodian border, Don Khon and Don Det were an important link for supply lines between Saigon and Laos during the French colonial era. In order to bypass the rapids and waterfalls in the Mekong River, the French built a narrow-gauge railway across the two islands, linked by an attractive arched bridge and terminating in concrete piers at either end. Boats from Vietnam and Cambodia offloaded their cargoes at the southern end of Don Khon onto railway cars, which transported the goods to boats waiting at the northern end of Don Det for the trip further upriver. The train hasn't run since WWII. The impressive bridge and piers are still intact but much of the rail line has been appropriated by the locals for use as footbridges over streams and gullies around the islands.

Don Khon, the larger of the two islands, is famous throughout Laos for the cultivation of coconut, bamboo and kapok. Some households still make their own incense from the aromatic wood of a local tree. In the main village, **Ban Khon**, there are several old French colonial villas. **Wat Khon Tai**, in Ban Khon Tai, towards the southwestern end of Ban Khon, is a Lao temple built on the former site of a Khmer temple of undetermined age – possibly from the Chenla era. Large laterite bricks used in the construction of the Khmer temple lie scattered about.

SIGHTS & ACTIVITIES

There are a few things to see while you're relaxing on the islands, all of which are best accessed on a bicycle. Bikes can be hired from many guesthouses, but the best are found about 250m east of the bridge on Don Khon. They cost between US$0.50 and US$0.80 per day. As you cross the bridge heading south you'll be charged US$0.50 for a day ticket, which is also good for Tad Somphamit, so don't lose it. Better value is the US$1 ticket that's valid for a week. The money goes toward the upkeep of the village.

Tat Somphamit
ຕາດສົມພະມິດ

About 1.7km downriver from Ban Khon is a raging set of rapids called Tat Somphamit (also known as Li Phi Falls). Water churns through here at a frenetic pace, and especially in May and June it's fascinating to watch local fishermen gingerly edging out to clear their bamboo traps. At this time, a well-positioned trap can catch half a tonne of fish a day. The falls can be reached via the main path heading southwest out of Ban Khon, or on a smaller path through the wat. There are a couple of small eat-drink shops at the falls.

Railway Hike

On Don Khon you can make an interesting 5km trek across the island by following the old rail bed. Rusting locomotives sit near either end of the line; the one about 75m from the south end of the bridge sits by what was once the rail service yard. As you head south you pass stretches of primary forest, rice fields, small villages and singing birds, eventually coming to the French loading pier. Across the river to the right is Cambodia. The rail bed is quite a rocky road and tough on a bike, tougher when you consider that many of the bridges along the way are fairly sketchy constructions and not for the faint-hearted. There is a welcome eat-drink shop at the south end. The return trip, with breaks, should take about three hours by foot.

Eastern Loop Hike

A less onerous walk or cycle takes you to the waterways at the eastern edge of Don Khon where the French built a series of concrete walls to form channels for logs being floated downstream. The logs, usually from forests in Sainyabuli Province west of Vientiane, were usually lashed together into rafts of three. To prevent them being lost, a Lao 'pilot' would board the raft and steer it through the maze of islands. When they reached the critical area at the north end of Don Khon, the pilots were required to guide the raft onto a reinforced concrete wedge, thus splitting the binds and sending the logs into the channels beyond. The poor 'pilot' would jump for his life moments before impact.

You can still see the walls if you go to the shaded village at the east end of Don Khon. To get there, head northwest from the bridge and turn south about 1km along, passing through a wat and following the path through rice fields to the river bank. As you continue south you'll see the walls, and eventually come to an area where trap-fishing is common. Coming back you can take another, more exposed path across the middle of the island.

Dolphins

Rare Irrawaddy dolphins can sometimes be seen off the southern tip of Don Khon in the late afternoon from December until May (during the rainy season the water is too murky and deep). The best dolphin-viewing area is a small sand island a bit further south of the island. Boats can be chartered from the pier area to the sand island for US$2.50. The fee must be paid whether or not any dolphins are seen. How-ever, most people charter a boat (US$6 per boat, maximum three passengers) from the beach at Kong Ngay. Whether you plan to view from Ban Hang Khon or the sand island, the best time of day to see the dolphins is early morning or late afternoon.

SLEEPING & EATING

Seemingly every farmer on Don Det has jumped aboard the bungalow bandwagon and there are now dozens of guesthouses around the edge of the island (see Not As Same, Same As They Look below). The greatest concentration is in Ban Hua Det at the northern tip of Don Det, which has become the place to be if you want to social-ise into the night. From here a quiet foot-path which has become known as Sunset Strip leads along the northwestern edge of the island to places which, not surprisingly, have good sunset views. The rest of the ac-commodation is spread along the pleasant eastern shore, which wears the tag Sunrise Boulevard. Note that things are changing especially fast on Don Det, so if the place you're looking at is not listed here, that doesn't necessarily mean it's no good; it might be newer and better.

Don Khon is home to a couple of more upmarket places, pleasant eateries on the water and a less-youthful atmosphere than Don Det; staying here is definitely a more 'Lao' experience.

NOT AS SAME, SAME AS THEY LOOK

'They're all the same, and they cost a dollar,' advised one traveller on Don Det. Well, not quite. While most bungalows on Don Det and Don Khon do look and cost basically the same, there are a few things worth considering when making your choice. If you know where you want to go, the boatman should be able to take you right there.

Bathroom While a few more guesthouse owners were starting to talk about attached bathrooms when we visited, currently they are few and far between. Most of the shared bathrooms are relatively clean, but these places are not palaces so don't expect to find too many thrones; prepare to squat.

Hammock(s) Most bungalows have balconies with hammocks, but if you're a pair it's worth checking if there is room to string up two hammocks, and if the guesthouse has a second one for you.

Location If you plan on sleeping in, avoid Sunrise Blvd or anywhere facing east, where the morning sun makes your bungalow pretty toasty by 8am.

Neighbours Bamboo walls are paper thin. If you need privacy, look for a detached, or at least semidetached, bungalow.

Roof Tin roofs are hotter than traditional palm-frond thatch roofs.

Window(s) With no electricity (yet) and, therefore, no fans or air-con, having two windows in your bungalow/room means that air circulation (and your night's sleep) is vastly improved. Sadly, most only have one window, or worse, none.

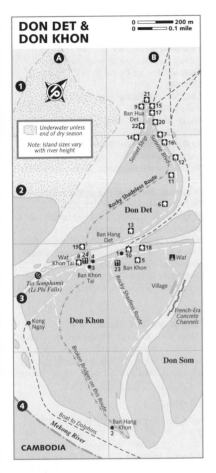

DON DET & DON KHON

0 ———— 200 m
0 ———— 0.1 mile

Underwater unless end of dry season

Note: Island sizes vary with river height

SIGHTS & ACTIVITIES	(pp233-4)
Bike Hire..	**1** B3
Rusted Locomotive............................	**2** B4
Rusted Locomotive............................	**3** A3
Ticket Booth.......................................	**4** A3

SLEEPING	(pp234-7)
Auberge Sala Don Khone...................	**5** B3
Guesthouse Mr Hom...........................	**6** B2
Khampong Guest House......................	(see 15)
Malay Thong.......................................	(see 20)
Mama & Papa's Guest House & Restaurant.........	**7** B1
Mama Dam Restaurant & Guest House.........	**8** A3
Miss Noy's Sunset Guesthouse & Restaurant......	**9** B1
Mr B's Guest House & Bungalows........	(see 9)
Mr Bounh's Guest House.....................	**10** B3
Mr Friends Bungalows.........................	(see 16)
Mr Man's Bungalows...........................	(see 7)
Mr Noi's Bungalows............................	(see 7)
Mr Phao's Guest House.......................	**11** B2
Mr Tho's Bungalows & Restaurant......	**12** B2
Mr Vong's Guest House Hang Det.......	**13** B2
Nar Place...	**14** B2
Nou Phit Guest House.........................	**15** B1
Oudomsok Bungalows.........................	**16** B1
Rasta Cafe Guest House......................	**17** B1
Sala Phae..	**18** B3
Santiphab Guesthouse........................	**19** A3
Seng Chan's Bungalows......................	**20** B1
Somphamit Guest House.....................	(see 10)
Souksan Hotel.....................................	**21** B1
Thon Don Family Bungalows & Sunset Cafe.......	**22** B2
Vixay Guesthouse...............................	(see 15)

EATING	(pp234-7)
Bamboo Bar & Restaurant..................	(see 18)
Chanthoumna's Restaurant.................	**23** B3
Restaurant Fleur de Mekong...............	**24** A3
Seng Ahloune Restaurant...................	(see 24)

SOUTHERN LAOS

Phan Don's best 'library' is here (books are loaned for US$1 and you are required to leave a deposit), and the **restaurant** (meals US$1-2) is worth visiting for its breakfasts, shakes, dhal and *làap*, all of which are delicious.

Miss Noy's Sunset Guesthouse & Restaurant (☎ mobile 020-2337112; bungalow US$1) The lovely Noy has been operating in this prime spot for years. The bungalows have good airflow, and the **restaurant** (meals US$1-2) does its Lao and mixed Asian food well.

Rasta Cafe Guest House (☎ mobile 020-2274293; Sunrise Blvd; r US$1) The rooms aren't flash and can be quite hot but the big communal balcony, inevitable Marley music and vivacious Mama (expect to be slapped for any insolence) make this place popular. The **café** (meals US$0.70-US$2) can be busy in the evenings.

Mr Vong's Guest House Hang Det (bungalow US$1) At the south end of Don Det, some bungalows here should have attached bathrooms by 2005 – and a US$3 price. There's a mostly Japanese travellers' book and the **riverside restaurant** (meals US$0.80-US$2) serves good Lao food.

Nar Place (Sunset Strip; bungalow US$1) This place has detached bungalows, each with two

Don Det

Souksan Hotel (☎ mobile 020-2270414; r US$3-10) A branch of Don Khong's Souksan Hotel located at the northern tip of Don Det, the sturdy bungalows with shared bathroom and rooms with private bathroom are the best on the island. All have fans, which run from about 7pm to 10pm. The **restaurant** (meals US$1.50-3.50) has the best view of the sunset, though it can get pretty hot. The food here is a mix of Lao and assorted other Asian cuisines and isn't bad.

Mr Tho's Bungalows & Restaurant (☎ mobile 020-2408576; Sunrise Blvd; bungalow US$1) Just south of the pier, these nine riverside bungalows and are well known for their relaxed atmosphere and super-friendly owners. Si windows, in a particularly attractive, quiet and shaded location.

Thon Don Family Bungalows & Sunset Cafe (Sunset Strip; bungalow US$1) This place is similar to Nar but less shaded.

Mama & Papa's Guest House & Restaurant (Sunrise Blvd; bungalow US$1) It's all about Mama here, who one traveller described as 'sweetness personified'. The atmospheric **restaurant** (meals US$0.80-1.50) serves some of the best food on the island – the dhal with lemongrass is recommended. Popular with solo women.

Santiphab Guesthouse (bungalow US$1) Beside the north end of the bridge, Santiphab has been around for years and has a deservedly good reputation. The **restaurant** (meals US$1-2.50) is a popular stop for hikers and cyclists, and is a cooler place for a sunset drink.

Mr B's Guest House & Bungalows (Sunset Strip; bungalow US$1) Around a large open yard, the huts here are less important than English-speaking Mr B's welcome and the food at his **café** (meals US$1-2.50) is wonderful (if a bit slow in arriving); the pumpkin burger has achieved legendary status.

Seng Chan's Bungalows (Sunrise Blvd; bungalow US$1) These four thatched-roofed and detached bungalows have two beds and two windows each and sit right on the river. It's a good choice.

Sunrise Blvd is home to many other lodgings. From north to south:

Khampong Guest House (Sunrise Blvd; r US$1) Cramped guesthouse near the beach (and the action).

Vixay Guest House (Sunrise Blvd; r US$1) Similar to Khampong.

Nou Phit Guest House (Sunrise Blvd; r US$1) Also similar to Khampong.

Malay Thong Guest House (Sunrise Blvd; bungalow US$1) Decent bungalows.

Mr Man's Guest House (Sunrise Blvd; bungalow US$1) Decent bungalows.

Mr Noi's Guest House (Sunrise Blvd; bungalow US$1) Decent bungalows.

Oudomsouk Bungalows (Sunrise Blvd; bungalow US$1) The bungalows here have two double beds in each.

Mr Friends Bungalows (Sunrise Blvd; bungalow US$1) The bungalows here are detached.

Mr Phao's Guest House (Sunrise Blvd; bungalow US$1) South of the pier, Mr Phao's has lounge chairs, multiple windows and multiple hammocks.

Guesthouse Mr Hom (Sunrise Blvd; r US$2.50) Rooms with attached bathrooms in a very quiet part of the island.

Don Khon

Auberge Sala Don Khone (☎ in Vientiane 021-242021; www.salalao.com; s/d with breakfast US$16/22) The three rooms in a French-era hospital are the choice for romantics (only the middle room has a double bed), while the sur-

---

CROSSING THE CAMBODIAN BORDER AT VOEN KHAM

While still not an internationally recognised crossing at the time of writing, this remote border has become popular with travellers seeking the exotic, or just to avoid the long detour via Thailand to get to Cambodia. It's possible to take a bus direct to Voen Kham from Vientiane, but most travellers come from Don Khong via Hat Xai (35km), or from Don Det or Don Khon via Ban Nakasang (US$0.80, 13km). In the mornings, *săwngthăew* leave frequently from these villages or you could arrange a door-to-border trip (about US$3) from any guesthouse on the islands.

The border itself is the Mekong River and is marked by small wooden buildings on both sides. Note that you cannot get a Cambodian visa here, so get it sorted in Bangkok or Vientiane. You'll be asked for a small 'processing fee' on both sides of the border, which ranges between US$1 and US$5 depending on how much you joke/flirt with the officials – stock up on US$1 bills.

Once through Lao immigration you'll have to face the cartel of Cambodian boatmen determined to rip you off. You'll be asked US$50, but should settle for US$40, for three or four seats in a jet boat to Stung Treng (90 minutes). You'll probably have to spend the night in Stung Treng before taking the 7.30am boat to Kratie (US$7) or Kompong Cham (US$15) the following day. The **Riverside Guesthouse** (r US$3-4) is the standout.

Coming north, jet boats from Stung Treng cost only US$4 or US$5 per person (yes, going south *is* a rip off). From Voen Kham, charter a jumbo or tuk-tuk to Nakasang (about US$1 per person). Stopping at Khon Phapheng (p237) is a good way to see the falls without paying for a costly tour later.

Details of this crossing are highly susceptible to change, so speak to fellow travellers or check the **Thorn Tree** (http://thorntree.lonelyplanet.com/) before setting out.

rounding sturdy wooden bungalows with terracotta tile roofs, verandas and attached cold-water bathrooms are nice, but perhaps a little overpriced; negotiation is possible and from May to September prices drop to US$14/16. A generator runs from 6pm to 10pm, longer if you pay for it. On the river's edge directly opposite is a **restaurant** (meals US$2-5; ☼ 7am-10pm) that serves decent Western and Lao food in a serene setting on the river. The owner speaks good English and is a mine of knowledge about the island.

Sala Phae (☎ mobile 020-2240325; luesakj@laotel .com; r about US$20) This 'raftel', as the owner puts it, was being finished when we passed. The bamboo rafts (*phae* means raft) each support two very comfortable rooms with bio-safe toilet in the hot-water bathroom, and small balcony. There are plans for 24 hour electricity from the 'hydroelectric power stations' underneath. The rafts are connected by a walkway to the **Bamboo Bar & Restaurant** (meals US$1.50-3; ☼ 7am-11pm), where the local speciality of fish roasted with Bolaven potatoes and salt (US$1.50) is recommended. It's a good place for a sunset cocktail.

Mama Dam Restaurant & Guest House (r US$1) These five rooms on the river's edge are nothing special, but the location looking up to the bridge is and the food in Mama's **restaurant** (meals US$1-2; ☼ breakfast, lunch & dinner) is special – the chicken *làap* and chicken with basil are mouthwatering.

Mr Bounh's Guest House (r US$5) Just south of the Auberge Sala Don Khone, these three bamboo-and-thatch bungalows have rooms with cold-water bathroom and squat toilet.

Somphamit Guest House (r US$3) Beside the river opposite Mr Bounh's, the battery-powered lights and two windows are probably not worth the extra cash.

Chanthounma's Restaurant (meals US$1-2.50; ☼ 7am-9.30pm) Chanthounma's offers 'good food to suit your mood', the Lao of which is, in fact, excellent.

Seng Ahloune Restaurant (☎ mobile 020-2207290; meals US$1-3; ☼ 7am-11pm) The Vietnamese spring rolls are just one of the very edible offerings on this epic menu; the curries and vegetarian meals are also recommended. Seating is on decking over the river.

Restaurant Fleur de Mekong (meals US$1-1.50; ☼ 7am-11pm) On a deck over the river and right next to the bridge, the Lao meals here are good value without being exceptional.

GETTING THERE & AWAY

The small boats ferrying passengers between Ban Nakasang and Don Det cost US$0.50 per person or US$1.50 charter. To Don Khon it's US$1 or US$3. Boats can be hired to go anywhere in the islands for about US$10 an hour.

For Pakse (US$2, three to four hours, 148km), buses or *sǎwngthǎew* leave Ban Nakasang at 6am, 8am, 9am and 10am. See p217 for buses from Pakse.

Khon Phapheng Falls

ນ້ຳຕົກຕາດຄອນພະເພັງ

South of Don Khong the Mekong River features a 13km stretch of powerful rapids with several sets of cascades. The largest, **Khon Phapheng** (admission US$0.90), flows between the eastern shore of the Mekong near Ban Thakho. A wooden pavilion on the Mekong shore affords a good view of the falls. A shaky network of bamboo scaffolds on the rocks next to the falls is used by daring fishermen who are said to have an alliance with the spirits of the cascades.

GETTING THERE & AWAY

Most people book a trip through a guesthouse to get to the falls, usually taking in both the falls and dolphins (see p234) and costing about US$4.50 from Don Det or Don Khon, or US$6 from Don Khong. If you're making the journey yourself, it's best to get to Nakasang and take a *sǎwngthǎew* from there. From Nakasang to Khon Phapheng Falls you can hire a motorcycle taxi for about US$3.50 or a jumbo for US$10 (this is a return fare for the whole jumbo and should include at least two hours at the falls). If the river is high enough a boatman can take you direct from Don Khon to the falls for about US$10 return.

SALAVAN PROVINCE

Like Sekong and Attapeu Provinces to the south, Salavan is notable as much for its remoteness as any traditional tourism draws. Salavan (also spelt Saravan or Saravane) is not on the way to anywhere and roads remain some of the worst in Laos, but it is these very qualities and the lure of tough travel that have begun to attract visitors looking to get well-and-truly off the beaten track.

There are, of course, attractions, and the ethnic diversity of the region is among the greatest. While more than half of the population of Salavan is ethnically Lao (Loum and Soung), none are native to this area. The remainder of the 295,000 inhabitants belong to 14 relatively obscure Mon-Khmer groups, including the Ta-oy (Tahoy), Lavai, Katang, Alak, Laven, Ngai, Tong, Pako, Kanay, Katu and Kado. For a taste of their lifestyle you can stay in the towns of Tahoy (Ta-oy people) and Tumlan (Katang); see p239.

Almost half the province is covered by natural forest and three areas have received protected status. The **Phu Xieng Thong NPA** covers 995 sq km adjacent to the Mekong River in the western part of the province (about 40km north of Pakse), the only NPA in Laos that encompasses the river's typical flats and sandbanks. The opposite bank is protected by Thailand's Pha Taem National Park; both sides are characterised by exposed sandstone ridges and outcroppings (some of which contain rock shelters with prehistoric paintings), interspersed with scrub and mixed monsoon deciduous forest. Rare beasts thought to inhabit this area (on the Lao side) include wild cattle (gaur and banteng), elephant, Douc langur, gibbon, Asiatic black bear, clouded leopard, tiger and Siamese crocodile. At this stage the **Se Xap NPA** in the far east and **Se Ban Nuan NPA** nearer to Rte 13, are very difficult to access.

Just about every major branch of the **Ho Chi Minh Trail** cut through Salavan at some point and UXO remains a serious problem. In Salavan town and most towns to its east you can expect to see plenty of rusted war detritus waiting for scrap merchants to cart it off to Vietnam. Meanwhile, clearance teams head out almost every day to continue the painstaking task of finding and neutralising these weapons of war.

Salavan also straddles the northern edge of the Bolaven Plateau and Tat Lo (p220), just 30km from Salavan town, makes a good alternative base from which to explore the province.

SALAVAN
ສາລະວັນ

☎ 034 / pop 76,493

Before it was renamed Salavan (Sarawan in Thai) by the Siamese in 1828, this area was a Champasak kingdom outpost known

as Muang Mam and inhabited mostly by Mon-Khmer minorities. The provincial capital of Salavan was all but destroyed in the Indochina War, when it bounced back and forth between Royal Lao Army and Pathet Lao occupation. The rebuilt town is a collection of brick and wood buildings with the post office being one of the few surviving colonial-era structures.

While Salavan is the best place from which to explore the province, a tranquil rural atmosphere is about all the town itself has to recommend it. For the most part Salavan serves as a supply centre for farmers in surrounding districts.

Information

The **Lao Development Bank** (🕒 8.30am-3.30pm Mon-Fri), a little west of the market, will change US dollars or Thai baht cash; if it's closed, try the market. The post office is around the corner from the market, and next door is a **telecom office** (🕒 8am-6pm Mon-Sat) where international calls can be made.

The unmissable large Municipal Authority building near the town centre is home to the **NTAL** (☎ 211528; Ground fl; 🕒 8.30am-noon & 1.30-4pm Mon-Fri), where the French- and English-speaking Mr Bounthone Sinachak is well worth chatting with if you plan on heading further into the province. If you ask nicely he might give you a handy booklet about the province. Alternatively, Tim Guesthouse & Restaurant in Tat Lo (p220) has plenty of information.

Sleeping & Eating

All the lodgings in Salavan have a mix of fan and air-con rooms with and without private bathrooms. There are several noodle shops in the vicinity of the market and at the bus station.

Saise Guest House (☎ 211054; r US$4-8; 🕸) On a rambling plot about 1km east of the market, the government-owned Saise has some of the best rooms in town, and some other not-so-good rooms. The newer 'Hotel' building has both huge and tiny air-con rooms, all for US$8. The older wooden building has airy but dusty fan rooms (US$4) with two or three beds.

Chindavone Guest House (☎ 211065; r US$4-7; 🕸) Near the market right in the centre of town, the bungalows here have large rooms with hot-water bathrooms, TV, and both fan and air-con. Less appealing are the steamy fan rooms with shared bathroom in the main house.

Sinsamay Guest House (☎ 211056; r US$3-7; 🗷) Not far from Chindavone, the rooms and shared facilities here are clean and spacious, the service friendly and the VIP rooms with air-con and bathroom are well worth a look.

Nong Vilaivane (☎ 211014; meals US$1.50-2.90) Beside the market, this attractive-looking place with bamboo walls and ceiling fans is probably the pick of Salavan's eateries. The menu includes Lao, Vietnamese and Chinese dishes.

In the same street as the Chindavone and Sinsamay are the **Thipphaphone Guest House** (☎ 211063; r US$3-7; 🗷), with a wide variety of rooms, some with satellite TV; and the **Miss Asim Guesthouse** (☎ 211062; r US$4-6; 🗷) where guests seldom stay the whole night; try the others first.

Getting There & Away
BUS & SĂWNGTHĂEW

For buses from Pakse see p217. Salavan's bus terminal is 2km west of the town centre where Rte 20 meets the rough Rte 15. Buses for Pakse (US$1.70, 115km) leave about every hour from 6.30am until 1.30pm. Buses or *săwngthăew* leave for Sekong (US$2, two to three hours, 93km) at 7.30am and 12.30pm, stopping at Tha Taeng (US$1, one to 1½ hours, 49km).

To get anywhere north or east of Salavan you'll need to take an infrequent *săwngthăew* along potholed stretches of earth that pretend to be roads. Contrary to the impression given on maps of Laos, unless you're in a 4WD the only way to get to Rte 9 is by going back to Rte 13. Rte 23 is not passable, and hasn't been since most of the bridges were obliterated during the Indochina War. It is, however, a very interesting road from the perspective of those interested in the local Austro-Asiatic tribes.

AROUND SALAVAN

Upcountry Salavan Province is an adventurer's delight, partly because getting to anywhere worth seeing is an adventure in itself. Northeast along Rte 15, which can be impassable for days during the wet season, is **Tahoy** (Ta-oy), a centre for the Ta-oy ethnic group, who number around 26,000 spread across the eastern areas of Salavan and Sekong Provinces. The Ta-oy live in forested mountain valleys at altitudes between 300m and 1000m, often in areas shared with the Katu and other Mon-Khmer groups. Like many Mon-Khmer groups in Southern Laos, they practise a combination of animism and shamanism; during village ceremonies, the Ta-oy put up diamond-patterned bamboo totems outside the village to warn outsiders not to enter. The Ta-oy people's distinctively patterned textiles are valued locally and by collectors in Vientiane.

Tahoy town was an important marker on the **Ho Chi Minh Trail** and two major branches lead off Rte 15 nearby. If you want to see war junk ask a local to take you; you might need to draw pictures of bombs or tanks to get your message across. If you come to Tahoy you'll likely have to stay. The government lets out **rooms** (US$3) in a simple building. Tahoy is tiger country and there's a good chance you'll hear them at night. There are so many, apparently, that leaving the town after dark is deemed too dangerous.

A *săwngthăew* leaves Salavan for Tahoy (US$1.50, three to four hours, 84km) every two days, though in the wet season this is not a guaranteed service. Alternatively, ask Mr Bounthone Sinachak at the NTAL (p238) about hiring a 4WD pick-up.

Nearer to Salavan is the Katang village of **Tumlan**, about 50km north along Rte 23. The area is famous for its weavings and Lapup festival (see The Katu & Alak Buffalo Sacrifice p218) usually held at the end of February. A bus leaves Salavan for Tumlan (two hours) daily at 2pm, returning the following day at 7am. You can stay in the simple government guesthouse.

The lake of **Nong Bua**, 14km east of town along a seasonal road near the source of the Se Don, is famous for its dwindling population of Siamese crocodiles (*khàe* in Lao). But as the population has dwindled to just two, and the journey is both difficult and hard to organise, it's hardly worth the effort for such a slim chance of seeing them. If you're still keen, the wet season is your best bet but at this time you'll need to take a boat. Phu Katae, a 1588m peak, is visible nearby.

SEKONG PROVINCE

Straddling the eastern edge of the Bolaven Plateau, this rugged and remote province is dotted with waterfalls and dissected by the impressive Se Kong river. By population Sekong is the smallest of Laos's provinces, but among its 70,000-odd inhabitants are people from 14 different tribal groups, making it the most ethnically diverse in the country. It's also one of the poorest, with basic infrastructure such as hospitals and schools rudimentary at best. Childhood mortality is distressingly high here and malaria is a constant killer in the lowland regions; see p281 for details on precautions.

It's perhaps no surprise, then, that this province of mountains, rivers and ancient slash-and-burn agriculture is one of the least visited areas in Laos. Those who come, however, are amply rewarded: waterfalls including the truly breathtaking Nam Tok Katamtok await…

The sparse population in Sekong consists mainly of Lao Theung or Mon-Khmer tribes, including the Chatong, Chieng, Laven, Kakang, Katang, Katu, Lawae, Nge, Suay, Talieng, Ta-oy (Tahoy), Yai and Ye. Many of these diverse tribes migrate between hilly Sekong and the Central Highlands of Vietnam (where they are known as Montagnards).

The largest groups are Katu and Talieng. The latter total about 25,000 and are found primarily in the district of Dak Cheung, east of the provincial capital and 1500m above sea level. Both groups tend towards monogamy but tolerate polyandry (two or more husbands); their belief systems mix animism and ancestor worship.

Note that in the wet season travelling anywhere off Rte 16 can be very difficult.

SEKONG (MUANG LAMAM)

ເຊກອງ (ເມືອງລະມັ່ງ)

☎ 038 / pop 18,000

With its rich ethnic mix and different sensibility from the larger Mekong River towns in southern Laos, Sekong makes an interesting base from which to visit more-remote villages, the surrounding waterfalls or to embark on a river trip down the Se Kong to Attapeu.

Carved out of the wilderness in the mid-1980s, the sprawling town features a group of government buildings in the centre, surrounded by areas of wood-and-thatch stilt homes among the cement and wooden ones.

The Se Kong river wraps around the town on the southern and eastern sides, while the Bolaven Plateau rises precipitously to the west. At the town market, border tribes trade cloth for Vietnamese goods. It's worth visiting the UXO Lao office opposite the Ministry of Finance office, just west of the market. These guys have been clearing UXO here for years and have built an interesting and educational installation in their yard, using some of the weapons they've rendered inert. Visitors are welcome.

Information

The only real information offered here is in the Pha Thip Restaurant menu, which has information on local ethnic groups, villages, handicrafts and travel, most of it prepared by a United Nations Development Programme (UNDP) caseworker.

The **Lao Development Bank** (⏰ 8-11am & 2-4pm Mon-Fri) is on the road directly behind Souksamlane Sekong Hotel; it changes cash Thai baht and US dollars for kip only. The **post office** (⏰ 8-11am & 1-4pm Mon-Fri) is beside the bank on the road behind Sekong Souksamlane Hotel; it offers a **telephone service** (☎ 8am-noon, 1-5pm & 6-8pm Mon-Fri) for local and international calls.

Sleeping & Eating

Several modest restaurants and fŏe shops can be found near the market. At sunset locals tend to gather at a no-name bar by the Se Kong, just down from the Pha Thip Restaurant.

Sekong Souksamlane Hotel (☎ 211039; r US$4.50-7.20; 🔀) The 16 rooms here are fairly decent; the fan rooms on the ground floor (US$4.50) and the air-con rooms upstairs (US$7.20) have hot water, but the service can be a bit too relaxed. The **restaurant** (meals US$1.50-4; ⏰ 7am-9pm) is not as good as it used to be. There is a handicrafts shop upstairs (see Shopping p241).

Sack Da Guest House (☎ 211086; r US$4-7; 🔀) This slightly dishevelled place just west of the market has decent rooms with TV

DOWN THE SE KONG BY LONGTAIL BOAT

With Routes 23 and 16 improved, boats down the Se Kong to Attapeu are hard to find these days. However, if you ask around in town – perhaps at the Pha Thip Restaurant – or at the river you should find a long-tail boat and boatman willing to take you for about US$30, depending on the river level and your bargaining skills. The scenic trip takes four to seven hours depending on the season and which direction you're going.

It's a wonderful journey; the river parallels the eastern escarpment of the Bolaven Plateau most of the way. During the late dry season, you may have to get out and walk along a path next the river while the boat pilot manoeuvres the craft through shallow rapids. The Se Kong is quite swift during the rainy season – if you're not a good swimmer, this journey may not be for you.

Remember that the cheapest boatman will not necessarily be the best – it's worth looking for someone with experience. Also, if a life jacket is provided be prepared to wear it; the last time a *falang* (Westerner) drowned on this trip (in very unlucky circumstances) the boatman got 10 years.

---

and cold-water bathrooms. Fan rooms cost US$4.

Somchay Guest House (r US$4.50-6.50; 🛱) At the north end of town, down a small lane off Rte 23, the rooms in the new Somchay are very clean, but a bit dark and pricey, with cold-water bathrooms.

Pha Thip Restaurant (meals US$1.50-2.50; 🕙 8am-9pm) Opposite the Sekong Souksamlane Hotel, this place offers a variety of tasty Vietnamese, Lao and Western dishes (the deep-fried fish with vegetables is a favourite), makes heavenly fruit shakes and has the most informative menu in Laos. Some English is spoken, there is a book exchange and simple **rooms** (US$3). Recommended.

Khamting Restaurant (🕿 mobile 020-5637945; meals US$1.50-2.50; 🕙 8am-9pm) Beside the Pha Thip, this place offers Vietnamese, Chinese, Lao and Western food and has some basic rooms to let.

Shopping

The cheapest place to buy tribal textiles is the market (where a sarong-sized textile of recent manufacture should cost no more than US$10), but the selection is not as good as in the following shops.

Sekong Ethnic Store (🕙 8am-6pm) A bamboo-thatch place on the street behind the Souksamlane Sekong Hotel and across from the post office, Sekong Ethnic a good range of textiles woven by the Alak, Katu, Nge and Talieng tribes, plus a few baskets and other tribal products. This is a good place to sort out the different colours and patterns of the various tribes. Katu cloth, for example, typically shows broad bands of red and black

with small white beads sewn into the fabric, while Alak designs use a more refined stripe. Rare Alak or Nge loincloths – long, narrow, heavy beaded affairs – can occasionally be found on sale for as much as US$200.

Lao Handicrafts Shop (🕿 211039; 1st fl, Sekong Souksamlane Hotel; 🕙 8am-4pm) Among the piles of textiles here you might find rare (though not necessarily expensive) examples of sarongs or blankets with stylised helicopter and fighter-jet motifs alongside traditional renditions of scorpions and lizards. If it's closed, ask reception to let you in.

Getting There & Away

BUS

Sekong's dusty/muddy bus station is about 2km north of town off Rte 23; a tuk-tuk there costs about US$0.40. Few buses actually originate in Sekong, rather stopping here between Pakse and Attapeu. For Pakse (US$2.50, 3½ to 4½ hours, 135km) expect buses every couple of hours from 7am until about 3pm. For Attapeu (US$1.50, two hours, 76km) they stop every two hours or so from about 9am until 4pm. Two buses a day go to Salavan (US$2, two to three hours, 93km); ask ahead for schedules.

Alternatively, simply park yourself on the main highway and flag down a bus or truck that's going in your direction. For transport from Pakse see p217.

Getting Around

Sekong has a couple of jumbos that will take you almost anywhere in town for about US$0.40.

AROUND SEKONG

Off Rte 16 south of Sekong there are several villages and waterfalls that could be visited as part of a day trip; you'd have to hire a bicycle or motorbike from someone in Sekong, or charter a tuk-tuk (US$6 for six hours). About 5km south of town, turn right along a rough dirt road immediately after a school. Follow the dirt road about 2.5km to the Tat Hia (Tat Hien) waterfall. A little further along Rte 16, another path heads southeast for about 3km toward the Se Kong and two Alak villages. The first is known for its fine *sín*s (border patterns on sarongs). Similar villages can be found at the end of dirt roads leading east 12km and 14km from Sekong.

The road at Km 14 also leads to **Tat Faek** (look for the sign). On the Se Nam Noi not far upriver of the Se Kong, Tat Faek is about 5m high and there are two pools in which you can swim. However, swimmers should use the one above the falls, as puffer fish are known to lurk in the pool below. Tat Faek is about 1.5km off the road; take the right fork after about 500m, then turn left at the T-junction another 800m on.

At Km 16 a long bridge crosses the Se Nam Noi and you enter Attapeu Province. Just south of the bridge a road leads east to **Tat Se Noi**, known locally as 'waterfall of the heads' (Tat Hua Khon) owing to a WWII incident in which Japanese soldiers decapitated a number of Lao soldiers and tossed their heads into the falls. The falls are about 100m wide and 7m deep, and you can jump from this height into a pool below.

Nam Tok Katamtok

ນ້ຳຕົກກະຕຳຕອກ

Running off the Bolaven Plateau, the Huay Katam drops more than 100m out of thick forest at the remote waterfall known as Nam Tok Katamtok. While not necessarily any bigger than Tat Fan, these falls are perhaps more impressive because you have to be something of an explorer to find them. Turn west along a laterite road 25km south of Sekong that, if it was passable, would eventually lead to Paksong. There are actually two falls to be seen from this road. The first is after 16km, where if you look off to the north (right) you'll see a large cascade in the distance. Nam Tok Katamtok is 2km further on; a short footpath leads off to the south and out of the jungle appears this spectacular drop.

ATTAPEU PROVINCE

Attapeu is the wild east of Laos. It's frontier territory in every sense, with the rugged and densely forested regions bordering Cambodia and Vietnam teeming with wildlife. Tigers aren't uncommon, and there's rumoured to be either Javan or Sumatran rhino near the Cambodian border. Like Sekong and Salavan, Attapeu is difficult to get around. Such remoteness has left border regions dangerously exposed to Vietnamese logging operations some of which are legal, others taking advantage of legal loopholes.

The Ho Chi Minh Trail ran through Attapeu and the region was heavily bombed during the Indochina War. Of the 11 ethnic groups found in Attapeu, Lave, Nge and Talieng predominate, with Lao Loum, Chinese and Vietnamese concentrated in the capital. There are less than 20 Buddhist temples in the entire province.

ATTAPEU (SAMAKHI XAI)

ອັດຕະປື

☎ 036 / pop 19,200

Officially known as Muang Samakhi Xai but seldom referred to as such, the capital of Attapeu Province is set in a large valley surrounded by the mountains of the nearby Bolaven Plateau, 1000m above, and the two rivers at whose junction it is located – the Se Kong and the smaller Se Kaman. Attapeu is famed in Southern Laos as the 'garden village' for its shady lanes and lush flora. While thoroughly deserved, this reputation is all the more remarkable given that Attapeu actually means 'buffalo shit' in Lao. Legend has it that when early Lao Loum people arrived they asked the locals what was the name of their town. In response, the villagers apparently pointed at a nearby pile of buffalo manure, known locally as *itkapu*. There was (hopefully) some misunderstanding, or perhaps the Lao Loum or even the villagers actually didn't like the place. Either way, with some subsequent adjustment in pronunciation, the town became Attapeu.

While Attapeu has little in the way of bona fide 'sights' it is a far from shitty town. The engaging locals, cheap accommodation and riverside 'sunset' drinking spots make this a good base for exploring the wild east, a job made simpler by the recent completion of a bridge across the Se Kong and ongoing work on new highway 18B to Vietnam.

Information

Attapeu Office of Tourism (☎ 212039; Provincial Hall) On the northwestern edge of town this office has guides (usually a staff member), though you'll find better value (less than US$20 a day) by asking around town. You can look at their large-scale map on the wall.

Lao Development Bank (about 500m southeast of the airstrip) Changes US dollars or Thai baht for kip at poor rates.

Metro Internet (☎ 211492; Rte 18; per hr US$4; 8am-7pm) There's only one terminal here, though more are said to be coming.

Post office (8am-noon & 1-4pm Mon-Fri)

Telephone office (7am-5pm, Mon-Sat) Beside the post office, these hours are not set in stone.

Sights

Attapeu is not renowned for its Buddhist temples. The most interesting is **Wat Luang Muang Mai** – usually known as Wat Luang – in the centre of town. It was built in 1939 and features some older monastic buildings with original *naga* bargeboards.

A couple of hundred metres west is an open field with an overgrown **bust of Kaysone Phomvihane** and a diminutive, rusting **Ferris wheel**. The latter will appeal to photographers on weekends, when children can often be seen scrambling all over it.

Tham Pha is a cave shrine containing Buddhist statuary located about 3km northwest of town in the foothills of the Bolaven Plateau.

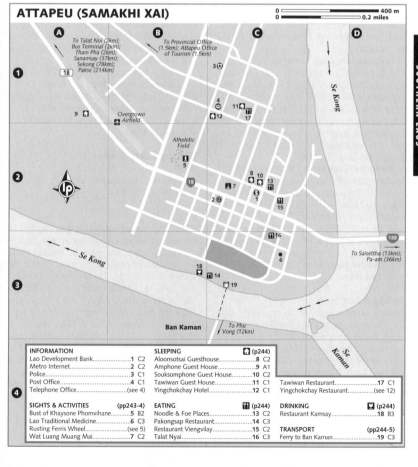

ATTAPEU (SAMAKHI XAI)

INFORMATION	
Lao Development Bank	1 C2
Metro Internet	2 C2
Police	3 C1
Post Office	4 C1
Telephone Office	(see 4)

SIGHTS & ACTIVITIES	(pp243-4)
Bust of Khaysone Phomvihane	5 B2
Lao Traditional Medicine	6 C3
Rusting Ferris Wheel	(see 5)
Wat Luang Muang Mai	7 C2

SLEEPING	(p244)
Aloonsotsai Guesthouse	8 C2
Amphone Guest House	9 A1
Souksomphone Guest House	10 C2
Tawiwan Guest House	11 C1
Yingchokchay Hotel	12 C1

EATING	(p244)
Noodle & Foe Places	13 C2
Pakongsap Restaurant	14 C3
Restaurant Viengvilay	15 C3
Talat Nyai	16 C3

Tawiwan Restaurant	17 C1
Yingchokchay Restaurant	(see 12)

DRINKING	(p244)
Restaurant Kamsay	18 B3

TRANSPORT	(pp244-5)
Ferry to Ban Kaman	19 C3

Activities

After a motorbike adventure (motorbikes can be hired from Souksomphone Guest House), sweat out the dust at the **Lao Traditional Medicine** (☺ 3-7pm Tue & Thu-Sun), which is actually a sauna place.

Sleeping

Yingchokchay Hotel (☎ 211031, mobile 020-5604679; r US$4-24.50; ☒) This unfeasibly large hotel two streets north of Rte 18 has easily the best rooms, and is the best value, in Attapeu. All rooms are clean, comfortable and spacious, and except for the economy fan rooms (US$4), all have fridge, hot water and satellite TV. VIP rooms (US$24.50) have a bathtub and are big enough to play football in. Breakfast is included in the rates of any room worth US$10 or more. The English-speaking manager is helpful, and gives guests a 20% discount in the restaurant.

Souksomphone Guest House (☎ 211046; r US$3-7.50; ☒) A block north of Rte 18, you won't miss the Souksomphone; it's the place with the mother-of-all hardwood staircases protruding from the front. The simple rooms are disappointing by comparison. The unflappable manager speaks some English and can arrange bicycle hire (US$2 a day) and motorbike hire (US$10).

Aloonsotsai Guesthouse (☎ 211250, mobile 020-5644385; r US$6; ☒) Just west of the Souksomphone, this two-storey aquamarine-coloured place has clean rooms with cold-water bathrooms and Vietnamese TV.

If these three are full, the **Amphone Guest House** (☎ 211069; Rte 18; r US$4-7; ☒) 1km northwest of town has simple, aging rooms; while the **Tawiwan Guest House** (Thavivanh; tw US$3) is your last resort.

Eating & Drinking

Noodle dishes and *fŏe* are available during the morning at the Talat Nyai, near the bridge, and other snacks can be had here at any time. There are a couple of cheap noodle and *fŏe* places just east of the Souksomphone Guest House that also specialise in tasty – though not always clean – barbecued pork, the repercussions of which prompted one traveller to ask despairingly: 'How can something so good be so bad?'

Restaurant Viengvilay (☎ mobile 020-5636266; meals US$1-2.50; ☺ 8am-8pm) The precooked food in this informal place is about the best Lao cuisine in town (the *làap* is delicious), but get here by 7pm or you might miss out.

Pakongsap Restaurant (meals US$2-4) This restaurant on the banks of the Se Kong specialises in fish dishes and does decent Lao and Vietnamese food. However, it keeps irregular hours and is often booked up for functions.

Restaurant Kamsay (☎ mobile 020-2337594; ☺ 2pm-10pm) Overlooking the Se Kong just west of the Pakongsap, this bamboo place is more about drinking than eating and is a favourite at sunset. If you do want food, the local speciality is barbecued goat (US$2 per plate), which you can wash down with Beerlao and fresh goat's blood (US$1).

Yingchokchay Restaurant (☎ 211031; meals US$2.50-6; ☺ breakfast, lunch & dinner) In the Yingchokchay Hotel, the food here consists of Korean barbecue, Asian dishes and a few European favourites.

Tawiwan Restaurant (meals US$1.50-3.50) This food is much better than the rooms in the adjacent guesthouse. The *kai nâm dąeng* (chicken in a red sauce) comes with boiled potatoes and is quite good. Ms Maniwan's son speaks some English.

Getting There & Away

BOAT

Attapeu can be reached by boat from Sekong via the Se Kong (see p241).

BUS

The long, slow process of upgrading Rte 16 between Sekong and Attapeu was almost complete when we passed. Because Rte 18 remains impassable to most traffic, all transport to or from Pakse goes via Paksong and Sekong. Buses leave Pakse (US$3.50, 4½ to six hours, 212km) at 6.30am, 8am, 10.30am and 1pm. From Attapeu, a 6am bus goes to Savannakhet (US$5, nine hours, one daily) via Pakse, and after that there are three other buses to Pakse (US$3.50, 4½ to six hours, 212km) at 6.45am, 7.30am and 10am. You can get off any of these buses at Sekong (US$1.50, two hours, 76km), and there is a 2.30pm bus that travels to Sekong only.

Gluttons for punishment might consider the 8.15am or 11am services direct to Vientiane (US$9.50, 22 to 24 hours, 812km). Most buses servicing Attapeu are older, naturally air-conditioned affairs.

The Asian Development Bank–funded road 18B, which is linking the Vietnam border to Attapeu and thus a new route between Vietnam and Thailand, is progressing though if recent form is anything to go by (and as long as the construction companies are allowed to log the surrounding areas while roadwork is underway) the remaining 65km to the Vietnamese border will not be finished for years to come.

The Attapeu bus terminal is next to Talat Noi at Km 3 northwest of town.

Getting Around

A jumbo trip around town should cost about US$0.20 per person. To/from the bus terminal costs about US$0.40.

AROUND ATTAPEU

To the east and southeast of the capital are the most heavily bombed districts along the Ho Chi Minh Trail, Sansai and **Phu Vong**. Here the trail splits into two, with the Sihanouk Trail heading into Cambodia, and the Ho Chi Minh Trail into southern Vietnam. Damaged and destroyed vehicles and equipment can still be seen lying about in the jungle, along with lots of UXO; don't attempt to explore this area without a local guide (ask at the government guesthouse). Phu Vong is an easy day trip from Attapeu; cross the Se Kong by passenger boat (US$0.05 per person and US$0.20 for a motorbike) to Ban Kaman, then take a *săwngthăew* (US$0.90, 30 minutes, 12km) to Phu Vong.

The northwestern part of the province near Sekong is home to some impressive **waterfalls**; for details see p242.

Attapeu Province has one NPA, **Dong Ampham**, a 1975-sq-km area which is wedged between the Se Kaman and the Vietnamese border. Timber poaching, even in protected and managed forests, threatens the pristine environment; Vietnamese loggers are believed to be working almost continuously in the area. Hydroelectric projects planned for the Se Kaman and Se Su also threaten the integrity of the Dong Ampham NPA. Until Rte 18B to the Vietnamese border is completed Dong Ampham is almost impossible to reach without a major expedition.

It's possible to take a boat down the Se Kong towards the **Cambodian border**, where the thick jungle meets the river like an impenetrable wall. If you fancy the road (or river) less travelled, then this might be for you. Apart from wildlife and untouched jungle, the border area has recently seen something of a gold rush, with dozens of Chinese and Vietnamese people panning by the banks of the river.

To get there, take a *săwngthăew* from the bus station to Sanamsay (US$1, 75 minutes, 35km) along Rte 18; *săwngthăew* leave Attapeu at 9am, noon, 2pm and 4pm, and the last one returns at 3pm. In Sanamsay find a boatman to take you to the border (about 30km, four to five hours). To get back to Sanamsay on the same day start early (hiring a jumbo or motorbike from Attapeu might be best). There is no guesthouse in Sanamsay, but you should be able to find somewhere to sleep if you can't get back to Attapeu.

Pa-am

ແປະ?

At this Alak village in Sansai district, about 35km east of Attapeu via the Rte 18B and another dirt road, a Russian surface-to-air **missile** (SAM) launcher – complete with an unfired missile stencilled in Russian and Vietnamese – has been left intact next to the Ho Chi Minh Trail. Other war junk can be seen in the village, though most has long ago been carted off to Vietnam as scrap.

Alak **textiles** can be bought in the shady village and you may be able to watch women weaving in their homes – ask first. There are several small cataracts in the Nam Pa where you can swim in the dry season, though plans for three Vietnamese dams in the area could put an end to that.

When coming from Attapeu you need to cross the Nam Pa to reach the missile launcher. An elderly man operates an improvised passenger and motorbike ferry, poling between the banks for about US$0.10 each way, US$0.30 for a bike. There is also a very rickety rope-and-bamboo footbridge.

GETTING THERE & AWAY

Passenger trucks to Pa-am (US$1.20, one hour, 35km) leave Attapeu every morning; you could also charter a jumbo or hire a motorbike from the Souksomphone Guest House (p244).

SOUTHERN LAOS

Directory

CONTENTS

ACCOMMODATION

The variety of accommodation in Laos continues to increase and in the three main cities – Vientiane, Luang Prabang and Pakse – you'll find places for nearly every budget. Elsewhere the selection is much more modest, typically restricted to budget-priced guesthouses and hotels, with the occasional mid-range offering.

It is almost always cheaper to pay in the requested currency rather than let the hotel or guesthouse convert the price into another currency. If the price is quoted in kip, you'll do best to pay in kip; if priced in dollars, pay in dollars. If you ask to pay a dollar-quoted

---

PRACTICALITIES

- The daily *Vientiane Times*, the only English-language newspaper permitted in Laos, cleaves to the party line.

- Francophones can read *Le Renovateur*, a government mouthpiece similar to the *Vientiane Times*.

- The LPDR's single radio station, Lao National Radio (LNR), broadcasts sanitised English-language news twice daily.

- Short-wave radios can pick up BBC, VOA, Radio Australia and Radio France International.

- Lao National Television has two TV channels with outdated American sitcoms and cartoons. Most Lao watch Thai TV.

- The LPDR uses 220V AC circuitry; power outlets most commonly feature two-prong round or flat sockets.

- LPDR follows the international metric system. Gold and silver are sometimes weighed in *bàat* (15g).

---

tariff in kip (or vice versa), you'll lose out to the hotel's mandated lower exchange rate. Because the kip is a soft, unstable currency, room rates in this book are given in the US dollar equivalent of the currency quoted by the particular accommodation.

Accommodation prices listed in this book are high-season prices for rooms with attached bathroom, unless stated otherwise. An icon is included to indicate if air-con is available; otherwise, assume that a fan will be provided. In this guide we include accommodation costing less than US$10 a night in the Budget category, from US$10 to US$40 in the Mid-Range category and over US$40 for Top End.

Guesthouses

The distinction between 'guesthouse', 'hotel' and 'resort' often exists in name only, but generally speaking a guesthouse in Laos has 10 or fewer rooms and rates run towards the budget side.

Guesthouses in Laos typically occupy large, two-storey homes of recent vintage, but occasionally you'll find them in historic homes. In more remote rural areas such as the island of Don Det in southern Laos or the village of Muang Ngoi Neua in northern Laos you may come across guesthouses consisting of simple bamboo-thatch huts.

The most inexpensive places to stay usually do not offer hot-water showers, but rather simple Lao-style bathing, where you wash yourself using a plastic bowl to scoop cold water from large jars or tanks. Hot water is hardly a necessity in lowland Laos, but would be very welcome in the mountains.

Rooms in most towns average between US$3 and US$5 a night per room with shared bathroom. In the more far-flung areas of the country rustic guesthouses with shared facilities cost as little as US$0.50 to US$1 per night per person.

Nicer rooms with attached toilet and hot shower tend to cost between US$6 and US$10 a night depending on size, condition and location. A few guesthouses may offer more upscale rooms in the US$15 to US$25 range.

Hotels

Hotel rooms in Vientiane, Luang Prabang, Savannakhet and Pakse offer private bathrooms and fans as standard features for between US$8 and US$15 a night. Better rooms with air-con and hot water cost between US$12 and US$30.

Small and medium-size hotels oriented towards Asian business and leisure travellers or the occasional tour group exist in the larger cities. In Vientiane, Luang Prabang, Savannakhet and Pakse these may be housed in charming old French colonial mansions. Whether modern or historic, tariffs at hotels such as these run from US$25 to US$60 for rooms with air-con, hot water, TV and refrigerator.

Top-end hotels with better décor, more facilities and personalised service, often occupying well-restored colonial villas, typically cost between US$40 and US$100, occasionally higher.

Resorts

The term 'resort' in the Lao context may be used for any accommodation situated outside towns or cities. It does not imply, as it usually does in many other countries, the availability of sports activities, spa and so on.

Lao resorts typically cost about the same as a mid-range hotel, ie from US$10 to US$40 a night. A few, such as those outside the city of Luang Prabang, come closer to the more international idea of what a resort should be, and these are priced well into the top-end category.

ACTIVITIES
Boating

The rivers and streams of Laos have potential for all sorts of recreational boating, particularly rafting, canoeing and kayaking. Tour agencies in Luang Nam Tha, Luang Prabang have recently begun offering guided rafting and kayaking trips, complete with the necessary equipment, along waterways in those areas.

As with bicycles, you shouldn't have any special customs difficulties should you decide to bring your own small boat to Laos. Because of the difficulties of overland transport, however, the smaller and lighter your craft is, the more choices you'll have for places to paddle.

For trained paddlers almost any of the major waterways draining from the western slopes of the Annamite Chain towards the Mekong valley can be interesting. In the north, the Nam Ou, Nam Tha, Nam Khan, Nam Ngum and of course the Mekong River are navigable year-round. In central and southern Laos the Nam Theun, Se Don, Se Set and Se Kong as well as the Mekong are safe bets. The upstream areas of all these rivers can be accessed by road, so drop-offs and pick-ups are limited only by the availability of public or private vehicle travel.

In the area between Vientiane and Tha Khaek, several tributaries that feed into the Mekong are smaller and less known than the aforementioned but very scenic since they run through rugged limestone country. In particular the Nam Xan, Nam Kading and Nam Hin Bun are wide and relatively clean rivers. The choices are somewhat limited by the availability of roads to take you upstream; see p193 and p194 for details. A company called **North-by-Northeast Tours** (www .thaitourism.com/tours.html), based in Nakhon Phanom, Thailand (directly across from Tha Khaek), offers river trips along the Nam Hin

Bun and other waterways in the Khammuan Limestone.

Between Champasak and the Cambodian border, the area of the Mekong known as Si Phan Don (Four Thousand Islands) is easily accessible and provides superior paddling possibilities among verdant islands and rapids.

Should you want to navigate in the local way, small new or used wooden canoes can be bought for between US$50 and US$100 without a motor; add from US$40 to US$60 for motors. Small Japanese outboard motors of 5.5HP to 11HP can be purchased in any of the larger cities along the Mekong River. These sorts of boats are suitable only for well-navigated waterways as their bulk prohibits portage around shallows or rapids.

Cycling

The overall lack of vehicular traffic makes cycling an attractive proposition in Laos, although this is somewhat offset by the general absence of roads in the first place. Bikes can be hired in the larger towns but they're generally not suited for much more than pedalling around town. For any serious out-of-town cycling you're better off bringing your own bike, one that's geared to very rough road conditions.

In terms of road gradient and availability of food and accommodation, the easiest long-distance ride is along Rte 13, which extends the entire north–south length of the country from Boten on the Chinese-Lao border south to Voen Kham on the Cambodian border. In the dry season this road may become very dusty even in the paved sections, and trucks – though nowhere near as overwhelming as in Vietnam or Thailand – can be a nuisance.

From Rte 13 you can easily hook up with newly sealed Rte 7 heading east from Muang Phu Khun to Phonsavan and beyond to the Vietnamese-Lao border.

Other cycling routes of interest – all of them currently unpaved and rough but due to be upgraded over the next decade – include: Luang Prabang to Muang Khua; Huay Xai to Luang Nam Tha; Pakse to Attapeu; Muang Xai to Phonsavan; and Sam Neua to Phonsavan. The last two routes are quite remote and require that you be prepared to camp if necessary along the way.

For routes to avoid, see p251.

Hiking & Trekking

The mountainous, forest-clad countryside makes Laos a potentially ideal destination for people who like to walk outdoors. All 13 provinces have plenty of hiking possibilities, although the cautious nature of the authorities means that overnight trips involving camping or staying in villages are viewed with suspicion. However, over the last five years the government has allowed a sprinkling of multiday trekking projects, so the situation is changing.

Many visitors trekking on their own have managed to spend the night in remote villages anyway. There doesn't appear to be any law forbidding this although it is somewhat frowned upon by the authorities in areas such as the provinces of Hua Phan, Sekong and Attapeu.

Day hiking is another story and you're free to walk in the mountains and forests almost anywhere in the country except the Saisombun Special Zone. See p251 for more information on this military-controlled district and for warnings on areas of eastern Laos contaminated by unexploded ordnance (see p252).

The provinces in Laos with the highest potential for relatively safe wilderness hikes include Bokeo, Luang Nam Tha, Luang Prabang, Vientiane, Khammuan and Champasak. In particular the 20 National Protected Areas (NPAs) should be rewarding territory for exploration. Of these Nam Ha NPA is the most geared towards organised group trekking. See p166 for more information.

Except at the occasional waterfall near towns or cities, recreation areas with public facilities are nonexistent in Laos.

BUSINESS HOURS

Government offices are typically open from 8am to 11.30am or noon and from 1pm to 5pm Monday to Friday. Some offices may open for a half day on Saturday but this custom was generally abandoned in 1998 when the official two-hour lunch break introduced by the French was reduced to one hour. Does this mean you can expect to find Lao officials back in their offices promptly at 1pm? Probably not.

Shops and private businesses open and close a bit later and either stay open during lunch or close for just an hour. On Saturday some businesses are open all day, others only

RESTAURANT HOURS

Business hours for Lao restaurants vary according to the type of clientele and type of food they serve.

■ Shops selling noodles and/or rice soup are typically open from 7am to 1pm.

■ Lao restaurants with a larger menu of dishes served with rice are often open from 10am to 10pm.

■ Tourist restaurants offering both Lao and *falang* (Western) food, and open for breakfast, lunch and dinner, usually open their doors around 7.30am and serve till 11pm.

■ Tourist restaurants that don't open for breakfast generally serve from 11am to 11pm.

half a day. Just about every business in Laos, except for restaurants, is closed on Sunday.

Most banks in Laos are open from 8.30am to 4pm Monday to Friday.

CHILDREN

Like many places in Southeast Asia, travelling with children in Laos can be a lot of fun as long as you come well prepared with the right attitudes, physical requirements and the usual parental patience. Lonely Planet's *Travel with Children* by Cathy Lanigan contains a lot of useful advice on how to cope with kids on the road and what to bring along to make things go more smoothly, with special attention paid to travel in developing countries.

Practicalities

Amenities geared towards children – such as high chairs in restaurants, child safety seats for vehicles, or nappy-changing facilities in public restrooms – are virtually unknown in Laos. Thus parents will have to be extra resourceful in seeking out substitutes or follow the example of Lao families. (which means holding smaller children on their laps much of the time).

Outside of Vientiane day-care centres are likewise unknown. The Lao adore children and in many instances will shower attention on your offspring, who will readily find playmates among their Lao peers and

a temporary nanny service at practically every stop.

Baby formula and nappies (diapers) are available at minimarkets in the larger towns and cities, but for rural areas you'll need to bring along a sufficient supply.

For the most part parents needn't worry too much about health concerns though it pays to lay down a few ground rules – such as regular hand-washing – to head off potential medical problems. All the usual health precautions apply; see p277 for details. Children should especially be warned not to play with animals encountered along the way since rabies is very common in Laos.

Sights & Activities

When younger children don't find the historic temples and French colonial architecture of Luang Prabang and Vientiane as inspiring as their parents do, the best thing is to head for the outdoors.

In Luang Prabang the waterfalls at Tat Sae (p136) and Tat Kuang Si (p135) can amuse most kids for days. Boat trips are usually good fun as well.

Most children also take to the unique Hindu-Buddhist sculpture garden of Xieng Khuan (p76) located on the outskirts of Vientiane.

Likewise the Plain of Jars (p145) invites the kind of fantasy exploration most kids are prone to.

CLIMATE CHARTS

The annual monsoon cycles that affect all of mainland Southeast Asia produce a 'dry and wet monsoon climate' with three basic seasons for most of Laos. The southwest monsoon arrives in Laos between May and July and lasts into November.

The monsoon is followed by a dry period (from November to May), beginning with lower relative temperatures and cool breezes created by Asia's northeast monsoon (which bypasses most of Laos), lasting until mid-February. Exceptions to this general pattern include Xieng Khuang, Hua Phan and Phongsali Provinces, which may receive rainfall coming from Vietnam and China during the months of April and May.

Rainfall varies substantially according to latitude and altitude, with the highlands of Vientiane, Bolikhamsai, Khammuan and eastern Champasak Provinces receiving the most precipitation.

Temperatures also vary according to altitude. In the humid, low-lying Mekong River valley, temperatures range from 15°C to 38°C, while the mountains of Xieng Khuang it can drop to 0°C at night. See p9 for comment on the best times to travel in Laos.

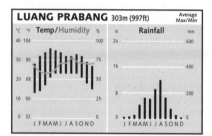

LUANG PRABANG 303m (997ft)

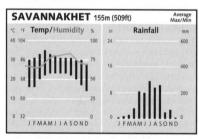

PAKSE 92m (305ft)

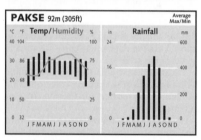

SAVANNAKHET 155m (509ft)

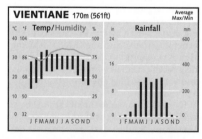

VIENTIANE 170m (561ft)

COURSES
Cooking
Tum Tum Cheng Restaurant & Cooking School (☎ 071-252019; Th Sakkarin) teaches Lao cuisine in Luang Prabang. See p79 for cooking courses in the capital.

Language
Short-term courses in spoken and written Lao are available at the following study centres in Vientiane:

Centre Culturel et de Coopération Linguistique (Map pp72-3; ☎ 021-215764; www.ambafrance-laos.org/centre; Th Lan Xang; ⊗ 9.30am-6.30pm Mon-Fri & 9.30am-noon Sat)

Lao-American College (☎ 021-900454; fax 900453; Th Phonkheng, Saysettha)

Vientiane College (☎ 021-414873; fax 414346; vtcollege@laopdr.com; Th That Luang) Opposite the WHO office.

Meditation
If you can speak Lao or Thai, or can arrange an interpreter, you may be able to study *vipassana* (insight meditation) at Wat Sok Pa Luang in southeast Vientiane. See p79 for details.

CUSTOMS
Customs inspections at ports of entry are very lax as long as you're not bringing in more than a moderate amount of luggage. You're not supposed to enter the country with more than 500 cigarettes or 1L of distilled spirits. All the usual prohibitions on drugs, weapons and pornography apply, otherwise you can bring in practically anything you want, including unlimited sums of Lao and foreign currency.

DANGERS & ANNOYANCES
Queues
The Lao follow the usual Southeast Asian method of queuing for services, which is to say they don't form a line at all but simply push en masse towards the point of distribution, whether it's ticket counters, post-office windows or bus doors. It won't help to get angry and shout 'I was here first!' since first-come, first-served simply isn't the way things are done here. Rather it's 'first-seen, first-served'. Learn to play the game the Lao way, by pushing your money, passport, letters or whatever to the front of the crowd as best you can. Eventually you'll get through.

TERRORIST BOMBINGS

Between March and December 2000 a string of small bombings or attempted bombings occurred in Vientiane, Savannakhet and Pakse. The first of these took place at a popular restaurant in Vientiane, and several foreign tourists were injured. No foreigners were affected in the subsequent 14 incidents. In almost all cases the incidents occurred in public places where large crowds congregated, such as the airport, post office and morning market.

Things stayed quiet after that till October 2003, when a small bomb placed at Talat Khua Din in Chiang Mai exploded; there were no injuries. The low incidence of injury across all of these bomb incidents suggest they were designed to promote an image of instability and danger in Laos, rather than to effect casualties.

Shortly after the October 2003 incident, two Lao military officers were arrested in conjunction with the Vientiane bombings. Although evidence is under the tight control of the Pathet Lao, third-party observers believe the two officers were paid to place bombs by a group called the Underground Government in Exile. Despite its claim of being based in Vientiane, observers speculate this is probably a small group of former Royal Lao aristocrats living in Thailand who are trying to discredit the Pathet Lao government.

So far in 2004 there have been no further reports of terrorist acts such as these, but you may want to check the latest situation with your embassy.

Road Travel

Hmong insurgency in Luang Prabang and Xieng Khuang Provinces continues to pose a slight security risk along Rtes 7 and 13, particularly in the vicinity of Muang Phu Khun and Kasi. These have been trouble spots more or less ever since the 1975 communist takeover, which left thousands of armed Hmong – previous allies of the Royal Government of Laos and its US and Thai supporters – in an embittered and embattled position. Despite the fact that both routes are now paved all the way, thus allowing Lao government troops to patrol Luang Prabang, Vientiane and Xieng Khuang Provinces more easily, violence still erupts from time to time.

Between 2001 and 2003 things were relatively quiet, but in February 2004, a Hmong attack on Rte 13 killed eight Lao bus passengers, plus two Swiss tourists who cycled into the situation.

That same month, after careful negotiations between the Lao military and Hmong leaders, around 700 armed Hmong insurgents surrendered in Luang Prabang and Xieng Khuang Provinces. Although it was widely hoped that this would mean an end to Hmong violence, in April 2004 another 12 died in a road attack in Muang Phu Khoun, at the junction of Rtes 7 and 13.

At the moment things seem quiet again, but it would be best to ask around in Vientiane or Luang Prabang to make sure the situation is still secure before embarking on any road trips along Rte 7 to Phonsavan or Rte 13 between Vientiane and Luang Prabang.

To the south of Rte 7, the Saisombun Special Zone, a relatively new administrative district, is another place to exercise caution. Carved out of eastern Vientiane, southwestern Xieng Khuang and northwestern Bolikhamsai Provinces in 1994, this 7105-sq-km district (larger than the province of Bokeo) is officially considered a 'troubled' area. The Lao government created the new zone with the intent of clearing up the guerrilla/bandit problem and has stationed two military battalions here to accomplish the task. Within the zone lies Long Cheng, formerly a CIA/USAF/Hmong army base during the Indochina War. In June 2004 seven Lao died in a Hmong attack in Saisombun.

The rugged mountains and upland valleys of the former Liberated Zones make as good a hiding place for anti-LPRP (Lao People's Revolutionary Party) organisations and other unruly sorts today as for the PL during the war.

ACCIDENTS

Despite the ongoing presence of an insurgency, the risk of road accidents remains by far the biggest danger plaguing the roadways of Laos. When riding in buses, you may be able to cut your risk of serious crash injuries

DIRECTORY

if you choose an aisle seat towards the middle of the bus. On your person, carry the number of your embassy in Vientiane and the number of **Aek Udorn Hospital** (☎ 0 4234 2555) in Udon Thani, Thailand, so that you can call for help if necessary.

Speedboats

In some areas of Northern Laos, particularly along the Nam Ou and Mekong River, a light and very fast type of boat called *héua wái* (literally 'fast boat', usually translated 'speedboat' in English) is a common form of riverine transport. Serious accidents, sometimes including fatalities, involving these speedboats seem to occur on an almost weekly basis. Usually they involve a boat striking a hidden rock or a tree limb, although occasionally contact with a standing wave is sufficient to capsize one of the light craft. Because of the high speed at which these boats travel, a simple capsize may have serious consequences for the passengers.

Although reliable statistics appear to be completely unavailable, our own observation is that the accident risk for this type of boat outweighs the potential savings in time they may represent over slower boat alternatives. In addition to the potential accident factor, these boats are tremendously noisy and disturbing to both animal and human life along the riverbanks. They also tend to be very cramped and uncomfort-

able. For all of the foregoing reasons, we recommend that you avoid all speedboat travel unless absolutely necessary.

Theft

On the whole, Lao are trustworthy people and theft is not much of a problem. Still, it's best if you keep your hotel room locked when you're out and at night. If you ride a crowded bus, watch your luggage and don't keep money in your trouser pockets. If you ride a bicycle or motorcycle in Vientiane, it's best not to place anything of value in the basket – at night thieving duos on motorbikes have been known to ride by and snatch bags from baskets.

We've also had a few reports of theft on buses between Vientiane and Luang Prabang, so watch your bags carefully and secure your valuables if you do this trip.

UXO

In the eastern portions of the country towards the Vietnamese border are large areas contaminated by unexploded ordnance (UXO) left behind by nearly 100 years of warfare. Despite heavy US bombing late in the Indochina War, the majority of UXO found today was left behind by ground battles and includes French, Chinese, American, Russian and Vietnamese materials, among them mortar shells, munitions, white phosphorus canisters, land mines and cluster bombs. US-made cluster bombs (known as *bombi* to the Lao) pose by far the greatest potential danger to people living or travelling through these areas and account for most of the estimated 130 casualties per year (in Cambodia, by comparison, the UN estimates 800 people per year are killed by UXO). Most of those injured or killed are Lao citizens, roughly 40% of whom are children. Large bombs up to 500kg dropped by US aircraft also lie undetonated in some areas, but it's very rare that one of these is accidentally detonated.

According to recent surveys undertaken by the Lao National UXO Programme (UXO Lao), financed by the UN under the auspices of the Ministry of Labour and Social Welfare, the provinces of Salavan, Savannakhet and Xieng Khuang fall into a category of most severely affected provinces, followed by Champasak, Hua Phan, Khammuan, Luang Prabang and Sekong.

Statistically speaking, the UXO risk for the average foreign visitor is low, but travellers should exercise caution when considering off-road wilderness travel in the aforementioned provinces. Never touch an object on the ground that may be a UXO, no matter how old and defunct it may appear.

DISABLED TRAVELLERS

With its lack of paved roads or footpaths (sidewalks) – even when present the latter are often uneven – Laos presents many physical obstacles for people with mobility impairments. Rarely do public buildings feature ramps or other access points for wheelchairs, nor do most hotels make efforts to provide access for the physically disabled (the single exception is the Lao Plaza Hotel in Vientiane, which has some ramping). Hence you're pretty much left to your own resources. Public transport is particularly crowded and difficult, even for the fully ambulatory.

For wheelchair users, any trip to Laos will require a good deal of advance planning. Fortunately a growing network of information sources can put you in touch with those who may have wheeled through Laos before.

Three international organisations which act as clearing houses for information on world travel for the mobility-impaired are:

Access Foundation (☎ 516-887 5798; PO Box 356, Malverne, NY 11565, USA)

Accessible Journeys (☎ 610-521 0339; www .disabilitytravel.com; 35 West Sellers Ave, Ridley Park, Pennsylvania, USA)

Mobility International USA (☎ 541-343 1284; info@ miusa.org; PO Box 10767, Eugene, OR 97440, USA)

Society for the Accessible Travel & Hospitality (☎ 212-447 7284; www.sath.org; Suite 610, 347 Fifth Ave, New York, NY 11242, USA)

EMBASSIES & CONSULATES
Lao Embassies & Consulates

Australia Canberra (☎ 02-6286 4595; fax 6290 1910; 1 Dalman Cres, O'Malley, Canberra, ACT 2606)

Cambodia Phnom Penh (☎ 023-426441; fax 427454; 15-17 Th Keomani, Phnom Penh)

China Beijing (☎ 010-6532 1224; fax 6532 6748; 11 Dongsie Jie, Sanlitun, Chao Yang, Beijing 100600); Kunming (☎ 0871-317 6624; fax 317 8556; Rm 3226, Camelia Hotel, 154 E Dong Feng Rd, 650041, Kunming)

France Paris (☎ 01 45 53 02 98; fax 01 47 27 57 89; 74 Ave Raymond Poincaré, 75116 Paris)

Germany Berlin (☎ 0 30 890 606 47; fax 890 606 48; Bismarckallee 2A; 14193 Berlin)

Myanmar Yangon (Burma; ☎ 01-222482; fax 227446; A1 Diplomatic Headquarters, Tawwin (Fraser) Rd, Yangon)

Thailand Bangkok (☎ 0 2539 6667; fax 0 2539 6678; www.bkklaoembassy.com; 520, 502/1-3 Soi Ramkhamhaeng 39, Th Pracha Uthit, Wangthonglang, Bangkok 10310); Khon Kaen (☎ 043 223473; fax 223849; 19/1-3 Th Phothisan, Khon Kaen)

USA New York (☎ 212-832 2734; fax 332 4923; 317 E 51st St, New York, NY 10022); Washington, DC (☎ 202-332 6416; fax 332 4923; www.laoembassy.com; 2222 S St NW, Washington, DC 20008)

Vietnam Danang (☎ 051-821208; fax 822628; 12 Tran Quy-Cap, Danang); Hanoi (☎ 04-825 4576; fax 822 8414; 22 Tran Binh Trong, Hanoi); Ho Chi Minh City (☎ 08-829 7667; fax 829 9272; 181 Haiba Trung, Ho Chi Minh City)

Embassies & Consulates in Laos

Of the 75 or so nations that have diplomatic relations with Laos, around 25 maintain embassies and consulates in Vientiane. Many of the remainder, for example Canada and the UK, are served by their embassies in Bangkok, Hanoi or Beijing. Opening hours for the embassies of neighbouring countries with valid border crossings are given here.

Principal consular offices in Vientiane (area code ☎ 021):

Australia (Map pp68-9; ☎ 413600, 413805; fax 431601; www.laos.embassy.gov.au; Th Nehru, Ban Phonxai)

Cambodia (Map pp68-9; ☎ 314952; fax 314951; Km 2, Th Tha Deua, Ban That Khao; ☷ 7.30-11.30am & 2-5pm Mon-Fri)

China (Map pp68-9; ☎ 315103; fax 315104; Th Wat Nak Nyai, Ban Wat Nak; ☷ 9-11.30am Mon-Fri)

France (Map pp72-3; ☎ 215258, 215259; fax 215250; Th Setthathirat, Ban Si Saket)

Germany (Map pp68-9; ☎ 312111, 312110; fax 314322; Th Sok Pa Luang)

Myanmar (Burma; Map pp68-9; ☎ 314910; fax 414406; Th Sok Pa Luang)

Thailand (Map pp68-9; ☎ 214581; fax 214580; Th Phonkheng; ☷ 8.30am-noon & 1-3.30pm Mon-Fri)

USA (Map pp72-3; ☎ 213966; fax 213045; http:// usembassy.state.gov/laos; Th That Dam (Th Bartholomie))

Vietnam (Map pp68-9; ☎ 413400, 413403; fax 413379; Th That Luang; ☷ 8-10.45am & 2.15-4.15pm Mon-Fri)

FESTIVALS & EVENTS

Festivals in Laos are mostly linked to the agricultural seasons or Buddhist holidays. The word for festival in Lao is *bun* (or *boun*).

JANUARY
International New Year's Day (1-3 January) Public holiday.

Bun Khun Khao (mid-January) During this annual harvest festival villagers perform ceremonies offering thanks to the land spirits that have allowed their crops to flourish.

FEBRUARY

Makha Busa (Magha Puja, Full Moon) This commemorates a speech given by the Buddha to 1250 enlightened monks who came to hear him without prior summons. Chanting and offerings mark the festival, which culminates in the candlelit circumambulation of wats throughout the country (celebrated most fervently in Vientiane and at the Khmer ruins of Wat Phu, near Champasak).

Vietnamese Tet & Chinese New Year (Tut Jiin) Celebrated in Vientiane, Pakse and Savannakhet with parties, fireworks and visits to Vietnamese and Chinese temples. Chinese- and Vietnamese-run businesses usually close for three days.

MARCH

Lao Women's Day (8 March) Public holiday for women only.

Bun Pha Wet This is a temple-centred festival in which the Jataka or birth-tale of Prince Vessantara, the Buddha's penultimate life, is recited. This is also a favoured time (second to Khao Phansa) for Lao males to be ordained into the monkhood. The scheduling of Bun Pha Wet is staggered so that it is held on different days in different villages. This is so that relatives and friends living in different villages can invite one another to their respective celebrations.

APRIL

Bun Pi Mai (Lao New Year) The lunar new year begins in mid-April and practically the whole country celebrates. Houses are cleaned, people put on new clothes and Buddha images are washed with lustral water. In the wats, offerings of fruit and flowers are made at altars and votive mounds of sand or stone are set up in the courtyards. Later, people take to the streets and douse one another with water, which is an appropriate activity as April is usually the hottest month of the year. This festival is particularly picturesque in Luang Prabang, where it includes elephant processions and lots of traditional costuming. The 15th, 16th and 17th of April are official public holidays.

MAY

International Labour Day (1 May) This public holiday honours workers all over the world. In Vientiane there are parades, but elsewhere not much happens.

Visakha Busa (Visakha Puja, Full Moon) This falls on the 15th day of the sixth lunar month, which is considered the day of the Buddha's birth, enlightenment and *parinibbana* (passing away). Activities are centred on the wat, with much chanting, sermonising and, at night, beautiful candlelit processions.

Bun Bang Fai (Rocket Festival) This is a pre-Buddhist rain ceremony that is now celebrated alongside Visakha Busa in Laos and in northeastern Thailand. It can be one of the wildest festivals in the whole country, with a great deal of music, dance and folk theatre (especially the irreverent *măw lám* performances), processions and general merrymaking, all culminating in the firing of bamboo rockets into the sky. The firing of the rockets is supposed to prompt the heavens to initiate the rainy season and bring much-needed water to the rice fields.

JULY

Bun Khao Phansa (Khao Watsa, Full Moon) This is the beginning of the traditional three-month 'rains retreat', during which Buddhist monks are expected to station themselves in a single monastery. At other times of year they are allowed to travel from wat to wat or simply to wander the countryside, but during the rainy season they forego the wandering so as not to damage fields of rice or other crops. This is also the traditional time of year for men to enter the monkhood temporarily, hence many ordinations take place.

AUGUST/SEPTEMBER

Haw Khao Padap Din (Full Moon) This is a sombre festival in which the living pay respect to the dead. Many cremations take place – bones being exhumed for the purpose – during this time, and gifts are presented to the order of monks (Sangha) so that monks will chant on behalf of the deceased.

OCTOBER/NOVEMBER

Bun Awk Phansa (Ok Watsa, Full Moon) This celebrates the end of the three-month rains retreat. Monks are allowed to leave the monasteries to travel and are presented with robes, alms-bowls and other requisites of the renunciate life. On the eve of Awk Phansa many people fashion small banana-leaf boats carrying candles, incense and other offerings, and float them in rivers, similar to Loy Krathong in Thailand.

Bun Nam (Boat Racing Festival) This is a second festival held in association with Awk Phansa. Boat races *(suang héua)* are commonly held in river towns, such as Vientiane, Luang Prabang and Savannakhet; in smaller towns these races are often postponed until National Day (2 December) so that residents aren't saddled with two costly festivals in two months.

NOVEMBER

Bun Pha That Luang (That Luang Festival, Full Moon) This takes place at Pha That Luang in Vientiane. Hundreds of monks receive alms and floral offerings early in the morning on the first day of the festival. There is a procession between Pha That Luang and Wat Si Muang. The celebration lasts a week and includes fireworks and music, ending in a candlelit procession circling That Luang.

DECEMBER

Lao National Day (2 December) This public holiday celebrates the 1975 victory over the monarchy with parades, speeches etc. Lao national and Communist hammer-and-sickle flags are flown all over the country. Celebration is mandatory, hence many poorer communities postpone some of the traditional Awk Phansa activities – usually practised roughly a month earlier – until National Day, thus saving themselves considerable expense (much to the detriment of Awk Phansa).

FOOD

Virtually all restaurants in Laos are inexpensive by international standards, hence we haven't divided them into Budget, Mid-Range and Top End categories except in the Vientiane chapter.

See the Food & Drink chapter, p52 for thorough descriptions of the cuisine and the kinds of restaurants in Laos.

GAY & LESBIAN TRAVELLERS

Lao culture is very tolerant of homosexuality although the gay and lesbian scene is not as prominent as in neighbouring Thailand. The legal situation is unclear, and there were reports of several arrests in the early 1990s. Public displays of affection – whether heterosexual or homosexual – are frowned upon.

HOLIDAYS
Public Holidays

These are official holidays when schools and government offices are closed.

International New Year (1 Jan)
Lao New Year (mid April) Five days.
International Labour Day (1 May)
Lao National Day (2 Dec)

INSURANCE

As when travelling anywhere in the world, a good travel insurance policy is a wise idea. Travel insurance is a way to regain your money if your flights are cancelled, for example. Read the small print in any policy to see if hazardous activities are covered or if certain countries are not covered by the policy. Laos is generally considered a high-risk area.

If you undergo medical treatment in Laos or Thailand, be sure to collect all receipts and copies of the medical report, in English if possible, for your insurance company.

See p277 for recommendations on health insurance and p274 for details on vehicle insurance.

INTERNET ACCESS

Cafés, cyber-centres and a few computer retail shops offer email and Internet access in Vientiane, Luang Prabang, Luang Nam Tha, Vang Vieng, Savannakhet, Pakse, Tha Khaek and Huay Xai. In places where there's plenty of competition – such as Vientiane and Luang Prabang – rates are low. In towns where there are only one or two places offering such services, rates will be higher.

PlaNet Online (a chain of cybercafés found in Vientiane, Luang Nam Tha, Vang Vieng and Luang Prabang) generally provides the most reliable machines and online access.

The Lao government controls the only legal access to the Internet through two government Internet service providers (ISPs), LaoTel and LaoNet. Both struggle for a very limited amount of available bandwidth, so can be excruciatingly slow. Some knowledgeable observers speculate that this slowness is exacerbated by Lao Telecom's attempt to block Internet voice transmission (which would cut into their revenues). The only private ISP is LaoPDR (linked to PlaNet Online).

Some private computer owners avoid the LaoTel/LaoNet logjam by logging onto LoxInfo and other ISPs in Thailand via long-distance dialling. Business centres in some hotels may be able to provide email via such systems, if you ask discreetly.

Nowadays most ISPs worldwide offer the option of web-based email, so if you already have an Internet account at home you can check your email anywhere in Thailand simply by logging onto your ISP's website using an Internet browser (such as Microsoft Internet Explorer or Netscape). If you have any doubts about whether your home ISP offers web-based email, check before you leave home. You may want to register with one of the many free web-based email services, such as MS Hotmail, Yahoo!, Juno or Lonely Planet's own eKit. You can log onto these services at any cybercafés in Laos.

Only top-end tourist-hotels have rooms with telephones, which almost always have standard modular phone jacks.

LEGAL MATTERS

Revolutionary Laos established its first national legal code in 1988, followed by a constitution two years later – the reverse order of how it's usually done. Although on paper certain rights are guaranteed, the reality is that you can be fined, detained or deported for any reason at any time, as has been demonstrated repeatedly in cases involving everything from a foreigner marrying a Lao national without government permission, to running a business that competes too efficiently with someone who has high government connections.

Your only consolation is that Lao officials generally don't come after foreigners for petty, concocted offences. In most cases you must truly have committed a crime to find yourself in trouble with the law. However, as documented by Amnesty International (and corroborated by local expats), you could easily find yourself railroaded through the system without any legal representation.

The message is clear: stay away from anything you know to be illegal, such as drug possession or prostitution. If detained, ask to call your embassy or consulate in Laos, if there is one. A meeting or phone call between Lao officers and someone from your embassy/consulate can result in quicker adjudication and release, though these are by no means guaranteed. On top of not wanting to hassle foreigners for misdemeanours, the Lao are not anxious to create international incidents by treating tourists unkindly.

Police sometimes hint at bribes for traffic violations and other petty offences. In such cases the police typically offer a choice along the lines of 'Would you like to come down to the station to pay your fine, or would you like to take care of it here and now?' Presented with such a choice, it's up to you whether to expedite matters by paying a bribe, or fight corruption in Laos by doing things by the book.

The legal age for voting and driving in Laos is 18.

Sexual Relationships

Sexual relationships between foreigners and Lao citizens who are not married are not permitted under Lao law. Permission for marriage or engagement to a Lao citizen must be submitted in a formal application to Lao authorities. Penalties for failing to register a relationship range from US$500 to US$5000, and possibly imprisonment or deportation.

Otherwise, the age of consent for sexual relations in Laos is 15.

MAPS

Good maps of Laos are difficult to find. The best all-purpose country map available is GT-Rider.com's *Laos*, a sturdy laminated folding map with a scale of 1:1,400,000. It's available at bookshops in Thailand and at many guesthouses in Laos, as well as online at www.gt-rider.com.

The **National Geographic Service** (NGS; Kom Phaen Thi Haeng Saat in Lao, or Service Géographique National in French; Map pp68-9; ☯ 8-11.30am, 2-4.30pm Mon-Fri) has produced a series of adequate maps of Laos and certain provincial capitals. These can be purchased direct from the National Geographic Service, which is on a side street to the north of the Patuxai in Vientiane.

The most detailed maps of Laos available, topographic sheet maps labelled in English and French and often seen on the walls of government offices, are based on Soviet satellite photography from the 1980s. The National Geographic Service reprints many of these maps, and will usually sell them to foreigners in spite of the fact that most are marked *En Secret*. Many of the place names are incorrect on these maps, however, and the roadways are not up to date.

The NGS' 1:500,000-scale topographicals number 11 in all, although only seven of these are available from the NGS, which claims that the missing four are out of print (but a more likely explanation is that certain border areas are deemed sensitive). Other topographical maps in the series decrease in scale to as low as 1:10,000, but anything below the 1:100,000 scale maps (for which it takes 176 to cover the whole country) is overkill unless you plan to drill for oil. Furthermore the NGS usually won't sell maps of 1:100,000 or less to foreigners unless they bring a written request on company letterhead.

The National Tourism Authority of Laos (NTAL) has published tourist-oriented city maps of Vientiane, Luang Prabang, Tha Khaek, Savannakhet and Pakse. These are reasonably accurate although not much beyond the larger hotels and government offices is marked on them and they are rather out of date. They may occasionally be available for sale at bookshops and gift shops in Vientiane, as well as at the NGS office. For all maps produced in Laos, including the city maps, the lowest prices are available through the NGS.

Map collectors or war historians may find American military maps from 1965 – now rather rare though they may still be available from the Defense Mapping Agency in the US – of some interest. These maps seem fairly accurate for topographic detail but they are woefully out of date with regard to road placement and village names. The same goes for the USA's highly touted Tactical Pilotage Charts, prepared specifically for air travel over Laos and virtually useless for modern ground navigation.

If you'll be travelling beyond Laos to Cambodia and Vietnam, Lonely Planet also publishes a full-colour *Thailand, Vietnam, Laos & Cambodia Road Atlas*. It contains over 100 map pages at a scale of 1:1,000,000 and includes topographic shading, city maps and a complete index.

MONEY

The official national currency in the Lao People's Democratic Republic (LPDR) is the Lao kip (LAK). Although only kip is legally negotiable in everyday transactions, in reality the people of Laos use three currencies for commerce: kip, Thai baht (B) and US dollars (US$). In cities such as Vientiane, Luang Prabang, Pakse and Savannakhet, baht and US dollars are readily acceptable at most businesses, including hotels, restaurants and shops.

In smaller towns and villages, kip or baht may be preferred. The rule of thumb is that for everyday small purchases, prices are quoted in kip. More expensive goods and services (eg long-distance boat hire) may be quoted in baht, while just about anything costing US$100 or more (eg tours, long-term car hire) is usually quoted in US dollars. In spite of the supposed illegality of foreign currency usage, a three-tier currency system remains firmly in place.

Because the kip is so unstable, and hence prices may change on almost a daily basis, prices in this guidebook are given in the US dollar equivalent.

The Lao kip is not convertible to any currency outside of the Lao PDR. Because of this, the only reliable sources of foreign exchange information are those inside the country.

See p9 for an idea of the ⟨ in travelling in Laos.

ATMs

There is one ATM in Vientiane located on Th Samsenthai. It accepts Visa.

Banking

Foreign residents of Laos are permitted to open US dollar, baht or kip accounts at several banks in Vientiane, including branches of six Thai banks. Unfortunately, if you already have an account at a Thailand-based branch a Thai banks, you won't be permitted to withdraw any money in Laos; you must open a new account.

A number of expatriates living in Vientiane maintain accounts at Thai banks across the river in Nong Khai because interest rates are higher and because more banking services – such as wire transfers – are available. Once a month or so they tuk-tuk down to the Friendship Bridge, hop on a bus to Nong Khai and take care of any financial chores. To do this, of course, you must have a multiple-entry visa.

Black Market

Vientiane had a flourishing black market for unofficial money exchange only a few years ago, but that's for the most part finished now. There are still a few unlicensed moneychangers around who can offer you marginally more kip per baht or dollar than the banks or licensed moneychangers, but it's not worth seeking these out unless you're changing huge amounts of cash. Even then the risk of being short-changed or worse is probably not worth the slightly more favourable rates.

Cash

Laos relies heavily on the Thai baht and the US dollar for the domestic cash economy. An estimated one-third of all cash circulating in Vientiane, in fact, bears the portrait of the Thai king, while another third celebrates US presidents.

Kip notes come in denominations of 500, 1000, 2000, 5000, 10,000 and 20,000 kip. The 20,000 kip notes are rarely seen outside of banks. For large amounts of cash, the dollar and the baht are favoured most of all for their relative portability. Five 1000 baht notes – about US$125 worth – are quite a bit easier to carry around than 125 10,000-kip notes, clumped in bundles of 10 by the bank.

Travelling in a country where the largest note amounts to only US$2 can be inconvenient. Hence if you plan on making frequent transactions of over US$20, you can save luggage space by carrying most of your cash in baht, along with smaller amounts of kip and dollars. A workable plan would be to carry half your cash in baht and a quarter each in kip and US dollars. But if you plan to make only small purchases (under US$20 per transaction) and you won't be travelling more than a few days, carry kip.

Towards the end of a lengthy trip it's best to spend all your kip and put aside some baht for your return to Thailand. Once you cross the Mekong no-one – except perhaps other travellers on their way into Laos – will want your kip.

Credit Cards

Many hotels, upmarket restaurants and gift shops in Vientiane accept Visa and Master-Card. In Luang Prabang there are also a few places that accept Visa and in Phonsavan the Maly Hotel does. Outside of these three towns, credit cards are virtually useless.

BCEL in Vientiane and Luang Prabang offers cash advances/withdrawals on Visa credit/debit cards for a 2.5% transaction fee if you take kip, or 3.5% for US dollars. Cash advances on baht are not available. Other banks may charge more. Depending on the amount you plan to exchange, you might save money by shopping around among the banks.

Exchanging Money

The kip continues to fluctuate, losing value against both the dollar and the baht at a sometimes alarming rate although for the last year or two it has been fairly stable. Still no-one can safely predict what the kip rate will be even a month from today, much less six months or a year down the road.

With some exceptions, the best exchange rates to be found are those available from banks rather than from moneychangers. At banks, travellers cheques receive a slightly better exchange rate than cash. The banks in Vientiane can change UK pounds, Euros, Canadian, US and Australian dollars, Thai baht and Japanese yen. Outside of Vientiane

most provincial banks will accept only US dollars or baht.

For many years now the best overall exchange rates have been those offered at the BCEL (Banque pour le Commerce Extérieur Lao; *thanáakháan kạan khâa taang páthêht láo* in Lao, or Lao Foreign Trade Bank in English). The Lao Development Bank (formerly Lane Xang Bank) has similar rates.

Licensed moneychangers also maintain booths around Vientiane (including the Talat Sao or Morning Market) and at some border crossings. Without exception their rates and commissions are not as good as BCEL or other banks; their only advantage is that they are open longer hours.

Once you get outside of the major urban centres of Vientiane, Luang Prabang, Savannakhet and Pakse, it can be difficult to change travellers cheques due to the relatively large amounts involved; even at Wattay International Airport the moneychanger is sometimes short of kip (be sure to ask whether they can cover your cheques before signing). Hence visitors are advised to carry plenty of cash outside Vientiane. If you plan to carry baht and US dollars along for large purchases (as is the custom), be sure to arrange your cash stash in these currencies before you leave the capital. Even in Luang Prabang, the most touristed town in Laos after Vientiane, it is difficult to get anything but kip at the bank.

So far all banks outside Vientiane are government owned. Exchange rates at these upcountry banks tend to be lower than what you'd get in Vientiane, despite the fact that the national bank mandates a single daily rate for all government banks. In a few cases we've been able to bargain a better exchange rate by pointing this out.

Laos has no restrictions on the amount of money you can exchange upon entry.

If you'd like to know the current exchange rate before you arrive in Laos, log on to www .vientianetimes.org.la – this website shows the latest Lao Foreign Trade Bank exchange rates. For a list of exchange rates as we went to press see the inside front cover.

Taxes

The only tax most visitors will be subject to is the one on hotel (but not guesthouse) rooms, which is 16%. Sometimes this is included in the room rates, sometimes not.

Tipping

Tipping is not customary in Laos except in upmarket Vientiane restaurants where 10% of the bill is appreciated – but only if a service charge hasn't already been added.

Travellers Cheques

Travellers cheques can be cashed at most banks in Laos, but normally only in exchange for kip. Cheques in US dollars are the most readily acceptable, and in fact outside Vientiane they are usually the only cheques accepted. Very few merchants accept travellers cheques, so visitors are advised to carry plenty of cash.

PHOTOGRAPHY & VIDEO
Airport Security

So far only the airports in Vientiane and Luang Prabang use X-ray machines to view luggage, so employ the usual protective procedures (eg lead-lined bags, hand inspection) if you're flying in or out of these cities and are worried about X-ray damage to film.

Film & Processing

Film is reasonably priced (available in Vientiane, Luang Prabang, Savannakhet and in Pakse), but the selection is generally limited to Fuji, Konica or Kodak colour print films in ASA 100 or 200. A few of the better photo shops in Vientiane and Luang Prabang carry slide films, typically Ektachrome Elite or Fujichrome Sensia. For B&W film or other slide films, you'd best stock up in Bangkok, where film is relatively cheap, before you come to Laos.

Processing is inexpensive but limited to negative and E-6 positive films.

Photographing People

In rural areas people are often not used to having their photos taken, so smile and ask permission before snapping away. In tribal areas *always* ask permission before photographing people or religious totems; photography of people is taboo among several tribes. Use discretion when photographing villagers anywhere in the country as a camera can be a very intimidating instrument.

Restrictions

Lao officials are sensitive about photography of airports and military installations; when in doubt, refrain.

Technical Tips

As in other tropical countries, the best times of day for photography are early to mid-morning and late afternoon. A polarising filter would be helpful for cutting glare and improving contrast, especially when photographing temple ruins or shooting over water. If you'll be in Laos during the rainy season (from June to October), pack some silica gel with your camera to prevent mould from growing on the inside of your lenses.

Camera batteries, especially lithium ones, can be difficult to find outside Vientiane and Luang Prabang. Bring spares or stock up in Vientiane before heading upcountry.

Lonely Planet's *Travel Photography* contains many useful tips on how to get the most out of your camera while on the road.

Video

Blank videotapes in popular formats, including DV, are readily available for sale in Vientiane and Luang Prabang, and to a lesser extent in Savannakhet, Pakse and a few other provincial capitals.

POST
Postal Rates

Postage from Laos is reasonable in price, although most people who plan to send parcels overseas wait until they reach Thailand since the Thai postal service is more reliable.

Sending & Receiving Mail

Outgoing mail is fairly reliable and inexpensive. The arrival of incoming mail is not as certain, especially for packages. Express Mail Service *(páisánii duan phisèht)* is available to many countries and is considered more reliable than regular mail. FedEx has a contract with the government-owned Enterprise des Poste (EPL) as well. When posting any package you must leave it open for inspection by a postal officer. Incoming parcels must also be opened for inspection; there may be a small charge for this mandatory 'service'.

The main post office in Vientiane has a poste restante service. Be sure that letters to you bear the country's full name – 'Lao People's Democratic Republic', or at least 'Lao PDR'.

The main post office is open 8am to noon and 1pm to 5pm Monday to Friday, 8am to noon and 1pm to 4pm Saturday, and 8am to noon Sunday. If you're moving to Vientiane, take note that there is no home mail-delivery service. Post-office boxes can be rented; the box areas are open from 8am to 6pm Monday to Saturday.

Throughout the country you can recognise post offices by the colour scheme: mustard yellow with white trim.

SHOPPING

Shopping in Laos continues to improve. Many of the handicrafts and arts available in Laos are easily obtainable in Thailand too, but some items – as noted below – are unique to Laos. Hill-tribe crafts can be less expensive in Laos, but only if you bargain.

Warning – there is a *total* ban on the export of antiques and Buddha images from Laos, though the enforcement of this ban appears to be very slack.

Bargaining

Like elsewhere in Southeast Asia, bargaining is a tradition (introduced by early Arab and Indian traders). Good bargaining, which takes practice, is one way to cut costs. Anything bought in a market should be bargained for; in some shops prices are fixed while in others bargaining is expected (the only way to find out is to try).

In general the Lao are gentle and very scrupulous in their bargaining practices. A fair price is usually arrived at quickly with little attempt to gouge the buyer (tour operators may be an exception to this rule). The amount they come down is usually less than what you see in neighbouring countries. Laos definitely has a 'two-tier pricing system' when it comes to quoting prices to foreigners, but it's nowhere near as evident as in Vietnam.

Remember there's a fine line between bargaining and niggling – getting hot under the collar over 1000 kip (about US$0.10) makes both seller and buyer lose face.

Antiques

Vientiane, Luang Prabang and Savannakhet each have a sprinkling of antique shops. Anything that looks old could be up for sale in these shops, including Asian pottery (especially porcelain from the Ming dynasty of China), old jewellery, clothes, carved wood, musical instruments, coins

and bronze statuettes. Because of the government's lax enforcement of the ban on the export of antiques, due to an overall lack of funds and personnel, you might be tempted to buy these objects. However, bear in mind not only that it is illegal to take them out of the country but that if you do so you will be robbing the country of its precious and limited heritage.

Carvings

The Lao produce well-crafted carvings in wood, bone and stone. The subject can be anything from Hindu or Buddhist mythology to themes from everyday life. Unlike in Thailand, authentic opium pipes seem to be plentiful in Laos and sometimes have intricately carved bone or bamboo shafts, along with engraved ceramic bowls. We've noticed, though, that the selection gets thinner every year.

To shop for carvings, look in antique or handicraft stores. Don't buy anything made from ivory; quite apart from the elephant slaughter caused by the ivory trade, many countries will confiscate any ivory items found in your luggage.

Fabric (Textiles)

Silk and cotton fabrics are woven in many different styles according to the geographic provenance and ethnicity of the weavers. Although Lao textiles do have similarities with other Southeast Asian textiles, Lao weaving techniques are unique in both loom design and weaving styles, generating fabrics that are very recognisably Lao.

Generally speaking, the fabrics of the north feature a mix of solid colours with complex geometric patterns – stripes, diamonds, zigzags, animal and plant shapes – usually in the form of a *phàa nung* (a women's wraparound skirt). Sometimes gold or silver thread is woven in along the borders. Another form the cloth takes is the *phàa bìang,* a narrow Lao-Thai shawl that men and women wear singly or in pairs over the shoulders during weddings and festivals.

The southern weaving styles are often marked by the *mat-mii* technique, which involves 'tie-dyeing' the threads before weaving. The result is a soft, spotted pattern similar to Indonesian ikat. *Mat-mii* cloth can be used for different types of clothing or for wall-hangings. Among Lao Thoeng and Mon-Khmer communities in the southern provinces there is a *mat-mii* weaving tradition which features pictographic story lines, sometimes with a few Khmer words, numerals or other nonrepresentational symbols woven into the pattern. In Sekong and Attapeu Provinces some fabrics mix beadwork with weaving and embroidery.

Among the Hmong and Mien tribes, square pieces of cloth are embroidered and quilted to produce strikingly colourful fabrics in apparently abstract patterns that contain ritual meanings. In Hmong these are called *pandau* (flower cloth). Some larger quilts feature scenes that represent village life, including both animal and human figures.

Many tribes among the Lao Soung and Lao Thoeng groups produce woven shoulder bags in the Austro-Thai and Tibetan-Burmese traditions, like those seen all across the mountains of South Asia and Southeast Asia. In Laos, these are called *nyaam*. Among the most popular *nyaam* nowadays are those made with older pieces of fabric from 'antique' *phàa nung* or from pieces of hill-tribe clothing. Vientiane's Talat Sao (Morning Market; Map pp72-3) is one of the best places to shop for this kind of accessory.

In general, the best place to buy fabric is in the weaving villages themselves, where you can watch how it's made and get 'wholesale' prices. Failing this, you can find a pretty good selection and reasonable prices at open markets in provincial towns, including Vientiane's Talat Sao. The most expensive places to buy fabric are in tailor shops and handicraft stores.

Jewellery

Gold and silver jewellery are good buys in Laos, although you must search hard for well-made pieces. Some of the best silverwork is done by the hill tribes. Gems are also sometimes available, but you can get better prices in Thailand.

Most provincial towns have a few shops specialising in jewellery. You can also find jewellery in antique and handicraft shops.

SOLO TRAVELLERS

Women should exercise the usual caution when travelling alone in remote areas of the country or when out late at night. Lao women almost never travel alone, so a foreign female without company is judged by most Lao – male and female – as being a bit strange. Lao men may interpret the fact that a woman is travelling alone to mean she wants company.

TELEPHONE & FAX

Telephone service in Laos, both domestic and international, has improved in recent years. International Direct Dialling (IDD) is widely available, and with links to IntelSat and AsiaSat, you can now dial over 150 countries from Vientiane.

You can make international calls from most Lao Telecom offices in most provincial capitals. Operators cannot place collect calls or reverse phone charges – you must pay for the call in cash kip when it is completed. All calls made at Lao Telecom offices are operator-assisted.

In towns that don't have a separate Lao Telecom office, the main post office usually has a calling booth or two. Where a separate phone office exists, hours typically run from 7.30am to 9.30pm or from 8am to 10pm.

International calls are also charged on a per-minute basis, with a minimum charge of three minutes. Calls to most countries around the world cost from US$2 to US$2.50 for the first three minutes.

Fax

At most Lao Telecom offices (or at post offices, where there is no separate Lao Telecom office) fax services are available.

Mobile Phone

Lao Telecom as well as three or four private companies offer mobile phone services in Laos on the GSM system. A government-affiliated company called Enterprise of Telecommunications Lao (ETL) provides coverage in every province but is also the most expensive. Least expensive is Tango Lao, but at the time of writing coverage extended only to Vientiane, Luang Prabang and Savannakhet.

Mobile phones are expensive in Laos so if you anticipate needing one while you're in Lao, and you have an unlocked mobile phone, bring it with you and buy a Laos-capable SIM card from one of the local service providers.

Phone Codes

Until a few years ago most cities in Laos could only be reached through a Vientiane operator. These days it's possible to direct-dial to and from many places in Laos using IDD phone technology.

The country code for calling Laos is ☎ 856. For long-distance calls within the country, dial ☎ 0 first, then the area code and number. For international calls dial ☎ 00 first, then the country code, area code and number.

See the inside front cover and under regional headings for area codes inside Laos.

Phonecards

Tholakham Lao (Lao Telecom), a private company, issues telephone cards (*bát thóh-lasáp*) which can be bought from any post or telephone office and used in special card phone booths in larger towns and cities.

Although the cards are supposed to come in five different denominations from 50 to 500 minutes, the only ones that appear to be available are cards of 100 (US$2.20) and 200 minutes (US$3.30).

TIME

Laos is seven hours ahead of GMT/UTC. Thus, noon in Vientiane is 10pm the previous day in San Francisco, 1am in New York, 5am in London, 1pm in Perth and 3pm in Sydney.

TOILETS

In Laos, as in many other Asian countries, the 'squat toilet' is the norm except in hotels and guesthouses geared towards tourists and international business travellers. Instead of trying to approximate a chair or stool like a modern sit-down toilet, a traditional Asian toilet sits more or less flush with the surface of the floor, with two footpads on either side of the porcelain abyss.

Next to the typical squat toilet is a bucket or cement reservoir filled with water. A plastic bowl or bucket usually floats on the water's surface or sits nearby. This supply of water has a two-fold function. Firstly, toilet-goers scoop water from the reservoir with the plastic bowl and use it to clean their nether regions while still squatting over the toilet. Secondly, since there is usually no mechanical flushing device attached to a squat toilet, a few extra scoops must be poured into the toilet basin to flush the waste into the septic system. The more rustic toilets in rural areas may simply consist of a few planks over a hole in the ground.

Even in places where sit-down toilets are installed, the plumbing may not be designed to take toilet paper. In such cases there will be the usual washing bucket nearby or there will be a rubbish bin where you're supposed to place used toilet paper – sometimes both.

Public toilets are uncommon outside hotel lobbies and airports. While you are on the road between towns and villages, it is perfectly acceptable to go behind a tree or even to use the roadside when nature calls.

TOURIST INFORMATION

The National Tourism Authority of Laos (NTAL) was established in Vientiane in the late 1980s as the government-sponsored sole travel agency and tour operator in the country. Following the privatisation of the travel business in the 1990s, its function as a travel agency declined, although the office can still arrange tours and guides for travel around the country. Private competitors (see p276) do a better job.

The bottom line is that you're better off going just about anywhere else in Vientiane *but* the NTAL if you're seeking accurate, up-to-date information on travel in Laos. The NTAL does not supply information by mail and does not maintain any overseas offices. In a few provincial capitals you may find nominal NTAL offices staffed by lone individuals whose major function seems to be extorting money from tour groups visiting the province; the general lack of information at these local offices can be profound.

Occasionally local travel agencies or guides will try to pass themselves off as NTAL officials or otherwise state that they are 'in charge of tourism' in the province, as has happened repeatedly in Phonsavan in Xieng Khuang Province. Remember that the NTAL has no official regulatory function outside Vientiane and that you are not required to use any services offered by its representatives, despite any claims to the contrary.

The **NTAL head office** (☎ /fax 021-212013) is on Th Lan Xang opposite the Centre du Langue Française.

VISAS

Visas for foreigners who want to visit Laos are of the types given below. For all types of visas, the Lao embassy requires that the official one-page visa application form be filled out in triplicate and submitted along with three passport photos and the appropriate fee.

When applying for a visa from outside Southeast Asia, you should allow at least two months for the visa process. This is because the embassies must wait for approval from Vientiane before they can issue them. In Southeast Asia, the process is much faster – for no apparent reason, since in any case all the embassy has to do is contact Vientiane.

TOURIST VISA (VISA ON ARRIVAL)

The Lao government issues 15-day tourist visas (VT) on arrival at all official international border crossings and at the international airports at Vientiane and Luang Prabang.

To receive this visa on arrival you must present the following: US$30 cash or the equivalent in Thai baht (travellers cheques and other currencies, including Lao kip, are not accepted); one passport-size photo of yourself; the name of a hotel you will be staying at in Vientiane (pick any one from this guidebook); and the name of a contact in Laos. Most people leave the latter blank with no problem but if you do know someone in Vientiane, by all means write the name in. For airport arrivals you're also supposed to possess a valid return air ticket, but so far they haven't checked ours and we haven't heard anyone else say they had their tickets checked either.

It's important to note that you must have US$30 (or the equivalent in Thai currency) cash in hand when you arrive at the Vientiane or Luang Prabang airports or at a border crossing. Moneychangers at these places are unlikely to be able to give you dollars in exchange for Thai baht or any other currency. We've seen several travellers get stuck in airport limbo because they arrived without cash to pay for their visas. In such cases the immigration officers may allow you to go into town and try to get dollars from another source. They will, however, keep your passport at the airport in the meantime.

PORTS OF ENTRY

These are the legal ports of entry to Laos, where tourists visas are available on arrival. Persistent rumours say that the border between Tay Trang, Vietnam (near Dien Bien Phu) and Tai Xang, Laos, will soon open as well.

Thailand

- Chiang Khong/Huay Xai
- Nong Khai/Vientiane
- Beung Kan/Paksan
- Nakhon Phanom/Tha Khaek
- Mukdahan/Savannakhet
- Chong Mek/Vang Tao

Vietnam

- Nam Can/Nam Khan
- Cau Treo/Kaew Neua (Nam Phao)
- Lao Bao/Dansavanh

China

- Mohan/Boten

The 15-day visa is extendible up to an additional two weeks.

VISITOR VISA

Lao embassies and consulates offer a 30-day visitor visa (B3) which you must apply for in advance. Officials can usually issue this visa in 24 hours if you leave your passport overnight for a cost of US$35 or the equivalent in the local currency of the country in which you apply. In Bangkok you can get your visa in a couple of hours for an additional 300B express fee.

You can also obtain 30-day visas through Laos embassies and consulates in other countries. Depending on the agency, it may take anywhere from 24 hours to four days to get your visa in this manner.

In Thailand, the Lao consulate in Khon Kaen issues 30-day visas for Laos in one to three days. You can also easily arrange Lao visas through travel agencies in Bangkok, Chiang Mai, Nong Khai, Udon Thani and Ubon Ratchathani. Generally speaking the cheaper services take up to five business days to issue a visa, while the more expensive services usually provide one within 24 hours or less.

The 30-day visa is extendible up to two months.

NONIMMIGRANT & BUSINESS VISAS

A person who has a short-term professional or volunteer assignment in Laos is generally issued a nonimmigrant visa that is good for 30 days and extendible for another 30 days. As with the visitor visa, the application fee is around US$35.

Journalists can apply for the journalist visa, which has the same restrictions and validity as the nonimmigrant and visit visas except that the applicant must also fill in a biographical form.

Business visas, also good for 30 days, are relatively easy to obtain as long as you have a sponsoring agency in Laos. Many brokers in Vientiane (and a few in Thailand) can arrange such visas with one to two weeks notice. The visa fee itself is 300B (US$12) at the Lao embassy in Bangkok, though brokers charge a fee on top of that to cover the cost of paperwork and the expense of contacting the Lao embassy in Bangkok.

Business visas can be extended from month to month indefinitely, although you will need a visa broker or travel agency to handle the extensions. After the first month's extension, the business visa can be converted to multiple-entry status, allowing you to leave and re-enter Laos as many times as you wish within the stated validity dates. Six-month business visas are also available.

While nonimmigrant and business visas may be collected in one's home country, the Lao embassy in Bangkok is a better place to pick them up since the staff are in daily contact with the appropriate ministries in Vientiane. Simply make sure that your sponsoring agency in Laos sends a confirmation fax to the Bangkok embassy; if you can present the fax date to the embassy it can find your fax and then issue your visa sooner.

TRANSIT VISAS

The transit visa is intended for stopovers in Vientiane only for people travelling between two other countries. It's common to ask for such a visa when travelling between Hanoi and Bangkok, for example. The visa is supposed to be granted only upon presentation of a visa for the country of final destination (eg Thailand), but often no-one asks to see such a visa. The maximum length of stay for the transit visa is five days, and no extensions are allowed. The fee for this visa is usually US$15.

VISA EXTENSIONS

Rules surrounding the extension of tourist visas seem to change from year to year in Laos. For a couple of years you had to apply for extensions at the NTAL office. Currently they're very easy to obtain at the immigration office in Vientiane for US$2 per day. Legally, only the Vientiane immigration office is authorised to extend your visa, but we have heard of travellers getting the occasional extension in remote provinces such as Phongsali or Sainyabuli. Most immigration offices, however, are adamant about refusing to extend your visa – they will simply tell you you must go to Vientiane. Two travel agencies based in the NTAL building can also extend your visa for you for between US$2.50 and US$3 per day. The service usually includes delivery of your passport to your guesthouse or hotel.

Nonimmigrant visas, journalist visas and business visas have to be extended through the sponsoring person or organisation. In these cases the extension fee is also highly variable; for consulting agencies the fee may be comparable to the fees charged for tourist visa extensions, although for long-term visitors – those people staying in Laos more than a month – the fees are usually more reasonable.

The transit visa cannot be extended under any circumstances.

OVERSTAYING YOUR VISA

If you overstay your visa, you will have to pay a fine at the immigration checkpoint upon departure from Laos. The standard fine at the moment is US$10 for each day you've stayed beyond the visa's expiry date. There seems to be little fuss over this.

WOMEN TRAVELLERS

Everyday incidents of sexual harassment are much less common in Laos than in virtually any other Asian country. In general, all visitors to Laos are treated with the utmost respect and courtesy.

One difference between Laos and Thailand is that prostitution is less common in Laos, where it is a serious criminal offence. While a Thai woman who wants to preserve a 'proper' image often won't associate with foreign males for fear of being perceived as a prostitute, in Laos this is not the case. Hence a foreign woman seen drinking in a café or restaurant is not usually perceived as being 'loose' or available as she might be in Thailand. This in turn means that there are generally fewer problems with uninvited male solicitations.

WORK

With Laos's expanding economy and the growing influx of aid organisations and foreign companies, the number of jobs available to foreigners increases slightly each year, although don't count on finding employment immediately. By far the greatest number of positions will be found in Vientiane.

Possibilities include teaching English privately or at one of the several language centres in Vientiane, work which pays about US$5 to US$8 an hour. Certificates or degrees in English teaching aren't absolutely necessary, although they increase your chances considerably.

If you possess technical expertise or international volunteer experience, you might be able to find work with a UN-related programme or an NGO involved with foreign aid or technical assistance to

Laos. For positions such as these, your best bet is to visit the Vientiane offices of each organisation and inquire about personnel needs and vacancies.

Liste du corps diplomatique et consulaire à Vientiane, published in French only by the Ministry of Foreign Affairs, has the addresses of the main UN organisations working in Laos. Another booklet, *Directory of Non-Governmental Organisations in Laos,* lists contact information as well as programme descriptions for over 100 NGOs registered in Laos. Either publication can be purchased in Vientiane. If you're thinking of launching your own aid project, note that all projects, whether UN, bilateral or NGO, must be approved by the government's Committee of Investment & Cooperation (CIC).

International companies hire locally in Laos on the rare occasion. A list of such companies in Laos is available from the Ministry of Foreign Affairs.

Once you have a sponsoring employer, a visa valid for working and residing in Laos is relatively easy to obtain. The most time-consuming part of the process is receiving ministry approval in Vientiane; depending on the sponsoring organisation and type of work, permission from more than one ministry may be necessary.

If your sponsor takes care of all the paperwork in Laos, however, this should culminate, in a day or two, in an order to a Lao embassy abroad to issue you the appropriate visa.

Transport

The transport infrastructure in Laos is barely recognisable from what existed a few years ago. The huge, foreign-funded road construction projects across the country are largely finished, and the smooth roads have brought a battalion of buses and scheduled services. Many travellers are choosing to come and go via Laos's many land and river borders, something we've acknowledged in this book by giving detailed descriptions of all border crossings that were open to foreigners when we visited (more are set to open). While there are many border options, flying into Laos is refreshing in that you can forget about shopping around – there are only five airlines flying into Laos and prices are usually the same.

THINGS CHANGE...

The information in this chapter is particularly vulnerable to change. Check directly with the airline or a travel agent to make sure you understand how a fare (and ticket you may buy) works and be aware of the security requirements for international travel. Shop carefully. The details given in this chapter should be regarded as pointers and are not a substitute for your own careful, up-to-date research.

GETTING THERE & AWAY

ENTERING LAOS

It's possible to enter Laos by land or air from Thailand, Cambodia, Vietnam or China. Land borders are often remote and the travelling can be tough either side, but actually crossing the frontier is usually pretty simple.

Passport

The only real prerequisites for entering Laos are a passport with six months' validity and, if you intend to stay longer than 15 days or are coming by boat from Cambodia, a visa. See p263 for full visa details.

AIR
Airports & Airlines

There are only three international airports in Laos. **Wattay International Airport** (VTE; ☎ 021-512165) in Vientiane; **Luang Prabang International Airport** (LPQ; ☎ 071-212856) and **Pakse International Airport** (PKZ; ☎ 212844). Lao Airlines is the national carrier and monopolises the majority of flights in and out of the country, though many are code-shares with the following:

Bangkok Airways (☎ 071-253334; www.bangkokair.com; hub Bangkok, Thailand) Code PG.

China Yunnan Airlines (☎ 212300; www.chinayunnanair.com; hub Kunming, China) Code 3Q.

Lao Airlines (☎ 212051–4; www.laoairlines.com; hub Vientiane) Code QV.

Thai Airways International (THAI; ☎ 222527; www.thaiairlines.com; hub Bangkok) Code TG.

Vietnam Airlines (☎ 217562; www.vietnamairlines.com; hub Ho Chi Minh City, Vietnam) Code VN.

Tickets

Unless you're in a country bordering Laos, your first mission is to find yourself a flight to Bangkok. There are plenty of flights to the Thai capital and competition is fierce, so expect fares to fluctuate sharply. Generally, airlines from third countries offer longer flights for cheaper fares. For example, if you're flying from the UK you'll probably get a better deal with Gulf Air, Emirates, Singapore Airlines, Garuda or other such

DEPARTURE TAX

The international departure tax is US$10, which can be paid in kip, baht or dollars.

airlines than you will with direct flights on either British Airways or Thai International Airways (THAI). Once you're in Bangkok, there are trains, planes and buses heading to Laos.

REGIONAL TICKETS

The **Asian Hip Hop Pass** (www.aseanta.org) is worth considering if you're flying all over Southeast Asia.

Asia

STA Travel proliferates in Asia, and has branches in **Bangkok** (☎ 02-236 0262; www.statravel.co.th), **Singapore** (☎ 6737 7188; www.statravel.com.sg), **Hong Kong** (☎ 2736 1618; www.statravel.com.hk) and **Japan** (☎ 03 5391 2922; www.statravel.co.jp). Another resource in Japan is **No 1 Travel** (☎ 03 3205 6073; www.no1-travel.com); in Hong Kong try **Four Seas Tours** (☎ 2200 7760; www.fourseastravel.com/english).

The only flights directly into Laos come from the following four countries.

CAMBODIA
Phnom Penh

There is at least one flight per day with Lao Airlines or, more often, Vietnam Airlines between Phnom Penh and Vientiane (US$133 one way, 1½ hours). On Monday and Saturday the flight stops at Pakse (US$73, 50 minutes). Book through either carrier.

Siem Reap

Lao Airlines flies between Cambodia's Siem Reap and Vientiane (US$123 one way, one hour) three times a week, with two of these flights stopping at Pakse (US$73, 30 minutes). The Pakse connection is prone to cancellation.

CHINA
Kunming

Lao Airlines shares two or three services a week between Kunming, China, and Vientiane (US$133 one way, 80 minutes) with China Yunnan Airlines (CYA). Book through either carrier.

THAILAND
Bangkok

THAI has one flight daily between Bangkok and Vientiane (5000B, 70 minutes), while Lao Airlines has two flights per day in each direction (US$73); discounts are available on THAI.

Some people save money by flying from Bangkok to Udon Thani in Thailand, then carrying on by road to Nong Khai and over the Friendship Bridge to Vientiane. Udon Thani is 55km south of Nong Khai and a Bangkok–Udon air ticket on THAI costs about US$45. The Thai-Lao International Bus runs from Udon to Vientiane (US$2.20, two hours, four times daily).

Bangkok Airways flies daily between Bangkok and Luang Prabang (5000B, 1¾ hours). Discounts are offered for booking online.

Chiang Mai

Lao Airlines flies three times a week between Vientiane and Chiang Mai (US$83, 1½ hours). The same flight stops over in Luang Prabang (US$68).

VIETNAM
Hanoi

There are eight flights a week between Vientiane and Hanoi – three on Lao Airlines (US$103, one hour), the rest on Vietnam Airlines for the same fare.

Ho Chi Minh City

Vietnam Airlines flies from Ho Chi Minh City (Saigon) to Vientiane (US$143 one way, three hours) daily, via a stop in Phnom Penh. Lao Airlines flies direct to Ho Chi Minh City on Tuesday for the same price.

Australia

Qantas, THAI, British Airways and a load of other airlines fly to Bangkok from Sydney, Melbourne and Perth, with discount fares starting at about A$950 return. For online bookings check www.travel.com.au. Other good agencies:

Flight Centre (☎ 133 133; www.flightcentre.com.au)
STA Travel (☎ 1300 733 035 Australia-wide; www.statravel.com.au)

Canada

Fares from Canada are similar to those from the US. **Travel Cuts** (☎ 800-667-2887; www.travelcuts.com) is Canada's national student

travel agency. For online bookings try www
.expedia.ca and www.travelocity.ca.

Continental Europe

Europeans can pick up discounted seats
from about €500. The following agents are
worth a look:

Lastminute (☎ 01805 284 366; www.lastminute.de)

Nouvelles Frontières (☎ 0825 000 747;
www.nouvelles-frontieres.fr)

OTU Voyages (www.otu.fr) This agency specialises in
student and youth travellers.

STA Travel (☎ 01805 456 422; www.statravel.de) For
travellers under the age of 26.

New Zealand

Both **Flight Centre** (☎ 0800 243 544; www.flight
centre.co.nz) and **STA Travel** (☎ 0508 782 872; www
.statravel.co.nz) have branches throughout the
country. The site www.travel.co.nz is recommended for online bookings.

The UK

It's not hard to find a bargain from London to Bangkok, with discount prices starting at £350. Gulf Air, Emirates, KLM and
Lufthansa are worth looking at. Check the
weekend broadsheet newspapers, *Time Out,*
the *Evening Standard* and the free magazine
TNT for other offers.

Recommended travel agencies:

Bridge the World (☎ 0870 444 7474; www.b-t-w.co.uk)

Flightbookers (☎ 0870 010 7000; www.ebookers.com)

North-South Travel (☎ 01245 608 291; www
.northsouthtravel.co.uk) North-South Travel donates part
of its profit to projects in the developing world.

STA Travel (☎ 0870 160 0599; www.statravel.co.uk) For
travellers under the age of 26.

Trailfinders (www.trailfinders.co.uk)

Travel Bag (☎ 0870 890 1456; www.travelbag.co.uk)

The USA

Fares from New York to Bangkok range
widely, with the cheapest (via places like
Moscow) starting at about US$800 return.
From Los Angeles it can be even cheaper,
and far more direct, with airlines such as
Philippine Airlines, China Airlines, Eva
Air and American Airlines. Nondiscounted
fares are several hundred dollars more. The
following agencies are recommended for
online comparisons and bookings:

Cheapflights.com (www.cheapflights.com)

Cheap Tickets (www.cheaptickets.com)

Expedia (www.expedia.com)

Lowestfare (www.lowestfare.com)

Orbitz (www.orbitz.com)

STA Travel (www.sta.com)

Travelocity (www.travelocity.com)

BORDER CROSSINGS

Laos shares land and/or river borders with
Thailand, Myanmar, Cambodia, China and
Vietnam; see the colour map at the start of
this guide for their locations.

In this book we give detailed instructions
for every crossing open to foreigners. These
details appear as boxed texts in the relevant
chapters – the information in this chapter
outlines the possibilities and points you to
the boxes. Of course, with so much detail
some of it is sure to change, so it's a good
idea to ask around or check the **Thorntree**
(http://thorntree.lonelyplanet.com/) bulletin board
before setting off.

Most crossings involve changing transport at the border, even when you've paid for
a 'direct' bus. There are, however, a couple
of exceptions, such as the direct bus between
Hanoi and Vientiane. Such long journeys are
possible, but they are not recommended for
anyone with a low pain threshold. Five of the
crossings on the western border with Thailand involve quick boat trips across the Mekong, as does the border with Cambodia.

It's possible to bring your own vehicle
into Laos from Thailand and Vietnam with
the right paperwork, (see p273), and Lao
customs doesn't object to visitors bringing
bicycles into the country.

In Thailand, trains run to the Thai-Lao
Friendship Bridge (see p269) and to Ubon
Ratchathani, three hours from the Lao bor-
der (see p269).

Unless stated otherwise, Laos issues 15-
day visas at all crossings that are open to
foreigners. For full visa details, see p263.

Cambodia

The border with Cambodia at Voen Kham
is open but neither Laos nor Cambodia
issues visas here. The border itself is the
Mekong, and on the Cambodian side you'll
need to take an expensive fast boat to Stung
Treng. See p236.

China

It is legal to cross between Yunnan Province
in China and Luang Nam Tha Province in
Laos at Boten. From Mohan on the Chinese

side it's a two- to three-hour minibus ride to Mengla, the nearest large town. See p172 for details.

Myanmar

There are no official border crossing points between Laos and Myanmar. With a valid visa you could try to cross at Xieng Kok, on the Mekong River north of Huay Xai, but success is far from guaranteed.

Thailand

The Mekong River forms much of Laos's western border and foreigners can use five crossings. We have noted here where Thai border crossings involve a boat ride across the Mekong.

VANG TAO & CHONG MEK

This border 40km west of Pakse is a popular and easy entry point in to southern Laos. Rapid and express trains from Bangkok's Hualamphong train station run three or four times a day to Ubon Ratchathani (sleeping berths from 771B, 10 hours, 575km), from where it's only about three hours to Pakse. See p217 for details.

MUANG NGOEN & HUAY KON

The remote border crossing between Muang Ngoen, in Sainyabuli Province, and Huay Kon, in Thailand's Nan Province, should be open to foreigners by the time you read this. Check ahead.

PAKSAN & BEUNG KAN

This is a river crossing from Beung Kan in Thailand to Paksan in Laos, about 120km from Vientiane. The Paksan crossing is rarely used by travellers. See p192 for more details.

THA KHAEK & NAKHON PHANOM

Another river crossing, further south than the Paksan crossing, takes you from Nakhon Phanom in Thailand to Tha Khaek in Laos. Travellers who use this border are usually crossing directly between Thailand and Vietnam. See p200 for more details.

SAVANNAKHET & MUKDAHAN

This southernmost river crossing between Thailand and Laos. A bridge across the Mekong near Savannakhet should be finished in 2006. See p207 for more details.

HUAY XAI & CHIANG KHONG

Crossing to or from northern Thailand is done at Huay Xai on the Laos side and Chiang Khong on the Thai side. This is the start point for two-day boat trips down to Luang Prabang and is very popular with travellers. There is accommodation on both sides of the border. See p179 for more details.

THE FRIENDSHIP BRIDGE AT NONG KHAI (FOR VIENTIANE)

The Thai-Lao Friendship Bridge is 25km east of the Vientiane (see p93). Buses run direct between downtown Vientiane and Nong Khai, and regularly between Nong Khai and Bangkok (380B, 12 hours).

Rapid and express trains from Bangkok's Hualamphong train station run daily to Nong Khai (11 hours). Overnight trains have sleeper carriages and make a convenient, comfortable and cheap way to get an early morning start across the border while saving on a hotel room. A berth costs about 780B. From Vientiane, the overnight train is popular, though you'll have to pay a little more to book it through an agent in Laos.

Vietnam

There are several border crossings between Laos and Vietnam but only three are open to foreigners. Laos issues 15-day tourist visas at the border, but the Vietnamese will not. Get a Vietnam visa in Vientiane or Savannakhet (see p263).

NAM PHAO & CAU TREO

The spectacular crossing through the Kaew Neua Pass, via the low-key border posts of Nam Phao on the Lao side, and Cau Treo in Vietnam, leads to Vinh and all points north, including Hanoi. It is, however, a very long trip, and while direct buses between the two capitals are convenient, they are also torturously slow and uncomfortable. If you can take the pain, buses leave Vientiane's Northern Bus Station (p93) every day for Vinh (US$16, 16 hours) and Hanoi (US$20, 24 hours), and occasionally for Hue (US$20), Danang (US$22) and even Ho Chi Minh City (US$45, too long: possibly up to 48 hours). For full details, see (p197).

DANSAVANH & LAO BAO

Crossing the border at Dansavanh (Laos) and Lao Bao, 255km east of Savannakhet, is much easier because of the newly resurfaced Rte 9. This is the place to cross if you're coming from or going to Hué, Hoi An or anywhere further south. For full details, see (p209)

NAM CAN & NAM KHAN
This border east of Phonsavan in Xieng Khuang Province was opened to foreigners in 2003. Even though you're a long way north of the Kaew Neua Pass crossing, the road on the Vietnam side runs so far south (almost to Vinh) before joining the main north–south Hwy 1 that this border is totally inconvenient. It's mainly for those looking to get well off the beaten track. See p147 for details.

NA MAEW & NAM XOI
In April 2004 the crossing between Nam Xoi, Thanh Hoa Province, Vietnam, and Na Maew, Hua Phan Province, Laos, was opened. From Na Maew it's a relatively short bus ride to Sam Neua, where there are buses and planes onward to other points in Laos. See p153 for details.

SOP HUN & TAY TRANG
The border at Sop Hun in Phongsali Province, just across from Tay Trang (32km west of Dien Bien Phu), is not yet open to foreigners, but is rumoured to be so soon. Stay tuned.

GETTING AROUND

AIR
Airlines in Laos
Lao Airlines handles all domestic flights with in Laos, with Vientiane as the main hub. The Laos Air Fares map (p271) details all Laos's scheduled air routes and prices, both domestic and international. Airline fare tables list several routes as 'suspended' (see the map), but many of these have been out of action for years; check schedules online (www.laoairlines.com) before making firm plans.

Prices have remained steady during the first few years of this century and are generally pretty good value. Except at Lao Airlines offices in Vientiane and Luang Prabang, where credit cards are accepted for both international and domestic ticket

> **DEPARTURE TAX**
> The domestic departure tax is US$0.50, payable in kip.

purchases, all payments must be made in US dollars cash.

Schedules are highly unreliable and during holiday seasons in particular it can be difficult to get a seat. It's best to book as far ahead as possible, then check with the airline in the days before you're due to fly to find out whether your flight has been cancelled. Delays and cancellations are frustratingly frequent.

It's uncertain whether the repackaging of the old Lao Aviation as Lao Airlines and the leasing of a new Airbus to service some international routes will have any effect on the airline's efficiency and safety. Safety records for Lao Airlines aren't made public, but many international organisations and Western embassies advise staff not to use the airline.

The international flights and busy domestic routes such as Vientiane–Luang Prabang and Vientiane–Pakse are safer, but flying into Sam Neua, for instance, where the descent is tricky and the conditions unpredictable, is not recommended if you're of nervous disposition. In most cases pilots must rely on visual flying techniques. When heavy cloud cover is present, pilots are forced to circle the area searching for a hole through which to descend. If none is found within the time allotted by fuel capacity, the pilots either return to the original departure point or land at another airport in the same region. After a short wait and a quick refuel, they give it another go!

BICYCLE
The light and relatively slow traffic in most Lao towns – and indeed on most of the highways – makes for favourable cycling conditions. Several tour agencies and guesthouses offer mountain biking tours, ranging in duration from a few hours to several weeks (see p276).

Hire
Basic bicycles can be hired in most main towns and tourist destinations, usually costing between US$0.50 and US$1 per

LAOS AIR FARES

CHINA

CHINA

MYANMAR
(BURMA)

VIETNAM

○ Hanoi

● Phongsali

Luang
Nam Tha ●
*35**
Udomxai
(Muang Xai) ●
*32**

Huay
Xai ●
*39**

Sam Neua ●

*48**

*47**

89

Kunming
133

74

● Luang Prabang

68

66

37

● Phonsavan

Gulf
of
Tonkin

81

● Sainyabuli

103

● Chiang Mai

57

*72**

44

46

83

Vientiane

THAILAND

TRANSPORT

Full one-way economy airfares in US$
* – Flights currently suspended

57

● Savannakhet

87

42

73

THAILAND

● Pakse

Phnom
Penh
133

Siem Reap
123

Phnom
Penh
73

Bangkok ○

Ho Chi
Minh City
143

Siem Reap
63

CAMBODIA

day. Mountain bikes can be hired in a few places, including Luang Nam Tha and Vientiane, for between US$1.50 and US$5 per day.

These Thai- or Chinese-made street bikes come in varying degrees of usability, so be sure to inspect them thoroughly before hiring. Common problems include loose seats or handle bars and broken bells.

Purchase

You can buy a new bicycle for between US$70 and US$90. The Chinese bikes are sturdier, the Thai bikes more comfortable. Low-quality Chinese or Taiwanese mountain bikes are available for between US$90 and US$140.

BOAT

More than 4600km of navigable rivers are the traditional highways and byways of Laos, the main thoroughfares being the Mekong, Nam Ou, Nam Khan, Nam Tha, Nam Ngum and Se Kong. The Mekong is the longest and most important route and is navigable year-round between Luang Prabang in the north and Savannakhet in the south (about 70% of its length in Laos). Depending on the season, this stretch of the Mekong can carry boats of between 15 and 140 tonnes. Smaller rivers accommodate traditional pirogues (dugout canoes) used both for fishing and transport.

Sealed roads and buses, however, mean the days of mass river transport are as good as finished. In the south, for example, there is almost no traffic on the Mekong at all between Vientiane and Pakse. Of the few remaining long-distance services, those favoured by tourists have seen the costs rise and the romance decline. Even so, no trip to Laos is complete without at least one river excursion.

River Ferry

The most popular river trip in Laos – the slow boat between Huay Xai and Luang Prabang (p179) – is still a daily event and relatively cheap at US$15 per person for the two-day journey. From Huay Xai, boats are often packed, while from Luang Prabang there should be plenty of room. Boats see very few passengers south of Luang Prabang. The only other regular long-distance service is the refreshingly local trip between Pakse and Si Phan Don (p228) via Champasak (see p215).

It's still fairly easy to charter a boat in Laos, for a price. Aside from the journey from Huay Xai to Luang Prabang, two of the most beautiful routes are Luang Nam Tha–Pak Tha (US$90, one to two days) and Nong Khiaw–Luang Prabang (US$65, five hours). Prices here are for whole boat charters, shared by up to 10 people.

River ferries were designed for cargo transport and facilities are quite basic. Passengers sit, eat and sleep on the wooden decks. The toilet (if there is one) is an enclosed hole in the deck at the back of the boat. It's a good idea to bring something soft on which to sit. Note that women customarily ride inside the ferries – the outside, front and especially the roof are considered 'improper' places to sit.

River Taxi

For shorter river trips, such as Luang Prabang to the Pak Ou Caves, it's usually best to hire a river taxi. The *héua hang nyáo* (longtail boats) are the most typical, though for a really short trip (eg crossing a river) a *héua phái* (rowboat) or one of the small improvised ferries can be hired. The *héua hang nyáo* are around US$3 to US$5 an hour for a boat with an eight- to 10-person capacity. Larger boats that carry up to 20 passengers are sometimes available for between US$5 and US$8 per hour, although higher tourist prices are often applied.

Along the upper Mekong River between Huay Xai and Vientiane, and on the Nam Ou between Luang Prabang and Hat Sa (Phongsali), Thai-built *héua wái* (speedboats) are common. They can cover a distance in six hours that might take a ferry two days or more. Charters cost at least US$20 per hour, but some ply regular routes so the cost can be shared among passengers.

BUS & SĂWNGTHĂEW

Long-distance public transport in Laos is either by bus or *săwngthăew* (literally 'two rows'), which are converted pick-ups or trucks with benches down either side. The public transport system in Laos is steadily improving, with more-regular buses and more options in terms of speed and comfort, at least on the main north–south road, Rte 13.

With the majority of highways in Laos now either in a reasonable condition or being upgraded, public transport by bus is booming. Places that were all but inaccessible a few years ago now see regular bus

---

KNOW YOUR BOAT

Following are some of the *héua* (boats) that you may encounter in your adventures along Laos's many waterways:

■ *héua sáa* – big, old, double-deck boats, almost extinct

■ *héua duan* (express boat) – roofed cargo boats, common on Huay Xai to Luang Prabang route; they're slow, but called 'express' because they're faster than double-deck boats

■ *héua wái* (speedboat) – these resemble a surfboard with a car engine strapped to the back; very fast, exhilarating, deafeningly loud, uncomfortable and dangerous (see p252)

■ *héua hang nyáo* (longtail boat) – boats (usually roofed but not always) with engine gimbal-mounted on the stern, found all over Laos

■ *héua phái* (rowboat) – essentially a pirogue; common in Si Phan Don.

services. Private operators have established services on a small number of routes – mainly along Rte 13 between Vientiane and Pakse – offering faster and more-luxurious air-con buses, known as VIP buses. Expect more routes to be added soon.

Despite these improvements, road trips in Laos can still be a test of endurance, especially in the northeast where there is barely a straight stretch of road to be found. Anywhere off the beaten (or sealed) track will also be a rough journey.

Passenger fares are very reasonable; less than US$1 per 100km on public buses but more on the air-con buses and minibuses that run the tourist routes. It's a good idea to book a day, or even a few hours, ahead if you want a little more luxury, or if there aren't many services on your route. You'll usually have to go to the bus station to do this, though some guesthouses can book tickets, for a fee. For an idea of prices, see Leaving Vientiane By Bus (p94).

CAR & MOTORCYCLE

Driving in Laos is easier than you might think. Sure, the road infrastructure is pretty basic, but outside of the large centres there are so few vehicles that it's a doddle when compared with Vietnam, China or Thailand. Motorcyclists planning to ride through Laos should check out the wealth of information at **Golden Triangle Rider** (www .GT-Rider.com).

Bring Your Own Vehicle

With a temporary importation permit it's possible to bring your vehicle into Laos through any border crossing with Thailand or Vietnam. Travel agencies on the Thai side can arrange the necessary permit for between 7000B and 8000B. In Chiang Khong this includes the cost of the ferry if you depart in the morning. Afternoon departures at Chiang Khong require chartering the large vehicle ferry for another 2000B.

From the Thai side you'll need to fill out an Information of Conveyance form to allow for the temporary export of a Thai-registered vehicle. On the Lao side you need to arrange a temporary export permit (usually referred to by the French term *laisser-passer*) and Lao vehicle insurance. For both sides you'll need photocopies of your driv-

er's licence, passport information page and vehicle registration papers.

Officially, the maximum initial permission you can obtain is for 15 days, even if you hold a visa valid for a longer period. However, some travellers have reported getting 30 days. If you can only obtain a 15-day permission, it's possible to extend the paperwork inside Laos. If you use an agency for the initial paperwork, it's a good idea to find out whether that agency has a representative in Laos in case you want to extend or if there are problems with the paperwork.

When you cross into Laos, be sure to stop at Lao customs and get your temporary import papers stamped. Failure to do this could result in a fine when you exit the country. Police in Laos will occasionally stop foreign-registered vehicles and ask to see your *laisser-passer*.

Driving Licence

To drive in Laos you need a valid International Driving Permit, which you need to apply for in your home country.

ROUTE 13: SAFE OR NOT?

In February 2004 an attack on a bus travelling Rte 13 north of Vang Vieng killed eight people, including two Western cyclists who came across the scene. Further attacks in 2003 killed and injured dozens more locals as a wave of violence swept the country, striking most regularly on Laos's busiest road. So is Rte 13 safe enough to travel?

There is no definitive answer. Rte 13 is certainly an easy target for those with intent, but between January and August 2004 there were no attacks whatsoever and traffic was flowing freely.

The identity and purpose of the attackers is a mystery, but the lack of recent action is encouraging. Some say the attacks are politically motivated (which means privately owned vehicles are theoretically safer); others, including the government, say it is banditry. Whoever is responsible, at the time of writing they were keeping quiet and Rte 13 was 'safe'. But until there has been at least a year without incident, 'safety' will be relative. If you're worried, take a plane. See p251 for more on road safety issues.

Fuel & Spare Parts

Fuel is relatively cheap at about US$0.50 a litre for petrol, slightly less for diesel. Fuel for motorcycles is available from drums in villages across the country. Diesel is available in most towns.

Spare parts are expensive and difficult to find, even in Vientiane.

Hire

Chinese- and Japanese-made 100cc step-through scooters can be hired for between US$5 and US$10 per day in most large centres. No licence is required. Try to get a Japanese bike (the ominously named Suzuki Smash, perhaps) if you're travelling any distance out of town. In Vientiane and Pakse 250cc dirt bikes are available for about US$20 per day.

It is possible to hire a self-drive vehicle, but when you consider that a driver usually costs no more, takes responsibility for damage and knows where he's going, it seems pointless. Informal charters can be arranged almost anywhere, with small Japanese pickups going for between US$40 and US$100

per day, depending on where you're going; the rougher the road, the higher the price.

The following companies have good reputations:

Asia Vehicle Rental (AVR; Map pp72-3; ☎ /fax 021-217493; www.avr.laopdr.com; 354-356 Th Samsenthai, Vientiane) The most reliable place to hire vehicles, with or without drivers. Offers 4WDs, vans, sedans. Recommended.

Lao Chaleun Hotel (Map p213; ☎ 031-251333; Th 10, Pakse) Cars, vans and 4WDs.

LaoWheels (☎ 021-223663, mobile 020-550 4604; laowheels@yahoo.com) One engaging man and his van. Christophe Kittirath speaks fluent French, good English, knows the country inside out and is a good driver. Highly recommended.

Insurance

Car-hire companies will provide insurance, but be sure to check exactly what is covered. Note that most travel insurance policies don't cover use of motorcycles.

Road Conditions

While the overall condition of roads is poor, work in recent years has made most of the main highways quite comfortable. Of the

Road Distances (km)

	Attapeu	Luang Nam Tha	Luang Prabang	Muang Khong	Nong Haet	Pakse	Phongsali	Phonsavan	Sam Neua	Savannakhet	Tha Khaek	Udomxai	Vang Vieng	Vientiane
Attapeu	---													
Luang Nam Tha	1400	---												
Luang Prabang	1133	267	---											
Muang Khong	186	1376	1109	---										
Nong Haet	1280	576	309	1256	---									
Pakse	212	1247	980	120	1127	---								
Phongsali	1547	359	414	1523	723	1394	---							
Phonsavan	1171	467	219	1147	109	1018	614	---						
Sam Neua	1346	446	375	1322	184	1193	593	175	---					
Savannakhet	411	1045	778	387	925	230	1192	816	991	---				
Tha Khaek	480	920	653	456	800	368	1067	691	866	125	---			
Udomxai	1294	106	161	1270	470	1141	253	361	340	939	814	---		
Vang Vieng	965	435	168	941	315	812	582	219	381	610	485	329	---	
Vientiane	812	676	384	788	468	659	811	374	612	457	332	578	153	---

main routes, only Rte 3 between Huay Xai and Luang Nam Tha, Rte 1 between Vieng Thong and Phu Lao Junction, and Rte 18, which cuts across the south to Vietnam, are still in poor shape; work on these is ongoing. Even the once-diabolical Rte 7 to Phonsavan and Rte 9 from Savannakhet to the Vietnamese border are now sealed and passable all year round. Rte 16 to Attapeu should be completed in 2005.

Elsewhere, unsurfaced roads are the rule. Laos has approximately 22,500km of classified roads and less than a quarter are sealed. Unsurfaced roads are particularly tricky in the wet season when many routes are impassable to all but 4WD vehicles. Wet or dry, Laos is so mountainous that relatively short road trips can take forever; a typical 200km upcountry trip could take from 10 to 18 hours, depending on conditions.

Road Hazards
Try to avoid driving at dusk and after dark; cows, buffaloes, chickens and dogs, not to mention thousands of people, head for home on the unlit roads, turning them into a dangerous obstacle course. Unsigned roadwork – often a huge hole in the road – is also a challenge in fading light.

Road Rules
Driving is on the right side, but Lao drivers use the left lane and then cross into the right lane – a potentially dangerous situation if you're not ready for it. Rather than stop and wait for traffic to pass, motorists usually merge into the oncoming traffic without bothering to look to the rear, reasoning that any big or fast-moving vehicle approaching from behind will sound a horn.

Every two-lane road has an invisible third lane in the middle that drivers feel free to use at any time. Passing on hills and blind curves is common.

HITCHING
Hitching is possible in Laos, but it's never entirely safe and not recommended for women, as the act of standing beside a road and waving at cars might be misinterpreted. If you are hitching, cars with red-on-yellow (private vehicle) or blue-on-white (international organisations and embassies) number plates might be the best ones to target. Long-distance cargo trucks are also a good bet.

LOCAL TRANSPORT
Apart from in Vientiane and, to a lesser extent, in Savannakhet and Pakse, you won't use local transport because Laos towns and cities are small enough to walk, if not cycle around.

Bus
Vientiane is the only city with a network of local buses (p95).

Pedicab
The bicycle *săam-lâaw*, known as a *cyclo* (*sii-khlo*) elsewhere in Indochina, is very much an endangered species in Laos. If you can find a *săam-lâaw*, fares are about the same as for motorcycle taxis.

Jumbo, Săam-lâaw, Sakai-làep, Tuk-tuk
The various three-wheeled taxis found in Vientiane and provincial capitals have different names depending on where you are. It can be quite confusing. Usually the larger ones made in Thailand are called jumbo (*jąmbǫh*) and can hold four to six passengers. In Vientiane they are sometimes called tuk-tuk as in Thailand (though in Laos this usually refers to a slightly larger vehicle than the jumbo), while in the south (eg Pakse and Savannakhet) they may be called *sakai-làep* (Skylab) because of the perceived resemblance to a space capsule! But wait, there's more…these three-wheeled conveyances are also labelled simply *thaek-sii* (taxi) or *săam-lâaw* (samlor or three-wheels). Whatever you call it, people will usually know what you're after.

Fares vary according to the city you're in and your bargaining skills. Locals generally pay about US$0.25 per kilometre on trips of not longer than about 20km.

Taxi
Vientiane has a handful of car taxis that are used by foreign businesspeople and the occasional tourist. The only place you'll find these are at the airports (arrival times only), at the Thai-Lao Friendship Bridge and in front of the larger hotels. They can be hired by the trip, by the hour or by the day. Typical all-day hire within a town or city costs between US$20 and US$40 depending on the vehicle and your negotiating powers. By the trip, you shouldn't pay more than US$0.50 per kilometre.

TOURS

Like so much in Laos, there is a growing number of tour operators running a wide variety of trips. Travel agencies in your home country will probably be able to book a tour of Laos, but it's cheaper to deal direct with the operators in Laos, cutting out the middleman. A common two-week tour might take in Vientiane, Luang Prabang, the Plain of Jars (Xieng Khuang), Savannakhet, Salavan and Champasak, although the better operators can customise itineraries. More specialised tours are also becoming more popular, with rafting, kayaking, cycling, trekking and motorcycling tours all available.

The following are worth investigating:

Adventurelao (☎ mobile 020-550 8719) On request, can organise 250cc motorbike rides.

Action Max Laos (☎ 071-253489; http://actionmaxasia .com; 02/169 Ban Xieng Muan, Luang Prabang) Trekking specialists.

Asian Motorcycling Adventures (www.asianbiketour .com) Hard-core motocross.

Diethelm Travel Laos (Map pp72-3; ☎ 021-213833; www.diethelm-travel.com; Nam Phu, Vientiane)

Exotissimio (Map pp72-3; www.exotissimo.com; Th Pangkham, Vientiane) Fairly new but getting good reports; mix of pure sightseeing tours and adventure tours.

Inter-Lao Tourisme (Map pp68-9; ☎ 021-214832; www.visit-laos.com/touroperators/Interlao/; 07/073 Th Luang Prabang, Vientiane)

Paddle Asia (www.laosadventure.com) Kayaking and rafting on a host of rivers, plus ethnic tours.

Sodetour (Société de Développement Touristique; Map pp72-3; ☎ 021-216314; sodetour@laotel.com; 114 Th Fa Ngum, Vientiane)

Spiceroads (www.spiceroads.com) Specialises in cycling tours. Very well organised.

Tiger Trails (☎ 071-252372; indochina1@yahoo.com; Th Phothisarat, Luang Prabang) Experienced trekking, rafting and kayaking outfit in Luang Prabang.

Wildside Green Adventure(Map pp72-3; ☎ www.wildside.com) Biggest adventure tourism operator in Laos. Kayaking, trekking, cycling, rock climbing, rafting…

Health

Dr Trish Batchelor

Health issues and the quality of medical facilities vary enormously depending on where and how you travel in Laos. Travellers tend to worry about contracting infectious diseases when in the tropics, but infections are a rare cause of serious illness or death in travellers. Pre-existing medical conditions such as heart disease, and accidental injury (especially traffic accidents), account for most life-threatening problems. Becoming ill in some way, however, is relatively common. Fortunately most common illnesses can either be prevented with common-sense behaviour or be treated easily with a well-stocked traveller's medical kit.

The following advice is a general guide only and does not replace the advice of a doctor trained in travel medicine.

BEFORE YOU GO

Pack medications in their original, clearly labelled, containers. A signed and dated letter from your physician describing your medical conditions and medications, including generic names, is also a good idea. If carrying syringes or needles, be sure to have a physician's letter documenting their medical necessity. If you have a heart condition bring a copy of your ECG taken just prior to travelling.

If you happen to take any regular medication bring double your needs in case of loss or theft. In Laos it can be difficult to find some of the newer drugs, particularly the latest antidepressant drugs, blood pressure medications and contraceptive pills.

INSURANCE

Even if you are fit and healthy, don't travel without health insurance – accidents do happen. Declare any existing medical conditions you have – the insurance company *will* check if your problem is pre-existing and will not cover you if it is undeclared. You may require extra cover for adventure activities such as rock climbing. If your health insurance doesn't cover you for medical expenses abroad, consider getting extra insurance – check **LonelyPlanet.com** (www.lonelyplanet.com) for more information. If you're uninsured, emergency evacuation is expensive; bills of over US$100,000 are not uncommon.

Find out in advance if your insurance plan will make payments directly to providers or reimburse you later for overseas health expenditures. (In many countries doctors expect payment in cash.) Some policies offer lower and higher medical-expense options; the higher ones are chiefly for countries that have extremely high medical costs, such as the USA. You may prefer a policy that pays doctors or hospitals directly rather than you having to pay on the spot and claim later. If you have to claim later, keep all the documentation.

HEALTH ADVISORIES

It's usually a good idea to consult your government's travel-health website before departure, if one is available:
Australia (www.dfat.gov.au/travel/)
Canada (www.travelhealth.gc.ca)
New Zealand (www.mfat.govt.nz/travel)
UK (www.doh.gov.uk/traveladvice)
US (www.cdc.gov/travel/)

Some policies ask you to call back (reverse charges) to a centre in your home country where an immediate assessment of your problem is made.

VACCINATIONS

The only vaccine required by international regulations is yellow fever. Proof of vaccination will only be required if you have visited a country in the yellow-fever zone within the six days prior to entering Southeast Asia. If you are travelling to Southeast Asia from Africa or South America you should check to see if you require proof of vaccination.

Specialised travel-medicine clinics are your best source of information; they stock all available vaccines and will be able to give specific recommendations for you and your trip. The doctors will take into account factors such as past vaccination history, the length of your trip, activities you may be undertaking, and underlying medical conditions, such as pregnancy.

RECOMMENDED VACCINATIONS

The World Health Organization (WHO) recommends the following vaccinations for travellers to Southeast Asia:

- Adult diphtheria and tetanus – Single booster recommended if you've had none in the previous 10 years. Side effects include a sore arm and fever.

- Hepatitis A – Provides almost 100% protection for up to a year; a booster after 12 months provides at least another 20 years' protection. Mild side effects such as headache and a sore arm occur for between 5% and 10% of people.

- Hepatitis B – Now considered routine for most travellers. Given as three shots over six months. A rapid schedule is also available, as is a combined vaccination with Hepatitis A. Side effects are mild and uncommon, usually a headache and sore arm. Lifetime protection occurs in 95% of people.

- Measles, mumps and rubella – Two doses of MMR required unless you have had the diseases. Occasionally a rash and flulike illness can develop a week after receiving the vaccine. Many young adults require a booster.

- Polio – In 2002, no countries in Southeast Asia reported cases of polio. Only one booster is required as an adult for lifetime protection. Inactivated polio vaccine is safe during pregnancy.

- Typhoid – Recommended unless your trip is less than a week and only to developed cities. The vaccine offers around 70% protection, lasts for two or three years and comes as a single shot. Tablets are also available; however, the injection is usually recommended as it has fewer side effects. Sore arm and fever may occur.

- Varicella – If you haven't had chickenpox, discuss this vaccination with your doctor.

Long-term travellers

These vaccinations are recommended for people travelling more than one month, or those at special risk:

- Japanese B Encephalitis – Three injections in all. Booster recommended after two years. A sore arm and headache are the most common side effects. Rarely, an allergic reaction comprising hives and swelling can occur up to 10 days after any of the three doses.

- Meningitis – Single injection. There are two types of vaccination: the quadrivalent vaccine gives two to three years protection; meningitis group C vaccine gives around 10 years protection. Recommended for long-term backpackers aged under 25.

- Rabies – Three injections in all. A booster after one year will provide 10 years protection. Side effects are rare – occasionally a headache and sore arm.

- Tuberculosis – Adult long-term travellers are usually recommended to have a TB skin test before and after travel, rather than vaccination. Only one vaccine is given in a lifetime.

Most vaccines don't produce immunity until at least two weeks after they're given, so visit a doctor four to eight weeks before departure. Ask your doctor for an International Certificate of Vaccination (otherwise known as the yellow booklet), which will list all the vaccinations you've received. In the US, the yellow booklet is no longer issued, but it is highly unlikely the Lao authorities will ask for proof of vaccinations (unless you have recently been in a yellow-fever effected country). See Recommended Vaccinations p278 for possible vaccinations.

INTERNET RESOURCES
There is a wealth of travel health advice on the Internet. For further information, **LonelyPlanet.com** (www.lonelyplanet.com) is a good place to start. The **World Health Organization** (WHO; www.who.int/ith/) publishes a superb book called *International Travel & Health*, which is revised annually and is available on line at no cost. Another website of general interest is **MD Travel Health** (www.mdtravelhealth .com), which provides complete travel health recommendations for every country and is updated daily. The **Centers for Disease Control and Prevention** (CDC; www.cdc.gov) website also has good general information.

FURTHER READING
Lonely Planet's *Healthy Travel – Asia & India* is a handy pocket-size book that is packed with useful information including pretrip planning, emergency first aid, immunisation and disease information and what to do if you get sick on the road. Other recommended references include *Traveller's Health* by Dr Richard Dawood and *Travelling Well* by Dr Deborah Mills – check out the website (www.travellingwell.com.au).

IN TRANSIT

DEEP VEIN THROMBOSIS (DVT)
Deep vein thrombosis (DVT) occurs when blood clots form in the legs during plane flights, chiefly because of prolonged immobility. The longer the flight, the greater the risk. Though most blood clots are reabsorbed uneventfully, some may break off and travel through the blood vessels to the lungs, where they may cause life-threatening complications.

MEDICAL CHECKLIST

Recommended items for a personal medical kit:

- antifungal cream, eg Clotrimazole
- antibacterial cream, eg Muciprocin
- antibiotics for skin infections, eg Amoxicillin/Clavulanate or Cephalexin
- antibiotics for diarrhoea, eg Norfloxacin or Ciprofloxacin; Azithromycin for bacterial diarrhoea; and Tinidazole for giardiasis or amoebic dysentery
- antihistamines for allergies, eg Cetrizine for daytime and Promethazine for night
- anti-inflammatories, eg Ibuprofen
- antinausea medication, eg Prochlorperazine
- antiseptic for cuts and scrapes, eg Betadine
- antispasmodic for stomach cramps, eg Buscopa
- contraceptives
- decongestant for colds and flus, eg Pseudoephedrine
- DEET-based insect repellent
- diarrhoea 'stopper', eg Loperamide
- first-aid items such as scissors, plasters (Band Aids), bandages, gauze, thermometer (electronic, not mercury), sterile needles and syringes and tweezers
- indigestion medication, eg Quick Eze or Mylanta
- iodine tablets (unless you are pregnant or have a thyroid problem) to purify water
- laxative, eg Coloxyl
- migraine medication (your personal brand), if a migraine sufferer
- oral-rehydration solution for diarrhoea, eg Gastrolyte
- paracetamol for pain
- permethrin (to impregnate clothing and mosquito nets) for repelling insects
- steroid cream for allergic/itchy rashes, eg 1% to 2% hydrocortisone
- sunscreen and hat
- throat lozenges
- thrush (vaginal yeast infection) treatment, eg Clotrimazole pessaries or Diflucan tablet
- urine alkalisation agent, eg Ural, if you're prone to urinary tract infections.

HEALTH

The chief symptom of DVT is swelling or pain of the foot, ankle, or calf, usually on just one side. When a blood clot travels to the lungs, it may cause chest pain and difficulty in breathing. Travellers with any of these symptoms should immediately seek medical attention.

To prevent the development of DVT on long flights you should walk about the cabin, perform isometric compressions of the leg muscles (ie contract the leg muscles while sitting), drink plenty of fluids, and avoid alcohol and tobacco.

JET LAG & MOTION SICKNESS

Jet lag is common when crossing more than five time zones; it results in insomnia, fatigue, malaise or nausea. To avoid jet lag try drinking plenty of fluids (nonalcoholic) and eating light meals. Upon arrival, seek exposure to natural sunlight and readjust your schedule (for meals, sleep etc) as soon as possible.

Antihistamines such as dimenhydrinate (Dramamine) and meclizine (Antivert, Bonine) are usually the first choice for treating motion sickness. Their main side effect is drowsiness. A herbal alternative is ginger, which works like a charm for some people.

IN LAOS

AVAILABILITY OF HEALTHCARE

Laos has no facilities for major medical emergencies. The state-run hospitals and clinics are among the worst in Southeast Asia in terms of the standards of hygiene, staff training, supplies and equipment, and the availability of medicines.

For minor to moderate conditions, including malaria, **Mahasot International Clinic** (☎ 021-214022) in Vientiane has a decent reputation.

For any serious conditions, you're better off going to Thailand. If a medical problem can wait until you're in Bangkok, then all the better, as there are excellent hospitals there.

For medical emergencies that can't be delayed before reaching Bangkok, you can call ambulances from nearby Nong Khai or Udon Thani in Thailand. **Nong Khai Wattana General Hospital** (☎ 0066 4246 5201; fax 4246 5210) in Nong Khai is the closest. **Aek Udon Hospital** (☎ 0066 4234 2555; fax 4234 1033) in

Udon Thani is better, but it's an hour further from the border by road. **Lao Westcoast Helicopter** (☎ 021-512023; fax 512055; Hangar 703, Wattay International Airport), will fly emergency patients to Udon Thani for US$1500, subject to aircraft availability and government permission. **Si Nakharin Hospital** (☎ 0066 4323 7602/6) is further away in Khon Kaen but is supposed to be the best medical facility in northeastern Thailand. From any of these hospitals, patients can be transferred to Bangkok if necessary.

Citizens of certain British Commonwealth countries have access to Vientiane's **Australian Embassy Clinic** (Map pp68-9; ☎ 021-413603, after hours 511462; ⏰ 8.30am-12.30pm & 2-5pm Mon-Thu, 8.30am-12.30pm Fri), reportedly the best medical facility in Laos.

Self-treatment may be appropriate if your problem is minor (eg traveller's diarrhoea), you are carrying the appropriate medication and you cannot attend a recommended clinic. If you think you may have a serious disease, especially malaria, do not waste time – travel to the nearest quality facility. It is always better to be assessed by a doctor than to rely on self-treatment.

Buying medication over the counter is not recommended, as fake medications and poorly stored or out-of-date drugs are common in Laos.

INFECTIOUS DISEASES
Dengue Fever

This mosquito-borne disease is becomingly increasingly problematic throughout Laos, especially in the cities. As there is no vaccine it can only be prevented by avoiding mosquito bites. The mosquito that carries dengue bites day and night, so use insect avoidance measures at all times. Symptoms include high fever, severe headache and body ache (dengue was once known as 'breakbone fever'). Some people develop a rash and diarrhoea. There's no specific treatment, just rest and paracetamol – do not take aspirin as it increases the likelihood of haemorrhaging. See a doctor to be diagnosed and monitored.

Filariasis

This is a mosquito-borne disease that is very common in the local population, yet very rare in travellers. Mosquito-avoidance measures are the best way to prevent it.

Hepatitis A

A problem throughout the region, this food- and water-borne virus infects the liver, causing jaundice (yellow skin and eyes), nausea and lethargy. There is no specific treatment for hepatitis A, you just need to allow time for the liver to heal. All travellers to Southeast Asia should be vaccinated against hepatitis A.

Hepatitis B

The only sexually transmitted disease that can be prevented by vaccination, hepatitis B is spread by body fluids, including sexual contact. In some parts of Southeast Asia up to 20% of the population are carriers of hepatitis B, and usually are unaware of this. The long-term consequences can include liver cancer and cirrhosis.

Hepatitis E

Hepatitis E is transmitted through contaminated food and water and has similar symptoms to hepatitis A, but is far less common. It is a severe problem in pregnant women and can result in the death of both mother and baby. There is currently no vaccine; prevention is by following safe eating and drinking guidelines.

HIV

According to Unaids and WHO, Laos remains a 'low HIV prevalence country'; Unaids reported a range of between 1000 and 1800 as of 2001. However, it's estimated that only about one fifth of all HIV cases in Laos are actually reported. Heterosexual sex is the main method of transmission in Laos.

The use of condoms greatly decreases but does not eliminate the risk of HIV infection. The Lao phrase for 'condom' is *thœng anáamái*. Condoms can be purchased at most *hâan khǎi yáa* (pharmacies). It is worth bringing your own condoms from home.

Influenza

Present year-round in the tropics, influenza (flu) symptoms include high fever, muscle aches, runny nose, cough and sore throat. It can be very severe in people over the age of 65 or in those with underlying medical conditions such as heart disease or diabetes; vaccination is recommended for these individuals. There is no specific treatment, just rest and paracetamol.

Japanese B Encephalitis

While a rare disease in travellers, at least 50,000 locals are infected with Japanese B Encephalitis each year in Southeast Asia. This viral disease is transmitted by mosquitoes. Most cases occur in rural areas and vaccination is recommended for travellers spending more than one month outside of cities. There is no treatment, and a third of infected people will die while another third will suffer permanent brain damage.

Malaria

For such a serious and potentially deadly disease, there is an enormous amount of misinformation concerning malaria. You must get expert advice as to whether your trip actually puts you at risk. Many parts of Laos, particularly populated areas, have minimal to no risk of malaria, and the risk of side effects from the antimalaria medication may outweigh the risk of getting the disease. For some rural areas, however, the risk of contracting the disease far outweighs the risk of any tablet side effects. Remember that malaria can be fatal. Before you travel, seek medical advice on the right medication and dosage for you.

Malaria is caused by a parasite transmitted by the bite of an infected mosquito. The most important symptom of malaria is fever, but general symptoms such as headache, diarrhoea, cough, or chills may also occur. Diagnosis can only be made by taking a blood sample.

Two strategies should be combined to prevent malaria – mosquito avoidance, and antimalarial medications. Most people who catch malaria are taking inadequate or no antimalarial medication.

Travellers are advised to prevent mosquito bites by taking these steps:

■ Choose accommodation with screens and fans (if not air-conditioned).
■ Impregnate clothing with Permethrin in high-risk areas.
■ Sleep under a mosquito net impregnated with Permethrin.
■ Spray your room with insect repellent before going out for your evening meal.
■ Use a DEET-containing insect repellent on exposed skin. Wash this off at night, as long as you are sleeping under a mosquito net. Natural repellents such as Citronella can be effective, but must be

applied more frequently than products containing DEET.

- Use mosquito coils.
- Wear long sleeves and trousers in light colours.

MALARIA MEDICATION

There are a variety of medications available. The effectiveness of the Chloroquine and Paludrine combination is now limited in most of Southeast Asia. Common side effects include nausea (40% of people) and mouth ulcers. It is generally not recommended.

Lariam (Mefloquine) has received much bad press, some of it justified, some not. This weekly tablet suits many people. Serious side effects are rare but include depression, anxiety, psychosis and seizures. Anyone with a history of depression, anxiety, other psychological disorder, or epilepsy should not take Lariam. It is considered safe in the second and third trimesters of pregnancy. It is around 90% effective in most parts of Southeast Asia, but there is significant resistance in parts of northern Thailand, Laos and Cambodia. Tablets must be taken for four weeks after leaving the risk area.

Doxycycline, taken as a daily tablet, is a broad-spectrum antibiotic that has the added benefit of helping to prevent a variety of tropical diseases, including leptospirosis, tick-borne disease, typhus and melioidosis. The potential side effects include photosensitivity (a tendency to sunburn), thrush in women, indigestion, heartburn, nausea and interference with the contraceptive pill. More serious side effects include ulceration of the oesophagus – you can help prevent this by taking your tablet with a meal and a large glass of water, and never lying down within half an hour of taking it. It must be taken for four weeks after leaving the risk area.

Malarone is a new drug combining Atovaquone and Proguanil. Side effects are uncommon and mild, most commonly nausea and headaches. It is the best tablet for scuba divers and for those on short trips to high-risk areas. It must be taken for one week after leaving the risk area.

Derivatives of Artesunate are not suitable as a preventive medication. They are useful treatments under medical supervision.

A final option is to take no preventive medication but to have a supply of emergency medication should you develop the symptoms of malaria. This is less than ideal, and you'll need to get to a good medical facility within 24 hours of developing a fever. If you choose this option the most effective and safest treatment is Malarone (four tablets once daily for three days). Other options include Mefloquine and Quinine but the side effects of these drugs at treatment doses make them less desirable. Fansidar is no longer recommended.

Measles

Measles remains a problem in some parts of Southeast Asia. This highly contagious bacterial infection is spread via coughing and sneezing. Most people born before 1966 are immune as they had the disease in childhood. Measles starts with a high fever and rash and can be complicated by pneumonia and brain disease. There is no specific treatment.

Melioidosis

This infection is contracted by skin contact with soil. It is rare in travellers. The symptoms are very similar to those experienced by tuberculosis sufferers. There is no vaccine but it can be treated with medications.

Opisthorchiasis (Liver Flukes)

These are tiny worms that are occasionally present in freshwater fish in Laos. The main risk comes from eating raw or undercooked fish. Travellers should in particular avoid eating uncooked *pạa dàek* (an unpasteurised fermented fish used as an accompaniment for many Lao foods) when travelling in rural Laos. The *pạa dàek* in Vientiane and Luang Prabang is said to be safe (or safer) simply because it is usually produced from noninfected fish, while the risk of infestation is greatest in the southern provinces.

A rarer way to contract liver flukes is by swimming in the Mekong River or its tributaries around Don Khong (Khong Island) in the far south of Laos.

At low levels, there are virtually no symptoms at all; at higher levels, an overall fatigue, a low-grade fever and swollen or tender liver (or general abdominal pain) are the usual symptoms, along with worms or worm eggs in the faeces. Opisthorchiasis is easily treated with medications. Untreated, patients may develop serious liver infections several years after contact.

Rabies

This uniformly fatal disease is spread by the bite or lick of an infected animal – most commonly a dog or monkey. You should seek medical advice immediately after any animal bite and commence post-exposure treatment. Having a pretravel vaccination means the postbite treatment is greatly simplified. If an animal bites you, gently wash the wound with soap and water, and apply iodine based antiseptic. If you are not vaccinated you will need to receive rabies immunoglobulin as soon as possible.

Schistosomiasis

Schistosomiasis (also called bilharzia) is a tiny parasite that enters your skin when swimming in contaminated water – travellers usually only get a light, symptomless infection. If you are concerned, you can be tested three months after exposure. On rare occasions, travellers may develop 'Katayama fever' – this occurs some weeks after exposure, as the parasite passes through the lungs and causes an allergic reaction – symptoms are coughing and fever. Schistosomiasis is easily treated with medications.

STDs

Sexually transmitted diseases most common in Laos include herpes, warts, syphilis, gonorrhoea and chlamydia. People carrying these diseases often have no signs of infection. Condoms will prevent gonorrheae and chlamydia but not warts or herpes. If after a sexual encounter you develop any rash, lumps, discharge or pain when passing urine seek immediate medical attention. If you have been sexually active during your travels have an STD check on your return home.

Strongyloides

This parasite, also transmitted by skin contact with soil, rarely affects travellers. It is characterised by an unusual skin rash called larva currens – a linear rash on the trunk which comes and goes. Most people don't have other symptoms until their immune system becomes severely suppressed, when the parasite can cause an overwhelming infection. It can be treated with medications.

Tuberculosis

Tuberculosis (TB) is very rare in short-term travellers. Medical and aid workers, and

SARS

In March 2003 the world's attention was drawn to the outbreak of an apparently new and serious respiratory illness that became known as SARS (Severe Acute Respiratory Syndrome). At the time of writing SARS appears to have been brought under control. Since the outbreak commenced, 8500 cases were confirmed, resulting in 800 deaths. The peak of disease activity was in early May 2003, when over 200 new cases were being reported daily. The outbreak started in the Chinese province of Guangdong in November 2002. By mid-March numerous cases of an unusually virulent respiratory virus were being reported in Hong Kong, Vietnam, Singapore and Canada. The World Health Organization (WHO) soon issued a global alert to health authorities and the public. Although this helped to bring the disease under control, it also resulted in widespread panic, and the cost of SARS to countries in the Far East as a result of lost tourism and trade was estimated as at least US$30 billion.

The cause of SARS was identified in April 2003 – a new virus unlike any other previously known in humans or animals. The symptoms of SARS are identical to many other respiratory infections, namely high fever and cough. The case definition of SARS is a person with fever and cough who has travelled to an infected area or had close contact with an infected individual within the previous 10 days. There is no specific quick test for SARS but certain blood test and chest X-ray results offer support for the diagnosis. There is no specific treatment available and death from respiratory failure occurs in around 10% of patients. Fortunately it appears it is not as easy to catch SARS as was initially thought. Wearing masks has limited effectiveness and is not generally recommended.

The risk of contracting SARS is extremely low. However, there are still fundamental questions to be answered about SARS – where did it come from, will it come back and can we develop a rapid test or treatment for it? At least another year will be needed to see whether SARS has become established in our ecosystem.

long-term travellers who have significant contact with the local population should take precautions, however. Vaccination is usually only given to children under the age of five, but adults at risk are recommended pre- and post-travel TB testing. The main symptoms are fever, cough, weight loss, night sweats and tiredness.

Typhoid

This serious bacterial infection is also spread via food and water. It gives a high, slowly progressive fever and headache, and may be accompanied by a dry cough and stomach pain. It is diagnosed by blood tests and treated with antibiotics. Vaccination is recommended for all travellers spending more than a week in Southeast Asia, or travelling outside of the major cities. Be aware that vaccination is not 100% effective so you must still be careful with what you eat and drink.

Typhus

Murine typhus is spread by the bite of a flea whereas scrub typhus is spread via a mite. These diseases are rare in travellers. Symptoms include fever, muscle pains and a rash. You can avoid these diseases by following general insect-avoidance measures. Doxycycline will also prevent them.

TRAVELLER'S DIARRHOEA

Traveller's diarrhoea is by far the most common problem affecting travellers – between 30% and 50% of people will suffer from it within two weeks of starting their trip. In over 80% of cases, traveller's diarrhoea is caused by a bacteria (there are numerous potential culprits), and therefore responds promptly to treatment with antibiotics. Treatment with antibiotics will depend on your situation – how sick you are, how quickly you need to get better, where you are etc.

Traveller's diarrhoea is defined as the passage of more than three watery bowel-actions within 24 hours, plus at least one other symptom such as fever, cramps, nausea, vomiting or feeling generally unwell.

Treatment consists of staying well-hydrated. Rehydration solutions like Gastrolyte are the best for this. Antibiotics such as Norfloxacin, Ciprofloxacin or Azithromycin will kill the bacteria quickly.

Loperamide is just a 'stopper' and doesn't get to the cause of the problem. It can be helpful, for example if you have to go on a long bus ride. Don't take Loperamide if you have a fever, or blood in your stools. Seek medical attention quickly if you do not respond to an appropriate antibiotic.

Amoebic Dysentery

Amoebic dysentery is very rare in travellers but is often misdiagnosed by poor-quality labs in Southeast Asia. Symptoms are similar to bacterial diarrhoea, ie fever, bloody diarrhoea and generally feeling unwell. You should always seek reliable medical care if you have blood in your diarrhoea. Treatment involves two drugs; Tinidazole or Metroniadzole to kill the parasite in your gut and then a second drug to kill the cysts. If left untreated complications such as liver or gut abscesses can occur.

Giardiasis

Giardia lamblia is a parasite that is relatively common in travellers. Symptoms include nausea, bloating, excess gas, fatigue and intermittent diarrhoea. 'Eggy' burps are often attributed solely to giardiasis, but work in Nepal has shown that they are not specific to this infection. The parasite will eventually go away if left untreated but this can take months. The treatment of choice is Tinidazole, with Metronidazole being a second line option.

ENVIRONMENTAL HAZARDS
Food

Eating in restaurants is the biggest risk factor for contracting traveller's diarrhoea. Ways to avoid it include eating only freshly cooked food, and avoiding shellfish and food that has been sitting around in buffets. Peel all fruit, cook vegetables, and soak salads in iodine water for at least 20 minutes. Eat in busy restaurants with a high turnover of customers.

Heat

Many parts of Southeast Asia are hot and humid throughout the year. For most people it takes at least two weeks to adapt to the climate. Swelling of the feet and ankles is common, as are muscle cramps caused by excessive sweating. Prevent these by avoiding dehydration and excessive activity in the heat. Take it easy when you first arrive. Don't eat salt tablets (they aggravate the gut) but do drink rehydration solution and eat salty food. Treat cramps by resting, rehydrating with double-strength rehydration solution and gently stretching.

Dehydration is the main contributor to heat exhaustion. Symptoms include feeling weak, headache, irritability, nausea or vomiting, sweaty skin, a fast, weak pulse and a normal or slightly elevated body temperature. Treatment involves getting out of the heat and/or sun, fanning the victim and applying cool wet cloths to the skin, laying the victim flat with their legs raised and rehydrating with water containing a quarter of a teaspoon of salt per litre. Recovery is usually rapid, though it is common to feel weak for some days afterwards.

Heatstroke is a serious medical emergency. Symptoms come on suddenly and include weakness, nausea, a hot dry body with a body temperature of over 41°C, dizziness, confusion, loss of coordination, seizures and eventually collapse and loss of consciousness. Seek medical help and commence cooling by getting the person out of the heat, removing their clothes, fanning them and applying cool wet cloths or ice to their body, especially to the groin and armpits.

Prickly heat is a common skin rash in the tropics, caused by sweat being trapped under the skin. The result is an itchy rash of tiny lumps. Treat by moving out of the heat and into an air-conditioned area for a few hours and by having cool showers. Creams and ointments clog the skin so they should be avoided. Locally bought prickly heat powder can be helpful.

Tropical fatigue is common in long-term expats based in the tropics. It's rarely due to disease and is caused by the climate, inadequate mental rest, excessive alcohol intake and the demands of daily work in a different culture.

Insect Bites & Stings

Bedbugs don't carry disease but their bites are very itchy. They live in the cracks of furniture and walls and then migrate to the bed at night to feed on you. You can treat the itch with an antihistamine. Lice inhabit various parts of your body but most commonly your head and pubic area. Transmission is via close contact with an infected

---

DRINKING WATER

- Never drink tap water.

- Bottled water is generally safe – check the seal is intact at purchase.

- Avoid fresh juices – they may have been watered down.

- Boiling water is the most efficient method of purifying it.

- The best chemical purifier is iodine. It should not be used by pregnant women or those people who suffer with thyroid problems.

- Water filters should filter out viruses. Ensure your filter has a chemical barrier such as iodine and a small pore size, ie less than four microns.

---

person, although body lice can come from contaminated bedclothes. They can be difficult to treat and you may need numerous applications of an antilice shampoo such as Permethrin, or in the case of body lice, with medicated creams or ointments. Pubic lice are usually contracted from sexual contact.

Ticks are contracted during walks in rural areas. They are commonly found behind the ears, on the belly and in armpits. If you have had a tick bite and experience symptoms such as a rash (at the site of the bite or elsewhere), fever or muscle aches you should see a doctor. Doxycycline prevents tick-borne diseases.

Leeches are found in humid forest areas. They do not transmit any disease but their bites are often intensely itchy for weeks afterwards and can easily become infected. Apply an iodine-based antiseptic to any leech bite to help prevent infection.

Bee and wasp stings mainly cause problems for people who are allergic to them. Anyone with a serious bee or wasp allergy should carry an injection of adrenaline (eg an Epipen) for emergency treatment. For others pain is the main problem – apply ice to the sting and take painkillers.

Parasites

Numerous parasites are common in local populations in Southeast Asia; however, most of these are rare in travellers. The two rules to follow if you wish to avoid parasitic infections are to wear shoes and to avoid eating raw food, especially fish, pork and vegetables. A number of parasites are transmitted via the skin by walking barefoot including strongyloides, hookworm and cutaneous larva migrans.

Skin Problems

Fungal rashes are common in humid climates. There are two common fungal rashes that affect travellers. The first occurs in moist areas that get less air such as the groin, armpits and between the toes. It starts as a red patch that slowly spreads and is usually itchy. Treatment involves keeping the skin dry, avoiding chafing and using an antifungal cream such as Clotrimazole or Lamisil. *Tinea versicolor* is also common – this fungus causes small, light-coloured patches, most commonly on the back, chest and shoulders. Consult a doctor.

Cuts and scratches become easily infected in humid climates. Take meticulous care of any cuts and scratches to prevent complications such as abscesses. Immediately wash all wounds in clean water and apply antiseptic. If you develop signs of infection (increasing pain and redness) see a doctor. Divers and surfers should be particularly careful with coral cuts as they become easily infected.

Snakes

Southeast Asia is home to many species of both poisonous and harmless snakes. Assume all snakes are poisonous and never try to catch one. Always wear boots and long pants if walking in an area that may have snakes. First-aid in the event of a snakebite involves pressure immobilisation via an elastic bandage firmly wrapped around the affected limb, starting at the bite site and working up towards the chest. The bandage should not be so tight that the circulation is cut off, and the fingers or toes should be kept free so the circulation can be checked. Immobilise the limb with a splint and carry the victim to medical attention. Do not use tourniquets or try to suck the venom out. Antivenom is available for most species.

Sunburn

Even on a cloudy day sunburn can occur rapidly. Always use a strong sunscreen (at least factor 30), making sure to reapply after a swim, and always wear a wide-brimmed hat and sunglasses outdoors. Avoid lying in the sun during the hottest part of the day (from 10am to 2pm). If you are sunburnt stay out of the sun until you have recovered, apply cool compresses and take painkillers for the discomfort. One percent hydrocortisone cream applied twice daily is also helpful.

WOMEN'S HEALTH

Pregnant women should receive specialised advice before travelling. The ideal time to travel is in the second trimester (between 16 and 28 weeks), when the risk of pregnancy-related problems are lowest and pregnant women generally feel at their best. During the first trimester there is a risk of miscarriage and in the third trimester complications such as premature labour and high blood pressure are possible. It's wise to travel with a companion. Always carry a list of quality medical facilities available at your destination and ensure you continue your standard antenatal care at these facilities. Avoid rural travel in areas with poor transportation and medical facilities. Most of all, ensure travel insurance covers all pregnancy-related possibilities, including premature labour.

Malaria is a high-risk disease during pregnancy. WHO recommends that pregnant women do *not* travel to areas with Chloroquine-resistant malaria. None of the more effective antimalarial drugs are completely safe in pregnancy.

Traveller's diarrhoea can quickly lead to dehydration and result in inadequate blood flow to the placenta. Many of the drugs used to treat various diarrhoea bugs are not recommended in pregnancy. Azithromycin is considered safe.

In the urban areas of Southeast Asia, supplies of sanitary products are readily available. Birth control options may be limited so bring adequate supplies of your own form of contraception. Heat, humidity and antibiotics can all contribute to thrush. Treatment is with antifungal creams and pessaries such as Clotrimazole. A practical alternative is a single tablet of Fluconazole (Diflucan). Urinary tract infections can be precipitated by dehydration or long bus journeys without toilet stops; bring suitable antibiotics.

TRADITIONAL MEDICINE

Throughout Southeast Asia, traditional medical systems are widely practised. There is a big difference between these traditional healing systems and 'folk' medicine. Folk remedies should be avoided, as they often involve rather dubious procedures with potential complications. In comparison, traditional healing systems such as traditional Chinese medicine are well respected, and aspects of them are being increasingly utilised by Western medical practitioners.

All traditional Asian medical systems identify a vital life force, and see blockage or imbalance as causing disease. Techniques such as herbal medicines, massage, and acupuncture are utilised to bring this vital force back into balance, or to maintain balance. These therapies are best used for treating chronic disease such as chronic fatigue, arthritis, irritable bowel syndrome and some chronic skin conditions. Traditional medicines should be avoided for treating serious acute infections such as malaria.

Be aware that 'natural' doesn't always mean 'safe', and there can be drug interactions between herbal medicines and Western medicines. If you are utilising both systems ensure you inform both practitioners what the other has prescribed.

HEALTH

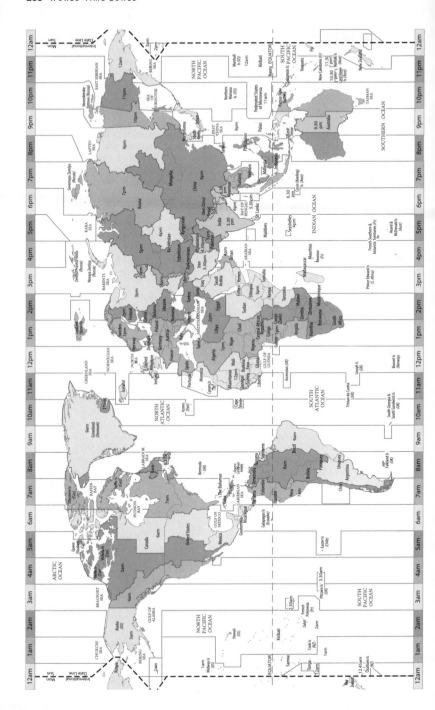

Language

CONTENTS

The official language of the LPDR is Lao as spoken and written in Vientiane. As an official language, it has successfully become the lingua franca (a universally understood linking language) between all Lao and non-Lao ethnic groups in Laos. Native Lao is spoken with differing tonal accents and with slightly differing vocabularies as you move from one part of the country to the next, especially in a north to south direction, but it is the Vientiane dialect that is most widely understood.

Modern Lao linguists recognise five basic dialects within the country: Vientiane Lao; northern Lao (spoken in Sainyabuli, Bokeo, Udomxai, Phongsali, Luang Nam Tha and Luang Prabang); northeastern Lao (Xieng Khuang and Hua Phan), central Lao (Khammuan and Bolikhamsai); and finally southern Lao (Champasak, Savannakhet, Salavan, Attapeu and Sekong). Each of these can be further divided into various subdialects; the differences between the Lao spoken in the neighbouring provinces of Xieng Khuang and Hua Phan, for example, are readily apparent to those who know the language well.

All dialects of Lao belong to the Thai half of the Thai-Kadai family of languages and are closely related to languages spoken in Thailand, northern Myanmar and pockets of China's Yunnan and Guangxi Provinces. Standard Lao is indeed close enough to standard Thai (as spoken in central Thailand) that for native speakers the two are mutually intelligible. In fact, virtually all of the speakers of Lao west of the Annamite Chain can easily understand spoken Thai, since the majority of the television and radio programmes they tune in to are broadcast from Thailand.

Among educated Lao, written Thai is also easily understood, in spite of the fact that the two scripts differ (to about the same degree that the Greek and Roman scripts differ). This is because many of the textbooks used at the college and university level in Laos are actually Thai texts.

Even more similar to Standard Lao are Thailand's northern and northeastern Thai dialects. There are actually more Lao speakers living in Thailand than in Laos, so if you're travelling to Laos after a spell in Thailand (especially the northeast), you should be able to put whatever you learned in Thailand to good use. (It doesn't work as well in the opposite direction; native Thais can't always understand Lao, since they've had less exposure to it.)

For information on food and dining in Laos, see p52. For a more in-depth guide to Lao than we have room for in this guide, get a copy of Lonely Planet's *Lao Phrasebook*. If you plan to travel extensively in any Lao Sung areas, Lonely Planet's *Hill Tribes Phrasebook* could also be useful.

OTHER LANGUAGES

In the cities and towns of the Mekong River valley, French is intermittently understood. In spite of its colonial history, French remains the official second language of the government and many official documents are written in both Lao and French. Shop signs sometimes appear in French (alongside Lao, as mandated by law), though signs in English are becoming more common. As in Vietnam, the former colonial language is increasingly viewed as irrelevant in a region that has adopted English as the lingua franca of business and trade, and among young Lao students English is now much more popular than French. Lao over the age of 50 may understand a little English, but to a lesser extent than French.

Many Russian-trained Lao can also speak Russian, though the language has drastically fallen from favour. The Russian Cultural Centre now offers more English courses than it does Russian, and the most popular event at the centre is an evening satellite TV programme of English-language shows. The occasional Lao who studied abroad in Cuba or Eastern Europe may be able to speak Spanish, German, Czech, Polish or even Bulgarian.

It pays to learn as much Lao as possible during your stay in the country, since speaking and understanding the language not only enhances verbal communication but garners a great deal of respect from the Lao people you come into contact with.

SCRIPT

Prior to the consolidation of the various Lao *meuang* (principalities) in the 14th century, there was little demand for a written language. When a written language was deemed necessary by the Lan Xang monarchy, Lao scholars based their script on an early alphabet devised by the Thais (which in turn had been created by Khmer scholars who used south Indian scripts as models!). The alphabet used in Laos is closer to the original prototype; the original Thai script was later extensively revised (which is why Lao looks 'older' than Thai, even though it is newer as a written language).

Before 1975 at least four spelling systems were in use. Because modern printing never really got established in Laos (most of the advanced textbooks being in Thai, French, or Vietnamese before the Revolution), Lao spelling wasn't standardised until after the Pathet Lao takeover. The current system has been highly simplified by transliterating all foreign loan words according to their sound only, and not their written form.

Lao script can therefore be learned much more quickly than Thai or Khmer, both of which typically attempt to transcribe foreign borrowings letter for letter, regardless of the actual pronunciation.

One peculiarity of the post-1975 system is that it forbade the use of the Lao letter 'r' in words where it was more commonly pronounced as an 'l', reportedly because of the association of the 'r' with classical Thai; although the 'r' was virtually lost in Laos (converting to 'h' in some cases and to 'l' in others), in many parts of Thailand it is still quite strong. Hence the names of former Lao kings Setthathirat and Phothisarat came to be rendered as Setthathilat and Phothisalat in post-1975 Lao script. Eventually the government loosened its restrictions and although the nasty 'r' is still not taught in the school system, it is once again allowed to be used in signage and in historical documents.

Other scripts still in use include *láo thám* (*dhamma* Lao), used for writing Pali scriptures, and various Thai tribal scripts, the most popular and widespread being that of the Thai Neua (which has become standardised via Xishuangbanna, China).

The Lao script today consists of 30 consonants (formed from 20 basic sounds) and 28 vowels and diphthongs (15 individual symbols used in varying combinations). Complementing the consonant and vowel symbols are four tone marks, only two of which are commonly used in creating the six different tones (in combination with all the other symbols). Written Lao proceeds from left to right, though vowel-signs may appear in a number of positions relative to consonants: before, after, above, below or 'around' (ie before, above *and* after).

Although learning the alphabet isn't difficult, the writing system itself is fairly complex, so unless you are planning to have a lengthy stay in Laos you should perhaps make learning to speak the language your main priority.

TONES

Basically, Lao is a monosyllabic, tonal language, like the various dialects of Thai and Chinese. Borrowed words from Sanskrit, Pali, French and English often have two or more syllables, however. Many identical phonemes or vowel-consonant combinations are differentiated by their tone only. The word *sao*, for example, can mean 'girl', 'morning', 'pillar' or 'twenty' depending on the tone. For people from non-tonal language backgrounds, it can be very hard to learn at first. Even when we 'know' the correct tone, our tendency to denote emotion, emphasis and questions through tone modulation often interferes with uttering the correct tone. So the first rule in learning and using the tone system is to avoid overlaying your native intonation patterns onto the Lao language.

Vientiane Lao has six tones (compared with five used in standard Thai, four in Mandarin and nine in Cantonese). Three of the tones are level (low, mid and high) while three follow pitch inclines (rising, high falling and low falling). All six variations in pitch are relative to the speaker's natural vocal range, so that one person's low tone is not necessarily the same pitch as another person's. Hence, keen pitch recognition is not a prerequisite for learning a tonal language like Lao. A relative distinction between pitch contours within your own voice is all that is necessary. Pitch variation is common to all languages; non-tonal languages such as English also use intonation, just in a different way.

Low Tone

Produced at the relative bottom of your conversational tonal range – usually flat level, eg *dǐi* (good). Note, however, that not everyone pronounces it flat and level – some Vientiane natives add a slight rising tone to the end.

Mid Tone

Flat like the low tone, but spoken at the relative middle of the speaker's vocal range. No tone mark is used, eg *het* (do).

High Tone

Flat again, this time at the relative top of your vocal range, eg *héua* (boat).

Rising Tone

Begins a bit below the mid tone and rises to just at or above the high tone, eg *sǎam* (three).

High Falling Tone

Begins at or above the high tone and falls to the mid level, eg *sâo* (morning).

Low Falling Tone

Begins at about the mid level and falls to the level of the low tone, eg *khào* (rice).

On a visual curve the tones might look like this:

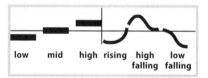

low   mid   high   rising   high   low
                            falling falling

TRANSLITERATION

The rendering of Lao words into the Roman alphabet is a major problem, since many of the Lao sounds, especially certain vowels, do not occur in English. The problem is compounded by the fact that because of Laos's colonial history, transcribed words most commonly seen in Laos are based on the old colonial French system of transliteration, which bears little relation to the way an English speaker would intuitively write a Lao word.

A prime example is the capital of Laos, Vientiane. The Lao pronunciation, following a fairly logical English-Roman transliteration, would be Wieng Chan or Vieng Chan (some might hear it more as Wieng Jan). Since the French don't have a written consonant that corresponds to 'w', they chose to use a 'v' to represent all 'w' sounds, even though the 'v' sound in Lao is closer to an English 'w'. The same goes for 'ch' (or 'j'), which for the French was best rendered 'ti-'; hence Wieng Chan (which means Sandalwood City) finishes up as 'Vientiane' in the French transliteration. The 'e' is added so that the final 'n' sound isn't partially lost, as it is in French words ending with 'n'. This latter phenomenon also happens with words like *lâan* (million) as in Lan Xang, which most French speakers would write as 'Lane', a spelling that leads most English speakers to incorrectly pronounce this word like the 'lane' in 'Penny Lane'.

Many standard place names in the Roman alphabet use an 'x' for what in English is 's'. This 'x' represents a Lao letter that historically was pronounced 'ch' but eventually became 's' in the Lao sound system. There's no difference in the pronunciation of the two; pronounce all instances of 'x' as 's'.

There is no official method of transliterating the Lao language (the government is incredibly inconsistent in this respect, though they tend to follow the old French methods). This book use a custom system of transliteration based on the Royal Thai General Transcription system, since Thai and Lao have very similar writing and sound systems. The only exceptions are where there may be confusion with terms that are already in common use (eg Vientiane vs 'Wieng Chan', Luang Prabang vs 'Luang Phabang').

The public and private sectors in Laos are gradually moving towards a more internationally recognisable system along the lines of Royal Thai General (which is fairly readable across a large number of language types).

PRONUNCIATION
Vowels

Lao vowels can be written before, after, above and below consonants – in the following vowel chart we demonstrate this by using 'x' to represent any consonant.

x̊	**i**	as in 'it'
x̂	**ii**	as in 'feet' or 'tea'
ໄx, ໃx	**ai**	as in 'aisle'
xາ	**aa**	long 'a' as in 'father'
xະ	**a**	half as long as **aa** above
ແx	**ae**	as the 'a' in 'bad' or 'tab'
ເx ະ, ເ x̆x **e**		as in 'hen'
ເx	**eh**	as the 'a' in 'hate'
ເx̂, ເx̂	**oe**	as the 'u' in 'fur'
x̂, x̂	**eu**	as in French *deux*, or as the 'i' in 'sir'
x̥	**u**	as in 'flute'
x̥	**uu**	as in 'food'
xາຍ	**aai**	as the 'a' in 'father' + the 'i' in 'pipe'
ເx̂າ	**ao**	as in 'now' or 'cow'
x̊	**aw**	as in 'jaw'
ໂxະ, x̂ x	**o**	as in 'phone'
ໂx	**oh**	as in 'toe'
ເx̂ອ	**eua**	diphthong of 'eu' and 'a'
xⅠx, ເx̂ຍ	**ia**	as the 'i-a' sound in 'Ian'
xວx, x̂ວ	**ua**	as the 'u-a' sound in 'tour'
xວຍ	**uay**	'u-ay-ee'
x̂ວ, x̂ວ	**iu**	'i-oo' (as in 'yew')
xⅠວ	**iaw**	a triphthong of 'ee-a-oo'
ແxວ	**aew**	as the 'a' in 'bad' + 'w'
ເxວ	**ehw**	as the 'a' in 'care' + 'w'
ເx̂ວ	**ew**	same as 'ehw' above, but shorter (not as in 'yew')
ເx̃ຍ	**oei**	'oe-i'
xອຍ	**awy**	as the 'oy' in 'boy'
ໂx̃ຍ	**ohy**	'oh-i'

Consonants

An 'aspirated' consonant is produced with no audible puff of air. An 'unvoiced' or 'voiceless' consonant is produced with no vibration in the vocal chords.

ກ	**k**	as the 'k' in 'skin'; similar to the 'g' in 'good', but unaspirated and unvoiced
ຂ, ຄ	**kh**	as the 'k' in 'kite'
ງ	**ng**	as in 'sing'; used as an initial consonant in Lao
ຈ	**j**	similar to 'j' in 'join' or more closely, the second 't' in 'stature' or 'literature' (unaspirated and voiceless)
ສ, ຊ	**s**	as in 'soap'
ຍ	**ny**	similar to the 'ni' in 'onion'; used as an initial consonant in Lao
ດ	**d**	as in 'dodo'
ຕ	**t**	a hard 't', unaspirated and unvoiced – a bit like 'd'
ທ, ຖ	**th**	as in 'tip'
ນ, ໜ	**n**	as in 'nun'
ບ	**b**	as in 'boy'
ປ	**p**	a hard 'p' (unaspirated and unvoiced)
ພ, ຜ	**ph**	'p' as in 'put' (but never as in 'phone')
ຝ, ຟ	**f**	as in 'fan'
ມ, ໝ	**m**	as in 'man'
ຢ	**y**	as in 'yo-yo'
ລ, ຫລ	**l**	as in 'lick'
ວ, ຫວ	**w**	as in 'wing' (often transliterated as 'v')
ຮ, ຫ	**h**	as in 'home'

ACCOMMODATION

hotel
hóhng háem
ໂຮງແຮມ

guesthouse
hăw hap kháek
ຫໍຮັບແຂກ

Excuse me, is there a hotel nearby?
khăw thôht, mĭi hóhng háem yuu kâi nĭi baw?
ຂໍໂທດ ມີໂຮງແຮມຢູ່ໃກ້ນີ້ບໍ່

Do you have a room?
mĭi hàwng baw?
ມີຫ້ອງບໍ່

How many persons?
ják khón?
ຈັກຄົນ

one person
neung khón (khón diaw)
ນຶ່ງຄົນ (ຄົນດຽວ)

two persons
săwng khón
ສອງຄົນ

How much ...?
... thao dąi? ... ເທົ່າໃດ
  per night
  khéun-la ຄືນລະ
  per week
  qathit-la ອາທິດລະ

air-conditioning
qe yén ແອເຢັນ
bathroom
hàwng nâm ຫ້ອງນ້ຳ
blanket
phàa hom ຜ້າຫົ່ມ
double room
hàwng náwn tíang khuu ຫ້ອງນອນຕຽງຄູ່
fan
phat lóm ພັດລົມ
hot water
nâm hàwn ນ້ຳຮ້ອນ
key
kájąe ກະແຈ
room
hàwng ຫ້ອງ
sheet
phàa pųu bawn náwn ຜ້າປູບ່ອນນອນ
single room
hàwng náwn tíang diaw ຫ້ອງນອນຕຽງດຽວ

soap
sábuu ສະບູ
toilet
sùam ສ້ວມ
towel
phàa set tŏh ຜ້າເຊັດໂຕ

(I/we) will stay two nights.
si phak yuu săwng khéun
ຊິພັກຢູ່ສອງຄືນ

Can (I/we) look at the room?
khăw boeng hàwng dâi baw?
ຂໍເບິ່ງຫ້ອງໄດ້ບໍ່

Do you have other rooms?
mĭi hàwng lîk baw?
ມີຫ້ອງອິກບໍ່

cheaper
théuk-kwaa
ຖືກກວ່າ

quieter
mit-kwaa
ມິດກວ່າ

CONVERSATION & ESSENTIALS

Greetings/Hello.
sábqai-dĭi ສະບາຍດີ
Goodbye. (general farewell)
sábqai-dĭi ສະບາຍດີ
Goodbye. (person leaving)
láa kawn pąi kawn ລາກ່ອນໄປກ່ອນ
Goodbye. (person staying)
sŏhk dĭi (lit: good luck) ໂສກດີ
See you later.
phop kąn mai ພົບກັນໃໝ່
Thank you.
khàwp jąi ຂອບໃຈ
Thank you very much.
khàwp jąi lăi lăi ຂອບໃຈຫລາຍໆ
It's nothing/You're welcome.
baw pęn nyăng ບໍ່ເປັນຫຍັງ
Excuse me.
khăw thôht ຂໍໂທດ
How are you?
sábqai-dĭi baw? ສະບາຍດີບໍ່
I'm fine.
sábqai-dĭi ສະບາຍດີ
And you?
jâo dêh? ເຈົ້າເດ

What's your name?
jâo seu nyǎng? ເຈົ້າຊື່ຫຍັງ
My name is ...
khàwy seu ... ຂ້ອຍຊື່ ...
Glad to know you.
dǐi-jai thii hûu káp jâo ດີໃຈທີ່ຮູ້ກັບເຈົ້າ
Where are you from?
jâo máa tae sǎi? ເຈົ້າມາແຕ່ໃສ
I'm from ...
khàwy máa tae ... ຂ້ອຍມາແຕ່ ...

DIRECTIONS

Which ... is this?
bawn nìi ... nyǎng? ບ່ອນນີ້ ... ຫຍັງ
street/road/avenue
thanǒn ຖນົນ
city
méuang ເມືອງ
village
muu bâan ໝູ່ບ້ານ
province
khwǎeng ແຂວງ

Turn ...
líaw ... ລ້ຽວ ...
left
sâai ຊ້າຍ
right
khwǎa ຂວາ

Go straight ahead.
pai seu-seu ໄປຊື່ໆ
How far?
kai thao dai? ໄກເທົ່າໃດ
near/not near
kâi/bạw kâi ໃກ້/ບໍ່ໃກ້
far/not far
kai/bạw kai ໄກ/ບໍ່ໄກ
north
thit něua ທິດເໜືອ
south
thit tâi ທິດໃຕ້
east
thit tạwén àwk ທິດຕາເວັນອອກ
west
thit tạwén tók ທິດຕາເວັນຕົກ

HEALTH

I'm not well.
khàwy baw sábqai ຂ້ອຍບໍ່ສະບາຍ
I need a doctor.
khàwy tâwng-kqan mǎw ຂ້ອຍຕ້ອງການໝໍ

EMERGENCIES

Help!
suay dae! ຊ່ອຍແດ່
Fire!
fái mài! ໄຟໄໝ້
It's an emergency!
súk sǒen! ສຸກເສີນ
Go away!
pai dôe! ໄປເຖີ

Call a doctor!
suay tqam hǎa mǎw hài dae!
ຊ່ອຍຕາມຫາໝໍ ໃຫ້ແດ່
Call an ambulance!
suay ôen lot hóhng mǎw hài dae!
ຊ່ອຍເອີ້ນລົດໂຮງໝໍ ໃຫ້ແດ່
Call the police!
suay ôen tam-lùat dae!
ຊ່ອຍເອີ້ນຕຳຫລວດແດ່
Could you help me please?
jạo suay khàwy dại baw?
ເຈົ້າຊ່ອຍຂ້ອຍໄດ້ບໍ່
I'm lost.
khàwy lǒng tháang
ຂ້ອຍຫລົງທາງ
Where are the toilets?
hàwng sùam yuu sǎi?
ຫ້ອງສ້ວມຢູ່ໃສ

I have a fever.
pẹn khài ເປັນໄຂ້
I have diarrhoea.
lóng thâwng ລົງທ້ອງ
It hurts here.
jép yuu nìi ເຈັບຢູ່ນີ້

allergic (to)
phǎe ແພ້
anaemia
lôhk lêuat nâwy ໂລກເລືອດໜ້ອຍ
asthma
lôhk hèut ໂລກຫືດ
diabetes
lôhk bạo wǎn ໂລກເບົາຫວານ
malaria
khài paa ໄຂ້ປ່າ
pregnant
thěu pháa-máan ຖືພາມານ
(mǐi thâwng) (ມີທ້ອງ)
toothache
jép khàew ເຈັບແຂ້ວ

LANGUAGE DIFFICULTIES

Can you speak English?
jâo pàak pháasǎa ǫngkít dâi baw?
ເຈົ້າປາກພາສາອັງກິດໄດ້ບໍ່

A little.
náwy neung
ໜ້ອຍນຶ່ງ

I can't speak Lao.
khàwy pàak pháasǎa láo baw dâi
ຂ້ອຍປາກພາສາລາວບໍ່ໄດ້

Do you understand?
jâo khào jǫi baw?
ເຈົ້າເຂົ້າໃຈບໍ່

(I) don't understand.
baw khào jǫi
ບໍ່ເຂົ້າໃຈ

Please speak slowly.
kálunáa wâo sâa-sâa
ກະລຸນາເວົ້າຊ້າໆ

Please repeat.
kálunáa wâo mai boeng dųu
ກະລຸນາເວົ້າໃໝ່ ເບິ່ງດູ

What do you call this in Lao?
ąn-nǐi pháasǎa láo waa nyǎng?
ອັນນີ້ພາສາລາວວ່າຫຍັງ

NUMBERS

0	*sǔun*	ສູນ
1	*neung*	ນຶ່ງ
2	*sǎwng*	ສອງ
3	*sǎam*	ສາມ
4	*sii*	ສີ່
5	*hàa*	ຫ້າ
6	*hók*	ຫົກ
7	*jét*	ເຈັດ
8	*pàet*	ແປດ
9	*kâo*	ເກົ້າ
10	*síp*	ສິບ
11	*síp-ét*	ສິບເອັດ
12	*síp-sǎwng*	ສິບສອງ
20	*sáo*	ຊາວ
21	*sáo-ét*	ຊາວເອັດ
22	*sáo-sǎwng*	ຊາວສອງ
30	*sǎam-síp*	ສາມສິບ

40	*sii-síp*	ສີ່ສິບ
50	*hàa-síp*	ຫ້າສິບ
60	*hók-síp*	ຫົກສິບ
70	*jét-síp*	ເຈັດສິບ
80	*pàet-síp*	ແປດສິບ
90	*kâo-síp*	ເກົ້າສິບ
100	*hâwy*	ຮ້ອຍ
200	*sǎwng hâwy*	ສອງຮ້ອຍ
1000	*phán*	ພັນ
10,000	*meun (síp-phán)*	ໝື່ນ(ສິບພັນ)
100,000	*sǎen (hâwy phán)*	ແສນ(ຮ້ອຍພັນ)
one million	*lâan*	ລ້ານ

| first | *thǐi neung* | ທີ່ນຶ່ງ |
| second | *thǐi sǎwng* | ທີສອງ |

PLACES & LAND FEATURES

Buddhist temple
wat ວັດ

cemetery
paa sâa ປ່າຊ້າ

church
sǐm khlit ສິມຄລິດ

forest
paa ປ່າ

jungle
dǒng ດົງ

mountain
phúu khǎo ພູເຂົາ

park/garden
sǔan ສວນ

rice field (wet)
náa ນາ

river
mae nâm ແມ່ນ້ຳ

sea
thaléh ທະເລ

stupa
thâat ທາດ

swamp
beung ບຶງ

trail/footpath
tháang thíaw/nyaang ທາງຫຍາວ/ທາງຢ່າງ

waterfall
nâm tók tàat ນ້ຳຕົກຕາດ

SHOPPING & SERVICES

Where is the ...?
... yùu sǎi? ... ຢູ່ໃສ

I'm looking for (the) ...
khàwy sâwk hǎa ...   ຂ້ອຍຊອກຫາ ...
   bank
   thanáakháan   ທະນາຄານ
   barber shop
   hâan tát phǒm   ຮ້ານຕັດຜົມ
   bookshop
   hâan khǎai nǎng sěu   ຮ້ານຂາຍໜັງສື
   hospital
   hóhng mǎw   ໂຮງໝໍ
   museum
   phiphithaphán   ພິພິທະພັນ
   pharmacy
   hâan khǎai yqa   ຮ້ານຂາຍຢາ
   post office
   pqi-sá-nii (hóhng sǎai)   ໄປສະນີ (ໂຮງສາຍ)

I want to change ...
khàwy yàak pian ...   ຂ້ອຍຢາກປ່ຽນ ...
   money
   ngóen   ເງິນ
   travellers cheques
   sek dôen tháang   ເຊັກເດີນທາງ

I'm looking for ...
   khàwy sàwk hǎa ...   ຂ້ອຍຊອກຫາ ...
How much (for) ...?
   ... thao dại?   ... ເທົ່າໃດ
I'd like to see another style.
   khǎw boeng ìik
   bàep neung   ຂ້ຳເບິ່ງອີກແບບນື່ງ
Do you have something cheaper?
   mii thèuk-kwaa nii baw?   ມີຖືກກວ່ານີ້ບໍ່
The price is very high.
   láakháa pháeng lǎai   ລາຄາແພງຫລາຍ

(latex) condoms
   thǒng yqang anáamái   ກົງຢາງອະນາໄມ
sanitary napkins
   phàa anáamái   ຜ້າອະນາໄມ
soap
   sá-buu   ສະບູ
toilet paper
   jǐa hàwng nâm   ເຈ້ຍຫ້ອງນ້ຳ
toothbrush
   pqeng thǔu khàew   ແປງຖູແຂ້ວ

telephone
   thóhlasáp
   ໂທລະສັບ
international call
   thóhlasáp lawaang páthêt
   ໂທລະສັບລະຫວ່າງປະເທດ

long distance (domestic)
   tháang kại
   ທາງໄກ
open/closed
   pòet/pít
   ເປີດ/ປິດ

TIME & DATES

today
   mêu nii   ມື້ນີ້
tonight
   khéun nii   ຄືນນີ້
this morning
   sâo nii   ເຊົ້ານີ້
this afternoon
   baai nii   ບ່າຍນີ້
all day long
   talàwt mêu   ຕລອດມື້
now
   diaw nii/tqwn nii   ດຽວນີ້/ຕອນນີ້
sometimes
   bqang theua   ບາງເທື່ອ
yesterday
   mêu wáan nii   ມື້ວານນີ້
tomorrow
   mêu eun   ມື້ອືນ

Sunday
   wán qathit   ວັນອາທິດ
Monday
   wán jqn   ວັນຈັນ
Tuesday
   wán qngkháan   ວັນອັງຄານ
Wednesday
   wán phut   ວັນພຸດ
Thursday
   wán phahát   ວັນພະຫັດ
Friday
   wán súk   ວັນສຸກ
Saturday
   wán sǎo   ວັນເສົ້າ

January
   dęuan mángkqwn   ເດືອນມັງກອນ
February
   dęuan kųmpháa   ເດືອນກຸມພາ
March
   dęuan miináa   ເດືອນມິນາ
April
   dęuan méhsǎa   ເດືອນເມສາ
May
   dęuan pheutsápháa   ເດືອນພຶດສະພາ
June
   dęuan mithúnáa   ເດືອນມິຖຸນາ

July
deuan kąwlakót ເດືອນກໍລະກົດ
August
deuan sǐnghǎa ເດືອນສິງຫາ
September
deuan kąnyáa ເດືອນກັນຍາ
October
deuan túláa ເດືອນຕຸລາ
November
deuan phajík ເດືອນພະຈິກ
December
deuan thánwáa ເດືອນທັນວາ

TRANSPORT

Where is the ...
... yùu sǎi?
... ຢູ່ໃສ
airport
doen bǐn
ເດິ່ນບິນ
bus station
sathǎanii lot pájąm tháang
ສະຖານີລົດປະຈຳທາງ
bus stop
bawn jàwt lot pájąm tháang
ບ່ອນຈອດລົດປະຈຳທາງ
departures/flights
thǐaw
ຖ້ຽວ
taxi stand
bawn jàwt lot thaek-sǐi
ບ່ອນຈອດລົດແທກຊີ

What time will the ... leave?
... já àwk ják móhng? ... ຈະອອກຈັກໂມງ
aeroplane
héua bǐn ເຮືອບິນ
bus
lot ລົດ
boat
héua ເຮືອ
minivan
lot tûu ລົດຕູ້

What time (do we, does it, etc) arrive there?
já pai hâwt phûn ják móhng?
ຈະໄປຮອດພຸ້ນຈັກໂມງ
Where do we get on the boat?
lóng héua yuu sǎi?
ລົງເຮືອຢູ່ໃສ

I want to go to ...
khàwy yàak pąi ...
ຂ້ອຍຢາກໄປ ...
I'd like a ticket.
khàwy yàak dâi pǐi
ຂ້ອຍຢາກໄດ້ປີ້
How much to ...?
pąi ... thao dąi?
ໄປ ... ເທົ່າໃດ
How much per person?
khón-la thao dąi?
ຄົນລະເທົ່າໃດ
May I sit here?
nang bawn nǐi dâi baw?
ນັ່ງບ່ອນນີ້ໄດ້ບໍ່
Please tell me when we arrive in ...
wéhláa hâwt ... bàwk khàwy dae
ເວລາຮອດ ... ບອກຂ້ອຍແດ່
Stop here. (lit: park here)
jàwt yuu nǐi
ຈອດຢູ່ນີ້

taxi
lot tháek-sǐi ລົດແທກຊີ
samlor (pedicab)
sǎam-lâw ສາມລໍ້
tuk-tuk (jumbo)
túk-túk ຕຸກ ຕຸກ

I'd like to rent a ...
khàwy yàak sao ... ຂ້ອຍຢາກເຊົ່າ ...
car
lot (ǒh-tǒh) ລົດ(ໂອໂຕ)
motorcycle
lot ják ລົດຈັກ
bicycle
lot thìip ລົດຖີບ

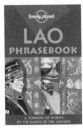

Also available from Lonely Planet:
Lao Phrasebook

LANGUAGE

Glossary

For a list of Lao words for different food and drink, see p58.

ąahaan – food
anatta – Buddhist concept of nonsubstantiality or nonessentiality of reality, ie no permanent 'soul'
anicca – Buddhist concept of impermanence, the transience of all things
Asean – Association of South East Asian Nations

bâan – the general Lao word for house or village; written Ban on maps
bąasii – sometimes spelt basi or *baci;* a ceremony in which the 32 *khwăn* (guardian spirits) are symbolically bound to the participant for health and safety
baht – *(bàat)* Thai unit of currency, commonly negotiable in Laos; also a Lao unit of measure equal to 15g
BCEL – Banque pour le Commerce Extérieur Lao; in English, Lao Foreign Trade Bank
bįa – beer; *bįa sót* is draught beer
bun – pronounced *bųn,* often spelt boun; a festival; also spiritual 'merit' earned through good actions or religious practices

corvée – enforced, unpaid labour

dhamma – (Pali) truth, teachings, the teachings of the Buddha, moral law; dharma in Sanskrit
Don – pronounced *dǫwn;* island
dukkha – Buddhist concept of suffering, unsatisfactoriness, dis-ease

falang – from the Lao *falang-sèht* or 'French'; Western, a Westerner
fǒe – rice noodles, one of the most common dishes in Laos

hǎi – jar
hǎw tąi – monastery building dedicated to the storage of the Tripitaka (Buddhist scriptures)
hét bun – 'making merit', mostly by almsgiving to monks
héua – boat
héua hang nyáo – longtail boat
héua phái – rowing boat

héua wái – speedboat
hùay – stream; written Huay on maps

jao – pronounced *jâo;* lord or prince
Jataka – (Pali-Sanskrit) mythological stories of the Buddha's past lives; *sáa-dók* in Lao
jęhdii – a Buddhist stupa; also written Chedi
jįin háw – Lao name for the Muslim Yunnanese who live in Northern Laos
jįntanáakąan mai – literally, new thinking; Lao form of *perestroika* (Russian economic reconstruction) introduced by the Lao government during the 1980s
jumbo – a motorised three-wheeled taxi, sometimes called tuk-tuk

kháen – a wind instrument devised of a double row of bamboolike reeds fitted into a hardwood soundbox and made air-tight with beeswax
khào – rice
khào jįi – bread
khào nǐaw – sticky rice, the Lao staple food
khào-nǒm – pastry or sweet; sometimes shortened to *khanǒm*
khúu-bąa – Lao Buddhist monk
khwǎeng – province
khwǎn – guardian spirits
kip – pronounced *kìip;* Lao unit of currency

láap – a spicy Lao-style salad of minced meat, poultry or fish
lák méuang – city pillar
lám wóng – 'circle dance', the traditional folk dance of Laos, as common at discos as at festivals
Lao Issara – Lao resistance movement against the French in the 1940s
lào-láo – distilled rice liquor
Lao Loum – 'lowland Lao', ethnic groups belonging to the Lao-Thai Diaspora
Lao Soung – 'high Lao', hill tribes who make their residence at higher altitudes, for example, Hmong, Mien; also spelt Lao Sung
Lao Thoeng – 'upland Lao', a loose affiliation of mostly Mon-Khmer peoples who live on mid-altitude mountain slopes
lingam – a pillar or phallus symbolic of Shiva, common in Khmer-built temples
LPDR – Lao People's Democratic Republic
LPRP – Lao People's Revolutionary Party

mae nâm – literally, water mother; river; usually shortened to *nâm* with river names, as in Nam Khong (Mekong River)

măw lám – Lao folk musical theatre tradition; roughly translates as 'master of verse'

meuang – pronounced *méuang*; district or town; in ancient times a city state; often written Muang on maps

múan – fun, which the Lao believe should be present in all activities

Muang – see *meuang*

muu bâan – village

náang síi – Buddhist nuns

naga – *nâa-kha* in Lao; mythical water serpent common to Lao-Thai legends and art

nâm – water; can also mean 'river', 'juice', 'sauce'; anything of a watery nature

néhn – Buddhist novice monk; also referred to as *samanera*

NGO – nongovernmental organisation, typically involved in the foreign-aid industry

nibbana – 'cooling', the extinction of mental defilements; the ultimate goal of Theravada Buddhism

NPA – National Protected Area, a classification assigned to 20 wildlife areas throughout Laos

NTAL – National Tourist Authority of Laos

NVA – North Vietnamese Army

pąa – fish

pąa dàek – fermented fish sauce, a common accompaniment to Lao food

Pathet Lao – literally, Country of Laos; both a general term for the country and a common journalistic reference to the military arm of the early Patriotic Lao Front (a cover for the Lao People's Party); often abbreviated to PL

pha – holy image, usually referring to a Buddha; venerable

phàa – cloth

phàa bjang – shoulder sash worn by men

phàa nung – sarong, worn by almost all Lao women

phàa salòng – sarong, worn by Lao men

Pha Lak Pha Lam – the Lao version of the Indian epic, the Ramayana

phansǎa – Buddhist Lent beginning in July, which coincides with the beginning of the rainy season; also *watsa*

phǐi – spirits; worship of these is the other main religion of Laos (and exists alongside Buddhism)

phúu – hill or mountain; also spelt phu

sǎa – the bark of a mulberry tree, from which paper is handcrafted

sǎaláa lóng thám – a *sala* (hall) where monks and lay people listen to Buddhist teachings

sǎam-lâaw – a three-wheeled pedicab; also written *samlor*

sabąi-dji – the Lao greeting

sǎinyasąat – folk magic

sakai-lèep – alternative name for *jumbo* in Southern Laos due to the perceived resemblance to a space capsule (Skylab)

sala – pronounced *sǎa-láa*; an open-sided shelter; a hall

samana – pronounced *sǎamanáa*; 'seminar'; euphemism for labour and re-education camps established after the 1975 Revolution

samanera – Buddhist novice monk; also referred to as *néhn*

sǎwngthǎew – literally, two-rows; a passenger truck; also written *songthaew*

se – also spelt *xe*; Southern Laos term for river; hence Se Don means Don River, and Pakse means *pàak* (mouth) of the river

shophouse – two-storey building designed to have a shop on the ground floor and a residence above

sǐi – sacred; also spelt *si*

sim – ordination hall in a Lao Buddhist monastery; named after the *sima*, (pronounced *siimáa*) or sacred stone tablets, which mark off the grounds dedicated for this purpose

soi – lane

tàat – waterfall; also *nâm tók;* written Tat on maps

talàat – market; *talàat sâo* is the morning market; *talàat mèut* is the free, or 'black', market; written Talat on maps

thâat – Buddhist stupa or reliquary; written That on maps

thaek-sǐi – taxi

thanǒn – street/road; often spelt Thanon on maps; shortened to 'Th' as street is to 'St'

tribal Thais – Austro-Thai (Tai) subgroups closely related to the Lao, who have resisted absorption into mainstream Lao culture

tuk-tuk – see *jumbo*

UXO – unexploded ordnance

Viet Minh – the Vietnamese forces who fought for Indochina's independence from the French

vipassana – insight meditation

wat – Lao Buddhist monastery

wihǎan – (Pali-Sanskrit vihara) a temple hall

Behind the Scenes

THIS BOOK
This is the 5th edition of *Laos*. Joe Cummings was the coordinating author, and also authored the two previous editions. Andrew Burke co-authored *Laos* 5. Dr Trish Batchelor prepared the Health chapter.

THANKS from the authors
Joe Cummings While travelling in Laos I received invaluable assistance from the Bill Tuffin and the Boat Landing; Greg Adamson; Greg Chapman; Oliver Bandmann and Baan Khily Gallery; John Demodena; Bill Weir; Korakot 'Nym' Punlopruksa; Sinlasone Soumpholphakdy and Vongxay Phongphanit of Sala Luang Prabang; Nicolas Pillet; Ivan Scholte; and Jo and Veomanee of OckPopTok.

I'd also like to thank all the readers who took time to send email, letters and postcards with helpful hints and corrections, most especially Susan Blick, Robin and Lizzie Hudson, Phil Dreith, Peter Todd, Susanne Rettig, Briana Bapty, Les Thompson, Chris Hayward, and Jenny Peacock.

Last but not least, thanks to co-author Andrew Burke for his admirable update of Southern Laos and Vientiane, and to editors Kalya Ryan and Suzannah Shwer for their fine work putting it all together.

Andrew Burke My biggest *khàwp jǫi lǎi lǎi* goes to the wonderful people of Laos – you are what makes this country so special. Among those locals and others who have come to call Laos home, Sisouphanh 'Christophe' Kittirath stands out for his good company and willingness to go the extra mile

(or 50) around Southern Laos. In Vientiane, thanks to Dr Klaus Schwettmann for being so passionate about Phu Khao Khuay NPA; Jan Dueker and especially Annette Monreal for sharing; George Ehrlich-Adam; and Virginia Addison. In Tha Khaek Jan Burrows, Ejnar Jorgensen and 'the Germans'; Jim Johnson in Savannakhet; Alan and Sririporn in Pakse; Leusak Soumpholphakdy on Don Khon; and Nikolai and Charlotte for their Sekong expertise. Among fellow travellers, Tom and Katrin the German-Aussies were especially helpful. Thanks also to Nicholas Bissel and Eve; Lucy Jenkins for her stimulating conversation; trailblazing Ponchai; and Karl Malakunas for his selfless dedication to pork in Attapeu. And to all those travellers who write with feedback, most notably Bill Weir, thanks. A simple thank you is insufficient for my family, who were even more supportive than usual. At Lonely Planet the saintly patience of Kalya Ryan and Corie Waddell was appreciated, and a special thanks to my ever-professional coauthor Joe Cummings.

CREDITS
Laos 5 was commissioned and developed in Lonely Planet's Melbourne office by Mary Neighbour and Kalya Ryan. Cartography for this guide was developed by Corie Waddell; the project was managed by Chris Love. Suzannah Shwer edited the book and coordinated proofing. Joanne Newell and Thalia Kalkipsakis proofed the book. Cartography was coordinated by Kusnandar and Emma McNicol, with assistance from Bonnie Wintle and Sally Morgan. The cover was designed by James Hardy and cover artwork was by Maria Vallianos.

THE LONELY PLANET STORY
The story begins with a classic travel adventure: Tony and Maureen Wheeler's 1972 journey across Europe and Asia to Australia. There was no useful information about the overland trail then, so Tony and Maureen published the first Lonely Planet guidebook to meet a growing need.

From a kitchen table, Lonely Planet has grown to become the largest independent travel publisher in the world, with offices in Melbourne (Australia), Oakland (USA), and London (UK).

Today Lonely Planet guidebooks cover the globe. There is an ever-growing list of books and information in a variety of media. Some things haven't changed. The main aim is still to make it possible for adventurous travellers to get out there – to explore and better understand the world. At Lonely Planet we believe travellers can make a positive contribution to the countries they visit – if they respect their host communities and spend their money wisely. Every year 5% of company profit is donated to charities around the world.

Sonya Brooke and David Kemp chose the colour images. Sonya also laid-out the book, with assistance from Steven Cann. Quentin Frayne compiled the Language chapter, and Bruce Evans brought his expertise to the script in the book.

THANKS from Lonely Planet

Many thanks to the following travellers who used the last edition and wrote to us with helpful hints, useful advice and interesting anecdotes.

A Gep Aadriaanse, Emily Adams, Jackman Adi, Michel Albregts, Lara Allen, Yorick Amerlynck, Simon Anderson, Kelly Askew, Warren Askew, Matthew Atherfold, Christine Atteneder, Alex Aziz **B** Chris Bain, Aaron Baker, David Baker, Martin Ballard, Cristiano Barberis, Mickey Barda, John Barnett, David Barr, Sarah Barrow, Natalie Bayliss, Steve Beatson, Mira Benes, Georgie Bennett, John Bennett, Nina Bert, Walter Bertschinger, Ferry & Annieke Bezem, Markus Bhnert, Matthew Glen Bigham, Tamzin Blair, Marc Blehert, Susan Blick, Rachel Bluck, Anthony Blythen, Michael Boller, Roger Bone, Julia Bonn, Roelien Booysen, Kees Botschuijver, David Boyall, Ernesto Braam, Kendal Bradley, Sophia Brickell, Joseph Brien, Alan Brocklehurst, Candice Kilpatrick Broom, Nick Broom, Cecile Brouwer, Alden Brown, Angus Brown, Chris Brown, York Bruijn, Werner Bruyninx, Mary Bryant, Roger Burrows, Marco Buschman **C** Kirsty Cambridge, Chris Carey, Susie Carr, Felicity Carus, Magnus Caullvine, Jean-Luc & Doris Chapatte, Lucy Chesser, Grant Cheung, Marjorie Chopin, Kinga Choszcz, Uwe Christner, Suwat Chumsri, Cristy Clark, Dean Clarke, Janette Clery, Kate Clifford, Hazel Colbert, Roberto Colombo, Annie Connolly, Richard Conway, Kay Cook, Trevor Cook, Erin Corry, Jean-louis Couderc, Philippe Coution, Luca Criscuoli, Gabor Csonka, Chris Custer **D** Jane Dancey, Markus Danhausen, Amanda Davies, Mike Davies, Sam Davies, Mark Dawson, Eddy de Bie, Gabriele de Gaudenzi, Georges de Graef, Peter de Ruiter, Barry de Vent, Steve Deadman, Andrea Dekkers, Peter Denton, Catherine & Richard Desomme-Koch, Fredrik Divall, Rosemary Dooley, Robert Dore, Alan Dowling, Phil Dreith, Jo Duthie, Mark Duvall **E** Helen Ebert, Christian Ebner, Yael Edrey, Oliver Eiss, Josie Ellis, Raz Elmaleh, Ranja Eloranta, Pernilla Engstrom, Richard Erb, Erik Eskin, James Evans, Paul Eveniss **F** Walter Falk, Erin Farnbach, Matt Farnholtz, Crists Fedryna, Erik Feenstra, Matt Feldmann, Lisa Ferguson, Luci Ferspal, Jamison Firestone, Jenny Fisher, Petra Fleck, Desirée Fleer, Mark Foley, Marco Fontana, Rebecca Frank, Triona Fry, Alexandra Fuchs, Andres Fukazawa **G** Sam Galloway, Dana Garrison, Frank Gaschen, Briseis Gatto, Sebastian Gee, Lia Genovese, Michael Geyerhofer, Bob & Eunice Goetz, Boaz Gofer, Christine Gordon, Mary Gorman, Professor F O Gorman, Chris Grabe, Joanne Griffin, Lewis Grove **H** Suzanne Hack, Mike Hagan, Andrew Hale, Sue Hall, Miranda Hamilton, Paul Hannon, Candida Hardenberg, Ed Hardy, Nick Harvey, Wendlandt Hasselle, Chris Hayward, Allan Healy, Susan Henderson, Claus Herting, Sonja Hilbrand, Michiel Hillenius, Jane Hollowell, Adrian Holman, Anne Hosking, Jug Hovi, Jill Ho-You, Petr Hruska, Robin Hudson, John Humble, Karen & Brian Humes, Martyn Humphreys, Quentin & Ann Hunter **I** Han Andre Iluk **J** Bastiaan Jaarsma, Danny Jacqmot, Jennifer Jakubowski, Lucy James, Anabelle Janier Clement, Sacha Jellinek, Richard Jones, Robert Jones, Karolien Joossens, Ejnar Jorgensen, Elmer Jutte **K** Anna Kaipainen, Line Kallstad, Tzvika Kanarek, Jennifer Karcher, Simon Karsties, Ancelikh Kaspinen, Yorgos Kechagioglou, Fiona Kendrick, Pamela Kiesselbach, Sarah Kinley, Susannah Kinley, Jay Klawier, Yvonne Kloepper, Ivo Kreiliger, Monika Kremser, George Kullmann **L** Vanessa Labossiere, Nina Laney, Roberto Latino, Liz Ledden, Konstantin Lederer, Sigal Lederman, Thomas Lehne, Iene Lemmens, Flo Lempp, Miki Lentin, Mikelson Leong, Elad Levi, Elton Levingston, Curt Lewis, Anna Liden, Angela Lingard, Tiffany Litzenberger, Marta Llorente, Danielle Loduca, Helen Lomas, Dirk Louwers, Traci Lund-Pederson, Maria Luptakova **M** Ian Macandrew, Jeff Mackinnon, John Maes, Andrea Malcouronne, Erin Mangurten, Michael Manivannan, Ariel Maor, Francois Margot, Susie Markham, Stéphane Martel, Holtz Martin, Benjamin Massen, Paul-Jack Mayska, Anna McEwen, JP McGuire, David J McLeod, Paul McTurk, Martin Meerkerk, Marieke Meijer, Ceciel Meys, Eithne Ni Mhorain, Robin Molenaar, Hans Mommer, Gavin Mooney, Nnenna Morah, James Morgan, Jane Morgan, Steffi Morgner, Sarah Morlok, Paul Morrison, Scott Morrison, Peter Morrissey, Dan Moshe, Phyllis Mui, Sonja Munnix, Ginger Muranaka, R H Murray-Philipson **N** Osnat Naor, Catherine Nauer, Dale Ne, Ruhama Neis, Chris Nelson, Udi Nir, Bruce Nisker, Sally Ann Northcliffe **O** Valentine Ockhuizen, Britta Oehler, Claire Olberding, Patrick Oldacre, Noey O'Rielly, Rachel O'Rourke, Carin & Jason Osburn, Ingvild & Jan Helge Ostensen, Paul O'Sullivan **P** Sarah Lynne Palomo, Aristea Parissi, Sarah Parsons, Jenny Peacock, Malcolm Pearch, Robert Sylvest

SEND US YOUR FEEDBACK

We love to hear from travellers – your comments keep us on our toes and help make our books better. Our well-travelled team reads every word on what you loved or loathed about this book. Although we cannot reply individually to postal submissions, we always guarantee that your feedback goes straight to the appropriate authors, in time for the next edition. Each person who sends us information is thanked in the next edition – and the most useful submissions are rewarded with a free book.

To send us your updates – and find out about Lonely Planet events, newsletters and travelnews–visitouraward-winningwebsite: **www.lonelyplanet.com/feedback**.

Note: We may edit, reproduce and incorporate your comments in Lonely Planet products such as guidebooks, websites and digital products, so let us know if you don't want your comments reproduced or your name acknowledged. For a copy of our privacy policy visit www.lonelyplanet.com/privacy.

Pedersen, John Peene, Kaj Pellberg, Llee Pennock, Lizzie Pettitt, Vithaya Phengsy, Ng Keng Phoy, Chaiya Pimrada, Jörn Pinnow, Sallo Polak, Michal Polat, Eva Poon, Adrian Portal, Robert & Alix Pratt, Kaori Prior **Q** Philippe Quix **R** Mark Ratter, Ann Reeves, Dietrich Rehnert, John Reid, Susanne Rettig, Felix Reychman, Jon Richards, Jonathan Richards, Scott Ridder, Lloyd Ridley, Francis Riezouw, Eduardo Robinovich, Irwin Robinson, Heikki Ronka, Barrett Ross, Markus Rossle, Stephanie Rummel **S** Jeni Sadler, Philip V Sale, Christopher Sap, Carmen Savella, Jo Scard, Michael Schäfer, Jeroen Schavemaker, Andreas Schepers, Gideon Schipper, Liz Schneider, Tom Schneider, Jeannette Schoenau, Dr Reuven Schossen, Wolfgang Seel, Pernille & John Seider, Gavin Sexton, Tina Shapiro, Harvey Shepard, Joe Shepter, Liz Shield, Pierre Simard, Jeroen Slikker, Alexander Slingeland, Todd Smith, Douglas Snyder, Mon Soen, Emma Soichet, Per Sonnvik, Lim Soon Ann, Flora Sproule, Ronit Srebro, Kristine K Stevens, Colin Steward, Rob Street, Klaus Streicher, Sander Strijbos, Jan Styblik, Linda Suen, Martin Svensson **T** Terence Tam, Bruce Tamagno, Chantel & Rubin Tankink, Takis Tap, Anna Tapp, Emanuela Tasinato, David Taylor, Paul Taylor, Sean Taylor, Genevieve Tearle, Tom Ternes, Pascal Teschner, N Thawee, Eva Theep, Nguyen Thi Viet, Barry L Thomas, Carolyn Thomas, Les Thompson, Dave Tih,

Jean-Luc Tinguely, Gregory T'Kint, Peter Todd, Luigi Toscano, Meryan Tozer, Werner Treipl, Tony Tu, William B Tuffin, Alexia & Paul Turner **V** Lauro Valera, Francisco Ballesteros Valero, Jelle van de Veire, Chris van den Broeck, Marieke van den Ham, Johan van den Hende, Suzan van Echtelt, Natalie van Eckendonk, Melissa N van Kirk, Teun van Metelen, Gerco van Vulpen, Roger Vanderbeek, Ben Verhoef, Pieter Verlinden, Giorgio Vintani, Chris Voaden, Manuela Volkmann **W** Graham Wade, Martina Wagner, Nathan Wales, Annie Walker, Clive Walker, Dawn Walsh, Ashley Wazana, Wolfram Weidemann, Peter Weiner, Bill Weir, Rachel & Andy Westnidge, Jake Wetherall, Perry Whalley, Caroline White, Nina White, Jeffrey Wicharuk, Dylan Wiliam, Kathleen Williams, Terry Williams, Timothy Willis, Sarah Wintle, Trudy Wong, Vincent Woo, Clayton Wood, Klaske Woolthuis, Joyce Wouters, Eoin Wrenn, Dave Wright **Y** Maureen Yeats, Jason Yeung, Chris Young **Z** Karina Zabihi, Nicholas Zdenkowski, Dirk Zeiler, Anat Zverdling

ACKNOWLEDGMENTS

Many thanks to the following for the use of their content:

Globe on back cover © Mountain High Maps 1993 Digital Wisdom, Inc.

Index

INDEX

MAP LEGEND

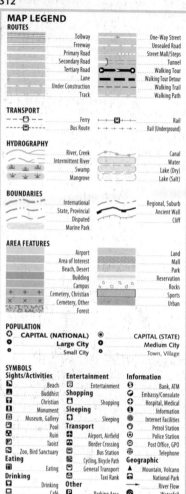

LONELY PLANET OFFICES

Australia
Head Office
Locked Bag 1, Footscray, Victoria 3011
☎ 03 8379 8000, fax 03 8379 8111
talk2us@lonelyplanet.com.au

USA
150 Linden St, Oakland, CA 94607
☎ 510 893 8555, toll free 800 275 8555
fax 510 893 8572, info@lonelyplanet.com

UK
72–82 Rosebery Ave,
Clerkenwell, London EC1R 4RW
☎ 020 7841 9000, fax 020 7841 9001
go@lonelyplanet.co.uk

Published by Lonely Planet Publications Pty Ltd
ABN 36 005 607 983

© Lonely Planet 2005

© photographers as indicated 2005

Cover photographs by Lonely Planet Images: Pha That Luang, Vientiane, Anders Blomqvist, (front); Novice monks at Mixaiyaram pagoda, Vientiane, Richard I'Anson (back). Many of the images in this guide are available for licensing from Lonely Planet Images: www .lonelyplanetimages.com.